INTIMATE ENEMIES

Pitt Series in Russian and East European Studies

Jonathan Harris, Editor

INTIMATE ENEMIES

Demonizing the Bolshevik Opposition,
1918–1928

UNIVERSITY OF PITTSBURGH PRESS

Published by the University of Pittsburgh Press, Pittsburgh, Pa., 15260

Copyright © 2007, University of Pittsburgh Press
Manufactured in the United States of America

Printed on acid-free paper

10 9 8 7 6 5 4 3 2 1

Library of Congress Cataloging-in-Publication Data

Halfin, Igal.

    Intimate enemies : demonizing the Bolshevik opposition, 1918-1928 / Igal Halfin.

       p.   cm. — (Pitt series in Russian and East European studies)

    Includes bibliographical references and index.

    ISBN-10: 0-8229-4329-8 (alk. paper)

    ISBN-10: 0-8229-5952-6 (alk. paper)

    ISBN-13: 978-0-8229-4329-7 (alk. paper)

    ISBN-13: 978-0-8229-5952-6 (alk. paper)

    1. Communism—Soviet Union—History.   2. Opposition (Political science)
—Soviet Union—History.   3. Communication in politics—Soviet Union—History.
4. Kommunisticheskaia partiia Sovetskogo Soiuza—History.   I. Title.

    HX313.H34 2007

    324.247'07509042—dc22   2006039175

To my friends from graduate school

CONTENTS

THE FIRST INTIMATE ENEMY

aled before the Supreme Tribunal in October 1918, Roman Vatslovich Malinovskii was an intimate enemy. While serving as the chairman of the Social
Democratic faction in the state Duma, he had spied for the tsarist secret police,
the notorious Okhrana.[1] The court described him as a provocateur, a "secret employee who systematically obtained information about the activities of revolutionary groups "with the aim of exposing them at the peak of their activity."[2] For the
Bolsheviks, Malinovskii had been not only a real traitor, but also the symbol of
treason. During the Great Purge, his name was almost interchangeable with those
of Judas and Trotsky. It became the link between the Judeo-Christian archetype of
betrayal and the more specific Bolshevik type of treason associated with internal
opposition.

In taking the trial of Malinovskii as the entry to our discussion of the Bolshevik notion of guilt we shall be starting with what must be considered an extreme
case, probably the most striking example of how conniving and sinister an intimate enemy could be. The recently unearthed transcript of the trial proceedings
conveys how early revolutionary courts conceptualized and prosecuted "treason"
(predatel'stvo). It is in some ways surprising that what took place less than a year
after Lenin seized power bears a striking resemblance to what was to take place
during the Great Purge. The accusations were similar: someone had infiltrated the
Party with the aim of subversion, and a strategy had been set in motion to lure the
innocent into the enemy's camp. The setting too was similar: once a Bolshevik was
declared a traitor, the Party refused to try him in a comrades' court and his case was
transferred to the state, which acted through a (typically ad hoc) juridical collegium. In 1918 Malinovskii faced the revolutionary commission of the Supreme Tribunal; in 1936–1938 the victims of the Great Purge were tried by the Supreme Military Collegium. And, most important, in both cases culpability was determined
according to the accused's personal record: the intention behind the crime was key,
and the object of investigation was the soul of the accused, its moral inclination, its
hopes and designs. To arrive at the soul, the investigators pursued the life history of

their quarry with great zeal: motives grew out of biography; without biography no verdict could be rendered.

Malinovskii strode into Smol'nyi, the Bolshevik headquarters in Petrograd, of his own accord and surrendered, despite the fact that he must have known that lesser provocateurs had been executed in previous months.[3] Court procedures were swiftly arranged and six justices were selected to oversee the proceedings, all of them Bolsheviks of some renown. The trial officially commenced in the Kremlin on November 5, 1918. A list of witnesses was drawn up—some had already been subpoenaed, while others were on the run—and soon a large volume of testimony had been heard: the evidence against the accused was overwhelming.[4] Malinovskii himself stated he "was not interested in denying his guilt."[5] He knew he was inculpated beyond hope by the testimonies of his Okhrana controllers, now in Soviet custody, as well as by the written depositions of the Bolshevik leaders to the Provisional Government's Extraordinary Investigatory Commission that had already dealt with his case in absentia in May 1917.

Just as it would do during the Show Trials, from the very beginning of the judicial process the prosecution demonized the accused. Much like the biblical Judas, Malinovskii was denounced for having "sold workers' interests for money." Illuminating excerpts from the indictment follow: "Malinovskii offered his services as a secret agent to the Okhrana police, aware all along that this would lead to comrades' arrest, exile, and persecution, to trials in tsarist courts and long jail sentences, also to the disruption of Party activity. . . . To achieve his goal, Malinovskii . . . penetrated the most important legal and underground Party institutions . . . and acted the part of agitator, propagandist and activist. This he did to deceive workers and to suggest that he was loyal to the socialist revolution." Taking advantage of the information that filled some fifty-seven reports on revolutionary pseudonyms, locations of Party meetings and storage placed for illegal literature, the Okhrana was able to interrupt almost all Social Democratic activity in Moscow during 1910 and 1911 worth speaking about.

The indictment went on to describe Malinovskii's next phase of treacherous activity, as he went abroad with the goal of "surveying and betraying revolutionary activity at its very top, the foundation of Party building—its foreign centers." When Malinovskii attended the 1912 Bolshevik Conference in Prague, he was, of course, on a special mission for the secret police. He relayed detailed information about conference attendance and deliberations, and about the plans made by the newly elected Central Committee. Finally, in his most extraordinary feat as a traitor, Malinovskii "penetrated the state Duma as the representative of Moscow workers." Thanks to political and financial assistance from the secret police, he passed along precious information on the leading representatives of the Social Democratic party organization.[6] Obliged at last to give up his place in the Duma, Malinovskii received six thousand rubles from the Okhrana and "ignominiously disappeared. In so doing, he disorganized the ranks of the revolutionaries, sowed confusion in the ranks of the working class, and by his treason profited the enemies of the workers' movement."[7]

A fundamental tenet of Bolshevism stated that intimate enemies enjoyed an extremely keen awareness of their own actions. Though theirs was a specifically evil role, they acted it as self-consciously as did the Party leaders their own roles. Writing in 1910, Aleksei Gastev, a prominent Bolshevik visionary, observed that he had never met "ignorant, illiterate provocateurs. No, these were the cream of the working class, coming from the heart of the movement."[8] Inesa Armand, Lenin's friend and lover, was scandalized when she learned that the intimate enemies often were drawn from the prestigious ranks of the "workers' intelligentsia." She granted that provocateurs were "class conscious: they are not driven by personal interests."[9] According to the prosecution, the money Malinovskii took from the Okhrana as remuneration for his espionage was not a symbol of weakness but the token of a premeditated decision to give up the revolutionary cause. Because the soul of this modern-day Judas and not his carnal form had been corrupted, he could not be re-educated. Malinovskii had enrolled in the ranks of secret agents "on his own initiative," driven by deliberate wickedness.[10]

Malinovskii's only hope for clemency lay in refuting the accusation that he had acted consciously. To this end he presented two texts, one written, the other oral. Both were very long. Accompanying the stenographic report of Malinovskii's testimony is a note that he spoke for over six hours. At the end of his written affidavit appear the following words: "I have written for twelve hours now (from eight o'clock on October 27, until eight in the morning, today) and I have no powers left. . . . If I have failed to reveal anything it is not because I wish to conceal something from you but because things happened a long time ago, almost five years now."[11]

The defense took the form of an autobiographical confession (*ispoved*'), proof that the very soul of the accused was on trial. Malinovskii spoke from a very weak position. His was the task of defending without seeming defensive, of conveying some understanding of his pitiful past without at any point seeking to play down his crimes. But he would insist on the attention and serious consideration of his judges, and in his remarks he sounded nearly self-righteous.

When I spoke before in this courtroom, the tribunal met my sincere words with laughter—this makes it hard to speak sincerely now. Still, I will struggle with my reserve, not because I want to justify myself before you, but to permit you to cast a glance at the psychological aspect of my case. Why did things happen as they did? How was I ensnared? Why has life presented me with no other way out than passing through this hall? I have to initiate you into my tribulations, the tribulations of a provocateur.

The terms for Malinovskii's defense were set. It was not to be a factual refutation; the case for the prosecution would not be dismantled point by point; this would be an apology. All the stages of the speech would reappear in the recantations of the oppositionists in the years to come: at the beginning lay a problem—unsympathetic parents and a family environment that was petit bourgeois or déclassé—over the course of the middle section the story of how the protagonist surrendered to the forces of evil would be told, and the conclusion would highlight a marvelous recovery and a return to the fold.

Malinovskii was born of Roman Catholic parents in the Russian part of Poland in March 1876. "I was an orphan," began the tale, "fatherless and motherless, from my early years. . . . My relatives wanted to make a salesman out of me. But I had always been attracted to hard labor, so I went to Warsaw and worked there for three years." Quite safe: the story of one who came from the lower middle classes but was instinctively smitten by the proletariat. Despite this promising beginning, no protagonist could rush to a happy ending before he had been distracted, had lost his way, had been misled.

In Malinovskii's case, the distraction had catastrophic consequences. "I became obsessed by an idée fixe: I wanted to travel around the world." He accompanied a friend to Germany with only three rubles in his pocket. "We entered an empty hut in a village near Plock, took bread and some money and went away. A mounted policeman caught up with us and we were arrested." Malinovskii admitted that in his youth he was no better than the "scum of society. . . . If I was prosecuted on only two occasions it was not because I was a minor criminal but because I didn't get caught more often." Police records showed that Malinovskii had been prosecuted for theft three times, in 1894, 1896, and 1899; he was sentenced to imprisonment for one and a half months, a year and a half, and two and a half years, respectively.[12]

While serving a sentence in Plits, Malinovskii worked in a button factory. "After my sentence was up, I went on working in the same factory, but only for a little while; soon I was drafted into the military." The defendant was drafted into the Izmailovsk Guards Regiment (1902). Luckily, his stint with the proletariat lifted his spirit. "If I'd never entered that factory, my life might have been very different." Because one day, while walking towards the barracks in which he was serving, he saw "workers in chains. Someone said that these were 'strikers.' I retorted that they were 'good people,' not criminals." Some soldiers got upset and Malinovskii was summoned to the regimental commander, who told him he would be tried for his "grave crime." Malinovskii managed to escape jail; his sentence was commuted to military service in the Far East.

Somehow Malinovskii managed to return to Petersburg in 1906, and it is to this period that he attempted to assign his first, very incomplete conversion. Working as a lathe operator in the Langenzipen factory Malinovskii was approached by Social Democratic activists, who urged him to leave the production line and assume the responsibilities of the secretary of the union of metalworkers.[13] Malinovskii showed considerable talent as a labor organizer and rose to be full-time secretary of the important Metalworkers Union. He recruited new members, edited the union newspaper, and participated in various political congresses legalized by the October 1905 Manifesto. "These were my first steps as a social activist. I need to say that during my three years in the union—until 1909—I worked in the only way I can, which is to say very conscientiously, with the passion natural to my character."[14] Here Malinovskii capitalized on his earlier narratological investment: was this not the same man who had taken up the cause of the shackled workers? Was this not a quite positive period in an otherwise somewhat dubious life?

No Bolshevik autobiographer could be satisfied with a dull chronicle of his life's main events, since a string of etiological dyads had none of the impact of a larger whole conveying an overarching moral message. Typically the author described the passage from the darkness of capitalism to the light of Marxism. Somewhere along the line the protagonist underwent a conversion, recognized the Party's righteousness, and united his life with the life of the movement. Of course, Malinovskii could not tell so simple a story. After all, much of his life has been spent in the service of the wrong side. Still, a fundamental feature of the genre made it useful to his needs: the autobiographer typically described a host of misdeeds, regardless of his overall ideological complexion; the key was proving that those misdeeds were committed unconsciously.

Malinovskii hoped to persuade the court to see him not as a wicked individual but as a man waylaid and misled by psychological circumstances beyond his control. He admitted his crimes, denying only that they reflected his inner world. During an acute spiritual crisis abetted by the Okhrana, the soul of Malinovskii split: one part remained with the revolutionary cause, while the other drifted temporarily to the clutches of the secret police. In time, the two halves had reunited and Malinovskii had eagerly presented himself to his Bolshevik judges, contrite and hopeful that he might become a decent revolutionary yet.

The Bolshevik discourse deployed two competing reconstructions of the primordial individual: Malinovskii's soul could be described as a field upon which good and evil vied for supremacy, or it could be seen as fundamentally good but temporarily under the sway of the forces of darkness. In the former case, conversion was a dramatic event, a victory for goodness and a leap into the light; in the latter, conversion was a more gradual process of enlightenment. Malinovskii wavered between the two narratives. While he knew that emphasizing his proletarian roots would have made his recovery a bit more plausible, pressing this point too hard would have made his vertiginous fall absolutely inexplicable.

Unforeseen circumstances changed the life of the defendant dramatically, and a promising beginning in a revolutionary service was spoiled. In November 1909 the police cracked down on the Metalworkers Union, arrested Malinovskii and expelled him from Petersburg. Now married with two children and unemployed, he went to Moscow, where he enrolled at Shaniavsk University. As he divided his

time between the factory and the classroom, Malinovskii made the acquaintance
of many different sorts, including Mensheviks and many other Moscow workers.[15]
By April 1910 his star seemed to be rising in the Russian Social Democratic movement.[16] It was during that month that he was approached by Viktor Nogin, a Bolshevik leader who asked Malinovskii to help run a Iaroslav Party cell and submitted
his name as a candidate for the renascent Social Democratic Central Committee,
one of his pet projects.[17] But almost immediately Malinovskii found himself arrested by the Okhrana. As we know, this was not his first arrest; it was, though, the
turning point of his life.[18]

From the date of his release on May 23, Malinovskii acted as a secret agent in
the employ of the tsarist state. He was given the cover name of "Tailor" and paid
between fifty and hundred rubles per month—a hefty sum for the time.[19] But Malinovskii wished to explain to his Bolshevik judges that "it was not as if I suddenly
decided to offer my services to the Okhrana, just like that, for no reason." When the
police, tipped off by some traitor, had seized him, he had initially refused their invitation to spy on his comrades. Having wrestled with his conscience, "I could not
accept the first offer, not because it disgusted me, but because I did not see how I
could lead a double life." More a matter of practical difficulty than of morality, he
presented his reaction as that of an individual not yet fully conscious, a consideration that must mitigate his guilt.

According to Malinovskii's 1918 testimony, the interviews had continued over
the ensuing days, as his jailers assayed a gamut of techniques. "They began by
threatening me, then cajoled me, treated me to tea and cigarettes, engaged me in
abstract conversations about my family life and the role of the Okhrana, told me
they were not against progress but that things should be done slowly. My God,
what was happening? I was facing human beings who, like spiders, tangled up my
soul and my body."[20] It was only when his interrogators told him that if he did not
agree to work for the Okhrana he could expect twelve years of forced labor for an
attempt to set up an illegal printing press in Iaroslav that he began to consider giving in. "It wasn't that I consented, but the thought crept into my mind."

Here the phenomenological dimension of Malinovskii's narrative leaps to the
eye. Like all those whose hearts are set not on pardon but on absolution, he showed
little concern for what had actually happened and wanted above all to provide an
accurate description of the inner movements of his soul. His decision to betray the
revolutionary movement, he insisted, was triggered by a crisis of faith. "It was the
impression that . . . the Party was surrounded by danger, that you could not tell
whether the people right next to you were conscientious activists or provocateurs,
that got me to join the Okhrana. I wasn't saying it yet, but internally I had already
made up my mind and was suffering because of my decision." Then finally "all of my
vacillations were over. I didn't feel any pangs of conscience, just the fear that they
would publicize my trial for theft."

This stage in the story, the capitulation to the enemy, would also feature promi-nently in all the recantations to follow during the purges. Every defendant would do time in the Trotskyist camp—generally for reasons that had no connection to his true identity—before he could return to the fold and once again embrace Stalinist orthodoxy. Though Malinovskii had converted to the counterrevolutionary cause, his narrative contained many moments of self-recrimination. A series of devices es-tablished a great distance between the narrator of 1918 and the protagonist of 1910, suggesting that this conversion lacked authenticity, that it only hinted at the con-version that would reveal his authentic moral self. Malinovskii wrote about his 1910 betrayal as if he were describing someone else.

Following the tips of this someone else, the Okhrana liquidated the Moscow Collegium of the Bolshevik Central Committee, as well as a similar body in the provincial city of Tula, and arrested the members of the underground meeting who attempted to create in Moscow a revolutionary "Renaissance" group. A delegate to the Prague Party Conference, Malinovskii transferred to the Okhrana detailed in-formation on the conference's agenda, evaluated the composition and activity of the newly formed Central Committee, and enabled the detection and arrest of all the conference's delegates who returned to Russia. His Okhrana file contains thirty signatures acknowledging the reception of 8,730 rubles for such "services" (uslugi). The deputy head of the tsarist police, Vissarionov, characterized Malinovskii as a "precious and hard working employee who knows his way in party affairs" and his deputy, Beletskii, described him as "the pride of our department."[21]

While the prosecution established that between July 1910 and October 1913 Malinovskii had betrayed eighty-eight men and women to the secret police, he ex-pressed contrition about only two of these, "my best friends, Sverdlov and Koba [i.e., Stalin]. These are my two real crimes: I knew they would be arrested, was ob-ligated as a decent human being to warn them but did not."[22] When the prosecu-tion expressed proletarian rage because the accused had communicated the delib-erations of the Bolshevik Central Committee to the tsarist police, Malinovskii did not understand all the fuss. "If you think about the angle from which my case is be-ing examined here, it seems pointless to introduce something so insignificant. The very fact that I served in the Okhrana speaks for itself: I committed a grave crime indeed." This peculiar touchiness continued with the claim never to have been "so ignoble as to insult Lenin's name by saying he had been an Austrian spy," and when this huffiness provoked snickering Malinovskii took offense. Was this not a revolu-tionary "court of honor" (sud chesti) rather than a common criminal court?[23]

In line with this distinction, Malinovskii refused to provide much detail about his treasonous career and insisted that the internal ramifications of his actions, but not the actions themselves, deserved scrutiny. "When I accept certain charges and reject others, it's not because I want to say that my crime isn't great, but because I want to establish the truth. If I didn't divulge that much [to the Okhrana], it wasn't because my conscience was torturing me, but because I myself knew very little and was not very active [in the Party]." As before, the point of so much wallowing in his own filth was to emphasize that at the time he was not a moral agent; this would make his eventual return to righteousness all the more impressive.

Throughout the period under discussion Malinovskii rose higher and higher in the Party hierarchy. Enjoying the support of the Okhrana and the Party, he was elected the chairman of the Duma workers' faction (1913).[24] Malinovskii moved to the capital, was renamed "X," and his pay was raised to 500, and sometimes even 700, rubles per month. The police knew why it was so generous: Malinovskii handed it Lenin's, Zinoviev's, and Krupskaia's personal letters, lists of *Pravda* subscribers, and the entire archive of the Duma workers' faction "so that a copy could be made."[25]

At the peak of both of his careers, Malinovskii became aware of a deepening sense of loss. "As crime followed crime, I begun to understand and feel with all my soul [*vsei dushoi*] just what it was I was doing." Malinovskii recapitulates the events the led him to assume his high post in the Duma. In January 1912 he showed up without a valid mandate at the Sixth Party Conference in Prague. Impressed by Malinovskii's reputation as a trade unionist and a good propagandist, Lenin insisted that he not only be elected to the Central Committee but also become a Bolshevik candidate for elections to the Fourth Duma from the Moscow workers' curia. Malinovskii denied that he had planned any of that. "The first time I heard about this idea was only when Lenin approached me at the conference." He tried to wriggle out of deepening his treason in such a profound way, but lacked the necessary resolve. "Here I was, having committed a conscious crime [*soznatel'noe prestuplenie*], a crime for which I am fully responsible and one that used to disturb my peace of mind. So I told Lenin that it was not a good idea to advance my candidacy to the Duma because I would harm myself and the Party. But Lenin did not ask for details and I limited myself to a few remarks."[26]

In his written affidavit he elaborated: "Many ask me now, 'Why didn't you run away? Why didn't you confess [*soznalsia*]?' But how can one escape himself? Had I known . . . the Party, its program, its goals, had I known Marx's teaching as I know it now, had I been the Malinovskii I would become later, I would have acted righteously without your guidance."[27] One faces his moral ordeal on his own, in solitude, and one does this only when the right time comes, once he had already learned to distinguish good from evil. Now, in 1918, Malinovskii was ready to take responsibility for his actions; in 1912 he was not. In the meantime, "I fooled myself into believing that I was not committing a grave crime. I distorted things because I wanted to believe my own distortions. . . . Flattered by the title 'member of the Duma,' I was living in my own fantasy world. . . . It was all a sham, the delirium of a sick man." The criminal was morally absent from the scene of the crime: "My conscience was asleep at the time."[28]

As one reads over the transcript from these legal proceedings, one encounters a wide array of seemingly incompatible discourses. But the value-free discourse of psychology and the value-laden discourses of ethics and religion did not admit any specific contradictions, nor did they legislate the domains of their respective applications. Quite to the contrary, the traditional moralistic vocabulary and the modern psychological vocabulary turned out to be compatible in important ways; psychology and sociology were intensively pursued precisely so that the Party could set its ethical judgments on Soviet science. And ethics in turn functioned as the ultimate referee between good criminology and bad criminology. Malinovskii's guilt had to be adjudicated with the help of procedures designed to evaluate moral states in a scientifically advanced vocabulary.

While he did not pose as a good Bolshevik, Malinovskii refused to be thought of as completely wicked. "I cannot say that I was fully sincere [iskrennii] in my dealings with the Okhrana. I did what I could to avoid saying certain things . . . because I found myself surrounded by pathetic individuals. I enjoyed taking a sort of vengeance for what I was going through." The accused emphasized that there had always been a certain distance between him and his controllers. After all, he said,

at the time I was "kin" to the Bolsheviks. I was not a Socialist revolutionary because I did not know [any of them], and I was not a Menshevik because I did not subscribe to their muddled position. . . . Nor could I join the Black Hundred—my father was in exile [on their account] and I hated them as a Pole. . . . If I sympathized with the Bolsheviks it was because I sensed their honesty. I said once in a conversation that the Bolsheviks smelled of the sweat of workers.[29]

The indictment against Malinovskii accused him of coveting the Duma membership he won, and while he would not deny that he had desired the position, he had to contradict the motives imputed to him by the prosecution. Rather, he had wanted to prove to his relatives, who had always looked down on him, that he enjoyed respect among the revolutionaries and could win the election. "I was lying to myself, and I half believed the lies, telling myself that I'd attain a high position and then resign. I had a lot of rubbish in my head and even thought of killing myself." If he sought to counter charges brought by the prosecution, it was not to prove his innocence but to prove that his guilt lay in his moral unsteadiness, not simply in his selfish ambition.

Despite his modest education, Malinovskii proved himself to be an eloquent parliamentarian and an undisputed leader of the Bolshevik Duma faction. Taking full advantage of his immunity as a Duma deputy he raised funds for the Party, promoted its publishing activity, and, ironically, even served on a commission seeking out Okhrana agents in Bolshevik ranks. At the same time, he was busy fulfilling police instructions to introduce divisions within the Party and was instrumental in splitting the united Social Democratic Duma faction in November 1913. Even though Malinovskii had been crowned with success, according to his 1918 narrative, he was assailed by doubts. "Here I was a Duma member, just as I had wanted. But what was I supposed to do next? What was my purpose?"

Among his troubles were problems with his new controllers who had set themselves "the utopian goal of directing the entirety of the Social Democratic party's activities through Malinovskii."[30] The accused testified that they so offended his conscience that he could no longer continue to deceive himself. The rules of spiritual dialectic could not be denied, and now that the turncoat had sunk to the very bottom of his pit of treachery he had to rise.

Their methods, their techniques were so exacting that they . . . began to destroy my psychology. At the same time there was the Duma, my political education. . . . It's not surprising that a whole range of events, my position of responsibility, all those trivialities I had to tolerate led to my personal transformation. . . . I found myself unable to think about working for the police anymore. It wasn't that I became better or purer as a person, or that I changed in some profound way. . . . The credit goes not to me but to their incompetence, since it was they who helped my conscience wake up.

So great did his internal turmoil grow that he begun revealing "signs of madness."

I was crying like a small child at the slightest thing; all it took was a long speech by a delegate from the [Social Democratic] faction and I would have to go to another room, where I shivered and sobbed. . . . The only thing that used to calm me down was biting my hands till they bled. No one knew why I had a bandage on my head for a week; at the time I said that a horse had run into me, but now you will know the truth: I had broken part of my skull by smashing my head against the wall.[31]

Without having passed through this excruciating period, Malinovskii could not have been reborn. "If you are capable of lifting yourself high enough to discard the nauseating disgust you must be feeling towards me, then believe me when I say I never wanted to be a provocateur. My situation deteriorated . . . because with every passing day I was becoming more conscious but I saw no way out."

Out of desperation Malinovskii told Beletskii that he could spy for him no longer and threatened suicide, but to no avail. If his controller would not release him, perhaps he could find another way out by quitting the Duma; quite considerately the government had just banned the "seditious" Social Democratic faction from the parliament's next fifteen meetings.[32] The public wanted to see a parliamentarian campaign against this measure but instead the weary spy stirred an all out row. "The Russian reading public got the impression that I suffered from a nervous illness."

What finally won Malinovskii his discharge from the Okhrana was the intervention of Dzhunkovskii, the new deputy minister of the interior. Arraigned by the Bolsheviks after the seizure of power, Dzhunkovskii told a 1918 court: "When I found out that Malinovskii, a member of the state Duma, was on the payroll of the chief of police, I decided that the two occupations were absolutely incompatible."[33] Malinovskii received a generous compensation grant (6,000 rubles) and was told to emigrate.[34] But Malinovskii presented a different picture: "Some say that I left the Duma at the behest of Dzhunkovskii. I suppose you have enough evidence to believe this claim, but it is erroneous. I quit my position in the Duma because my suffering had surpassed the levels of my stamina."[35]

But though he had resigned from the Duma, Malinovskii had yet to begin his convalescence. "I will say sincerely—though it does not do me any good here—that I was not capable of sacrificing myself for the Party back then. Socialism became a religion for me only while I was in German captivity. Only there did my soul go through a profound spiritual transformation [korennoi, dushevnyi perelom]."[36] In other words, Malinovskii asked the reader/listener not to judge too harshly the actions and inaction that immediately followed. Even at this late stage of his activity, he was still not conscious enough to embrace the Bolshevik truth in full.

On May 31, 1914, the Bolshevik central committee published a resolution to the effect that "leaving his post as a Duma deputy without notifying the Central Committee and without explaining himself to his voters or to his comrades Malinovskii committed a monstrous [chudovishchnoe] breach of Party discipline."[37] His sudden and utterly unexplained resignation provoked not only anger but also suspicion, so Malinovskii went to Poronin (Galicia) to explain things to Lenin.[38] Though the interview soon became a formal arraignment, and though the word provocateur rang through the court of comrades, no accusations could be substantiated and the humbled ex-spy managed to wriggle free.[39] A Bolshevik tribunal concluded that Malinovskii's "political honesty" was not in doubt but removed him from the Party for having deserted his post in the Duma.[40] He could not bring himself to reveal the whole truth, he now explained: "people trusted me too much."[41] After all, his days of deception had ended, and now he simply hoped that his activities on behalf of the Okhrana would remain unknown to his comrades. Had not his controllers promised him that every shred of paper that might reveal the truth would be destroyed?

Then came the First World War. Malinovskii fought in the tsarist army for four and a half months, was wounded and taken prisoner by the Germans in 1915.[42] From his prisoner-of-war camp he got in touch with Lenin in Switzerland and contributed to spreading Bolshevik propaganda among his fellow prisoners. "While in captivity, I met individuals who didn't understand politics and were unaware of even the most basic truths. I conversed with them and was intrigued, so I began a speaking tour." For the first time Malinovskii was "truly calm. In captivity there was none of the bickering found elsewhere, no intra-Party conflict, just a steadily increasing enlightenment. You cannot add those years to the list of my crimes; those were my taintless years. . . . In 1914–1916, I acted as only the most conscientious human being can act." Malinovskii's dedication came "not just from my brain but from my heart and my soul as well. I believe that had I first entered the Okhrana hell in such a state of mind, I would have spit into their mugs just as hundreds and thousands of comrades had done."[43]

At the time that the documents revealing his prerevolutionary treachery were made public by the provisional government in 1917, Malinovskii was still a prisoner of war in Germany. "Since I was working in the village I found out I'd been unmasked only in the end of May or the beginning of June. Only then did I understand what weight had been off of my shoulders. . . . [During my imprisonment] I had become a different human being, a normal human being." If his fellow prisoners did not quite forgive him on hearing his confession, they understood him. "As they'd watched me for two, three, four years, they'd witnessed my loyalty every day, had seen how I loved my [revolutionary activity], had seen my happiness and my suffering, whether caused by events in the camps or in Russia. This was the most luminous, the most cherished time of my life. I may be a criminal, but there I worked conscientiously and others came to imitate my purity [chistota]."[44]

At the conclusion of his confession, Malinovskii sketched a quite extraordinary scene of true conversion. "Please listen to me: you may find this interesting. One day in 1916, while doing farm work in the fields, I lay down in the grass and became fascinated by the hundred and thousands of small insects there who lived just as I did." Instinctively driven by a need to find a difference between men and these creatures, he began to assess himself.

What have I accomplished? What have others accomplished? What is the balance sheet of my life? Does it match the balance sheet others have for me, official and unofficial? In addition to my work as a provocateur a number of other crimes came to mind. I have done all sorts of things that I presently regard as crimes. I could acknowledge all this as crimes because mine was the view of an individual for whom—you may be offended to hear me say this—socialism has become a religion.

Though this final declaration could have easily been regarded as atavistic, it found many echoes in the official discourse that carried on to 1918 and far later. The modern sciences of man on which the Bolshevik jurists leaned relied heavily on Christian vocabulary: the traditional notion of the soul and the Marxist notion of consciousness turned out to be complementary in important ways. The eschatological master plot, with its focus on the movement of individuals from darkness to light, was assimilated into Bolshevik socialism: thus "comrades" and "the faithful" enjoyed many parallels, as did "illumination" and "awakening," "classless society" and "paradise."[45]

At the outset the prosecution expressed a certain resistance to Malinovskii's talk about the soul. It was not the purpose of the present court "to evaluate moral qualities," stated Nikolai Krylenko. "Rather, we work from the point of view of the Revolution to judge the danger to the Revolution and the defense of Revolutionary achievements."[46] Krylenko contrasted the Marxist preoccupation with the science of objective truth with the Christian tradition's insistence that individual intentions were all important. Since history was an objective process, he could disregard subjective intentions; the Marxist studied the unchanging laws of the universe, not the conscience of the historical actors. Judged from the point of view of historical utility, Malinovskii was guilty. Krylenko directed special attention to the "impact of his unexplained departure from the Duma and the terrible blow this meant for the Revolution. . . . Workers who had held this individual in high regard were stabbed right through the heart."

Devoted as he was to objective facts, Krylenko could not give up the soul-judging framework. No Bolshevik had done any better than his Christian or his liberal predecessors in separating jurisprudence from the discourse on the soul. Krylenko himself had successfully argued for granting judges the option of forgoing any prolonged judicial inquiry when the accused confessed to his crime. The concept of "revolutionary legality" popularized during the Civil War explicitly included not just criminal acts, but plans as well.[47] Krylenko stated in July 1923: "To us, a counterrevolutionary act is one which the perpetrator 'knew full well' [zavedomo] would undermine the Revolution."[48] During the 1925 trial of alleged terrorists, Krylenko ridiculed the distinction between intention and action: "Jurisprudential cretins would most likely build their defense on the following argument: 'Well, let us grant that the accused intended to perpetrate a terrorist act. Since they committed no actual crime they remain as innocent as the lamb of God.'" No, according to Krylenko, the distinction between the disposition towards a crime and the crime itself had to disappear.[49] Instead, the Cheka-GPU-NKVD were guided by a distinction between crimes perpetrated with "evil intention" (zloi umesel) and inadvertent crimes, so familiar to every Christian. In a word, the Bolshevik legal system addressed not crimes but criminals and judged not isolated acts but complete moral creatures.[50]

This explains the energy Krylenko devoted to dismantling Malinovskii's tale of conversion in 1918. The prosecution had to prove that the same Malinovskii who sat facing his accusers had committed terrible acts of treason; the defense hoped to convince the judges that the traitorous Malinovskii had been cast off in the German prison camp, like an old skin.

Since Krylenko was obliged to show that the accused had been politically conscious at the time he perpetrated his crimes, he attacked Malinovskii's contention that in 1910 he had known nothing of politics. Was it conceivable, Krylenko asked, that a trade union activist, "a secretary in one of the largest professional organizations of the working class during the Third Duma," would know nothing of socialism? Additionally, "Malinovskii was invited to join the Central Committee, and since such invitations were sent only to those who had won great trust, this contradicts the statement of the accused that he was not involved in politics as such."

Was the accused a self-aware Social Democrat in 1910? The judge posed this question to Valerian Pletnev, hoping that Malinovskii's erstwhile comrade could help assess the consciousness of the accused. "Yes, he was a Marxist," Pletnev responded.[51] The prosecution now had sufficient grounds to reject the plea that circumstances had forced the accused to become a provocateur.[52] According to Krylenko: "The picture of moral tribulations the accused has tried to draw, with its sense of coming to a dead end, searching for a way out—all this is nice and commendable, but it does not correspond to the documents at our disposal." Krylenko concluded with a moral reproach, not with a factual condemnation: from 1910 to 1913 the accused had displayed "adaptability" (*prisposobliaemost'*), "chameleon-like behavior" (*khamelionstvo*), and "sycophancy" (*ugodnichestvo*), not innocence and spiritual suffering.[53]

Malinovskii's legal counsel accepted the transformation of the legal proceedings into a trial of the inner soul. It seemed to him appropriate to examine the soul of the accused, for did not the judges insist that the Bolsheviks were not the kind of people "for whom a document, a certain scheme, is more important that a living person"? The trial would become, as the public defender put it, a "political sacrament" (*politicheskoe tainstvo*), a procedure that further developed the Bolshevik system of trials of the soul rather than one that relied on a liberal legal framework. During this period few rules of the game had been established, and their applicability to the current trial amounted to guesswork. A series of questions opened by the Bolshevik jurists in 1918—What evidence is pertinent? What constitutes guilt? What is fit punishment?—was still being debated when Stalin's Show Trials were staged almost twenty years later.

If the bourgeois court treated the soul as an ahistorical given, the revolutionary court regarded it as a work in progress. Before they underwent true conversion, individuals were treated as the objects of history, not its subjects. Bringing psychology and sociology to bear, Malinovskii suggested that not he but the old regime had been responsible for his actions. The mixture of medical terminology and spiritual language he used to describe his condition in 1911 suggests the tension between a strictly mechanistic realm where no judgment can be made and a realm of free agency eminently subject to evaluation: "My double game permeated my organism. I was myself only during those sleepless nights when I experienced the pangs and sufferings of my soul, itself hidden away in a remote corner."[54] When Malinovskii deployed a moralistic vocabulary, he seemed to be hinting at the self to come, a morally mature and responsible self. By contrast, when he spoke of himself as a provocateur, he described a self wrecked by illness. Should a madman be punished or healed? Such was the question implied by Malinovskii's descriptions of his struggles with insanity. The answer was obvious.

Whatever was implicit in Malinovskii's apologia became explicit in the speech of the public defender. The latter presented his client as a Bolshevik Raskol'nikov: "Unless my ears deceived me, the accused was quite sincere when he said that he was led to treason not by free will [*dobrovol'noe zhelanie*] or personal initiative [*lichnaia initsiativa*] but by the cursed conditions [in which he found himself]." It was as though he had been hypnotized. "When asked why he first slipped, what introduced the first crack into his conscience, the accused tells us that it was the general system used by those subtle speculators [of the Okhrana], experts in hollowing out the human soul." Having said that much, the public defender sent Dzhunkovskii in the same direction: "Have you had a chance to hear what was involved in snaring victims, how they were drawn . . . into their clutches?" "It is not easy to describe how this was done," Dzhunkovskii answered. The public defender explained that "besides the facts, I am interested in the motives behind Malinovskii's behavior. I want to know whether something that might be called psychological torture was used."[55] Malinovskii, he believed, had been seized by the "tentacles of policemen armed with a knowledge of inquisitorial psychology. . . . Inquisitorial methods can turn a thoroughly sincere individual, someone dedicated to ideals, into . . . a tortured, depraved, and powerless person."

Somewhat paradoxically, the court privileged the voice of the accused, reasoning that the inner workings of his soul were directly accessible to him alone. "How do we know what he brooded on? Much as the public prosecutor would like to open up his brain for inspection, we can't."[56] According to the defense, the criminal story that the court had convened to hear was overshadowed by a more significant psychological story involving fateful personal encounters and bad influences. "Perhaps the great misfortune of the accused is that he never met the person who could lead the way for him."

The science of psychology, the defender went on, and not the court system, would have to be the final arbiter of Malinovskii's crimes. "Malinovskii has a flaw [*nadlom*] in his will, a flaw we frequently encounter . . . in unfortunate individuals. Such individuals come from the world of the psychiatrist and the historian. . . . Caught in the net spread by the Okhrana police, Malinovskii could not extricate himself." The passive construction is noteworthy here. Only when an individual was made whole did he and his actions begin to speak in the active voice. The defender implied that Malinovskii served as a provocateur not "of his own volition" (*dobrovol'no*), but because he had been "coerced" (*prinuditel'no*).[57]

"So how would you summarize the personality of Malinovskii?" the defender asked the deputy head of the tsarist department of police, Vissarionov. "I had the impression that Malinovskii found himself in his situation due to an intersection of circumstances," Vissarionov replied. "During his speeches in the Duma, the Party activist in him would wake up, the activist he had been in the beginning, the activist that continued living in him somewhere. An emotional person, he would get excited and reembark on the path circumstances had driven him from."[58] Later, during his concluding remarks, the public defender was to say, "We all heard here how Malinovskii . . . was tortured by his duality [*dvoistevennost*']. . . . Within him a constant struggle went on: on the one hand, a socialist; on the other, a traitor to socialism, a provocateur." Such a spiritual agon directly preceded the emergence of a responsible moral agency.

A question arises, the public defender pointed out. Why did he return from Germany and give himself over? "Malinovskii must have been searching for death." But this, according to the defense, was not the proper punishment in his case.

I hope that the verdict will be different and I shall explain why: the living human soul of a socialist provocateur is wracked with torment as it starts to comprehend the degree of its guilt. . . . Every clod of earth that falls on his grave, on the other hand, renders the provocateur more indifferent: he is released from his suffering. Citizen judges, now that weapons advance the socialist cause, death at the front is understandable. But in the tranquillity [of this court], socialism and death do not go hand in hand; as a public defender and a human being I ask that the accused be treated with humanity.[59]

To one who had endured the suffering described in the testimony of the defendant, would not a death sentence be meaningless? Would not all crimes against the Revolution be expiated by a man born again so that he might join his comrades in the trenches of the Civil War?

Malinovskii himself explained that no other motive than the need to face his accusers had brought him back to Russia. "I was deeply conscious of my crimes and realized that if I failed to turn myself in, my life would be meaningless."[60] The accused noted that as a Pole he could have arranged to be sent to Poland, but he had chosen to return to Russia despite the certainty that he would be convicted. During his second interrogation, he stated, "As early as 1917 I had sent the minister of justice a request for a trial."[61] Then, on reaching Petrograd, Malinovskii learned that "for agent provocateurs, there is no other sentence but execution—that is the reality." Even then, he had no desire to conceal his identity. "I could not, would not hide anymore."[62]

To surrender was to be reborn—though this birth might only take place a moment before death. "Never before could I sacrifice myself, but at that time I thought about it very calmly. If I am a bit agitated, it is because I am unfolding before you my soul's sufferings, and not because I am anxious about your verdict."[63]

Thinking of himself now as part of a larger movement, Malinovskii was "internally overjoyed" to realize that even if he died, the disciples he had taught Marxism during the last few years would fight for the Revolution. "I may be gone, but they will remain and will replace me."[64] Then, in closing, he said, "Now that you have listened to me, give me my just deserts—you see yourselves that there is no alternative, the verdict is clear to all of us. And believe me, I will accept it calmly because I do not deserve anything else!"[65] Malinovskii's individual self may perish, but joining Bolshevism, he would live on with the Revolution.

But the state prosecution could not think of forgiving Malinovskii even posthumously; in view of his treacherous record, he was an emblem of an irredeemable soul.[66] His was not to be the death of a hero but of a mad dog.

Unanimously the six judges found the accused guilty and ordered his execution. The verdict was carried out almost immediately, at 12:30 a.m. on November 6, 1918.[67]

INDIVIDUAL TRUTH AND PARTY TRUTH

Could two people be more dissimilar than Malinovskii and Trotsky? The first had stolen, lied, and betrayed his fellow Party members for money; the latter had dedicated his life to returning the Party to the truth. Though in 1918 they looked quite different from one another, provocateurs and oppositionists would become, to all intents and purposes, identical by 1936, the year when the Trotskyists were declared subhuman. As it moves from the relatively amicable intra-Party debates of 1918–1921 to the demonization to which the opposition was subjected in the late 1920s, this book documents in detail the process by which these two concepts gradually fused.

In a secret letter circulated by the Central Committee following Kirov's assassination in December 1934, Malinovskii is mentioned in the same breath as the Trotskyists and the Zinovievists who were trying to undermine the Party "from within." Weaving manifold connections between the "liars," "provocateurs," and "Judas-traitors" of the prerevolutionary era and the oppositionists who had allegedly tried to undercut the Party, the letter drew heavily on the concept of the intimate enemy. "It might appear strange and perverse that the role of the agent of terror, the last resort of the dying bourgeois classes, was assumed by individuals who came from our own ranks, but was not Malinovskii a scion of the working class? Was this agent provocateur not a former member of the Bolshevik faction in 1913?" Widely considered the trigger of the Great Purge, the letter, apparently drafted by Stalin himself, was clear: the real enemy had to be sought inside the Party.[1]

It is impossible to understand the ferocity of the Stalinist onslaught against the opposition without studying the fear surrounding those Party members regarded as more dangerous that the imperialists, the fascists, or even the White Russian immigrants. Once a legitimate criticism of the Party line, the opposition evolved gradually in the official perception into an act of "apostasy" (*otstupnichestvo*).[2] As the case of Malinovskii amply shows, the Party suspected its own people from the beginning. If they were pronounced traitors, their fate was harsh. In the early years, though, the Bolsheviks were largely forgiving. While the population at large suffered immense losses at their hands, Party members were always spared. Almost no blood was spilt in the Party until the mid-1930s, and even Trotsky, who was judged to be a dangerous political instigator, was spared. In the mid-1930s, by contrast, many in the Party expressed an open regret that he was not put to the wall when still within reach. To understand why judgment during the Great Purge (1936–1938) became so severe, why almost every suspected Communist ended up being shot, we have to look into how the Party dealt with its intimate enemies over the years.

An entire vocabulary had to be drawn up to capture the essence of the intimate enemy. In a letter received by the Social Democratic activist Lidia Dan after one of her friends had been denounced, provocateurs were described as "friend-foes" (*drugo-vragi*).[3] In the context of the political struggles among Bolsheviks in 1923, there was talk of "the enemy in our own camp" (*vrag v sobstvennoi srede*).[4] At first, "oppositionist" and "provocateur" appeared to be very different terms, the former indicating ideological apostasy while the latter suggested treason for the sake of treason—yet they shared something important: much like the spies and provocateurs whom Stalin's henchmen saw everywhere, the Trotskyist "renegades" (*renegaty*) had been born within the Bolshevik camp.[5]

What distinguished intimate enemies from other, more regular foes—the aristocracy, the bourgeoisie, liberal political parties—was their familiarity with revolutionary theory, revolutionary practice, and the revolutionary thought process. Such knowledge was reckoned to make the intimate enemies doubly dangerous: the well-meaning but gullible working class could be seduced, lulled by the superficial similarity between the language of the Party and the language of the inner enemy into the belief that the Party's greatest foes were its saviors. Had not the Trotskyists, for example, toiled to undermine the Party when the conflict with Hitler's Germany became inevitable? Had they perhaps studied Malinovskii, who had tried to hand over the entire Bolshevik Central Committee to the Okhrana? Trotsky and Malinovskii alike presented themselves as scions of the working class, concerned only about the Revolution—this made them doubly dangerous.

How could an intimate enemy be told apart from a loyal comrade? Might virtuous activists not innocently err from time to time? Ought a single error doom one to being cast out of the Bolshevik brotherhood? In order to be able to tell apart the souls of the befuddled comrade and the true provocateur, the Party developed a quasi-judicial practice I shall call the Bolshevik hermeneutics of the soul.[6] Because the inner recesses of the mind could not be read directly, the Bolshevik hermeneuts searched for the signs of dispositions that would permit them to gauge the private thoughts of each and every Party member, to "elucidate his or her character, to bring him or her into the open [*vyiavit*']."[7] Consider the following ruminations, from 1925, of a rank-and-file member on the difference between essence and appearance in the Bolshevik hermeneutics: "In judging people, we Communists should adduce external evidence least of all. . . . Instead we should monitor our comrades' internal inventory very closely. . . . Indeed, the Party's first duty is to expose the putrid insides of its members."[8]

As part of their investigation, the Bolshevik hermeneuts hoped to determine whether subjects acted intentionally or out of ignorance. When an oppositionist decided to recant, he always maintained that he had fallen into error thanks to "ideological backwardness" or "political shortsightedness," not because of something done deliberately. "There are mistakes and then there are mistakes," a Bolshevik columnist explained in 1924. "Unintentional mistakes, stemming from insufficient knowledge of the issue or from insufficient attention—this is one thing. But conscious mistakes must be combated with all our might, so that revisionism is nipped in the bud."[9] Once one knew why a mistake had been made one knew how to pass judgment. Questions of scientific truth and moral judgment, of consciousness and conscience, were intimately linked.

Without an understanding of the demonizing discourse that elided all differences between the oppositionist, the traitor, and the provocateur, no one can hope to grasp Stalin's cleansing campaigns, during which the Bolshevik notion of guilt— how it was established and punished—underwent a thorough revision. Over the years, tolerance for the type of defense that presented the accused as a comrade in error shrank and then nearly vanished. To understand this severity, to understand why nearly every Communist suspected of anti-Party activity was purged, we have to investigate the conceptual preconditions framing the Bolshevik search for the intimate enemy.

Despite the outcome of his appeal, Malinovskii's confession provided the model for the oppositionists' recantations of the 1920s and the 1930s, including the recantations of those arraigned for the Show Trials. They too confess to terrible crimes, express deep regret over their treacherous thoughts and actions, and go on to declare their undying devotion to the Revolution. On the day of his execution, August 24, 1936, Lev Kamenev, a major leader of the New Opposition from 1925, wrote: "I deeply regret my enormous crimes against the Proletarian Revolution and implore the presidium [of the Supreme Court] to spare my life, if this is not found to be at odds with Lenin and Stalin's enterprise."[10] Early in the morning of the same day Grigorii Zinoviev, the other leader of the New Opposition, had scribbled a note, reading in part: "I have told the proletarian court everything about the crimes I committed against Soviet power. I ask you to believe me, believe that I am no longer an enemy and that I want to contribute what remains of my life to the socialist motherland."[11]

Coolly considered, Malinovskii's 1918 trial and the Moscow Show Trials exhibit important differences. For example, while Malinovskii committed many of the crimes attributed to him, the Bolshevik oppositionists were largely innocent.

Threats and, possibly, torture drove Kamenev and Zinoviev to accept the indictment brought against them, but as we have seen, Malinovskii pleaded guilty from the outset. Yet in the context of the Great Purge these distinctions were elided.

If we are to understand how the confessions sounded by Kamenev and Zinoviev could be openly printed and how they could make sense to the Soviet populace, we must consider the genre of recantations that developed during the intra-Party struggles. After each defeat, oppositionists submitted "recantations" (*zaiavleniia ob otkhode*). Addressed to the bureau of the cell, the provincial Party committee, or the Central Committee, depending on the author's seniority, recantation letters stated that the author disassociated himself from the opposition, regretted ever joining it in the first place, and promised to stick to the Party line in the future. As oppositionists recanted, they typically did their best to show that they succeeded in fully purging themselves of all counterrevolutionary thoughts. Reapplying the poetics of Malinovskii's defense, a well-executed recantation traced the spiritual history of the offender's consciousness. The crux of the narrative was the attempt to explain and somehow justify the oppositionist lapse; generally this meant depicting the act of defiance as fleeting. The identification with the position of the Central Committee's majority allowed the penitent to claim that he had returned to the bosom of Party orthodoxy.[12]

The inquisitional character of interrogation, so prominent in Malinovskii's trial of 1918, dominated Soviet jurisprudence throughout. The prosecutors were interested in material facts only to the extent that these could be used as hermeneutical signs illuminating motives, and punishment was tailored to correspond to subjective guilt, not to objective injury. A pardon was forthcoming if Party members offended "unconsciously." Deliberate crimes, even if they led to little harm, had to be heavily punished.

The Bolshevik comrade courts can be described as legal institutions for a number of reasons. First, they had the trappings of court proceedings: true, there were no official prosecutors or defense counselors, but it is easy to identify individuals assuming these roles as cases were examined by the Party collective. Second, the accused was always present during hearings and was given the opportunity for self-defense. Indeed, he or she had the right to a final word and to an appeal. Third, deliberations always ended with some kind of censure—"reprimand," "warning," "purge"—that strongly resembles a court's verdict. Finally, and most importantly, the procedure was geared to assess culpability.[13] Party courts sought truth not in the formality of the judicial process but in the acumen of their hermeneuts; but that does not diminish their perception of themselves as judges establishing individual guilt.

The centrality of hermeneutics of the soul to the everyday functioning of the brotherhood of the elect suggests that notions such as revolutionary justice, intra-Party debating, deviation, and oppositionism, to name just a few, have to be examined against a new background. Events such as the ban on factions in March 1921, Lenin's Testament from December 1922, and the formation of Trotskyism in 1924–1925 will appear in a new light. Stalin's defeat of Zinoviev in 1926 and the purge of the leaders of the United Opposition in the autumn of 1927 also require a fresh interpretation. The protracted contest between the Central Committee majority and the various factions and groupings that challenged it will be shown less as a political battle and more as an ethical agon.

Bolsheviks understood opposition to be not so much a political platform as a spiritual predicament—a dangerous infirmity of consciousness. Because emancipatory truth was supposed to speak in a single voice, to be in opposition to the Central Committee meant to challenge proletarian truth, to become a source of discord in the brotherhood of the elect. "I know one cannot be right against the Party," Trotsky avowed in 1924, "for history has created no other way for the realization of its right."[14] Mikhail Pokrovskii agreed three years later that "If in our midst two opinions are encountered, then for us it is completely clear that one of them is undoubtedly wrong. Thank God, all of us are sufficiently Marxists, Leninists, and Communists" to accept this proposition, he noted with evident relief.[15]

Given this set of premises, the Party theorists found it difficult to explain how dissent could originate within a Bolshevik soul. How did the Party come to terms with this anomalous fact, the perseverance of dissent inside the Bolshevik camp? The hermeneutical diagnoses evolved over the years until a category was created, not this or that minority platform, not a current of opinion, a grouping, or a faction, but the opposition as such, a source of dangerous contamination that had to be contained. If in the early part of the decade the Party believed it had to cure the opposition, by the end of the 1920s, the opposition was declared to be deliberately treasonous and its supporters were arrested and exiled. During the Trade Union Discussion (1920–1921), support of a minority view was still compatible with Party affiliation, and the term "opposition" was not yet applied to all expressions of political freethinking. Oppositionists were reassured, given advice, and pardoned. Emerging on the scene six years later, the United Opposition (1926–1927), led by Trotsky, Kamenev, and Zinoviev, was already accused by the Stalinist leadership of violating sacred revolutionary principles. Allegedly setting up a second party, an anti-Party that was the Party's sinister shadow, the opposition was held guilty of intentional subversion.

I hope that the motif of the Black Mass—an image turned concept that is crucial to this book's argument—conveys something of the transformation of the opposition from an illness into a demonic crime. Christians described the Black Mass as a carefully conceived inversion of the sacred order. Instead of elaborating an independent set of rituals to suit their faith, Devil worshipers mocked God by styling their worship after orthodox Church rituals. Since it assumed that the Opposition related to the Party in the same way the Devil relates to God, the Stalinist leadership recognized in the nascent oppositionist organization a diabolical perversion of official Party ceremonies.[16] Even as it replicated orthodox Party trappings, the opposition deliberately inverted their meaning: Party cells became "oppositionist cells," Party conferences "factionalist gatherings," Party agitation departments "Trotskyist propaganda agencies," and all of this anti-Soviet activity was masterfully concealed behind emphatic calls for a return to true revolutionary values. Far from being innocuous and well-meaning comrades who temporarily lost their way, the worshippers of the oppositionist Black Mass were proclaimed in the late 1920s to be virulent and dangerous—a wicked cabal that had to be isolated. An excellent indication of the increasing identification of the opposition with the intimate enemy was the condemnation of Trotsky on the basis of paragraph fifty-eight of the penal code, specifically directed against "counterrevolutionaries."[17]

The transformation of the Bolshevik humor during the 1920s—another major theme in this book—gives us an additional angle from which to observe the growing demonization of the opposition. In the early days, bickering at Party congresses included a lot of mockery and ridicule, yet no one behaved as if he was irreparably humiliated. What amused the oppositionists made the Central Committee supporters sulk, and the reverse, but laughter seemed to have relaxed the atmosphere and eased anxieties. In teasing each other and scoffing at each other the contending groupings and factions suggested that the Bolshevik camaraderie remained intact. Since at the early stages no supporter of Trotsky or Zinoviev was indeed treated as an inveterate counterrevolutionary, speakers were clearly not attributing a serious meaning to these labels.

But the Bolshevik humor also had a more and more sinister ring, one that was amplified with the intensification of the intra-Party struggles. If in the early 1920s Party meetings devoted a great deal of energy to assaying different interpretations of revolutionary language, towards the end of the decade speakers were more and more interested in claiming they were the ones who incarnated that language. Debate over interpretation allowed for dialogue and persuasion, but there could be no compromise over who personified revolutionary lore. When the mirroring logic obtained and the warring parties made identical and yet mutually exclusive claims, the blows they exchanged struck more fiercely. The anxiety that the working class might be confused by the similarity of languages and mistake the wrong side for its true spokesman provoked some nervous giggles, not a hearty laughter. Humor became derogatory, completely indistinguishable from malice.

How could the oppositionists themselves make sense of their heterodox, defiant stance? Did they not agree that there could be only one truth and the Party was supposed to speak in a single voice? And if so, why would they willingly take on themselves the role of pollutants, the source of dissention in the proletarian camp? An inquiry into the Bolshevik ethics might hint at an answer. The Bolsheviks defined their moral worth through their individual response to the Party's emancipatory call: the truthful identified fully with the laws of history and yoked themselves to the revolutionary project.

What mediated between individual truth and collective truth and allowed the brotherhood of the elect to function was Lenin's famous principle of "democratic centralism" (*demokraticheskii tsentralizm*)—the alpha and omega of Bolshevik political theory and practice. "Democratic centralism" involved the election of officials responsible for running the Party's affairs but excluded the possibility that the decisions made by these officials would be challenged. The governing body was elected on a democratic basis. From that point on, however, centralism applied: everyone had to comply with the governing body.[18] The tension between the democratic and the centralist tendencies inherent in democratic centralism created the discursive space for the opposition phenomenon. On the one hand, opposition was abnormal since it went against centralism; on the other hand, opposition was a necessity because it instigated the democratic debate crucial for the hammering out of the Party line.

According to the Trotskyist narrative, opposition to the Central Committee had its origins in the safeguard of values that were supposed to be the concern of every Bolshevik but were for some reason neglected, or even betrayed. In such cases, dedicated comrades were supposed to prefer their consciousness to institutional authority: elections and support of numbers proved nothing since, according to the first principle of democratic centralism, the opinion of every comrade had to be reckoned with.

Had the opposition ranked comrades' individual judgment over the judgment of the central Bolshevik institutions? Was every comrade supposed to act as his own Party? Time and again, we will see the opposition throwing full responsibility for political judgments back onto the conscience of the individual. Time and again, oppositionist groupings would argue that in times of crisis, regular authority had to be replaced by charismatic authority. In 1904 Trotsky pointed to the tension between discipline and consciousness that cropped up in democratic centralism: "If the minority is compelled to violate what the majority calls discipline because it suppresses the vital interests of the movement, only one conclusion is possible: to hell with such 'discipline'!"[19] From this followed the first systematic defense of the right of the minority. "If a number of us in the Party have a separate point of view, we, the minority, will organize into a force," even if this meant doing away with centralism. Truth was more important. Trotsky asked:

Is it so difficult to understand that any movement obliged to choose either silence and self-obliteration for the sake of discipline, or a struggle for existence, will take the second road, so long as the movement is even slightly serious and important? This is so because discipline makes sense only when it secures the ability to struggle for what we think is right. . . . In the last eventuality, the representatives of the heretical current (*kramol'noe techenie*) either bring about a schism in the Party, thus rating discipline for the sake of their own principles above the "principles" of formal discipline, or they remain in the Party and try to . . . maximize their freedom to resist what they believe to be detrimental tendencies.[20]

Far from being a prerevolutionary idiosyncrasy, this defense of individual self-expression found support among a number of Bolshevik leaders, including Trotsky's opponents after 1917. Speaking in the name of Workers' Opposition, Aleksei Kiselev, a trade union leader, set truth before discipline at the Ninth Party Congress (1920): "There is a tendency on the part of our centers to diminish, weaken, and destroy the thinking of the Party's grass roots. . . . This is too bad: there are moments when an expression of independence [*samostoiatel'nost*] can play a decisive role in history."[21]

During the New Course Discussion (1923–1924) the tensions within democratic centralism surfaced again. Still a majoritarian, Kamenev stated in a speech given on January 1924: "There are comrades who believe that . . . the line of the Central Committee is wrong. Do they have the right to think so? Yes, they do. . . . And the one who thinks that the Central Committee line is wrong must, of course, begin an attack on the apparatus that implements that line."

A voice cut in: "So opposition is possible?"

"Of course it is possible," Kamenev answered.[22]

Trotsky, by then already an oppositionist, agreed: "A Bolshevik is not merely a man of discipline: he is a man who in each case and on every question forges a firm opinion of his own and defends it courageously and independently, not only against his enemies but also within his own Party."[23] Finally there was Lenin's widow Nadezhda Krupskaia, who reminded the delegates at the Fourteenth Party Congress (1925) that "for us Marxists, truth [*istina*] is what corresponds to reality," and that "there have been congresses in which the majority was in error." Individual responsibility in the pursuit of truth could not be overestimated: "Precisely because the congress must be the expression of collective thinking, every delegate must evaluate every question himself."[24]

Within the framework of democratic centralism, there could be no strictly constitutional solution to the crises of authority engulfing the Party from time to time. Trotsky, Kamenev, and Krupskaia could always beseech a comrade to trust his consciousness rather than his Party secretary, urge him to act in the name of revolutionary justice as he saw it. Oppositionists of various stripes claimed repeatedly that no one could predict who, of whatever status, would turn out to be speaking the proletarian truth.

So often did the interrogations of oppositionists return to conflicts between epistemological individualism and Party authority that this tension must be treated as the book's main axis. In the earlier chapters, we will see the Party attempting to negotiate the tension between the consciousness of individual members and its institutional structure without sidestepping "Party regulations" (*partiinyi ustav*). The Central Committee accepted a modicum of criticism; the opposition, for its part, bowed before the decisions of the Party congresses. Later on, however, a group of oppositionists felt compelled to break out of the institutional straitjacket by asserting the priority of their consciousness over what they perceived to be the degenerate Party leadership. A watershed in this connection was the readiness of some supporters of Trotsky to accept the title "oppositionist" as their own (1926–1927) and create an alternative political organization: they preferred to release the anchor of the Party, guaranteeing their collective emancipation, in order not to violate their own conscience.

Bolsheviks could not conceive of themselves outside the heroic framework of action, which initially involved a readiness to sacrifice one's life for the Revolution.[25] During the underground period (1898–1917), all Bolsheviks were heroes of sorts: did they not give up their personal security and the comforts of cozy bourgeois life for the sake of justice and equality? Were they not ready to rot in Siberian exile or even lose their lives in the battles of the Civil War so that the proletariat won? More than any other motif, "self-sacrifice" (*samopozhertvenost'*) featured in their self-presentation. Once tensions within the Party surfaced, and especially as the persecution of critics of the Central Committee began, the more radical among the oppositionists took on the colors of martyrs. Zuev, a student at the Tomsk Technological Institute, was described in 1927 as a "typical oppositionist, one affected by the spirit of heroism and selflessness [*samootverzhennost'*]." Chastised for his failure to report the wide dissemination of oppositionist literature at the school to the authorities, another oppositionist, Gorsunov explained that he was ready to risk everything "for the sake of the Revolution." According to the official report, one oppositionist at Leningrad Communist University had the temerity to present herself as a "martyr to the truth."[26]

Standing on the side of discipline, the majoritarians mocked such heroic posturing. The oppositionist, wrote Vasili Slepkov, a prominent youth activist, in 1926, "is always pompous, always messianic. He who betrays the proletarian cause always claims that he will save that cause, that he and he alone represents the interests of the proletariat."[27] Emel'ian Iaroslavskii, one of the heads of the Party's ethics police, was "scarcely inclined to kowtow before . . . the oppositionists' supposedly heroic, critically thinking personalities." Iaroslavskii ridiculed oppositionists' attempts to cover "a petit bourgeois deviation . . . behind their big names and their past revolutionary achievements."[28] Under this onslaught, the opposition asserted even more fiercely its right to the mantle of true Bolshevism.

There were many important disagreements within the Party over the course the Revolution should have taken. The wrangling sides agreed on so many common premises, however, that I will focus not only on the fierce debates separating the sides but also on shared premises. This search for discursive cohesion involves a partial erasure of the political persuasion of this or that comrade and the specific ideological context in which he spoke in favor of treating the fundamental discursive similarities and repetitions that outlined the accepted preconditions of speech. No one wanted to give up his membership in the epistemologically omnipotent proletarian vanguard, and everyone was fond of characterizing his rival's position as "unscientific," "backward," and therefore illegitimate. Stalinists and their rivals agreed that the proletariat was the sole arbiter of truth and that only Party members could speak in the name of the revolutionary movement as a whole. When viewed from this perspective, the opposition, in all its manifestations, hardly seems to be the comprehensive conceptual alternative to Stalinism it has been called.[29]

While some historians ask their readers to believe that the study of archival materials would convince anyone that "all that could justly be criticized in Stalinism had already been stated by the Communist oppositionists,"[30] and that "a Trotsky regime would have been much less hard on Russia,"[31] I will show that the examination of recently unearthed documents suggests that the presuppositions on which the opposition's argument was founded did not deviate in its core assumptions from what is normally identified with Stalinism. Both the Central Committee majority and the opposition maintained that there was only one path to the light and only one platform that could show correctly what that path was—and claimed that the adversary undermined proletarian emancipation. The belief in the singularity of history explains the refusal of the sides to compromise. The battle between the oppositionists and the Stalinists was then hardly a savage repression of the conscientious, democratic part of the Party by the merciless and totalitarian part. What really happened was more like two heroic groups, the supporters of the opposition and the supporters of the Central Committee, involved in simultaneous self-fashioning in a hall of distorting mirrors: self-representation, the transmission of that image to the other, and a reflection of the image in aggrandized, distorted form. "Two rival and quasi-messianic beliefs seemed pitted against one another," comments Isaac Deutscher.[32]

■

Focusing on the form of Bolshevik politics, not its contents, I have not set out to document the secret history of the Politburo, Lenin's illness and the fierce succession struggle that followed, or to review the Byzantine intrigues that accompanied Stalin's rise to power. Little space will be dedicated to economics, international relations, the army, propaganda, and so on. I do not say much about why the Bolshevik debating evolved so that the opposition was delegitimized over the course of the 1920s but only trace the linguistic shifts that heralded this process.

Is it possible to discuss the Bolshevik discourse of the 1920s without incorporating the social context into analysis? Political rhetoric may be important, some scholars would say, but it does not exist in a vacuum and does not operate independently—language is spoken by living people with their own backgrounds, interests, and circumstances. However, my analysis does not presuppose the existence of a multilayered social structure so that language somehow expresses the social interests lurking behind it. Instead, I treat language as a constitutive force that brings society into being in the first place. I show how the meaning of political language was activated by other meanings and how political behavior was modified in and by the political process itself.[33]

In fact, a question mark might be put before the notion of society itself—the sacred cow of so much historiography.[34] For society is too often interpreted as something fixed, a field where social agents vie for power and privilege. No matter how fluid and heterogeneous society is, or how complex and conflicted its constitutive components are said to be, society remains a totality in such accounts. According to this approach, the historian is supposed to place himself, at least temporarily, outside the society he studies and examine it dispassionately from an external vantage point. While some scholars tend to ignore the fact that society is not a reality but a construct—a discursively mediated notion that never fully actualizes itself—I suggest that many imaginary societies coexist within a single political discourse hoping to be realized, and that the historian cannot, and should not, totalize his knowledge.

While the surge in intra-Party violence has been studied within the context of Soviet economics, politics, and society, I suggest that this phenomenon is better addressed through the examination of a set of messianic ideas and practices that the Russian Revolution implemented. By examining how the revolutionary discourse was embodied, put to work, and contested at the various levels of the Party apparatus, I hope to transcend the reductive understanding of language widespread in current scholarship. Sidestepping high politics and the decision-making process within the Bolshevik elite, I focus on how the official discourse—the language and ritual of the Communist Party in the 1920s—was appropriated at the grassroots level.[35] A series of microstudies undertaken below enable me to examine the daily interactions between the Bolshevik rank and file, provincial and central Party organs, and official discourse on the opposition. The archives unfold before us the minutes of endless discussions, edifications, and heated arguments, as well as a series of autobiographies and recantations in which individuals spoke about themselves, their values, and their opinions openly and in great detail.

Drawing material not only from the minutes of the Moscow Party congresses but also from institutions of higher learning in Petrograd-Leningrad and Siberia, the focus below will be on how ideology was interpreted by the grass roots, not on how Party policy was conceived by the center. While I do not ignore the peculiarities of the regions from which the material is taken, my aim is to provide a set of microstudies—not regional studies. Rather than comparing specific geographical areas and their social relations, I intend to examine the ways in which Bolshevik political identities were negotiated in specific arenas—imagined communities in the process of self-purification.

What follows, then, is not a history of the Party, its institutions, personnel, and internal politics, but what might be termed an archaeology of the Bolshevik discourse on the opposition.[36] I am interested in the particular sets of practices and language games that brought about and assigned to Party members different subject positions and that claimed to adjudge who is playing by the rules and who is not, who should be promoted as a loyal Bolshevik and who should be cast out as a repeat offender.[37] "Party Discussions"—the official deliberating periods that preceded a Party congress—are treated here as an institutionally embedded ritual filled with rhetorical maneuvers, innuendos, victories, and losses.[38] My analysis takes the form of an interactional ethnography of the ways of speaking that were used by Party members in enacting their encounters and in which they mutually construct their political identities.[39] And politics emerges as a discursive enterprise, a struggle over the coining of political terms, their interpretation and embodiment. I am interested here not in the why of Soviet history but in the what and the how—not why certain things happened to certain oppositionists at certain times but how the opposition was construed and how it was treated.[40]

Nowhere is the work of the new discourse more evident that in the Party meetings–the base of the Bolshevik institutional life and the main source for the present study. In describing the struggle over who gets to implement Party policy and how, protocols document the process through which new political rituals were constituted and elaborated. Every Party meeting, not only at the central Party congresses but also at the primary Party cells, was carefully recorded by a stenographer. These thick folders contain a considerable number of transcripts, sometimes a number of pages long. Many of the turbulent and intense beliefs of the revolutionary era emerge from these transcripts, which were abbreviated and condensed by the stenographers to keep up with what must have been very animated and contentious debates. The attentive student of these records soon becomes familiar with the language Bolsheviks used in addressing each other and can trace fine shifts in terminology. The transcripts detail the perceptions of comrades and foes, trust and suspicion—I sometimes feel I am reading not Party documents but the field notes of an anthropologist.[41]

Remaining at the level of the phenomena, I treat the language of these transcripts with utmost seriousness. The reader might in fact be struck by a certain congruence between Bolshevik metahistory and my own reconstruction of Soviet history, for I argue that the Bolshevik perception of their own historical conjuncture—where they were in their revolutionary quest and what had to be done to bring it to conclusion—had very tangible effects. Indeed, what drives events forward in both narratives—the principles of eschatological time reckoning—appears strangely similar. Of course, such an approach stands the risk of being dismissed as historical naiveté: taking what he finds in the archive at face value, the historian, so the charge would go, does not approach sources critically. Focusing on what the archive reveals, he is blind to what the archive supposedly conceals—intrigues, passions, real people. Should we not assume that, at least from time to time, documents mean something other than what they say? Is there a point in writing history, if we do not distinguish between saying and meaning, the statement and the intention behind it? No wonder that historians who adopt this interpretative skepticism tend to pride themselves on the distance they achieve vis-à-vis the source base they study. It is true that I am reluctant to employ a principle of historical causality extrinsic to the one used by the Bolsheviks. It is equally true that I take very seriously not only what contemporaries were doing but also what they were saying they were doing. Indeed, instead of establishing a critical distance from the Soviet sources, I opt for a good measure of intimacy with them. The Bolshevik language, as it were, contaminates my narrative.

It is my claim, however, that the approach I take has its benefits: by remaining at the level of the contemporary discourse itself, I am trying to show how discourse operates and with what consequences. An effort is made herein to transcend the self-understanding of contemporaries by showing that these consequences were unknown to those who "spoke Bolshevik."[42] Neither language producers nor language consumers are always fully aware of what is implicit in the language they use. What is often said of human economic and social activity can also be said of language, namely, that language use has unintended results.[43] The Bolsheviks ended up committing hair-raising acts that they hardly expected would follow from the humanistic principles that, they were convinced, shaped the revolutionary project. But once entrenched in the tissue of power relations that structured the Bolshevik discourse, providing it a frame of reference and setting standards of conformity, messianic dreams could not be easily curbed, even when some of their horrific implications became evident.

To be sure, human intentions and a certain manipulative approach to language cannot be completely ignored—Party members used language as a tool to achieve their goals.[44] At the same time, it is imperative to penetrate their language and make it, as it were, speak against itself. Certain slippages are symptomatic because intention is always subverted. We do not have to postulate some kind of a radical separation between identity and discourse against which the speaker was constantly dissimulating. Rather, the forces that shaped the Bolshevik public sphere constituted a field of play delimited by a set of beliefs and practices. The speaker was neither an actor essentially possessed of agency, nor a puppet of language. And agency was produced in the course of practices under a whole gamut of more or less explicit disciplinary constraints.[45] There can scarcely be an identity outside language: I discard the notion of an agent whose sense of selfhood remains unchanged to advance the notion of a self that comes into being in different ways, depending on a changing linguistic context.[46]

If historians have in the past been inclined to view the human species as a given, explaining differences in terms of reactions to varying social, political, and cultural contexts, recent research suggests that subjectivity can be a fascinating agenda of research in its own right.[47] No longer must we imagine a universal self putting on a range of disguises based on its environment; revolutionary discourse helps the self reflect upon itself, articulate itself, and assume its concrete outline.[48] The identity of the Bolsheviks examined over the course of this book becomes a locus of discourse, not of a fixed selfhood.[49] Because the self is always in flux, constantly reinvented, the personal narratives are treated below as something that encompasses radical discontinuities and ruptures. Self-presentations constantly changed not because Bolsheviks were exceptionally self-seeking and opportunistic, but because at moments of crisis the revolutionary discourse called on them to rethink and retell their life stories, adding new insights into why they behaved the way they did.[50] No one entered the 1920s as a Trotskyist, a Zinovievist, or a Stalinist. Individuals emerged as such following long and complicated negotiations, sometimes embracing their new identity, other times forced into it.

Verbal formulas are voiced below by rather abstract name-bearers, usually without first names and almost always also without intentions, material circumstances, and so on. To identify the oppositionists in personal terms I have to rely on the biographical information my protagonists provided to Party authorities and to their peers and the denunciations their opponents launched against them. Unfortunately, we simply do not have a broader spectrum of documents pertaining to the lives of our protagonists.[51] On a deeper plane, however, I want to emhasize that it is futile to search for the oppositionist's true self or to attempt to return his voice to its pristine condition—one cannot escape the filter of the official language that produced the voice in the first place. The context I am interested in is in the text—the discursive presupposition of the protagonists' speech. What I emphasize is not personal background and interests but the rhetorical strategies historical figures employed, the institutions and rituals they enlisted to have their definition of reality prevail.[52] To the extent that biographical information is treated here, it is regarded as a discursive category, a part of an already existing though never stable regime of self. What is important is not whether this or that figure revealed the truth about his life according to our present-day criteria, but how and why the genre of recantation and the ritual of the hermeneutical interrogation constructed every deposition as the revelation of an interior truth.

Diverse institutions and practices that went into the Bolshevik hermeneutic of the self allowed the creation of pragmatic typologies that made it possible to distinguish between the good and the wicked, the loyalists and the oppositionists. The Party cell was a place of systematic and coded observation of the individual

—a practice informed by the ideological propagandist, the medico-psychological expert, and the judge. The general framework of this enterprise remained remarkably stable over the years—Party hermeneuts always obsessed by the relations between errant comrades and wicked foes. The same fundamental question that animated comrade trials went on to haunt the Party's Central Control Commission's hearings, and prosecutors might have phrased it thus: Is the accused corrigible or irredeemable? But if we are to account for the changes that did occur between 1918 (the first cleavages in the Bolshevik government) and 1928 (Trostky's forced exile) we must look within the discourse itself, and there we find that as the Bolshevik perception of the present evolved, hermeneutical judgments became harsher and harsher. At first the opposition was construed as an illness to be healed; by the late 1920s it became a wickedness that had to be extirpated. Stalin's apparatus diagnosed opposition as a hopeless mental predicament, one that transcends a political position per se, and assimilated it into the stereotype of the intimate enemy, along with Malinovskii and the rest of the traitors who threatened to undermine the Party from within. Guilt was relocated from a person's background and upbringing to the heart of his being—the moral self.

CHAPTER I

OPPOSITIONISM AS A MALADY OF THE MIND

The Authority of the Party Congress

During the first years of the Soviet regime, Party congresses, "the brain of the organized proletariat," met annually to set policy and to act out the range of Bolshevism's fraternal rituals in full regalia.[1] Kamenev, the chairman of the Moscow soviet, called the congresses "the only arena where a politically responsible individual can say what he thinks about how the Party and the country can be helped."[2] The right to speak out belonged to any delegate who "is in the Party ranks and suffers the same hardships the Party suffers."[3]

The minutes of the Bolshevik congresses merit close study precisely because in them we can observe Party discourse in the making. The delegates could communicate through language because they believed that what they meant was directly embodied in language as the medium of discussion. But to understand the effect of Bolshevik speech it is not sufficient to comprehend to what the words refer. It is also necessary to grasp the pragmatic force of the utterance, which may be expressed solely in the tone of voice or the grammar of the utterance, sometimes unbeknownst even to the speaker. To understand how language led the Bolsheviks by the nose, we have to steep ourselves in their political vernacular and give voice to premises too often unspoken. Once we have articulated these shared assumptions—which often concern society, politics, and history—we shall be in a better position to spot the connections between seemingly discrete and unrelated notions and to appreciate their significance in the Bolshevik discourse.[4]

One could hardly imagine a better view into what may be called the Bolshevik public sphere than the Party congress. Of course the application of this term to Bolshevism is rather problematic.[5] If by public sphere we mean a venue to which all are free to come to exchange ideas without state intrusion, then a Bolshevik public sphere is an oxymoron. In revolutionary Russia state and society were fused, and the right to participate in political deliberations was restricted to Party members. However, the term "public sphere" can also refer to that public site where a struggle breaks out over the new forms of political language, where contests determine a pecking order of speakers and opinions, and where men and women teach one another what can be said and what cannot. Every word uttered was carefully weighed: after all, delegates were aware that the printed proceedings were being sent even to the most remote Party organizations, read aloud, and analyzed at endless political literacy lessons.[6]

As we examine the records, we must constantly be alert to who is speaking and when.[7] Which of the delegates used language with the greatest authority? How did he or she exploit the right to mount the podium, and from there to advance criticisms, articulate countertheses, and announce rebuttals?[8] The tension between the ingrained equality in the brotherhood of the elect and the rank imposed by function and Party seniority played a role in determining what happened during a given session.[9] One could say that there was, on the one hand, revealed doctrine, and on the other there were those whose personal or institutional authority commanded attention, but in fact, the line between the two sides was swept away. Political decision making relied not only on criteria of knowledge and ideology but also on Party regulations, ethical imperatives, and procedural norms—the constituent elements of the Bolshevik political ritual.[10]

No "discussion" (diskussiia) was supposed to begin with agreement; enforced unanimity was described at the Twelfth Party Congress as "non-Marxist."[11] In prerevolutionary times, Lenin wanted to see "normal relations between Party members who think differently [nesoglasno mysliashchie]."[12] And after the seizure of power, Alexander Lozovskii was still proud that "passionate discussions characterize our party. Whatever we do, we do with a fury."[13]

The individual at the peak of the pyramid held no absolute monopoly on truth; rather, truth emerged from a complex and highly ritualized series of exchanges between the various Bolshevik strata. Naturally, Lenin's words carried more weight than the words of other Central Committee members, the words of the Central Committee members carried more weight than the words of the provincial delegates, and so on. And yet a statement drew its force not only from the authority of the speaker but also from his or her mastery of political language. Without discourse, there can be no power: this is particularly so under an ideologically based regime. How can we explain the long hours consumed by innumerable Party meetings unless we take the Bolshevik culture of debate seriously?[14]

The Bolsheviks were committed to giving the greatest power to the rank and file, and no regulation expressed this more clearly than the supremacy of the congress and its power to elect the Party leadership. Guided not by local prejudice but by a general commitment to the Revolution, the delegates gathered in Moscow resembled not at all an assembly of agents aching to promote particularist interests. Though every delegate had been chosen by a particular Party organization, he or she was free to decide what promoted the interests of the Revolution as a whole.

"What should we do when delegates were instructed to vote in a certain way?" wondered a member of the presidium of the Ninth Party Congress. He was informed that the "Party's established practice is that at the congress delegates know no constraints, no mandates, and they are obligated only to explain later on to their home organizations what arguments convinced them to vote as they did."[15]

Between the congresses, which were supposed to be convened annually, authority was vested in the Central Committee elected by the congress.[16] At the outset, the Central Committee, a body saddled with the task of "resolving questions of world importance," was elected in a rather ad hoc fashion at a regular meeting of the Party congress, and was expected to meet twice a month at the so-called plenary session.[17] Watched over by the spirits of those earlier Russian legislators who had assembled in Moscow's Kremlin before them, the members of the Central Committee debated and hammered out the major policies of the day. Kollontai defined this body as "the main political and ideological organ, leading the way for our Soviet institutions, correcting their ideological orientation, regulating their class spirit."[18] "No organization in the nation has more prestige and power than the Central Committee," Grigorii Zinoviev, the chairman of the Petrograd soviet, agreed. "This is because for the last twenty-five years it has been absorbing everything in the Party with any authority."[19]

The excellence of the Central Committee members had little to do with position or expertise—it resided in their superior revolutionary spirit. In his obituary for the legendary Party secretary Sverdlov, Nikolai Krestinskii spoke of a comrade who "introduced comradely unity, personal love and intimacy into our party."[20] Aleksandrov, a delegate to the Eighth Party Congress from Orel, trusted Central Committee members "intuitively" since he had been impressed with their theoretical acumen.[21] Even while bitterly criticizing the Party leadership, Vladislav Kosior, a trade union activist, noted that he was not suggesting that the Twelfth Party Congress "look for better Central Committee members. Where would we find such people?"[22]

As awe-inspiring as a position on the Central Committee may have appeared at certain moments, it was not unassailable. Should a member's consciousness prove inferior, his will at odds with the true will of the proletariat, demotion instantly followed. "You have probably noted that every congress replaces about one-third of the membership of our Central Committee," Zinoviev said at the Ninth Party Conference. "The Party is evidently still looking for its true Central Committee."[23] At the following Party Congress, Ivar Smilga, a prominent member of the Revolutionary Military Council who had recently lost his seat on the Central Committee, insisted that the body was no "House of Lords"—no one was a member for life. "The Party keeps in the Central Committee only those comrades who reflect its convictions and attitudes most clearly and precisely."[24]

Official policy never escaped criticism at the Party Congresses; in fact, the abuse many heaped on the official line throughout 1918–1921 attests to a great openness of debate. Lenin's willingness to accept the humiliating German peace terms at Brest-Litovsk in 1918 came under severe criticism at the Seventh Party Congress held later that year: Trotsky, the head of the Red Army, and Nikolai Bukharin, the editor of *Pravda*, assumed an ultra-leftist position and declared their preference for revolutionary war to this humiliating pact with the German barons.[25] According to Krestinskii, "things came to a near schism [*poluraskol*]. We had to fight hard for the ideological unification of the Party after the congress ended ... [and] for the return to activity of the major comrades from the opposition."[26]

In 1918–1919, the Central Committee majority was challenged again, this time by the Group for Democratic Centralism (*gruppa demokraticheskogo tsenrtral-izma*).[27] These men certainly acknowledged Lenin's authority, but they did not fear it—and all were highly respected Bolshevik veterans. Vladimir Smirnov, for example, had presided over the armed uprising in Moscow in 1917 and served on the Council on Labor and Defense; Timofei Sapronov, another name that will crop up frequently in the following pages, was the head of the Small Sovnarkom. Finally, there was Nikolai Osinskii, perhaps the most outspoken Democratic Centralist, a renowned economist and the deputy head of the Commissariat of Agriculture in the early 1920s.[28]

Shrewdly drawing the name of their group from the organizational principle Lenin had described long before 1917, the Group for Democratic Centralism called on the Party to return to the organizational principles it had recently abandoned.[29] Without "freedom of opinion," Sapronov argued, the dictatorship of the proletariat would not last.[30] Time and again the leaders of the Democratic Centralist group assailed the Central Committee for its failure to develop good communications channels between the center and the grassroots Party organizations. Pointing to the need to curtail authoritarian elements in the proletarian dictatorship, they argued that "the principle of one-man management encourages arbitrariness and personal ambition."[31] At the Eighth Party Congress (1919), Sapronov criticized Lenin for a "lack of collegiality in Party and state activity" and proposed that lower-ranking Party members be admitted to the Central Committee, "so that this organ will benefit from better connections to the masses."[32] And when his suggestion was not immediately taken up, Sapronov repeated it: "Take into account the experience of the local areas—this will make our Revolution invincible."[33]

At the Ninth Party Congress (March–April 1920) Lenin again found his plans harried by the Democratic Centralists.[34] He was challenged by "co-reporters" (*so-dokladchiki*), a sort of Bolshevik devil's advocates whose right to criticize official policy was stipulated in Party regulations.[35] Osinskii was the co-reporter for economic issues, while Vladimir Maksimovskii, the deputy head of the Narkompros, held the analogous role for organizational issues; both essentially repeated already familiar criticisms.[36] The bureaucratically constituted "political departments" had to go; a crucial element of the Democratic Centralists' plan was the freeing of local Party committees from the direct control of the Moscow Secretariat—a body registering and assigning Party personnel.[37]

Toward the end of the Civil War, critical voices mounted. Now that the immediate danger to the young regime had been throttled, many Bolsheviks wanted to resist the centralizing trend of Soviet politics. A group that shared some of the concerns of the Democratic Centralists was the Workers' Opposition (*rabochaia oppozitsiia*), and it soon became the most outspoken of the oppositionist groups.[38] The leaders of this group were Aleksandr Shliapnikov, one of the heroes of the direct action taken by the working class in 1917, and Aleksandra Kollontai, the doyenne of Bolshevik feminism; they and their followers targeted the noticeable retreat from the important achievements won for the Russian working class during the Revolution.[39] The growing "chasm" between workers and the party that claimed to speak in their name drove the Workers' Opposition to urge the masses on to a greater range of activities.[40]

Shliapnikov's theses, together with Kollontai's articles, became the programmatic documents of the Workers' Opposition.[41] The main demand articulated in these documents was the immediate transfer of the running of the national economy into the hands of the trade unions.[42] No wonder that among the leaders of the Workers' Opposition were Ivan Kutuzov and Sergei Medvedev, the heads of the textile and metal trade unions, respectively.[43] Because the economy, according to the scheme, was supposed to be run by a "national congress of producers," the Workers' Opposition demanded that the Party withdraw from the direct management of industry.[44] Furthermore, the leaders of the group had conceived of measures to reduce the bureaucracy in Party and state institutions, partly by purging from the Party all nonproletarian elements, and partly by paying closer attention to the well-being of the masses.[45]

Party regulations helped to ritualize and defuse clashes of opinion. Before each congress the Central Committee distributed its newest set of "theses" (*tezisy*) around the country to persuade Party members of the soundness of its policy over the previous year. In a parallel move, opposition groups advanced "countertheses" (*kontrtezisy*) voicing their criticisms. Communists could sign any number of theses that were subsequently presented to the Party congress as policy suggestions. "I have a habit," Shliapnikov noted: "if I agree with a program I read, I sign the document."[46]

But the distinction between the Central Committee and the opposition— whether in terms of policy, organization, or personnel—was usually arrived at only ex post facto: the Central Committee could split into any number of groups, each of which would drum up support for its own position. Especially in the early years, no one really knew which group had majority support. "Comrades point out that we are in opposition," Bukharin noted at the Eighth Party Congress (1918). "True, we are in the minority now. But only a few days ago we were certain that the majority ... was following our lead."[47]

In terms of Bolshevik political theory there was nothing terribly threatening about a clash of platforms as such.[48] In fact, heated debate served the crucial role of keeping the Party on the alert. According to Nikolai Skrypnik, a Bolshevik leader from the Ukraine, "the importance of the discussion resides in everybody's license to express his point of view." Before the congress stated otherwise, disputes were generally held to be not only tolerable but actually advisable.[49] In his review of the "animated debates" of 1919, Trotsky praised the Bolshevik contentiousness: "Questions were not glossed over, and a principled battle raged around key issues."[50] How extensive the discussion should be was a question posed in stark terms at the Ninth Party Congress. Should opponents only state their points, or should the pros and the cons of each point be belabored in detail, "comrades speaking for and against," as Osinskii and the Democratic Centralists insisted?[51] Such a procedure appealed to Karl Radek, a Central Committee member who was himself on the "defiant Left" during the Brest debates of 1918, since he believed that when all was said and done the oppositionists would admit defeat: "We got the extensive discussion of our proposals we wanted at the congress and it was proven to us that our position was mistaken."[52] Anatolii Lunacharskii, the commissar of enlightenment, was also in favor of a "wide and absolutely sincere discussion."[53]

Given the wide array of venues that the Party made available, including the Party cell meetings, district and provincial conferences, in addition, of course, to the supreme Party congress itself, Bolsheviks were expected to express themselves in full. "Hearing little from the congressional tribune but a great deal of backstage criticism," Shliapnikov did not hesitate to "provoke Party members into talking. After all, the sight of a displeased Communist audience sitting quietly is eerie."[54] The Bolsheviks wanted all mediation between the individual and the Party torn down so that the conscience of the individual and the messianic goals of the Party would naturally coincide. The Central Committee demanded absolute submission to its decrees but not blind acceptance. Few things were worse than "blindness," a frequent metaphor for capitalist obtuseness, and all comrades were expected to see clearly.

Only discussion could lead one to a conscious acceptance of Party policy. To disseminate news about the debates in Moscow and draw the ranks in, the Ninth Party Congress instituted the so-called *Discussion Sheet* (*diskussionnyi listok*), a periodical published by the Central Committee beginning in January 1921.[55] In Zinoviev's words, this was supposed to be produced by "a Central Committee press organ to permit every Party member to express his point of view on the burning issues."[56]

An opportunity for the rank and file to speak out in a widely publicized forum, the Party Congress marked the heyday of "workers' democracy."[57] Given the Bolshevik axiom that political participation would broaden with the expansion of consciousness, the role of democracy in historical progress could not be doubted. The opposition insistently tugged the Party towards democratization. Osinskii, the chairman of the Tula soviet at the time, feared that a center that could be quite "arbitrary" would derail these efforts and urged a "shift away from military discipline."[58] The need for a broad democracy, other Central Committee speakers insisted, was evident "not only during relaxation but, especially, at a time of danger."[59] Noting that "workers refuse to serve as voting machines or beasts of burden," Korzinov, a delegate from Orenburg, wanted to see the rank and file "collectively hammering out the Party line."[60]

With the cessation of the Civil War, the Party had to "turn their faces to the masses"—in this the leadership of the Central Committee agreed with its critics.[61] "We have to learn to distinguish between democracy and a chain of military command," Bukharin urged. "In the first case every issue is put to discussion, in the second case we have a top-down transmission system—the two could hardly be more different from one another."[62] But woe betide he who would tip the delicate balance too far in the democratic direction, warned the Central Committee. While it certainly was an important Bolshevik value, "democracy was not always applicable." It was Radek who pointed that out at the Tenth Party Congress (March 1921) and went on to insist that "delegates returning home must be instilled not so much with the idea that democracy has to be preserved . . . as with the idea that the Party has to gather its energy for the defense of the Revolution."[63] Quite regretfully, Smilga seconded this opinion, noting that "democracy has to be mitigated"; he maintained that the Party had to continue relying on its political power rather than counting on the weak consciousness of the population.[64]

What side of the equation was supposed to be emphasized, democracy or centralism? It was impossible to be sure. Democracy pulled in the direction of epistemological individualism: every rank-and-file Party member could potentially undergo a personal enlightenment, and every Party leader could turn out to be a conduit for petit bourgeois interests. Centralism, on the other hand, would tend to insist on obedience to the most recent decisions of the Party Congress. Every majority decision, even if misguided or shortsighted, would have to be carried out. Consciousness superseded and eclipsed all other criteria, or to put it slightly differently, there were no formal criteria. No procedure could distinguish the democratic, legitimate opinion from the others; it was strictly a matter of revolutionary inspiration.

Of course, to suggest that the Bolsheviks totally disrespected formal stipulations would be to go too far—violation of the procedures called for in the Party regulations (*ustav*) was strictly interdicted.[65] Even when the rules of the game were moot or changing, it was assumed that rules existed and should be followed.[66] In the debates of the early 1920s, the argument often focused on degree: the members of the Central Committee granted that victory in the Civil War had to go hand in hand with grassroots initiatives but added that utopian times were not yet upon them and that a good deal of centralism should therefore be retained. Some official spokesmen regarded the vote of the majority sacrosanct; others were more interested in how "the mature [*zrelye*] comrades voted."[67]

There were arguments and more arguments: the key was to know when to argue, about what, and for how long. "In the distant past, while deep underground, we used to have heated disputations ," Mikhe Tskhakaia, a Georgian Party veteran recalled. "We argued for whole nights, to white heat. But in the morning we would have tea together and return to our practical work in a comradely fashion."[68] Lutovinov, a delegate from the Donbass who sided with the Workers' Opposition, explained that defeat could be swallowed if it arose as the result of a due process: "As long as no resolution had been issued . . . we defended our principles. But a decision was reached and we now have a law. We have never contemplated sabotaging a decree issued by the congress or the Central Committee."[69]

The discussion was an orderly debate within the brotherhood of the elect, not the public washing of dirty linen. When Party etiquette was breached, when hard words were spoken and the uninitiated became embroiled, this was generally perceived as a serious setback. On one occasion Lenin distinguished between two forms of discussion, "exchange of opinions," which was not only acceptable but encouraged, and "political struggle," utterly prohibited.[70]

To appreciate the true variety in the Party's landscape during the 1920–1921 discussion, let us briefly review election campaigns to the Tenth Party Congress that sparked considerable disputatiousness, one in the center (Moscow) and two in the provinces (Ekaterinburg and Samara).[71] A range of different groups crowded the Party arena, where various platforms clashed. With the Central Committee formally acknowledging the "right of every organization to have its own opinions and to nominate its own reporters," Bolshevik politics looked almost liberal: opinions proliferated, leaders switched sides, and votes cut several ways.[72]

A heated precongress discussion was played out against the backdrop of a deepening split within the Central Committee itself. It was during the plenary session of November 8–9, 1920, that three factions within the Party leadership emerged: one led by Trotsky, who called for the militarization of the trade unions;[73] a group headed by Lenin known as "The Ten"[74] (Kalinin, Stalin, Rudzutak, and others) and identified with support for their relative independence; and a "buffer group" (Zinoviev, Kamenev, Rykov) that more modestly advocated the absorption of the trade unions into the state structure.[75] And then there was the Workers' Opposition.[76] Because no support from the Central Committee was forthcoming, Shliapnikov and Medvedev spread their gospel through the Union of Metal Workers, which supported them almost unanimously.[77] The union's central committee sent a directive to all its branches urging the election of as many supporters of the Workers' Opposition as possible.[78]

Such vigorous campaigning lent Party meetings a febrile intensity.[79] No less than eight Party platforms competed for the vote of the Moscow Communists.[80] When three hundred delegates met at the Moscow Provincial Party Conference (February 19–21, 1921) to elect delegates to the Tenth Party Congress, "harsh words" were exchanged.[81] Though the Central Committee repeated incessantly that including all its "variants" (*raznovidnosti*) the Moscow opposition did not exceed one-sixth of the local membership, tensions ran high. Three speakers took up the question of Party building. Kamenev expressed the view of the Moscow Party committee (gentle balance between the top and the bottom), E. N. Ignatov advanced the position of the Workers' Opposition (more power to workers), and Andrei Bubnov defended the position of the Democratic Centralists (democratization); they received 251, 57, and 30 votes respectively.[82] Because elections to the local and national Party bodies were based on platforms, the vote was divided (see table 1). A highly fragmented election by later Bolshevik standards, this four-way Moscow outcome actually reflected a simplification of the political landscape: it had been achieved only after two consolidations: the buffer group with Trotsky, and Korzinov's group with Ignatov's.[83]

A myriad of platforms, programs, and individuals had competed for the vote during the 1920–1921 discussion, and Trotsky's minority views attracted widespread enthusiasm in the Urals.[84] He had traveled to Ekaterinburg as a delegate of the Council of Labor and Defense and ended up taking an active part in the local discussions. The best-known Communists in the region attached their names to his platform, which went on to be adopted by the Ural bureau of the Central Committee. Still, when the decisive showdown took place at the Fifth Ekaterinburg Provincial Party Conference (February 18–22, 1921), Lenin's group managed to turn the tide, wining 159 out of 226 votes.[85]

Although the Workers' Opposition did very well in the east of the country and in the Ukraine, Samara was the only province it managed to take over; out of

TABLE 1. The Outcome of Party Elections in Moscow (1920)

Platform	Seats on the Moscow Party Committee	Delegates to the Tenth Party Congress
"Ten"	28	27
Trotsky's proposal	6	6
Workers' Opposition	6	6
Democratic Centralism	2	2

Sources: *Kommunisticheskii trud*, February 19, 20, 22 and 23, 1921; *Pravda*, February 24, 25, and 27, 1921; G. Zinoviev, *Sochineniia*, vol. 6, pp. 618–24; *Moskovskaia gubernskaia konferentsiia RKP(b): Kratkii otchet i rezoliutsii* (Moscow, 1921), p. 5.

twenty-five newly elected members of the Samara provincial Party committee, sixteen were supporters of the Workers' Opposition.[86]

In sum, noted Lenin at the Tenth Party Congress, "we had the most open, wide,
and free discussion possible. The platform of 'Workers' Opposition' was reproduced in 250,000 copies by our central printing press."[87] "The Central Committee
satisfied our request that everyone be acquainted with what we have to say," Medvedev granted Lenin's point.[88] According to the Petrograd Party organization, the
decision to allow platform-based elections ensured that "different shades of opinion receive proportional representation at the congress."[89] There would be forty-
five delegates supportive of the Workers' Opposition platform at the Tenth Party
Congress.[90]

The fact that the staffing of the presidium, a body responsible for procedure,
was carried out in accordance with the view that every opinion deserved to be represented is another indication of the pluralistic nature of the Tenth Party Congress.[91] "All currents and shades existing in our party have to be included in the presidium," said Yakov Drobnis, the delegate from Odessa.[92] When it turned out that
Democratic Centralism received no representation after all,[93] Dmitrii Manuil'skii, a
Ukrainian commissar of agriculture who served on the organizational committee,
apologized: "First, the list of presidium members was drawn up by looking at the
candidates as individuals—we tried to include those with the highest Party prestige. Second, we had to keep the principle of territorial representation in mind, so
the presidium includes representatives of all the major provincial Party organizations. Finally, the principle of combinatorics had to be applied and slots assigned to
members of the Workers' Opposition."[94]

What makes the winter of 1920–1921 remarkable is that fractious politics was
perceived as a normal state of affairs—the election results laid out above were official and were publicized as such in the Party press.[95] The pattern of the campaigning just outlined, which included a plurality of platforms and a great emphasis on
alliances between factions, was not to be repeated in the years to come. We should
carefully assess how things were done in those early years not only because the discussion preceding the Tenth Party Congress stuck in the Party's collective memory,
but also because such an assessment may allow us to gauge the effects of the ban
that this congress imposed on factions.

Doing Things with Words in Bolshevik Politics

During wartime the Bolsheviks had a good sense of where their opponents lay: the
proletariat fought on their side, the bourgeoisie fought on the side of the Whites—
it all boiled down to class loyalties.[96] With victory, however, the picture became considerably more complex.[97] "During the war we gnaw at our enemies," Moscow officials maintained, "but now that the war is over we begin gnawing at each other."[98]

The Bolshevik leadership had lost the simple criterion that would determine political loyalty, since many elements from the "petit bourgeois swamp" had been allowed to join the victors.[99] After all, a Party card carried more and more benefits, without the risks its carriers used to run. Class aliens now wormed their way into the Party in search of spoils.[100] In many ways, a covert enemy was worse than an open one.[101] "Remember," Lenin said immediately upon the hurried departure of the last White detachments from the Crimea in 1921: "the danger within is, in a sense, more menacing than Denikin or Iudenich."[102]

It is within this context that the opposition came to be seen as so dangerous; the Party leadership feared that it would become the voice of the politically backward segments of the population, reflecting the objective pressures they placed on the Party.[103] The opposition's readiness to criticize the Party could turn it into a tool in the hands of conniving counterrevolutionaries, Bukharin warned at the Tenth Party Congress. "Our enemies look for allies inside our party, attempting to recruit supporters from various groups."[104]

The pressures and anxieties of peacetime were only mounting just as the Tenth Party Congress was about to convene.[105] Soviet power was on the brink of collapse: faced with growing peasant unrest and a wave of industrial strikes, the Bolsheviks felt an urgent need to liberalize economic policy at least somewhat.[106] But what about the Marxist tenet that every economic concession finds its expression in the political sphere? The need to assert strict political control called for tightening up the intra-Party regime. "Our party splintered . . . into different parts, each with its own psychology, its own deviations," Bukharin noted with alarm. "Our present task is to bring the Party together, to unite it ideologically, to iron out deviations."[107]

The writing was on the wall: the range of possible interpretations of the canon must be narrowed. Tskhakaia, a Party veteran who had seen many a platform, explained at the Tenth Party Congress that no longer would diverse platforms be tolerated. "Asked a fortnight ago which platform I planned to support, I replied, 'None, except the Communist Party program.'" To adopt the opposition's debating strategy would mean succumbing to "submerging myself in the 'swamp' . . . of bourgeois parliamentarism." Others besides Tskhakaia also felt their "heart sink" at the sight of the so many theses and counterheses.[108] "Should we really reduce the discussion to a struggle between platforms?" Trotsky demanded. No, this was a "sin."[109]

A number of additional speakers claimed that platform-based elections introduced turmoil. For example, David Riazanov, one of the main Party's theoreticians, was amazed "to see the same Central Committee sending Trotsky and Krestinskii to the provinces with one platform and Kamenev and Lozovskii with another." He concluded that it would be best simply to select delegates individually, thereby doing away with "a practice that inexorably leads to the creation of factions even before the congress assembles." Platforms undermined true democracy, creating "unnatural groupings"; delegates tended to enter into alliances based on only one of the issues under debate, a situation that prevented the free discussion of the other issues.[110]

Lenin was not sure the Party could implement Riazanov's suggestion. "We cannot deprive the Central Committee members of the right to appeal to the Party when an important issue gives rise to disagreements. What are we to do if we run into a problem of the magnitude of Brest again?" The "extraordinary" Seventh Party Congress, Lenin reminded the delegates, had been convened to discuss this crucial peace treaty. "Clearly in such a case we will have to vote on a platform basis."

"On one issue?" asked Riazanov, clearly startled.

"Of course," Lenin answered. "We cannot prohibit platform-based elections. If we . . . manage to consolidate our ranks, elections based on platforms will not persist. But if circumstances give birth to significant disagreements, issues must be thrashed out by the Party."[111]

Lenin wanted to make sure that the Central Committee could present important questions to the grassroots directly. Yet, as the exchange with Riazanov suggests, he was in favor not of platforms covering a variety of issues (what would be described as a "factionalist platform" later in the decade) but of a single issue policy document.[112]

Eventually, platforms of both types became synonymous with partisanship and exclusiveness. "On Party Unity," a resolution adopted by the vast majority of the delegates to the Tenth Party Congress, anathematized platforms:[113]

It is essential that every Party organization be very strict in seeing to it that the unquestionably necessary criticism of Party shortcomings, the analyses of the general Party line, the surveying of the results of practical experience . . . not be submitted for discussion by groups formed on the basis of some "platform" or other. . . . All class-conscious workers must clearly realize the harmfulness and inadmissibility of any factionalism whatsoever; it inevitably leads . . . to repeated and intensified attempts by enemies of the ruling party—who have attached themselves to it under false pretenses—to deepen divisions and use them to incite counterrevolution.[114]

A secret clause in the resolution stipulated that the Central Committee should not hesitate to expel undisciplined Bolshevik leaders who refused to bow down before the Party line.[115] Lenin referred to this highly sensitive clause—it both undermined the congress's power to determine the composition of the Central Committee and granted it a mandate to purge it own members—as an "extraordinary measure" and suggested it not be published.[116]

Even delegates with serious reservations, not to say premonitions, supported the ban on factions at the Tenth Party Congress. Destined to meet a grim end as a convicted Trotskyist, Radek noted towards the end of the proceedings that when he first heard that the Central Committee had been granted the right to purge its own members, "it was my sense that a rule was being established here . . . that could be turned against us as well." Kamenskii, a Democratic Centralist, also feared the resolution: "Who can determine what is dangerous and what is not? What about comrades who innocently fail to understand that something is dangerous?" Since Lenin's supporters had the required two-thirds majority in the Central Committee, Kamenskii mentioned that "they would be able to oust any faction at will, thereby rendering null and void the explicit desire of the congress to provide representation for the various currents." But, like the others, Kamenskii and Radek ultimately gave their support to the efforts to improve discipline. Facing a great threat, "the Central Committee must take whatever measures it deems expedient, even against the best of comrades. We need a clear line—it is better to be mistaken than to waver."[117]

The Central Committee still encouraged comrades to speak out, urged them to openly state their views at Party gatherings and in newspapers. Disagreeing with this or that aspect of official policy, a Party member could seek others who would share his view and possibly elect him to representational institutions. Opposition understood as "a short term union of comrades on a given issue" was judged to be "not so dangerous," and the tradition of vibrant precongress discussions remained alive.[118] But the dissenters were not supposed to articulate a comprehensive alternative to official policies. Carefully articulated policy templates indicated a persistently negative state of mind. "And oppositionist moods had to be eradicated."[119] If oppositionists were upset with practically everything the Party leadership was attempting to do, if they linked their misgivings regarding Party structure, foreign policy, and agricultural policy, into a wide-ranging platform, they fostered the formation of alien, divisive bodies within the Party. What really scared Smilga most about Democratic Centralists was that "this group appears with its own resolution projects on all issues."[120]

"Secluded" groups and "organized" factions were dangerous because they threatened the Party with a "schism" (raskol)—the Bolsheviks' main fear throughout the 1920s.[121] The Central Committee vowed to put an end to "fractious discussions" in the future.[122] Even Shliapnikov acknowledged that the latter were associated with "certain inconveniences" and promised to prevent the creation of factions before the Eleventh Party Congress.[123] Sapronov, Smirnov, and Evgenii Preobrazhenskii will complain in 1923 that a sweeping ban on groupings means "we cannot even meet in pairs and exchange opinions." But such complaints, the majoritarians retorted, were, "of course, rubbish. Get together as much as you want. Defend your views but do not form solid leagues."[124]

One of the most important and celebrated Bolshevik documents of its time, the resolution "On Unity" drew on every theme that animated the intra-Party debates: the working class, centralism, and consciousness. Terms such as "unity," "expression," and "vanguard" also advanced into the spotlight. If we retrace our steps and unpack some of these terms we discover a certain ambiguity underlying the Bolshevik intra-Party debate. Specifically, the competing resolutions exhibit remarkable parallels in their basic frameworks and many of their propositions. Everyone advocated "centralism" and "workers' democracy." Everyone shared a deep contempt for any bourgeois political framework.

A careful reading of these debates suggests that at the center of many of the most vigorous struggles lay the contested meaning of Bolshevik terminology. All agreed that the state was under siege, which made unity the most important Bolshevik ideal, and so the most loaded term.[125] Even Trotsky, later a steadfast oppositionist, made clear in 1918 that he was ready to sacrifice his opinions for the sake of unity. "One thing is obvious to me," he said at the Seventh Party Congress. "Whatever we decide . . . , we have to have complete unanimity in our ranks."[126] A day or two later Trotsky added: "by abstaining when the Brest Peace Treaty was put to a vote, my supporters demonstrated their great self-restraint. We sacrificed our 'I' to preserve Party unity at a decisive moment."[127]

While "unanimity" (edinodushie) had always been a supreme Bolshevik value, it had not been considered an attribute to be looked for in an electoral system.[128] Unlike the British Parliament, the Party congress aimed to represent not the gamut of social classes but the conscious proletariat alone.[129] The delegitimization of the representation of interests entailed the delegitimization of pluralism and heterogeneity.[130] The Bolsheviks maintained that unity could not be mechanical—political compromises were futile.[131] The truth, Tskhakaia argued, could not be embodied by the whole unless each and every particle of that whole embodied it individually:

If all the cells of a living organism are healthy and united, if they work in agreement, each executing its functions in solidarity with the others, then the organism will be healthy. The same is true for the Party, with all its cells and all of its members. Of course, there are various opinions and shades. The collective is precious precisely because individuals introduce something of "their own" into the common pot, the common arsenal of Party thought. The result of an exchange of opinions is not what Ivan thinks and what Peter thinks, but what the collective thinks.[132]

In this account, true unity was a fusion of heart and mind, an ecstatic experience which leads the Bolsheviks to the "truth" (istina) and not some sort of compromise, as the liberals would have it. Emel'ian Iaroslavskii, a member of the Siberian Party bureau, could not agree more: "The congress should make clear that the Party is not a conglomerate but an indissoluble whole."[133]

The Tenth Party Congress called on the Workers' Opposition to "accept Party discipline."[134] While this faction was obliged to disband, its supporters would remain legitimate comrades. In fact, unity demanded that leading oppositionists not retire. The recent inclusion of a comrade from the Workers' Opposition in the Central Committee, Lenin intoned, "is a token of comradely trust."[135] Seats were reserved for its representatives Shliapnikov and Kutuzov.[136] This gesture did not go over too well, however. Kutuzov ironically described the composition of the new Central Committee as "coalitional."[137] Shliapnikov was equally dismissive of mechanical unity: while he acknowledged that "discipline was necessary" he also wanted to see "the sort of ideological and organic links that existed previously in our party."[138]

Terms such as "coalition," "combination," and "association" belonged to the lexicon of liberal politics and were anathema to true Bolsheviks, the Workers' Opposition reminded the majoritarians. "Lenin's resolution demands unity so as to put an end to the harsh crisis within the Party," noted Medvedev. "But he proposes to achieve that aim by means of formalistic declarations."[139] There were two types of unity, unity in essence and unity in form, said speakers for the opposition. "While we need the first kind of unity, I believe that the resolution 'On Unity' is an attempt to implement the second kind of unity. Unity cannot be decreed and imposed on adults, especially if they are Party activists."[140]

The leaders of the Workers' Opposition declared Lenin's assault on their group unfair and demagogic; they bitterly complained that many of the crucial details of the intra-Party debates had been papered over.[141] Were Lenin's proposals even consistent? How could positions be both "ferreted out" and "condemned outright"? Lenin was introducing "not unity but schism," said Shliapnikov.[142] Advanced on behalf of the Workers' Opposition, a resolution authored by Medvedev affirmed the need for better cohesion in the Bolshevik ranks. "In order to meet the challenges it faces," stated the preamble, "the Party must be better united than heretofore." But how? In Medvedev's resolution, "unity" had less relevance for the Communist brotherhood proper than it did for the bonds between the Party and the working class it was supposed to represent.[143] "No matter how small and disorganized the proletariat is, no matter how little Communist education the proletariat possesses, it is the only basis for our struggle, for the Revolution and for Communism."[144] Only once the Bolsheviks had acted on Medvedev's suggestions could the "creativity" (tvorchestvo), "initiative" (initsiativa) and "self-expression" (samodeiatel'nost') of the workers ripen.[145] In his view, true unity could be obtained only through the "elimination of the distrust between the masses and the leading Party bodies."[146]

The Workers' Opposition warned that the Party was losing authority with the worker grass roots.[147] According to Perechenko, "replacing the initiative of the grass roots with the initiative of bureaucratic apparatuses is not an isolated phenomenon but a system, a policy."[148] Ignatov echoed him: the Soviet apparatus "is metamorphosing into a bureaucracy before my very eyes."[149] The Party could not continue basing itself on the motley petit bourgeois elements. Rather, posts in the Soviet administration had to be filled by advanced workers subject to recall at any time by the electors.[150] "Only individuals who have worked with their hands should be elected to positions of authority," Aleksei Kiselev, chairman of the miners' trade union, argued. "If everyone who spent a year [in an administrative position] then was assigned to manual labor ... we would be able to diffuse the hostility of worker-Communists towards the Party's non-worker element."[151]

Since according to their schema the Party leaders and the Party ranks could be exchanged at will, the heads of the Workers' Opposition denied that they were acting as "leaders" (*vozhdi*)—a title that could turn them into bureaucrats in their own right.[152] A price had to be paid for this modesty: Medvedev complained at the Tenth Party Congress that "our platform attracted few votes because ... it contradicted other platforms bearing famous signatures." Trotsky, he noted, told workers more than once: "You must not call the official platform the 'Platform of the Ten' but 'Lenin's Platform.'" This, much to Medvedev's chagrin, turned a position a Bolshevik occupied, rather than his ideas, into a magnet for votes.[153]

Stung, the Central Committee retorted that the Workers' Opposition failed to appreciate the role of the political vanguard in making revolution.[154] And the suggestion that the group was leaderless struck Lenin as "attesting to the false modesty of Kollontai, Shliapnikov, and Medvedev."[155] In its resolution, "Against the Syndicalist-Anarchist Deviation in Our Party," the Tenth Party Congress condemned the opposition for incorrectly formulating the relations between the Party and the broad non-Party masses.[156] "Marxism teaches that the only political party of the working class, namely the Communist Party, is capable of unifying, teaching and leading ... the mass of toilers, and constitutes a vanguard capable of countering the mass's inevitable petit bourgeois wavering."[157]

Bolsheviks never saw the Party as a mundane political body formed to reflect the popular will.[158] At the Eighth Party Congress Lenin had insisted that the Party program be built on a "scholarly foundation."[159] The model was the modern scientist rather than the ancient politician, permitting the Party to extract from history its hidden meaning through the application of Marxist sociology.[160] This meant excluding class aliens from the political process and preventing workers from engaging in politics outside the Party framework.[161] The great failure of the Workers' Opposition, according to Lenin, was its inability to see that the Central Committee was most concerned about the proletariat's historical task, not the mundane interests of the actual Russian workers.[162] "Our Party," Bukharin followed suit, "does not aspire to unite all workers directly, physically; it is uniting the vanguard of the working class, its leading part."[163] No matter what the worker whispering at Shliapnikov's ear had to say, the question set before the Party remained, What is the proletariat? And what is the proletarian mission? "Yes, we are sometimes obliged to take a stand against certain layers of the proletariat," Preobrazhenskii explained. "Our line has to be strictly implemented even if certain proletarian layers, having lost their head, resolutely resist us."[164]

Few things upset the supporters of the Workers' Opposition more than the charge that their slogans were the voice of the backward layers in the working class.[165] "Referred to as syndicalist or anarchist before," Medvedev noted at the Tenth Party Congress, "Workers' Opposition is now being called petit bourgeois."[166] "Who has shown anything of the sort?" Kollontai wanted to know. "At the very moment when the Party is under siege by petit bourgeois elements from without, we are attempting to . . . clearly formulate proletarian ideas."[167] Because the proletarian consciousness in the factories yielded a far headier elixir than did the fast-growing Central Committee machinery, the Workers' Opposition demanded that the Bolshevik leadership heed its voice and readjust its priorities.[168] Might the Party, asked Medvedev, lose its class basis altogether?[169] If you want to detach yourself from the proletariat, Shliapnikov told the Central Committee majority, "if you want to sever your ties with the revolutionary element, then just go on closing your eyes to the plight of the working class."[170]

This was the opposition's most daring gambit. Whence did the Workers' Opposition draw its own legitimacy? From the industrial workers, not from the Party's institutional structure. Shliapnikov's reliance on the "hundreds of thousands of Communist workers who sent us to the tribune" did not need to be interpreted as an attempt to come between the working class and Lenin. Still, the Party leadership would warn soon enough that it could not close its eyes while "criticisms presenting the working class as antithetical to the Party . . . assumed a distinctly counterrevolutionary character."[171]

Charges and countercharges mirrored each other, each side insisting that while it advocated a universalistic truth the other spoke for the particularist, interest-driven part of the working class. Agreeing that the litmus test for true leadership was consciousness, not whether one had calluses on one's hands, the Workers' Opposition's programmatic brochure insisted that "it is the class united, class conscious, and class disciplined part of our industrial proletariat that is behind us."[172] While Lenin conceded that the working class and the Party had recently struggled to redefine their relations, he refused to consider that something fundamental could be wrong with the Central Committee leadership. Instead, he proposed that the working class had suffered a setback.[173] "Due to the vicissitudes of our revolution," Zinoviev explained, "the working class is declassed, its hard core is destroyed and it is scattered all over the country." With the Workers' Opposition as his subtext, he warned that "one does not serve the working class by flattering it. . . . To deny the declassification of the working class, to see it as something different than what it is, amounts to preventing the Party from gaining a proper orientation."[174]

It was a Bolshevik truism that the working class and the Party defined each other. Zinoviev never really demythologized Shliapnikov's or Kollontai's reliance on the proletariat; he countermythologized it. Whereas the Workers' Opposition claimed that the Party had degenerated, he reversed the argument and claimed the working class itself had suffered a setback. Mutual recriminations at the Party congresses only intensified animosities, so that, rather than functioning to keep the two sides in equilibrium, movement and countermovement rendered the pitch of the debate ever shriller.

According to the majoritarians, the suggestion made by a number of delegates to the Tenth Party Congress that the economy ought to be managed by an "all-Russian congress of producers" emerged from an inability to appreciate that the working class had not attained a state of perfection.[175] Had the Workers' Opposition lost all sense of the necessary progression of historical stages? Lenin argued that it had, otherwise there would have been no talk of an economic order in which the Party played a secondary role. "When he talked about 'producers,' Engels was thinking of a Communist society, a society without classes. Do we have classes now? Yes we do. Do we have a class struggle going on? Yes, a wild one! The current talk of producers' conferences," Lenin concluded, "constitutes a syndicalist deviation that has to be decisively condemned."[176]

Oriented towards the future, the Bolsheviks viewed the present as a stage in the universal progression toward a Communist society.[177] Insofar as Marxists deployed a linear concept of time, outlining a series of stages that would convey the proletariat from the "darkness" of capitalism toward the salvation of a classless society, their thought can be described as eschatological.[178] Constantly preoccupied by temporality and narrative—those structuring themes of eschatology—Bolsheviks wanted to know whether the present was an age of "state capitalism," "socialism," or "Communism," and they made this one of the poles around which intra-Party debate revolved.[179]

In 1921, Kollontai saw conditions fit for a "resolute march towards Communism."[180] Two years later Martynov, a Menshevik recently converted to Bolshevism, was celebrating: "We have already made the transition from the kingdom of necessity to the kingdom of freedom. The important thing is that the Communist Party directs the economic life of Russia according to a plan. While capitalism is run by blind economic powers, socialist economic life is directed by an intelligent will."[181] More cautiously, Zinoviev defined the social regime the Bolsheviks instituted as the "first step. . . . Full Communism, where everyone is equal, will be achieved only after a long struggle."[182]

Such divergent views of the achievements of 1917 call to mind the tension in Christianity between the idea that the messiah has "already" come and the idea that salvation has "not yet" arrived. At the core of the eschatological hope was the faith that with Christ, salvational time had made a great leap forward and entered into its final phase. The decisive event had already taken place, and the End was sure to materialize. "As long as the fundamental conviction of the 'already' is dominant, the belief in the coming end loses nothing of its intensity," theologians explain, though the period of the "not yet" may be quite extensive indeed. This confirmed that eschatological hope planted its faith in the Bolshevik seizure of power and in the tension of the intermediate period which went with it, and that the post-1917 present was properly defined neither by a one-sided emphasis on the "already," nor by a one-sided emphasis on the "not yet."[183]

According to Lenin and Zinoviev, one of the major failings of the Workers' Opposition was its inability to appreciate the "not yet" aspect of the situation. "We are far removed today from the view that on a certain day, at a certain hour, at a single stroke we will dethrone the bourgeois order and create a proletarian order," Zinoviev noted. "No: Revolution is a process."[184] The Workers' Opposition had yet to grasp the true tempo of social transformation: "You do not give the masses time to talk, to absorb, to think through the issues," Zinoviev further charged. "You hasten things, exaggerate, create formulations that run contrary to theory."[185]

The good Bolshevik could determine with uncanny precision where the country lay along the route towards Communism and what that meant in terms of policy making. The appearance of utopian oppositionist platforms at a time "when vestiges of capitalism linger in the pores of Soviet institutions indicates an obvious syndicalist-anarchist deviation."[186]

For the Bolsheviks, political concepts made sense only in a temporal context—only bourgeois metaphysicians attempted to define things in the abstract.[187] "Time," Trotsky explained, "has a tremendous importance in history. Even the dictatorship of the proletariat is a temporary institution."[188] Zinoviev derided the Workers' Opposition for its failure to appreciate that the form of a workers' hegemony depended on the historical epoch:

In 1895 the hegemony of the proletariat led to the creation of the Union for the Emancipation of the Working Class; in 1903 it led to the founding of an organization of professional revolutionaries; in 1912 it meant the preservation of the Bolshevik center in the face of counterrevolution . . . ; in 1917 it meant an uprising; in 1918–1919 it provided the basis for organizing the Red Army and learning to fight; in 1920–1921 the hegemony of the proletariat meant contact with and help to the peasant . . . ; and in 1930 it can take the form of us, Russian communards, fighting shoulder to shoulder with foreign workers on the streets of Europe.[189]

A realization about timing led the Tenth Party Congress to make a sharp turn in its economic policy and introduce what became known as the New Economic Policy (NEP)—this was the realization that Russia was not yet ripe for Communism.[190] While some sort of a "transitional period" (perekhodnaia stadiia) was necessary, Marxist thought barely left an opening of hair's breadth for a program such as NEP.[191] Justifying economic decentralization and the resurgence of private entrepreneurship posed a major challenge to the Bolshevik understanding of its eschatological trajectory.[192]

"Is NEP a maneuver?" Trotsky wondered. "NEP is the totality of the measures of a class which, striding towards socialist revolution, began, naturally enough, by pushing itself forward but, having seized control of the government, correctly evaluated the balance of power. Does retreat mean the negation of our program? No. Does it mean serious changes? Yes, it does."[193] Apprehensive lest some comrades, confused by the zigzags in official policy, should lose track of historical time, Smilga explained at the Twelfth Party Congress: "True, NEP is not everlasting—it is only a stage—but NEP has not yet moved beyond its initial stages: it is a mistake to conflate the point of departure and the point of arrival."[194]

Every true Bolshevik bore a revolutionary chronometer in his bosom. It was of course very difficult to translate abstract eschatological road maps into a concrete timetable, but M. Kharitonov, the secretary of the Perm' provincial committee, was fearless: "The Party knows how to regroup, reexamine its practical measures and reformulate its tasks to suit the NEP transitional epoch."[195] To a Bolshevik versed in Marxist theory it would have been evident that while the "epoch of NEP," which involved a provisional revival of capitalism, may have stood for the "not yet," the "already" of 1917 could not be forgotten.[196]

The Central Committee's majority and its critics from the Workers' Opposition agreed that all of the days after the Revolution belonged to a time already fulfilled even if not yet fully consummated, and were utterly different from the tsarist days.[197] What distinguished the sides was the "appraisal of the present moment" (*otsenka tekushchego momenta*)—in this case the Workers' Opposition's insistence that classless society lay so close that the working class could run the Party unassisted.[198] But Lenin complained that his rivals were acting too hastily; due to Russia's economic backwardness, the separation between the working class and its vanguard would last for a long time to come.[199]

"Opposition": The Emergence of a Term of Abuse

The pages that follow amount to a linguistic inquiry, in which I trace the genesis of the term "opposition" and the semantic field around it.[200] Though the term seems a quite natural one, it was hardly used to designate a political group working against the Central Committee majority before the advent of the New Course Discussion (1923–1924).[201] When used at all, its implications were hardly dramatic. But that all changed, so much so that it is hardly an exaggeration to say that the story of how "opposition" became the linchpin of the political discourse is the story of the origins of fratricide in the Bolshevik camp.[202]

To refer to the critics of the Party line who spoke out in the early postrevolutionary years as "oppositionists" involves a great deal of hindsight, possibly anachronism insofar as it adopts the Bolshevik usage of the late 1920s and the 1930s.[203] More problematic still has been the assumption that a single and united front challenged the Party leadership, for this is precisely the construct it took Stalin's ideologues years to fabricate. And if we consider the words of those implicated we find that very few speakers were referred to as "oppositionists" during those years; more often they were described as adherents of "currents," "factions," or "groups."[204] These terms were not all synonymous and interchangeable; neither were they exclusively linked to oppositional discourses. They were, instead, employed strategically and continently, interweaving meanings and implications.

At the Ninth Party Congress (1920) a set of very mild terms referred to those who would subsequently be called the opposition—we are here in the semantic universe that preceded the ban on factions. Preobrazhenskii wanted to acquaint the delegates with a certain "nonconformity" (*raznomyslie*) among Party members in the provinces; and Riazanov talked about a new "tendency" (*tendentsiia*) he did not care for.[205] Trotsky called ideological disagreements "grumblings" (*briuzhanie*) and "chatter" (*boltovnia*).[206]

Neither he nor any other majoritarian used the term "faction" at the Ninth Party Congress; when those who supported differing positions formed alliances it was still a matter of "currents" (*techeniia*). Bukharin detected two currents in the Party, neither too homogeneous, as is evident from his readiness to refine his taxonomy and speak about "shades of opinion" within each current.[207]

The vocabulary of the Tenth Party Congress contained a number of important linguistic innovations, and the synonyms for dissent coined in those weeks would remain. Classifying the various challenges to the Party leadership that cropped up during the preceding months, Viacheslav Molotov, then the secretary of the Ukrainian Central Committee, noted that the Party was dealing not only with an "opposition" but also with "groups" and even "factions." Note the hierarchy: "factions" appear as the worst threat, "opposition" the mildest.[208]

Let us take a closer look at those terms. At first, the term "faction" (*fraktsiia*) eluded any consistent moral judgment.[209] Party groups in civic, non-Party institutions could be called factions without a trace of censure. If there were Communist factions on a university board of administration or in a trade union, they were the pure kernel that one day was to grow to take over the institution, remove the chaff, and recreate it as a uniform and exclusively Communist body.[210] When the Party itself was at stake, however, a faction could only be a pollutant, a negative entity in a mass supposed to be absolutely pure and homogeneous.[211] Note how delegates to the Tenth Party Congress dodged the label and tried to pin it on their rivals:

ZINOVIEV: Just before I mounted the dais I received a printed note that looks like yet another list of factionalists, whose ideas differ from ours.

VOICES: The list is not factionalist.

ZINOVIEV: I'm sorry, but it is factionalist. . . . Let us not prepare our platforms like pancakes, comrades, and bad ones at that.[212]

Factions were defined by the Eleventh Party Congress as an "impermissible" force that "obstructs collective activity and plays into the hands of our enemies, who wish to deepen divisions within the Party."[213] Since such "self-enclosed" troops were said to enforce internal "discipline," since their institutional base made them far more redoubtable than mere currents, they were certainly more dangerous than "opposition" assemblies.[214] A Politburo letter of 1923 explained that factions did more than just advance sporadic criticisms—"they fomented disorder."[215] "Factions—now this is a serious thing indeed," Kalinin wrote to Stalin in August 1924. "Here you have a fundamental disagreement, an antithetical approach to each and every issue. When you have factions Party policy is formed in different ideological centers."[216]

An equally direct threat to the Bolshevik sense of camaraderie, "groups" (*gruppy*) and "groupings" (*gruppirovki*) could also be very detrimental.[217] But here too a temporary association designed to promote a certain view of proletarian needs did not have to be immediately condemned.[218] When Lenin, for example, spoke of "groups in the Central Committee," he did not appear to have been overly concerned about such alliances. At the Tenth Party Congress he made a distinction between legitimate and illegitimate groupings: the latter erred by placing opinion above Party discipline and thus introducing an illicit political dimension into the discussion. Trotsky and his supporters, according to Lenin, were an example of the former type of grouping, the Workers' Opposition of the latter.

The subtle but very important difference between the two groupings was thrown into sharp relief at the Second Congress of Miners. According to Lenin's account, the miners found three different "points of view" (*tochki zreniia*) vying for their attention—his own, Trotsky's, and Kiselev's—but only two real political groupings. The Workers' Opposition accepted Lenin's bifurcated universe: "Trotsky and Lenin will eventually unite [and form a block opposing us]," Kiselev predicted. What appeared to this speaker as unprincipled behavior was seen by the Central Committee leaders as the honest implementation of Party discipline. "Anyone who does not understand that we have to unite is not Party-minded," Trotsky stated. Lenin agreed: "Of course, Trotsky and I do not see everything eye to eye. But when more or less equal groups emerge in the Central Committee, the Party adjudicates and they eventually unite to execute its instructions and its will." This, according to Lenin, was how every decent Communist had to behave, and this was the reason why Trotsky, no matter how prone to go wrong on the concrete issues, shared Lenin's understanding of the rules of the game. "By contrast, the Workers' Opposition states, 'We will make no concessions, but we do intend to remain Party members.'" Lenin closed by protesting, "No, this trick cannot work!"[219]

During the Tenth Party Congress a new term was added to the lexicon of heterodoxy: "deviation" (*uklon*).[220] The word occurs in the title of an important resolution, "Against the Syndicalist-Anarchist Deviation in Our Party," and Lenin himself explained that the resolution had been drawn up to propose an appropriate attitude towards certain "deviations of thought." To account for the introduction of a new political term, Lenin explained that: "When we speak about 'deviations' we are trying to say that a new political orientation has been recognized and has to be carefully evaluated by the Party. It must be clear, though, that in these deviations we see nothing fully formed, unequivocal, and determined."[221]

In coining the term "deviation," Lenin boasted that he was not the sort of coward who was "afraid to call things by their real names."[222] The Party had to have a vocabulary articulating the dangers of divisiveness.[223] This did not mean that terminology could not be challenged: "Let anyone find a more suitable word in Russian than 'deviation'—I am eager to hear it. The presidium will be happy to revise the resolution and employ a gentler formulation." Though neither Shliapnikov nor Medvedev had made a lexical counterproposal, Lenin conceded that "deviation" might have been a bit too harsh; in any case, "an even stronger term was out of the question."[224]

Everybody knew what deviants were deviating from: the straight line the working class traveled to salvation.[225] The Bolsheviks maintained that only one line connected the here and now with the classless society to come, that the Party had been charged with finding this line, and that the writings of Marx and Engels offered the Party invaluable help with that endeavor. Some overcontentious comrades had forgotten all this, Smilga told the Tenth Party Congress; they had lost track of the truth and were challenging the authority of the Central Committee. Before any irreparable damage befell these comrades the congress had to act, to explain how the two factions, "Workers' Opposition and Democratic Centralism, constitute deviations from the true path of Marxism and Communism."[226]

Lenin could not maintain a monopoly on the term "deviation," and as each group asserted that it held the keys to universal emancipation it abused the others for deviating. Fairly damning was the Party's distrust of workers, and it led Kollontai to wonder "in what way the Central Committee deviates and what is the origin of its deviation?"[227] In other critical remarks, Medvedev commented on the "deviations of leading Party organs."[228] "If the congress dismisses our program," he stated, "the nail stuck in the boot of the Party will remain where it is. As it limps along, the Party will be slowed in advancing our Revolution."[229]

The Workers' Opposition said that slowdowns and "deviations" would result from the Central Committee's one-sided theses. To deviate means to digress, to diverge, but not to abandon the main road. Returning the favor, Lenin reiterated that the term "deviation," opprobrious to be sure, was not that terrible. "We are talking here about comrades who have begun to lose their way (*sbilis' s dorogi*) but who can still be led to the correct path." Delegates were told that "this condition is not permanent: a deviation can be easily mended."[230] Indeed, the Tenth Party Congress was treating Bolshevik deviants with kid gloves. This, in any event, was how Radek saw things: "We rebuked . . . the Workers' Opposition in a brotherly spirit. . . . Under the prevailing circumstances, I can imagine no gentler response."[231]

Because deviations always had a certain direction, it became common to refer to them as "right" or "left."[232] (Searching for unity, Lenin punned, "The party is not a goose, it does not have to have a right and a left wing.")[233]

The history of the right-left divide in the Bolshevik worldview curiously mirrors the history of the term "opposition." During the period when Bolsheviks met only surreptitiously, in small numbers, they deemed themselves "in opposition" to the tsarist regime.[234] The emphasis was on the layout of the body politic: the Bolshevik opposition was coming "from the left," in the best Jacobin tradition. A temporal dimension was added to the spatial tropes after 1917. Groups that "slowed the pace of the revolutionary process" by assailing the Central Committee were a retrograde force. It was of little moment which direction that force came from if it slowed the Party, and the "left" exercised nearly as much deviational force as the "right."[235]

The pangs that accompanied the decision to give up leftism as an unqualified good can be made out in the speech made by Smilga at the Tenth Party Congress. Even as he waved the Party banner, Smilga could not quite relinquish the mantle of leftism: "The danger to our Party comes from the right," he stated boldly. "For me there can be no question that Workers' Opposition and Democratic Centralism have come from the right wing and not the left wing."[236] But even Smilga knew that the left had been delegitimized. When Lenin amiably referred to the leftists as good revolutionaries in an interview with the *Observer*, Stalin gently scolded him. In his letter of November 13, 1922, Stalin noted that comrades "maintain that now that the Communist left has been eliminated—including Workers' Opposition—it is dangerous and futile to present the left as a legitimate phenomenon fully licensed to compete with official Party Communism."[237]

The "right" and the "left" functioned as abstractions, markers in the Bolshevik cosmology. A great deal of talk about "left deviation" and "right deviation" preceded the emergence of the specific platforms conventionally associated with these labels (the Trotskyist and the Bukharinist platforms, respectively). A sway leftward meant a deviation in the direction of the "lumpen proletariat," while a sway rightward meant a deviation in the direction of the "petit-bourgeoisie."

In the early 1920s Party members tossed the epithets "right" and "left" at one another almost casually and no harm came of it. For example, after he had "listened very carefully" to a series of objections provoked by the report Zinoviev gave at the Ninth Party Congress, Mikhail Tomskii came away with the impression that "although the right and the left appeared to differ from the speaker, they essentially repeated his very words." One might conclude that as long as deviation, rightist or leftist, remained bounded by the Party program, it was ultimately viewed as harmless.[238]

No one took seriously the idea that an assemblage as pure and consistent as the Bolshevik camp might be rent by divisions deep enough to prompt political reinvention along the lines of liberal parliamentarian forms. Listen to Zinoviev: "'There is,' Larin says, 'a right deviation in the Party, with Kamenev as its main representative.'" By implication, Zinoviev himself emerged as a leftist in Larin's scheme. "When Larin described me as unsusceptible to rightist deviations, I thought to myself, 'Could it be that I was flirting with leftism and that this is why Larin gives me such good marks?'" The ironic tone is heavy: Larin's own propensity to think of the Party in spatial terms attests to a slight left deviation of his own.[239]

What about the term "opposition" itself? We have seen that even when the line of the Central Committee came under bitter criticism, it was not immediately called "opposition." In the early Bolshevik discourse a sustained and, even more important, ideologically grounded objection to the official line could be designated as either "heterodoxy" (*inakomyslie*) or "heresy" (*erest'*), depending on the context. "Heterodoxy" referred straightforwardly to ill-advised criticism of a sound position; "heresy" was more of a metaphor deployed to excoriate illegitimate mouth shutting of the opposition by tacitly comparing the Central Committee's majority with the Inquisition.[240]

Early uses of "opposition" (*oppozitsiia*) were sporadic and inconsistent.[241] Though he carped on misbegotten ideologies as much as any other writer, Lenin does not appear to have used the word before the Revolution.[242] It did crop up in the speech he gave at the Seventh Party Congress (1918), but his tone was amicable, if slightly condescending. Lenin directed a few hard words towards his "young friends from the opposition." Although two of the "leftists" at the congress, Radek and Bukharin, grudgingly identified themselves as "oppositionists" (Bukharin would become a "rightist" only in the mid-1920s), this label bore none of the resonance it would later acquire.[243]

In any case, the 1918 oppositionist must not have been viewed as too threatening, since they were described as "infantile." The majority saw their objections to signing the peace treaty with Germany as an emotional outburst more than an ideological stance. Zinoviev scorned Moisei Uritskii, the leftist head of the Petrograd Cheka, for "longing to return to the prehistorical epoch where feelings ruled." Bukharin was the reverse: since there could be only one truly rational resolution of any political disagreement, Zinoviev was confident that his attempt to "evaluate policy guided by his mind, not his heart" was a "signal" that "Bukharin was moving closer to the official position."[244]

Before the ban on factions the right to oppose the Central Committee majority was explicitly acknowledged. At the Eighth Party Congress (1919) Zinoviev stated unequivocally: "The opposition is legitimate. . . . Any comrade who believes that the Party and the Soviet ship have to be set on a new course may say so—such is his right."[245] Latsis, a Ukrainian delegate, was respectful of "comrades arguing on behalf of the opposition," and Iurenev emphasized "how significant a temperate opposition [*vyderzhannaia oppozitsiia*] is for . . . reanimating Party life."[246] A number of prominent Bolsheviks suggested that "the opposition is the watchdog of proletarian democracy."[247] "Those who say that the opposition is artificial are wrong," Min'kov said at the Ninth Party Congress (1920). Policies often contained flaws, and should these go unnoticed and unspoken they could not be corrected.[248]

According to the Democratic Centralists, when the opposition sowed discord, this was a necessary evil. "As long as the Party fails to implement the resolutions made by the congress," wrote Maksimovskii, "oppositionist groupings that want to correct this anomaly will have to appear."[249] And Rafail' promised that: "We will celebrate when the Party is such that no type of opposition has a place."[250] But in the meantime, the opposition was a magnetic needle of sorts, a precious political compass that corrected the leadership when it veered off the main road. Yet another Democratic Centralist, Osinskii, sketched out his ideal: "Without gloating or doing anything to burden its conscience a true opposition ensures the purity and the forward motion of the Party."[251]

Expressing his disappointment that Osinskii had mounted the dais in order to present no more than "his own personal observations," the Ukrainian delegate to the Eighth Party Congress, Lev Sosnovskii, hoped for a long-lived political opposition, something "serious" and "profound."[252] But even by the standards of 1919, his enthusiasm for a steadfast bunch to nag the Central Committee seems to have been unusual. Osinskii, for one did not wish to be seen, à la Sosnovskii, as a standard-issue oppositionist. "We have no such thing as an acrimonious opposition group here," this leader of the Democratic Centralists stated. Did not the willingness of the official speakers to adopt theses presented by the Democratic Centralists prove that there were no two camps at the congress?[253] Democratic Centralists tried to co-opt the Central Committee majority at the Ninth Party Congress. The Novgorod delegate who sided with this group, Meshcheriakov, wanted to make clear that "we are in no way Krestinskii's rivals [protivniki]." Meshcheriakov was not "objecting" to the Party secretary; he was "supplementing" what Krestinskii was saying.[254] At the same congress two other dissenters, Osinskii and Rykov, announced that their own theses were not "counterposed" to the theses of the Central Committee but offered as "corrections."[255]

Impressed with the olive branch that Democratic Centralists were extending to him, Zinoviev denied the existence of "any serious opposition" within the Party at the Ninth Party Congress (1920). In the process of delivering his argument he provided an early definition of the term: "We do not have a group of comrades presenting antithetical [protivopolozhnye] suggestions regarding each and every item on the agenda. . . . What we do have are small streams of discontent flowing into each other."[256] Sapronov, explicitly allied with Democratic Centralism at that conference, agreed that "within the Party there are no disagreements on matters of principle."[257]

Both speakers downplayed the opposition, because for both a true opposition was a group of consistently defiant comrades who opposed not this or that aspect of the official line but everything the Central Committee advocated, precisely because the Central Committee advocated it. Zinoviev and Sapronov appeared to have both been committed to interpreting language to facilitate a modus vivendi. Neither was so threatened by the other that the gloves had to come off, and so they agreed to adopt the following rule: let's define opposition in terms so extreme that what has been going on cannot possibly be described as opposition.

The extent to which the linguistic atmosphere changed at the Tenth Party Congress should not be exaggerated. To be sure, for Lenin the schizophrenic peek-a-boo of Shliapnikov and Kollontai as carping critics and, seemingly moments later, the Party's best friends was beyond endurance: "The time is not ripe for the sort of theses the opposition advances! Either you are with us or you are out there [with the anti-Bolshevik rebels], continuing the discussion with rifle in hand—but you must not stand in opposition."[258] Others agreed that the Party cannot afford the "luxury" of having an opposition.[259] "I am certain," Loginov explained, "that every opposition is the enemy of the Party."[260] Smilga, a harsh disciplinarian, found the activity of the opposition at times "anti-Marxist" and "anti-Communist," but he was the only delegate except Lenin to refer to the opposition without quotation marks and use the term with a more or less stable negative connotation.[261]

So long as the opposition was something other than traitorous, various constructions remained open. On the one hand, Danishevskii, a delegate from Siberia who was perhaps the harshest critic of the deviant groups, stated that "the Workers' Opposition has assumed a leading role in shaping the attitudes of counterrevolutionaries who oppose the Communist Party."[262] On the other hand, even the least sympathetic depictions of the opposition presented it as a naive force. On a second reading, Lenin appears to be chiding and reprimanding rather than castigating and scourging. Most of all he was unhappy with what he regarded as the opposition's infantilism. By "casting aspersions on us," some comrades, he noted sorrowfully, "show how much they like to play the part of the opposition."[263]

Another reason few took the opposition seriously was the widespread feeling that political disputes had more to do with personal feuds than with ideology. Thus a Central Committee document from 1921 traced the intra-Party struggles to "personal vendettas," "misunderstandings" and individual "clashes."[264] At the Ninth Party Congress, Lenin described Lutovinov and Tomskii, both major organizers of the Bolshevik trade unions, as participants in a "noisy squabble."[265] Zinoviev's brief mention of the situation in the provinces was similarly spirited. "An opposition formed itself in Rostov: I see no point in trying to understand who is right and who is wrong." By "opposition" Zinoviev was referring to a petty "personal feud there."[266]

If squabbles gave rise to opposition groups, association with petty quarrels drained the word "opposition" of vigor—it could be used as a mundane and quite apolitical term.[267] NEP was believed to have something to do with this. Occupational categories now divided Bolsheviks into distinct, unconnected, and often incompatible groups. When Matvei Shkiriatov spoke on behalf of the Moscow Party organization at the Eleventh Party Congress, he said that in some Party districts, "groupings lacking any principles have popped up."[268] These groups did not unite around principles, political or otherwise; around what, then? A year later Shkiriatov returned to the point: "During my three trips to the provinces this last year I discovered that squabbles have nothing to do with ideology, everything to do with materially oriented quarrels."[269]

At the Twelfth Party Congress Zinoviev insisted on a distinction between "political and apolitical factions." Of a rubric in his notes he said, "'Groupings, Tensions, Squabbles'—not a very parliamentarian caption, perhaps, but it comes closer than any other to capturing the reality . . . in many Party organizations." Zinoviev emphasized that what he had in mind were not such "purely political groupings as the Workers' Opposition," but something "more prosaic."[270]

One might say of the competing interpretation offered by the Workers' Opposition that it relied on a similar analytic framework but emphasized different elements: for this group, the factional squabbles marring Party meetings had to be blamed on the willingness of the Party heads to live and work in isolation from the people. Considering that local initiative was suffocated, no wonder internal strife ensued. Stukov demanded that "a hole be punched in the wall separating the Party heads from the Party masses—the law of diffusion will necessitate an exchange of essential fluids."[271] The Workers' Opposition frequently accused Party leaders of erecting "no barrier against personal influence."[272] The result was a leading group in the Central Committee that pushed a particularist agenda "in many ways at odds with Party interests."[273] The "intriguing leaders" (*intriguiushchie verkhushki*), so said the Workers' Opposition, "spread careerism and toadying."[274] Additional critics accused the Central Committee of "basing its policy not on ideas but on alliances among groups."[275]

When delegates suggested at the Tenth Party Congress that some oppositionists were being persecuted for reasons that had nothing to do with the soundness of their proposals, Lenin finally flared up: the official attitude to the Workers' Opposition, he asserted, had nothing to do with interest-driven "politicking" (*politikanstvo*) and everything to do with a carefully developed "politics" (*politika*).[276] Smilga turned the linguistic guns around: "Instead of committing themselves to stand by the Party in its struggles with the dangers to come, the Workers' Opposition is engaging in political intrigues."[277]

According to the Central Committee, their critics could not see beyond their noses. To hear Iaroslavskii tell it, all the opposition did was fuss and grumble about workers' salaries and so on: "Suggestions put forward by Workers' Opposition and by Democratic Centralism resemble the very familiar formulas advanced by the grassroots opposition." He ironically added that grassroots groups had never found it necessary to give themselves lofty titles. Such modest "oppositions" presented themselves in the lowercase, and were so presented; for example, "the peasant opposition . . . has the same roots as the Workers' Opposition: to wit, the evident exhaustion being felt by the masses because of the difficulties of the transitional period."[278]

Semantic regularities had been disturbed, and the meaning of the word "opposition" had lost all stability—the variety in its usage rendered it almost meaningless. According to Lenin, the changeable vocabulary of those who criticized the Central Committee suggested that the whole thing was a prank. "They voted for certain platforms identified sometimes as 'the Workers' Opposition platform' and at other times by other names."[279] In a fascinating maneuver, Lenin's critics turned the unstable taxonomy he had ridiculed to their own advantage. Some of them performed a remarkable feat of semantic prestidigitation, a Chinese box trick in which the Central Committee majority and the opposition traded places. Maksimovskii, for example, ridiculed Lenin's supporters, referring to them as "the group for the 'analysis of the opposition.'"[280] Only a linguistic environment of great mutability and playfulness could permit the identification of Lenin's group as an intra-Party formation.

Milonov, the delegate from Samara, talked about what he called "the Central Committee current [*techenie tsentral'nogo komiteta*]," a tendency among the employees of the apparatus to approach every issue with blinders on. By applying to Lenin's followers the loaded term "current," Milonov placed the Central Committee on the same footing with oppositionist formations. "Until now," he noted, "we had three groupings jockeying for position in our party: the Central Committee grouping, the 'Democratic Centralism' grouping, and the 'Workers' Opposition' grouping." Implying an equality of sorts among the three groups, Milonov opted for an awkward but interesting term: "The Central Committee opposition [*oppozitsiia TsK*]."[281]

Having brought a dazzling stratagem to bear, Milonov attempted to shatter the orthodoxy/heterodoxy dichotomy and strip the Central Committee majority of all special and exclusive claims to doctrinal insight. In his vocabulary, the opposition was just one position, no more and no less. Positions tend to clash, and inasmuch as the Central Committee's view clashed with Milonov's, it too could be designated as an "op-position." In Milonov's linguistic universe, each of these "oppositions" represented a legitimate, albeit partial view of reality. If anything, it was "much easier" to see all kinds of problems "from below," which was where Milonov placed himself and the Workers' Opposition.

"The opposition," singular and devoid of epithets, appears very few times in the minutes of the Tenth Party Congress. The plural form was more widespread: Smilga stated, "Yes, comrades, my relations with the so-called oppositions (*oppozitsii*) in our Party are tense." "We can mend the situation only if we understand that we have to put an end to factions and oppositions," declared Murakhin, the delegate from Stavropol'. The plural form, "oppositions," does not refer to chronological plurality but to a synchronic one; the Party had to reckon with not an essence given form—the Opposition—but a variety of mutually discordant ad hoc currents opposing the majority line.[282]

References to "Workers' Opposition" cropped up frequently in 1920–1921. Does such a use of the singular form vitiate my argument? Let us note that the quotation marks never disappear.[283] In this particular linguistic construction "workers'" receives the emphasis, not "opposition."[284] When congressional discussion took a genealogical turn, none of the delegates outlined the history of the Opposition—that would happen only in 1925–1927, when the Party would construct a time sequence with one opposition replacing another—they turned instead to the current state of the workers' thought.[285] True enough, some "backward" workers had chosen to assume an "oppositionist" stance toward Soviet power: within the Party that meant joining one of the various "oppositions," while outside the Party it meant complaining about food shortages, but that was all.[286]

So long as the majoritarians refrained from essentializing the opposition, the intra-Party debates did not assume a Manichaean form, a clash of two mutually exclusive forces. In the middle of a peroration in the ferocity of the 1920 discussion, Trotsky hastened to qualify himself: "But it was not like we stood at loggerheads [*stena k stene*]."[287]

A random sampling of some of the rhetorical skirmishes that took place on the floor of the Tenth Party Congress suggests that the delegates were far from coalescing into discrete camps. There was no immediate linking of arms by all opposition delegates, and the Democratic Centralist delegate from Khar'kov, named Rafail', reckoned Workers' Opposition far more misguided than the Central Committee itself—he yearned to begin "destroying the grounds that generated the Workers' Opposition" and spoke acidly of its "intelligentsia-cannibalism" (*intelligenstvoedstvo*).[288] Maksimovskii, a Democratic Centralist from the Ukraine, would not tolerate any "currents that lead to the dismemberment of the Party" and was quite certain that "the activities of the Workers' Opposition cause damage."[289] Perechenko managed a retort: "It is evident that what they really want is to make a straw man of the Workers' Opposition. Democratic Centralists are moving in the same direction of bureaucratism and centralism that they have sworn to contend with."[290]

Opinions were so diverse that an observer at the Tenth Party Congress might have concluded that there were more factions present than individuals. When Zinoviev said that "Workers' Opposition showed two faces today, one belonging to Kutuzov, the other to Medvedev and Shliapnikov," he was stressing the wide range of heterodox opinion rather than its convergence.[291] The differences among Bolshevik leaders struck Zinoviev as annoying but ubiquitous—he had a few terse words to say "to our friend Bukharin, who found nothing better to do than fabricate a disagreement between me and Lenin. I would rather see him find common ground with Trotsky first!" Trotsky intervened from the bench: "Back then we [he and Bukharin] were not yet in agreement."[292] Few could follow this bickering.

In the early 1920s, factions were individualized; this was a very different phenomenon from applying the names of leaders to the factions themselves. Having noted that "we have received corrections to the various resolutions and they are signed by Rykov, Sapronov, Tomskii, and Miliutin," the chairman of the Ninth Party Congress knew that "certain groups stand behind these individuals." But at this date names were not used as emblems for platforms.[293] What was called in 1920 "Ignatov's group" differed profoundly in type from what in 1925 was called "Zinovievism"; the former was perceived as the fruit of trivial quarrels among individuals, while the latter conveyed the impression of a highbrow ideological stance.[294]

Encouraged to seek historical parallels, the Bolsheviks were fond of turning names into types, be they negative (e.g., "our Guizots") or positive (e.g., "our Babels"). At a Central Committee conference in 1923, Sakhibgarei Saidgaliev underscored the notion that some individuals were not only unique selves but also instruments fated to play a predetermined role: "If I mention the name of [Mirsaid] Sultangaliev [who had turned oppositionist], it is not a personal name [*imia sobstvennoe*] but as a pejorative type [*naritsatel'noe*]. . . . We should be talking not about Sultangaliev but about *Sultangalievshchina*." (The suffix *-shchina* is appended to words to convey a generalized way of thinking or "ism," but one strictly negative in its connotation.)[295]

But at this stage, typological constructions of this kind were reserved almost exclusively for non-Communists. "Trotskyism" was not in wide use before 1925, in part because Trotsky continued to present his minority views in utterly apolitical terms. "Lenin believes that we must sign a peace treaty today," he stated at the Seventh Party Congress. "The other wing, to which I belong, believes that [continuing the war] is our only chance to influence the German proletariat."[296] Three years later, in 1921, Trotsky showed no inclination of giving his position an ideological coloring. The "endless disputes about the role of the trade unions," disputes in which he played a major part, found an easy explanation, "in the rift that had opened up within the presidium of the central trade union."[297] What separated the "professional half" from the "productive half" was an occupational bias, not ideology.[298] His Central Committee rivals, among them Stalin, Kalinin, Kamenev, Tomskii, and Zinoviev, responded in kind: "though we have disagreements on the question of trade unions, we protest any attempt to see in this declaration anything offensive to Comrade Trotsky."[299]

Speaking at the Tenth Party Congress, Trotsky drew a fundamental distinction between a "big politics" and a "small politics." The latter consisted of intra-Party "agreements" and "compromises," and Trotsky assigned it the belittling title "maneuvers"—it was the realm to which the occasional bickering between the Central

Committee and the opposition belonged. "Big politics" involved more serious is-sues such as administration of the national economy and general relations between classes, and it was there that the Party attention was supposed to be focused. One slight misstep could send practitioners of small politics reeling into personal clashes and petty oppositionism, and Trotsky was trying to avoid this misstep.[300]

The Opposition Medicalized

Many delegates to the Party Congresses of the early 1920s described the intra-Party struggle as a bizarre illness threatening the brotherhood of the elect.[301] Few speak-ers were prepared to say whether the opposition was a symptom, a source, or a cure of this "illness" (*bolezn'*).[302] Whatever the answer to this question, the prominent metaphors of disease suggested that the disagreements among the Bolsheviks were sometimes taken more seriously: the "health" (*zdorovie*) of the party organism was at stake.[303]

From the late 1910s to the mid-1920s, the opposition sounded the theme of ill-ness at a higher and higher pitch. As early as the Eighth Party Congress (1919), Osinskii found the Party "lifeless: the dregs of society are pouring in, people with Party cards but without any intellectual equipment."[304] At the Ninth Party Con-gress Andrei Bubnov, a member of the Ukrainian Central Committee, observed "symptoms of dissolution."[305] Sapronov and the group for Democratic Centralism used more specific medical metaphors, speaking of an "ulcer [*iazva*] eating away at our Party" and "an abscess [*naryv*] on its body."[306] Grigorii Belen'kii, the secretary of Moscow's Krasnopresninsk Party district committee, mentioned "chronic ailments" (*boleznennye nedugi*).[307] In the alarmist picture painted by Perepechko, an opposi-tionist from the southern trade unions, at the Tenth Party Congress, the Party was akin to a "decomposing" carcass.[308]

The Central Committee retorted with metaphors of illness and nervous break-down of its own. Vikto Nogin, from the commissariat of trade, noted at the Eighth Party Congress that "the thin layer of the proletariat has had its nerves shat-tered."[309] A year later Lenin compared the defiant speeches of some hawkish com-rades to neurotic outbursts. "Though critics such as Lutovinov and Bubnov speak too much, I would not say that this is demagogy. It is just that some comrades are exhausted and have become hysterical."[310] "The atmosphere in which we work," con-curred Tomskii, "is nervous, unhealthy. Deviations and excesses are becoming more pointed, now that the very finest among us have exhausted themselves to no end."[311] Such identifications between the opposition and illness found a resonance in the readiness of Manuil'skii, from the Ukrainian Central Committee, to alternate be-tween the terms "unhealthy [*nezdorovye*] attitudes" and "oppositionist [*oppozitsion-nye*] attitudes."[312]

The rhetoric of the majoritarians and the oppositionists converged around ideas of decay. Historically the human propensity to contract not only physical but also moral diseases had been explained by recourse to the idea of "degeneration" (*vyrozhdenie*), and the official discourse equated deviation from proletarian truth with moral breakdown.[313]

The origins of the Bolshevik usage of degeneration appear to be closely related to the discourse of late-nineteenth-century western European medicine. Charles Darwin may be said to have translated the Judeo-Christian idea of man's fall into modern scientific language when he described, in his late writings, the physical decline of a species as degeneration. Engels's expanded notion of degeneration, "no longer occurring at the racial level, but at the level of societal analysis,"[314] appealed to Bolsheviks, and they began to talk about "decay" (*razlozhenie*) and "decadence" (*upadochnichestvo*) when referring to the ideological decline of their comrades.[315]

Having exhausted itself towards the end of the nineteenth century, capitalism had entered, in Engels's view, a "retrogressive state," forcing humanity back into a primitive animalistic state.[316] The Bolshevik leadership found that this model squared with its perception of postrevolutionary Russia.[317] A full proletarian consciousness had supposedly been achieved for the first time in history in 1917, and for a moment the proletariat had appeared in its full glory, self-aware and omnipotent, but bloody battles and the deprivations of the Civil War had sapped the vital energy of the masses, and many proletarians had tumbled back into the state of nature.

NEP ratcheted up the anxieties about illness. Trotsky presented the logic of NEP as the logic of inoculation: "We introduced a 'new' economic policy in order to beat capitalism with its own methods."[318] The Party expected the body popular to respond to the introduction of the bourgeois vaccine with mild disease. Zhakov, a delegate to the Eleventh Party Congress, could refer to petit bourgeois attitudes as an "infection" (*zaraza*) responsible for an "unhealthy atmosphere," a sordid trail that oppositionists "would happily have rejected if they only had known how."[319]

But while NEP was a necessary evil, infighting among the Bolsheviks was not. If Communism was not yet possible and the Party had to go on fine-tuning society, a healthy subject was a necessity, and not one wracked by internal illnesses. Though the heterogeneity of the population at large could not be denied, this could not be permitted within the Party—patients could be ill, doctors could not. Identifying health with unity and oppositionism with discord, the Central Committee blamed the opposition.[320] Molotov, now a Central Committee secretary, talked in terms of finding "symptoms of factionalist activity." Here opposition was an elusive disease.[321] According to Danishevskii, comrades' urgent search for "historical solutions" caused them "fever" (*likhoradka*). "Disease . . . finds its organizational expression in oppositionist groups such as the Democratic Centralists and the Workers' Opposition."[322]

While the Workers' Opposition agreed the Party was seriously ill, it traced the cause to official policy. The "organic illness" (*organicheskaia bolezn'*) observed in the

Party, Shliapnikov maintained, "has to do with the growing separation between the apparatus and the laboring masses." The vector of this illness was very clearly identified "within the Central Committee. The accusation that we . . . infected the Party with syndicalism has to be directed back at its sender."[323] Explaining that their group had not caused this illness, that it was, in fact, the remedy, Medvedev insisted that he had devised many valuable "medications" that could "rejuvenate" (*ozdorovit'*) the Party.[324]

Everybody liked to compare the workers to red blood cells, without whom the Party organism would falter and perish. Preobrazhenskii, then still a majoritarian, put it thus: "Only full-blooded organizations, those enjoying a constant influx of youthful vitality, lead a normal life. Other organizations grow thin; life in them subsides."[325] Speaking for the other side, Kollontai used similar tropes: "we are losing our red blood cells. It is only natural that, without the working class, the Party becomes lymphatic, fatigued."[326]

The Workers' Opposition claimed that workers were fleeing the Party in droves because they could see how ill it was.[327] "The best proletarians leave," Medvedev lamented, "those who had sacrificed everything for the Party." The oppositionists blamed the Central Committee for draining all the oxygen from the political atmosphere, choking democratic impulses. "Workers felt they had been reduced to voting puppets."[328] Kosior maintained that "a proletarian whose health has been eaten away packs his bags because he cannot get used to an environment where he loads lumber, sweeps the streets, . . . but decides nothing."[329]

But Manuil'skii wondered whether it might be the case that workers were leaving not because the Party was corrupt but because they themselves had been corrupted? "It is wrong to present the old workers who have been giving up their Party cards as romantics. . . . Let's create instead an atmosphere where anyone who would do that is made out to be a Judas renouncing his own class."[330] Shortly before the Eleventh Party Congress, a bunch of oppositionist workers responded to losing in the Kostroma elections by renouncing Bolshevism. What most bothered Aron Sol'ts was that the explanations offered by the malcontents offered medical excuses such as "exhaustion." Sol'ts was confident that, "even when tired as hell," true workers "will always choose to remain in the Party."[331]

At the beginning it had seemed as though Party unity could be wrought by talking things out; now some more effective measures had to be brought in. Driven to desperation by the failure of the local leaders to take up a broad discussion of the sources of workers' discontent, Ogorodnikov, a middle-tier provincial functionary, deplored during the Ninth Party Congress the apathetic expectation that the Central Committee would do all, and demanded to know the "recipe" for the drug that would heal all decline, all degeneration. Listen to an extended web of tropes woven by this spokesman for the mid-level Party apparatus, as he shuttled between religious and medical-scientific discourses.

Not only is the Central Committee ill, we too are ill. . . . To pin the illness [*bolezn'*] on others—this is a sin [*grekh*]. . . . If we just take a close look at ourselves we will have to say, "Yes, it is myself I have to correct." . . . Once we realize we are not only patients but also doctors at the patient's bedside, once we learn to take healing seriously . . . and deal with the problems faced by the lower orders of our Party, the sick man will get up on his feet. Gradually he will grow stronger, will breathe with the full capacity of his lungs, and eventually he will become as tough and healthy as he once was.[332]

Demanding drastic measures, Lutovinov preferred to stick to the medical register. "Instead of concealing the abscesses that eat away at us we must burst them open and substitute radical healing [*lechenie'*] for superficial treatment [*zalechivanie*]."[333] "We have spent quite a bit of time in discussion, trying to heal our illness." "What do delegates propose now?" Lenin asked at the Tenth Party Congress, also preferring medical language.[334] According to the Central Committee, the 1921 restrictions on Party enrollment and the purge in the fall of that year—two measures taken to curtail the size of the brotherhood of the elect—amounted to a colossal, albeit necessary, "bloodletting."[335] Two years later, Trotsky was even more resolute: "even extreme reactions to threats to Party unity . . . must be considered as a symptom of our revolutionary willingness to protect our political and moral health."[336]

Overall, however, the Party leadership was concerned about the choice of medicine in the early 1920s: if it proved too strong, the patient could die.[337] Riazanov advocated tender care. "If, instead of exacerbating our wounds, we . . . limit the activities of the bosses that intimidate workers, 'Workers' Opposition' will dissipate."[338] For Lenin, the "so-called opposition" evidenced a "psychological crisis" within the Party, and he called "to apply to its supporters a carefully individualized approach. . . . We should give them advice and counsel."[339] With the corrupting influences of NEP in full view at the Twelfth Party Congress (1923), Zinoviev spoke even more compassionately: "Each and every oppositionist must be healed politically. There are not so many of us that we can afford to toss comrades out just like that."[340]

Such sensitivity to the well-being of the opposition seems apt, given the rather mild challenge to the majority made by Workers' Opposition. According to Milonov, its spokesman from Samara, the drawbacks evident in the work of the Central Committee "are of course not the result of a concrete individual's personal, subjective distress [*personal'naia, sub"ektivnaia beda*] but of an objective set of problems that beset our entire party."[341] Returning the favor, Bukharin did not present the opposition as deliberately wicked; rather, it was a "frivolous" force unwittingly expressing less than ideal objective conditions.[342] Lenin was also disinclined to invest the Workers' Opposition with political maturity: "they cry like babies."[343]

He maintained that those who had drawn up the oppositionist theses should be blamed "not for a conscious decision to take the unrighteous path, but for a theoretical mistake . . . resulting from their inability to think things through."[344] "You would agree that blaming our economic difficulties on Larin's wicked design [*zloi umesel*] is a ridiculous argument," Sosnovskii told the delegated to the Eleventh Party Conference.[345] The Central Committee granted that factions often formed along lines "quite different from what their participants had in mind."[346] No wonder, Lenin noted at the Eleventh Party Congress, the Workers' Opposition was stunned to realize where it had ended up: "They just discovered that they gone into one door and come out of another."[347]

Lenin thought he saw a way to put an end to the oppositionist malady: quarantine. He called on the Party "to separate at all costs the healthy part of the opposition from the ill."[348] And so long as the Workers' Opposition made only "healthy demands," Lenin and Smilga promised to do the maximum to accommodate it.[349] As a whole the Party organism longed for recovery—and it could recover! Its affected parts had to be healed, not amputated. When the Central Committee called on all comrades to prepare a "prophylactic vaccine" (*predokhranitel'naia privivka*) against the opposition, no one wanted to assign blame. Quite explicitly: the vaccination would address breakdowns stemming not from anyone's "evil will" but from "grave malady."[350]

Camaraderie of the Party Leadership

1. "Soviet Leadership from 1923 as a Soccer Team. Forwards: Radek, Sosnovskii, Trotsky, Riazanov, Bukharin; Halfbacks: Chicherin, Lozovskii, Zinoviev; Defense: Lenin, Kamenev; Goalkeeper: Marx." Note that Stalin is missing from the lineup. Only two players, Lenin and Chicherin, who both died early on (and Karl Marx, of course), will not be accused of oppositionism. *Krasnyi perets*, 1923, no. 14, p. 7.

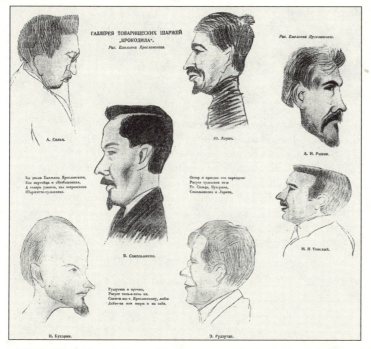

2. "*Krokodil*'s Gallery of Comradely Caricatures [*druzheskie sharshi*]" drawn by Emelian Iaroslavskii, himself a member of the Central Control Commission and a prominent Bolshevik leader, who thus proves he can make fun of his comrades without humiliating them." (Top from left to right): A. Sol'ts, Iu. Larin, A. Rykov; (middle): V. Sokol'nikov and M. Tomskii; (bottom from left to right): N. Bukharin, E. Rudzutak. *Krokodil*, 1924, no. 16, pp. 6–7.

3. "The Bolsheviks Writing a Reply to the Englishman Curzon." "Budennyi, Rykov, Kamenev, Kalinin, Radek, Krasin, Bukharin, Lev Kamenev, Chicherin, Trotsky, Rakovskii, Demian Bednyi, Litvinov, Stalin, Zinoviev." Based on *The Reply of the Zaporozhian Cossacks to Sultan Mahmoud IV* by the Russian Realist painter Ilya Repin. The original painting shows the cheering Ukrainian Cossacks composing a challenging letter to the mighty Sultan of the Turkish Empire. Here, Lord Curzon, the oppressor of nowadays, is a pompous representative of the English bourgeoisie, while the Bolshevik leaders come from the people. They are cheerful and iconoclastic, bringing a new style of political leadership. *Krasnyi perets*, 1923, no. 6, p. 7.

Images of the Eschatological Journey and Deviation from the Path

The Bolsheviks believed that history is unidirectional and that they were its vehicle. The opposition was seen as deviating from the true road. It is difficult to exaggerate the consequences of the discursive shift that turned "deviators" (*uklonisty*) into "counter-revolutionaries." "Straight-liners" (*priamolineinye*) and "deviators" had much in common: they traveled along the same roads, and oppositionism was simply one of the most ill-advised, lengthy, and hazardous routes. Nothing, however, united straight-liners with counterrevolutionaries; their journeys moved in completely opposite directions.

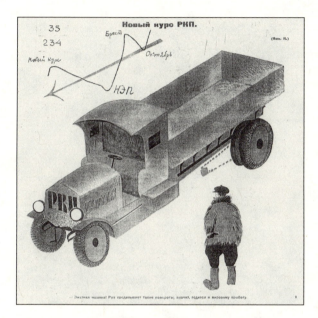

4. "The Party's New Course." "A noble car: making such turns it is capable of the international run." Bolshevik eschatology animates the drawing: the messianic vehicle may make all kinds of zigzags, adapting to circumstances, but the driver never loses track of the final destination. *Krasnyi perets*, 1924, no. 1.

5. *(below)* "Those Lost Along the Way." "When the Party makes a sharp turn there are always a number of confused leaders who fall out." Below: "They do not like hills." The opposition leaders, Trotsky and Zinoviev, cannot hold on to the truck moving fast towards socialism and industrialization. The implication is that it is physical illness or weakness of character, not their evil will, which precludes them from joining the Central Committee. *Rabochaia gazeta*, no. 281, December 9, 1927.

НАШ ПАРОВОЗ ЛЕТИТ ВПЕРЕД

ВКП(б)

оппозиция

Пигмею не столкнуть его с ленинских рельс.

6. "Our Train Flies Forward." "A pygmy cannot remove the Party train from the Leninist track." Here Trotsky is a saboteur, but he does not have a line of his own to follow. *Krasnoe znamia,* no. 281, December 9, 1927.

Рис. К. Елисеева

ОППОЗИЦИОННАЯ ЛИНИЯ

К БОЛЬШЕВИЗМУ

К МЕНЬШЕВИЗМУ

ПЛАТФОРМЫ: 15 тыс. экз. 83ж. ВДОВЬЯ

1927   1927

АНТИСОВЕТСКИЙ ЭЛЕМЕНТ:— Хоть и без билетов, но как-нибудь доедем,—нам эта линия по пути!..

7. "The Opposition Line." Ignoring the opportunity to take the train in the direction of Bolshevism, Trotsky drives the train in the opposite direction: towards Menshevism. Below: "Anti-Soviet element—even without tickets, we will get there somehow. 'This train goes our way!'" Zinoviev (as a female) and Kamenev (in the train) are also depicted. Here the opposition deliberately abandons the revolutionary journey and becomes the fellow traveler of the bourgeoisie. *Krokodil,* 1927, no. 42, p. 12.

Images of Trotsky and Stalin through the 1920s

In the early 1920s, Trotsky was a Civil War hero, the bearer of Lenin's legacy; at the end of the decade he is a pathetic impostor unmasked by the working class. Stalin's trajectory is opposite Trotsky's: in the beginning of the decade, he is a minor member of the leadership and it is possible to describe him humorously. When he emerges victorious over the United Opposition his image is solemn and not at all distorted. This is the beginning of the personality cult.

8. "On the Threshold of the Year Nineteen Twenty-three." Drawing on the traditional Russian theme of three kings reaching a crossroad and trying to determine which way to go, the drawing depicts the Soviet leadership: Lenin in the center, Chicherin, the commissar of foreign affairs, on his right, and Trotsky, the commissar of defense, on his left. The prominent position of Trotsky made him a natural heir once Lenin became incapacitated. Stalin and even Kamenev and Zinoviev are nowhere near. *Krasnyi perets*, 1923, no. 2, p. 1 (drawing by Min).

9. *(left)* Trotsky. "No one can become Lenin, but everyone must become a follower of Lenin." (From Trotsky's speech at a parade on May 23.) Trotsky is shown as leader, towering above the Party's rank and file. *Krasnyi perets*, 1924, no. 12, p. 1.

10. "The Coup Failed." "Lenin has been, is, and will be our banner." Falling, Trotsky failed to substitute Leninism with Trotskyism. *Krasnoe znamia*, no. 291, December 21, 1927 (drawing by M. Cheremnykh).

11. "Comrade Stalin: 'There Are No Mensheviks!'" In connection to the lively debate in Menshevik congresses regarding the possible dispersal of this party, newspapers run a questionnaire: "What will be the future of the Menshevik party?" Below: "Stalin stamps an envelope addressed to the Menshevik party: 'Return to sender due to the absence of the addressee.'" Stalin's mustache and other rough Georgian attributes are emphasized. Here he is the Party secretary, a person ruling in matters of manpower and procedure, not substance. *Krokodil*, 1923, no. 40, p. 1133 (drawing by D. Moor).

12. "You Face the Wrong Direction" (a play on the slogan of the mid-1920s "face to the countryside"). Bottom: "Comrade Stalin: Face to Moscow . . . And what about the countryside?" Provincial functionaries went out of their way to tailor reports, tables, and diagrams instead of truly improving the situation in the countryside. Stalin, the Party's general secretary, appears as a clerk seated behind a table—a far cry from the Bolshevik ideal of a speaker-activist. *Krokodil*, 1925, no. 7, p. 1 (drawing by B. Efimov).

13. Stalin emerges as the only leader, towering above the party masses. He holds in his hand the "Results of the Pre-Congress Party Discussion." The banners state: "To the Fifteenth Party Congress, the True Keeper and Intransigent Defender of Lenin's Legacy—Our Warm, Proletarian Greeting!" and "Into Lenin's Party." *Pravda*, no. 278, December 4, 1927 (drawing by Deni).

CHAPTER 2

KILLING WITH WORDS

Do Words Carry Meaning?

Much as they celebrated the bonds of Party camaraderie, this did not stop the Bolsheviks from criticizing each other, taunting each other, even scorning each other. As we have seen, the minutes of the Party congresses overflow with mutual accusations and harsh words bordering on derision and mockery. Did lasting bruises ever result from such verbal scourging? On the face of it, the answer must be resoundingly negative: since they trusted each other, since their minds and hearts were filled with nostalgic memories from the underground years, the Bolsheviks could not have brought any harm to their comrades.[1] Now that the Civil War was won and Bolsheviks could take their ease, they found that the Party congress surrounded them with like-minded friends with whom they could engage in lighthearted banter. Their language could finally become a game, played a bit roughly at the edges, but nonchalant and blithe overall.

And yet, there is no better time to remind ourselves that most of the speakers cited in these pages, if they were not among those lucky enough to die relatively young, perished at the hands of their erstwhile comrades. The quips and barbs that amused so many at the time looked macabre fifteen years later. If someone was threatened enough by Shliapnikov and his friends to kill them, should we perhaps take the fulminations against the opposition more seriously?

What can we say about the Bolshevik attitude towards their own language? Of course, no theoretical treaty on the subject was written at the time: Party leaders lacked both the time and the inclination to dedicate themselves to such a task. If we want to understand Bolshevik assumptions about the relation between words and deeds, we have to inspect those comments they let drop about their own language by accident, unthinkingly; we need to read their words against themselves.

It is impossible to understand the Party skirmishes without understanding the Bolshevik conception of rhetoric. Oratorical excellence per se was never a target for Bolshevik barbs. "Infatuated with talking," the Bolsheviks developed a whole revolutionary lexicon, with its special similes and double meanings, its own comic tradition.[2] They were masters of invective, diatribe, peroration, and an extravagant verbal vendetta. Indeed, their enjoyment of their own invective jumps out at the reader from the page.[3]

Although speech was supposed to be transparent, in fact tone was noticed and delivery mattered. Mar'iasin, an observant delegate from the provinces, noted at the Ninth Party Congress that "Krestinskii is making tender speeches, Bubnov angry ones."[4] And Rafail, a seasoned Party veteran, had the impression that if the majoritarians "have a high pitched voice; the opposition is a bass."[5]

Semantics had to be placed above pragmatics: since language had to embody the truth, its referential function had to prevail over its communicative function. Expressiveness, facility with words and masterful oratory were acceptable, even commendable if—and only if—all of these words were the direct expression of the working class's political will. Woe to the "empty talkers" (*govoruny*) who substituted eloquence for responsible words. "Instead of substantive arguments all we hear is spiteful polemics," complained Mashatov, a Red Army delegate to the Tenth Party Congress. "Different groups trade polemical blows to the backs of each others' heads."[6] Ivanov was similarly displeased at the Twelfth Party Congress: "What we see here, at the center of our Communist culture, is not a discussion of the issues but personal exchanges between random speakers. . . . If a comrade is going to speak, let him be precise, truthful, and straightforward."[7]

Among the worst things that the Central Committee could say of the opposition in 1920–1921 was that it had a cavalier attitude towards language. Kamenev dismissed the "big words" (*krupnye slova*) hurled by the critics of the Central Committee.[8] Lenin's dislike of flowery elocution is evident in his hope that "we should not argue over words but over substance."[9] And Tskhakaia was unhappy that Kollontai "applies all her rhetorical skills to dividing the Party."[10] On matters of substance the opposition defended itself energetically, but it had no quarrel with official assumptions about the form revolutionary language should take. Speakers for Workers' Opposition denounced "polemical maneuvering," and speakers for Democratic Centralism excoriated the "gap between our words and our deeds."[11]

Lutovinov described Zinoviev's speech at the Twelfth Party Congress as having left out all the real causes for the emergence of the opposition. "Was it really true, as Zinoviev had claimed, that following the ban on factions groupings evaporated into thin air? Of course not. Zinoviev, the daydreamer, had been trying to alter reality with verbal bans." Driving his point home, Lutovinov invoked the highly unflattering image of Kerenskii, "who, in the old days, would bellow and browbeat everyone, yelling, 'We will not tolerate this' and 'We will annihilate that.'" This lampoon of the prime minister from 1917 made Zinoviev, by juxtaposition, appear in a ridiculous light—surely there could be no substance to the ravings of such crackpots. And yet Lutovinov did not denigrate speech completely; he had not lost hope in a "responsible way to vent opinions and points of view in our party."[12]

Even as they cast great rhetorical thunderbolts, Bolsheviks now and then took a step back, retracting their arguments, claiming that they did not mean exactly what they said, that their inflammatory declarations should have been understood in a polemical context. The chasm between words and reality had gaped a bit threateningly. The delegates examined their own speeches as though disinterestedly and from a distance, interpreted themselves for themselves and for others, asked their listeners to think twice before deciding what intention lay behind their words. Immediately after leveling harsh charges at the official policy, Iur'ev, speaking at the Ninth Party Congress, qualified himself: "It is not my intention to offer malicious criticism of the Central Committee; rather, I am just trying to point out our blunders in comradely fashion."[13]

Early on, a certain decorum prevailed, and a comparison with the late 1920s reveals that many terms of opprobrium slung at the opposition were of fairly late vintage. What criticisms did turn up were only "reproaches" (*upreki*) or "objections" (*vozrazheniia*).[14] What in a few years would turn into an intra-Party "struggle" (*bor'ba*) was still only a "disagreement" (*raskhozhdenie*) or a "difference of opinion" (*raznoglasie*).[15]

Of course, venomous tongues were not always curbed. An "extraordinary spate of vituperation [*rugan'*]" broke out at the opening session of the Ninth Party Congress.[16] A survey of the obloquy to which critics of the Central Committee were subjected suggests that the level of linguistic violence escalated even further at the next congress: Lenin described the Workers' Opposition as "indecent" (*neprilichnaia*); Riazanov called it "absurd" (*nelepaia*); Minin used the word "hideous" (*urodlivaia*).[17] The opposition answered with the language of trampled honor. Medvedev complained about the "campaign of provocation against Workers' Opposition."[18] And Sapronov was offended by the "venom" (*iadovitost'*) and "scoffing" (*nasmeshlivost'*) directed at the Democratic Centralists.[19] When Lenin called Democratic Centralism "foolishness" (*glupost'*), Osinskii took it quite personally. Lenin retracted: "My words were distorted."[20]

But when asked to apologize for his derogatory comparison between Workers' Opposition and Pugachevshchina, the violent eighteenth-century peasant rebellion, Osinskii himself confessed he was not a defender of a polite, clean metaphor. "Sure, I know how to swear [*rugat'sia*]. Who does not?" But Osinskii compared himself with Aleksei Tolstoi's princess, who said,

> If not for my maidenly shyness,
> That bars me from outright unkindness,
> The curses I used, you simpering ass,
> Would have struck you with infinite brass.

[Kaby ne moi devichii styd
cho slovechka inogo skazat' ne velit,
ia b tebia, proshchelgu, nakhala,
i ne tak by eshche izrugala.]

The moral of the ditty was that delegates must know how to distinguish between the metaphorical and the literal, "between the vile language we direct at our class enemies and the kind of polemics permitted at a Party Congress."[21]

Other delegates, however, bridled when language was treated so lightly. Had not the Bolsheviks' commitment to communicating the truth to the proletariat won them the great victories of 1917?

When Shliapnikov charged Aleksandr Tsiurupa with "criminal bureaucratism" and demanded he be prosecuted by a revolutionary tribunal, he failed to honor a highly respected Bolshevik who had joined the Party in the year of its formation (1898) and currently served as commissar of supply.[22] True, Tsiurupa's economic management may have been questionable.[23] Equally true, workers may have suffered as a result. But to threaten Tsiurupa with the type of treatment counterrevolutionaries were receiving violated all sense of proportion. Livid, Lenin demanded that Shliapnikov be curtailed: "He bandies about words he himself does not believe in, words he cannot substantiate. . . . Why is he not prosecuted for the kind of speeches he makes?"

Though he had a concrete issue before his eyes, Lenin was unwittingly calling attention to the implications of language. "If Shliapnikov is correct and we are guilty of failing to bring Tsiurupa to trial, then we should be tried ourselves. If not, if his speech is demagogic, . . . his anarchistic words should be answered with bullets." And yet, in the end, Shliapnikov was not prosecuted for getting carried away with "phrases," and Tsiurupa was not tried for mismanagement. This was, according to Lenin, an anomaly: "words cannot be flung about just like that!"[24]

In his rebuttal, Shliapnikov reminded Lenin and his supporters that the crime of rhetoric taken to excess had been committed by others besides the Workers' Opposition. Supporters of the Central Committee, he said with some indignation, were fond of "smearing their antagonists": he reminded them of a secret meeting held in 1919 during which Tomskii offered to speak to workers in the "language of machine guns" (*pulemetnyi iazyk*). Now it was Shliapnikov who was calling for a language police: "I want to say loudly and clearly: we cannot talk to workers that way."[25]

Firing squads, apparently a recurring motif during the Civil War, would deal with those comrades who violated the ban on factions. It may be that Lenin's use of this threat—in the context of debates among Party leaders—pushed his critics beyond the edge.

A freshman Central Committee member, Kiselev, took up the image with gusto.[26] "Vladimir Il'ich said figuratively [*obrazno*] that 'machine guns will have to be rolled out and put in a combat position.' Well, I reckon that I will be one of the thirty or forty-five Central Committee members expected to operate these machine guns and we'll probably have to open fire."

Instant uproar. A sarcastic voice came: "Aha! We have a Tolstoyan [read: pacifist] in our midst!"

Kiselev went on with his line of thought: "I will be expected to shoot first not at comrades from the 'Ten,' but at those from 'Workers' Opposition' or the representatives of other opposition-minded groups."

Drama blossomed into melodrama; the hubbub in the hall became outright pandemonium. "Comrades, I cannot accept the role of 'machine-gunner,'" Kiselev could still be heard pleading. "Under the circumstances, I must remove my candidacy for the Central Committee . . ."

Lenin responded immediately and announced his "regrets at having mentioned machine guns. I hereby solemnly swear not to use such words in the future. They needlessly scare people." In any case, Lenin assured his auditors that his metaphors would remain metaphors. "No one intends to use machine guns. I am quite certain that neither Kiselev nor anybody else will have to shoot anyone."[27]

But soon enough the dire effects of NEP drove Lenin to pull his machine guns out of mothballs, and during his opening report at the Eleventh Party Congress he insisted that those groups inciting panic would have to have their mouths shut. "A retreat is a complicated thing, especially when we are talking about revolutionaries who have gotten used to advancing over the last few years. . . . If an entire army was retreating and it was not obvious when this would stop, a few panicky voices can put everybody on the run. Because the danger here is grave, machine guns are brought in. If the retreat becomes disordered the command is 'Fire!' And rightly so."[28]

Lenin and Shliapnikov were at it again, and the leader of the Workers' Opposition reacted with typical vehemence.[29] Advising comrades "to refrain from communicating by means of machine guns," Shliapnikov drew up his conclusion: "Let us be more serious about what we say. . . . After all, we know how badly previous revolutions ended up"; the terror of the French Revolution was on the minds of all Bolsheviks.[30]

Earlier, Lenin had demanded of Shliapnikov that he speak more straightforwardly. Now the roles were reversed, and Lenin complained that his words had been interpreted too literally.

Shliapnikov pretends he does not know what I mean when I speak about machine guns and panic-stricken individuals. . . . What I had in mind—and Shliapnikov certainly understands this—was aiming machine guns at today's Mensheviks and Socialist Revolutionaries, who claim that we are sliding back into capitalism and that this is a welcome thing! . . . To those who were always in retreat, to those who say, "The Revolution went too far," the Bolsheviks reply: Either refrain from expressing your political views or . . . be ready to be shot like the worst of the Whites.[31]

When Lenin threatened the opposition, on the other hand, his threats should have been understood "metaphorically" (*v perenosnom smysle*). What he was really talking about here was "what sort of censures [*mery vozdeistviia*] Communists can exert on one another, not machine guns as such."[32]

Speaking about his feud with Shliapnikov at the Second Congress of the Union of Miners (January 22–24, 1921), Lenin demanded, with a measure of frustration, "Do I 'attach labels automatically'?" "What grown-up would believe such stuff?" "'You terrorize us!' Shliapnikov says. But it would be ludicrous to try and terrorize seasoned revolutionaries who had already been through so many ordeals in their lives."[33] Lenin ridiculed his oversensitive and easily offended opponent: "Shliapnikov's complaints are nonsense! Just look at him! What a wretch he is! Lenin, you see, intends to fire at him!" These comments were met with applause and laughter.[34]

At the Eleventh Party Congress, Shliapnikov tried to quip that he had been tried many times, certainly more times than he could remember.[35] Precisely because Lenin recognized this as a strategy designed to play down the seriousness of the matter, he was deeply annoyed. "Comrades," he retorted, "some things must not be joked about: Party unity is a case in point." Shliapnikov's giddiness has become, at least in Lenin's estimation, a "sad affair."[36]

The axis of interpretation was loose, and words—threats in this case—acquired their precise meaning only once the identity of their recipient had been specified. It was up to Shliapnikov to decide whether he would put himself alongside the participants in the Bolshevik rhetorical game (a role demanding greater personal reserve) or in the camp of those whose language had to be taken literally (a position that might levy a great tax on his utterances). By maintaining an ambiguous position, Shliapnikov could exploit the floating signifiers of the Bolshevik discourse and laugh heartily at Lenin's threats. But at any time the signifiers could be frozen, the threats taken quite literally, and an awareness of this potential left a sinister undercurrent visible not too far beneath the surface.[37]

As long as NEP was on and the population was in flux, language could not surrender its flexibility. Those who had mastered the subtlety of Party congress speech making understood the shades of meaning associated with given words and the political universe transmuted through them, and exploited this alertness to brilliant rhetorical effect.[38] Far from one another were the words the delegate used and the things he referred to; meaning was assigned through interpretation, and the range of legitimate interpretations was quite wide. A highly polysemic, highly metaphorical discourse, Bolshevik speech precluded overserious reading, as if the full realization of its potential was out of the question. So, for a while, strong language could be interpreted as a verbal pirouette—exaggeration designed to enhance the effect of speech, but ultimately of no real significance.[39]

But the ontological premises of Bolshevism rendered the place of rhetoric intrinsically unstable. With the realization of the revolutionary project, irony and allusion would gather dust as the meaning of every statement shrank to singularity. At the moment of enlightenment, rhetorical violence would have no meaning save real violence. Though few delegates saw their words in these terms as they spoke them, the eschatological underpinnings of Bolshevik language would prove to be stronger than human intentions. When laughter filled the chamber as Shliapnikov or Osinskii tried to defend their position against Lenin, was it a light laughter at the absurdity of a delegate who falsely belittled himself by asking for mercy? Or was it gallows humor, the nervous titters provoked by a prophetic glimpse of an oppositionist standing alone in an NKVD cellar, universally forsaken?[40]

Laughter

While our knowledge of the Show Trials of the 1930s makes it hard to imagine them as a funny affair, we must not dismiss the possibility that this was precisely how wranglings among Bolsheviks were perceived fifteen years earlier or so.[41] Even in the midst of the bitterest altercations, the language of the Party congress retained a certain lightheartedness. Delegates laughed, sometimes quite heartily.[42] At the Tenth Party Congress Osinskii pleaded: "If a joke cannot be spoken, even to lighten one's spirit; if no one has the wit to parry a pun with a pun, then there is only one way out: to drown oneself."[43] Lenin had to agree that "a joke is, of course, a very good thing; we cannot make speeches without cracking a joke here and there. Our meetings are long, people are human and they get tired."[44] Mitrofanov, who represented Novgorod at the Eleventh Party Congress, recalled that "a sly smile [lukavaia ulybka] appeared now and then on Lenin's face. If the speaker made a good joke, Lenin laughed heartily, simply, openly, sincerely. His laughter was contagious."[45]

In these comments, laughter is a side issue, a diversion, marking that brief respite when delegates are allowed to forget that it is up to them to decide the future of the Revolution.[46] Since the frequent chuckles and titters convey an informal atmosphere, a certain looseness, they indicate that language was used in jest. When laughter abounded, words were not subjected to a literal interpretation: much of what was said was taken indirectly, figuratively.[47]

Littering the minutes of the Party Congresses one finds the standard comment, "laughter in the hall."[48] Laughter emerged out of the willingness of both sides to give as good as they got, often snatching up an opponent's discarded club to beat him with it.[49] Bukharin appears to have enjoyed relating lighthearted anecdotes that reflected the attitude to rhetorical violence among the Bolsheviks in the early

1920s. "Let me tell you a story," he told the delegates of the Twelfth Party Congress. "I ran into a comrade from the periphery and asked him, 'What's new?' 'Not much,' he replied. 'We are busy strangling the nationalist opposition these days.'" This was met with appreciative chuckles. As long as the reality remained distant from the words, the blackest of jokes inspired bright laughter.[50]

Osinskii treated the Central Committee's disciplinary measures lightly, and suggested at the Twelfth Party Congress (1923) that Zinoviev was linking subversive platforms to him "just like mischievous boys tie a tin can to a cat's tail." Still, the leader of Democratic Centralism took umbrage at the recent newspaper articles, in which Zinoviev

sounds like a "priest" entitled to yell unrestrainedly at his critics. When Vladimir Il'ich "whips" me, you may believe, comrades, that I take no offense. Although, both in terms of my Party standing and in terms of my general development, I have long since passed the age when I could be "whipped," I am at times subjected to this treatment by my spiritual father. I stand below Lenin: he is taller than me, in terms of human height, by something like two meters. But when Zinoviev adopts Lenin's language I say to myself, [after Koz'ma Prutkov, a well-known satirical figure] "If the sign on the cage says 'Lion' but the lion is nowhere to be seen, do not believe your eyes."[51]

Zinoviev responded to the levity in this speech with humor of his own. "I can fully appreciate Osinskii's feelings: if you must get flogged, get flogged by the master."[52] Sorin also made flippant remarks: "If Lenin found out that Osinskii was calling himself his 'disciple,' he would have echoed Marx's dictum that 'I sowed dragons, but reaped a harvest of fleas.'" These comments both provoked laughter—perhaps from the same people who had laughed at Osinskii's jibes.[53]

Even when bitter judgments were meted out, humor did not always disappear.[54] Iu. Larin, a prominent member of the Vesenkha (Supreme Council of the National Economy) collegium, was ridiculed at the Eleventh Party Congress for his long-winded criticisms of the Central Committee's planning. "Larin embraces me, laughs, makes jokes," Lenin said. "In this he is truly marvelous!" Then, as if asking the delegates to judge his own sharp barbs in such an amicable context, Lenin spiced his evaluation with ridicule: "Fantasy is very precious—what a stupid prejudice it is to think that only poets need such talents! . . . The trouble is that Larin possesses it in excess. I reckon that if we could divide his reservoirs of fantasy among all the members of our Party, everyone would have just the right amount. [Laughter.]"[55] Zinoviev took up Lenin's sarcastic tune: "Larin excessively admires the role of personality in general, and of a concrete personality, his own, in particular. [Laughter.]"[56]

But humor could boomerang, as Larin ably demonstrated by skewering his critics' claims to infallibility. "You see, 'the Party always correctly predicts the course of events, and possesses the greatest accumulation of talent, wit, and character.'"[57]

This set off chuckles among the delegates, and Larin now advanced to thrust home his sword: "It is not as though we are terrified when scary words are directed at us, especially given the proverb that runs, 'His words are scary, but let's see what his actions are like.'"[58]

Or consider the clash between the flamboyant Marxist theoretician, Riazanov, and the Party's head disciplinarian, Sol'ts.[59] A few years after these events, a summons to appear before the Central Control Commission—the Party's supreme disciplinary body—would set the soul of the accused to shaking. But at the Eleventh Party Congress the verbal give and take amounted to trivial, ad hominem exchanges:

RIAZANOV: Just let me speak the way I'm used to. We don't have to be afraid of governesses in skirts or the ones in pants [read: the control commission]. [Laughter.]

SOL'TS: I am not sure what type of governess Riazanov needs. [Laughter.]

Sol'ts chaired the control commission, but this did not intimidate Riazanov. "We have all seen what becomes of the control commission when it's faced with serious matters," he laughed.[60] He clearly relished transforming so serious and masculine a body into its feminine opposite. "Someone has said that the British parliament can do anything except turn a man into a woman. Well, our Central Committee appears to be much more resourceful: it managed to turn more than one revolutionary male into a *baba* [i.e., an old, supercilious woman]. [Laughter.]"[61]

In a carnivalesque atmosphere the accuser and the accused, the loyalist and the oppositionist, switched roles, turning now and then to the delegates, who obliged them with approving laughter.

When Sol'ts asked Riazanov why he often made "irresponsible" and "demagogic" speeches, Riazanov blamed his untamed character. "You see," Sol'ts commented, "Riazanov has the temperament of a Party jester [*shalun*]." Like any good jester, Riazanov laughed at authority—in this case, that of the Party's disciplinary court. "Following the trade union congress . . . I found myself in a tragic situation . . . in the dock, an accused facing the Central Control Commission." This bit of ironic self-mockery earned laughter.[62]

These clashes between Larin and Lenin and between Riazanov and Sol'ts were only two among many mock duels that took place at the congresses of the early 1920s. No one emerged a clear victor or loser, and, judging by the ease with which roles were reversed, the opposition was not yet resigned to the role of accused.

A frequent victim of derision, the opposition groups often found humor the best form of self-defense. What, for example, was meant by all this talk about deviations? "Trotsky has been trying to figure out the degree of our deviation," Shliapnikov noted. "His findings: two degrees at most. Lenin will probably say that the angle of our deviation is greater. [Laughter.]"[63] According to Milonov, "the reason why delegates laugh when I say that 'Workers' Opposition' relies on healthy working-class elements is that their own perspective is nonproletarian. . . . Recall the old proverb: 'He who laughs last laughs best.'"[64]

Bolsheviks thought nothing more amusing than the profanation of Christian values, and in the early 1920s religious language, comedy, and the carnivalesque all overlapped. Accusations of heresy were frequently deployed—supporters of Workers' Opposition were described as "sinners" (*greshniki*). Kiselev from Workers' Opposition returned the favor accusing the Central Committee of acting "sacrilegiously" (*sviatotatstvo*). He claimed that the accusers were the true "apostates" (*otsupniki*).[65] Bukharin denied accusations that he was "preaching" (*propoveduet*) Party schism, to which Stalin jeeringly responded that the speaker was clearly in a "penitent mood" (*pokaiannoe nastroenie*).[66]

A few years earlier, Gol'tsman's jeremiad about "the application of the lash to those workers who drag us backward" drew heavy fire and this second echelon Bolshevik was compared to a religious fanatic. Lenin could not bring himself to repeat Gol'tsman's sacrilegious threats, but neither could he second Trotsky's description of the unfortunate speaker as "possessed by the Devil. You see, the word devil calls to mind something frightening while Gol'tsman calls to mind something nice—so no one can be said to have been possessed here." Gol'tsman was small fry and innocuous, and Trotsky should really not have taken him and his language so seriously.[67]

Grotesqueries indeed occasionally appeared in Bolshevik humor as small things were presented as enormously large and menacing and large things were presented as overinflated. Majoritarian speakers ridiculed the opposition for pretending to be more threatening than it actually was. Before the Eighth Party Congress was convened, Zinoviev was told that the opposition was planning to make the congress a "bloodbath." Only very "minor criticism" stood behind this mighty challenge, he noted with an ironic sigh of relief.[68] Oppositionist bravado disposed Iosif Vareikis, the delegate from Vitebsk, to laughter more than anything else: "I don't exactly shake like an aspen leaf before 'Workers' Opposition'; . . . they only leave blisters on my ears."[69] And Lenin compared Shliapnikov to a chicken who is "hatching disagreements" during a Party meeting in Moscow suburb—the audience generally found such belittling of the Central Committee critics amusing.[70]

Speakers wishing to point out that the opposition was more menacing than it let on also found the grotesque handy. When Osinskii suggested in 1920 that "two cultures are clashing within our Party, civil culture and military culture," Bukharin retorted, "I want to remind Osinskii that there is also a culture of germs,"—these creatures from the opposition are very small but very menacing.[71] A year later, Zinoviev was determined to warn all good Bolsheviks that the Democratic Centralists had been lying low to lull the Central Committee to sleep. Drobnis, one of the leaders of the Democratic Centralists, had claimed that "my platform is quite tame [*ruchnaia*]." "The baby," Zinoviev parodied him, "is miniscule, you see" but it could grow into a dangerous giant.[72]

Most classically, irony combines incompatible images and emotions.[73] By juxtaposing Kiselev's serious crime and his own concern not to offend this sensitive chairman of the Union of Miners, Bukharin produced an ironic moment at the Tenth Party Congress: "Kiselev speaks like a lamb, a kind of Madonna. 'Have mercy!' he demands. 'Can't you see how pure we are?' . . . As I gaze upon these Madonnas . . . tender emotions [*umilenie*] engulf me and tears begin to fall from my eyes."[74] How incongruous, these efforts on the part of the Workers' Opposition to appear pure and innocent!

Language was the turf on which the Bolshevik did battle. Notoriously fierce and merciless, Party politics was always discursive, always achieved through words: before anyone was defeated and expelled from the brotherhood of the elect he had to be labeled, defamed, castigated. Rejecting the liberal concept of legitimacy with its constituencies and voting booths, the Bolsheviks were very sensitive to ideological critiques.[75] Mockery and jokes could kill. "Laughter," Lunacharskii explained, "is not an expression of power, but power in itself."[76]

Linguistic politics, especially in the Bolshevik case, went beyond ideological controversies. Paradoxically, when warring parties employed a similar vocabulary, the blows they exchanged struck more fiercely. In these cases the stakes had ceased to be form (everybody subscribed to the same linguistic nomenclature) or content (interpretations of key terms could vary, but seldom radically); the battle was waged over the right to embody the revolutionary language.

Who had the right to use certain words? This issue lay at the center of a quarrel that took place at the Tenth Party Congress. Medvedev demanded that the quotation marks be dropped from "workers' opposition."[77] "The workers' opposition stands for what is written in the program of our Party," he exclaimed in 1921, and nothing else.[78] The quarrel had developed around the right to identify the man behind the marker. Who spoke in the true voice of the working class, Medvedev or Lenin?

In a fascinating speech given at the Tenth Party Congress, Tskhakaia struggled to understand the names chosen by the different opposition groups, revealing in the process aspects of Bolshevik linguistic practice that normally remained unarticulated.

How am I to understand the name "Workers' Opposition"? Are workers not in essence always in opposition, consciously or unconsciously? Should they not be in opposition to alien classes, which are not their own, and to enemy parties, also not their own? . . . The Workers' Opposition should not choose new names . . . dividing themselves from the Party or confusing the Party.

The name "Democratic Centralism" was equally puzzling.

What are these comrades trying to say by choosing that name for themselves? Did we not struggle for at least twenty-five years for democratic centralism? And if it's just a matter of playing with words, why don't we name yet another current, say, the "Current for the Expropriation of Expropriators," since the Party and Soviet power have not yet completed their implementation of this policy?

Tskhakaia concluded that "this sort of wild naming is unacceptable in the Bolshevik workers' party."[79]

Struck by the undeniable affinity between his own words and the words of Medvedev, Bukharin, Lenin's staunch supporter at the time, decided that "Workers' Opposition" was playing a diabolical trick on the Party: "You say, 'The Party should be cleansed,' and we say, 'The Party should be cleansed.' You say, 'Workers' needs should be systematically advanced,' and we say, 'Workers' needs should be systematically advanced.'" The stance of the Workers' Opposition reminded Bukharin of a "famous passage from Goethe in which Margaret says to Faust: 'You say the same things our pastor does, but what you say is slightly different.'"[80]

The fear that the opposition was a Trojan horse set to overtake the Party from within elicited some nervous chuckles from the delegates of the Tenth Party Congress. Passionate that "Workers' Opposition" would make no compromises, Kollontai insisted that this is no incitement to a schism. No, "our task is different: even if we are defeated at the Party Congress, we will have to remain in the Party and defend our point of view step by step, saving the Party and straightening its line."[81]

"'Even in case of a defeat . . . !'" Lenin jeered. "How farsighted!"

Kollontai proposed an inversion: Central Committee out, Workers' Opposition in; Lenin found the fantastical substitution of heterodoxy for orthodoxy eerie. "You'll pardon me, I hope, if I allow myself the liberty of asserting with some confidence that it is the congress that will decide whether you stay in the Party or not!"[82]

By claiming key symbols, the opposition was stripping the Central Committee of its revolutionary mantle. While there could be only one vehicle of salvation, numerous camps had hoisted identical flags and were making identical promises. What could be more terrifying than a host of messiahs, all of whom claimed to be the authentic one and labeled the others false prophets? Indeed, majoritarians found such a situation "monstrous" (chudovishchno).[83]

A monstrosity possesses the uncanny characteristic of being sometimes comical. On the face of it, there was nothing funny about the mutiny in Kronshtadt, a challenge coming from the previously impeccable naval fortress, that forced delegates from the Tenth Party Congress to go in person to participate in its suppression (March 1921).[84] Indeed, it is at first sight surprising, perhaps even baffling, that the following exchange regarding Kronshtadt between those who remained in Moscow provoked the delegates' laughter.

KOLLONTAI: Comrades, do not forget that "Workers' Opposition" is broadly linked to the working masses. . . .

VOICE FROM THE BENCH: And to Kronshtadt. . . .

KOLLONTAI: We were the first to respond to the Party's call and volunteered to battle Kronshtadt. It was not the Red general staff that went there, but members of "Workers' Opposition." [Laughter.]

Why "laughter"? To the ear of the uninitiated, this was a ridiculously repetitive, totally redundant exchange. The Central Committee contended that the constant grumbling of the opposition had inspired the Kronshtadt mutiny. The opposition retorted that, quite to the contrary, the Central Committee's erroneous policies had been the trigger: in its own version of the events, the opposition had been the first to warn of the possibility of a mutiny. The two sides shared ideological assumptions: the Leninists venerated the working class, and so did Kollontai; the Leninists regarded Kronshtadt as a counterrevolutionary uprising, and so did Kollontai. The Leninists believed that counterrevolutionary uprisings had to be put down through armed struggle, and so did Kollontai. All this has been stated and restated ad nauseam, so that the response one would have expected to this sort of line was yawning, not snickering.[85]

And yet, there is something funny that jumps out at the reader from these minutes. The obstinate, absolutely wooden quality of the debate amuses. Precisely because the language duplicates itself, there is no room for real argument here. An argument, an attempt to persuade, has to be a disagreement, but in this case all meanings were agreed upon. Clashing head to head, delegates wanted to settle who incarnated the Revolution and who deserved to be identified with its enemies. By describing Lenin's supporters as nonchalant about the working class, Kollontai presented them, at least implicitly, as traitors. Returning the favor, the Central Committee majority linked Kollontai with an anarchist outburst. The amusement of the audience grew out of the childishness of the exchange: "I'm the real Bolshevik!" "No, I'm the real Bolshevik!"

The congressional echoes may have sounded hilarious, at least in terms of the Bolshevik sense of humor, but the implications were sobering. How long could both positions be maintained? If one side was speaking the truth, the other side had to be pretending, speaking in what Bukharin termed the language of Mephistopheles. Discussions of interpretation allowed for dialogue, persuasion, discursive maneuver, but there could be no compromise over who personified revolutionary values.

Which camp, then, was one with the Revolution? Determined to delegitimize the claims made by the Workers' Opposition at the Tenth Party Congress to speak for the workers, Lenin insisted that the group's very name was "polemical."[86] At the following Party congress he went a bit further, saying that he did not think "this title corresponded to reality."[87] The workers could no longer be certain who deserved their allegiance, and the insistence of the Workers' Opposition on retaining their name—nay, their very existence—dismayed the Central Committee leaders.[88] "When you were proofreading the galleys of Kollontai's broadside, *Workers' Opposition*, you already knew about the events in Kronshtadt," Lenin stated. "How could you come up with the name 'Workers' Opposition' at such a moment?"[89] Later in the decade, charging the opposition with violating the unity of the working class, Stalin would refer to its attempt to split the Party organizationally. What Lenin seized on in 1921 were the linguistic prerequisites of this highly subversive strategy: the appearance of impostors claiming to be the workers' true representatives.[90]

Drawing up a final balance sheet for Workers' Opposition in 1923, Zinoviev made a pun. "We have to obliterate even that name. That was not a *'workers'* opposition,' but, objectively speaking, an *anti-workers'* opposition" [emphasis in original].[91] And Trotsky said of Workers' Truth (*rabochaia pravda*), an offshoot of Workers' Opposition to be discussed below, that it was more accurate to call this group "Workers' Falsehood" (*rabochaia krivda*).[92]

As one reads over the protocols of the Tenth, Eleventh, and Twelfth Party Congresses one is struck by the slow, inexorable process used to push the opposition beyond the threshold of legitimacy.[93] Over time the claims to good faith laid by the opposition were dissolved, and the following set of opposed dyads was deployed:

Central Committee	Opposition
theses	platform
legal	illegal
revolution	counterrevolution
proletarian	petit bourgeois
Party	anti-Party

It is difficult to exaggerate the significance of bipolarity in the Bolshevik discourse. A Manichaean view allowed someone like Karl Radek, for example, to call the Workers' Opposition platforms "anti-Party" (*antipartiinaia*) and relegate their supporters to the "enemy underground."[94]

Battle Lines Harden

The discourse on the opposition was a strange thing. Did the opposition present an increased danger because of NEP, or was oppositionism forgivable for that same reason? Were the numbers of the critics of the Central Committee rising or dwindling? One would have expected the opposition, puffing up its chest, to claim that it stood on the brink of taking control, and the Central Committee to promise that at the next congress the Party would at last be totally united. But roles sometimes reversed, with the official leadership obsessing about growing internal danger and the opposition priding itself on being small in numbers but pure and devout. The

Bolshevik truth was a slippery thing, and multitudinousness of supporters could be as much of a burden as an asset.

Many Party spokesmen patted one another on the back after sampling the effects of the famous ban on factions. "We are on much firmer ground than a year ago," Lenin stated at the Eleventh Party Congress.[95] "Today we can declare with confidence that the main groupings and currents have been expunged," Molotov agreed.[96] The opposition told a different story. "Unity still eludes us," said Shliapnikov. "One could even say that we were more united a year ago—and I say that in the face of the significant ideological skirmish that took place in this hall then."[97]

The majoritarians blamed the opposition for cleavages. The Central Committee's annual report for 1921–1922 stated that although issues discussed at the Tenth Party Congress had lost much of their relevance, "we cannot call our disagreements utterly insignificant."[98] Overt and covert struggles broke out over the control of the leading Party organs.[99] At the conference of the metalworkers' union, oppositionists allegedly "agitated for a schism."[100] The opposition agreed that the tendency to present intra-Party disputes as technical and inconsequential was waning. "Up to now there were no principled disagreements in the Party," Shliapnikov noted. "Now, however, the attitude towards the working class is at stake and disagreements can no longer be papered over."[101]

The language of the Party Congress suggests that a binary picture of the Party had begun taking root. Sol'ts's virulence was unprecedented: "We have a group in the Party that does not believe all is right. What is crucial now is that this group is an opposition to the Party, not an opposition within the Party!" Speaking from the other side of the fence, Kutuzov lamented: "Comrades, since the Tenth Party Congress there has been a division into 'ours' and 'theirs.'"[102] How distant such talk was from the majoritarians' ironic but amicable "our opposition" (nasha oppozitsiia).[103]

Semantic polarization moved in both directions. Consider Medvedev's use of pronouns: "Despite all we have done to build confidence, someone wants to kick us out of the Party."[104] A high degree of ambiguity infused his use of "us" and "we": at times the reference was inclusive, referring to all Party members, at other times it was exclusive, designating members of the Workers' Opposition alone; in one reading, Medvedev believed he was part of the Party, while in the other, the Workers' Opposition was, in his view, the only true Party.[105]

Still a spokesman for the Central Committee, Trotsky took note of such subtleties. When Shliapnikov complained that "they do not give us a chance," Trotsky was more upset with the language of Shliapnikov's complaint than with the complaint itself. "In this division into the 'we' and the 'they,'" Trotsky bellowed, "lie the principal sin and the principal political crime." Next, he turned directly to Shliapnikov: "You talk in terms of 'us' and 'them'—as if you had a party to spare!"[106]

Whereas at the Tenth Party Congress it was often said that little separated the Central Committee from its critics, no bridge could possibly cross the divide between the two after the Tenth Party Congress. "He who has the courage to point to shortcomings," Kosior complained, "is immediately relegated to the opposition."[107] "Where is our united front?" Kutuzov wondered. "We have begun regarding each other as enemies [*smotriat drug na druzhku kak chert na petrushku*]."[108]

Had the "stifling intra-Party regime" set the Party sliding down this slippery slope? Responding to such concerns, some delegates to the Twelfth Party Congress proposed that the ban on factions must be rescinded. The ban, Kosior declared, which was "originally dictated by exceptional circumstances—Kronshtadt and our internal crisis—has since become something like the alpha and omega of our Party system. . . . Today, in a period of calm and peaceful construction, why do we need extraordinary measures?" Some delegates laughed at Kosior, while others hurled abuse—clearly the ban was fast becoming the cornerstone of a new orthodoxy. Kosior balked: "All I meant was that we cannot set up a process of a collective opinion making . . . without some sort of exchange of opinions."[109]

To be sure, Lutovinov granted the Party disciplinarians their main point, "everything suggests that groupings did not disappear—they live on underground." But such secrecy was a reasonable reaction to the intimidating tactics employed by the majoritarians. "Zinoviev does not seek the real causes of the abnormalities in our Party in a proper Marxist manner. . . . His threats only prove that the Central Committee . . . buries its head in the sand like an ostrich. . . . The Politburo regards itself as an infallible pope."[110]

The Central Committee's rejoinder was dismissive. "Lutovinov is very disappointed with my speech," Zinoviev taunted. "Well, I am very disappointed with his. [Laughter.] He says I threaten comrades. No, I threaten deserters."[111] Stalin spoke scornfully of what he regarded as the opposition's wish to turn the Party into a "discussion club." "Lutovinov wants to have the entire Party participate in the deliberations of each and every issue. . . . Given that we have 400,000 members and 20,000 cells, we will constantly talk, never decide."[112] Shouldering the brunt of the Central Committee's rejoinder, Bukharin insisted in an uncompromising, urgent tone that nothing could be more abnormal than "the demand that we institute a normal way to voice anti-Bolshevik positions. No, our old revolutionary virtues must be preserved. . . . Some comrades apparently do not like all discussion to come to an end after we reach a decision and before the implementation stage begins. In other words, they do not like the principles of democratic centralism, the basic structure of our Party as, precisely, a Bolshevik party."[113]

Insofar as it represented alien interests—and Lenin never tired of reiterating that politics reflected economics—the opposition threatened to subvert the Party from within. However, if it could be sufficiently weakened, the opposition could be exploited: whenever infiltrators were unmasked, comrades' hermeneutical acumen was sharpened. "Something good came out of the Discussion after all," Lenin noted in 1921. "While diverting our attention from the urgent battle with the petit bourgeoisie," it taught the working class how dangerous an inner enemy might be.[114]

Iaroslavskii boasted that not a single organization, not a single cell joined the Workers' Opposition after the ban on factions was introduced. "If we feel that we have to tell its story in detail, this is because we want to inoculate the younger generation with an antidote [*protivoiadie*]." Hopeful, Iaroslavskii was also anxious: even the smallest heterodox group called into existence by NEP—an antibourgeois vaccine in its own right—could, if not carefully monitored, take over the entire body politic. "You know how an organism can be infected by a tiny germ. . . . It is when the Party organism is most isolated and weak that it is most likely to contract an illness."[115]

By the mid-1920s, the oppositionists became the crucial element separating the insiders from the outsiders of the brotherhood of the elect. But this separating function could not function statically; the "heterodox" had to be constantly pointed to, "revealed" (*vyiavit'*), or "unmasked" (*razoblachit'*).[116] "Plenty of alien elements penetrated our ranks after the end of the Civil War, and a purge was necessary," Party officials stated in 1921. "But the task of purifying [*ochistit'*] cannot be solved with one stroke.[117] "I have no doubt," Kalinin wrote to Lenin in 1922, "that the Party lives by constant selection. . . . The process of removing alien elements can never stop."[118]

The Communist hunt for internal enemies was enacted on the boundary line between the inside and the outside, tracing and retracing this boundary repeatedly. The source of pollution and division, the oppositionist represented evil both introjected and projected. Hence the endless rhetorical repetition of the ban on factions. Speaker after speaker addressed various Central Committee plenary sessions and lesser Party meetings in 1921–1923 to emphasize the newfound Party unity, only to warn against the danger of the multiplying oppositionist forces. Whether a speaker described the opposition as negligible or ubiquitous, the increased preoccupation with splinter groups was a part of a larger process: talking endlessly, eternally, inexhaustibly about the inner enemy.[119]

Although intra-Party discussion was still welcomed, its justification changed somewhat. Kamenev reproduced the language of those who maintained the Central Committee was obsessing with its critics in a withering response. "All the disputed points are 'blown out of proportion,' or so say some comrades who believe it would have been better not to raise such points at all. 'So what if this or that pen pusher made this or that mistake in this or that article! Big deal!'" According to Kamenev, such a position was "absolutely wrong": The oppositionists had to be provoked into talking, not because there was a chance they had something useful to say, but primarily because their criticisms were indicative of the moods "taking shape in the depths of our Party."[120] The Party performed an inventory of the symptoms of oppositionism, noting not only what the opposition explicitly said, but also what it involuntarily let slip. The likes of Krasin, Larin, and Osinskii had unwittingly expressed views that normally remained implicit, and now the Central Committee could "sound the alarm bells."[121]

At that point the intentions of the oppositionists hardly mattered. "Things have their own inner logic," Radek pointed out, "independent of the logic people do or do not happen to apply.'"[122] Keep those words in mind while reading part of Kamenev's address to Osinskii, a Democratic Centralist, and Safarov, one of the leaders of the "military opposition" at the Eighth Party Congress and Komsomol functionary at the present, from the floor of the Twelfth Party Congress (April 1923).

I suppose you did not write the anonymous platform and that its authorship is erroneously attributed to you. Let's say that that's so. But a Marxist who went through twenty-five years of schooling must know that the question should not be examined only in personal terms, that connections between ideas are important. . . . Because it represents a certain political line, your platform gave our class enemies the right to enroll you in their church, in their congregation [zachislit' v svoiu tserkov', v svoi prikhod].[123]

Caviling in some respects, circumspect in others, Kamenev's criticism is indicative of the discourse at that time: the opposition groups were rejected for their theories, but their supporters were not necessarily condemned as moral selves—no one had given up calling leading oppositionists "comrades."[124] Radek noted: "Everybody is said to be deviating—deviating from this, deviating from that. It will be funny if some comrades take this sort of reproach as a personal insult."[125]

The Central Committee still worked on the assumption that the aims of most oppositionists were decent, that these were fundamentally honest comrades; Kamenev did not agree with a word Krasin was saying but he applauded his "sincerity."[126] What we have in the year 1922–23 is not a case of the negation of the soul but its absolution; at this point it simply did not occur to the leaders of the Central Committee that there could be something intrinsically wrong with their critics, all of whom were distinguished Bolsheviks who had proved their ideological valor on more than one occasion. To join the opposition was to err, and while the error was condemned, the errant comrade was forgiven. "We will continue to do things precisely as Lenin taught us," Zinoviev promised: "we will be intransigent in terms of our ideological principles and flexible with individuals."[127]

Repressive Practices

From the Tenth Party Congress on, the Party leadership searched for the means to dissuade the oppositionists from their opinions, to convince them to return to the fold. Early measures designed to reduce the unbrotherly infighting were very mild; they developed piecemeal and without a directing hand. These policies evolved in

tandem with the construction of the opposition as a noun—an entity to be unearthed and disarmed. Different measures had to be applied to quell acrimonious
personal feuding (definition of the problem in 1919–1920), to arbitrate in rambunc-
tious organizational disagreements (definition of the problem in 1921–1922), to
censure moral weaknesses (definition of the problem in 1923–1925).

Who had the mandate to decide who overstepped the line separating orthodoxy from heterodoxy and how violators were to be treated? From very early on,
the opposition groups began complaining about repressive activity following intra-
Party disagreements. Standing for any illegitimate punishment, "repressions" (re-
pressii) had been a vague catchall term that could refer to the arbitrary transfer of
a functionary from one locality to another, or to a purge without due process.[128]
The opposition groups specifically claimed that their adherents were systematically removed from leadership positions because of their views. Such demotions
were generally called "transfers" or "relocations" (perevody, perebrosy).[129] As early as
the Ninth Party Congress, Sapronov maintained that "our Party discipline has assumed the ugliest forms imaginable: whenever a comrade ventures a criticism, he
is transferred to another organization, then to a third one and so on."[130] Kollontai
echoed this observation: "critics who articulate all of our woes are 'sent off to eat
peaches in warm climes.'"[131]

Some Bolsheviks ventured a principled justification of transfers. "People who sit
in the same place for too long make local connections and their personal and family life grow too comfortable," stated Iosif Khodorovskii from the Omsk Party organization at the Ninth Party Congress.[132] Enforced relocations, he believed, could
reduce the squabbles without tarnishing the political record of the official affected.
While Zinoviev agreed with Khodorovskii that the Party could and should move
errant comrades, he insisted that the procedure should be absolutely transparent.
"We must guarantee that the transfer of cadres is not done on a whim and that relocations do not turn into a method for the removal of unpleasant individuals."[133]
The Central Committee just elected by the Tenth Party Congress promised to "put
an immediate end to . . . transfers motivated by a factionalist struggle."[134]

Despite all of these promises, the opposition's reproaches grew only more bitter
with the passage of the years. In April 1921, the Central Committee received an official complaint from the Workers' Opposition concerning "persecutions" (goneniia)
of its former members.[135] "The identity of each oppositionist," Kosior protested at
the Eleventh Party Congress, "is being recorded and, when it seems necessary, he is
taken out of circulation."[136] In Kosior's opinion, the Party leadership was acting in
bad faith. "The path to the top is barred to our best comrades not because they are
incompetent Communists but only because, at different times and for different reasons, they challenged the Central Committee."[137]

In extreme cases, Moscow did not stop before cutting oppositionist organizations off. Their funds were confiscated and their members cast out. Certainly am-

putations were intrusive, but, according to the Party leadership, they were medical steps intended to heal, not repressions intended to punish. For example, the Central Committee did everything possible in 1921 to help oppositionist Samara "through palliative measures."[138] Legates such as Nikolai Kuibyshev were sent to revive Party life there—to no avail. Sedoi, envoy from the Central Committee, finally had to announce the complete disintegration of the Samara Party organization; anyway, 35 percent of its members had already turned in their Party cards.[139] All this justified the removal of the entire local leadership and the nomination of Minkov from the Moscow Party organization as the new head of the Samara Communists.[140] "This was a unique but necessary step," the Central Committee stated. It was inclined to think of the opposition as a cancer spreading through one of the Party's limbs; it was imperative that the cancerous tissue be wholly removed from Samara and healthy tissue grafted on. Indeed, with the help of Antonov-Ovseenko, Minkov, and other disciplined Communists, "the Samara Party organization finally emerged from its crisis."[141]

Because one of the responsibilities of the Central Committee was the supervision of local Party organizations, at any time it might step in to override their decisions. If their behavior contradicted the official resolutions of Party congresses, provincial Party organizations were dispersed; this was construed not as a violation but as an implementation of democratic centralism. The center would typically convene an extraordinary Party conference, conduct an orderly reelection of the local committees and reenroll their members.[142] Moscow was not ashamed to admit it intervened in the staffing of the provincial Party organs when necessary. While the Central Committee declared itself committed to fair play in demotions and transfers, it certainly would not "entrust the implementation of its line to individuals who object to it."[143] "What we have are not 'repressions' [repressii] but 'relocations' [perebroski]," Molotov explained; any type of political vendetta was "out of the question."[144]

I will devote later chapters to the Party's membership-screening practices; let it suffice to note here that, by and large, purging carried positive connotations for the Bolsheviks.[145] It was purges, not the process of consensus building, that were, in Trotsky's eyes, a sure road to unity.[146] "Because we did not fear division and did not hesitate to remove elements threatening to Party unity," Iaroslavskii explained, "we managed to remain pure [chistye]."[147] Lenin agreed: "Unity is a great thing and a great slogan, but our cause requires the unity of Marxists, not the unity of Marxists plus the enemies and distorters of Marxism."[148] According to Smilga, purges and unity were complementary, not mutually exclusive: "It is better that our party's ranks be smaller in number, but tight-knit. When the numbers decrease, this redounds to the benefit of the actual political leadership of the masses."[149]

Though they were threatened with purges on many occasions, the members of the opposition never called the basic principle of the purge into question—many of them seemed to be purges' greatest fans. "Once the Party's house is cleaned, unity will naturally follow," Kollontai said at the Tenth Party Congress.[150] Other oppositionists backed Kollontai: "We want a purge." "We want to make the Party homogeneous [*odnorodnaia*]."[151] Oppositionists and majoritarians carried on a protracted argument over who deserved credit for the idea. "Our opposition lays claim to having first come up with purges," Zinoviev noted at the Eleventh Party Congress. "This is untrue. Following the report delivered by your humble servant, the Party decided to conduct a 'serious purge' as early as the Eighth Party Congress, that is, in 1919!"[152]

No doubt, purges provoked a number of major controversies in the 1920s. But the question of whether a purge was a fair sort of censure never played a part in any controversy. The Central Committee pointed at the unruly factionalists and suggested that they be shown the door.[153] Workers' Opposition also dreamed of a Party relieved of its chaff, although in that scenario the first to be cast out would be the majoritarian bureaucrats. Ignatov thought it only right that "those who in their slovenliness failed to mend breakdowns in Party life be the first to go."[154] The issue was not procedural (what formal operation ensures justice?) but ethical-hermeneutical (who deserves to be a judge? who should be accused?).[155]

The "control commissions" (*kontrol'nye komissii*) handled the cleaning of the Party's house.[156] Still a novelty in 1921–1922, these bodies were the prerevolutionary Bolshevik courts of honor recast for a new set of functions.[157] A bridge between the Party's hermeneutical courts and the legal institutions of the state, the control commissions make an excellent case for the impossibility of separating politics and ethics in the Bolshevik discourse. As they provided finer and finer analyses of the violations of the opposition, these institutions highlighted the ambivalence of heterodoxy: a crime of honor or a state crime? An obfuscation or outright treason?

The need for a court of that nature was felt as early as the Civil War. Zinoviev wondered at the Ninth Party Congress how many "conflicts" reached the Central Committee's organizational bureau, a center for resolving disputes among Communists set up before the control commissions. Preobrazhenskii replied that in his briefcase at that moment were about five hundred cases awaiting scrutiny—"a very large harvest indeed."[158] Zinoviev believed that a "special Party organization that can be called the 'control commission,' or the 'court of proletarian honor' [*sud proletarskoi chesti*] ought to be created."[159]

Determined to enforce moral standards, the Ninth Party Congress created a network of control commissions, one at the center and one for each provincial Party organization.[160] It was some time before control commissions developed a serious apparatus. "Effectively," Sol'ts reported in 1921, "we have only five individuals at the disposal of the Central Control Commission."[161] Office space was makeshift at the outset, and quarters were so cramped that papers lay stacked in every corner. Nogin depicted the situation his inspection team encountered in Gogolian terms. The single room where work was carried out was bustling with activity, the investigators "interrogating [*doprashivaiut*] four individuals simultaneously." A huge number of old Party cards lie around on top of the general chancellery's closets in which papers are supposed to be kept; registration sheets are pilled up in different boxes, all covered with a thick layer of dust. On the windows of the meeting room a large pile of paper can be found, with a document pertaining to some unfinished business lying on the top of the pile."[162]

When Riazanov proposed the abolition of the Central Control Commission at the Eleventh Party Congress ("It was created at a difficult moment and should now be replaced by a more regular body"), he envisioned the institutional succession with a certain degree of detail: "If a comrade commits a private, criminal offense, he should be sent to the people's court; if, on the other hand, he commits a crime in the Communist milieu, he should be sent to the Party court."[163] Iu. S. Myshkin, the secretary of the Stavropol' Party committee, maintained that the provincial control commissions were even less expedient. "They should be dissolved, for they needlessly duplicate the Party structure."[164]

Sol'ts, who earned the nickname "the political judge" (*politicheskii sud'ia*), furiously launched into a defense of the network of the control commissions, which he considered "doubly important, considering that NEP represents a threat to the least stable and temperate Party members."[165] Other speakers agreed that the provincial control commissions "helped to defeat all attempts to import bourgeois habits into the Communist ranks."[166] Though Lenin had backed the control commissions,[167] the vote to determine their status held at the Eleventh Party Congress was close by Bolshevik standards: Myshkin's proposal received 89 votes, Sol'ts's received 223, and over half of the delegates abstained. Someone even cracked a joke: "Since both resolutions received a substantial number of votes, I suggest we find a way to reconcile the two. [Laughter.]"[168]

With their organization streamlined and their responsibility more clearly defined, the control commissions were supposed to take a comprehensive view of the causes of unhealthy phenomena and (1) improve the conduct of individual Party members as well as of those organizations whose actions were undermining Party unity and authority; (2) eliminate conflicts and the settling of personal accounts; (3) combat deviations; (4) struggle against careerism, bureaucratism, and other "office holders' crimes"; and, finally, (5) purge the Party of degenerate elements.[169] Oppositionists could find themselves challenged on the basis of any of these items. Summoned to the control commissions, they were asked about their biographies, their habits, their sexual mores. Even if their politics were less than orthodox, this was but a symptom of general moral breakdown.[170]

Whatever fell in the realm of what the Bolsheviks called "political ethics" (*politicheskaia etika*) was the domain of responsibility of the control commissions.[171] Overall, their work was not supposed to take the form of legal inquiry.

Such routine police methods as house searches, surveillance, and arrests were out of the question.[172] In fact, the comprehensive examination of a Party member could not be regarded as successful unless a "comradely atmosphere" ensured "mutual trust." Whether evidence was overwhelming or inadequate, the control commissions thought it important to review the case in the presence of the accused.[173] This, Shkiriatov explained, was done to prevent mistakes: "Frequently comrades were purged by a provincial control commission without any idea why. In the presence of the sides the situation always clears up—we find out about the atmosphere of workplace of the accused and about his moral identity [*moral'nyi oblik*]."[174] Rather than judging a discrete act, control commissions judged the entire personality of the actor behind that act.

Because they could not excel in their work unless the members of the control commissions "enjoyed prestige among the masses," their Party standing was meticulously examined. In 1923 a member of the Central Control Commission had to have been a Communist for a minimum of ten years; those who served at the provincial level were required to have Communist histories dating at least to the October Revolution. Only those who had awakened early to the Party's message could possess a superior consciousness, and only those endowed with such a consciousness could have a good understanding of the faults of other comrades.[175]

To enhance the authority of the Central Control Commission, its members were nominated not by the Central Committee but directly by the Party Congress.[176] The local control commissions also enjoyed some autonomy.[177] The members of their investigative teams were relieved of all other obligations and given the right to attend whatever Party meeting they wanted.[178] (But control commissions had no executive authority. Because their decisions were implemented by the local Party committees their sense of autonomy was somewhat weakened.)[179]

Should control commissions intervene in the Party discussion if it got out of hand? Speaking at the Tenth Party Congress, Sol'ts insisted that "control commissions have to ensure that intra-Party arguments adhere to proper Party guidelines, since otherwise a state of agitation characteristic of internal war could result."[180] But this did not mean that the control commissions should act as the supreme judges in intra-Party disputes.[181]

The Eleventh Party Congress dedicated much attention to the role of the control commissions in implementing the ban on factions. Many delegates of an oppositionist bent claimed that instead of defending their rights the new institution was biased in favor of the majority. "Should we conclude," Sol'ts retorted, "that the Central Control Commission has nothing to say about a looming Party schism?" When Medvedev stated, "We do not trust you at all," Sol'ts spread his arms: "How is that possible? Do you not recognize that we are a body elected by the congress? . . . It seems like Medvedev doesn't care about Party decisions, only about his own individual 'I.'"[182]

Medvedev mounted a vigorous rejoinder:

Sol'ts is portraying me as someone who places his ego above all else. If he was right, everyone would already have noticed. And yet, I've been in the Party for twenty-two years, never . . . pushing myself forward. . . . All there is to back up Sol'ts's contention that I do not trust the Central Control Commission is my reluctance to appeal to this body. But after all, have you not said yourself that political issues lie outside its jurisdiction?[183]

The authority of the Central Control Commission to curb oppositionism was challenged in connection with the Riazanov affair as well. The origins of this skirmish lay in the Fourth Trade Union Congress (May 1921), convened largely to address the status of unions in the overall structure of government—a bone of contention between the Central Committee and Workers' Opposition.[184] At the congress Riazanov had presented a resolution calling for a degree of autonomy for unions, which was preferred to the resolution drafted by the Central Committee— something that aroused the ire of Lenin's supporters.[185] Personal appeals by Lenin and Stalin, both of whom made extraordinary visits to the congressional hall, were required before the congress reversed itself and endorsed the official line. Upon his return from a meeting with the trade union Communists, Lenin, to whom Riazanov's behavior appeared appalling, said: "For the first time I felt like I was speaking not to Communists but to people who did not belong to the Party." After roundly criticizing Riazanov, the Central Committee plenary session resolved on May 18, 1921, to deprive him of all official authority in the trade union movement.[186]

Riazanov was officially reprimanded by the Central Control Commission shortly before the Eleventh Party Congress. Accused of making destructive suggestions regarding workers autonomy, Riazanov, who was not happy to find himself in Sol'ts's office in the first place, was defiant: "If this is a trial, I am leaving." "It is not a trial," said Sol'ts, "but a comradely conversation. It is the duty of the Central Control Commission to strengthen the will of the Party."[187]

When he eventually recounted these events at the congress, the recollection of Sol'ts's insolence left Riazanov beside himself: "Can anyone tell me what are the limits of the Central Control Commission's mandate?"[188]

How can the Central Control Commission bar a Party member from trade union activity? Am I a drunk? a debaucher? . . . What, may I ask, is my crime? Suppose I had advanced outrageous proposals along the lines of "We must depose the Central Committee," or "We must change the principles guiding Party policy." What could have been done to me? My resolution could have been rejected, of course. But to summon me to the Central Control Commission—this is nonsense of the highest order, tantamount to prosecuting someone for something he said at a Party Congress.[189]

A fundamental idea united the speeches given by Riazanov and Medvedev: both argued that in interfering with the process of Party deliberation, the Central

Control Commission was trespassing on territory outside its jurisdiction. All sorts of misdemeanors required the intervention of the newly formed body, but not the voicing of opinions. Since he had made no moral errors, since he had not "defiled [*oporochil*] himself in any way," Riazanov claimed he could not be censored.[190]

Despite appearances, the attack on the Central Control Commission involved far more than procedural issues. Ultimately the following question was at stake: Was one's political and ideological stance a matter of one's explicit convictions and beliefs (something for the Party Congress to look into), or was it an expression of one's deep-seated moral self (the domain of the Central Control Commission)? Riazanov and Medvedev were determined to convince their hearers that regardless of what the majoritarians thought of their views, their ethics were beyond reproach. Since they were good Communists, their intentions should not have been subjected to humiliating investigation. Excommunicating a veteran Bolshevik was ridiculous in their eyes: an oppositionist was not a criminal.

But what if they belonged to an enemy contingent that had wormed its way inside the Communist camp? Should the control commissions not be entrusted with the most sensitive task of detecting the anti-Party within the Party?[191] No one was telling them so to their faces yet, but when the cases of Riazanov and Medvedev were moved to the Central Control Commission, that indicated that the moral probity, if not the basic goodness, of some oppositionists had been thrown into dispute—the first suspects were those who had violated the ban on factions.[192]

The *Appeal of the Twenty-Two*

The widely publicized events triggered by the *Appeal of the Twenty-Two* (named after the number of its signatories) fairly gauged the position of Workers' Opposition after the ban on factions. Delivered by Kollontai to the executive committee of the Komintern on February 26, 1922, this document bitterly and exhaustively lamented the suppression of criticism in all national Communist parties.[193]

The authors of the Appeal demanded redress from the Komintern, a body that, at least in theory, stood above the Russian Communist Party. The *Appeal of the Twenty-Two* contended that "not everything is right . . . not only in the country at large but even within our Party itself." The authors vehemently protested the "struggle the apparatus conducts against anybody with independent opinions."[194] Choice words were also reserved for rampant Party bureaucratization and the failure to implement democratization. In addition, the Appeal contained numerous complaints of violations of comrades' rights by the Central Committee.[195] Examples included the illegal search of Shliapnikov's apartment and the interception of the oppositionists' private correspondence.[196] "True, the Central Committee decided to open an investigation of the matter," but this proved to be only a decoy; "in any case, nothing materialized." Finally, the Appeal addressed the question of "provocations." Thus it contained a story about Rubinov, a Cheka agent, who suggested to Shliapnikov and Kollontai's secretaries that they create a nucleus of the Fourth International. This was allegedly done to suborn the secretaries so that they might be purged.[197]

The Workers' Opposition soon found itself on the defensive again, as the heads of the Komintern labeled the *Appeal of the Twenty-Two* subversive and inimical to Party discipline. Those who had signed the document were warned that the continuation of their struggle against the resolutions of the Tenth Party Congress was "at odds with the tasks of the Russian proletariat."[198]

The Central Committee investigated the origins of the Appeal. The leaders of Workers' Opposition did have a "statutory right to ask the Komintern to intervene," as Trotsky admitted.[199] The problem was that Shliapnikov, Kollontai, and Medvedev "had presented unsubstantiated facts regarding the relations between the Party and the working class," shamelessly "distorting" reality.[200] A special commission named by the Eleventh Party Congress to look into the matter further concluded that the Workers' Opposition had advanced far enough along the road to heterodoxy to consider calling for a full-blown Party schism, a motion allegedly postponed "only because conditions were believed not to have ripened yet."[201] Having examined all of the material at its disposal and having questioned the majority of the signatories to the Appeal, in the process "carefully comparing comrades' words with the materials in our hands," the Central Control Commission arrived at a grave conclusion: this was no "accidental grouping" but an "illegal" and "factionalist" organization.[202]

Sol'ts emphasized that several of those quizzed about their role in the drafting of the Appeal refused to treat the Central Control Commission as a comradely institution, behaving instead as if they were in the hands of an alien body. "So they conducted themselves as if they were being questioned by a bunch of bourgeois legal clerks," blamed much on "forgetfulness," and refused to mention names. In view of the accumulated evidence, Sol'ts maintained, the *Appeal of the Twenty-Two* could not be regarded as a routine criticism of the Party's defects. Several factors indicated that the document was prepared in utmost secrecy and that "its signatories were approached selectively." Some sort of conspiratorial activity must have taken place: specific individuals were brought into the secret based not just on Party membership but on partisan, oppositionist sentiments.[203]

One of the Central Control Commission's more important tasks was establishing the "degree of consciousness" (*stepen' soznatel'nosti*) each of the signatories brought to the affair. The first category included Shliapnikov, Medvedev, and Kollontai: these were the leaders, "the individuals who had coordinated the 'Appeal' and whose self-awareness had to be estimated as high." This attempt to rank the oppositionists according to their role in the Appeal affair drew prompt protests from the signatories. This, they alleged, was an old military trick: "Figure out who the officers are and who are the rank-and-file soldiers." While she claimed to have been flattered by the title of "high commander," Kollontai rejected it "most categorically; all twenty-two signatories are highly conscious. Not only is there no question of my leading such seasoned Communists as Kopylev, Mitin, Tolkontsev, and others, but I learned a great deal from them myself."[204] Medvedev flatly refused to cooperate with his interrogators, noting: "Sol'ts, who knows half of the signatories personally, must agree that we are not talking about individuals who can be worked over . . . like young boys."[205] Shliapnikov's argument developed along similar lines: "We were moved, all twenty-two of us, by nothing but the wish to strengthen, fortify, and reinvigorate the Party. You vainly separate us into goats and sheep."[206]

Tellingly, while Shliapnikov denied possession of a consciousness superior to other signatories, he did not question the hermeneutical presuppositions of the investigation: what lay at the bottom of his heart, he agreed with his interrogators, was what really mattered. Intention was key, but "when you speak of my supposed aspirations to divide our Party, you are all wrong. My desire is to see the Party united—the Party that we, acting together with thousands of workers, created with our own hands during the underground days and in 1917. It is not that easy to give that up and seek a schism. Anyone who says I would do this is an unworthy comrade."[207]

Shliapnikov resisted all attempts to frame the signatories of the Appeal as conspirators.[208] The Appeal, he argued, "was born from, literally, a few hours of conversation. I scribbled it on the edge of the table with my own hand, as comrades stood around, dictating to me.[209] Medvedev picked up where Shliapnikov left off. Nothing extraordinary was done to prepare the Appeal and "it was not designed to be consumed by the general masses. Most of us are close personal friends anyway, the result of a decade of working together in the underground. Now that we live here in Moscow, we are linked by telephones and work meetings."[210] The rest of the signatories were good friends of the original group who happened to arrive to Moscow on the occasion of the Fifth Congress of the Metalworkers' Union.[211] Before the Appeal was drafted, each signatory had come either to Medvedev or to Shliapnikov and complained about how things were with the Party at the grassroots level "so that the situation prompted serious concerns regarding the fate of the proletariat and the Revolution." At a certain point, Medvedev stated, it no longer made sense to continue meeting in pairs—a general meeting had to be convened. "We said to ourselves: 'Since we know each other so well we can talk frankly. With luck we will realize that the shortcomings one person sees in his locality don't exist everywhere.'" But it quickly became obvious that everyone had similar misgivings about Party policies.[212]

Sol'ts contested every detail of the story. To begin with, he rejected as an obvious lie the idea that the *Appeal of the Twenty-Two* had been "prepared in half an

hour. Look at what Tolkontsev is confessing to. He came to us and found the proletarian courage to say, 'Yes, we made a mistake.' Yes, Tolkontsev may have been
Kollontai's teacher, but she turned out to be a bad student." The entire operation,
Sol'ts went on, was closed up with seven seals of secrecy. "When asked under what
circumstances he had signed the Appeal, Bekrenev testified that the leaders had enlisted a messenger who went around signing everyone up. In view of this testimony,
are we expected to believe that they met accidentally?"[213]

The Central Control Commission identified a second group among the signatories of the Appeal: important provincial activists of the Workers' Opposition.
This group, the commission opined, had nothing to do with the "lower orders" of
the Party it claimed to be representing—its members occupied "important managerial posts." Half a political subversive and half an ordinary crook, Kuznetsov was
charged with pruning the record of his past to remove the unsavory moments. According to his indictment he was an "unstable and alien element" who fraudulently
signed illegal oppositionist documents in the name of the proletariat. In actuality,
this was a petit bourgeois individual who had taken work in a factory "in order to
dodge military duty."[214]

A more interesting oppositionist was Mitin, a prominent Communist from
Donbass. Although his questionnaire stated that he had been with the Bolsheviks
since 1902, in the Central Control Commission's account this erstwhile Menshevik
had not joined the Party until 1920. "Prior to that date he had been on Denikin's
side"—clearly not a sign of proletarian consciousness.[215] But there was more to Mitin's case: some of the material therein linked provincial chiefs to the Moscow oppositionist leaders, substantiating the claim that Workers' Opposition had woven a
clandestine political network of national scope.

A letter from Mitin to Shliapnikov and Medvedev proved beyond a doubt that
a factionalist organization had developed an independent political program. Mitin
wrote: "At our last meeting you, Shliapnikov, were handed the task of evaluating
NEP and drawing the appropriate conclusions." Mitin himself assumed responsibility for seeing to it that "our guys" were named to every factory committee, "so that
later they could take over the factory cells." This stratagem was supposed to lead to
the conquest of district committees and the Provincial Party Conference. "If I manage to accomplish that," Mitin concluded, "Donbass is ours."[216]

The Central Control Commission wondered what exactly Mitin meant by
"ours," and what was to be made of the ideological "world outlook" (*mirosozertsanie*)
undergirding his letter. These, of course, were rhetorical questions: "Only individuals who belong to a grouping alien to our Party . . . can write in such a way."[217] Mitin's letter demonstrated "what depravity this malicious [*zlostnyi*] disorganizer dis-
seminated in the Party milieu."[218] Armed with its own secretariat and a mailing list,
a Workers' Opposition group had allegedly taken form in the midst of Party activ-

ity and had sent circular letters to its supporters across the country. As one might imagine, the majoritarians felt that the "attitude of this underground organization to the Central Committee was anti-Party, uncomradely, and scandalous."[219]

A special commission established by the Eleventh Party Congress called for purging Mitin and Kuznetsov.[220] A precedent had been set: the decision inaugurated a practice of purging by means of an ad hoc body endowed by the Party Congress with supreme disciplinary authority (as opposed to purging by the local party organizations, as stipulated in the Party regulations).

The Central Control Commission allocated the remainder of the signatories to the third and least self-conscious group.[221] No hard evidence could be provided to implicate anybody from this group in factionalist behavior: the only charge was participation in the meeting held by Shliapnikov and Medvedev.[222] Punishment was designed accordingly. Sol'ts suggested that these accused go uncensored, "but apprised of the resolution of the Komintern concerning the Appeal of the Twenty-Two."[223]

The Bolshevik hermeneutical apparatus honed and applied to the opposition over the course of its investigation of the Appeal would see much use in following years. Not only would the opposition be accused endless times of failing to bow to Party authority and of advocating a schism in the Party, but there would be no more challenges to the authority of the network of the control commissions in prosecuting political heterodoxy. Guilt would be assigned based not on the acts actually committed but on the divination of the intent behind them, and, perhaps most importantly, the oppositionists deemed most intransigent in their positions would be purged.

Counterrevolution within the Party?

Some time in the months between the Eleventh and the Twelfth Party Congresses the "opposition groups" metamorphosed into the opposition. This in two senses: the plural became the singular—there was much less mention of "opposition groups" after 1922, and even less emphasis on their triviality—and the adjective became a noun. If before some delegates were said to be "oppositionists," now the official press argued that some oppositionists managed to become delegates. The disappearance of quotation marks announced the naturalization of a neologism of recent vintage and the similar begun to replace the dissimilar as the Central Committee gazed out upon its critics. What once appeared as a heterogeneous assortment of groups, coteries, currents, and factions was now in the process of being amalgamated—still very sporadically and inconsistently, to be sure—into more or less one piece. Oppositionism had begun the long trek from political mood into tangible conspiratorial essence.

Official commentators indicated that some oppositionists had turned to breaking the rules of the game: they not only denied that the Central Committee majority truly represented the working class but intimated that the Party may have become irredeemable. The calls to the workers to exit the Party and join an alternative organization violated the fundamental Marxist tenet that only one vehicle could be the bearer of the emancipatory truth. Part of the opposition, asserted official spokesmen, had burrowed so far underground that not only did it refuse to share its membership lists with the official Party organization, it aimed at becoming a militant revolutionary force; if necessary it would violently overthrow the Bolshevik leadership.

The Workers' Opposition had advocated the formation of a second party, an anti-Party of sorts, or so Bukharin concluded after listening to a discourse that mirrored and yet subverted the official message. "Ignatov claims that 'The Party . . . stands apart from the masses.' Who, then, needs such a party? . . . The present party," continued Bukharin, extrapolating the opposition's thinking, "should be tossed away and another party should be set up to replace it, without its shortcomings. If I had taken Ignatov's arguments seriously"—namely, that the Party did not defend the proletariat—"believe me, I would have exited the Party and begun organizing a new party immediately."[224] This, according to Iaroslavskii, was exactly what a segment of the Workers' Opposition was doing: "I believe—and I could be wrong—that a petit bourgeois party is taking form in the bosom of our party."[225]

Speakers for the Workers' Opposition flew into a rage over the accusation that they longed for organizational independence. "Workers' Opposition is no different than the group called 'the Ten,' the group called 'the Eighteen' and other groups," intoned Shliapnikov: "it wants to implement policy through the Party, not outside the Party or against the Party."[226] Medvedev explained in heartfelt tones how loyal the Workers' Opposition had always been: "When our party experienced a massive outflow of members, comrades used to come to our flats . . . and ask us, 'What should we do?' Time and again we deemed it our duty to respond, 'Don't leave the Party. Don't take the most damaging, most dangerous step.'"[227]

To further the rhetorical denigration of the opposition, the Party leaders had to show that its legitimate and acknowledged wing had consciously allied itself with underground elements. To this end, it was suggested in 1922–1923 that the licit opposition had entered the walled city of Bolshevik camaraderie as a Trojan horse. Workers' Truth—perhaps the first Communist splinter group actually described as "counterrevolutionary"—was a case in point.[228] According to the findings of the official investigation commission, this group coalesced within the Party in the spring of 1921 with the goal of revising the character of the Russian Revolution and the role of the Party therein.[229] Like every other "conspiratorial" (*zagovornicheskaia*) formation, utter secrecy surrounded the group. Iaroslavskii said that he possessed materials proving that Workers' Truth was "using Party information for its own ends and was carrying out underground activities with the aim of blowing the Party up from within."[230]

In 1922, Workers' Truth circulated an *Appeal to the Revolutionary Proletariat of Russia*.[231] Addressed to "all revolutionary elements that remain loyal to the working class," the leaflet excoriated the Bolsheviks for having degenerated into a "new ruling class." "The Communist party, which during the Revolution was the party of the working class, has transformed itself into the party of state managers."[232] *An Appeal to the Twelfth Party Congress* by Workers' Truth blamed the Central Committee for "the renaissance of regular capitalistic relations ... and the annihilation of the working class as a political force."[233] According to the group's spokesmen, "NEP stands not for 'New Economic Policy' but for 'New Exploitation of the Proletariat.'"[234]

The Central Committee was shocked that the Workers' Truth denied the socialist character of the October Revolution, "maliciously depicting our economic and political order as a dictatorship of the bourgeoisie."[235] Iaroslavskii inveighed against the new heresy: "The main task confronting the international movement—namely the revolutionary dismantling of the bourgeoisie—is minimized in the thinking of Workers' Truth." Worse, the Workers' Truth challenged the teachings of Marx, setting against his "materialism" the views of Bogdanov.[236]

Aleksandr Bogdanov, a revered left-wing Bolshevik theorist who had quit the Party well before 1917 over a dispute with Lenin, was widely believed to be the founding father of Workers' Truth, ideologically if not organizationally.[237] Though he repeatedly denied any direct links to the group,[238] the ideas set forth in Workers' Truth's appeals resonate strongly with Bogdanov's: a full-blown socialist society will not be achieved in Russia unless proletarian culture is developed.[239]

What put Bogdanov and the Workers' Truth beyond the pale was their open contention that the Bolshevik Party cannot carry forward the idea of cultural revolution and that it is imperative that a true workers' party be founded in Russia.[240] This was a blatant violation of a taboo. Yes, we have shortcomings, Iaroslavskii granted, "but one can treat shortcomings in a comradely way, as shortcomings of his own class and his own state, and one can invest his power in correcting them. Or one can treat shortcomings as derived from an alien class, an alien state, devoting one's efforts not to correcting these shortcomings but to sharpening dissatisfactions with the Party and laying blame at its feet."[241] According to the official Party line, Workers' Truth did not perceive the Party as the vanguard of the proletariat at all, but saw it as the organizer of "state capitalism" and therefore was interested in taking over the Soviet state and not correcting it.[242]

Here we witness an early appearance of the Black Mass motif: through the lure of a pseudo-Party, the Workers' Truth supposedly threatened a diabolical dispossession of Bolshevism and assumption of control over proletarian souls. The most menacing feature of this radicalized opposition was its condemnation of the Central Committee majority in the name of the very same doctrinal principles on which the latter's legitimacy rested. The Bogdanovist supporters of Workers' Truth were presented in the official press as true apostates.[243] Unlike the Mensheviks or the Social Revolutionaries, the socialist parties that opposed the Bolshevik seizure of power in 1917, "seeking support for their pseudorevolutionary slogans among the petite bourgeoisie," Workers' Truth had carried the name of the working class itself and did so in vain.[244]

Bolsheviks were not easily scared by counterrevolutionaries. Official newspapers featured stories about GPU unearthing and eliminating enemy plots on an almost daily basis. The trouble with the new type of illegal formations, Zinoviev explained, lay elsewhere.

It has been demonstrated to my satisfaction that under normal conditions "Workers' Truth" would have functioned as a normal social democratic group.... This group could easily have turned out to be quite harmless—and yet, it became quite important. Why? Because it does not act in isolation, as an independent group, but attempts to act under our aegis [pod nashei firmoi]. They want to enter our Party, to nest in it, to insert themselves into it.[245]

Provocation was the most sinister weapon of all, and Workers' Truth was said to have employed this device to seduce "the least experienced comrades."[246] Naive workers might mistake the political vocabulary of Workers' Truth for their own; when they heeded such a call they would end by attacking their own government. "If somebody openly non-Party or anti-Party stood up in front of the broad masses to make counterrevolutionary speeches," Zinoviev said, no one would listen to him. But imagine "calls for a repetition of January 9—a procession to the Kremlin, everyone carrying a portrait of Lenin, demands for wage increases, and so on. ... Though they are done in the name of our party, such steps would lead to its disintegration."[247]

"Temptation" (iskushenie) seemed to be the heart of the problem.[248] "Hiding behind our banners, trying to present themselves as 'pure' Communists and spokesmen for 'truth,' ... the adherents of Workers' Truth are disseminating disguised Menshevik ideology."[249] Workers' Truth, in the official view, was nothing but "treason" (predatel'stvo), an intimate enemy, dangerous precisely because it spoke words some workers mistakenly recognized as their own.

Indeed, whom did the true workers support? A Workers' Truth broadside of October 1923 bragged: "Within a short time our banners gained wide popularity among workers.... Now that the claim that workers follow the Party has been disproved, the ruling groups have realized that their final hour is fast approaching."[250] Naturally, the official view was the contrary: while conscious workers supported the Central Committee, it was the degenerated part of the working class that stood behind Workers' Truth, "a group that formed following the intensification of class struggle under NEP."[251] A new discursive reality was shaping up: the reality of two parallel universes, each excluding the other.[252]

As if to add insult to injury, the Workers' Truth looked for allies in the Party. During that period when its appeals were causing a stir, many good Bolsheviks assumed that the faction had ties to the Workers' Group, a similar "illegal counter-revolutionary group," that distributed the so-called "anonymous platform" to the delegates of the Twelfth Party Congress (April 1923), calling for the removal of specialists and managerial authority and the ouster of Zinoviev, Kamenev, and Stalin.[253]

The case of Gavriil Miasnikov, a Bolshevik since 1906 and the leader of the Workers' Group, became a Bolshevik cause célèbre.[254] Every step of the case, the identification of a threat to the Party and the categorical elimination of the threat, would become a template for many similar prosecutions in the years that followed—from the Central Committee's proclamations that it had done everything in its power to return Miasnikov to the correct path, to its claim that the culprit openly violated Party discipline, and finally to the charge that Miasnikov had sent his followers to infiltrate the regular Communist cells.[255]

Though he had been warned in August 1921 that, "in view of the clash between his theses and the interests of the Party, he should not propagate them publicly," Miasnikov published a brochure, *To Party Members*, controversially demanding "freedom of the press, from the monarchists to the anarchists."[256] Lenin chastised Miasnikov, who resided then in the provincial city of Perm': "eager to heal the Party you got hold of a medicine that ensures certain death."[257] Undeterred, Miasnikov drafted a letter of protest against the local Party committee and instigated a walkout of almost the entire Motivilikhan delegation from the Perm' Party conference. Workers, he explained, trusted him as someone who had organized a workers' soviet at Motovilikha, an industrial village on the Kama River and as "one of the leaders of the 1905 uprising."[258] As if that was not enough, Miasnikov sent his tentacles to the capitals; thus he urged his Petrograd friends to unite all the dissatisfied Bolsheviks under one banner so as to take over "at least two Party districts."[259]

On February 20, 1922, a Central Committee commission found that Miasnikov had used his Party membership "solely to facilitate his struggle against the Party" and resolved to expel him.[260] Zinoviev defended this harsh punishment: "'What,' you ask, 'have you done with Miasnikov? A worker spoke out against us and without stopping to think we expelled him.' . . . But this is rubbish, comrades! I personally spent a year talking to Miasnikov, doing all I could to change his mind."[261]

In the summer of 1923, as Workers' Truth and the Workers' Group penetrated more deeply into the factories, the GPU stepped in, and Miasnikov as well as a handful of other activists were arrested.[262] As he prepared the case against the accused, Jan Dzerzhinskii, the head of GPU, found that even reliable Communists continued to see them as "comrades" and refused to testify against them. Out of desperation, Dzerzhinskii had to ask the Politburo to announce that it was the duty of every loyal Party member to denounce to the GPU all those who had taken illegal actions against the Party.[263] Condemning Workers' Truth and the Workers' Group as "anti-Communist," the September 1923 Central Committee Plenary Session defined adherence to these groups as incompatible with Party membership.[264]

How large were these oppositionist-turned-counterrevolutionary underground organizations? In the 1920s the Central Committee tended to belittle the size of these illegal groups.[265] With the roundup of the Workers' Truth activists operating in Moscow, it became apparent to Iaroslavskii that "we are dealing not with an organization made up of a few thousand—as its members stated . . . but a group of about twenty individuals, including sympathizers."[266] "There is no reason to present Workers' Truth as a huge many-headed hydra," Bukharin agreed.[267] In the 1930s this approach was reversed, as Stalin's followers inflated the numbers to prove how menacing these groups had been, and how deserved their punishment.

It is doubtful whether anything can be gained by taking sides in this debate, by declaring the early numbers more or less accurate than the later ones. Let us instead focus our attention on the evolution of the Bolshevik concept of political support itself. Indeed, if we define adherence to Workers' Truth or the Workers' Group as participation in its underground cells, attendance in most of its meetings, perhaps even some agitation in the factories on its behalf—these were the criteria used by the Central Control Commission and GPU in 1923—we will get very small numbers.[268] If, on the other hand, we apply the later criteria, adding up all expressions of solidarity with slogans associated with the Workers' Truth platform—even when the individual in question had no organizational allegiance to the underground and possibly did not even know that it existed—then the numbers would skyrocket.

Be that as it may, the Central Committee leaders believed they had cause for concern already in 1923. Jealous of the Party's drive towards unity, the oppositionist underground called on all the elements grouped around defeated platforms to join forces and attempt to correct the Party's course. Kamenev alerted the Party to the existence of a "new alliance" (*novoe ob"edinenie*), and Zinoviev was also worried by platforms that "attempted to amalgamate previous platforms, calling on former groupings to unite and create a non-Party organization that would strive to correct our Party, as it were. Let me make a suggestion of my own to these groups," he commented sardonically: "better correct yourselves first!"[269]

To prove his point about the continuity in the oppositionist movement Zinoviev reported the results of a careful comparison between the tenets of Democratic Centralism and the manifesto of the Workers' Group: "Although areas with anything to do with NEP are incomparable because Democratic Centralism's manifesto was written before the advent of NEP, 99 percent of the ideas in the two documents are the same. I will be happy to show the notebook in which the comparison is detailed to anyone who has doubts about my conclusions."[270] Bukharin traced all of the new groupings to "the same single divinity, a holy trinity [*odin i tot zhe gospod' v trekh litsakh*]"—Democratic Centralism, Workers' Truth, and the Workers' Group. Those who kept at their subversive practices and combined into a "united block" had to be driven from the Bolshevik camp. "Gentlemen," Zinoviev said, "hit the road [*skatert' vam doroga*]!"[271]

The Twelfth Party Congress urged comrades who wished to preserve their integrity to dissociate themselves from underground opposition groups.[272] Picking on a quite visible fence-sitter, Zinoviev challenged Lutovinov: "Are you with us or with traitors like Miasnikov?" Anyone who returned to bad old habits after having been warned suffered from incurable oppositionism. "I am not making any personal accusations," Zinoviev clarified. "This is not about remembering yesterday's lapses; it's about not repeating them."[273]

Alarmed by the insinuation that they had become an illegal underground movement, the erstwhile supporters of Democratic Centralism voiced a lusty rebuttal: "The supposed link between us and this anonymous platform is a calumny!" But the Central Committee insisted that supporters of Democratic Centralism had to "dissociate themselves openly from the 'anonymous' platform."[274] It was during the Twelfth Party Congress that a leading oppositionist chose to offer a public recantation. Though the letter Bubnov sent to the Party presidium on April 19, 1923, would serve as a model of contrition for many to follow, it took the form less of an apology than of an attempt to dispel a misunderstanding:

Many comrades present here probably recall that I was among those who signed the "Platform of Democratic Centralism" at the Tenth Party Congress. Since Zinoviev apparently links all Democratic Centralists to the anonymous platform, I must state that I had nothing to do with it. I had always thought that no Party member who knows me would be capable of linking my name to this unsigned anti-Party platform. In recent years I have proved many times, through words and deeds, that for me, Party unity is not an empty phrase. . . . Any attempt to organize an opposition goes, in my opinion, against the Party and is therefore criminal.[275]

Bubnov's recantation crystallizes an interesting transitional moment. On the one hand, when he states, "I regard any type of opposition as a harmful act [*vsiakaia oppozitsiia eto vrednoe delo*]," he implies the verbal form ("opposing") rather than the noun form ("opposition").[276] Bubnov is talking here about a lower case opposition, a contingent event, and not about the opposition as a camp—a group of individuals to whom oppositionism is second nature. Another way of approaching Bubnov's declaration is to see him maneuvering to get his name stricken from a list of politically dubious leaders; this must be based on the supposition that he knew something about the control commissions' registry of souls.

A reasonable supposition, since the Bolsheviks had kept lists of the politically alien from the early stages of the Civil War. For the Cheka, these could become death lists or simply lists of those in need of monitoring.[277] The extension of such practices to suspected Party personnel gained momentum only subsequent to Stalin's nomination as Party secretary.[278] Not everything about this process took place behind closed doors in the chancelleries of the Party Secretariat. It was during the Tenth Party Congress that the named vote of each delegate was recorded for the first time. The Central Committee demanded individual responsibility for political stance and would not hesitate to judge according to the record.[279]

A short skirmish over procedure had led to the decision. This was one of those events that appeared trivial in 1921 but assumed colossal significance later on. Hoping to "save time," an anonymous voice from the bench suggested that those who did not endorse Lenin's resolution "On Party Unity" jot down their proposed amendments and submit them to the presidium. Riazanov offered an alternative: "Revolutionary precedent permits us to dispense with the name vote and record [only] the names of those who object to Lenin." Trotsky observed that Riazanov's proposal was difficult to implement "because many comrades had already left Moscow anyway." Setting a precedent that was to cost his later supporters dearly, Trotsky insisted that all voters be tallied. He proposed that the secretariat prepare a list of all the delegates and send ballots to the provinces, "where the vote of all absent comrades must be registered. . . . We need a vote with names attached. To forestall future false finger pointing . . . comrades should be able to say, 'You voted on this occasion in such and such a way.'"[280]

The congressional stenographers recorded the names of the twenty-five people who voted against the Central Committee's majority. It is a fact that the vast majority of those twenty-five were shot during the Great Purge.[281]

But no one thought of presenting bookkeeping measures as tantamount to blacklisting at the time. Perepechko, a member of the Workers' Opposition, praised such measures as "registering names as people come and go from meetings" and publishing in the press the names of censured Communists—he thought that they would contribute to the process of healing the Party.[282] In this one area oppositionists and the Central Committee agreed: the strict monitoring of voters would enhance the sense of political responsibility.

The Opposition and Hermeneutics of the Soul

Few Bolsheviks saw oppositionism as a personality type in the early 1920s. Some leaders of the Central Committee majority sporadically applied the hermeneutics of the soul to their critics, but their attempts to elucidate intentions took place outside juridical framework. Nobody expected the confrontation between an oppositionist and a majoritarian to resemble a man accused facing his accuser. The character of erring comrades might be discussed in an article, at a Party meeting, or in a letter of personal evaluation, but rarely did inner qualities come under close scrutiny in a disciplinary context.

The cases of Larin and Osinskii, two major Party economists who were responsible for the creation of the Soviet planning apparatus, are exemplary.[283] Commenting at the Eleventh Party Congress on the possibility of forgiving their recent miscalculations, Lenin displayed real charity. "Cut off their misguided desires," he noted, "and we will benefit tremendously from their talents." In 1922 Lenin considered Osinskii and Larin worthy comrades who, if admonished properly, could contribute greatly to the revolutionary cause. Over the following pages, as we sit in on some of the classes Lenin taught on hermeneutics, let us pay close attention to the master's unspoken assumptions, his language and his tone.[284]

Lenin discussed Osinskii first: "Osinskii has a real strength: he knows how to take up his work energetically." But this had failed to compensate for an ingrained character weakness: Osinskii felt compelled to oppose the Central Committee at every turn. Lenin took a condescending tone: "had I wanted to take a polemical approach to Osinskii's case, I would have said that the most damning material that could have been used against him is the speech he has given today: I'd have printed up a copy and hung it on the bulletin board." But this would have placed the judge and the defendant on the same level. Lenin's matter-of-fact attacks on Democratic Centralism had thundered through the hall on previous days and at previous congresses. The time had come to judge the character of its followers.

Lenin asked himself how Osinskii could be saved. "We need to arrange it so that his strong side is expressed and his weak side is curtailed.... Otherwise Osinskii will be lost as an activist.... Sometimes we need to limit an individual's freedoms, even when that means subjecting him to, as it were, a circumcision." Lenin hoped that if Osinskii learned to follow a series of simple precepts he would attune his inner self to Party values. "One has to seek advice from comrades ... who will show one how to stick to the majority line.... Unless Osinskii ... applies his talents in a controlled way and learns how to restrain himself, he will end up in the swamp."[285]

Much like Osinskii, Larin resisted the call to apply his considerable abilities to the Party's enterprise and so missed the chance to shine. He, too, needed the help and guidance of his comrades.[286] "No one," said Lenin, "could doubt Larin's loyalty or his knowledge for a moment. And yet, ... because he is out of step with his comrades, Larin has provoked tensions and resistance." It is strange, Lenin noted, "that while the institution of the dictatorship of the proletariat and the forceful use of terror have brought us victory over all the armies of the world, they have not brought a victory over Larin. In this battle we have been completely routed!" In Lenin's estimate, Larin was not a bad Communist. When he had done wrong, it had been "against his own will."[287]

On the face of it, Lenin's judgments emerged from the same set of presuppositions as liberal politics. Indeed, what is so special about politicians commenting on one another's personal qualities and drawing psychological portraits, some more flattering than others? Even when Lenin adopted a patently inquisitorial language, one could dismiss it as metaphorical. The sorry fate of the individuals he discussed suggests how deadly serious was the issue of judging their deepest selves: ideological stance was inseparable from moral persona.

To more fully answer the question we must reconstruct the concept of the self implied by the Bolshevik discourse. A language of modern science grafted onto ethical Judeo-Christian soul-searching dominated Party discourse at all levels. Bolshevik hermeneutics of the soul was embodied in a wide gamut of practices, among which comradely discussions, purges, and campaigns of self-criticism were the most prominent. The individuals words used to account for a comrade's thoughts and desires were taken as clues to or symptoms of some vaster reality—the individual's intimate, moral disposition—which replaced it as its ultimate truth. Indeed, functioning as a meeting place between traditional, Judeo-Christian soul-seeking and modern psychology, Bolshevik hermeneutics involved probing into the deepest recesses of the individual. Even Bukharin, perhaps the most scientific among the Party leaders, often referred to the "soul" (*dusha*) with its "vices" (*poroki*) and "sins" (*grekhi*).[288] And when Sol'ts conducted an investigation into the "personality" (*lichnost'*) of a certain Bolshevik, "bringing his figure into the open [*vyaivit' figuru*]," who could say whether he had adopted the idiom of a scientist or a confessor?[289]

It was an unstated Bolshevik assumption that every individual was characterized by a basic disposition: each tended to either accept or reject the emancipatory call. A moral kernel—referred to as "physiognomy," (*fizionomiia*), "inner part" (*vnuterennost'*), or "essence" (*sushchnost'*)—defined the individual.[290] Seeking new means of reaching one's innermost core, the Party attempted to recast as a scientific challenge the ancient inquisitorial question: Who was good deep down inside his soul, and who was evil?

Although I just presented them separately, the detection of wickedness and the perfection of goodness shared the same language. This led to some degree of ambiguity between inquisitorial and virtue-oriented language of the self, and to a variety of hermeneutical interpretations. When he evaluated his comrades' souls, Lenin may well have assumed that they were all essentially good. His concerns were those of a pastor: how far had Larin and Osinskii come and how much more guidance did they need if their Communist personalities were to be perfected? But so multifaceted was the hermeneutical discourse that the same statements used to rebuke Osinskii in 1922 could be cited almost verbatim to justify his irrevocable condemnation fifteen years later. Had Lenin not pardoned Malinovskii in 1914 as an erring friend only to learn three years later that he was a conniving foe? The Bolshevik history can be presented as the history of the gradual transformation of the kind-hearted psychologist's vocabulary into the lexicon of demonology.

Having said that much, let us examine Lenin's "Testament," a document famous for its unflattering characterization of Stalin. As we shall see, this address to the delegates of the Twelfth Party Congress, dictated by Lenin on December 22, 1922, played an important role as a weapon in intra-Party debates.[291] Hastily composed, the Testament addressed the "serious disagreements within the Party" in hopes of securing at least "short term stability." Lenin suggested that his comments about the personalities of Central Committee members arose out of his determination to stem possible divisions. He wrote: "Having become the general secretary, Comrade Stalin concentrated unlimited powers in his hands. I am not sure that he will be able to use this power carefully enough." He added in the appendix:

Stalin is too coarse. While this shortcoming may readily be tolerated in our milieu, considering how we Communists are accustomed to interacting with each other, it is intolerable in a general secretary. This is why I suggest that comrades look for a way to remove Stalin and replace him with somebody who would be more patient, more loyal, more polite, more attentive to comrades, less capricious, and so on and so forth.

Historians often cite this passage as evidence that Stalin's sinister disposition betrayed itself early on. They are wont to lament the tragedy of contingency: had Lenin lived just a little bit longer, Stalin could not have consolidated his power.[292] But is such reasoning not an example of getting caught in the terms of the phenomena one studies? Taking sides in Lenin's trial of the Central Committee from 1922 leaves us blissfully unaware of the implications of the hermeneutical framework that made such trials possible in the first place. Lenin's judgments were mild; ill results followed "unmindfully" (nenarokom), he noted. But the question he focused on, namely whether the schism was intentional or not—was not that far from the categories deployed during the Show Trials of the 1930s.

There was more to Lenin's Testament than just a condemnation of the general secretary. When he "characterized" (kharakterizoval) the members of the Central Committee core according to their "personal qualities" (lichnye kachestva), Lenin was evaluating Stalin alongside six other Bolshevik leaders. He faulted Stalin's arch-rival, Trotsky, whom he considered a "most talented individual," for being "excessively confident." He who supposedly did everything in his power to avert the degeneration of the world's first socialist revolution into an Asiatic dictatorship, was portrayed by Lenin as arrogant, authoritarian, and not necessarily much better than the coarse Stalin. Lenin was quite clear that as much as he respected both Trotsky and Stalin, "the two outstanding leaders of the present Central Committee" were equally dangerous: "Their qualities can unmindfully lead to a schism."

Lenin gave his underlings rough treatment not because he thought the Central Committee was hopeless, but simply because he wanted to alert the Party to some weaknesses in the personas of its leaders. "Suffice it to remind you of the October episode involving Zinoviev and Kamenev," he went on, making a reference to their betrayal of the Bolshevik plans to seize power in 1917. "This, of course, was not an accident."

Finally, there were the "youngsters," Bukharin and Piatakov. "With respect to these most outstanding individuals, we should bear in mind the following: while Bukharin . . . is rightly considered the Party's sweetheart, one can't help doubting that his theoretical convictions can be regarded as fully Marxist—there is something scholastic about him." As for Piatakov, "this individual doubtlessly possesses outstanding will power and talents, but he . . . cannot be trusted with serious political issues." Again Lenin was lenient, almost paternal. "Of course, my comments pertain only to the present; I suppose that these two outstanding and loyal activists can find a way to learn and rectify their one-sidedness."[293] Once again, the judgment handed down during the Moscow Show Trials was very different. But the nature of the enterprise—an attempt to unlock the secrets of one's soul, to assess one's abilities, inclinations, and loyalties—was a fundamental that animated Party activities throughout Soviet history. Lenin's Testament was also a testament to the Bolshevik soul judging mind-set.

Bolshevik hermeneutics did not always turn an amiable countenance towards oppositionists, even in those early years. This is shown by the case of Mirsaid Sultangaliev, a member of the second Red Army's revolutionary soviet during the Civil War and an active participant in the Bolshevik war effort in Tataria (1920–1921).[294] When he appeared at the Twelfth Party Congress to demand equality for the national republics within the structure of the emerging Soviet Union, the official press lionized him.[295] As a result, his arrest less than a week after the congress had adjourned was headline news. When the Central Control Commission had reviewed a ciphered letter intercepted by the GPU, it accused Sultangaliev of counterrevolutionary activities aimed at instigating an anti-Soviet rebellion in Central Asia.[296]

Sultangaliev denied most of the charges. In an explanatory note written to Stalin on May 19, 1923, he contended that he had only organized a "group of comrades who share my views on national and colonial issues. If we struggled for anything, it was for the enhancement of the authority of the Party among the eastern peoples."[297] Having realized that Sultangaliev had managed to rally certain individuals to his "nationalist opposition," the Central Committee decided to consult the representatives of the periphery regarding possible countermeasures. Quite interesting for us are the minutes taken at the secret meeting organized by the Central Committee (June 9–12, 1923) "to show where the logic of the secret anti-Party work is leading": over the course of the meeting a debate was waged over the theory and practice of the Communist hermeneutical procedure.[298]

As we scrutinize the inquiry into Sultangaliev's self, we cannot help noting that, as with Malinovskii's trial, it is difficult to distinguish legal discourse from inquisitorial discourse, a characteristic trait of Party justice standing at the crossroads of competing concepts of culpability.

One of the speakers who discussed Sultangaliev's case, Khodzhanov, drew an important distinction between the sort of question that might be asked in a court of law—for example, should Sultangaliev be acquitted or condemned—and the sort being asked by comrades—for example, how was Sultangaliev's activity to be characterized in terms of his inner dispositions. Mikhail Frunze, one of the leaders of the Red Army, pointed out that "the juridical aspect is hardly worth our time: the facts have already been clearly established." Turar Ryskulov, a Bolshevik from Turkestan, agreed that the stakes in the debate were "not Sultangaliev's guilt but our entire national policy."[299]

Khalikov, the chair of the Bashkir soviet, took a different view; he did not want the hearing to move beyond a police investigation. Sultangaliev deserved to be considered a traitor and remain in the hands of GPU—end of story. "If we treat the question as an issue of internal policy deliberation and begin asking ourselves whether Sultangaliev deviated leftward or rightward, we exclude the possibility of settling the question in court."[300] But Trotsky tipped the scales in the direction of Party hermeneutics. The crux of the case, he pointed out, was "how Sultangaliev evolved, how his position hardened and how he eventually crossed the boundary separating a factionalist struggle from state treason." The last thing Trotsky was interested in was "the specific clause of the penal code that gave rise to Sultangaliev's arrest."[301]

The Bolsheviks defined "deviation" as a political crime and "counterrevolution" as a state crime. Punishments were designed accordingly: "Had Sultangaliev's mistake taken place within the confines of the Party, had he created an intra-Party group or a faction, a purge could have sufficed," Khadyraliev explained. "But since he suggested contacting Validov, the treacherous chairman of the Bashkir revolutionary committee, our censure has to be harsher."[302] In his letter of recantation, Sultangaliev himself admitted that he deserved to die: "My actions were indeed criminal. . . . I believe that my arrest is legal and that the application to me of the most stringent punishment—death by firing squad—will be legal as well. I say this in all sincerity."[303]

Still, Sultangaliev was hoping for a chance to explain himself. The thought of facing a Party interrogation must have been decidedly less ominous and less humiliating for Sultangaliev than appearing before a revolutionary tribunal. An interrogation would not necessarily result in disenfranchisement, but a tribunal would almost certainly apply the strictest measures. Seeking to understand rather than to condemn, the Party's hermeneutical courts permitted the accused to stage an elaborate defense and to introduce character witnesses. Most important, at these hearings the defendants often gathered support from within the Party, which went far to legitimize their voices, something that was not permitted to counterrevolutionaries. Since the procedure investigated intentions and inclinations, not actual acts, a certain amount of interpretive flexibility could not be avoided: because the inner workings of the soul could not be divined with absolute certainty, the judge might always harbor sympathetic doubts. By contrast, the man facing a revolutionary tribunal had already been classified as a traitor or a provocateur. The accused had only a slim chance of acquittal, and he certainly could not negotiate the nature of the charge.

As we have seen, when Malinovskii confronted the courts in 1918, he learned very late that his hopes of being understood in no way reflected the goals of the institution. He had hoped to face his comrades, but the request he submitted to the Russian Social Democratic party in Stockholm was declined, and he was told, "You are subject to prosecution by a state court, not a Party court."[304] Five years later, when Sultangaliev found himself in the same situation, the Central Committee accepted his case—apparently understanding and clemency were possible.

Taking the hermeneutical high road, the tenor of the 1923 Central Committee that discussed Sultangaliev's behavior in his absence (he was still in GPU custody) alternated between psychology and sociology. What was denied to Malinovskii's advocate—namely, an examination of his client through a scientific and not a legalistic lens—was granted to Sultangaliev's benefactors. To determine whether his mistake was an unprecedented and accidental lapse or just another step on the treacherous road he had long trod, Sultangaliev's life story was subjected to close scrutiny. Ibragimov, the chairman of the Crimean autonomous republic, had no hope that Sultangaliev could be reeducated. Once a traitor, always a traitor. "Yes, there is such a thing as intrinsic [*prirozhdennyi*] nationalism!" Sultangaliev was a case in point:

before the revolution he worked at Baku's monarchist newspaper, *The Caspian*. True, in 1917 he did enroll in the Party. But what were his subsequent activities? . . . In 1919, he advanced a program for the creation of a separate Communist Party of the East. Why? Because he had already come to distrust the Russian Communist Party. Thus we should not be surprised today to find Sultangaliev conducting counterrevolutionary political activities.[305]

When Kamenev reminded comrades that Sultangaliev had "fought valiantly in our ranks," Ordzhonokidze, a Georgian Bolshevik, offered a prompt rebuttal: "This proves nothing. Any member of the progressive . . . intelligentsia would have opposed Kolchak's terrible regime."[306]

Anyone with "eyes to see," sputtered Nimvitskii, perhaps the most indefatigable among the detractors, had to see that treason ran like a "red thread" through the activities of the accused. "Sultangaliev's connections with Validov prove that . . . these are systematic and carefully thought out steps—aimed at tearing apart our ranks." Nimvitskii offered to present a mountain of evidence to prove that "Sultangalievshchina is not a right or a left current in the Communist party but conscious counterrevolution." Having warned against the possible consequences of failing to provide a lesson to the countless traitors, he concluded his philippic: "Do not to be softhearted: . . . Bear in mind that Sultangaliev is influential with young Communists who admire his Party experience and even hang his portrait alongside Lenin's."[307] Shamigulov, a member of the Bureau of the Communist Organizations of the East, agreed that treating Sultangaliev gently would only lead to more trouble: "He does not believe in Communism . . . and is bound to move against the Soviet power sooner of later. . . . Those who believe they can reeducate such people had forgotten the wise Russian proverb: 'Only the grave can cure the hunchback' [*gorbatogo tol'ko mogila ispravit*]."[308]

The worst came to pass: speakers condemned Sultangaliev's soul. The accused had always been evil but only belatedly had he been diagnosed as such. According to Ibragimov's and Shamigulov's exacting judgment, recent events had not precipitated any change in Sultangaliev's behavior: he was as he had always been. Others were more forgiving. A. Enbaev, the deputy chairman of the Tatar Agricultural Commissariat, refused to accept that there could have been anything intrinsically wrong with Sultangaliev. "What is this thing called innate nationalism?" he wondered. "Is it a new category of human being? No biological theory has ever proposed anything of the kind!"[309]

Enbaev saw the accused as a "former comrade who made a mistake and broke down" and claimed that Sultangaliev had been an innocent victim of NEP. Given the sort of strenuous political work he had handled in a difficult environment, surely it was not hard to see why "one of our best comrades stumbled. . . . The history of our Party is familiar with such lapses, especially during transitional periods. Consider the uprising of the Left Socialist-Revolutionaries and what happened at Brest and Kronstadt. We saw the strongest comrades topple very quickly, and they took a hard knock." Enbaev diagnosed Sultangaliev's "nervousness" for quite some time: "A while ago he showed me his poems. . . . I told him that his foul mood will not land him in a good place thus turning out to be a prophet."[310]

The chairman of the Tatar soviet, Mukhtarov, also offered an essentially positive reading of the life story of the accused:

Until recently, Sultangaliev was known and popular among the Tatars because of his revolutionary and Bolshevik commitments. He occupied the highest positions in the Red Army and in many other proletarian institutions . . . and was always above suspicion at the most decisive moments. . . . For years Sultangaliev advanced in step with the

Party: he not only established friendly relations between Tatar Communists and their Russian comrades but also obtained from the backward Tatar peasants a modicum of conscious support for our policies. . . . The Central Committee would surely agree that it detected no expressions of counterrevolutionism in Sultangaliev's activity in the past, and we certainly did not see any either.[311]

Mukhtarov concluded that "the atmosphere of frenzy" among local Bolsheviks who saw themselves threatened by Russian chauvinism had triggered Sultangaliev's crimes. "Sultangaliev found himself on the spot and . . . lost his path and his head [svikhnut'sia s puti]." Mukhtarov called attention to the unique conditions of the territory under consideration—a national republic: "To show that Sultangaliev succumbed to the rightist, nationalist temptation was not the same as showing that he actually crossed over to the enemy."[312]

Granting that Sultangaliev's deviation was unusually deep, Skrypnik, the number one Communist in Ukraine, still classified it as a deviation and nothing more: "The Central Control Commission acknowledged that a nationalist deviation exists in the eastern republics and that Sultangaliev's case amounts to a new phenomenon: an exacerbation and a stony-faced expression of this deviation." Since the environment was the ultimate source of the trouble, the remedy was a policy shift, not the punishment of an individual. "If the soil that generates national deviation should disappear . . . distortions will disappear as well."[313]

Kuibyshev, a representative of the Central Control Commission, also hoped the accused would be pardoned. "It must be allowed that conditions in the periphery are such that it is not entirely evident to certain comrades that links with [the counterrevolutionary nationalist] Validov are a grave sin [bol'shoi grekh]. Although reactions to the 'Great Russian Chauvinism' sometimes take the form of an ugly nationalist deviation . . . the actions of local leaders should be understood in terms of the vestiges of national inequality."[314] In any case, simply to investigate the culprit's person was not enough. "Sultangaliev's fall [padenie] is not some mental aberration. . . . The trouble is that counterrevolution is born from much more complicated phenomena than personal breakdown [proval], the seemingly sudden psychological leap. . . . Sultangaliev's leap actually bespeaks deep historical economic and social causes."[315]

Even as Kuibyshev maintained that "the Soviet republic stands to lose nothing at this stage by releasing Sultangaliev from jail"—after all, he had "confessed" (soznalsia) and "repented" (raskaialsia)—he denied that "comrades placed in difficult psychological circumstances made similar mistakes in the past."[316] Kuibyshev criticized Enbaev's analogy between the Left Opposition of 1918 and Sultangaliev: "True, the Left Opposition was mistaken, but it was nonetheless a current that kept within the Party framework, a current that bowed to Party discipline, and it certainly had nothing to do with treason. To compare what happened then to what is happening now is, de facto, to absolve Sultangaliev." While Sultangaliev was not irredeemable, Kuibyshev strongly opposed his reinstatement: "Let him continue his miserable existence outside the Party."[317]

The Central Control Commission's nuanced approach prevailed. In the report he sent to Stalin on June 6, 1923, Menzhinskii, the head of the GPU's operations, stated that while Sultangaliev was "guilty of creating an illegal group that obstructed our policy in the East . . . the allegation that he . . . supported the Basmachi struggle against the Soviet power appears to be questionable." The committee handed down a political condemnation but found Sultangaliev innocent of treason. Could the hearing have ended more differently than it had opened? In time, the reversal was to be reversed: arrested again in 1928, Sultangaliev spent years in prison camps and was finally executed late in 1939 as a "counterrevolutionary."[318]

Both in 1923 and in 1939, Sultangaliev was judged to have succumbed to oppositionism because of a certain constitutional inability to "stick by the general line." But how different the two cases! At the earlier date, Sultangaliev—by most contemporaneous accounts a well-meaning Bolshevik—had been unable to restrain himself. When soft-liners such as Enbaev and Mukhtarov referred to a natural weakness, they directed their criticism at the superficial traits that prevented the accused from making an appropriate contribution to the Party. In 1939, the harsh interpretation of Ibragimov and Ordzhonikidze (both already executed) would prevail, and Sultangaliev would be condemned and put to death as a wicked, irredeemable soul.

CHAPTER 3

HEALING OPPOSITIONIST SOULS

The Petrograd Communist University: A Microcosm of Bolshevik Politics

The New Course Discussion (December 1923–January 1924) took place during the last two months of Lenin's life. At the time, no one believed that Bolshevism could exist without Lenin.[1] One of the many who had come to accept him as the Communist Party's paramount leader said of his genius that it "was especially evident in his ability to predict how the barely discernible processes would evolve, what prospects and dangers they harbored."[2] Whether one considered his solitary determination to see the Bolsheviks seize power in November 1917 or his advocacy of what proved to be an exceedingly farsighted concession to Germany in the Brest peace treaty of 1918, Lenin's vision of the shape of things to come had trumped his critics time and again. Zinoviev unstintingly lauded him: "It is primarily thanks to Lenin's genius that we have solved the main problems posed by the Revolution."[3]

Who could replace the ailing leader at the helm of the Party? After many signs of feuding within the Central Committee, the succession struggle burst out into the open in the spring of 1923.[4] Trotsky seemed to think that at any moment laurels would be placed on his brow.[5] Only one man, so his supporters reckoned, had the right to succeed to Lenin's position, "because one man stood head and shoulders above the other claimants, and could depend upon our unswerving loyalty. That man was Trotsky."[6] At that moment Trotsky appeared to have stood at the zenith of his glory. Radek talked about "the Party and its leader, Lev Davydovich Trotsky" and Nevskii described him as "Lenin's primus inter pares."[7] In some ways, Lunacharskii dared to suggest, Trotsky outdid Lenin: "It would be wrong to think that the second great leader of the Revolution is in all respects inferior to the first. Trotsky is more brilliant, more dazzling, more exciting than Lenin."[8] Children were named in his honor: Ledat, Troledav, El'da.[9]

But try as Trotsky might to play the part of the resplendent hero of the Civil War and Lenin's anointed successor, many were unconvinced. Stalin, Kamenev, and Zinoviev allied themselves in a famous triumvirate—a temporary but effective maneuver to fend off the charismatic pretender.[10] "Now that Lenin is gone," the triumvirs stated, "certain persons are laying claim to a monopoly on Leninism. This is quite ridiculous! Today no source of authority exists except for the Central Committee and the Party Congress; only they can provide legitimate interpretations of the Leninist line."[11] "While Trotsky may have traits that make him superior to other Politburo members, those traits are also his weaknesses," Party observers noted. "Trotsky is an individualist, incapable of team work, of singing in a choir."[12]

The bitter contest for Lenin's mantle cannot be appreciated without an understanding of the widespread belief in the Revolution as a revelation. While Marxist theoreticians would forever continue to interpret 1917, the signposts guiding future generations to the truth had to be drawn from the testimony of a carefully defined elite—such disciples of Lenin as Trotsky, Stalin, Kamenev, and Zinoviev.[13] If repeated scrutiny of Lenin's written corpus had any value, it was as a technique that ensured the transmission and dissemination of a unique inspiration. But unique as the source was, all Party leaders participated in the interpretation of Lenin's message, offering their own definitions of what could only become a manifold Leninism. To make authoritative accounts of the Revolution widely available, the central Soviet publishing houses embarked in the mid-1920s on the publication of the collected works of Lenin, Trotsky, and Kamenev.[14]

Engendered by NEP, the economic and political crisis that engulfed the country in 1923 would provide the testing ground for the claimants to Lenin's position. The government concentrated production in the most efficient plants and curtailed credit to nationalized enterprises; with the rise of unemployment and decline in real wages a wave of strikes swept the country in August and September.[15] A Communist uprising in Germany failed dismally, dashing hopes for economic assistance from abroad.

How would a robust and vigorous Lenin have reacted?[16] As this question and many others were bruited about, more and more voices began to allude to a crisis of leadership in the Party.[17] Trotsky lashed out: "The Party is to a significant degree ceasing to be that self-acting collective that really embraces living activity. . . . The regime that has been set up is absolutely intolerable."[18] In his letter to the Central Committee and the Central Control Commission of October 8, 1923, Trotsky criticized the "methods used in the staffing of the Twelfth Party Congress." He referred to the well-known fact that the majority of the delegates were elected by the provincial Party conferences on the recommendations of the local Party secretaries. This meant that they were, de facto, nominated by Stalin operating through the Central Committee's Secretariat.[19]

Calls for opening the floor for criticisms and suggestions came from all corners. By now, important segments of the Party came to support the abrogation of the ban on factions. Many were of the opinion that Lenin insisted on the ban in a time of an acute crisis and that the ban was obsolete as it only obstructed the Party's growth.[20] Trotsky was determined to present his diagnosis of the Party's ills to all the Bolsheviks who were "sufficiently conscious, mature, and self-restrained" and he sent a slew of motions and proposals to the Central Committee. In that, Trotsky was not alone. On October 15 a second oppositionist document had arrived at the Central Committee—the Proclamation of the Forty-six, named after the number of its signatories. This programmatic statement charged the Party apparatus with "top-down approach to decision-making" and demanded that central executive bodies of the Party release their grip on local Party life.[21]

Rejecting most of the charges, the triumvirate dispatched a strongly worded communiqué to the Central Committee and the Central Control Commission on October 19 in condemnation of the opposition. A joint session of these two bodies met on October 25 and resolved to cast aspersions on Trotsky's statements as well as the Proclamation of the Forty-six. The latter was described as a "concerted factional outburst incapable of solving the Party's difficulties." The triumvirs maintained that Trotsky's criticisms deviated from Democratic Centralism and flirted with a Menshevik conception of the Party as a heterogeneous organization which gives voice to petit bourgeois classes and subclasses.[22]

The first phase of the internecine warfare ended on December 5, 1923. The meeting of the Politburo and the Presidium of the Central Control Commission approved a compromise resolution "On Party Building," jointly drafted by Stalin, Trotsky, and Kamenev. While criticizing any attempt to divide the Party, this resolution stated that "Party functionaries who should naturally be the link between the Party and the non-Party masses are almost entirely absorbed in administrative and managerial work," thus conceding that Trotsky's warning that the Party was on the wrong course had some merit.[23]

Very shortly thereafter, the Petrograd Party organization violated the truce. In a series of speeches Zinoviev, the chairman of the Petrograd soviet who turned the northern city into his fiefdom, charged Trotsky with criticizing the resolutions to which he himself had been a signatory.[24] The Nineteenth Petrograd Provincial Party Conference (December 1923), which Zinoviev presided over, approved the "Open Letter of the Petrograd Party Organization"—a strongly worded manifesto aimed at "Trotsky's factionalism."[25]

At first, the Central Committee was reluctant to launch a discussion, especially as the preparations for the Thirteenth Party Congress were stalled. Lenin's illness contributed to the anxiety. "During previous discussions," Kol'tsov, a second-tier Bolshevik leader, noted, "we knew when we reached the limit. Vladimir Illich would knock on the table, and that was that. But now Illich is gone. Who would prevent a platform based discussion now?"[26] But once a number of local Party organizations demanded to conduct a deliberation of official policy on a national level, the discussion was unavoidable.

During the eventful months of the autumn of 1923, the student-dominated Moscow Party organization became home to the bulk of the country's supporters of Trotsky. It was clear that the university Party cells would play a paramount role in determining the outcome of the Party discussion in the capital, as they accounted for almost one third of local Party organization.[27] In the Sverdlov Communist University, students attacked Stalin for tarnishing the name of Trotsky and the central press for its "partisan coverage of the debate." Castigating the Central Committee majority for "usurping Party opinion" they managed to pass a resolution calling for reelection of the entire Party apparatus. While oppositionists were warmly greeted at the university Party cells, Kalinin, a speaker for the Central Committee, was physically kept off the floor at the Moscow Mining Academy.[28]

Having achieved considerable success in Moscow universities, the opposition rethought its original intention of "conceding" the old capital to Zinoviev.[29] In mid-December 1923, a team of Moscow students arrived in Petrograd. They had chosen the Communist University as the locus for their propaganda work because of what they believed to be the advanced theoretical level of its students.

In the pages below we will enter the Uritskii Palace, home to the Petrograd soviet for much of 1917 and now the location of the Petrograd Communist University. This specific place, observed between the years 1923 and 1926, provides us with the focus we need for a case study that will enable us to examine in detail the interrelationships among individuals, institutions, and political language. Unlike the traditional academic establishments still very much active in the old capital, the Communist University was a child of the Revolution.[30] Founded in the summer of 1918 by the Executive Committee of the Northern Commune as the Worker-Peasant University, it now carried the name of Zinoviev, the celebrated Bolshevik leader. The founding covenant of the university maintained that this "highest Party school was to teach the theory and practice of Communism under the direct leadership of the Central Committee." Only Party members could enroll; the academic program was designed for trusted Bolsheviks who had distinguished themselves during the Revolution and the Civil War.

The local Party organization, almost a thousand members strong, was supervised by the rector of the university.[31] The eminence of Semen Kanatchikov, the famous worker turned Bolshevik ideologist who had for two years served as rector, transcended his status at the university: a member of Leningrad's Party committee, he was nominated directly by Smol'nyi—the Party's municipal and regional headquarters.[32]

A glance at the internal structure of the enormous organization reveals a vast pyramid of student bodies divided into ever smaller units, each of which comprised both leaders and led. An annual student conference elected a Party committee of twelve to fifteen comrades who in turn elected the Party secretary, the head of the university propaganda department, and the university journal's editorial board. To streamline decision making, the Party committee selected a single executive to run the Party's daily affairs: the university Party bureau. This was the real seat of power: control of the bureau meant control of the local Party organization and its personnel decisions. In addition, the bureau was authorized to deal with violations in the dormitories and actions unbecoming to a student at a Communist University.[33]

The student body was divided among a large number of circles (*kruzhki*).[34] Each circle comprised approximately twenty students, with the same major and the same matriculation year. The circle was run by a presidium and a Party organizer charged with ensuring that all circle members performed their Party responsibilities.[35] But, complex as it was, the university's organizational hierarchy amounted to only one block in the larger pyramid of the state's Party apparatus. The Communist University was linked to the Central Petrograd Party District and thus to the Leningrad provincial Party organization; this series of vertical links led all the way to the Smol'nyi. One can speak of a Party, understood as a nationwide political order, intruding on the university, understood as a microcosm of Bolshevik power. Constantly on its guard, the apparatus had to attack whatever solidarities formed within smaller units, ensuring that they remained transparent to the center. As we shall see, whenever the university deviated politically, the center effectively intervened, sometimes to replace the entire university leadership.

The considerable success of Moscow emissaries at the Petrograd Communist University was the talk of the town for a few weeks. Especially noteworthy was the careful exploitation of an unpublished letter of Trotsky's from October 8, 1923, that lambasted the Central Committee majority.[36] "All copies were to be immediately turned in," decreed the university Party bureau. But to no avail: the letter was widely known to students "who read secondhand and thirdhand copies."[37] "The forbidden fruit is always desired," explained the supporters of the triumvirate.[38]

In the meantime, record numbers of Petrograd Communist University students responded to the Central Committee's appeal of December 1923 for discussions of the changes that should be introduced into Party structure and policy.[39] Every circle dedicated at least two meetings to the discussion. Despite the pleas of frustrated chairmen to put matters to a vote after three, four, or five hours of violent debate, arguments often lasted until the early hours of the morning. Day after day, students came to their lecture halls bleary eyed; no real studying was happening. In late December students noted that "we finally got into the thick of the discussion, found its pulse."[40]

We have seen in previous chapters how the idea of "oppositionism" came into being and how this term gradually grew in importance. But to be real, to have an impact, the official discourse had to be embodied. Now we are in a position to link the debates at the Party Congresses with the nuts and bolts of the "struggle against the opposition" at the grassroots level. We will see that the discourse on the inner enemy cannot be understood as a language imposed from above or as a freely expressed set of opinions; rather, it has to be seen as a complex interaction between the various tiers of the Party hierarchy—at one and the same time a hierarchy of consciousness and a hierarchy of power.

Examining the way that the student discussions took place and considering the unwritten rules governing the interactions between antagonists should answer a range of questions: how was the "opposition question" turned into a set of practices and set in motion? What rituals of Communist life sustained these practices? How much interpretative leeway did the rank and file have? How did statements made in disagreement interlock with or challenge each another? Who delivered the official reports? Who presented the countertheses? Who was shouted down after uttering only a few sentences, and who rose to speak time and again? Disputants relied on the ability of various state and Party institutions, official and unofficial, to legitimize their opinions and endow them with a binding force. Indeed, if eloquence and persuasion did influence the outcome of the endless debates to some extent, success could not be won without a firm grasp of the newest statutes and regulations emanating from the Central Committee and the Central Control Commission.

By and large students defended their right to take a stand on the issues, and the discussion went some way towards suspending Party hierarchies. The voices of Bolshevik dignitaries mingled with those of the rank and file and, while authorities were generally respected, a certain equality prevailed. No one had a monopoly on truth: a rank-and-file comrade could understand the specifics of a certain place at a certain time better than could Zinoviev or Kanatchikov. A considerable involvement with the fate of the Party leaps to the eye from the discussion protocols: the attentive reader can discern a sense of satisfaction, even of pride, alternating with a sense of rage, of derision. The discussants were clearly given to reformulating the issues introduced by the reporters: broad policy statements were honed into questions relevant to university affairs, and "equality," "democracy," and "camaraderie" took on meanings associated with everyday student life.

Communist consciousness served as the only touchstone for truth and the shared frame of reference throughout the discussion. Only politically up-to-date comrades could claim the right to speak and to persuade; only they could vote and decide on the issues. Spiritual teleology reigned supreme: everybody was talking about the awakening of the mind, the incomplete, ongoing growth of consciousness. The selfhood of every Party member had to be scrutinized: all were expected to reach a personal, resolute decision on crucial issues that would either further or halt their personal evolution. The criteria employed in evaluating consciousness were numerous and often contradictory; the discussion inspired conflicting strategies of self-presentation and political argumentation and, most importantly, made it possible to introduce the same set of concepts into a range of different rhetorical games.

During a key meeting held on December 19, 1923, the Communist University examined the party-building resolution advanced by the Central Committee, the "Open Letter of the Petrograd Party Organization," and Trotsky's programmatic letters, collectively entitled "The New Course." Assorted newspaper clippings criticizing Party policy and their official rebuttals were distributed among students.

Kanatchikov, the rector, asked the Party headquarters to send in its best reporters. When Petr Zalutskii came to deliver the main report, his presence lent the occasion a certain luster. Arrested five times and exiled twice before the Revolution, Zalutskii had risen to fame as a member of the Petrograd military-revolutionary committee during the Bolshevik seizure of power, and as a brigade commissar during the Civil War. Thirty-five years old, he was currently a member of the Central Committee.

The growth of Party democracy, Zalutskii stated at the outset, "will doubtlessly do much good" and "the Party will emerge out of the discussion more cohesive, better unified." Then he admitted that in Moscow "the discussion took an unhealthy form. The sorties by the supporters of the former oppositionist currents should not have been allowed." The Party assumed that debates would, at a certain point, exhaust themselves, "but it turns out that the further we go, the worse the situation gets [chem dal'she les tem bol'she drov]." Zalutskii was proud of Petrograd's special animosity towards Trotsky's irresponsible stance. "Our position is even more uncompromising than that of the Central Committee," he stated. "When Party unity is at stake, the Petrograd Party organization does not hesitate to take action."

Zalutskii alluded to Trotsky's unfair methods in Moscow universities, where Central Committee reporters had been booed off the stage. Taboos were broken and there was no end in sight. The opposition had not yet begun revising Lenin's teachings in earnest, he commented, "but if the discussion continues this way, I fear it won't be long." And what about the Central Committee? "We do not deny that we have made certain practical mistakes, but no one should be advocating a complete revision of the Party line."[41]

Initiated by the local teaching staff, the co-report presented by a veteran university lecturer named Karpov may communicate some of the intensity of the discussion. Step by step, right under the nose of Zalutskii, Karpov drove home an attack on the triumvirs. He found much in the official report that was "biased" or so vague as to be meaningless. "No one is questioning the importance of unity. We know that the Paris Commune failed because of petty bickering." The co-reporter was not a naive liberal: he accepted that factionalism was dangerous, but by factionalists he meant those who plotted against the Party, groups such as Workers' Truth and the Workers' Group, and not Trotsky, since he offered helpful pointers.[42]

Karpov's speech was argumentative and sharp, and Zalutskii grew increasingly frustrated with the applause he received. When Karpov lashed against Zinoviev and Kamenev, "who committed treason during the October days and now are hiding behind Lenin's back," Zalutskii yelled back: "You were not born yesterday, were you? Where have you been, comrade Karpov, after the defeat of the 1905 Revolution [when Kamenev and Zinoviev saved the Party]? . . . What contribution have you made to the proletarian cause then? First learn who is who and then open your mouth, or else your words will be classified as libel of the worst kind."[43]

The wrangling sides presented an ever more polarized picture of Lenin's relations with Trotsky. Zalutskii strongly differentiated the two, insisting that at no point did their thinking converge. He was fond of giving a great deal of attention to Trotsky's oratorical style, which he said was "affected" and polluted by "floridity and extravagant verbiage. Trotsky's verbal slapstick can be of benefit in one respect only, as an example of rhetoric and style. But as a political worldview, as a school and a method it will soon vanish from the historical scene."[44] A decent Communist had to be against every kind of obfuscation. Just as Avakkum had called on the Christian believer to cast aside the pagan fondness for rhetoric so that the soul's truths might be directly spoken, Zalutskii demanded that speech be absolutely unambiguous, rendering the speaker transparent. "Karpov's birdsong is very sweet," he brought the point home, "but what branch he will land on is not so clear yet."[45]

But Karpov did not accept that he was a big talker who excelled in playing to the gallery. Trotsky's Civil War speeches, he argued by juxtaposition, had in fact held entire fronts together—they were an asset rather than a liability. The truth is that Trotsky had been "Lenin's most consistent disciple. . . . Remember that when Lenin could not attend the Twelve Party Congress he entrusted the report on the economy to Trotsky." And Trotsky's words were as inspiring as usual. If anyone was to be accused of anti-Leninism, it ought to be the triumvirs. "Trotsky was the first to endorse Lenin's April thesis . . . while those who today are calling themselves Leninists were wavering."[46]

While no criticism could be leveled at the Leninist Central Committee per se, the character of the triumvirate, and its accession to control of the Party apparatus due to Lenin's illness, drew much criticism.[47] Karpov cited Trotsky's New Course letters extensively to show that the recent decisions by the Central Committee could not be implemented without grassroots support. "The center of gravity which the old course mistakenly placed in the apparatus has now been transferred by the new course to the energy and initiative of all Party members."[48]

The co-reporter found in the circles an interested audience. "The Party masses don't participate at all in deliberations," Filatov complained. "The higher-ups prepare all resolutions ahead of time."[49] Others wanted to see an increase in the frequency of provincial and national Party conferences. "If the Central Committee policy is to be fully implemented, the Party masses must be yanked out of stagnation and drawn into active participation in discussions."[50] "The Party must bring in new blood," Karpov's supporters said. "The apparatus has to be rebuilt from scratch, this time in adherence with the ascending line, from the bottom up."[51] "Nominations must be reduced to a minimum."[52]

Vasilli Ivanov, the secretary of the Petrograd Communist University Party organization, was a case in point. In some respects, the authority of this young worker equaled the authority of the rector. The Twelfth Party Congress has just upgraded the status of the Party secretary from that of a "technician primarily involved in clerical work" to a "Party organizer guiding the work of his organization." To fulfill his expanded role, the secretary had to be an "educated" and "temperate" comrade with a long Party record—Ivanov's extended back to 1915. True to his calling, Ivanov aspired to guide the conscience of the students. He kept watch on each and every one of them so as to gauge their academic and political performance. From shaving in the morning to late-night study, whatever a student did was done under his penetrating eyes.[53]

Relieved of all other professional responsibilities, Ivanov was allocated an annual salary of 124 golden rubles, an offense to the egalitarian bent of Karpov's and many other students, whose stipends were only a fraction of this amount.[54] "If you want to see how bureaucratic the Petrograd organization has become, look at our Party secretary," they sardonically noted. "Ivanov is constantly running to the Leningrad Party committee for instructions."[55] "As soon as one of us breathes one word of criticism, the secretary takes his Party card away."[56]

Zalutskii rejected outright the notion that Party leadership, locally or nationally, was perverting democracy. "We operate not in some abstract realm but under a specific set of circumstances, and we cannot transform the Party into an arena for dueling currents."[57] Speaking at the first circle, the student Kudriavtsev echoed those words: "Questions about democracy cannot be examined outside the context of time and space. During the underground period, democracy was one thing, during war, Communism it was another, during NEP, a third."[58] Other supporters of Zalutskii could only repeat that Lenin talked about democracy "not as an end in itself but as a necessary means to advancing the Revolution."[59]

But the young faculty Garin and Gorokhov, whose indictments of the triumvirs were among the harshest, would have none of it. "It was during the Tenth Party Congress that Lenin made his remarks about factions and groupings," Gorokhov noted, "but now the Thirteenth Party Congress is around the corner. If each congress does nothing but repeat the resolutions drawn up at the preceding congresses we will go down the drain [*vyletim v trubu*]!"[60] What made Garin's and Gorokhov's stance truly provocative was their reliance on Sapronov and Preobrazhenskii to suggest that the strict enforcement of the ban on factions would lead to stagnation in Bolshevik thought. The former, by now widely perceived as an extremist, argued that the Party was desperate for free election "without preliminary 'arrangements'" with the apparatus.[61] The latter, also a hypercritic, warned that the "system of military command" hindered the transition to the "new forms of Party structure."[62] Shying away from demanding that factionalism be legalized, Preobrazhenskii and his followers asked for freedom of groups.

Zinoviev's apparatus ridiculed such scholastic distinctions: "Factions? No! Groups? Yes! Who needs those word games! Even if Preobrazhenskii demands the legalization of the tiniest of groupings,' he must be rejected. No matter how tiny the baby is, someone has to sin in order to bring it into the world."[63] Preobrazhenskii thus became a sexual transgressor, but Garin and Gorokhov ironically noted, "they at least stuck to a firm position on the issues."[64] In a trenchant speech in the fifth circle against the suffocating Party regime and the growth of bureaucracy, Savko suggested that the only remedy lay in completely subordinating the apparatus to the Party grassroots.[65] In the sixth circle, Taraskin repeated the unsayable: "Within limits, groupings should be allowed."[66]

Even students who otherwise sympathized with much of what the opposition was saying found such ideas unacceptable. Some were even outraged: "Preobrazhenskii is stating loud and clear that since the Tenth Party Congress Party policies have been ill-conceived"; "this is nothing less than an attempt to revise Leninism!" Golodaev declared.[67] Kogan, a member of the sixth circle, chimed in, "Preobrazhenskii's medicine will heal none of the Party's ills." Promoting democracy was one thing, fragmenting the Party another. "As I understand it," stated Zhukova from the second circle, "democracy means elections and freedom of discussion, not carte blanche for factions."[68]

At the end of the day, even Karpov admitted Preobrazhenskii and his local followers had gone too far: "While the ideal of a workers' democracy includes the enjoyment of freedom of discussion by all Party members . . . it does not imply the freedom to form factions or groupings." He called the Party apparatus "self-engrossed" but maintained that the solution to this problem lay not in destroying the apparatus, à la Preobrazhenskii, but rejuvenating it, à la Trotsky. Nothing could be further, he asserted, from Trotsky's agenda than launching a comprehensive attack on the Party. Others joined their voices to Karpov's: "Even if Trotsky's opinions do not square fully with those of the Central Committee, this does not mean that he should be put in the same basket with Preobrazhenskii."[69]

Clearly, Bolshevik politics in the age of the New Course Discussion centered on individual personalities. Only seldom were Preobrazhenskii, Sapronov, and Trotsky perceived as parts of a larger whole—namely, the opposition.[70] While the supporters of the first two were said to have an "oppositionist itch," symptoms of Trotskyist sympathies did not necessitate summary expulsion from the orthodox camp—everything depended on one's evaluation of Trotsky's recent writings. When the student Kirilov claimed during the debates in the third circle that "Trotsky's views were not as extreme as Sapronov's," his peer, Russkova, ridiculed him: "You may not see any difference between Trotsky and the Central Committee, but the truth is that the difference is vast. Trotsky calls Party leaders 'degenerates.'"[71] Ivanov also flatly rejected the idea of "reconciling the irreconcilable. If we examine Trotsky's writings as a whole, there is no way to avoid the conclusion that they are factionalist."[72]

Students examined Trotsky's letters and *Pravda* articles through a magnifying glass. There they found out that Trotsky had controversially proposed that the Party take its lead from the youth.[73] Far better the "flexible minds" of Communist students than the "ossified minds" of the apparatchiks; Trotsky wrote in one of his New Course letters that "youth is the barometer of the Party. . . . Fresh and receptive, it embodies the pluses and the minuses of our society in a lively form." With his complements to the young as the "barometer of the Party," Trotsky gave his program a generational twist. The wish to see revolutionary victory over bureaucratism and the renewal of Party spirit were central to Trotsky's imagination.[74]

His appeal to the youth soon became popular at the Communist University. Kursakova, a member of the second circle, stated: "Trotsky's separation of the Party into the young and the old is right on the mark." Speaking at the sixth circle, Ardashirov agreed: "Bureaucratism is felt by young people more strongly."[75] The majoritarians countered that students were too new to class struggle to serve as the Party's barometer. They had never been obliged to grapple with the rude realities of life, a fact that prevented them, it was said, from matching theory and practice.[76]

Zalutskii denounced Trotsky's veneration of students. "We should not forget that the young are more susceptible to alien influence . . . and that the theory of alleged Party degeneration was invented by the Mensheviks. Callow youths receive these vague, abstract ideas without penetrating their substance."[77]

The petit bourgeois, philistine putridity [*obyvatel'sko-meshchanskaia gnil'*] of some lecturers infected our ranks. Every academic institution has half a dozen or a dozen of such lost souls. . . . Recall the popular saying, "I recognize my sweetheart by her gait": the lifestyle of these fellow travelers, their habit of muddling things and wreaking havoc, jumps forth. . . . If you ask them, they are all ripe and ready to assume posts in the Politburo, the Komintern, you name it. . . . You mustn't believe these types: . . . They could not care less about Party policy, and their goal—of course, an unconscious one—is to show off, not to beat our enemies.[78]

Zalutskii pointed out that the lifeblood of the Party pumped through the occupants of factory shop rooms, not academic hallways, and the worker at his bench rarely gave a moment's thought to Trotsky except to scorn and deride him. Indeed, about a hundred worker-students called Zalutskii's attention to the fact that Karpov, Gorokhov, Garin, and their likes "never learned to understand the true soul, the aspirations and the wishes of the working masses, never learned, with the help of Marxism, what class struggle is all about." Trotsky's popularity in the universities "only reflected the objective pressure of petit bourgeois elements on the Party." According to Ivanov, to whom the above judgment belonged, some university lecturers indulged in endless criticisms of the Central Committee because their detachment from the working class did not predispose them to fully appreciate the importance of unity in the Bolshevik ranks. "Swayed by their psychology, utterly convinced of the importance of their own opinions, Trotsky's supporters waste their days split-ting hairs."[79]

Yearning to leave the mark of their class politics, the intelligentsia hoped to force the workers from the seat of power, or so Zalutskii argued. "The petite bourgeoisie joined us not because they had absorbed proletarian ideology but, quite to the con-trary, because they believe they know how to run the country better than us." This is a subtle and elusive foe. "If during the Civil War we always had the enemy in clear view, now [under NEP] the enemy remains under cover. In order to battle against the petit bourgeois intelligentsia the proletariat can rely only on state power; cul-ture is outside its reach at the moment." So the Bolsheviks had to show even more discipline, even more centralization. Democracy came second to the need for eco-nomic and political controls. The Party must build a strong apparatus capable of directing the "elemental processes." And what was the opposition doing? Instead of helping the Party to stay on course "it makes all kinds of unreasonable demands on the Central Committee." Zalutskii had no other name for it but sedition. "Things reached a point where the 'Workers' Group' and 'Workers' Truth' groups organized [anti-Party] processions."[80]

But many in the Communist University remained skeptical that Zalutskii had found the root cause of all the problems. Unsatisfied with what he had to say about the sources of social and political unrest, students demanded more information about the state of the national economy. Karpov expressed grave concern about a so-called "scissors crisis": he felt that unusual irregularities in pricing could de-stroy the economy. A sharp decline in the volume of grain peasants were selling to the cities worried him; because the price of industrial goods had risen, in real terms, three times faster than the price of agricultural products in the decade since 1914, the village had little incentive to sell its goods on the urban market.[81] Discus-sants were keenly aware of the claims by Osinskii, Piatakov, Preobrazhenskii, and Smirnov that the disorder in the work of the Central Committee had created the prospect of a serious economic breakdown (the "Resolution of the Four").[82] In the lecturers' circle, debates kept returning to questions such as who had to foot the bill for the recent economic setbacks. Iseki, a young lecturer, credited the Central Com-mittee for putting the issues on the table. Others lecturers, like Nenadykh, insisted that without the opposition, the Party would have remained complacent even to-day, at great risk to the economy.[83]

In Nenadykh's view, nothing could be done before taking steps to shore up the worker-peasant alliance. "If we leave things as they are, it will be Kronshtadt all over again. The inability of Soviet industry to satisfy the peasant consumer cannot be explained only by our alleged inability to trade. Our bloated economic apparatus is a more likely explanation." Tselikov, another critical-minded lecturer, identified the Central Committee as responsible for the scissors crisis. "Our fiscal policy has yielded unfortunate results: a contraction in sown acreage and pauperization of the village." If only the poor peasants were given a chance, they would prove themselves as consumers; taxes would have to be lowered while competition between factories was encouraged, yielding a drop in the price of finished goods.[84]

Barabash, a cynic among the young scholars, sounded an ironic note soon followed by others. "At the end of the day, the peasants will still have to carry a heavy burden. We should not be promising them relief and relief alone." Stepanov, a partisan of the triumvirate, developed this idea: "Yes, if state industries are planned, production will become rationalized. But no plan can cover everything because agriculture is in the hands of small-scale producers and therefore is not susceptible to state regulation." Had the "four economists" taken this objective factor into consideration, they would not have been so critical.

Whatever their differences, everybody agreed that peasant support was the beginning point of sound economics. Resolving the economic crisis would involve not the intensive development of heavy industry, but the stabilization of currency and the promotion of prosperity in the countryside; these would provide the basis for a domestic market for industrial products, which would in turn produce the capital for industrialization.[85]

With the discussants' voices quieting down a notch, neither of the resolutions that competed for the vote at the lecturers' circle on January 20, 1924, presented itself as oppositionist. When the dust settled, the doctrinaire reporter's resolution had prevailed, five votes to three. "The Central Committee line is adequate to meet the challenges of socialist construction." The defeated resolution had stressed the "need for a directing hand in our economy" and added, quite appositely, that "weakness of planning is one of the sources of our current crisis."[86]

In 1923, one could choose between Trotsky, Zinoviev, Preobrazhenskii, and Stalin, or one might have been able to synthesize from among them. A vote against the letter of the Petrograd Organization did not necessarily imply belief in all the opposition stated, particularly when students were laying claims to a unique position of mediation between the Central Committee and the dissenters. "We should not base our position exclusively upon Zinoviev's statements," said one student in the sixth circle; "Trotsky's letters also have some basis in reality." According to his friend, "The Central Committee's resolution is correct, but Preobrazhenskii's suggestions are also partially correct."[87]

Indeed, not all the resolutions adopted by the circles at the Communist University fit readily into a category. When the members of one particularly agitated circle found themselves almost hopelessly divided over two proposed resolutions on economic policy, they devoted a great deal of energy to refining the nuanced differences in the two texts. The official resolution, which ultimately obtained sixteen votes, read as follows: "The circle fully endorses the decisions of the Central Committee and the Central Control Commission; Party democracy must be advanced." Six students had suggested a controversial addition: "We must also reinvigorate the

Party apparatus, encourage healthy criticism and discard intimidation." An even smaller group, five students strong, exhibited the fiercest defiance: "We deny the accusation aimed at Trotsky, one of the most respected comrades, that he has betrayed the interests of our Party." Yet not even this brave quintet wanted to be identified at oppositionists.[88]

Nenadykh, responsible for a polemical and much-discussed co-report in the lecturers' circle, also denied that he systematically defended heterodoxy: "Some comrades believe that to make a co-report is automatically to advance oppositionist views. This is not the case at all. My task was simply to sharpen some points." Among his sententious declarations was Nenadykh's repeated assertion that he hoped to stimulate debate, not to push the circle's members into one camp or another.

No one appears to have been keen on launching a pitched battle across sharply demarcated lines, and "oppositionists" still appeared in quotation marks in the official press.[89] Some speakers claimed that the triumvirs had nothing to distinguish their position by and that they had stolen their economic policy from Trotsky. Others described an array of economic platforms distinguished by infinitely subtle variations. As one lecturer noted, "Everyone seems to have a pet plan, and the differences are only a matter of what should be planned and to what degree."[90]

It was only when the bureau of the Petrograd's Central District Party organization expended Herculean efforts over the whole of 1924 that the records of the New Course discussions were reexamined, ideological fluidity was shut, opinions classified, and two opposing camps identified. In the margin of a copy of Karpov's desiderata, an unknown hand added the words: "a resolution proposed by the Trotskyists." Once the apparatus imposed the dividing question of belief, students and faculty were confronted for the first time with the demand to align themselves on one side or the other.

After a run of about five weeks, the discussion at the Petrograd State University drew to a close towards the end of January. Ivanov, the secretary of the Party organization, announced the end of the debates and forwarded the documents produced by the various circles to the district committee. Even though during the debates critics of the triumvirate may have overwhelmed the university bureau through their theoretical sophistication, this was rendered moot when Ivanov served as the only voice of his organization before the district committee, following the dictates of his own mind as he underlined or undermined the circles' resolutions. In fact, he quite flatly claimed in his summary that the university Party organization had endorsed the position of the triumvirate.[91]

Now that he could finally refer to the discussion in the past tense, Ivanov spoke of it as a phase in the life of the university: "The last three months witnessed intense arguments and serious explorations. . . . Party building was hotly debated." Certainly this had been the hour of democracy, "and legitimately so," but Ivanov unabashedly described his own interventions: "Never choking off the initiative shown by his comrades, the Party bureau still did not leave things to inertia; our representatives were sent to every circle." The justification for such measures lay in Ivanov's characterization of some students as potentially demagogic. "The opposition was as opportunistic here as anywhere else, of course. At times I felt as if I was speaking to alien elements who needed proof that Soviet power is indeed the power of workers and peasants and not just another version of an oppressive state machine."[92]

Indeed, Ivanov could not forget that strains of heterodox music had been struck up many times during the remarkable bureau meeting at which Zalutskii and Karpov clashed as well as during the minor rhetorical skirmishes at the circle level. Even a very conservative estimate put the number of heterodox speeches in the university at no less than 50 percent of the total. According to the official summary completed on February 6, 1924, "The state of mind of the student body left a lot to be desired. While their ranks varied in commitment and quantity, oppositionists turned up in all the circles; one out of every two students was sympathetic to the opposition in one way or another."[93]

The report broke the student body into three parts. The first group (thirteen circles) came down heavily on the side of the Central Committee. "Even here, however, in the healthiest part of the student body, about 30 percent of the comrades turned out to be oppositionists." The second group (twelve circles) endorsed what were described as "halfway resolutions." Eight of the circles in this group stated that "we do not oppose the Central Committee but simply believe that the recent opposition makes the Party even better." Finally, there were three stubbornly rebellious circles: "These students repeatedly demanded the widest democracy possible and wanted to debate things endlessly."[94]

Judged in terms of their factual accuracy, such ex post facto political characterizations are clearly simplistic and tendentious. But one may almost reject such judgments as irrelevant, since the task of recording the complex state of current political opinion had never been a goal of the Manichaean Party apparatus, which instead set out to reveal the ultimate political disposition of each and every comrade—how each would vote at the end of time, given ultimate knowledge. This approach to polling assumed, and in a sense brought about, a black-and-white version of reality. When the opinions of students who spoke of nuances were not completely effaced, they were inserted between two antagonistic camps and framed as a "buffer"—a term always used in connection with the baleful, politically spineless middle expected to disappear once NEP had been successfully phased out.

Oppositionism as a Character Flaw: The 1924 Party Screening

Soon, however, the subject of political belief had to be examined more closely. Convoked just after the discussion, the Thirteenth Party Congress of January 1924 concluded that the opposition was a "clearly expressed petit bourgeois deviation."[95] Zinoviev noted that alien classes exerted their influence on the Party primarily through the student milieu.[96] To be sure, the majority of the academic Party organizations in Petrograd supported the triumvirate. Still, according to the official statistics, institutions of higher education accounted for a disproportionately large number of Trotsky's sympathizers, when compared to all centers of Party registration: among the 300 "oppositionist activists" tracked down by the Petrograd provincial Party committee, 108 were reported to be registered in universities and 57 in military academies.[97]

Because it isolated them from the factory, the academic environment was said to have transformed even proletarian students into worthless "grade grubbers."[98] Even in the Communist University, considered a relatively pristine environment free of non-Party students and conservative professors, workers stood the risk of losing their class identity. "A worker who has enrolled at the university is no longer a worker," stated Troshchenko, an expert on such matters. "Once he has been separated from the production line, he is declassed."[99]

Oppositionism was presented in medical terms. Majoritarian students claimed that "Party illness expresses itself through groupings."[100] To rid the universities of their "decayed" (*razlozhivshikhsia*) and "estranged" (*otorvavshikhsia*) elements, the Central Committee announced a "verification of Party membership."[101] Limited in scope, the 1924 housecleaning involved primarily educational Party cells that, in Iaroslavskii's words, "had to be purged of their decadent elements."[102] A specially nominated committee drew up lists of candidates for the verification commissions, seeking in particular "steadfast Bolsheviks," industrial workers whose commitment to the Party might date back to 1904–1905.[103]

According to Moscow, the purge did not target "comrades who became embroiled in accidental misunderstandings."[104] Only individuals who "degenerated as a result of NEP" would be culled from the Party's ranks.[105] The Party had explicitly announced that it did not consider oppositionists a lost cause. A 1923 directive categorically forbade the GPU from conducting surveillance of student Communists without the consent of the Central Control Commission, and then only when "ties with anti-Party organizations were suspected."[106]

There were those at the Leningrad Communist University who wanted to see as thorough a purge as possible. Ivanov, for instance, maintained that the discussion had revealed the presence of large numbers of unreliable comrades. "Not everyone can be enlightened," agreed members of the local Party bureau. "In many cases, expulsion is the only solution." A milder note was sounded by Kanatchikov: "a purge must take the form neither of punishment [*karatel'naia mera*] nor of revenge [*rasprava*] against the opposition." The principle endorsed by the rector was class: "Those comrades who did not come here directly from the bench must go first." Class purists marshaled masses of data proving that workers accounted for a distressingly modest percentage of the university's student population. "I would perhaps not go so far as to say that students from the intelligentsia are in the majority here," Bondarev from the university presidium noted, "but the university is teeming with declassed elements." Rumors circulated that the verification troikas were instructed to reduce the share of the intelligentsia at all costs.[107]

A complaint sent to the university Party bureau on March 3, 1924, directly linked oppositionism to class background. "We, the undersigned workers," the text read, "demand that the bureau censure the intelligentsia and lumpen proletarian students responsible for the motion against Zalutskii"—this was a reference to a highly controversial student petition from the previous fall that subjected the head of the Leningrad Party organization to terse criticism and obtained a number of signatures, now described as oppositionist.[108] The denunciation was signed "the workers"—an autograph that should be understood not so much as an index of the authors' social origins as evidence of a widespread conviction that true proletarians were best positioned to unmask unsavory social and political elements. Denunciations coming from true workers—the universalist agents supposedly incapable of ulterior motives—were not seen as a source of internal strife in a Party organization but as a remedy to it.

Unlike any of the other educational purges of the time, the cleansing procedure at Petrograd Communist University was largely conducted by the students themselves.[109] For a few weeks in March 1924, students met after classes and discussed one another. Each student in turn presented an autobiographical synopsis, and then the other members of the circle launched into a brief interrogation. Next, the circle typically turned to a discussion of the student "as a Communist" and, finally, "as a comrade." Straightforward cases did not take long to conclude; more controversial cases might lead to protracted investigations—always the student in question was present and retained the right to speak. Eventually, the circle drafted an evaluation of the student's strengths and weaknesses, drawn up in a more or less formulaic language. The circles had been instructed "neither to condemn nor to vindicate, but to characterize"; their evaluations would serve as the basis for the judgments handed down by the purge commission.[110]

But even the task of drawing up balanced personal evaluations cannot have been easy, given the frequently passionate disagreements that arose in the circles. Opportunities for polemical oratory were seized by students as likely to shoot questions at one another as at the subject of the interview. Originally intended as a comradely conversation, the give and take became an adversarial procedure. While the individual under scrutiny could be counted on to dwell on purity and dedication, the process would have been incomplete without denunciations.

When pleading their case, students operated within a strict universe of truth, statute, and canon. The smallest evasion or omission would leave a stain on their reputations, possibly forever. Casual slurs about the verification process, such as the ironic comments comparing it to a religious confession (*ispoved'*), were rare, and offhand remarks generally indicate that procedural norms were honored. The student Turkin, for example, noted: "We must not pick on comrades; instead we must consider a wide range of questions and only then make a careful final assessment."[111]

Party hermeneuts sought as objective a judgment as possible. Gordeev urged his fellows "to live not by impressions but by reason."[112] Many students opened their comments with the words, "Objectively speaking . . ."[113] At the same time, discussants were aware that the purges were a creative process, and as they interpreted one another's stories they necessarily offered interpretations. After an especially intense series of criticisms from the members of her circle, Sashanova asked what facts they had against her; Diakin scolded her: "Facts do not just lie there in a pile. One has to know how to point to them."[114] Bolshevik hermeneutics was a technique requiring a "hunch" (*chut'e*). The Central Control Commission did not make a secret of the fact that "it is impossible to compose a circular specifying what constitutes an offense and how to punish each different offense."[115]

Once deliberations on the case were completed, the members of the circle voted on their comrade's personal evaluation. Often the group split into nearly equal halves, and the purge commission generally received written opinions from the circle's minority as well as the majority. If a student was to be censured, the circle that sat in judgment had but two options, the assignment of additional readings and practical work, or, far worse, expulsion from the university and the transfer of the case to the control commission. While circles could not actually purge anybody, students knew that if they drew a damaging personal evaluation of a colleague, the Leningrad Control Commission would almost certainly expel that person from the Party.[116]

None of the cases examined by the verification commission focused exclusively on ideology or politics. When oppositionism came up, it did so in a wide biographical context involving class origins, attitude towards comrades, commitment to Party life, and so on. Oppositionism did not necessarily arouse the greatest concern. One student told another, "We should not say that if one is in the opposition one must be intemperate." Even when mention of heterodoxy occurs in the verification protocols, it does not appear as a monolith. It is clear, for instance, that in 1924 many dissident views had nothing to do with Trotsky; students criticized the Party leadership for different reasons and in different keys, sometimes including Trotsky in the elite and holding him responsible, too. Nor was every expression of sympathy with Trotsky identified as a serious deviation. No eyebrows were raised when Nikolaev stated that he "supported the line of the Central Committee but defended Trotsky as a personality against unfair accusations and slurs."[117] "The opposition is a scary thing indeed," Avantin agreed, but there was no reason "to castigate students for speeches demanding that the Party actually implement its own decisions."[118]

To be sure, some of the events of the discussion months would be reconsid-ered in the light of the Central Committee resolutions on oppositionist narrow-mindedness and occasional factionalism.[119] Once they had been identified with the petite bourgeoisie, most manifestations of oppositionism were frowned upon. But what constituted insubordination, and what was to be done about it? Mos-cow did provide some guidance: those who refused to implement the decisions of the Thirteenth Party Congress had to be purged. So had those who sought clan-destine oppositionist material. What about the petition lampooning Zalutskii and the Leningrad apparatus? A ruling came down: "The letter should be regarded as contradicting the line of the Central Committee" and its signatories were to be rel-egated to the category of the "undisciplined."[120]

Was Zhezlov, a student from the third circle, a hard-core oppositionist? Ac-cording to some, not informing the members of his circle that he supported the motion against Zalutskii was "dishonest." But Zhezlov refused the mantle of het-erodoxy: "Though I regarded the protest petition as an impractical measure, I be-lieved that nothing in it was anti-Party." Even if Zhezlov had lately exhibited some unfortunate inclinations, said Mikhailov, this was but a symptom of a more general disorientation at the university: "Zhezlov's mistakes are not a deviation—they sim-ply come from a certain unsteadiness [shatkost']," he said. "This may be assigned to his naiveté [naivnost']."[121]

Of a comrade named Nikolaev, who was "rather taciturn during the discussion," it was simply said that as a member of the intelligentsia he had not yet acquired "Party spirit" (partiinyi dukh). Nikolaev admitted that political questions some-times stymied him. "I haven't yet developed a proletarian psychology."[122] Another student, Mikhailov, strongly supported the opposition in the fourth circle, but no-body worried overmuch about his heterodox stance, which was dismissed as un-serious, almost waggish. "Mikhailov adopted Trotsky's slogan that 'Youth is the ba-rometer of the Party' because it is so flattering," his adversaries claimed. "He wants to believe that the Party will measure itself against him!"[123]

All in all, the leniency shown students by the 1924 screening attested to great confidence in the young people who had earlier proven themselves worthy of being sent by their mother organizations to study in Petrograd. Whatever shortcomings they had exhibited during the discussion were regarded as temporary breakdowns. Even when they decided to expel them, their fellow students still exhibited a be-nign attitude, especially by the standards of later purges. "We should not engage in persecution," one student purger argued. "Be demanding, but do not go overboard," another added. The Party was afflicted by the diseases of NEP, and perfection was still remote.[124]

At this stage, oppositionism had to do not with intentions but with the ability to follow them through. If students had wandered onto the wrong path, quite likely their "character" (kharakter) was to blame, but character meant here little more than a collection of idiosyncrasies induced by the pressures of the transitional period. Every student was supposed to conduct an endless struggle with his "psychology," a force that pulled him back, reactivating old, long-superseded negative habits. "Psychology" (*psikhologiia*) related to "convictions" (*ubezhdeniia*) as potentiality relates to actuality.[125] Eventually, ideology was to bring psychology to the surface, subjecting it to the rule of the comrade's will.

During the winter a student named Voronov expressed misgivings about the official policy, which annoyed many of his comrades. But steadfastness far outweighed anything else, and the unshakability of Voronov's opinions led his questioners to overlook his opinions themselves. Voronov stoutly said: "During the discussion, I was firm. No one has yet proved me wrong on the economic issues."[126]

Another case, that of Petrova, shows that those who conformed enthusiastically to the official line could fall if their stance did not reflect deeper persuasion.[127] Extreme and perpetually self-contradictory, "Petrova has no opinions of her own." Shkliarovskaia went on to say, "Due to her husband's influence, she has come to believe that Trotsky is a counterrevolutionary." This led to some questions from the other members of her circle, who had clearly grown a bit tired of her anti-Trotskyist harangues and had begun to wonder whether that flimsy political attitude betokened Petrova's indecisiveness or her overconfidence. What bothered the students were not so much Petrova's views but that it was nearly impossible to make them out. A contrite Petrova did not cavil: "Because of my hot temper I treated certain issues too lightly. My views were shaped impulsively."

Political opinions lay on the surface; the purge had been initiated to dig a bit deeper, moving from actions to intentions. As they discussed one another, comrades talked about this or that feature "finding its expression" (*nakhodit svoe vyrazhenie*) in a specific action. This suggests the hermeneutical logic underlying the purge: seeking to decipher each other's nature, students assumed that everyone had a secret to reveal. Every word might be a clue, and beneath all the words lay a design that accounted for every action. Behind the formulaic language of the protocols a hunt for the students' selves was going on.

As part of the file moved up to the purge commission, the circle drew up personal evaluations (*kharakteristiki*); in these, students' trustworthiness was assessed, but little was said about political opinions as such.[128] Rather, general disposition stood at the heart of the document. This is evident from the main questions that had to be answered: "What are the student's personal abilities [*sposobnosti*]?" "How steady [*ustoichivost'*] is he or she?" "What are his or her inclinations [*sklonnosti*]?"

Suitability for the Party was discussed in terms of character traits. As one student put it, the one who was "not a resolute person could not be a resolute Party member either." Censures often took the form of moral exhortations: "do not be so smug" (*posbav' spes'*); "do not be so lax" (*razviazan*); "be less chatty" (*mnogorechiv*); or "eradicate dandyism" (*frantovstvo*).[129]

"Vices" (*poroki*) came in clusters in the Bolshevik world, and they were believed to reveal something about the essence of the person who engaged in them. The Party control commissions called them "misdeeds" (*prostupki*) and "flaws" (*nedostatki*). Vices were a deplorable manner of talking or a fond devotion to a bad habit, and were thought to reveal the psychology of a person. One vice always implied another, ultimately leading to a series of bad habits. If someone was an individualist, it was unlikely that he would not dodge a *subbotnik* or some other Party duty when given the opportunity. It was as unlikely that one bad habit would not automatically lead to another as it was improbable that talking in an opinionated manner in a student circle would come without trying to patronize workers in a study group. At the extreme end of the range of vices was engagement in trade, reading of unauthorized literature, and dealing with ardent oppositionists. But vices were not only accumulated and collected around certain weak comrades. They were also attributed to entire categories of people seen as naturally prone to them, especially children of kulaks and merchants or degenerate Party bureaucrats.

What character traits corresponded to the Bolshevik ideal? Generally admired was "steadfastness" (*tverdost'*), for which Rogoznikov drew praise as he showed himself "willing to bear heavy responsibilities."[130] Self-control was among the qualities for which another student, Stasiuk, was praised; he was seen as one "who knows how to make rational use of his time."[131] Other character traits were clearly negative. Authoritarianism, for example, violated the basic values of equality and camaraderie, so dear to the Bolsheviks. Of Kolchinskii it was said that "he lacks Communist sensitivity [*chutkost'*]; . . . he slights comrades."[132] An "aloof" (*zamknutyi*) individual, Savinov was particularly reviled for his "boastfulness" and "ponderousness."[133]

Borderline cases cropped up, and when, for example, Nasulenko faced his questioners, his good and bad points could not be readily distinguished. "True," Mikhailov noted, "Nasulenko is sensitive, but this is a virtue rather than a vice"— the intelligentsia's refinement could not be just thrown overboard.[134] Another borderline trait, "directness" (*priamota*), meant openness and sincerity, but could also verge on rudeness; it was generally used to describe a worker who was still somewhat uncouth. Petrova "used to insult comrades," which meant, in Maron's judgment, that she was "undisciplined." Interpreting her categorical language as a sign of her proletarian essence, others were more forgiving: "True, Petrova can be tactless and coarse. Yet she is a good comrade overall."[135]

How could anyone with a bad character be a good Communist? Members of Shkliarovskaia's circle called her "crafty" and "posing," and insisted she had no backbone: "She not only wavers in Party affairs—in her personal life she also tosses hither and thither." Voronov was even harsher: "Shkliarovskaia is a bit of a toady: she has no opinions of her own and simply repeats the words of others."

Shkliarovskaia attempted a rebuttal: "I am simply attentive and respectful towards people who are smarter than I am." Though it was finally decided that she ought to be permitted to continue at the university, the circle noted: "Shkliarovskaia needs to be completely reformed."

A faithful supporter of the Central Committee, Fedulaev also got into trouble because of his negative character traits. The opposite of the insecure Shkliarovskaia, Fedulaev was overconfident. A need "to demonstrate his superiority" drove him to declare that "I find studying in the circle utterly unsatisfying." Confronted, he soon admitted his duty to work on himself. "Yes, I am far too individualistic. . . . But now I know my aim: to become a Communist, a Marxist working actively in production."[136]

The Communist ethical register displayed the subtlety and range of its colors and pitches over the course of a long debate concerning Rogoznikov's actions and their connection to his inner sensibility.[137] An evident problem was "lack of discipline" (nedistsiplinirovannost'). When he had first obtained a copy of Trotsky's unpublished letter, Rogoznikov had stated defiantly, "Do with me what you like but I will not give it up!" The shocked members of his circle said, "Can you believe this is a Party member speaking?" and, "This individual cannot be described as disciplined."

But Rogoznikov insisted that he had not violated the proper rules of conduct: "I told you all I knew; it would be foolish to purge me just for possessing the letter."

Did such claims sway many of the circle's members? Absolutely not. "From time to time, Rogoznikov launches another attempt to prove that he is correct," testified his ill-wishers. "He cites Trotsky on his right to cling to his opinions and to try to persuade others, both of which fly in the face of the official resolutions."

Perhaps Rogoznikov exhibited discipline—some comrades were not convinced—but was he "temperate" (vyderzhannyi)? Party members could not live on discipline alone: this other trait, which captured the Communist determination to engage the individual's most inner self, was at least as important. A truly dedicated Party member had to embrace the Communist mission as his own. Integrity, consistency, a certain openess—these were the constituent elements of "Party temperance."

Somewhat apologetically, Kozlov said, "It is difficult to evaluate Rogoznikov. Take the most recent period, for example: even though fundamental questions were raised, he still would not reveal his true colors." Mikhov expressed a similar view: "Rogoznikov would not forcefully take on the issues. He said it was not worth it!" And Gordeev too: "What is strange about Rogoznikov is not so much the specific position he took, but the fact that he took no clear position at all." His decision to absent himself from both of the circle meetings devoted to considering the Party's political program had obviously ruffled some feathers.

Fel'dman harped on the issue: "The discussion was a trying time for the Party. Everyone was supposed to get involved. Rogoznikov, however, spent the time who knows where. . . . Even when he did attend a meeting he would not say a thing. Only at the very end, when asked point-blank what he thought of the opposition, did he make a passionate speech criticizing the official reporter."

A long-term view, students suggested, might help decipher Rogoznikov's soul. First of all, his more straightforward comments had to be ignored, "for in them he had simply tried to find a theoretical explanation for the economic crisis." But by carefully considering his body language, demeanor, and manner of speech, one could see the "bitter spirit" (gor'kovatyi dukh) that had always been there: "Rogoznikov behaves like a lumpen proletarian." "During the discussion, he [mentally] went underground—such must be his 'nature.'"

The time had come for Rogoznikov's supporters to speak. "There is no basis for saying that Rogoznikov did not speak clearly," said one of them, opening the case for the defense. "Rogoznikov often argued about economics," added another, going on to ask, "Where is his alleged lack of self-revelation?" A third felt strongly that those who accused Rogoznikov of "indeterminacy" (neopredelennost') were not fair or Party-minded. "Rogoznikov supported Trotsky's line on Party building and economic planning; in fact, he said exactly what was on his mind. But no one should be forced to make speeches on every issue."

Rogoznikov tried to add substance to the defense offered by his partisans. Above all, the reluctance he had shown to public speaking had been due, so he said, to his need to avoid mechanically echoing the official spokesman, and to arrive at his own conclusions. "Yes, it took me a while to do that; I am not about to hide my shortcomings." While each disciplined Communist had to implement Party decisions, this did not mean that he had to give up independence of thought: "Take the question of the origins of the present economic crisis. The issue was theoretical, so Communists could cling to this or that Marxist point of view. Since I believed that the problem had arisen from a lack of planning . . . I said as much to the circle. . . . If I still hold to my opinions, well, no one has the right to take them away from me!" Rogoznikov's claim to independence proved a shrewd strategy: he was adjudged a "temperate and steady Party member."

As students adopted attitudes they hoped the Party might find convincing, they were making their way across a thickly planted minefield. Somewhere between naked coercion and the rule of law lay a third force, "authority" (avtoritet). On the one hand, students had to respect Party leaders at the local and certainly the national level. On the other hand, they were also supposed to think for themselves. "If I am susceptible to persuasion," Fadin from the sixth circle proudly announced, "it would not be that of the authorities but that gained by a personal study of the materials."[138] A measure of independence could be quite laudable, then, but the determination shown by Bogatyrev "to prove he had an original mind" was considered "rawness" (neoformlennost') and even "mischievousness" (mal'chishestvo). Such glibness and an abundance of self-assurance were better avoided.[139] Kudrin, another student, was taken to task for veering in the opposite direction: "His weak spot is resignation before authorities."[140] For these mine dodgers, balance was everything.

Decipherment of character exercised hermeneutical skills to the utmost, because a manifest, objectively verifiable way of judging the individual was lacking. Because character was a tricky thing, often buried behind appearances, students developed what might be called hermeneutics of suspicion. Sometimes testimony was taken at face value, but quite often the surface meaning of a student's words had to be inverted.

Kondrat'ev was suspected of changing his mode of behavior to save his skin. But Frolov was not a fool: "Watching how he became such an ideal Communist I wonder, is it the same person? In my heart I suspect that he must have heard that a purge would follow the discussion." Or take the case of Bogatyrev from the seventh circle. "Before the discussion of his case, he kept quiet and lay low [tishe vody, nizhe travy], out of fear that his reputation would suffer." After his comrades had figured out what he was up to, Bogatyrev revealed his true colors and began calling his fellow students "boors" (khamy) and "country bumpkins" (muzhich'e). His manners could finally be diagnosed as "typical of the servile ideology instilled in him by his previous work as a waiter."[141]

The case of Sal'kovskii, the head of the fourth circle, stirred the university.[142] The report Sal'kovskii delivered to the circle during the opening day of the discussion created the impression that he was leaning towards Trotsky. But then he experienced an inexplicable change of heart. Kapustin was frustrated: "I simply do not understand Sal'kovskii. I tried to talk to him but he would not give a clear answer to a single question. He criticizes the opposition one moment, and the next moment he's criticizing the Central Committee." Or perhaps Sal'kovskii was shifty and hypocritical. "There are people who do not know how to hide their mistakes and blunders, and there are also people who know how to camouflage them well," commented Grigor'ev. "Sal'kovskii belongs to the second category." According to Kapustin, "Sal'kovskii likes to have his cake and eat it too [i volki syty i ovtsy tsely]." Mironov was equally ironic: "I truly admire Sal'kovskii's diplomatic flexibility; he is a match to [Georgii] Chicherin [the Soviet commissar for foreign affairs]."

A number of speakers suspected that Sal'kovskii was a political chameleon, even self-consciously deceitful. Having changed his pose at the most convenient time, charged Mironov, Sal'kovskii became a tool of the official line. "We all heard him swear that he was a majoritarian. But in the club, before the discussion session began, I also witnessed him besieging Zelinkov for his support of the Central Committee. . . . Furthermore, he confided to me the contents of Trotsky's letter at his place over a cup of tea. Should a circle organizer be distributing forbidden literature?"

Highly sensitive to duplicity, the Bolshevik language deployed a number of words to refer to a person who spoke in two voices. Whereas his bitterest adversaries described Sal'kovskii as "two-faced" (*dvulichnyi*), a term hinting at deliberate deceit, the majority of the circle's members preferred the gentler "two-minded" (*dvoistvennyi*), that is, someone who was truly tossing hither and thither in desperation, unable to decide what side to choose. The harshest epithet of all, "double-dealer" (*dvurushnik*), was saved for an individual who not only kept his true thoughts to himself but also surreptitiously acted on them; in 1924 the term was not applied to oppositionists.

Kipiatkov refused to see his Party organizer maligned as a fraud. "Sal'kovskii is being accused here of two-facedness but no one can say how it has expressed itself. . . . Certainly he experienced no vacillations [*shatania*] during the discussion. If he fell prey to hesitations [*kolebaniia*], well, didn't we all? . . . If some of his points are unclear we should not be amazed, since he poses his questions with heat and excitement. This lack of clarity is typical of our circle."

Fadin went the furthest in defending Sal'kovskii's loyalist credentials: "In my view, even before the discussion he supported the Central Committee. When I mistakenly took up the line of the opposition, he even yelled at me, saying, 'You are not an oppositionist, only a troublemaker. You yourself do not know what you are defending!'"

According to the above-cited speakers, Sal'kovskii may have been an ideological charlatan, but he was certainly not an ideological foe. Many saw in him a middle-of-the-road opportunist: "Having failed to develop a proletarian ideology, he simply adjusts to the moods and wishes of others." Students found Sal'kovskii's ideological neutrality dispiriting. They did not want a dispenser of labels—this one oppositionist, that one official—but a leader committed to sincerity and fairness, and Sal'kovskii refused to act as this leader. Katushkin maintained, "Sal'kovskii does not care what resolution passes as long as his authority is preserved." By a vote of eleven to five (with two abstentions) Sal'kovskii was expelled from the university for lacking sufficient proletarian "sensitivity" (*chutkost'*).

Screening Autobiographical Narratives

The pivotal role played by autobiographies during the purge also points to the pursuit of the ethical kernel of the individual. Both readers and writers of these narratives focused not on actions per se but rather on how actions had shaped individual consciousness. The student was expected to narrate in some detail what influences were exerted on him during childhood, when he was first introduced to socialist ideas, what he did during the Revolution and the Civil War, and to what views he adhered "during the conscious stages of his life."

The brief, handwritten autobiographies found in every purge folder—sometimes written by the student himself, sometimes by the circle's stenographer—were informed by the eschatological motifs that permeated the Bolshevik discourse. A student typically claimed that he had reached a mature Communist consciousness and narrated his life up to the current moment as a process of spiritual growth. That decisive moment when the autobiographer claimed to have seen the light of Communism was presented as a conversion of sorts; at that moment his individual mind and the Party line embodying the suprapersonal proletarian consciousness merged.

What a student stated in his autobiography was compared to the material in his personal file and the documents he deposited with the university bureau. The elaborate process of examining student autobiographies led to quite a rigmarole in the fourth circle. Grigor'ev charged that members of the presidium searched for compromising details when examining the records of students with whom they had "antagonistic relationships." But while Ergenpreis admitted that "we examined autobiographies with an eye towards determining who should be purged and who should be spared," he stoutly insisted that "this does not mean we somehow colluded." Kipiatkov also defended this practice. "Once it became clear to us that we were not sufficiently acquainted with the student questionnaires and autobiographies, four of us secluded ourselves late to examine their materials. True, we paid more attention to certain comrades ... and less to others, but there is nothing wrong with that." The presidium was simply preparing materials to buttress its recommendations.[143]

The discussion of every case was opened with the organizer reading the autobiography in question aloud. The short sessions of questions and answers that followed suggest that it was not the dry information that the circle was after—for that the data in the questionnaire sufficed. Much more interesting was the issue of student openness and sincerity. After a certain Lutkina had presented her self-portrait, students complained that they were left feeling that they knew her no better than before she had spoken. "She's trying to conceal herself."[144] Seeking indications of political trustworthiness, students tried to determine the student's suitability for the Party. They assigned importance to actions performed in the immediate past, especially conduct during the discussion, but were concerned primarily with the general life trajectory, the connections between all of the actions that provided a coherent picture of the student's self.[145]

Autobiographical detail was of course open to different and even contradictory interpretations. Military service can serve as a test case here: many comrades came to the Communist University straight from the Red Army—their life narratives could be bent in opposite directions depending on how the Civil War was presented. While anyone who had served the Red cause might claim to have proved his loyalty, those who harped interminably on their experience at the front could come off as blindly devoted to Trotsky, the celebrated military commissar. More generally, the Bolsheviks feared that the Red Army bred authoritarianism, which in turn encouraged oppositionism.

One of those who came to the university soon after demobilization, Boitsov himself embraced this diagnosis: "The military world deformed me, encouraged me to play the dandy and left me with a streak of haughtiness [*vysokomerie*]." Though Boitsov did not give any "sign of instability" during the discussion, his experience as a military commissar was said to have left "negative marks" on his character, fostering indolence, profligacy, reckless extravagance, and overbearing bossiness and irritability. The "crudeness" (*grubost'*) of Voronov, who had served as Zinoviev's personal guard during the years of fighting, was said to have "exceeded all bounds." Even those who offered kind words seemed to be alluding to a problematic military past: "Hardly perverted, . . . Voronov just tends to be nervous sometimes"; "Voronov is a good comrade but there are flickers of a rude lack of restraint [*nesderzhannost'*] in him."[146]

In 1924 the purge process considered family background preeminently important. No amount of detail could sate a hunger for information about past and present parental income, parental education, and social standing prior to the Revolution. Disgruntled, a circle might very well vote to revise the "social position" the bureau put down in his personal evaluation. But the apparent social determinism underlying such attitudes did not always prevail. Fadin, for example, angrily rebutted those who "derived my oppositionism from my petit bourgeois village background. If something of my former life has stuck with me, it's my revolutionism, which I absorbed in the Red Army. No schools taught me; I was taught by life itself."[147]

While class origins could raise certain suspicions, they could also provide precious clues as to how one's shortcomings could be mitigated. Those who assessed the lineaments of Zavilovich's political outlook provided a remarkably flexible reading of his class background.[148] Born to a dentist and having attended a gymnasium, Zavilovich could hardly lay claim to proletarian roots. Efimov was resolute: "Because he comes from a family of the intelligentsia," Zavilovich, who had been inactive while the decisions of the congresses were being analyzed, "must leave the university." Others, however, were willing to entertain the possibility that class could be transcended. "Social origins do not tell the whole story," Kazachenko noted. "I detect no trace of the intelligentsia in Zavilovich's makeup. His activities in the Komsomol definitely cultivated a proletarian psychology in him, as I understand it." Here class was a psychological type, a matter of Zavilovich's own attitudes, and was not related to his social origins. Another who objected to the vulgar equation between one's political outlook and the background of one's parents was Filipov: "I believe that his family played no role in Zavilovich's life. If anything, it was the Komsomol that influenced his family: Komsomol activists used to come to the house every day and Zavilovich's young sister was eventually drawn into the Bolshevik ranks." Most of his comrades appear to have believed that Zavilovich transcended his class origins without great effort; this suggests that the social and the ethico-political concepts of class were constantly engaged in a dynamic interaction.

Of course, there is no denying that the family remained important in the Communist universe. A routine part of any interview held during the purge involved the relatives' political outlook. Petrova was proud of her kin. "During the Revolution, I was a Bolshevik by virtue of family relations: Father has been affiliated with the Party since 1902." Mikhailov displayed a bit less pride. "My father and sister lack a revolutionary temper; I have nothing to do with them."[149]

Construed as a relapse to an old, interest-driven mode of thinking, political heterodoxy could be a family-transmitted disease. While one's explicit political orientation was a conscious matter that might be directly repaired, one's relations with parents or spouse involved a deep-seated, subconscious mental stratum, not easily transformed. And loyalty to the family, reactionary or not, might imperil one's commitment to the Party. "Love always sins," Bolsheviks said. "This is because when the thoughts and feelings of 'two loving hearts' are absorbed in one another, that same love isolates the pair, separates them from the collective."[150]

Some marriages could be read as deviations: one might as well join the opposition as wed a class alien. Students attributed Boitsov's oppositionism to his marriage to a "bourgeois lady" (burzhuika).[151] The politically undecided Nasulenko was accused of retreating into private life on account of his wife. She taught Nasulenko to adjust to political fashions—or so it was said by those who accused Nasulenko of withholding his opinions until one side had prevailed in the discussion. Nasulenko himself did nothing but sing her praises: "We had a church wedding simply because we needed a marriage certificate. A daughter of a poor peasant . . . my wife was once arrested for revolutionary activity." One could hardly wish for more compelling proof of her ideological virtue.[152]

Peasant Oppositionism

Intertwined with character and political persuasion, social origins were a double-edged sword. A source of pride, especially in case of workers, class could turn into an impediment as well. Some students were said to be lured by heterodoxy because their peasant origins asserted themselves, others because they came from the uncommitted intelligentsia. A peasant named Savinov, for example, was constantly reminded of his roots—and not by those who would praise him. This self-styled oppositionist had, when the discussion turned to the question of democracy, supported the Central Committee, but on economic questions he was in full agreement with Osinskii.

Comrades saw in Savinov's "intemperance" a clear indication of his "peasant deviation." Through some hermeneutical arithmetic—roughly, "middle peasant origins plus preoccupation with agrarian policy equals self-interest"—they concluded that "when he joined the Party, Savinov must have been seeking economic benefits for his class," a damning evaluation.[153] Instead of struggling against the local kulaks, Savinov had reportedly "fled the village. . . . No wonder the Komsomol had protested his dispatch here." Though there was little support for the harsh view that "in the resolution of fundamental issues he expresses oppositionist deviation," the majority decided to expel Savinov from the university as an unreformed peasant.[154]

By objecting to the Petrograd Party organization's letter condemning Trotsky, another student with a rustic background, Potapov, had also earned an undesirable reputation.[155] Comrades thought that Potapov's peasant orientation deprived him of confidence and conviction when it was time to vote. The economic interests of his village allegedly outstripped other considerations when he evaluated official policies. A fable by no other than the venerate Zinoviev himself explained why peasants such Potapov were welcome in the Party but peasant political identity was not:

Let us take two comrades, A and B, both prominent, disciplined, and excellent comrades in every way. Comrade A came to Bolshevism at a different time and by a different route than Comrade B. A's origins are in the peasant movement that formed a mighty wave following October and the Civil War. By contrast, B came from the workers' movement and joined Bolshevism over twenty years ago. Both comrades are precious to our Party and the final victory of the Revolution depends on the complementarity of their qualities. . . . And yet, if comrade A suddenly began demanding that the Party policy orient itself not towards workers but towards peasants, if he demanded, following Trotsky, that the Party headquarters become a bloc representing the interests of different social groups, what then would our Party have to say to him?[156]

Still very much attached to the village and his kulak father (and "probably a Socialist Revolutionary" to boot), "Potapov hardly boasted a proletarian psychology," hence his penchant to nepotism. "Potapov's acquaintances joined forces to advance his career," students noted. Sapozhnikov recalled being told by Potapov "how he went to work in a bank and then was dragged by his cronies into the Komsomol." In a word, NEP had done its nefarious work on this peasant: he was unable to break out of his milieu. "Having thought about Potapov all night long," Nudel'man reached a sad conclusion: "he is simply using the system."

Off balance, dazed by the torrent of accusations, the best reply Potapov could muster was patchy and disjointed. "There are no grounds," he said, "for the accusations against me. I disagreed with the Petrograd Party organization's letter because at first I didn't know what Trotsky stands for. . . . Sure, there are problems with peasants, but what have they got to do with me?"

Jumpy as it was, this speech launched the defense. Reztsov insisted that "judging by his psychology" Potapov was "proletarian" after all. Fel'dman agreed: whatever his opinions, "Potapov is evolving in a positive direction." Sounding a bit irritated by what he took to be trivial criticisms, Andreev wanted to know whether "we're asking Potapov to shower us with smiles, or what?" Several others confirmed this view, Agatov among them. "It is impossible to describe Potapov as a fellow traveler. Fellow travelers are alien elements with a foreign ideology. If Potapov had looked for more money in a new job he would have answered this description," but he did not.

There appear to have been several Potapovs, one an opportunistic and selfish peasant, the other a serious Communist, "one who always looks at the heart of the problem."

The majority of the circle, however, clung to the view of Potapov as a degenerate peasant. "Last year Potapov was a good comrade," Mataladze noted, "but now I see changes: his relations with comrades are not as good as they used to be." And, with greater precision: "There was a time when Potapov did not pontificate. Rather, he wanted to examine every issue from all angles." But employment on the provision commission revived the selfish peasant in him: "because of his eagerness to get ahead, he became uncommunicative, authoritarian."

Time went on, opinion followed opinion, the stenographer was hard at work and there would be no vote on a resolution anytime soon.

Feuds, Vendettas, and Personal Networks

With Potapov, ulterior motives, personality clashes, and competition for spoils came to be so central to the discussion that they deserve commentary. At the time of his interrogation it had been suggested that some of his critics might have had "biased opinions" that led them to make "many exaggerations and overstatements of various sorts."[157]

"Why is this circle always against me?" Potapov exasperatedly exclaimed. "If no one cared for my speeches, which were brief enough, why wasn't I told? . . . What we have here is an attempt at undermining [podkatyvanie]." An outsider, Mataladze, made a controversial statement: "My impression is that the examination of Potapov is unfair." Then Aleksandrov spoke up: "Kudilevskaia picks on Potapov. Potapov was being sincere about his past and she was just digging for something else. . . . To accuse Potapov of the crime of self-seeking is a crime in itself." Perhaps Feld'man went the furthest: he spoke of conspiracy. "Comrades must have agreed in advance to look for ways to scuttle Potapov. The accusations against him have no inner logic."

Clearly there would be no reconciling of the competing assessments of Potapov's character:

Kuznetsova's suggestion: "Potapov considers his personal interests before the Party's" (3 for, 11 against, 3 abstentions).

Nikitin's suggestion: "Potapov is two-faced" (1 for, 17 against, 5 abstentions).

Rybakova's suggestion: "Potapov is haughty" (3 for, 17 against, 3 abstentions).

Gaidamak's suggestion: "Potapov is a good comrade; he has no shortcomings." (10 for)

Lipova's suggestion: "Potapov treats his comrades with contempt" (9 for).

The judgment that ultimately won out was Rogoznikov's: "Potapov is an undisciplined, intemperate, and unsteady Party member" (14 for, 8 against, 1 abstention).

Appalled by personal evaluation they considered utterly baseless, two dissenters, Fedorov and Gaidamak, submitted an "extraordinary statement" to the university authorities:

his former circle would never have endorsed such a view: they known Potapov much better. We believe the evaluation is wrong and prejudiced, and feel that the conclusion had been reached in advance of today's debates. Trivial faults are cited while everything of real importance is silently omitted; captious objections [*pritsepki*] make up the bulk of Potapov's personal evaluation.... Since the vote was split and considering the seriousness of the charges, Potapov's case should be moved to the control commission.

Remarkably, another minority opinion was submitted through this process, articulating a view of Potapov less generous even than the official evaluation. Nudel'man wrote that, "judging by the material in our hands, I suggest that Potapov be downgraded to Party candidate for a year or two."[158] In the moment of extremity, two cliques had viciously attacked one another, pushing the members of the circle into two polarized camps.

Following the regulations, the university authorities ordered the case reexamined—this time in the presence of comrades from Potapov's old circle. As Potapov had no doubt expected, this round yielded an opinion far more favorable to his reputation. Stasiuk stated: "During the year and a half we studied together I came to know Potapov as a truly talented and steadfast comrade"; and Boitsov added, "I know Potapov as a comrade free of any deviations and philistine moods." All this to no avail: on April 4 the purge commission ruled against Potapov and he was expelled from the university.[159]

Should we conclude that personal enmity played a key role during the purge? While the historian claims to read against the grain, to adjust his interpretation in light of alleged biases in the sources, he often does little more than repeat the language of the primary documents. Imperceptibly, he takes sides in the debate: if ideological claptrap is dismissed as concealing more than it reveals, other utterances, especially those that conform to the interests of utilitarian politics, are pronounced genuine and, in fact, revelatory. The historical methodology that summons us to dig beneath the surface of the source to the passions and the interests that supposedly shaped it turns out to be a projection of the liberal outlook onto the Communist universe.

A careful inquiry into the politics of Bolshevik identity requires consideration of how personal ambition was justified, and the student purges provide us with remarkably complete records of countless varied justifications. To be sure, biases were frequently mentioned—but they were construed as vices, indications of the degeneration wrought by NEP.[160] The point here is not that personal relationships did not have a role to play but that they could not be construed outside discourse; even the most intimate aspects of life depended on official self-fashioning to make sense of them.

If Potapov's benefactors cleaved to the codes of the orthodox Bolshevik autobiography and described a conscientious comrade, the aim of those who brought charges was just the reverse: to prove that the targeted student was not a conscious Communist but a petit bourgeois hanger-on. Schematically speaking, denunciations were inverted autobiographies. Where an autobiography depicted true Communist consciousness, the denunciation found only petit bourgeois narrow-mindedness. Nothing was private; a summons to comment on a comrade's behavior might lead to questions about personal "attitudes" (*nastroeniia*) and "habits" (*navyki*) as well as public declarations.[161] An anecdote about some dormitory prank, a remembered conversation—to repeat these to the investigating circle would raise no eyebrows; ordinary conduct was habitually brought to the attention of the collective and cannot constitute the locus of truth for the historian. Slanderous and calumnious accusations, though, would not be tolerated, since they fomented squabbles within the collective. But the denunciations leveled by trustworthy students served as bulwarks against discord, not as incitements to conflict.

As the example of the fifth circle shows, attempts to distinguish the personal roots of paralyzing disagreements from the ideological roots often prove vain.[162] Smotriaeva responded to her expulsion from the university by petitioning the university Party bureau to review her case as soon as possible, "before April 7, 1924, when the material drawn up by my circle is transferred to the purge commission." She provided a lengthy argument, excerpted here:

While my circle's purge protocol presents me as a troublemaker, I believe that the true source of the trouble is Kisel', who started it all to settle personal accounts.... Kisel' and I lived in the same room for quite some time and we used to have bitter arguments. At least twice I brought her attention to tactless, what I would even call non-Communist, things she did and told her she tried to pass herself off as what she wasn't.... At the end of an argument with me on the morning [of the purge], Kisel' threatened to make sure I got expelled and listed almost all the comrades who used to adhere to the opposition— she told me these would be my accusers.... What gossip she told the circle, playing on the feelings of mistrust incited by the Party discussion, no one would tell me (except Smirnova, who passed me a little note in the reading room), but the fact remains that in the evening my comrades were against me. Kisel' got her way and the circle trashed me—rightly or wrongly is for the purge commission to decide.

Smotriaeva accused her enemy of using politics as a facade for furtively carrying on personal feuds—this much leaps to the eye. On closer reading, though, one notices that even when the argument was clearly personal and students called each other names, they employed the official jargon. Politics informed any assessment of personality: to wound an opponent, call her ideologically alien. Smotriaeva linked oppositionism and corruption, but she made no effort to call one cause and the other effect.

The Intelligentsia: A Vulnerable Self

Able to elevate itself above self-seeking and petty feuding, the intelligentsia, in the Bolshevik perception, tended to behave in a dignified manner. But the intelligentsia had other shortcomings, perhaps even graver ones, and was certainly less susceptible to reform. The Bolsheviks' ambivalent attitude towards this class, social stratum, or profession, depending on the theorist, is well known. On the one hand, the intelligentsia had betrayed the Revolution in 1917, and on the other hand, it was believed to be indispensable to the task of enlightening the workers. Many thunderbolts were cast against the intelligentsia, but caveats abounded as well. The educated class could do good by teaching Marxism, but deep-seated suspicions that it was the agent of the petite bourgeoisie would not soon dissipate.[163]

According to the Bolsheviks, the intelligentsia's predilection for reflection subjectivized the world, transformed the brute actuality of class struggle into mere ideas existing for the thinker alone. In addition, it regards the individual as simply a thinking intellect rather than an experiential, worldly entity in active interaction with society. If members of the intelligentsia, like other human beings, are subject to the influences of their social milieu, it is not hard to see how a number of their core traits—their asocial turning inward, lack of spontaneity, detachment from emotion, and exquisitely vulnerable sense of self-esteem—might be exaggerations of tendencies fostered by their role in the division of labor.

Students identified with the intelligentsia experienced great frustration as they labored to acquire talents for which they would only be derided. Born in the city of Kerch to a Jewish boot maker, Kolchinskii was sent as a boy "to study the Talmud and the Torah."[164] Soon, however, he turned to a different set of sacred texts. "My family," Kolchinskii maintained in his autobiography, "has always illegally harbored Social Democrats. During the Civil War, I was in the Crimea, and was kept in the White Army." Then in late 1919 he entered an underground Komsomol organization; the police harassed him, often searching his house. Somehow Kolchinskii survived until the advent of Soviet power and served in the Sevastopol' propaganda department before being sent to Petrograd to study. Here was a transitional figure, his locus somewhere between the petit bourgeois shtetl and the revolutionary city.

Naturally attracted to the opposition because of his sense that the Revolution was nothing so much as an intellectual game, Kolchinskii delivered a series of sophisticated speeches that left all who heard them convinced that he had fallen for Trotsky. Generally appreciative of Kolchinskii's abilities (he was called "a capable guy") his circle mates pointed out a "bunch of shortcomings" in his character. Turgenev's Rudin and this Jewish smart aleck in the big city had a lot in common, said some. Kazachenko explained the comparison: "Since his arrival at the university, he has terrorized us with memorized phrases from Plekhanov. Each article, each phrase, sends him into ecstasies and he turns everything into an aesthetic pleasure." Avrutin had the impression that "Kolchinskii hovers in the sky. Since he has no real life experience ... he turns every stupid thing into a philosophy."

It was all a game. "Kolchinskii does not come to grips with the bowels of the Revolution," Gorokhov believed; "instead he only sees its external aspect. He states his opinions but ... does not take Party affairs to heart." But, after all, was this not quite natural? The Bolsheviks spoke for the workers, not for intellectuals like him. Efimov rubbed it in: "From the first days after his arrival here, one could sense that he was contumacious and arrogant. When we took him to task for neglecting to pay his membership dues he even threatened to commit suicide." Note that the Bolsheviks viewed suicide as a repellent capitulation and saw a "link between suicide and self-flagellation of the intelligentsia."[165]

Could Kolchinskii be reeducated, and if so, was the Communist University the place for it? The suggestion, made rather meekly, that Kolchinskii had recently been making changes for the better drew instantaneous rebuttals. Gorokhov spoke out with remarkable bluntness: "If he has changed anything it's only superficial. Sure, he behaves more carefully, but inside he's just the same."

Moments before the curtain fell, Kolchinskii was permitted a rejoinder: "The transformation [perelom] I have undergone is not just external. . . . Back home I was believed to be one of the best; this may have had a negative influence on me: and it accounts for my haughty treatment of comrades here. . . . Even when flashy words catch my attention, I never put form over content." Though the circle strongly recommended expulsion, the purge commission reversed the verdict.[166]

When Gorokhov took his turn as the focus of the circle's probing eyes, his affinities with Kolchinskii became apparent.[167] First there was his distinguished Bolshevik record. His autobiography, captured by a stenographer as he spoke, presented a series of events narrated in the present tense: "A twenty-three-year-old son of the agent of a company that makes bread for export takes part in underground activities in the Ukraine while it is ruled by the hetman, periodically embarks on treks to communicate with partisan detachments and joins an underground detachment. Later he becomes a Cheka interrogator, a warrior in the conflict with Makhno, and, at the time of Antonov's mutiny, a peacemaker."

How did somebody with this sort of Party record lose his way? According to Avrutin, Gorokhov's outbursts during the discussion stemmed from his "nervousness," characteristic of the intelligentsia. Conditions in the Ukraine, others explained, "can produce only people like Gorokhov. The social environment encourages enormous cheekiness." Tkachenko concluded, "Gorokhov's hot temper has evolved into ambition, individualism."

But the partisans of the Ukraine piped up. "It is not true," insisted Efimov, "that the Ukraine produces nothing but anarchists and rebels. To be sure, thirty to forty changes in government would affect anyone, wouldn't it? . . . But the Ukraine gave us many revolutionaries, and anyone who does not know that should just shut up! Gorokhov has been a Party member since 1918, and has held positions of responsibility all along—his is certainly a proletarian psychology!"

As the circle labored to determine what to do with Gorokhov, Leznikov formulated the questions thus: "He may be an able student and a good revolutionary, but Gorokhov is volatile and intemperate. Where will be better at toughening him and ridding him of all oppositionist temptation, the university or practical activity?" To Brandt the answer was obvious: "A revolutionary background, important as it is, is insufficient in itself. . . . Gorokhov is precious to the Party, but if he is to increase his value further and perfect his psychology, the factory is the place for him, not the university."

Divided over Gorokhov's character, the circle could not agree about what to do with him. "How do we rein in Gorokhov?" Kazachenko wondered. "It is too late for him to work in production. . . . It would be a crime to put a broom into the hands of this sort of Party member!"[168] This was seconded by Efimov, who believed he was stating a "simple truth" when he said, "The factory is not a purgatory: not everyone has to go through it. We should always ask ourselves what the factory can give and to whom. What is the point of sending Gorokhov to production, if in two or three months he'll just be assigned administrative work there, too?"[169]

Among the various treatments of oppositionists available to the Party authorities, an enforced term at the factory bench was often presented as a remedy rather than a penalty—was not the proletarian locus a field of Communist activity rather than a place of exile?[170] A stint at the factory promised a return to a healthy, "primordial condition" (pervobytnoe sostoianie).[171] Manual labor did not spell loss of honor. The reverse was closer to the truth: to work meant to forge the soul. When it sent Savinov to the factory, the circle permitted him to return one day, "provided he toughens up."[172] This does not mean, however, that students eagerly pursued that route: none returned to production save those known to have degenerated. Zavilovich and Kolchinskii were both sent off to factories, the first "to end his seclusion," the second to refresh his "knowledge of workers."[173]

The True Heretics?

We have considered so far only those comrades whose committed quest for illumination suffered setbacks during the discussion, and have left until now any consideration of the others, the turncoats who remained Bolsheviks in name only. During the 1924 purge at the Communist University, accusations of the latter type fell only on lecturers. The better educated a comrade, the more intense the suspicion directed towards him. Unlike their rank-and-file students, lecturers would win no sympathy by claiming to have spoken unwittingly. After all, these men and women had won their positions thanks to their theoretical expertise, and their redoubtable understanding of Marxist science left them particularly vulnerable to charges of heresy. No one believed that the heretics were confused.

Those who had embraced the ideas of Bogdanov came under the heaviest fire. Many responded with surprise, since Bogdanov had enjoyed an excellent reputation as a socialist theoretician, and his followers had been seen as true Bolsheviks. Though he had been forced from the Bolshevik ranks before the Revolution, this unfortunate event had failed to taint his political biography. In a land desperate for indigenous Marxist thinking, leading publishing houses continued to publish Bogdanov's difficult books, while Party schools included these works in their curriculums.[174]

All of this changed in 1923. In those tense times, Party historians recalled the bitter rivalry that had raged between Lenin and Bogdanov. Suddenly Bogdanov's ideas stood exposed as subversive tracts, and his teachings were rechristened *Bogdanovshchina*—with the peculiar suffix *-shchina* indicating opprobrium. Formerly a part of the canon, Bogdanov's theories were now pronounced "a far cry from Marxism."[175]

On February 21, 1924, about one month before the student purges would begin, the university lecturers met to address mounting accusations of oppositionism lodged against some of their number. According to the university bureau, the lecturers' circle dedicated to teaching the "history of the West" made up part of a buffer group. And some reflection on earlier criticisms of the Central Committee made by university lecturers, circumscribed though they had been, suggested the possible presence of die-hard dissenters within the faculty. Well after the Party had identified Bogdanov's writings as heterodox, many of the university's instructors not only continued to study them intensely but seemed to be disseminating them at the command of the "Moscow syndicalist."[176]

These were the days following the New Course Discussion, and the possibility that the enemy had managed to introduce a Trojan horse into the Party's house could not be lightly dismissed. "The time is ripe for a thorough examination of what went on here," one of the instructors noted. "Bogdanov has been thrown out, but *Bogdanovshchina* has persisted." Those acquainted with Bogdanov's followers described them as tight-lipped, uninterested in mixing with orthodox faculty, and devoted to intense discussions among themselves.

Ivanov, the aforementioned secretary of the university Party organization, led the charge. He collected denunciations, asked the most embarrassing questions, intimidated the defendants, and usually recommended the sternest censure. "We have to see the matter through and battle *Bogdanovshchina* mercilessly," he noted. "It is quite possible that an undesirable element is dwelling among us, trying to sap our Party from within."[177]

Vozdvezhenskii, an instructor with three years of Party standing, appeared to be the leader of the local Bogdanovists.[178] Ivanov mentioned that this had been confirmed by information "sent to us from all kinds of places."

To save himself from the accusation of heresy, Vozdvezhenskii had to redefine his political self and justify his former interests, even as he renounced them. Compared to the onus borne by the student accused of waywardness, this teacher's task involved a great deal of explaining: charges had less to do with his more or less accidental personality traits, more with his moral core as such. In this context, character flaws were a plus, not a minus: if one was obliged to explain why one had succumbed to temptation, pointing to weakness of character could absolve one's innermost self of blame.

The review panel still expected to devote much attention to the biography of the accused, but not to, say, Vozdvezhenskii's social origins or his extensive service in the Red Army. Instead of the question "Have you already arrived at the light?" the verification commission would ask "Have you joined those in quest on the light in the first place?" If in the student examples we have considered, unfortunate experiences often served as excuses for missteps, here his whole life story was appropriated by Vozdvezhenskii's adversaries to show that he had never been a true Bolshevik, or that if he had converted, it had been to Bogdanov's philosophy, not Lenin's. "Bogdanov helps me find my way in the discussion," a teacher named Stalina recalled him saying; this was apparently an oblique reference to the Bogdanovist heretical view that disagreements among the Bolshevik heads reflected a struggle within the new ruling class.[179]

In an effort to unearth useful information, Ivanov urged comrades "to voice whatever is on your minds regarding Vozdvezhenskii's persona."

Kreger spoke up first: "We all suspected that he had succumbed to *Bogdanovshchina*, but no solid information was available. But recently we noticed that he never gives his own opinion and just sprays irony in the direction of the Central Committee as well as Trotsky." Medvedev made a telling point: "It's not just that

Vozdvezhenskii studies *Bogdanovshchina*—he completely absorbs it." Those who took a passing interest in Bogdanov's ideas could not be faulted, and even some sympathy with a tenet or two could be forgiven, but woe unto him who embraced Bogdanov's philosophy as a personal dogma. Lecturers recalled that Vozdvezhenskii liked to lock himself in a room to read his beloved Bogdanov undisturbed, that he traveled to the Petrograd's Astoria Hotel to discuss Bogdanov's ideas, and that he insisted that his banned mentor was "the most eminent expert on questions of religion and philosophy." Vozdvezhenskii's devotion to Bogdanov had led him to organize a faculty reading group that met five or six times in Youth Village, a summer retreat managed by the university, to discuss "tectology," a central concept at the heart of Bogdanov's thinking.

Over the course of the discussion, Vozdvezhenskii had been assigned the task of preparing a report on Party politics; what he delivered struck all who heard it as an unnecessarily bleak and blackly exaggerated picture of degeneration within the Party. Vozdvezhenskii explained: "I wanted to lay it on thick about discord in the Party to provoke a lively discussion. I told Kudinov I planned to make my report contentious."[180] Medvedev was not accepting this excuse: had Vozdvezhenskii just wanted to be provocative, he would not have gone around giving out heterodox tracts. Kanatchikov too found Vozdvezhenskii's explanation unsatisfactory: "Since the study of *Bogdanovshchina* was not part of the curriculum, why were you paying so much attention to Bogdanov, searching out his books and so on?"

Vozdvezhenskii tried to account for his fascination: "Bogdanov's organizational science, known as tectology, struck us as very interesting: we saw in it an attempt to transcend philosophy." Also original were "Bogdanov's theses about the world situation and about imperialism." Given the Marxian axiom that the world economy could not return to capitalism once 1917 had moved it beyond, there were only two alternatives: "regression to barbarity or further development." Distinguishing Bogdanov's analysis was his contention that class struggle in the present era was in many ways a struggle over cultural hegemony, and only the development of robust proletarian culture would secure the victory of the working class.[181] Indeed, Vozdveshenskii used to claim during the discussion that "ideology plays an important role" and that religion must be supplanted with a new, more rational set of beliefs.

As the group turned to investigating Vozdvezhenskii's application of this analysis to the current situation in Soviet Russia, he offered the opinion that the native proletariat was culturally too underdeveloped to rule on its own, and that a "technocratic intelligentsia" (*organizatorskaia intelligentsiia*) was running things for the time being. Vozdvezhenskii admitted that he "had always had difficulty fully understanding" Bogdanov's position on this new group. All he could say for certain was that it had something to do with a "counteraction of equal forces," the bourgeoisie and the working class somehow "nullifying" each other and thus giving birth to a new class.

The possibility of such an articulation between the social base and the political edifice was outlined in the foundational texts of Marxism. Vozdvezhenskii recalled an occasion during which Bronshtein, a Bogdanovist from Moscow, pointed to a place in Ludwig Feuerbach's writings where the philosopher said that sometimes leaders who come into power were "compelled to execute the will of another class." Given his conviction that the Revolution would only be completed once the consciousness of the workers had been considerably refined, we can understand why, during a brief visit to Vozdvezhenskii's room, lecturers found on his table many articles on proletarian education. "Yes," said Vozdvezhenskii, "we used to talk a great deal about the role new culture would play in accomplishing a true social revolution."

Again and again statements such as this showed how fully Vozdvezhenskii had adopted Bogdanov's model of revolution as a multilayered and continuous process, something utterly different from the all-enlightening cathartic experience Lenin had described quite early, before 1917. While Lenin believed that revolution reversed the course of history (hence his famed "love of dialectics") Bogdanov believed that historical growth, by and large, took place in small increments. With this difference in mind, Mikhailov was hardly surprised that Vozdvezhenskii shunned Lenin: "I do not recall his exact words, but the day Lenin died he said to me something like, 'We used to be Lenin's political rivals.'"

These increasingly perilous revelations eventually led Vozdvezhenskii to admit that "an old but vibrant revolutionary tradition asserted itself in me: the rejection of hero worship." Communist society, he believed following Bogdanov, had to be based on scientific principles. "So many people around me indulge in the fetishization of personalities," he complained, making an oblique reference to the nascent Lenin cult.

More questions led to a discussion of Vozdvezhenskii's familiarity with Marxism. He was asked, "How can you reconcile your Party membership with your lament about the prevalence of the technocratic intelligentsia and your rejection of the socialist nature of our revolution?" Rather lamely, he explained: "Back then I was not well versed in Marxist literature." Almost as an aside, he added, "When it came to politics I could never really clarify to myself what I was thinking."

It appears that Vozdvezhenskii intended to plot a path of personal development from utter ignorance to a future point of full ideological maturity—he just was not quite there yet. As to Bogdanov versus Lenin, he rejected the very premise: Bogdanov had simply been Vozdvezhenskii's first real theoretical interest, and in any case he had never become a true adept. "I used to look for Bogdanov's publications, which I found engaging. . . . But I never really read all he wrote. And since *Tectology* is quite an abstract book and since I don't know much about natural science or the social sciences, I couldn't really absorb all that much. Eventually I settled for a few articles from *Empiriomonism*, which is much simpler." The next stage of evolution, rejection, took place "when Bogdanov's definition of matter no longer seemed convincing," and it was at that point that Vozdvezhenskii began considering other theoretical approaches.[182] By claiming a course of intellectual development that ran from Bogdanov to Marxist theory more generally, rather than the unforgivable trajectory that began with the orthodox Marxist canon and ended in the exclusive veneration of Bogdanov, the embattled lecturer presented a self-portrait he hoped might save him.

But key details had been left out of the picture, and they could very well tip the balance. What made Vozdvezhenskii's narrative questionable was his involved connection with Workers' Truth, an organization that had recently received plenty of negative attention in the central press, its Bogdanovist worldview fully exposed. The official discourse ridiculed the notion that this group of Workers' Truth supporters might claim to be the true voice of the working class: "The vast majority of the adherents of Workers' Truth come from a petit bourgeois milieu" (and so did Vozdvezhenskii). "No wonder they deviated from Lenin's path."[183]

Though Party officials eagerly asserted that the influence of Workers' Truth on Party policy had been negligible, the movement had seized the attention of many students and teachers in the Communist universities of Moscow and Leningrad, and the connections between Bogdanov's ideas and Workers' Truth became apparent as students organized circles for the study of tectology.[184] The majority of the Workers' Truth activists arrested in 1923 had been drawn from the ranks of Moscow faculty members: active at the so-called Workers' Truth Center were a lecturer at the Socialist Academy and a prominent instructor at Sverdlov Communist University named Moglin.

Vozdvezhenskii and Moglin had often discussed political theory, and now Moglin had been seized for his part in instigating workers' protests. During the time he taught political theory in the Youth Village (1922–1923), Moglin had infected his listeners with enthusiasm for Bogdanov's social analysis. "The members of my study group never decisively rejected the theses of Workers' Truth, but we never completely accepted them either," Vozdvezhenskii explained. "Eventually we reached the conclusion that our revolution was socialist, not bourgeois after all," thus dropping Workers' Truth's most important tenet. But all Ivanov cared about was that "Vozdvezhenskii does not deny that he used to correspond with Moglin: this proves that they saw things the same way."[185]

Kanatchikov was amazed that Vozdvezhenskii "did not make more of an effort to rehabilitate himself after Moglin's arrest. Didn't you know that he is affiliated with an anti-Party grouping?"

Until his arrest Moglin had been a well-respected Party instructor. "Everybody knew that Moglin was a Bogdanovist," Vozdvezhenskii noted, "including the university academic board." Had not Kanatchikov himself referred to him as a "comrade"? As to the rumors that Moglin had translated Bogdanov's theory of the new intelligentsia into a counterrevolutionary platform, and that guided by such a platform he had attacked leadership—absurd, said Vozdvezhenskii. "I completely reject the suggestion that we ever intended to struggle against the university's administration."

The time had come to split hairs: speakers proposed a sharp demarcation between die-hard Bogdanovist activists and those who had read some of Bogdanov, were perhaps even taken by some of his arguments, but never violated Party discipline. No one denied Bogdanov had cast a spell over much of the university. "We were advised to read this eclectic thinker," Usik noted. Even Konstantinov, a redoubtable Bolshevik, was reported to have said not long before that "many of Bogdanov's propositions have yet to be refuted." Vozdvezhenskii (and this was his main sin) "was among those who had recruited supporters to his views."

But how far had he gone? Kisilev wanted to know whether the Bogdanovists had employed a secret password, and wondered whether the university had a Bogdanovist underground. "I never attempted . . . to organize any cells," said Vozdvezhenskii. He had steered well clear of the infamous supporters of Workers' Truth and their schemes. "Moglin did not have to go so far as to give out assignments. He was told that we had already begun reading Bogdanov on our own."

Kanatchikov decided to set a trap: "You knew that Moglin was affiliated with Workers' Truth: what are his principles?" Vozdvezhenskii elegantly sidestepped the steel jaws: "These are not 'principles' in the sense of 'principles of practical organization,' but 'organizational principles' presented in Bogdanov's tectology—a set of theoretical principles, nothing more." Vozdvezhenskii consistently presented himself throughout the questioning as a misguided but quite innocent intellectual, whose curiosity had gotten the better of him.

Nonetheless, his testimony prompted howls of rage and incredulity again and again. When Kisilev talked about some special materials Vozdvezhenskii had requested for the preparation of his discussion report, Kruger had confidently declared that these had been Workers' Truth theses, spicy ideological blasphemies with which he had hoped to regale his young pupils. Ivanov proposed that Vozdvezhenskii's house be searched, only to reject the plan immediately as "too awkward."[186]

Eventually Vozdvezhenskii was obliged to confess to having Workers' Truth theses in his possession. Bronshtein, his Moscow lover and Moglin's collaborator, "got them for me," he said, humiliated. Capitalizing on their victory, his ill-wishers presented him as somebody who was trying to win souls for the new anti-Bolshevik creed. Zuev stated: "Thanks to Vozdvezhenskii our political economy circle was divided." Others testified that this lecturer "used to walk around looking for a milieu receptive to his ideas," connecting cell to cell in a web of Bogdanovist complicity.

Vozdvezhenskii was doomed. According to Ivanov, "a truly contrite Party member would have written that he had given up *Bogdanovshchina*. Vozdvezhenskii has not done anything like that." Others agreed: "Vozdvezhenskii will never be able to unite with us organically." The final verdict was incontestable: "An objective examination has established that Vozdvezhenskii is a follower of Bogdanov in questions of theory as well as in questions of policy. Under the circumstances, allowing Vozdvezhenskii to prolong his affiliation with our Party would mean contributing to our degeneration from within." By a vote of eleven in favor, two opposed and two abstentions the case was sent to the purge commission "with a purge recommended."[187]

The interrogation of Vozdvezhenskii can be seen as an early anticipation of important elements in the persecution of opposition during the Great Purge; the treatment of an individual as a self-conscious, wicked counterrevolutionary. His case suggests that the change in approach that was to come in later years was not the inevitable consequence of bureaucratic infighting or economic deterioration, nor of a change in the higher echelons of power. A demonization of a seasoned Party member was possible in 1924; that it was not widely used until later in the decade has to be understood as a matter of discursive change and discursive power, not an inevitable social or economic process.

Vozdvezhenskii was not the only Bogdanovist among the teachers to draw fire, though he certainly was the most prominent. "It seems to me," mused Kudinov, "that Bogdanov had other supporters who tailed along in the rear: I'm thinking of Frumkina." The suggestion failed to rouse the circle to immediate action. "Let's not go that far," Stepanov urged. "Frumkina did not side with the opposition." Heterodoxy had failed to stir her soul for long. According to Kreger, "to call Frumkina an ideological Bogdanovist, to say that she grasped his theory, would really mean assigning her far greater honors than she deserves—she never made heads or tails of the matter. Yes, Frumkina was interested in Bogdanov; yes, she exhibits vacillations and deviations; but they do not amount to *Bogdanovshchina*." Martynenko concurred: "It's wrong to suggest an identification between Frumkina and Vozdvezhenskii. The first understands nothing about any of that, while the second is a spiritual follower of Bogdanov." [188]

"Still," Kalei intervened, "When we all lived in the dormitories on Znamenskii 41, Frumkina and Vozdvezhenskii were inseparable." Whatever Bogdanovist conspiracy was afoot at the Communist University, Frumkina must be an integral part thereof. Ivanov remained in character as prosecutor: "While it's somehow tolerable that Frumkina was in a Bogdanov reading group, it's quite another thing that she knew about Bronshtein's ties to our students and hushed it up. Smart people should know better. Frumkina is the head of a circle, so she should not play the fool here."

Kanatchikov argued decisively: "Let us assume that Frumkina did not understand what was going on around her. That would reflect poorly on her general aptitude. The alternative assumption, that she was in the thick of things but pretended otherwise, is equally worrisome. In either case, such an individual has no place in our ranks"—and she was purged.

No case did a better job of bringing the hermeneutics of the self into sharp relief than that of Ruzikas, who had acted, to the amazement of many, as Vozdvezhenskii's right hand throughout his love affair with Bogdanov's theories.[189] Furthermore, Ruzikas's conduct during the Discussion had left something to be desired. "He joined Trotsky's supporters," Konstantinov reminded those who might have forgotten.

Still, the members of his circle seemed inclined to describe the recent deviation of this worker turned lecturer as an expression of little more that difficulties adapting to the discouraging realities of NEP. After all, was this not a steadfast Bolshevik, who had distinguished himself during the Civil War by taking on very dangerous and thankless political missions? To one person, at least, the answer to this seemingly rhetorical question was not so obvious—Ruzikas: "I cannot accept the circle's laudatory words. Issue me a carefully researched personal evaluation, not a perfunctory letter of praise. I am not trying to ingratiate myself with anyone."

Making exceptionally full use of the right to participate in his own interrogation, Ruzikas directed the investigation into his character from beginning to end. Such a situation derived from the Communist notion of the self as something that could only be articulated at the nexus of the individual and the community. Since one's moral properties were a private affair, the circle had to rely on the stories told by Ruzikas about himself for the clues to his soul. Ruzikas had to interrupt whenever his examination took what seemed to him to be a wrong turn, so that he might insert a recollection that might get things back onto the right track.

At the same time, the Party expected its members to dissolve themselves into the brotherhood of the elect. However indispensable his effort at introspection, Ruzikas could not form a view of himself without the active participation of his peers: the circle would provide him with the model for his self-construction. The ideal of liberalism—an autonomous and self-sufficient self—was a sin in the Bolshevik universe. The highest praise that can be bestowed upon a Communist, Bolsheviks used to tell one another, is to say that he has no "private life," that his life has fused completely with History.

One is tempted to see in the remarkably dialectical soliloquies through which students delivered their testimony the proof that the barriers between the private and the collective had collapsed. "Do I have a proletarian psychology?" one student asked himself. "I think I proved beyond any doubt that the answer to this question is positive," he answered his own question, playing out the parts of interrogating circle and cooperative defendant.[190] So disinterested was the student supposed to be in discussing himself that if he "assumed the voice of a lawyer, constantly defending his interests," this was adjudged "intemperance."[191]

Carried out with the utmost seriousness, the debates on Ruzikas's self lasted for almost an entire day (February 20, 1924). As they considered the matter closely, the members of the circle found themselves at loggerheads. At one extreme stood Gordiakov and Patrushev: the first noted that "everybody remembers Ruzikas recently defending the opposition," while the second could not get over "what an avid supporter of Trotsky's letters Ruzikas had been." Others, such as Konstantinov, insisted that Ruzikas was a model Bolshevik. Serebrov occupied an intermediate position: "Ruzikas was an eclectic and certainly not a steadfast oppositionist."[192]

Somewhat halfheartedly Ruzikas played the part of the penitent. "During the discussion, I'd criticize either side whenever it made a demagogic move. Perhaps I sounded more like a 'Menshevik apparatchik' than a firm Bolshevik." But time had taught him the folly of such gestures, and "today I see there are die-hard oppositionists in our Party." Without restraint Ruzikas spoke of "oppositionist physiognomy"—he knew well that by excoriating and essentializing those who questioned Party practices, and by using the orthodox terminology, he stood a good chance of clearing his name. And then, immediately, he offered his own declaration of innocence: "I was never affiliated with the real opposition concealing itself within the Party's bosom . . . and I agree that this opposition has to be eradicated."

Unmoved by the self-portrait Ruzikas had presented, a number of speakers insisted he be held responsible for his recent mistakes. According to Serebrov, "During the Discussion, Ruzikas was a convinced oppositionist." The word "convinced" (*ubezhdennyi*) carried a special weight here, and suggested that Ruzikas's stance was consciously patterned on the "Declaration of the Four Economists." Serebrov recalled that, after the circle had already ferreted out the question of economic planning, Ruzikas had showed him an article by Preobrazhenskii. Not only had Ruzikas been quite familiar with the problematic texts that haunted his resolution, he had insisted on reproducing Preobrazhenskii's tainted ideas even when he was challenged.

Ruzikas's undeniable revolutionary exploits had to be juxtaposed with his recent lapses "with the utmost care," stated Grezhunov. Overall, he tended to explain Ruzikas's recent conduct in terms of infantile leftism. "Given to orienting himself towards the rank and file," Ruzikas had succumbed to Trotsky's criticisms of leaders. True, he sometimes went too far in attacking all authority, even the Party. "Painting with a wide brush, Ruzikas did not hesitate to call somebody like Zinoviev a demagogue when he felt that Zinoviev was in the wrong. . . . But if someone was oppressed before the Revolution it was likely that his character would lose all restraint and that he would grow contemptuous towards authority." If Ruzikas had often been inflexible and painfully blunt, these were typical proletarian traits, indicating sincerity and commitment.

Konstantinov claimed that the incident of the winter was a single atypical slip. "Ruzikas only set himself against the administration while at the university." This defender felt that Ruzikas's positive personal example easily compensated for his uncouth ways. During the struggle with Makhno's Anarchist bands in the Ukraine "he was quite cruel to those who ignored the Party's instructions." The elder teacher's uncompromising tenacity in the battle against banditry during the Civil War had been an unforgettable lesson for the young instructor. "I am very much indebted to Ruzikas for teaching me how to treat the Cossacks," who were exterminated en masse by the Red Army during the Civil War.

Things were hardly that simple, however. "What we say about him should combine an assessment of his discipline with an assessment of his worldview," students noted. And as Gordiakov pointed out, Ruzikas had not always been "a model Party veteran. . . . We no longer live in the past. State power is now in the hands of the workers and criticism must always be constructive—if a real worker like Ruzikas does not know this, who does?"

And what of the relationship between Ruzikas and Moglin, and what had Ruzikas done to further the cause of Workers' Truth? "Last Christmas I paid a visit to Moglin," so went the crucial part of his somewhat prolonged account. "After Moglin read me his article *On Trade*, the two of us went to meet Bogdanov in person. Moglin wanted to discuss his article and I was curious to see for myself what Bogdanov was like. When we met, Bogdanov scolded Moglin for 'mysticism.'"

Papering over the details of his acquaintance with Bogdanov and switching back to Moglin, Ruzikas played down the episode. "Knowing Moglin only superficially . . . I never participated in the circles he led . . . and sat down with him to discuss Bogdanov's philosophy on only two occasions. I did all I could to show him Bogdanov's errors. Moglin could only respond by reiterating points from *Tectology*. He was quite incapable of countering my criticisms." In short, the Bogdanov enthusiasts were never a coherent and united group. Far from being the charismatic leader of a sect, Moglin was a parrot unable to rebuff his guru's most elementary arguments. Nor was Bogdanov himself infallible—Ruzikas had always known that.

But an anecdote told by Gordiakov proved that Ruzikas was anything but innocent. The events had taken place just before Christmas, the time not only of the discussion but also of the debates concerning the origins of religion. While walking along a dormitory corridor Gordiakov had overheard a heated argument taking place in Ruzikas's room. Out of curiosity he had knocked at the door. Without mincing words, the attendants had drawn him into the thick of things: "Tell us, Gordiakov, would you call Bogdanov's view on the origins of religion scientific? In your opinion, wouldn't it be a good idea to use it in our antireligious propaganda?" Other voices also presented Ruzikas as a jealous Bogdanovist. During the readings of one of the articles directed against heterodoxy, Grezhunov recalled, "Ruzikas protested the unfair attacks on Bogdanov and called him a 'martyr' [*muchenik*]."[193]

Ruzikas insisted again that his Bogdanovist sympathies belonged to the past. "At first I was taken in by Bogdanov but later I reached the conclusion that Bogdanov's teaching had nothing to do with materialism." Then, in a move no less surprising than it was contradictory, he essayed a radically different defense: "Even now I have no grasp of the schemes and principles Bogdanov propounded." Rather than a Bogdanovist who changed his heart, he had never been a Bogdanovist at all.[194]

A number of instructors were generous: "We should say that Ruzikas is 'disciplined and self-controlled.'" But Serebrov was more captious: "Individuals with his sort of experience usually rise to a higher level of temperance." Carefully weighing these suggestions, Konstantinov searched for a middle course. "We have to take into account our comrade's evolution," he argued. If Ruzikas had shown a certain ideological instability, he had eventually overcome his weakness. As to Ruzikas's ideological affiliation with Workers' Truth, Gordiakov admitted that it was finally impossible to know the truth: "I can't get into his head, can I?"[195]

At this point Ruzikas made another effort to assist with the hermeneutical process. "After a prolonged study of Bogdanov I determined that *Bogdanovshchina* is a brand of liberal-bourgeois empiricism. . . . Yes, I have shortcomings. But, tell me, have they turned me into somebody who could join Workers' Truth?"[196] Gordiakov did as he was asked. "When I think to myself that Ruzikas is an old Party member, I simply can't imagine him joining Workers' Truth. Could one really accommodate such contradictions within one's personality?"[197]

Things had begun to look better for Ruzikas, though the members of the circle agreed that no conclusive judgment could be made until a fuller picture of his activities had been drawn up. The text of the personal evaluation follows: "Ruzikas's stance during the Party discussion suggest that he is not always a self-controlled Marxist theoretician. However, this shortcoming failed to express itself in practice, suggesting he is a disciplined Party member."[198]

■

How did the 1924 screening cope with heterodoxy? Was ideological free thinking punished? On May 26, 1924, in a special session of the Thirteenth Party Congress, a heated debate broke out on the subject. Leading the counterattack, the much-maligned Preobrazhenskii protested:

Once the Central Control Commission had passed a resolution forbidding the purging of comrades solely because of heterodox beliefs, purge commissions were obliged to employ formulaic explanations unrelated to their true motivations. Comrades, it would have been much better to state openly that the purpose of the purge was to expel oppositionists. Then anyone purged would have left the Party as an "oppositionist," not as a morally or politically stained individual, a careerist, a self-seeker (*shkurnik*), or an inciter (*sklochnik*), and might preserve some hope of being readmitted later, with honor.[199]

This charge was rebutted by Iaroslavskii, a stalwart champion of the Party line, who accused Preobrazhenskii of slandering an honorable Party procedure. "When he claims that we purge oppositionists, the speaker is feeding on rumors, not on facts. Preobrazhenskii is trying to discredit a purge of alien and detrimental elements, people who clung to us only because they hoped for personal gain—this was a purge aimed at resuscitating our Party." According to Iaroslavskii, "individuals devoid of principles were expelled even when they had voted along with the Central Committee majority."[200]

While Iaroslavskii admitted that many heterodox cells had been rigorously purged, he maintained that the purge commissions had been searching for petit bourgeois, not oppositionists. In his view, alien elements had to be removed regardless of their vote during the New Course Discussion, as a sort of social prophylactic. Though he was speaking from the other side of the barricades, Preobrazhenskii was not inclined to take issue with the linkage between political opinion and its class underpinnings. But beginning with the precept that the opposition, not the Central Committee, was the conscience of the proletariat, he quite logically concluded that the 1924 verification was a setback in the struggle against the nascent bureaucracy. "I have no quarrel with those who would purge abusers," he insisted. "But I take exception to the use of a purge to combat the opposition; I object to the launching of a purge by interested parties."

Oppositionists and majoritarians differed not in terms of the basic premises of Bolshevik discourse, which they shared, but in terms of dividing the good guys from the bad in Soviet society. When the Central Committee majority blamed Trotsky for his "reliance on the petite bourgeoisie," Trotsky turned the tables. "It is worrisome," he said, "that the same comrades who persistently argue that every disagreement, every divergence of opinions, no matter how fleeting, represents a difference in class interests, do not wish to apply the same criterion in evaluating bureaucratism.... If apparatchiks threaten to separate the Party from the masses, it follows that our struggle against the apparatchiks cannot be 'non-proletarian.'"[201]

No one was questioning the link between class and ideology; the debate turned on whose ideology truly reflected the interests of the working class. Trotsky did not oppose the use of purges; what upset him was unfairness, and this recent verification struck him as deeply unfair, since what threatened his supporters threatened the proletariat.[202]

The logic underpinning the intra-Party debate remained consistent throughout the 1920s: each side accused the other of retreating from a purely proletarian line and slipping towards the petite bourgeoisie. The Party majority and the opposition both hoped to purge their rivals. As if to prove that their Stalinist opponents had no monopoly on housecleaning procedures, the Trotskyist students who briefly seized control of the Khamovnik district in Moscow in 1923 replaced the local secretary with their own nominee.[203] As they handed over the helm of the local Party organization to oppositionist leaders and put their own men in charge of local agitprop, they supported their actions with the claim that they were snatching the local apparatus away from the petit bourgeois supporters of the Central Committee majority. "The opposition needs an apparatus too—there is no other way to influence the Party—but it needs the apparatus to implement factionist policies," loyalists noted. "Only that they want everything arranged under a democratic guise, disguised as wholesale reelections, removal of the apparatchiks."[204]

The celebration of the purge, the belief that it was the only procedure able to secure Bolshevik purity, is attested by the scattered utterances of anonymously polled students. A Leningrad State University oppositionist explicitly linked the de-proletarianization of the university to its degeneration. The student wrote: "Every year the percentage of proletarian students falls and riffraff makes up the difference, . . . promoted at the expense of the real proletarians, who used to come here from the factories and the fields. The result is plenty of anti-soviet students . . . who are inclined towards entrepreneurship and careerism. This is a disgrace!!!" Another oppositionist took full advantage of the anonymity guaranteed by the form, declaring that only purging petit bourgeois students from the cells would rejuvenate them: "Because it is dragged down by spineless petit bourgeois intelligentsia elements, our Party organization cannot fulfill its function as the 'school of Communism.' . . . Down with opportunism! Down with leaders who have completely lost touch with reality! Long live the truly Bolshevik Leningrad State University!"[205]

Trotskyist Opposition

The cartoons from 1923–1925 include a lot of mockery and puns, but none of the discussions' participants took home any deep wounds to his pride. The contending factions ridiculed and sneered at each other; clearly they could not take each other too seriously. Even when the accusations grew more severe, the tone remained playful. What amused the loyalists made the oppositionists frown, and the reverse, but laughter seems to have brought the sides together.

14. "A Pre-Congress Discussion Sheet." Osinskii, Preobrazhenskii, Larin, Kamenev, Stukov, and Krasin compose all kinds of projects and policy proposals. Everyone is opinionated, everyone pontificates, but Central Committee supporters and oppositionists are on a par, equally ponderous, equally opinionated. *Krasnyi perets*, 1924, no. 5.

15. (*left, above*) The title, "Preobrazhenskii Regiment," is ironic in that it invokes both an elite tsarist regiment and the name of one of the leaders of the opposition, Comrade Preobrazhenskii. Does the opposition have regiments of its own? Top: "Osinskii, Ivan Smirnov, Riazanov, Mdivani, Sapronov, Preobrazhenskii." Bottom: "Comrade Preobrazhenskii commands: 'Run in place! Forward!'" The drawing makes fun of the oppositionists preference for formulating endless resolutions. *Krokodil*, 1924, no. 1, p. 5.

16. (*right, above*) "In the Party School." "Comrade Trotsky decided to give 'Lessons of October.' He will have to take lessons in Leninism first." *Krokodil*, 1925, no. 1, p. 8 (L.M.).

17. (*opposite, top*) The "Scissors Crisis." Top blade: "Prices on city fabric." Bottom blade: "Prices on agricultural fabric." The opposition warned that because the price of industrial goods had risen much faster than the price of agricultural products, peasants had no incentive to sell their goods to the proletarian. Sokol'nikov, the Commissar of Finance, is helped by the other heads of Soviet economics, Rykov, Krasin, and Kamenev; they all use the gold-based ruble (*chervonets*) to close the scissors. *Krokodil*, 1924, no. 1, p. 5.

18. (*opposite, bottom*) "Discussion Meetings Turn into a Nightmare." Zinoviev: "In leading the country, the Communist Party cannot turn itself into a Noah's ark with seven pure-impure pairs." The ark drifts in the water aimlessly, as should be expected from a vessel displaying a banner reading "Live and Let Live" over a pierced heart. The cartoon pokes fun at the opposition's alleged penchant for pluralism, warning that this might jeopardize revolutionary purity. The pairs in the drawing are: Budennyi and Wrangel (Red Army general and White general); Kamenev and Miliukov (a Bolshevik leader and a counter-revolutionary leader of the Kadet party); Sosnovskii and Esenin (a Bolshevik famous for his astute political writings, versus the Soviet decadent poet); Iaroslavskii and Father Tikhon (the head of the anti-clerical campaign and the head of the Russian Orthodox Church); worker and NEPman; Chicherin and Curzon (Soviet foreign minister and British foreign minister who threatened the Soviet Union in his notorious note); Zinoviev and Dan (Bolshevik leader and Menshevik leader). *Krokodil*, 1924, no. 1, pp. 8–9.

The Émigré Perspective

Figures 19-24 are taken from the émigré newspapers *Rul'* and *Poslednie novosti*, 1924–1925.

19. (*left*) A reworking of Pushkin's famous duel. Bukharin and Preobrazhenskii are dueling; Zinoviev and Piatakov are their seconds. Pushkin's text: "The foes! How long had they been parted . . . ?" (*Evgenii Onegin*, chapter 6, 28.) Note that violence at this stage is symbolic only: the Bolshevik leaders are dueling with paper resolutions; the guns in their hands are only metaphoric.

20. (*below, left*) Trostky as Onegin, "I see how justly now I am afflicted." (*Evgenii Onegin*, chapter 8, 32.) The booklet *Lessons of October* is discarded at his feet.

21. (*below, right*) "A Medical Concilium." From the newspapers: "Possibly, Trotsky will be ill again." Zinoviev (with Kamenev standing beside him): "We don't like the look of your tongue!" The best speaker among the Bolsheviks, Trotsky had to be silenced.

Троцкій: — Я такъ ошибся, я такъ наказанъ!

— Намъ не нравится вашъ языкъ!

— Дальше ѣдешь, — тише будешь!

Тов. Троцкій поселится на островѣ св. Елены.

22. (*above, left*) "The farther you go, the quieter you get!" (a Russian proverb). The members of the triumvirate part with Trotsky, who is leaving for unofficial exile. The opposition groups claimed that their adherents were systematically removed from leadership positions because of their views. Such demotions were generally called "transfers" (*perevody, otkomandirovki*).

23. (*above, right*) "Trotsky will be sent to the Island of St. Helena" (reference to Trotsky's Bonapartist ambitions—a widespread explanation of his demise).

Зиновьевъ: — Паду ли я, стрѣлой пронзенный?

24. "The arrow leaping, may pass me by or pierce me through." (*Evgenii Onegin*, chapter 6, 21.) Zinoviev as Lenskii, contemplating his future moments before he is killed by Onegin in a duel.

25. "The Horse Got Dizzy in the Steep Mountains." "The Leningrad Party activist comrade Sarkis found eight 'deviations' in the Party. Comrade Sarkis gets too much mileage from the term 'deviation.'" Below: "The boy went too far ..." *Rabochaia gazeta*, no. 282, December 10, 1925 (drawing by Ganfa).

26. "Face to the Countryside à la Safarov." "Some Leningrad comrades claim that the weight of the kulak in the village is covered up. Inflating the importance of the kulak they rub the village's central figure clean—the middling peasant." Bottom: "How is it done? One needs a magnifying glass and a strong will." *Rabochaia gazeta*, no. 283, December 11, 1925.

27. "Champion Marksmen." "Not a single hit." Zalutskii, Safarov, and Sarkis shoot at *Pravda*, the Central Committee's newspaper, but all their arrows miss the target. Note the absence of the opposition's main ideologue, Zinoviev, still a Politburo member, from the drawing. Only his underlings are ridiculed. *Rabochaia gazeta*, no. 289, December 18, 1925 (drawing by K. Rotov).

28. "Where Is Right, Where Is Left?!" "Comrade Sarkis found nine deviations in Party policy" (from the speech of Comrade Rykov). Bottom: Sarkis (with wisdom and restraint): "I am the only one without a deviation." *Rabochaia gazeta*, no. 292, December 22, 1925.

"Party Building"

These two cartoons from 1925 and 1927 do not so much capture the dissolution of unity in the Central Committee as make this fact public. Despite the denigration of Trotsky and the already evident rift between Stalin and Zinoviev, in 1925 the entire leadership is still depicted as participating in Party affairs; two years later the opposition is clearly excluded—its purge from the Central Committee and later from the Party itself is imminent.

Рис. К. Елисеева

ОДНИМ—РАБОТА, ДРУГИМ—ДИСКУССИЯ.

29. (*opposite*) *Krokodil's* illustration of the Central Committee's political and organizational report. Trotsky (fixing a lamp) is on a par with Stalin (working with a spade) and Bukharin (carrying bricks at the bottom). Zinoviev and Kamenev are not ostracized either, putting the upper floor together along with Rykov and Molotov. *Krokodil*, 1925, no. 47, p. 11, p. 8 (drawing by Rotov).

30. (*above*) "To Each His Own." "To some—work, to others—discussion." The United Opposition is presented clearly as a disruptive force. Its policy suggestions, officially described as counterrevolutionary, were no longer openly printed. *Krokodil*, 1927, no. 38, p. 4 (drawing by K. Eliseev).

CHAPTER 4

THE EMERGENCE OF "TROTSKYISM"

AND "ZINOVIEVISM"

Lessons of October

To judge by the language Soviet leaders used in talking about the opposition, the years 1924–1925 were transitional. Hermeneutical judgments were still fairly lenient during the Second Discussion with Trotsky and the Discussion with Kamenev and Zinoviev. While "opposition" became increasingly imbued with a specific history and essential character, no one had yet suggested a necessary link between the opposition and counterrevolution. Among all these shifting political labels, no matter how loosely an oppositionist identity was constructed, there was always an impetus to medicalize and psychologize errant behavior, to heal, not to purge.

Oppositionism is in focus in the pages below not so much as an ideological position, although a few words will have to be said about that as well, but as a mental predicament diagnosed by the Party's hermeneuts. What is at issue is the unfolding relation between the political battles in the Party and the soul-judging framework that resulted in the gradual loss of legitimacy of the various opposition stances and their adherents. Still a respected member of the Politburo, Trotsky disassociated himself from Shliapnikov and Sapronov as hard-core oppositionists, only to find the same pejorative applied firmly to himself once he challenged the Central Committee majority for the second, if not the third time. Kamenev and Zinoviev, two pillars of the triumvirate that did so much to identify Trotsky as oppositionist, will also turn into oppositionists before this chapter ends.

"Oppositionist fever" (*oppozitsionnaia likhoradka*) reappeared briefly in the fall of 1924. At the center of the new discussion was an essay by Trotsky published on the seventh anniversary of the October Revolution and entitled *Lessons of October*.[1] There Trotsky portrayed himself as Lenin's chief collaborator and suggested that some of his political rivals had behaved ignobly in 1917. Conflict among the Bolsheviks, according to Trotsky, had peaked before October 25, the day power was seized. Anxious that the suitable moment for a revolutionary uprising might

slip away, Lenin had pressed the Central Committee to prepare an armed insurrection as soon as possible. While Trotsky wholeheartedly agreed with the Bolshevik leader, Zinoviev and Kamenev had refused to fall into line. In "On the Present
Situation," a letter dispatched to local Bolshevik organizations on October 11, they
objected to any use of force, preferring to bank on the "excellent prospects of our
party in the Constituent Assembly elections."[2] All this, Trotsky claimed, was relevant today: the same hesitation, the same cowardice, had already fatally undermined the leadership of Zinoviev's Komintern during the German Revolution in
1923 and threatened to stifle the initiative of the native proletariat as well. Was not
the triumvirate, with its repeated calls for moderation and a slow pace of construction, essentially reverting to the position taken by Kamenev and Zinoviev in 1917?
Would not this Menshevik-inspired willingness to compromise with NEP cripple
the Revolution?[3]

Discussion of the *Lessons of October* brought Party history and Party biography to the forefront of the Bolshevik public sphere. Those who proved adept at
incorporating the story of their conversion to Bolshevism into the universal epic
of proletarian emancipation crowned themselves with considerable revolutionary
mystique. As it grew clear that policy proposals had to be evaluated in terms of
their authors' biographies, everyone acknowledged the strong connections between
politics and the hermeneutics of the self. Always the speakers emphasized their
dedication to the cause, their skill in getting their bearings with the aid of a Marxist compass. It was as important to know what the Bolshevik leaders had done in
1917—and in 1903 and 1905—as it was to study their present-day political and economic suggestions.

Participants in the discussion agreed that Lenin had established the standard
of historical perspicacity. Measuring themselves against his towering figure, each of
the contestants in the succession struggle had to concede that at some point in the
past they had disagreed with him. But not all mistakes were the same. Some were
brief, others protracted; some singular, others repetitive; some deliberate, others almost inadvertent.

Coming at a very sensitive time, Kamenev's and Zinoviev's attempts to denigrate Lenin in 1917 were quite embarrassing. Zinoviev admitted that he erred in
November 1917. "If my mistake was not immediately confessed, if Lenin was not
around, even such a short-lived but acute disagreement in the Bolshevik leadership could yield serious repercussions."[4] But his supporters cited Lenin's declaration that "there is no need to recall mistakes that have been fully corrected."[5] Stalin
was charged with blunders as well. "True," he admitted in an apology of his own,
"I was slow to advance the new slogan, 'All power to the Soviets!' I did not completely shake off this mistaken attitude until the middle of April 1917, after I had
subscribed to Lenin's theses."[6]

If the guilt of Kamenev, Zinoviev, and Stalin was brief and accidental, the guilt of Trotsky—a newcomer to the Party who had often feuded with Lenin—was something quite different, or so argued the official historiography of the 1920s. When he attacked their own record, the triumvirs made a sustained effort to expose Trotsky's theoretical and political clashes with Lenin, and his alleged refusal to make amends for striking a quite independent pose before the Revolution.[7] By concentrating on the days and months preceding the Bolshevik seizure of power, Trotsky had conveniently forgotten that Lenin had rehearsed for his brilliant stand in October during earlier battles for the cause of Russian social democracy. Had the Bolsheviks adopted the conciliatory views Trotsky had trumpeted during the preparatory period, there would have been no victory in October.[8]

It was in this context that "Trotskyism" as the obverse of "Leninism" began to take root.[9] The Komsomol organized discussion groups on the subjects of "Trotskyism before October," "Trotskyism after October," and "Trotskyism and Leninism."[10] The term "Trotskyism" itself was first used by Lenin in a letter he wrote to Gol'denberg on October 28 (Old Style), 1909.[11] Once Trotsky joined the Party the term was retired; it was revived by the triumvirs in 1925, with its meanings ranging from a "variety of Bolshevism" to a "variety of Menshevism."[12]

Plenty of evidence was dug up to document Trotsky's rivalry with Lenin.[13] The suggestion he made in 1904 that "Lenin is the leader of the reactionary wing of our Party" was mentioned.[14] And Stalin was quick to quote from the letter that Trotsky addressed in 1913 to Nikolai Cheidze, a Georgian Menshevik: "The whole edifice of Leninism," Trotsky had written, "is built on lying and falsification." If that was not enough, Trotsky described Lenin as an "exploiter of every imaginable backwardness in the Russian working-class movement."[15] When the letter had been found in the archives of the tsarist police in 1921, Ol'minskii, president of the Bureau of Party History, asked Trotsky whether it could appear in print. Trotsky replied that the publication would only rekindle long-forgotten quarrels, adding, "I by no means consider that I was entirely wrong in the dispute I had with the Bolsheviks back then."[16]

Such comments cost Trotsky dearly in 1924–1925. The triumvirs presented *Lessons of October* as a political document, a Trotskyist attack against Leninist theory.[17] Zinoviev and Kamenev expressed shock that Trotsky "set himself the task of healing Leninism and Leninists with Trotskyism."[18] Bukharin described "Trotskyism" as "dynamite under the foundations of our Party."[19] The Central Committee did not long debate the question: "Our next banner will read 'Down with Trotskyism! Long live orthodox, Leninist Bolshevism!'"[20] One year earlier no one seemed certain as to whether Trotsky or the collective leadership ought to replace the convalescing leader; now Trotsky was struggling for the right to be numbered among the elect.[21]

How could Trotskyism be defined in theoretical terms? According to the triumvirs, Trotskyism meant three things, all diametrically opposed to Lenin's teaching:

advocacy of the so-called permanent revolution, neglect of the peasant movement, and disregard of the monolithic nature of the Party organization.[22] The core tenet of the theory of permanent revolution advanced by Trotsky in 1905–1906 was that Russian social democracy would not be able to stop at its intermediate, bourgeois face; the revolution would charge ahead to its proletarian stage. Whereas Trotsky maintained that "a direct line links the theory of permanent revolution with Lenin's theses of April 1917"—both called for an all-out attack on the bourgeois government—the triumvirs responded that Lenin found Trotsky's theory to be "semi-anarchist."[23] Trotsky's predilection for permanent revolution was linked to his other theoretical blunder—"underestimating the peasantry."[24] While Trotsky had set out to show that the proletariat would be unable to consolidate a bourgeois republic in Russia due to the inherent conservatism of the native peasantry, the triumvirs claimed that his pessimism contradicted Lenin's teaching about the importance of revolutionary democratic dictatorship of the proletariat and the peasants.[25]

Whatever the merits of the theory of permanent revolution, these debates belonged largely to the past. If it was true that in 1917 Trotsky abandoned his former views to embrace those of Lenin wholeheartedly, his former views no longer mattered much. Thus it was incumbent upon his detractors to show either that Trotsky's conversion to Bolshevism was incomplete, or that he had converted not to Bolshevism but to something else. This is a case of the politics of naming: Trotsky was charged with appropriating "Bolshevism" to himself; as he used it, the term meant nothing other than "Trotskyism."[26]

While Trotsky contended that he had joined Lenin in 1917 without ever looking back, the triumvirs tried to show that his conversion was not a true change of heart, but a surreptitious, hence all the more dangerous, attempt to convert the Party to his own teachings. Nominally, Trotsky was a Bolshevik, but in reality "he remained a Trotskyist."[27] In switching to Bolshevism, the triumvirs said, "Trotsky did not find it expedient to renounce his own views on the fundamental questions of the Russian Revolution in favor of our common ideology."[28] The Central Committee candidate, Vareikis, was ringing the alarm bells: "In reality, Trotsky's approach to Leninism is revisionist. . . . Some say . . . 'Trotsky himself could not "muster up the courage" to oppose Leninism!' But is that so? It seems to me that a certain political naiveté conceals itself behind such a spineless position—utter ignorance of the differences between Trotskyism and Leninism."[29]

Trotsky vehemently denied that his conversion had been less than complete.[30] In a letter to the Central Committee dated January 15, 1925, he wrote, "I have rejected the charge that I have a line of my own, this so-called Trotskyism, or that I am somehow attempting to 'develop Leninism.' . . . It never occurred to me during the last eight years to examine any issue from the perspective of so-called Trotskyism—I consider that to have been politically liquidated long ago."[31]

In an essay entitled "On Our Disagreements," Trotsky scrutinized and refuted each of the interpretations his past quarrels with Lenin had inspired, "interpretations based on misunderstandings and biases." Since his political past was coming under such close scrutiny, Trotsky offered some proleptic "clarifications." He admitted that in the years succeeding the failed 1905 revolution his view of political necessity had differed from Lenin's:

I claimed then that it was imperative that Bolsheviks and Mensheviks unite in one party. Lenin, on the other hand, believed it was important to deepen the schism in order to cleanse the Party of the main source of bourgeois influences on the proletariat. . . . Having failed to understand how crucial the difference between Bolshevism and Menshevism was, . . . I believed that the development of the Revolution would eventually push both factions to take the same route—a very mistaken perspective that made me think that a schism was a needless waste of revolutionary energy.

Trotsky did not deny that his error was rightfully dubbed "Trotskyism" but took issue with those who turned Lenin's old polemical thrusts at him into a "timeless personal evaluation."

Confronted by his record of attacks on Leninism proper, Trotsky encountered real trouble. "The term 'Leninism' itself," he explained, "was not used by the Bolshevik faction. Lenin would not have allowed it. . . . Before the Revolution, only detractors spoke of 'Leninism,' referring to everything they saw as negative and detrimental in Bolshevism. While at the time I stood for conciliation, Leninism stood for divisiveness and factionalism." But Trotsky had renounced his old positions and no longer recognized his former vocabulary as his own. "My old texts sound just as wild to me as they do to any other Party member."[32]

To prove he had changed, Trotsky detailed the circumstances of his conversion. In his narrative, it occurred sometime between 1914 and 1916. "My outlook shifted with the outbreak of the imperialist war. Since 1907, I had expected that a European war would create a revolutionary situation, but in reality, war meant the wholesale betrayal of social democracy. I had begun a painstaking reassessment of my thinking on the relations between the class and its party and finally reached the conclusion that an organizational rupture with Menshevism was necessary." As he looked out upon a changed political landscape it dawned on Trotsky that the Bolsheviks had been correct all along. "From the moment it became evident that we needed an all-out struggle against defensism [the belief that the working class should support the tsarist war effort during World War I], Lenin's position began beckoning to me. What had looked like 'divisiveness' . . . was now revealed to be an exceptionally farsighted struggle for the organizational independence of the revolutionary party." Until then a rival, Lenin became Trotsky's hero. "Not only his political and organization methods, but his entire personality—in the political and the human sense of the word—appeared to me in a new light, the light of Bolshevism, that is, the true,

Leninist light." The term "Leninism" underwent, as it were, a conversion of its own; Trotsky scraped off its former taint and unfurled its positive attributes.[33]

Most members of the Central Committee treated Trotsky's narrative with suspicion. Competing reconstructions of his biography were drawn up, incorporating elements of Trotsky's own reconstruction of his past while emphasizing details he would not have emphasized. Vareikis, the head of the press section of the Party secretariat, for example, regarded the "history of Trotskyism as a peculiar drama of an insulated revolutionary in the Russian revolutionary movement."[34] Molotov, the secretary of the Central Committee, concurred, "Trotsky could not become a true revolutionary of the proletarian sort."[35] Instead he was a "classic example of the radical from the intelligentsia, making sharp leaps, vacillating, turning now to the left, now to the right."[36] Trotsky was hanged with his own rope: he had accused the triumvirate of reluctance to storm the provisional government in 1917 and by implication, of petit bourgeois vacillation, and now, a few months later, he was condemned for his equally petit bourgeois, Menshevik outlook.[37]

In order to evaluate Trotsky's crimes, the Party had to return to the Second Party Congress (1903), the moment of the parting of the ways for Bolshevism and Menshevism and thus the decisive ordeal for any veteran Russian Marxist.[38] As the majoritarian propagandist Babakahn reminded his comrades, "Lenin predicted that the position each revolutionary took there would determine his political line for the years to come." The decision Trotsky made was hardly accidental. "When the time came to reveal his true political physiognomy . . . and clarify in his own mind where to place his loyalty, Trotsky abandoned Lenin and went with our enemies."[39] In the same vein, Kamenev wrote that "from the birth of Menshevism in 1903, Trotsky played the part of an agent of Menshevism within the working class."[40]

The trouble with erstwhile Menshevik sympathizers was that their life stories never fit the model for a proper conversion narrative. Properly, those who came to the Revolution via non-Bolshevik organizations were not political novices but "ripe" (zrelye) individuals; their political minds had already matured. So Trotsky had entered into all of his political misalliances with his eyes wide open. Having opted for a position opposed to Lenin's, he could not make conventional claims and describe his path to Bolshevism as normal and unidirectional.

"Of course, one can reproach me for not having correctly understood Menshevism earlier," Trotsky conceded. "This means reproaching me for not becoming a Bolshevik in 1903. Yet no one chooses the way he grows." There was no room for a plea of innocence in this framework, and Trotsky agreed to "take political responsibility for my tangled development." But had he not acted in good faith? "Although my road to Bolshevism was long and complex, I was moved by no interests but those of the proletariat and the Revolution."[41]

The triumvirs and their supporters expressed skepticism. "No doubt good Bolsheviks can be found among those who used to struggle against Bolshevism," Va-reikis stated. "We do not care how anyone found his way to Lenin, as long as one did." But while the convert could not look back, "when Lenin forced him to his knees Trotsky did not hand over his weapons. . . . Thus we accuse him not of com-ing to Bolshevism in battle but of remaining in the Party even as he battled it."[42] According to Stalin's sardonic interpretation, Trotsky divided the history of Lenin-ism into two periods: "an objectionable period before the October Revolution, fol-lowed, thanks to Lenin's embrace of Trotsky's theory of permanent revolution, by a praiseworthy post-October period."[43]

The Hungarian Communist leader Bela Kun informed the triumvirate that Trotsky had insisted in Khar'kov that Bolshevism had embraced him, and not vice versa. "Asked in 1920 how he had come to join the Bolsheviks, Trotsky had an-swered: 'It is an open question who joined whom!'"[44] Kamenev explained in this context: "Trotsky came to us as an individualist accustomed to thinking that he and not the Party was correct. 'I came to Lenin because Lenin brought the Party to me': such was the foundation of Trotsky's attitude."[45] This testimony suggested that Trotsky never converted to anything. He always remained true to himself, a crypto-Menshevik. As the Party historian Gonikman put it, "Trotsky snuck onto Lenin's train and under his coat he concealed his Menshevik baggage."[46]

Trotsky Judged by His Peers

As an articulated ideological position, Trotskyism could not be a naive deviation, the triumvirs maintained. An ism, Trotskyism was an ideology, not just a social reflex. But was it a full-blown heresy or only a deviation induced by NEP, a de-liberate attempt to undermine the Party or an innocent mistake? It is possible to distinguish two lines of attack used against Trotsky in 1925 and therefore two somewhat distinct interpretations of Trotskyism, one psychological, the other ideological. The first reading, highlighting Trotsky the individual, presented him as an unsettled type who should have found his natural place in the camp of the Menshevik vacillators.[47] Here Trotsky was cast as an ambitious individual eager to take over Lenin's post. Zalutskii thought that Trotsky had joined Lenin on a whim. "If the political atmosphere in 1917 had been different, Trotsky could as easily have evolved into some sort of a Menshevik."[48] Kanatchikov, then at the peak of his popularity as a Party publicist, mentioned "Trotsky's political impressionability" and his "individual, fleeting moods."[49] Babakhan explained that Trotsky was a manic-depressive: "When in good spirits, he sides with the Bolsheviks. When in decline, he . . . makes himself the focal point of all the despondent 'proletarian groups.'"[50]

In this reading, "Trotskyism" was not a full-fledged theoretical stance, an anti-Leninism, but a decadent form of Leninism, Leninism as espoused by weak, irresolute Bolsheviks. "Trotsky is not a conscious leader," Babakhan claimed, "but a leader who reflects and extols the elemental psychology of the masses around him."[51] Goloshchekin, another Central Committee candidate, described Trotsky as more an object of history than its subject. "After October, Trotsky began to drift," he noted, succumbing to the tides of the petit bourgeois sea.[52] Whereas good Bolsheviks had always known how to "swim against the current, toward a determined goal,"[53] Trotsky was more like a "chip carried by the wave's crest."[54] Could it be that Trotsky was more a helpless victim than a conniving foe? "History played a joke on Trotsky by turning him into a toy of the oppositionist forces struggling against Bolshevism."[55]

Others spoke of Trotsky's deliberate and conscious attack on the Party. Here too, Trotsky was linked with Menshevism, but this time with Menshevism as an ideological current and not a hyperindividualist personality type. In the official political vocabulary, Menshevism was an ideological rallying point for all the petit bourgeois forces seeking a faction within Bolshevism that would defend their interests.[56] Was Trotsky not driven by his "febrile factionalist imagination" to try to legalize groupings, "sincerely convinced as he was that the old methods of Leninism cannot cope with the widening spectrum of the Party's operations?"[57]

There were those among the triumvirate's supporters who perceived a carefully designed system lurking behind Trotsky's inconsistencies and vacillations. Vareikis observed, "Although one can speak of a variety of intra-Party discussions during which a variety of groupings have coalesced in a variety of combinations around Trotsky, this does not rule out the relative stability of Trotsky's principal political position."[58] Zinoviev suggested the following metaphor:

Take an arch of electric bulbs: the picture one sees is very bright, all the colors of the rainbow, red, green, blue, white—they all appear. And yet the color of the bulbs is a secondary thing. A single matter underpins everything—electricity. The same is true of Trotsky's position. Externally, it too radiates all the colors of the rainbow. Our task is to find out what the substance is here, what the source is. My contention is that the basis here is a certain "negative matter"—everything that is non-Bolshevik, everything that is non-Leninist.[59]

Trotsky's recurrent lapses were noted by several during the discussion of 1924. "Trotsky's 'Lessons of October,'" wrote Babakhan, "should be seen as a continuation of his former sorties."[60] "Trotsky serves as an irritant to the Party almost every year," others elaborated, "appearing as part of periodically appearing circles with sturdy underpinnings. At every key moment—Brest, the trade union discussion, the so-called New Course—Trotsky served as the leader of the opposition, the person with a 'special line of his own.'"[61] Bukharin even cracked a joke: "True, history repeats itself. Unfortunately, however, tragedy is not always followed by farce."[62]

Hard-liners spoke of a sinister plot, an unusual approach to the opposition by the standards of the mid-1920s. Diman, an especially zealous vigilante, suspected Trotsky of hoping that his faction would eventually take over the Party. "Trotsky is deeply convinced that the objective course of history has yet to prove him wrong and the Party right. Hence he concludes: 'The number of my supporters will grow every year; historical development must invest me with power.'" According to Diman, though, Trotsky was preparing not for a discussion but for war. "It is naive, even juvenile, to think that Trotsky, an experienced politician familiar with the importance of calculations and plans, would not know that by writing *Lessons of October* he would be striking a great blow against the Party. It was not lack of knowledge or some sort of mistake that prompted Trotsky to violate Party discipline. No, he is acting in full consciousness, with a certain political aim in mind. He is sending 'his people' a 'signal': 'Do not lose hope!'"[63]

This severe interpretation of Trotsky's motives won over the Leningrad Party leadership. Evdokimov, the chairman of the Petrograd Soviet, described Trotskyism as a dangerous current which set itself the goal of "revising Leninism,"[64] and Safarov maintained that Trotsky's ideas followed the subversive line already charted by the Workers' Opposition.[65] So strong was the expectation in Leningrad that Trotsky would explicitly repudiate all of his political writings that D. A. Sarkis, chairman of Leningrad's Moscow-Narva district Party committee, actually outlined the sort of apology he hoped to hear. "Trotsky must state that he considers the main ideas he developed in the years 1904, 1905, and 1906 as having nothing to do with the true essence of Leninism, that the theory of permanent revolution does not coincide in any way with the main strategy of Bolshevism . . . and that he is aware that his writings contain an attempt to 'leap over the peasantry.'"[66]

Much to the chagrin of Sarkis and the rest of the Leningrad leadership, Trotsky refused to say what he was supposed to say "and remained, from head to toe, the Trotsky from the epoch of Trotskyism, in other words, an enemy of Leninism."[67] Of course, the immediate effect of so abject a recantation would have been the erasure of all of his revolutionary achievements to date from the annals of Party history. A renewed conversion would mean starting a Bolshevik career all over again.[68] This would have had disastrous consequences for Trotsky's position in the Party's hierarchy, and he was in no rush to demote himself and bow to Sarkis, Evdokimov, and the rest.

When drafting the resolution of the January 1925 Central Committee plenary session, "On Trotsky's Sortie," the Leningrad leadership contemplated hard measures: "Trotsky's incessant outbursts against Bolshevism are obliging the Party to choose between abandoning its tough-as-steel unity and putting an end once and for all to these outbursts."[69] Evdokimov urged the immediate removal of Trotsky from the Politburo.[70] Resisting these demands, Stalin showed Trotsky clemency. "The policy of cutting off heads," he explained, "is liable to be 'infectious': you cut off one head today, another tomorrow, a third the day after, and then what will remain of the Party?"[71] The Muscovites maintained that Trotsky was still "precious to the Party" and that his soul might be redeemed.[72] Separating the man from his theory, a number of Bolshevik literati expressed the hope "that Trotskyism can be unmasked strictly on the ideological plane" as an objective ramification of the petit bourgeois pressures he had unwittingly absorbed. If only the Party could wait until Trotsky's personality had fully matured it would be well rewarded—his Civil War exploits proved he had great promise as an organizer, if not as a theoretician.[73] "If Trotsky understands that he has become a symbol of everything that is directed against our Party, if he draws the appropriate conclusions," Kamenev promised, "things will return to their place."[74] Voroshilov stated that following its successful rebuttal of Trotsky's *Lessons of October*, the Central Committee decided to leave the author in all his posts and see what personal conclusions he would draw from the harsh lesson given him by the Party. "If he does not misbehave, if he straightens himself out and performs his assigned tasks assiduously, . . . there will be hope for a thorough rectification [*vypravlenie*]."[75]

"It would be a monstrous fable by philistine old ladies from the political bazaar to see in the *Lessons of October* discussion a scuffle instigated by personal animosities."[76] As that contemporaneous commentator suggested, Trotsky's travails of 1924–1925 should not be viewed as an example of Bolshevik intrigue. If the period was marked by important events in the struggle over Lenin's succession, the struggle was not a personal affair carried out by power-thirsty leaders but a struggle for the control of Bolshevik language. It was not enough to control the Party apparatus and place one's people in positions of authority. The victor also had to know how to turn public discourse to his advantage and how to turn himself into a source of ideological inspiration.

Trotsky was becoming less and less effective both as an organizer and as a propagandist. Although the Party had to work through the issues he put on the agenda in an outwardly proper manner, grassroots opinion was already turned against him. Even the young ears once so sympathetic to his appeals had been stopped up.[77] When, on December 3, 1924, the Party bureaus of Moscow's universities met in a special plenary session, every one of them condemned Trotsky's "new sortie."[78]

In Leningrad, where Trotsky was especially maligned, Zinoviev's apparatus systematically removed his supporters from whatever positions of authority they still held early in 1925. Two elections for Party cell bureaus were held in January and in April; thirty-four new cell secretaries entered office (an 80 percent turnover) as well as 191 new bureau members (a 72 percent turnover). Few, if any, were willing to even listen to the opposition.[79] The Leningrad Party organization had already observed in November 1924 that "support for Trotsky in the universities is insubstantial nowadays."[80] "Trotsky's accusations in his *Lessons of October* are groundless," a local student meeting declared in December. "Kamenev and Zinoviev may have committed mistakes, but these were not deviations."[81] "We defeated the revisions attempted by Trotsky, who tried to rely on the Party youth," the heads of the academic institutions triumphantly stated. "We wish to inform Trotsky," one resolution sarcastically noted, "that the student youth, the 'Party's barometer' as he liked to call us, now foresee bad weather and advise him to recant his pamphlet."[82]

The Communist University bureau reported late in 1924 that "the political situation in the collective is generally healthy. We have no more than six or seven students still clinging to the opinions espoused by the oppositionist block."[83] If during the New Course Discussion "there were comrades asking themselves, 'Should I support the opposition or the Central Committee?' no one vacillates here at the present." Circles for the study of Leninism, the best antidote to Trotskyism, clearly proved their effectiveness.[84] Having endorsed Evdokimov's condemnation of Trotsky's recent historical writings, the attendees announced on November 23, 1924: "Trotsky's distortion of the history of the October Revolution, his attempt to substitute Leninism with Trotskyism, is nothing else but the continuation of the struggle with Leninism, which he has been conducting for decades now."[85] In a landslide that was especially remarkable considering the balance of power less than a year earlier, Evdokimov's strongly worded resolution castigating the opposition was endorsed by an overwhelming majority.

When the Moscow-Narva district committee (Leningrad) held a high-profile Party meeting, not a single member spoke in Trotsky's defense; out of 6,780 Communists enrolled in the Vasilevsk Island Party organization, only 3 voted for Trotsky.[86] The same phenomenon repeated itself elsewhere in the city. When Victor Serge, a well-known Russian-Belgian Trotskyist, drew up an eyewitness account, the tone of his record was quite different from these triumphal declarations, but even he had to concede that "the youth had turned in upon itself. Meetings are hardly noticed by the apathetic public."[87] No doubt, the students faced a variety of pressures; any oppositionists who dared to appear were booed and forced to leave the meeting before the vote was cast.[88] In the estimation of Smirnov, another prominent oppositionist, Trotsky's silence and the threat of repression created, for the first time in Party history, a situation where comrades "voted with their feet." For all intents and purposes, the opposition was made illegal.[89]

How meager student support for Trotsky had been during the *Lessons of October* Discussion is evident from the data collected by the agitation department at the Leningrad provincial committee, shown in table 2.

Strikingly different than the summaries of the Trade Union Discussion from 1920 (see chapter 2), the table serves as an excellent illustration of the emergence of what would become known as Stalinist voting patterns. So minuscule was the number of dissenters that one wonders: Why did the provincial committee bother to record—and with such care—that, say, 3 out of 1,147 student Communists in the Central district supported Trotsky? Or that two students abstained during the vote in the Moscow-Narva district? An inkling of an answer can be obtained if the

TABLE 2. Student Communists' Conduct during the *Lessons of October* Discussion (by Leningrad city districts, Fall 1924)

	Central	Petrograd	Moscow-Narva	Vasilevsk island	Vyborg
Student Communists attending at the meetings	1,147	634	612	941	1,261
Made speeches	36	35	24	56	28
Defended Trotsky	3	6	2	—	8
Objected to harsh condemnation of Trotsky	1	7	—	—	6
Abstained	6	13	2	4	16

Source: TsGA IPD, f. 16, op. 5, d. 5378, ll. 157–60.

table is read not as a statistical map of the political moods but as a text reflecting Bolshevik assumptions regarding the body politic. In the Bolshevik imagination, ideological maturity meant political unity—each implied the other. The nearly unanimous rejection of the opposition at the polls was viewed as the outcome of a definite mental and spiritual maturation of the rank and file. The further the brotherhood of the elect had progressed in its eschatological journey, the keener was its sense of itself as a single collective.

This was definitely not a liberal reading of Party politics. The true liberal celebrates closely contested elections because such occasions permit citizens to take advantage of their basic right to express differing opinions by casting ballots; narrow electoral margins make sense here because they reflect the natural plurality of interests in society. In the Communist mind, however, the proletarian truth is unitary. The members of a well-functioning Party were supposed to agree in their assessment of the truth, and the outcome of elections would be consistently unanimous. Unanimity meant purity and homogeneity, and dissent revealed the presence of infiltrators or saboteurs. Even one infiltrator represented a danger and had to be unmasked and rooted out. Failure to do so could lead to the growth of a rival faith.

Though during NEP the political consciousness of the nation was undergoing constant purification, it remained impure in the official perception. In order to deal with this condition, tables were drawn up to analyze the composition of the general student body—an entity that should not be confused with the select group of Communist students. Fundamental tools of analysis included a range of categories reflecting the heterogeneity of students' class backgrounds and levels of political development. Since the Party cell prefigured the pure proletarian society of the future, it had, by contrast, to be presented as completely unified. The Leningrad Party tables show the fulfillment of this ideal over and over again in the form of unanimous votes during the discussion of *Lessons of October*. At least at the level of the local Party organization, the ideal was realized.

Leningrad Contra Stalin

With the Bolsheviks being in power a number of years, it became evident that alliances in the Party's collective leadership were highly unstable. Friendships were betrayed, and mutual condemnations meant that the elite had become too crowded. The members of the triumvirate denounced Trotsky in unison and a few months later sank their teeth into each other. After Trotsky was ousted from every influential position, Kamenev and Zinoviev felt free enough to smear their ally of yesterday as a conservative and theoretically uncouth power seeker. Stalin struck back with enormous force and denounced Zinoviev as an infantile and irresponsible troublemaker. The carousel of intra-Party struggles kept spinning, the intervals between rotations becoming shorter and shorter. Soon the contours of Stalin's one-man rule became discernable and Kamenev and Zinoviev had to swallow the same bitter pill they only recently dished out to Trotsky.

Relations within the triumvirate went bad already during the course of 1925.[90] NEP reached the apex of moderation. The Central Committee encouraged private initiatives among peasants with the aim of raising productivity and the standards of living in the rural society.[91] Stalin maintained that a "diligent peasant will ensure our agricultural upswing," and Molotov elaborated a scheme of concessions to the village that included tax relief, liberalization of the terms of leasing land, improved machinery supplies, and organization of agricultural cooperatives.[92] An outraged Zinoviev described all this as a slide to the right. NEP, he pointed out, was supposedly introduced as a "strategic retreat"; in principle, the policy of creating a prosperous stratum of smallholding peasants was a violation of Leninism. According to Zinoviev, Soviet industry was socialist only in terms of the ownership of the means of production, not, however, in its relations of production.[93]

In September 1925, Zinoviev, the head of the Leningrad Soviet; Kamenev, his Moscow counterpart; Gregorii Sokol'nikov, the commissar of finances; and Lenin's widow, Nadezhda Krupskaia, summarized their point of view in a letter to the Central Committee that earned the name *Platform of the Four*.[94] The new policy document demanded that the socialist component of the nationalized economy be strengthened by means of wage equalization.[95] Sarkis, one of Zinoviev's closest allies, accused the Central Committee of "syndicalism," that is, encouraging the existence of peasant organizations outside government control.[96] He demanded an immediate proletarianization of the Party and wanted to see 90 percent of its membership consist of "workers from the bench."[97]

The Central Committee majority joined the battle. Dzerzhinskii, the iron head of the Cheka, spoke in terms of a "conspiracy of the heads of the Leningrad organization," a "new Kronshtadt."[98] According to Mandel'shtam, a majoritarian propagandist who got tired of the opposition, Zinoviev's outbursts echoed Trotsky's pessimism. "How ironic! The leaders of the new opposition just renounced everything they have been saying [against Trotskyism] for the last two years!"[99] Tomskii, the chairman of the central trade union, ridiculed Zinoviev's claims that he had inherited Lenin's extraordinary historical perspicacity: "Would you believe it? Zinoviev hears the steps of history. We, the other members of the Politburo, hear nothing, though we sit nearby."[100] If the arguments with Trotsky had been something like a duel—the challenger being an outsider—the battle with Zinoviev was described as a family affair. "The new opposition exposed disagreements at the core of the Central Committee itself!"[101]

Rejecting Zinoviev's request for a national discussion at the autumn 1925 Central Committee plenary session, Stalin saw no reason to allow publication of the *Platform of the Four*.[102] Before he would join the ideological battle, the general secretary took some administrative measures. By now effectively in control of the Central Committee's secretariat, Stalin was busy cleansing the Party institutions of his rivals. The first one to go was Zelenskii, an important ally of Zinoviev on the Moscow Party committee, dispatched to Central Asia already in the autumn of 1924. In the early months of 1925, Stalin purged the Komintern executive—Zinoviev's key bastion on the national scene. Another prominent Zinovievist, Safarov, departed his prominent position in the Komsomol later that year.[103]

The Twenty-second Leningrad Party Conference (December 1–10, 1925) took place at the zenith of the tension. In his opening address, "On the Activity of the Central Committee," Zinoviev dwelled on the difficulties that lay along the path of socialist construction. "Some comrades do not see that the kulak is raising his head, and they pay no attention to what is happening in Siberia and in other provinces. We must decisively take on this deviation." NEP has socialist as well as capitalist elements, he noted, "but is it not the duty of the proletarian dictatorship to help the former rather than the latter?"[104]

The next fifteen speakers developed Zinoviev's themes. Some argued that the Party did not take firm enough measures against social stratification in the village. Safarov's wake-up call was especially blunt: "A kulak is a kulak. Lenin taught us this is a nasty beast!"[105] Others preferred to criticize blunders in foreign policy. In a long and inspired speech, Minin, Kanatchikov's replacement in the Communist University and the secretary of the present conference, contrasted Zinoviev's internationalist interpretation of Leninism with Stalin's parochialism. He defended the honor of the northern city against Moscow's attacks and claimed Leningrad to be responsible for distilling the pure proletarian line. A Bolshevik since 1905, famous for his role as the chairman of the Tsaritsyn Party committee in 1917–1918, and the organizer of the Red's war effort in the south, Minin received long applause.[106]

The rift between the two largest Party organizations in the country was exacerbated once the opinion expressed during the simultaneous Fourteenth Moscow Party Congress became known.[107] Lomov, prominent on the Moscow Party committee, spoke of Leningrad's attempts to give up NEP. "The link with the main mass of the peasantry has to remain the main goal of our policy," his friends reportedly agreed. "Neglect of the middle peasant will undermine the worker-peasant alliance."[108] Even more insulting was Moscow's characterization of "Zinoviev's indiscriminate attacks on the Party apparatus" as a pitiful rehash of old oppositionist slogans.[109]

By mid-December, rumors spread in Leningrad that "Moscow is urging the Party to beat us up." Zinoviev argued that future historians will divide the work of the Twenty-second Leningrad Party Conference into two halves: "before Moscow's resolution and after. When word of Lomov's aggressive speech reached us, our conference adopted a contentious tone."[110] Sokol'nikov agreed that it was Lomov who created a wedge within the Leninist camp, setting members of the Politburo and the Central Committee on two opposing sides. "The Moscow conference," others added, "cast its shadow on our own. . . . In his polemics with an organization as large and as important as ours, Lomov stooped to reviving the tricks of the left Communists of 1918 and the Trotskyists of 1923–25. . . . Accusations of 'liquidationism,' 'pessimism,' and of 999 other deadly sins flared about."[111]

Extending its deliberations for a few more days, the Leningrad Party Conference flung Moscow's words back at them. A polemical rebuttal was issued: "In view of the whole range of Moscow resolutions directed at our organization, . . . we state that the allegations that we do not believe in the strength of the working class, that we are snivelers, would have been funny had they not been so sad."[112] The charge against Zinoviev and Kamenev, "Lenin's closest disciples, that they 'defend in the Politburo the view that we will not be able to overcome internal difficulties because of our technical and economic backwardness' and that 'international Revolution is our only savior,' are absolutely monstrous."[113] "Instead of condemning us for panic," so Leningrad claimed, "Moscow should do something against the professors of economics who kowtow to the kulak."[114]

In this behind-the-scenes skirmish (all these exchanges were not published until the following year) the last word belonged to Moscow: "We see in NEP more than just a retreat, as Zinoviev, Safarov, Sarkis, and others do. We believe that its framework will soon allow us to stop retreating and launch an all-out attack. Capitalist resistance is sometimes fierce, but we advance nonetheless." "Zinoviev is calling for a war against the Muscovites," Stalin's men commented. "We are ready to join the battle."[115]

The doctrinal disagreements at the top left their mark on the Communist University. In the week before the Fourteenth Party Congress opened, a number of political rallies took place on its premises. First, there was the meeting of the circles' presidiums, convened "to discuss ways of introducing students to the issues." With the Leningrad provincial Party conference taking up all Minin's time, this meeting was chaired by Rybin. "We were struck by Rybin's strange approach," majoritarians claimed in retrospect. "The secretary of the university Party organization seemed agitated, unsure what to do. Clearly, there was something on his mind, yet he restrained himself trying to gauge students' attitudes."[116] In this scenario, the university leadership was aware that the Central Committee was divided but refrained from alerting the rank and file.

The importance of the Communist University in this period is evident in the fact that its graduation ceremony, held shortly before the Leningrad delegation departed for Moscow to attend the Fourteenth Party Congress, turned into a political rally. Speakers were stumbling over each other in their efforts to condemn Stalin. The first speaker was Evdokimov, recently nominated as secretary of the Leningrad Party organization, who stressed the need for the proletarianization and democratization of the Party.[117] Next spoke Zinoviev himself. Introduced as "our main theoretician" and "our main ideologue," Zinoviev declared that the heart of the controversy with Moscow was the need to face up to the breakdowns in socialist construction. He stressed the need to combat the petite bourgeoisie and rejected accusations that he did not believe in the capabilities of the working class.[118] Minin bid farewell to the fledglings flying out of his nest: "Wherever you are assigned, do not forget Leninism! . . . Remember that while we register victories everywhere . . . many difficulties still lay ahead."[119]

A meeting of the Communist University, convened on December 16 to review the resolutions of the Leningrad Provincial Party conference (650 students were in attendance, including visitors from the Krupskaia Institute), gave Minin more time to do justice to Zinoviev's stand. His main cavils were reserved for Moscow's

dubious intellectual sources of inspiration, dished out to us as the essence of Leninism. . . . When we point to the fact that already at the Tenth Party Congress Lenin said that "dangers exist and will exist in the years to come," we hear in response that, "You have panicky moods." How is it, then, that we had to scale down our plan for industrial imports? We overestimated the harvest. Where is the wheat that the peasant was supposed to give us?[120]

To prove that the Stalinist leadership jeopardized the hegemony of the proletariat, Minin cited an anonymous complaint that had reached his Smol'nyi office. "Is the proletarian dictatorship fair?" a disgruntled peasant demanded to know. "Should the Bolsheviks not share with the peasantry?"[121] Bukharin's notorious banner, "Peasants, Enrich Yourselves!" unfurled before Moscow Communists on April 17, 1925, was the backdrop for these protests. "Was this simply a matter of 'poor phrasing?" Minin and Rybin did not think so. "Did Bukharin forget how to formulate policy? Despite his later disclaimers, his banner played an anti-Party, negative role."[122]

The Zinovievist leadership of the Communist University was not immune from challenge. A number of speakers rejected the accusation that the kulak rules the village or that agricultural cooperation somehow translated into state capitalism. "What Lenin understood by state capitalism is a link between small producers and socialist industry," Brenner pointed out. "Cooperation is actually the high road to socialism." According to Anfalov, another member of the university bureau who supported Bukharin, the letter from the peasant cited by Minin "must be a typical. Comrades exaggerate problems and go after flies with sledgehammers." The rest of Anfalov's comments were pure sarcasm: "Minin demands we discuss the issues like true Bolsheviks, clearly and directly. And yet, despite my utmost attention, I did not understand a thing he said. Or did I hear correctly that kulaks control 60 percent of our economy?!"

"Where socialism is growing, capitalism cannot be born," Minin agreed. He was not saying that the Central Committee had given up on building socialism, but that it should be building socialism internationally. "You would ask, 'And how many years remain until the world revolution?' I cannot say, though the tempo has clearly slowed somewhat." The sooner the Party returned to Lenin the better. "Some say even today that Lenin said nothing new on economics and philosophy and that if he contributed anywhere, it is only in politics and in his theory of the state. In fact, he gave us plenty.... Lenin talked about ten to twenty years of meticulous work solidifying the unity between workers and peasants."[123]

All three resolutions put to vote following the speechifying expressed support of the Leningrad leadership. If compared, however, they reveal important differences. Minin's resolution stated: "We shall always go in step with the Leningrad Party organization . . . that leads the struggle against distortions of Leninism." The vast majority of students expressed full solidarity with the view that "Moscow's accusations against Leningrad are baseless." Another resolution, drafted by Vavilin, a young instructor of history, also denied that "the Leningrad organization does not believe socialism can be built in the Soviet Union." But Vavilin refrained from criticizing the Party line: "It is fundamentally wrong to describe our economic system as state capitalism. . . . NEP ensures the working class reaches socialism" (for, 106 votes). Brenner, in a third resolution, was the only to cross swords with Zinoviev, though his criticism was faint: "certain leaders of the Leningrad organization must admit their mistakes regarding socialist building, just as Bukharin did regarding his own mistakes on the village question" (for, 8 votes).[124]

Just before packing for the Fourteenth Party Congress (December 18–31, 1925), Zinoviev moved every supporter of the Central Committee majority from the Leningrad delegation.[125] The organizing committee honored his special request that the guests from Leningrad should stay in a fancy hotel (the one in which they stayed during the Thirteenth Party Congress), while the majority of the delegates, coming from less illustrious strongholds, were accommodated in dormitories.[126] Arriving several days before the congress opened, the Leningrad delegation toured Moscow, bringing with them a catalogue of political literature. The Zinovievists promoted their views at the semiofficial conferences of the provincial delegations and, even before the Congress officially opened, talked privately with the other delegates. Judging by the fact that a number of delegations criticized Leningrad's "schismatic activity," these efforts were only a partial success, at best.

On December 15 the divided Politburo met for the last time before the Congress. A compromise proposal, offered by Stalin, Kalinin, and Dzerzhinskii, was put on the table: the Leningrad delegation will avoid public criticism of official policies and disassociate itself from the extremist positions of Sarkis and Safarov.[127] In exchange, the Central Committee will soften the resolution it intended to propose and honor the personal prestige of Leningrad leaders. Each side suspected the other of dishonesty and the attempts at a truce came to naught.[128]

When the congress officially opened in the Andreev Hall of the Kremlin's Great Palace, the tensions surfaced. The first bone of contention was the question of location. Zinoviev wanted to move the seat of the congress to Leningrad, "for at least the first few sessions." His request rejected, he asked that his trustee, Badaev, replace Komarov on the presidium. Again, he was turned down.[129] In a clear signal of his ascendancy, Stalin delivered the Central Committee report (during the previous Party Congress this honor had fallen to Zinoviev). Stalin called for full reconstruction of the native economy based on the imperatives of industrialization. The growth of the middle layers in the village, he maintained, proves that the worker-peasant alliance had emerged from the scissors crisis fully recovered and that the toiling peasantry supports the soviet state. In the polemical section of his speech, the general secretary charged that the left deviation's systematic exaggeration of the kulak danger tempted localities to revert to military methods of grain extraction as in the Civil War.

The contest over the role of the voice of the conscious proletariat proved to be a highly combustible issue. Everybody acknowledged that in delivering a co-report, Zinoviev did not violate Party norms. He had three votes more than the forty required to be allowed to deliver an extended rebuttal of Stalin's speech. Still, Zinoviev's defiance evoked strong protests. "We have here, in fact, an organized faction," Martymian Riutin, the secretary of the Krasnopresninsk Party committee (Moscow), stated. "Our enemies could not wish themselves anything better," Postyshev, the secretary of the Kiev provincial Party committee, agreed. Anastas Mikoian, the secretary of the North Caucasian Party committee, was even more sarcastic. "Let Uglanov and Evdokimov [the heads of the Moscow and Leningrad Party organizations respectively] quarrel. . . . But we cannot have leaders of the caliber of Zinoviev and Bukharin at each others' throats before the eyes of our enemies, can we?!"[130]

But nothing could distract Zinoviev from addressing his nightmare: the rise of the village bourgeoisie. Social differentiation in the countryside, he said with evident distress, was growing. Worse, the kulaks had counterparts in the cities: the NEPman, the new bourgeoisie in general, and the white-collar elite. Zinoviev controversially claimed that "the banner of Socialism in One Country smacks of nationalist parochialism." The relatively backward Soviet economy had to seek salvation from the hands of the international proletariat.[131]

Speaking for almost as long as Zinoviev did, Kamenev also justified the challenge issued to the Central Committee. "We present a co-report here because we deeply believe that an erroneous theory guides the Party: 'Bukharin's school.' . . . And Stalin fell straight into Bukharin's trap. [Laughter.]" Of course, the general secretary was not exactly a novice to Bolshevik politics, and Kamenev had to be more serious in his dealings with him. Criticizing the consolidation of power in Stalin's hands, Kamenev called for a restoration of freedom of opinion in the Party. "We oppose this 'Duce,' we oppose the secretariat, an administrative body that usurped political functions."[132]

Stalin's rejoinder to the last point was cautious but firm. Agreeing that "with Lenin gone, only a collegium can lead the Party," he reminded Kamenev and Zinoviev of their own former arguments against Trotsky, to the effect that "in the eyes of the Bolsheviks, formal democracy is just a code word."[133] "We are not liberals," Stalin pointed out. "For us, the interests of the Party stand above formal democracy." Old truisms had to be reiterated: the suppression of minority positions "is the only way to secure class unity. Any alternative notion of leadership is syndicalism, anarchism, you name it, but not Bolshevism, not Leninism."[134]

Uglanov offered a resolution endorsing Stalin's report. Complaining that it was informed of the resolution only two hours before the vote and that it was not invited to participate in its drafting, the Leningrad delegation demanded that the resolution be sent to a commission for further deliberation. This demand was rejected and Moscow's draft was accepted, 559 for, 65 against. The opponents were given the title "schismatics."[135]

Additional points of friction were revealed during debate over the activities of the Central Control Commission. Delivering the main report on the subject on December 26, Kuibyshev declared that "the responsibility for the intra-Party struggle falls on the shoulders of the Leningrad leadership."[136] In his finest hour in national politics, Minin from the Communist University answered that the Central Control Commission violated the principle of impartiality. "Kuibyshev, for example, participated in drafting the resolution of the Moscow Party Conference"—was this not a token of partisanship? Furthermore, the Central Control Commission relied on a system of denunciatory letters—"this introduced unhealthy, heretofore unheard-of habits into our Party."[137] Minin's accusations were informed by the highly controversial removal, in September 1925, of Zalutskii, the man who had nominated Minin to be rector of the Communist University, from his position as the first secretary of the Leningrad Party organization.[138]

Iaroslavskii's speech at the congress shed additional light on the affair. "The entire Party now knows about the letter by Leonov telling us how the secretary of the Leningrad provincial committee, Zalutskii, besmirched the Central Committee majority."[139] In that letter (a "denunciation," in Minin's terms), Leonov informed the Central Control Commission of his private conversation with Zalutskii and attributed disparaging remarks of policy makers in the center to the Leningrad secretary: "Zalutskii said that 'state officials exert pressure on the Party. . . . The petit bourgeois Moscow Party organization does not protect the grass roots from this pressure and the result is the isolation of the proletarian Leningrad.'"[140] Tomskii could not leave Zalutskii's truculence unanswered. "Mind you," he laid it on thick, "Zalutskii said all that in his own office, not while drinking tea somewhere! He was not attacking the Central Committee as such, so he justifies himself, only Stalin, only Molotov, only Bukharin, only and only. . . . As the saying goes, "Danylo did not die, it is the illness that smothered him [*ne vmer Danylo, a boliachka ego zadavila*].'"[141]

A duel in the press that lasted throughout December reflected the split at the Congress. *Pravda* presented Moscow's point of view: "Finding itself in the minority at the Congress, the opposition uses Leningrad as a bulwark for an offense against the Bolshevik party. . . . The opposition praises the conduct of Zinoviev and Kamenev as a 'standard the rest of the Party should emulate.'"[142] But *Leningradskaia pravda* did not agree that this was a case of insubordination. If anything, the opposite was true: "Comrades, please end your pointless worries about how to heal our Party organization. We can tell you safely: physician, heal thyself!"[143] Safarov reminded Moscow: "In 1923, we helped your organization to rid itself of the Trotskyist fever. . . . Later, we played a major role in confuting *Lessons of October*. Surely, the Leningrad organization can get by without a governess from Moscow!"[144]

December 24–30: Turmoil in Leningrad

Events in Moscow were closely followed in Leningrad. As the word of the vote at the congress reached the city, Stalin's protégés on the Leningrad provincial Party committee, Komarov, Lobov, Shvernik, and Moskvin, immediately demanded a condemnation of the scandalous behavior of the Leningrad organization.[145] Since the extraordinary plenary session of the provincial Party committee refused to consider their demand, the Moscow-oriented functionaries issued a remonstrance arguing that "Zinoviev had not informed the Twenty-second Leningrad Conference of the true extent of his disagreements with the Central Committee majority," and his electoral victory was therefore meaningless.[146]

Unusually vitriolic, the institutional and rhetorical battles that followed presented, at least in the eyes of most Leningrad Communists, the imposition of an alien stand. What is remarkable is that this time, the supporters of the Central Committee successfully utilized techniques normally associated with oppositionist activity: they signed Party members to letters of protest, challenged the authority of the legally elected Party institutions, and so on. Circumventing the local power pyramid, Stalin's supporters were referred to as "factionalists" in Leningrad in the second half of December and early January. Another anomaly must also be noted. In claiming that the Leningrad rank and file had changed their minds and deserved new leadership, it was the victors and not the vanquished who emphasized the "democratic" aspect of democratic centralism. Drawing on Lenin, the defeated side sought to draw legitimacy from the more "centralist" aspects of democratic centralism. Thus, Zinoviev's supporters constantly reiterated how the official Party institutions, that is, the Leningrad Party district committees that they controlled, were alone allowed to wield power.

When the Fourteenth Party Congress adjourned for a short recess on December 24, a substantial part of the Leningrad delegation went home. The delegates maintained that they never intended to challenge the Central Committee, only to promote decisive measures against Bukharin and the right deviation.[147] Zinovievists talked about the honor of the Leningrad organization and called on the grass roots to support its leadership "at this difficult hour."[148] An internal document entitled "How Things Unfolded" presented the Zinovievist version of events:

In his report at the Congress, Stalin called to attack those who warn the Party against the kulak. . . . A co-report was necessary; whereas our suggestions were constructive. . . . Moscow responded with a squabble. . . . For the first time in Party history we were not invited to participate in drafting the resolution on the report of the Central Committee. Our delegation voted unanimously against it (except Alekseev). . . .

The political outcome: The Congress created an atmosphere of heated animosity toward Leningrad. An attempt is made to set the lower ranks of our organization against the higher-ups.[149]

Sarkis, Minin, and other Leningrad delegates toured Party organizations and addressed audiences in several key Leningrad factories during the last week of December.[150] Resolutions in support of the Leningrad delegation were adopted in at least two hundred Party organizations and in four of the city's seven district committees.[151]

On December 26 the Leningrad provincial Party committee officially banned discussion of Stalin's theses prior to the return of all the delegates from the capital.[152] On the following day, the plenary session of the Central District's Party committee was convened in the local club Komintor. Toivo, the Party secretary of the Central District, reported "on the ongoing Party Congress" to the heads of the Party cells

under his jurisdiction (including the Communist University). He denounced violations of the Leningrad Provincial Committee's instructions and called for a "resolute struggle against attempts at disorganization."[153] Speakers protested against "inflaming disagreements. . . . We reject the description of the Leningrad organization
as opposition, faction, or grouping—our organization does not intend to pit itself
against the Party. In introducing its corrections to the official resolutions it acted
not as a faction but as one of the largest proletarian organizations, determined to
take part in articulating the resolutions of the Congress."

In the minority for the time being, Moscow's supporters answered with a set of
countermeasures.[154] One anonymous "combatant against the opposition" read Stalin's report to the Congress at a private gathering already on December 25.[155] On
the same day, he was told to begin majoritarian activity in the Leningrad State University and the Hertzen Pedagogical Institute.

Joining forces with a few friends, this Stalinist zealot helped establish "initiative
groups" (*initsiativnye gruppy*) across the city, improvised bodies geared to disseminating the Muscovite version of events. A pro-Moscow activist, Chechkovskii, met
Nikolaev, who was in charge of the local GPU, and Antonov, the secretary of the
Volodarsk textile factory. Constituting the core of the initiative group at the Central District, this trio was soon joined by Bystrianskii, later a professor of Leninism at the Communist University, and several other local potentates. The activities
of the initiative groups were guided by the Northwestern Party bureau, the center's outpost in Leningrad, and by Ivan Moskvin and Nikolai Shvernik, who represented Stalin on the Leningrad provincial Party committee. The initiative group at
the Central District met every other day in private, which is suggestive of the conspiratorial nature of the enterprise. The group was greatly aided by a list of all Party
cells in the district that included the names and addresses of the leading activists, a
list obtained by Basuev, who had defected from the district bureau.[156]

A veritable information war went on in Leningrad during those momentous
days. According to the recollections of Goilo, the head of *Pechatnyi dvor* (the main
printing house), Moskvin phoned him during the early days of the congress and
demanded that steps be taken for distributing the Central Committee stenograms.
"We worked for days without ever leaving the press. I used to bring the printed
bulletins myself to Moskvin's office in Smol'nyi, being very careful lest Evdokimov's
people intercept us."[157] The material of the congress, which was illegal in Leningrad, was usually brought from Moscow to the GPU offices and then passed out
across the Central District. According to official reports, 140,033 copies of Stalin's
report and related papers were distributed in five days (December 29–January 2).[158]
Because the official circulation of the Moscow press was effectively blocked, the
Northwestern Bureau handed out copies of *Pravda* free of charge.[159]

As the majority of the Fourteenth Party Congress saw it, Leningrad needed to
be saved from the plague of the opposition.[160] Antipov, the secretary of the Ural

Party organization and a onetime Petrograd Bolshevik, spoke with pathos: "It pains me that the best proletarian organization . . . finds itself in such an absurd position." When Andreev declared that the Party must send its best propagandists to Leningrad, the response received was that "We shall all go there!"[161] Departing for Leningrad on December 29, a delegation from the Congress's presidium that included Ordzhonikidze, Kirov, Podvoiskii, and Mikoian were instructed to study the situation, establish direct links with activists loyal to the Central Committee, and begin explaining the resolutions of the congress in Zinoviev's stronghold.[162]

Stalin's legates met with a hostile response. "They sent Kalinin and Tomskii to Leningrad and ordered Zinoviev to shut his mouth," Levenson from the Enukidze Institute of Eastern Languages remarked. "Is this the best way to clarify issues?!"[163] Others were dissatisfied with the one-sided representation of "our delegation, chasing us into rat holes [medvezhie ugolki]."[164] A delegation of five students from Moscow's Sverdlov Communist University was also booed.[165] "Here, there, and everywhere," Leningradskaia pravda commented, "the subservient Moscow emissaries spread bulletins with 'basic information about the Congress.' We are supposed to accept what they say on command, without deliberation and discussion."[166]

Taking advantage of the fact that the entire Party leadership was gathered in Moscow for the Congress, Stalin convened an extraordinary meeting of the Central Committee on December 28 to discuss ways to bring the campaign against the Leningrad apparatus into a higher gear. While Zinoviev claimed that his followers were persecuted, Dzerzhinskii argued that it was the Leningrad delegation that had violated Party regulations first by openly rebelling against Party unity. Catching Zinoviev off guard, Kalinin rose to the dais immediately after the former completed his report on Komintern activity and, speaking in the name of eleven Party delegations, read an "Appeal to the Leningrad Organization."[167]

The heart of the "Appeal" addressed a disjuncture between the Leningrad Party organization and its delegation to the congress: "The opposition waited until the Congress to fully unmask itself. At the district Party conferences and even at the Leningrad Party conference its leaders refrained from mentioning any disagreements with the Central Committee. . . . The Congress has no doubt that the Leningrad Party organization, always in the forefront of the Party, will know how to correct the mistakes committed by the Leningrad delegation."[168]

Without effective means for bringing it to the attention of the Leningrad audience, the "Appeal" was an empty gesture. Stalin's supporters knew that. In a carefully prepared, complementary initiative intended to give the appeal the necessary muscle, they proposed that the Congress "improve the editorial board of Leningradskaia pravda." The Zinovievist Bakaev remonstrated: "The nomination of an editor who objects to the line of his own Party organization is tantamount to an extirpation of this organization."[169] But a cable signed by Stalin reached the newspaper offices on the night of December 29: "In view of the fact that the Leningrad provincial committee did not take any steps to prevent the violation of the Party regulations ... the Central Committee hereby relieves Zaks-Gladnev of his responsibilities as the editor of *Leningradskaia pravda* and nominates Skvortsov-Stepanov as his replacement."[170] One of the founders of Soviet censorship, Skvortsov-Stepanov was no newcomer to monitoring the Party press. From 1918 to 1924 he had been on the editorial board of *Pravda* and served as the deputy head of Gosizdat, the state publishing house.

The December 30 issue of *Leningradskaia pravda* was already signed by the new editor and duly carried the text of the congress's "Appeal to the Leningrad Organization."[171] Skvortsov-Stepanov was emphatic in his editorial: "Leningrad workers must ask themselves: Is it likely that the situation in our party is so catastrophic that the Leningrad organization alone defends Lenin's true legacy? Must we think that the entire Party has decayed, degenerated, that it is already dead? Surely, this cannot be!" Insisting on its bleak view of things, the Leningrad delegation, according to Skvortsov-Stepanov, "turned itself into an opposition to the Party. Do they need a reminder that the Congress is the highest Party organ and that its resolutions must be implemented, not debated?!"[172]

Unwilling to forfeit control over their main propaganda asset, the Zinovievists stormed the editor's premises and demanded that the newspaper return to its previous tone.[173] Skvortsov-Stepanov sent a hurried telegram to the presidium of the Congress: "Filing in one after another, people remain in my office for several hours, besieging it from 5 p.m. until 2 a.m. ... They label my staff 'spies' and 'provocateurs' and threaten to beat them up. The atmosphere is crazy."[174] The newly arrived employees of the newspaper were followed around and barred from using the phone.[175] The Central Committee instructed Skvortsov-Stepanov "not to give in to threats and to refuse the opposition's ultimatums. ... We will take measures to bring the disorganizing actions of the factionalists to an end."[176]

December 30–December 31: The Communist University Is Torn Apart

Having received the news about Zinoviev's provocative stand in Moscow, Communist University students became agitated. For two weeks the political situation there remained a seesaw. Due to a truly staggering volume of documentation, it is possible to follow events in the university with a unique degree of precision. Furthermore, the contentious nature of what transpired and the existence of competing narratives offer an opportunity for analysis of the nexus between politics and poetics during the 1925 discussion. We must appreciate the complicated relationship between institutional and rhetorical maneuvering, namely that Bolshevik politics was based on the accumulation of ideological authority and prestige and so was dependent on the ability to use words.

Although Zinovievist in its general orientation, the university Party bureau was not without dissenting voices. Brunin, Zhuk, and Anfalov, who were respected Bolsheviks (and Party members since 1914, 1915, and 1917, respectively) declared that Minin's conduct was "disgraceful." By December 25 or 26, the three had already created a local initiative group, explaining that "no decent Bolshevik can keep quiet in the face of the tension between us and the rest of the Party resulting from the activity of the Leningrad delegation to the Congress."[177] Searching their souls and determining for themselves "what side defends true Leninism," the initiative group resolved that it desired that the entire Party know that they "accept the Appeal of the Congress to the Leningrad organization."[178] The initiative group turned the history department into a rallying point for the supporters of the Central Committee majority. Vavilin later recalled how he personally carried the first batch of Congress bulletins from Dzerzhinskii Street to the Uritskii Palace on December 30, "despite every effort by the Zinovievists to confiscate them." "A pilgrimage to the Party cabinet was begun by students who wanted to know the truth about the Congress," as the self-congratulatory Stalinist version of events had it.[179]

Functioning as a shadow university bureau, the initiative group raised the profile of its activities in the last days of 1925. Its leaders approached Rybin on December 27, 1925, and requested that a general Party meeting be convened. "Such a meeting will allow us to reveal the overall physiognomy of our organization." Bobrikov, who belonged to the initiative group, elaborated: "Our student body is split: some of us believe that the decision of the meeting on December 16 that endorsed the Leningrad delegation does not reflect students' true point of view."

Rybin objected: "Most of the students are on vacation now anyway. Furthermore, did they not already express their position regarding the provincial Party conference [that supported Zinoviev]?"[180] The line of the University leadership was clear: "We must wait until the return of our representatives from Moscow and see what they tell us."[181]

"Deprived of our right to express our views," the initiative group told Rybin it was left with no choice but to send a "terse letter criticizing the conduct of the Leningrad Party organization" to the press. "Do what you like," Rybin snapped back.

The letter assured the presidium of the Fourteenth Congress that "Our delegation did not have a mandate to present its co-report, directed against the Central Committee, as the views of the entire Leningrad Party organization. The collective of the Communist University would like to stress that the report on the Twenty-second Leningrad Provincial Party Conference was one-sided. Polemical and tendentious, highlighting only deviations in the Party, the resolution adopted by the Communist University did not reflect the opinion of all the students."[182]

Without wasting much time, Zudov, one of the heads of the initiative group, made copies of the December 30 letter. "Collecting as many signatures as possible, such a letter puts comrades' true views on record," he explained. After eight copies were already prepared, Ivanov, who had been the cornerstone of loyalism in the

university two years earlier, suddenly showed up and, claiming to be acting on Rybin's instructions, confiscated all the copies of the letter. "Writing such a letter and
signing students to it is illegal," he explained. But the initiative group persisted: The
next day, six new copies of the letter made their way to the Moscow press, with 116
students expressing written support of its contents.[183]

The bureau of the Communist University protested what it called "disorganizing
activities by assorted groups addressing students over the head of the Party organization."[184] Minin, the university rector, described the initiative group as "Trotskyist"
insofar as "it goes against the actions of our own delegation to the Fourteenth Party
Congress and revives the old Trotskyist groans about the alleged separation between the upper and lower echelons in our Party." The existence of assorted groups
within the collective, Minin continued, "goes against Party regulations and under-
mines discipline. . . . Students have no mandate to place in *Pravda* a letter stating that 'we condemn the new opposition.'"[185] Summoning Anfalov, Borovkov, and
Vavilin to his office, he and Rybin confronted them with pointed questions: "Do
you acknowledge the authority of the University Party bureau? Do you acknowledge the authority of the Central District Party committee? Do you acknowledge
the authority of the Leningrad provincial Party committee?" The Zinovievist bureau made an effort to portray the members of the initiative group as insurgents.[186]

The initiative group formulated a line of defense. "We obey the decisions of the
superior Party organs but only insofar as they do not contradict the decisions of
the Fourteenth Party Congress." "We do not seek to replace elected Party organs,"
Stalin's men argued, "only to assign ourselves the responsibility for disseminating
the decisions of the Congress." This was the duty of each Communist and each
Party organization. "Furthermore, we do not formulate any binding resolutions, do
not speak in the name of the University, but only prepare meetings where students
can determine their opinion of events in Moscow by themselves." In its own terms,
then, the initiative group not only acted in the spirit of Party democracy, but actually promoted democracy by inviting the rank and file to participate in the political
process.[187]

In the face of vociferous protests, the initiative group convened the Party meeting it so desperately desired on December 31. According to Moscow's spokesmen, 323 students were in attendance, constituting about half of the student body.
Kornilov, from the Sverdlov Communist University, was a watchful eye for the
Central Committee. When Rybin declared that the meeting was "unauthorized"
(*ne pravomochno*) he was met with deafening noise and shouts of "clear out!" and
barely managed to finish his statement. Increasingly confident about his authority, Anfalov, a member of the meeting's presidium, asked for silence. "The initiative
group is perfectly able to rebuff Rybin by itself," he said, trying to calm his overea-
ger supporters.

"This meeting is illegal," Rybin continued to protest. "First, with so many students on vacation, there is clearly no quorum here. Second, the meeting is sponsored by the so-called initiative group. Could anyone tell me what the hell this is?!"

After several exchanges, Minin urged those who thought like him to leave the hall. "Disgrace! Disgrace!" his supporters heard as they filed out. While the Zinovievists claimed that 106 students followed the rector, the Stalinist sources scaled the number down to "39 at most."[188]

The fact that the initiative group reported on these dramatic events in a memorandum sent directly to the Central Control Commission in Moscow shows that the Leningrad apparatus was still very much in Zinoviev's hands. The memorandum was suffused with irony.

The brave protectors of the Leningrad delegation rose and staged a flashy exit. Positioning himself at the rostrum's corner, Minin turned toward the meeting's chairman and began moving his arms. With the airs of someone set out to commit a great exploit, this magnanimous hero gestured toward students who were saying good-byes, apparently with the intention of emphasizing that the unalloyed remained loyal to him. We were told that Minin convened his supporters in an adjacent room. Making a speech there, he called us "self-seekers" and added other improper imprecations.

While the pretentious rector was "swearing," "posing," and degrading himself in every imaginable way, the initiative group, according to its own account, retained the high moral ground: "We branded Minin's behavior as 'dishonorable.'"[189]

With the Zinovievists out of sight, the field was finally clear for the castigation of the old leadership. "Allow me to say a few words about the 'alien' [*potustoronnie*] bureau," Borovkov sarcastically commented. "It has much powder, but no real bullets."

Anfalov also sought to call things by their real name: "The demonstrative departure of some students should be appraised as an effort to debunk this meeting. An attempt is made here to prevent us from expressing our true opinion regarding the conduct of our delegation at the Congress. Hiding behind our old resolutions, the bureau simply wants to help the opposition." Anfalov insisted that "the present meeting is perfectly legal. . . . Yes, many students are away, but this does not mean we must cease functioning as a legitimate collective. The trouble is that Rybin could not care less about what students really think."[190]

Zhuk joined in the effort to show that the initiative group did not violate regulations: "The new opposition will not succeed in throwing sand in our eyes: we just saw how out of touch the bigwigs are. We will force our oppositionists to show their true face. . . . Minin's and Rybin's actions deserve no better name but 'cheap politicking.' It is not we who initiate a factionalist struggle. We only protest against the methods of those who embarked on a divisive course of action at the Congress."[191]

Now that the meeting had legitimized itself, Sten outlined its agenda. "Our main task today is to explain the political line of the Central Committee to the masses." Heretofore an oddity in the university, the Moscow view of things was now presented by Zorin for judgment by the students. "The Congress began in a difficult atmosphere: delegates were caught unawares of the attitudes the Leningrad delegation brought with it. Judging by the resolutions of our district and provincial Party conferences the delegation was supposed to go shoulder to shoulder with the Central Committee. Of course, other sources indicated that subversive efforts were under way." Zorin recounted to the audience how Stalin offered compromises, but that factions nevertheless insisted on dividing opinion. "The build-up to Zinoviev's co-report was enormous, but what he actually said revealed the political impotence of the opposition."

According to Zorin, the new opposition had been so scatterbrained that it did not even manage to speak in one voice: "Krupskaia declared that NEP put shackles on our proletarian government. Sokol'nikov went further, calling our government state capitalism. And Zinoviev made baseless charges that there are comrades who believe that the present economic order is a true socialism." The speaker concluded that Zinoviev and Kamenev must be in pursuit of personal power.

Kamenev went far in revealing the true intentions of the opposition when he denounced Stalin. With his demand for a "sovereign Politburo," Sokol'nikov did not lag behind. Mind you, no one restricts the Politburo! Is Kamenev himself not its chairman?! . . . The opposition applies the following syllogism: if the leadership is in the hands of Kamenev and Zinoviev then we have a collective leadership; if Kamenev and Zinoviev are in a minority then we do not have a collective leadership.[192]

And what was the University rector doing when all this nonsense was being spread around? "He was making speeches on Zinoviev's behalf throughout the capital." Having attended one such performance—Minin's appearance at the Skorokhod shoe factory—Agapov, the next speaker, turned him into a butt of ridicule. Instead of withdrawing support from the Leningrad delegation, Minin launched irresponsible criticisms at the organizers of the Fourteenth Party Congress. Agranov was beside himself:

Comrades, we all know how we should treat the Party Congress—Lenin told us that a number of times. And how Minin taught workers to treat the Congress? "You see," he said to the workers, "all types of scandalmongers were invited as guests! Mensheviks and semi-Mensheviks address us from the rostrum. We have to listen to lowbrow intimidations, to grovel before the mighty of this world [read: Stalin]. Disguising its anti-Leninist outbursts with Lenin's name the Congress—so Minin—went dumb [oboldel]."[193]

What Minin had to say about the Central Committee was no better. "The disagreements," he reportedly argued, "began when we, Leningrad Communists, demanded Trotsky's purge. Minin judged him to be a near-Menshevik, and demanded his expulsion from our ranks. Yet, the majority went against us—attacking us because we steadfastly defend the true, Leninist positions." Agapov was outraged by the opinionated rector and his insolence. "Instead of explaining to workers why it makes sense to retain Trotsky in the Party, Minin tells them that Trotsky must be purged, and that the Leningrad delegation alone sticks by this correct demand!" Continuing in this sprit, Minin made the insidious claim that "Moscow is teeming with the old Trotskyists, gossips, careerists, and economic bosses.'" This conduct was "utterly demagogic. Minin's anti-Party behavior must be interpreted as an attempt to take advantage of workers' disgruntlement."[194]

"Shame on him!" pro-Moscow students clamored. The stage was set for Tishkin to draw the obvious conclusions: "In view of the fact that Minin distorted the position of the Congress he lost any authority among us. We must request his demotion as the university rector." The majority decided to "brand Minin with infamy."[195]

Another thirteen students asked for the floor, but "because no one intended to defend the opposition" debates came to an end. Zorin stated in conclusion that "we are temporarily still a minority in Leningrad; the bosses try to intimidate us—note the exit of Minin and others. But comrades, do not fear. Move to the mills and factories and disprove the current one-sided picture of the Congress they made current there."[196]

Voting a lack of confidence in the bureau, the meeting instructed the presidium to prepare a general Party meeting as soon as the vacationing students returned. The resolution echoed the letter of the 116: "We condemn the conduct of our delegation. . . . The statement that the delegates obey Congress's decisions is insufficient: true Leninist unity demands not outward obedience but public recognition of mistakes." Sending greetings to the new editor of *Leningradskaia pravda*, Skvortsov-Stepanov, the majoritarian resolution stressed that "the newspaper should turn itself into a venue explaining the errors of the opposition."[197]

After singing the *Internationale*, the students dispersed and the meeting's secretary, Vavilin, signed the protocol.[198]

December 31 to January 8: The Pendulum Swings Stalin's Way

In Moscow, things were drawing to a close. On December 30–31 a number of Leningrad representatives arrived in the capital to attend the final sessions of the Congress and express their solidarity with the Central Committee majority. Zinoviev's supporters also returned to Congress to participate in elections for the central Party organs, their cohort beefed up with what they described as workers' representatives. Party institutions were crisscrossed with inner tensions. Cleavages in the center played themselves out in Leningrad and vice versa.[199]

When the Congress was officially adjourned late at night on December 31 it was clear who enjoyed the upper hand and who would be paying a political price for intransigence. Five key oppositionists (Zalutskii, Kharitonov, Zorin, Kuklin, and Safarov) failed to be reelected to the Central Committee. Komarov, Lobov, Skvortsov-Stepanov, and Shvernik, Stalin's men in Leningrad, took their place.[200] On January 1 the Central Committee plenary session nominated a new Politburo and secretariat. Zinoviev retained most of his posts for the time being, but Kamenev had to part with his Politburo seat and Sokol'nikov with the commissariate of finances.[201] Evdokimov, the secretary of the Leningrad Party organization for only three months (he replaced Zalutskii in late September), was included in the Central Committee's secretariat. Thus moved from Leningrad to Moscow, he was detached from his source of support.[202] A Central Committee telegram from January 13, 1926, however, remarked that "the group of Party members who were in the opposition should not be deprived of the possibility of participating in responsible Party activity."[203]

The Central Committee plenary session from January 1, 1926, instructed Leningrad to implement the resolutions of the Fourteenth Party Congress to the letter. Issuing a call for the "elucidation of the mistakes committed by the Leningrad delegation," Stalin and Bukharin were poised to go on the offensive. The length and breadth of the Leningrad Party apparatus clung to Zinoviev, however. A substantial part of the opposition's troops mobilized during the January battles in the city would come from the Komsomol; many of its young leaders, among them Rumiantsev, Katalynov, Tolmazov, and Tseitlin, went strongly against the Party secretary.[204] The Zinovievists prepared their own digests of Congress materials (banned by the Central Committee, which claimed it was "the only lawful editor of the official stenographic record") and began preparations for an extraordinary Provincial Party Conference where they expected the Leningrad Party organization to support their unyielding stance.

The Zinovievists' trump card was control of the Leningrad Party apparatus.[205] Essentially dethroned, the bureau of the Communist University Party organization sought support from the leadership of the Central Party District. Having complained on January 2 that he was losing control over the students, Rybin got the resolution he wanted: Toivo, secretary of the district committee, declared that members of initiative groups were "violators of Party regulations." What about the demand, repeatedly voiced by the initiative group, to have fresh elections to the University Party bureau? Here, too, Toivo gave Rybin firm backing: "It is inadmissible to conduct elections without our sanction," he stated. "We are not some 'faction' or some 'opposition' but the official Party committee of the Central District."[206]

Toivo instructed his organizational department to collect materials concerning the anti-Party activity of the initiative group and to transfer its findings to the Leningrad control commission.[207] In its January 14 session this body discussed "the case of Zhuk, Borovkov, Anfalov, Zudov, and Vavilin," accused of acting against the advice of the bureau of their Party collective, and issued them a "warning."[208] Moscow called these measures against the initiative groups "persecution" and "oppression," and Molotov charged that the Leningrad control commission was resorting to "undignified, bureaucratic pestering of comrades."[209] On February 18, 1926, the Leningrad control commission was to annul the censure of the new leadership of the Communist University and rule that creation of the "initiative group" was expedient, a reversal made possible due to the reelection of the commission's membership on January 20.[210] In the meantime, the heavily pro-Stalin Northwestern Party bureau collected materials concerning "violation of Party democracy in Leningrad" on the part of the Zinovievists, turning them over to the Central Control Commission.[211]

During the afternoon hours of January 4, the bureau of the Leningrad provincial Party committee met to discuss the working through of the Congress resolutions. In normal times, this was a standard campaign involving a report on the proceedings and elucidations of the principal decisions.[212] The secretary of the bureau, Kuklin, a staunch Zinovievist, chaired the meeting. "The situation here," he commented, "is highly abnormal. Protocols of the speeches of Stalin, Bukharin, and Molotov are distributed illegally." Kuklin demanded strict censure of unsupervised propaganda operations. His nemesis on the bureau, Komarov, a Moscow supporter, retorted: "Whatever repressive steps you take, comrades will always find ways to express their criticism of the opposition."[213] In command of a clear majority and eager to present the center with accomplished facts, the Zinovievists declared that the plenary session of the Leningrad provincial committee would open within half an hour despite Komarov's loud remonstrations.

Just as they were heading toward the conference room, a disturbing cable reached Smol'nyi: Stalin notified Leningrad that official reporters on behalf of the Central Committee were making their way to the city. This included Kalinin, Molotov, Tomskii, Kirov, and others. "Surely, the plenary session can be postponed until their arrival tomorrow." But Stalin's men had an uphill battle. Anti-Muscovite sentiment was running high and facts had to be established on the ground as fast as possible. The plenary session of the Leningrad provincial Party committee adopted a controversial resolution to the effect that, "In view of the official termination of the discussion, all attacks on the Leningrad delegation must end. . . . We cannot turn a blind eye to the fact that a group of comrades created a parallel provincial Party committee in Leningrad, convening their own meetings, distributing their own literature, creating so-called initiative groups. The unity of the Leningrad Party organization is threatened not by disagreements at the congress . . . but by disorganizing activities that . . . undermine elementary discipline."[214]

Moscow's rebuttal was swift. On the morning of January 5 Stalin's second cable arrived. Stalin was in a rage: "The Leningrad provincial committee erred in refusing to postpone its plenary session by one day. Its demand not to criticize the Leningrad delegation . . . does not accord with the Central Committee's resolution from January 1." Stalin insisted that provincial Party committees do not have the right to dictate to the rank and file. "Party collectives must be allowed to put forward their own resolutions." The Leningrad newspapers were instructed to publish all grassroots resolution proposals, "except those that contain elements of insubordination toward the Congress."[215]

The contest over the makeup of the Leningrad Party secretariat was a decisive test of force. Determined to find a replacement for Evdokimov, the first secretary of the Leningrad Party organization, without Moscow's intrusion, the bureau suggested to the plenary session of the Leningrad provincial committee the candidacy of Badaev (January 4). But twenty minutes before the plenary session started, the aforementioned cable signed by Stalin, the general secretary of the Party and, as such, the master of ceremonies, demanded that, in addition to Evdokimov, Kuklin must also be replaced. (The official reason for this demand was that "Kuklin has just lost his position on the Central Committee," though the Zinovievists immediately pointed out that no regulation stipulated that a member of a provincial Party committee bureau must also be a Central Committee member.) This meant that two out of three Leningrad Party secretaries were to be replaced, a move that presented Zinoviev with the prospect of losing control over his Party organization.

Composition of the Leningrad Party secretariat became the subject of urgent deliberations at yet another extraordinary meeting of the bureau of the Leningrad provincial Party committee held on January 5 and attended by Safarov, Sarkis, Minin, and other Zinoviev enthusiasts. Leningrad's hopes to settle the issue before Stalin's emissaries appeared were foiled: Tomskii, Molotov, Kirov, and Andreev had arrived on the morning train and were already in attendance. Deliberations lasted all night but no compromise was achieved. Zinoviev still enjoyed a comfortable majority. The proposal to include Kirov, Komarov, and Badaev (the first two being Stalinists) in the secretariat obtained only four votes. The competing slot, listing the names of Badaev, Kuklin, and Shvernik (the first two being Zinovievists) won the support of thirteen votes (a clear majority).[216] Casting all decorum aside, the Central Committee moved to reshuffle the entire Leningrad secretariat, which had been elected only three week earlier, as it pleased. Kirov replaced Evdokimov as the first secretary of the Leningrad provincial Party committee and Komarov replaced Kuklin as the head of its organizational department.[217] A few days later, the plenary session of the Leningrad provincial Party committee voiced objections to Moscow's coup. "Nomination of Komarov for the secretariat against our will cannot add to the unity of the Leningrad Party organization." Ninety were in favor of this resolution, twenty against. But the Central Committee remained steadfast, and Stalin's nominees emerged as the undisputed heads of the Leningrad Party organization.[218]

Moscow was determined to clear a legal pathway for the activity of its supporters. When the bureau of the Leningrad provincial Party committee urged the grass roots on January 7 to ignore the instructions of Stalin's emissaries, the Central Committee struck back.[219] Kirov, Shvernik, and Skvortsov-Stepanov conferred by phone with the members of the Northwestern Party bureau and agreed by 2 a.m. that night on a document entitled "Some Clarification Regarding Intra-Party Democracy."[220] The right of Party members to convene Party meetings "even without the permission of the district committee" was reaffirmed, and initiative groups were de facto legitimized.[221] In answer to a query asking whether elections of Party bureaus are valid if they were not initiated by the superior Party organs, Kirov pronounced: "A plenary session of any collective can decide on reelection if it believes that its bureau does not reflect the attitudes of the rank and file."[222]

The Central Committee insisted that the Party must speak in one voice, its own. Toivo and the Central District received instructions to lift the ban on criticisms of the Leningrad delegation and allow distribution of Stalin's report at the Congress. "What Does Democracy Stand For?" Ivan Skvortsov-Stepanov's editorial asked on January 7. "Repeating a thousand times that they submit to the authority of the Congress, the opposition fakes naiveté and says, 'What else do you want from us?' Well, plenty! The acceptance of the decisions of the Congress will not be conscious . . . unless the rank and file understand how it came about that Red Leningrad ended up with an oppositionist representation at the Congress." An earlier editorial proclaimed: "Leningrad workers must find out the truth, the entire truth, about the new opposition."[223]

Workers were doing so, and at a rapid pace. On January 7–8, the decisions of the Fourteenth Party Congress were ratified by twenty Party organizations at the Central District alone.[224] Molotov boasted of the success of Moscow's tactics: "When we got to Leningrad we found out that the bureau of the provincial Party committee decided to convene a meeting of the local leading cadres. It was there that we were supposed to deliver our main report."[225] Voroshilov picks up the story in his letter to Ordzhonikidze: "The local chiefs were ready to surprise us at the leadership meeting, but we went to the factories and mills first. The troublemakers were trashed before they had time to recover. . . . Our success is not really surprising: we realized that, luckily, the opposition attracted only the higher-ups, no more."[226]

Staying first at the Evropeiskaia Hotel, the Central Committee emissaries soon moved to Smol'nyi, which symbolized their transformation from a conquering force to the legitimate rulers of the city. Ignoring local functionaries, they won over more and more rank-and-file support. "The district committee turned itself into the house for groupings," a typical voice at the Electropower factory stated. "One can find anything there, except normal Party activity."[227] One after another, Party organizations declared their unwillingness to remain affiliated with their (Zinovievist) committees and petitioned to be subsumed under the jurisdiction of the (pro-Stalin) Northwestern Party bureau.[228] Organizing their supporters from the bottom up, Moscow legates created a structure mirroring the official Leningrad Party organization. Leningrad was divided into a number of counties and an ad hoc administrative map of the city was created in the process. Co-reporters were sent to each district committee, and close links were maintained with Moscow loyalists in the Party collectives.[229]

The battle over control of the Leningrad Party apparatus transcends issues of routine politics. Rather than view such battles as fulcrums in the leveling of blind power, the institutions that took part are better understood as embodied discursive formations. Competing organs—the Central Committee versus the Leningrad Party committee, the official Party bureaus versus the initiative groups—all claimed to be representative. The various administrative bodies were doing their best to enforce on the Leningrad Party rank and file their own specific interpretation of the Party hierarchy. Whereas Moscow wanted all power to be absorbed into the vortex, and thus pressed for full submission to the Central Committee, Zinoviev's apparatus defended the autonomy of "one of the most distinguished Party organizations"—Leningrad's.

Legitimacy depended on what branch of the Party invested this or that body with authority and what aspect of the official language this body emphasized. The "Northwestern Party bureau," for example, was a meaningful institution with a right to intervene in Leningrad affairs since the Bolsheviks assumed that regional Party organizations must coordinate their work with the national center. By contrast, the talk about the "legally elected Leningrad Party secretariat," or "legally elected district committees" suggests that the Zinovievists justified themselves in terms of locally based support. If Stalin was torn between the imperative to assert the prerogative of the center and the respect he owed the Leningrad dignitaries, who had proved themselves so valuable in the recent battles with Trotsky, Zinoviev's stand was no less contradictory. Making claims at the Congress in the name of universal revolutionary truth, even when he was in the minority, he denied minority rights to his rivals in Leningrad.

Having just delivered the political report at the Congress, some saw Stalin as embodying the Party. According to others, Zinoviev was the first Bolshevik among equals, since he was the head of the Komintern. The discourse of official legitimization was multifaceted enough to be used to opposite effect. Whether at the level of a primary Party organization or at the level of the provincial Party committee, speakers jockeying for position employed a rhetoric that highlighted their assumptions regarding proper procedure. According to Zinoviev's supporters, only Leningrad Communists could enroll in the presidiums of key Party meetings. Everything else would be an imposition from above and a violation of Party democracy.

According to Stalin's supporters, only comrades who embraced the resolutions of the Congress could direct Party life. Everything else would be a violation of Lenin's centralism.

Because neither side wished to yield any part of the Bolshevik vocabulary to the other, this rhetorical dichotomy was also sometimes inverted: the Stalinists claimed that the Zinovievists never bothered to find out what the Leningrad rank and file really thought and thus were authoritarian themselves; the Zinovievists claimed that their Party organization, which was generally considered to be more proletarian than its Moscow counterpart, deserved the mantle of the vanguard of Bolshevik consciousness. In this scenario, the real center of the Party had to be in Leningrad, not Moscow, and the Soviet government's move south, carried out by Lenin seven years earlier in the face of the advancing German army, was only temporary. If Moscow prided itself on being the home of the Central Committee, which was the heart and mind of the proletariat, Leningrad saw itself as the cradle of the revolution.

January 9–21: The Takeover Is Complete

The growing legitimacy of the Moscow-oriented institutions did not go unnoticed at the Communist University. Stalin's supporters were poised to don the garments of the university Party bureau, if not yet in theory, certainly in practice. The initiative group convened a meeting of the presidiums of the circles on January 9 to discuss candidates for the new leadership. A short debate took place over the question of who should open the proceedings. Since the official Party secretaries refused to renounce Zinoviev, their names were set aside—a clear sign that the pressure of the center was bearing political fruit. On the semantic level, the Zinovievists were not doing much better. Increasingly described as "oppositionists," their own attempt to identify their rivals as Trotskyists did not stick.[230]

Functioning as an ad hoc Party secretary, Zudov delivered the opening report. "Our work is being obstructed by a loud oppositionist cohort," he said. "The Party secretary no longer expresses the real position of the bureau: a number of bureau members admitted their mistakes, others resigned, and there are those who have just returned to Leningrad and we do not know what their actual position is. It follows that the work against the opposition in our organization was conducted by [what can be described as a de facto] bureau majority." The awkward title, "initiative group," could now be safely discarded.[231]

Suddenly, Minin, Rybin, and Ivanov stormed in. Minin reminded students and staff that he was still their rector. "I deem myself in charge here by virtue of the authority vested in me by the Central Committee and the Leningrad Provincial Committee. How is it that despite my position as the head of the academic program and the administrative owner of the university building, no one asked me for permission to convene this extraordinary meeting?" The majoritarian rejoinder was instantaneous: "An owner who does not know what is happening in his domain is a bad owner indeed; besides, when given the chance to speak all you do is abuse our time making all sorts of accusations."[232]

A rhetorical duel around the subject of authority and legitimacy took another turn, this time with Minin protesting Zudov's effrontery. "Though you disgrace me in every way, infamy will not stick to my name. You point fingers at me in a million copies of the national newspaper and today you give me just fifteen minutes to defend myself—surely, you must be doing that because you realize that you dug yourself into a hole (*popal v prosak*)!" Ideological credibility was measured in the ability to count: "You state in the press that 35 comrades left the hall with me, but I counted 106 comrades leaving. You must hate arithmetic! You better study arithmetic first and only then move to politics—politics is the algebra of Revolution!"

Bobrikov thundered back: "About arithmetic Minin is mistaken yet again: our last meeting was attended by the majority of students." The audience applauded. In retreat and losing supporters by the minute, the Zinovievist university leadership was fighting a desperate rearguard battle.

Almost the entire Party organization of 605 students was present during the bureau elections in the Communist University two days later. Powerless to influence the meeting's presidium and get a proper hearing, Minin turned to sentiment: "Not to allow me to voice my grievances—this is no way to have an argument among Bolsheviks! Just because you reneged on your views does not mean that our delegation should have also been disloyal to the decisions of the Twenty-second Leningrad Party Conference."

Ivanov also refused to back off: "Though you decided I am an oppositionist, . . . I state openly here that the decisions of the Congress are obligatory to all of us. It was the initiative group that drafted a letter in hiding. When you say that I used physical power in confiscating it, you lie!"

Rybin also portrayed the Zinovievists as the legitimate side in the controversy. "The minority has a perfect right to express its point of view at the Congress: there is no crime in that! We are not against the distribution of the Congress material in principle, but we are against the way it is being done here. It is impermissible that, circumventing the district committee and the bureau, a GPU organizer would bring a truckload of literature to the Khalturin factory, for example." The leading newspapers refused to give Rybin a voice. "We wrote a letter protesting the improper convocation of students on December 31—can a Party meeting be legal when only 236 comrades out of 726 participate?!—but *Pravda* declined to publish."

Still the secretary of the university Party organization at least in theory, Rybin flatly refused to follow standard procedure and present an official summary of the bureau's activity in recent weeks. Like Minin, he employed the language of honor: "I have no intention of doing so in view of the distrust you expressed toward me during the recent Party meetings: you covered me with disgrace and you must remove the stigma if you want me to resume my duties."

But Rybin was clearly on his way out. With the shadow bureau taking more and more official responsibilities, Borovkov accused him of "blatant factionalism" and offered a detailed report of his own "about the work of the initiative group." The old bureau was entirely delegitimized. "We still did not hear our leadership state plainly that the resolutions of the Congress are correct," Anfalov remarked. "Is this a normal state of things in a high Party school?! I believe that we, the bureau minority, were correct throughout and that comrades will approve of our activity." Zhuk took on the entire university leadership, name by name:

Ivanov claims he is not an oppositionist; facts, however, tell a different story: it is he who bars our way to the Red Putilov [factory] and boasts about that. "You guys enjoy success in student collectives," he tells us, "but just go to the factory and you will be whistled down." Is this what is called, in Ivanov's language, "implementing the decision of the Congress?"

Rybin is offended that we do not let him speak. Yet it is the same Rybin who takes the liberty of ignoring the decisions of our Party meeting. His present refusal to report to his electorate proves how the principles of Party democracy refract in his mind. Rybin thinks that he can ignore comrades' will, but when comrades ignore him, this, you see, is "improper Bolshevik behavior."

Minin states that they, not us, are loyal to the official resolutions of the Twenty-second Leningrad Party Conference. How is it, then, that we do not recall any resolution stating that our Party organization objects to the line of the Central Committee? Minin does not dare to openly state that he opposes the Central Committee because he knows very well that its authority is unassailable!

Deciding the line of the bureau to be "deeply erroneous" and "clearly factionalist," the meeting declared that the work carried out by the initiative group "must be applauded. It reflected the view of the majority of the students." With only twenty-one dissenting votes, the meeting resolved to reprimand Minin and Rybin for their dismal behavior.[233]

Finally, the university Party organization turned to elect a new bureau. The results, achieved through a vote by show of hands, were predictable: the leaders of the initiative group were elected while Zinoviev's supporters were severely beaten. Minin, for example, received only five votes in his favor, against forty that wanted to see him out of office (January 11, 1926).[234]

In one last, desperate countermove, the old university Party bureau, the only legitimate one in the eyes of Toivo and the local apparatus, declared the results of the elections null and void and again urged the initiative group to come to its senses and disperse. Two members of the Leningrad Party committee who were in the hall endorsed this demand. While the Zinovievist hold over the university was slipping, their control over local control commission made it possible for them to threaten organizational sanctions up to a purge.

But, given the changing political atmosphere in Leningrad, these threats were empty. On the next day, the new, pro-Stalin university leadership convened yet another general Party meeting, this time having an especially high profile: Molotov, the secretary of the Central Committee, attended and was incorporated into the meeting's presidium as a honorary member.[235] The Communist University was clearly recognized as one of the keys to the city: Zinoviev, Zalutskii, Evdokimov, and other leading Bolsheviks addressed its students at one point or another during the intra-Party debates of the mid-1920s. Yet, if heretofore the main report was always delivered by a Leningrad luminary, the January 12 event was held in the shadow of Moscow's takeover. An outsider delivered the official report on the Fourteenth Party Congress.

The first thing Molotov sought to establish was that Zinoviev, the vanquisher of Trotsky and the symbol of orthodoxy in the eyes of so many Leningrad Communists, had switched sides and become an oppositionist himself. "The fact that a Politburo member insisted on a co-report on the political line suggests a new opposition has been formed."

Highbrow and dully theoretical, the bulk of his address was well attuned to the ears of the future Party propagandists. Assessing the internal and external situation of the Soviet Union, Molotov elucidated the controversy.

Following the stabilization of capitalism in the West what are the chances for building socialism in one country? We had disagreements in the Politburo on this cardinal question. Kamenev and Zinoviev denied socialism is feasible due to the technological backwardness of our economy. . . . Questions regarding cooperation, industry, and state capitalism were examined through this lens. Kamenev, and even more so Zalutskii, tried to subsume our state industry under the rubric of "state capitalism"—but the Central Committee was able to prove them as wrongly relying on Lenin. With private owners gone, with exploiters gone, our state industry cannot be considered capitalist.[236]

Molotov dismissed the opposition's pessimistic class analysis. "Under close scrutiny, Sarkis's famous proposition that 90 percent of the Party should consist of workers from the bench is nonsense, a case of 'Aksel'rodovshchina'"—a reference to the prerevolutionary attempt by a Menshevik leader, Pavel Aksel'rod, to create a party not only for the working class but also of the working class, and convene a Social-Democratic Conference exclusively based on factory delegates. The reporter concluded with a condemnation of the "violation of Party unity by Leningrad" and a demand for the immediate reelection of the Leningrad Party committee. "No longer expressing the comrades' will," Zinoviev's nominees had to go—this was Stalin's agenda and the intended outcome of Molotov's embassy to Leningrad.

Still vocal, Zinoviev's supporters besieged the reporter from all sides. Tuntul charged against Moscow's authoritarianism: "It is impermissible to set up two city committees in the same Party organization. The methods employed against the minority—selection of hearsay statements drawn from intercepted documents—must also be condemned." "Tell me, Molotov," Govokov carried on the assault, "should the majority not try to change our minds instead of demanding that we publicly recant?" Ivanov allowed himself a quibble: "You are in the majority now—so what are you afraid of? Why do you not let us speak freely? Molotov, do you really think that creating 'initiative groups' and ignoring official bureaus is fair? Is that how you want to contribute to Party unity?"

Or consider the sharp and biting quality of Rybin's diatribe: "the present hunt on the Leningrad Party organization is absolutely impermissible. What do we learn from the fact that during the New Course Discussion university collectives supported Trotsky and now they are the first to [switch sides and] support Moscow? What do we learn from the fact that the Red Putilov and other large factories do the opposite and support us?"

The new bureau rushed to Molotov's rescue. "There is nothing I am more proud of than my contribution to the creation of the initiative group," Anfalov stated. Under the circumstances, he had no choice but to seek original ways to enlighten students. "Do Tuntul or Rybin recall a period in the history of our Party when delegates were not allowed to distribute the congress bulletins here in Leningrad?!"[237] "Perhaps the most characteristics feature of the new opposition," Goldenberg followed suit, "is its hypocrisy. Note what the opposition does at the grassroots level: in the Moscow-Narva district, for example, Party schools are not supposed to function between January 8 and January 15," lest issues will be vented out and the opposition exposed. "The Party can forgive theoretical mistakes, but not such unprecedented mouth shutting."[238]

Only nine lone votes were cast against Molotov's resolution—clearly Zinoviev's generals had little army left. "We hereby affirm that the Fourteenth Party Congress worked in a true, Leninist spirit," the university resolution stated. "In presenting a co-report the new opposition displayed its opportunism, defeatism . . . and additional perversions of Leninism." The methods by which Stalin seized Leningrad were fully legitimized: "We approve the resolution adopted by the students who remained at the meeting of December 31 [organized by the initiative group]." The meeting concluded with, "Long live the Leninist staff of the Central Committee elected by the Fourteenth Party Congress!"

Caught between the pressure of Moscow and student rebellion, the university leadership was crushed. Two parallel organizational structures, two parallel sources of legitimacy, two competing narratives—this was no more. The university keys were officially handed to Stalin's men on January 13: Brunin became the new secretary of the Party organization and Zhuk the plenipotentiary of the control commission.[239] The university bureau selected a list of thirty-nine delegates—all Moscow supporters—to the Seventh Extraordinary Conference of the Central District (February 5–6).[240] Those were already fighting for the university's good name: "Though some castigate us as oppositionists, we reject this brand of shame. True, there are in our collective about forty comrades who support the minority position, but our entire collective should not be judged negatively on their account. We will not bear responsibility for isolated individuals!"[241]

The ground was ready for the removal of Toivo and the Zinovievist apparatus of the Central District. Local activists wrote to Petrovskii, one of Stalin's emissaries, on January 14: "This is not the time to sleep. . . . The opposition must be banished."[242] When the plenary session of the Central District Party committee met on January 18, Molotov's "organizational conclusions" indeed topped the agenda: "we must stuff our leading organs in such a way that the barriers . . . separating leaders and rank and file disappear."[243] Speakers took Toivo to task for doing exactly the opposite. One of them recalled his "dictatorial manners: 'You would vote exactly as I tell you,' you said to Antonov, who objected to the resolutions of the Twenty-second Conference."[244]

Toivo was bad enough, but he was only the tip of the iceberg. "Unhealthy phenomena are all around us," others droned on. "Our leaders are ailing, having no idea how to deal with NEP."[245] The plenary session of the Central Party District officially disowned the Leningrad delegation to the Party congress (forty-one votes against twenty-two) and removed the Party bureau that supported it.[246] The sporadic Zinovievist voices who dared to hold ground risked everything: they entered the books as "unrepentant" (neotoshedshie).[247] (Dug up during the Great Purge with deadly consequences, this list included forty-four names of Communist University students.)[248]

Taking over the large Leningrad factories required additional effort.[249] Kirov wrote to Ordzhonikidze in a letter from January 10: "We were received here not too well, especially as we immediately went to the large factories and began trying to turn collectives around. . . . The atmosphere is heated, we must do lots of screeching and yelling."[250] On January 16, Kirov wrote to the same addressee: "I do not remember such Party meetings since the revolutionary days. Who could imagine: fistfights erupt here and there—I am not exaggerating. . . . We have been making speeches for two weeks now saying pretty much the same thing. My head spins."[251] On January 17 Stalin was triumphant: "All important factories in the city said their word against the opposition," he informed his colleagues. "The Red Putilov remains alone. . . . Things went better than one could imagine."[252]

The Red Putilov factory was indeed Zinoviev's last bastion. Party workers in the plant claimed that "for any conference or congress we elect reliable people, not idiots. Likewise, for the Fourteenth Party Congress we selected comrades we trust, some of the best, and it is wrong to hurl accusations at our delegation. If our delegates are guilty then we are guilty too."[253] Minin was spending more and more time in Red Putilov, less and less in the university, where he realized his case was lost.[254] "Our stronghold and pride" remained loyal to the Leningrad delegation, the frustrated rector told students who stayed with him, implying that Stalin's triumph in the Communist University was obtained on the strength of petit bourgeois sentiment. The majoritarians saw things differently. "We were shut out from the Red Putilov," they complained, "only because we had congress bulletins in our hands. Others, who supported the opposition, were told, 'Sure, Welcome!'"[255] In this scenario, these were students who clung to Zinoviev, while workers clearly preferred the Central Committee. "Students and Red professors," Moscow grumbled, "agitate against the Leningrad Party committee, inflaming differences of opinion."[256]

Violence was in the air. Having heard that in the Tobacco Factory the Zinovievists tore down the door of the shop where an initiative group was holding a meeting and hit its leader, Turovskii, with the butt of a revolver, Stalin's supporters at Red Putilov asked for weapons of self-defense. "We fear that we will be shot from a blind corner," they noted.[257] Weapons or no weapons, Minin's workers could not withstand political pressure for much longer. Rumors that authorities decided to cut off electricity to the factory were disturbing.[258] Besides, Stalin's propaganda machine had the GPU muscle at its disposal: vans drove though the factory premises at full speed and dropped loads of pro-Moscow material.[259]

On Kirov's insistence, the decisive factory meeting was convened on January 20; up to 2,000 members were in attendance. The presidium was mixed: Kalinin and Voroshilov, the chairman of the Supreme Soviet and the war commissar respectively, represented the Central Committee. Minin and Kuklin spoke for Zinoviev. Judging by the Party protocols, however, words were not the main weapons. Kirov replaced the guards with men on the payroll of the Party apparatus, who were supposed to push back individuals without passes from the Leningrad secretariat "so that there will be no sabotage." Using a battering ram, the Zinovievist managed to break the factory wall and admit a few hundred Komsomol members who interrupted "this illegal meeting." Eventually, however, even here things did not go Minin's way: the Central Committee won the floor and the vote.[260]

Zinoviev's best protected nests, the Moscow-Narva and the Vasilevsk Island Party committees, proved impossible to take from below. Resorting to direct administrative action, Kirov replaced the secretaries of these organizations in a top-down action on January 21. The new bureaus did not enjoy grass-roots confidence—even Moscow supporters had to admit this was a violation of Party democracy, "albeit one necessitated by extraordinary circumstances."[261] "It is obvious that the contending sides do not have the same rights, that the contest is uneven,"

Bukharin admitted. "But the entire situation is abnormal: it never happened in history that the largest Party organization went against resolutions adopted by the Party congress."[262]

Despite residual resistance, Stalin's men managed to convene an extraordinary Twenty-third Leningrad provincial Party conference (early February).[263] Molotov summarized the results of the discussion in Leningrad: 60,228 Party members approved the resolutions of the Fourteenth Party Congress: 96 percent of the participants.[264] He admitted, though, that "the decisive break with the opposition happened only recently." Another unsettling fact was that "among the 2,244 supporters of the opposition there is a large percentage of top-ranking Party functionaries."[265] "Having lost the party ground underneath their feet" they "got confused" on a number of cardinal questions.[266]

"With the voice of what social groups does the opposition speak?" Molotov wondered aloud. "We have capitalist elements growing (in absolute terms, of course, not in relative terms) . . . and they influence certain parts of our Party."[267] According to the Central Committee, the rank-and-file Leningrad Communists were naive, even gullible; most of them joined the opposition under "psycho-moral pressure."[268] But recovery was quick. "Elementary access to information revived the proletarian bent of the Leningrad organization." In any case, according to Molotov, the naive workers of Leningrad were led into sin by the local leadership, which manipulatively "imposed its will on the Party masses."[269]

Though someone like Safarov tried to joke that this was the "bad pastors theory," humor was a weapon mainly in the loyalists' hands. Hilarity and laughter still pervaded Party meetings, but they covered less and less the menacing implications of the official speech. With the victory of the Central Committee becoming apparent, metaphors became more and more threatening, more and more sanguine, though they did not yet lose their function as figures of speech.

In his remarks as keynote speaker at the Eleventh Extraordinary Vyborg Party Conference held in late January 1926, Bukharin made a number of jokes at the expense of the opposition. "When we talk about the imperialist war," he noted early on, "it is really not essential that we know which side initiated hostilities"—after all, there were voracious capitalists on both sides of the barricade. But the recent Party disagreement was "no imperialist war, so it was important to establish the identity of the aggressor and the defender. In this case, a chronological investigation, determining who said 'A' first and who answered with 'B,' is not superfluous [Laughter]."[270] It would be a mistake to linger over Bukharin's insinuations that the opposition opened war against the Central Committee, though they were probably the cause of the giggles in the audience. If there had been a quarrel, it was a family affair. Both sides were now embracing and recalling with relief and amusement each other's offensive words.

This was all the more reason for Bukharin to scorn the local Party organization as hysterical. The opposition appeared to agree that the Soviet Union must build socialism on its own, but this forecast somehow "will not be valid if capitalists tickle us to death with their bayonets." The audience laughed again and the speaker stepped up his ridicule. "If we cannot impede foreign intervention [so the opposition says] there is no guarantee that we will not find ourselves hanging from telegraph poles for a few days. [Laughter.]"[271] Worries about the isolation of the proletarian dictatorship were so exaggerated that Bukharin's jocular recapitulation of its apocalyptic predictions was only a slight distortion of Zinoviev's utterly serious pronouncements of gloom and doom.

Was Bukharin mocking oppositionists who remained firm in their wrongheaded opinions, or the entire Leningrad Party organization? This ambivalence was deliberate. However tense, the dialogue had to be maintained: humor was used to relieve tensions, not to exacerbate them. To restore a sense of camaraderie, Bukharin invited laughter at his own expense. "I made the following mistake," he confessed: "when formulating my ideas about trade . . ., I told the peasants, 'Accumulate! Enrich yourselves!'" Now this was the language of a petit bourgeois, but who in his right mind would have taken Bukharin literally? Indeed, laughter sounded again. Bukharin was the first to admit that his choice of words was silly. "'Enrich yourself' doesn't smell good, and various parties capitalized on my words. . . . Generally, my ideas were correct, but in using this unfortunate expression I spoiled a barrel of honey with a spoonful of tar [*lozhkoi degtia isportil bochku meda*]. [Laughter.]"[272] The Zinovievists were invited to enjoy Bukharin's linguistic incontinence. He was not infallible, and one might even get away with calling him a "kulak."

To be sure, Bukharin feigned offense: "The opposition keeps hammering away at the same point. It portrays me as a kulak chief who tried to lure the Party . . . right into the arms of the bourgeoisie. [Laughter.]"[273] The emissary from Moscow seemed to be suggesting that language can trip one up, but when one is among comrades everyone must assume that one means well. His slips of the tongue were funny, that much Bukharin granted. The Central Committee had sent a message: the vanquished Zinovievists could poke fun at the official speaker, trade jokes perhaps, but they could not continue to question official policy.

At times Bukharin was laughing at the opposition; at others he was laughing with it.[274] In Vyborg, he used humor to draw the two sides together. When he spoke to local Communists at the Leningrad Party Organization's Twenty-third Extraordinary Conference a fortnight later, his tone changed somewhat. He still was eliciting giggles, but now his words were more derisive, closer to the sardonic humor of a victor toying with his vanquished rivals.

Yet if Bukharin was to be believed, it was the opposition that suffered from overseriousness. Its overweening pretentiousness had rendered it preposterous. Zinoviev's followers eagerly put forward their learned criticisms but, cowards that they were, could not stand behind their allegations. Consider the note oppositionists sent to the meeting's presidium: "It shows some learning," Bukharin stated contemptuously;

too bad the author is not literate enough to write his signature clearly. [Laughter.] This attests to his enormous erudition and his not-so-enormous courage. Why fear adding one's name to the end of a note that contains nothing criminal, or, more significantly, nothing politically reprehensible? Apparently caution is our comrade's principal virtue. [Laughter.] . . . Only one comrade sent a note expressing misgivings about the official Party line. "I reckon we must apply to him the good Russian aphorism 'Don't hit a man when he's down' [lezhachego ne biut]." [Laughter.][275]

Upset with the opposition's conspiratorial tactics, Bukharin was less forgiving; violence could be read figuratively and trigger snickering in the audience, but here it is difficult to believe Zinoviev's supporters joined in.

In his next philippic, Bukharin cited a classic—the grotesquery constructed around the tension between the enormously solemn (sublime poetry) and the ridiculously low (the opposition's ravings) had a macabre effect. "We had a famous tiff, a spat, and, quoting the words of a poem, we can say of those we argued with, 'Alas, some now are distant / Some are no more [odnikh uzh net, a te daleche].'"[276]

The audience burst into hearty laugher—Bukharin had cited Pushkin (Evgenii Onegin, canto 51), but the world he invoked was not the genteel and polished one of the great poem, much as Bukharin loved, or pretended he loved, his Zinovievist brethren. He evoked the values of Bolshevik camaraderie only to mock them: the time for harsh reprisals against opportunists was fast approaching, and his mention of death indicated that the opposition was on its way to becoming a living corpse.

The Administration of Hermeneutics

In the wake of the Discussion with Leningrad, the Central Committee took further steps toward the delegitimation of the opposition. If two years earlier support of Trotsky could have been considered as an acceptable expression of opinion, now any pro-Zinoviev sentiment was regarded as a breach of discipline.

The fact that recalcitrant students were barred from propaganda activity was a telltale sign that opposition came to be perceived as a dangerous doctrine, hence the urgency with which the new Party bureau of the Communist University stripped Zinovievists of their teaching positions. On January 20, the four heads of specialists' seminars, Kofman, Pavlova, Minikainen, and Tuzhilkin, were sacked.[277] Ivanov was released from his duties four days earlier—a glorious career came to an infamous end.[278] Taking care of the bigger fish, the Central Control Commission examined the "Case of the Grouping in Leningrad Party organization (Safarov, Toivo, and others)," and the "Case of the Moscow-Narva District Committee (Sarkis and others)," and censored a number of Leningrad apparatchiks. Only one Zinovievist, though—Baranov—was actually purged; he was guilty of "physical violence."[279]

Blacklisting became an integral part of the work of the Party apparatus in 1926. At the Communist University, the hunt for turncoats cut both ways. For most of January a battle was waged between the 116 students who had signed the letter condemning the Leningrad delegation and the students who had stormed out of the hall in a show of solidarity with the rector. As the war of words escalated, both groups called the other "undisciplined." For a while Stalin's supporters worried that the Zinovievists were "in cahoots with the local control commission." They portrayed Gorgacheev, for example, as a "dangerous type" (*opasnyi tip*), because he was "actively gathering information on us."[280] When the tide began to turn in the middle of January and the heads of the initiative group ceased to be the pursued and became the pursuers, they piled up their own inventory of schismatics. The new bureau called for a "list of oppositionists who made up a faction under the leadership of Minin."[281]

Under the circumstances, the "individual vote" (*poimennoe golosovanie*) that had been taken at the crucial Party meeting of December 31, assumed a remarkable significance—students could now be classified on an individual basis.[282] Voting records from the factories, by contrast, show that workers could still vote by roll call: at the Skorokhod shoe factory supporters of the Central Committee went to one corner of the hall, Zinoviev's supporters to another—a voting procedure that indicates that the Party could live without knowing what was in the heart of each and every worker.[283] If the consciousness of workers could remain unscrutinized at the individual level for a time, since it was certain to mature, thanks to the process of industrial labor, the shortcomings of university students were not likely to be remedied (because of the degenerating nature of academic work) and the Party had to determine what stuff they were made of here and now.

Stalin's apparatus applied increasingly sophisticated means to documenting students' political attitudes. Not that the names of Trotsky's enthusiasts were unknown during the discussions of 1923–1924—we have seen clear evidence to the contrary. But political persuasion, even when publicly known, had not yet become part of the information collected at the bureaucratic level. But in 1926 lists flew to the chancelleries of the Party district committees and the control commissions—tallies of names, Party card numbers, and political labels.

The interest in how each oppositionist came to terms with Zinoviev's defeat points to the hermeneutical agenda behind the list making. An entry in one such list indicated that a certain Vinnikov subscribed to the resolution of the Fourteenth Party Congress, "but deep in his soul he remains distrustful."[284] A "dedicated oppositionist until some time ago," a student named Burakovskii was described as somebody who "had evidently grown pessimistic. He has given up serious studies and spends most of his time playing chess and basketball." Indifferent to his Party duties, a blacksmith-student named Bordon "has become apathetic and slothful [*nepovorotlivyi*]." The peasant-student Pavlov had sunk into a depression: "It is apparent that he is aware of having been beaten during the discussion: hence a certain passivity and less attentiveness in school."[285] Each such entry identified the symptoms exhibited by oppositionists and the mental condition that triggered the symptoms: the repetitive etiologies invited the apparatchiks to participate in the deduction from causes to effects.

In April 1926, Kirov's apparatus asked university authorities to submit supplementary personal evaluations on its personnel. This was not done to classify students in terms of their outward actions, since the identity of all the Zinovievists was well known. The new evaluations tackled deeper questions. Why did students move to the oppositionist camp? Did they fully understand what they were doing? The oppositionism of a student named Depsosnogal'skii, for example, was characterized as an "unconscious mistake." The writer went on to note, "This Bulgarian Communist speaks Russian poorly: when his compatriots explained to him what was what he changed his mind."[286] While a certain Kazina enrolled "out of solidarity," a student named Kotin did the same "out of misunderstanding."[287] "Soft-hearted" (*miagkotelaia*), Smoliak found herself among the heterodex because she obeyed a herd instinct: loyalty to Zinoviev, not deviant consciousness, landed her in the wrong camp. A supporter of the Leningrad delegation due to "the influence of others," Chugin was another schismatic who "has no will of his own. A sop, he embraces the opposition one day, only to abandon it the next." The same, however, could not be said of all students: "It is quite possible that Korotkov entangled himself in the affair quite consciously. Even after the Fourteenth Party Congress, he continues to cling to his opinions."[288]

The Party officialdom was careful not to generalize the oppositionists' personal abilities. If Panchenko was "underdeveloped" and Romanenko "a twaddler," Elagin was a "top-notch fellow" and Maznin "unquestionably talented." Of Bel'kevich it was even said that "he is one of our best students."[289] Ideological acumen was not used as a straightforward hermeneutical criterion. How one used knowledge depended on one's moral inclination: theory could open one's eyes or turn one into an inveterate heretic.

Was there such a thing as an oppositionist self? There are many indications that interest in such typologies picked up in 1926. Of course, most of the Zinovievists had not been even remotely involved with Trotsky two years earlier; the enmity between the two camps was notorious.[290] Still, the university authorities prepared a list of students who had voted for Trotsky in 1923–1924 and checked to see whether any of the new oppositionists had made that earlier error.[291] Although most of the champions of the New Course had graduated, some individual trajectories could be traced. Of a student named Gubanov, for example, a university official wrote, "In 1923 he was a Trotskyist and today he is an ardent oppositionist." Another, named Bordon, "vacillated during the Trotskyist discussion. Now he is vacillating again. This is not a man but a seesaw."[292] The case of a certain Smel', on the other hand, presented stark discontinuity: "Smel' was a Trotskyist, but he opposes the new opposition today."[293]

While the summary drawn up during the New Course Discussion of the fifth circle's reaction to the issues noted that "a student named Savko was a loquacious champion of Party democracy," a note added two years later was designed to protect him. Suchak, the circle's former secretary, wrote at the bottom of the page: "On my instructions, Savko presented a co-report and advanced the point of view of Trotsky and Preobrazhenskii, an attempt to provoke comrades into participating in the discussion. He himself was by no means an oppositionist. April 5, 1926."[294]

Determined to improve their understanding of deviation, the apparatus turned the pursuit of oppositionism into a process of gathering, collating, and naming. Without hermeneutical classifications the university could not assess how its manpower could be deployed. But hermeneutics was seldom easy. How was a wavering student such as Nikonov to be diagnosed? Could he still be a good propagandist? "I doubt that anything good will come of Nikonov," his supervisor reckoned. "He often fails to get to the point and his words are sometimes absurd. Still, my appraisal is not final. Nikonov's teachers are in a better position to evaluate him from all sides—I could be wrong."[295]

Other officials, such as the secretary of circle number ten, did not hesitate to make sweeping judgments.

It is quite difficult to figure out just how steadfast each individual comrade is and what his attitude toward the Central Committee is. Overall, the circle is healthy—except for the five comrades . . . who are threatening us with degeneration. One of them, Seliverstov, confides in me. During a personal conversation he told me more or less the following: "The struggle in the Party is waged solely over portfolios; everything else is a smoke screen." I must also mention Seliverstov's agreement with Zalutskii's criticisms of the workers' living conditions.

In addition, one cannot but note that the circle's presidium member, Dergunov, is hiding his true face: he did not show up for the reading of the Politburo stenograms. He speaks little.

Regarding the two students who were transferred to our circle from other Communist universities—I have not had sufficient time to get acquainted with them. We must make inquires regarding Kuchak at the district committee where he did practical work. When I instructed him to prepare a report for our next meeting he begged off, saying, "I haven't finished my previous obligations."

This is all I can say about the circle. October 13, 1926.[296]

The last thing the new authorities at the Communist University wanted was to be held responsible for infecting the factories under their ideological supervision with wrongheaded propagandists.[297] Kirov's apparatus instructed the Party secretaries to go over the lists of students and establish who could be retained for this sensitive duty and who "must be used elsewhere." In a communication to the Vyborg District Party committee, Brunin highlighted some of his worries regarding students only recently considered "the best of the best in terms of theoretical preparation." The letter began, "Find attached a list of students at the Zinoviev Communist University who were in the opposition during the recent discussion and who will be dispatched to practical activity upon graduation this June." The new head of the Party organization at the Communist University hoped that his flock could be brought to heel if they were made to attend the Party meetings at the shops. Close interaction with the industrial proletariat was certain to rekindle their revolutionary spirit. One Glagolov had wavered "just a bit" during the early days, only to join the majority—he was judged reliable. A certain Ul'ianov also "vacillated at first but soon expressed his ideological solidarity with the Party."[298] While the university bureau did not advise that he be assigned sensitive Party work, he could be used in an administrative capacity.[299] "For the moment," Brunin declared forty students completely unfit for propaganda work: eighteen of them were classified as "ardent oppositionists," thirteen as "oppositionists," five as "vacillators," and four as "renouncers."[300]

Having acted as an oppositionist did not doom a student to excommunication: seventy-three were kept on to do practical work despite their imperfect records. Brunin's memorandum talked about contagion but also about healing. At this stage hermeneutics was used not to condemn souls but to determine how to deploy them best.[301]

If they wanted to clear their names, Zinovievists were advised to recant and submit a "statement of departure from the opposition [*zaiavlenie ob otkhode*]."[302] Usually addressed to the bureau of the Party collective, such recantations eventually landed in the chancellery of the Leningrad provincial committee, turning it into something like an archive of souls.[303] Recantations were drawn up with the gaze of the hermeneutical bureaucracy in mind: authors wanted their names crossed off the official lists of oppositionists.[304] In their recantations, they tried to show that though they might have had "doubts" (*somneniia*) in December, by the time Molotov had completed his work in Leningrad, they had succeeded in fully cleansing themselves of all Zinovievist urges.[305] Leaving the opposition could be described as "disassociating" (*otmezhivatsia*)[306] or "sobering up" (*otrezvliatsia*).[307]

As he tried to establish the state of mind of any given oppositionist, the Party hermeneut regarded recantation as conclusive evidence. Contrition was supposed to manifest itself in a recantation that was more ritualistic than juridical, a beginning of reconciliation rather than an end to investigation. To the Party authorities, confession in the sense of admitting an action was inefficacious; a confession without apparent contrition and an abjuration of oppositionism meant recalcitrance. Kirov's men knew perfectly well that a student's recantation might result from fear or evasion, and that it might consequently lack the genuine change of heart they sought. But the act of writing itself was thought to produce intrinsic modifications in their authors, purifying them and improving their ideological orientation. A willingness to condemn Zinoviev and Kamenev in public and read the right kind of theoretical literature further helped make manifest the confessant's sincerity.

Some recantations were very brief. Here is the entirety of the statement given by a student named Glazkov in early January: "Now that I have examined all the details of the congressional materials I can see that my original position was erroneous." The recantation of another student, Chuchin, was only slightly longer: "I confess to having defended the position of the Leningrad delegation. When I acquainted myself with the congressional materials, I grew convinced that I had made a mistake. I hereby disassociate myself from the opposition."[308] If it was to convince its skeptical readers of the author's remorse, the text had to be absolutely credible. The letter of a student named Vinnikov was judged to be insincere. Although Vinnikov had voted to approve the resolution of the initiative group, the hermeneut concluded that "deep down in his soul he does not trust us."[309]

Recanting students had to prove that they fully understood their crimes and had come to deeply regret them. The reader will recall Golodaev's acrimonious rebuffs of Trotsky during the New Course Discussion. Two years later, Golodaev was still loyal to Zinoviev, but this time his allegiance turned him into an oppositionist. His recantation of January 8, 1926, was especially contrite, the new self edifying the old:

It is futile to deny my mistakes—I want instead to correct them. . . . I hope that with every passing day those who were mistaken will disassociate themselves from the opposition, not just in words but in deeds. . . . Teaching us to look truth in the eye, Lenin said that it was not the one who made mistakes and then admitted them who was wrong, but the one who did not confess them. If I set my hand on my heart and ask myself how oppositionism can be rectified, I am compelled to answer that by denying one's mistakes one aggravates them.[310]

A member of the old bureau named Borovkov also admitted that he had originally sided with the Leningrad delegation. "Not fully, only in part. I was tempted because this was not the attitude of just any Party organization—it was the Leningrad organization." He recognized his error quickly and, a few days after the Fourteenth Party Congress concluded its work, Borovkov provided an account of what had led up to his error: "During the bureau meeting of December 30 I was feverish and flat on my back in bed. When my absentee ballot was cast in favor of the opposition, it was practically an unconscious act. As soon as I recovered, I realized how profoundly wrong I had been."[311]

Borovkov had turned to the solar eclipse line of defense, the only apology in the poetic arsenal that could absolve a repentant Communist. Just as the sun could be obscured by the moon, so even a perfect mind could be tainted by a physical malady. The solar eclipse defense allowed a repentant oppositionist to claim that his lapse had been ephemeral—the sun reemerges after the eclipse just as Borovkov's consciousness recovered once his fever subsided. Guilt depended to a large degree on whether injury had been done "intentionally" or as a result of bodily weakness—character being something natural in this context, more a part of the body than of the mind. If an errant Communist was able to prove that he had beaten back the animalistic forces within him and that his predicament was only temporary, he could hope for forgiveness. Borovkov claimed that he had erred through "thoughtlessness." He had suffered a passing illness and had never seriously considered challenging the Central Committee while well.

Indeed, in 1926, oppositionism was still often medicalized. Take the long and contested meeting of the Skorokhod factory Party organization bureau that took place on January 13 and ended with a split vote. In the "turmoil" (*sumiatitsa*) that followed, a certain Leonova was said to have "lost her nerve" and voted for Zinoviev. Also in a state of a nervous shock, Gubanov, a member of the Leningrad control commission, "smashed the glass set in the door and run out cursing and swearing." He received medical attention and on the next day was sent off to a resort.[312] "Tempted by the provocations of schismatics," female workers at the Red Triangle factory exhibited similar symptoms, going on a "hysterical rampage and hurling insults at those who supported the Central Committee."[313] Those who opposed Moscow's emissaries were depicted in official reports as effeminate, witless oppositionists. When Kalinin arrived at the Egorov car factory "one of the female oppositionists had a hysterical fit and started sobbing and screaming."[314]

Oppositionism appears here as temporary insanity, a certain alienation from the self, a condition very different from the premeditated wickedness it would be recast as in later years. It would take the Discussion with the United Opposition (1926–1927) to begin the gradual transformation of the opposition from a group of mistaken and deluded but forgivable sorts to a threatening conspiracy bent on the downfall of the Bolshevik dictatorship.

CHAPTER 5

FROM A WEAK BODY TO A WICKED MIND

Semantic Battles

In the late 1920s, intra-Party struggle escalated further. The most powerful challenge to Stalin's leadership grew out of the wedding of a pair of former rivals to form the "United Opposition." Despite the claim in January 1926 of Stalin's close ally Kaganovich that "the one who wrote 'Lessons of October' cannot unite with Zinoviev," a Trotskyist-Zinovievist Central Committee had begun to hold meetings.[1] The alliance became public when Trotsky, Zinoviev, and Kamenev openly expressed regrets about past disagreements—this was a joint plenary session convened in July 1926 by the Central Committee and the Central Control Commission.[2] The United Opposition stood for the "restoration of Party democracy" and the "defense of the working class against NEP bourgeoisie" and against "Stalin's tyrannical regime."[3]

The discussion with the United Opposition marked the beginning of a new epoch in Party politics. Never before had conflicting views been aired so brutally; never before had so much been riding on the outcome. At first, the charges leveled against the opposition appeared to be identical to those of the New Course controversy: dusting off the old arguments of 1923–1924, the Central Committee majority characterized Trotsky's ideal as the "dictatorship of one faction within the Party";[4] yet again Stalin presented the opposition as a "petit bourgeois deviation." In his 1926 report on the Fifteenth Party Congress, he excoriated the opposition with such familiar catchwords as "opportunistic" and "Menshevik" but never "treacherous" or "malevolent." The fact that the head of the Central Control Commission, Sergo Ordzhonikidze, was investing great effort in personally persuading oppositionists to remain in the Party also suggests that the heterodox were not undergoing automatic ostracism.[5]

But the intensifying administrative and political pressure coming from the Central Committee's majority prompted the United Opposition to advocate formation of an independent party of its own—a step that created a vicious circle of organizational measures and countermeasures and deepened the rift between the sides during the course of 1926–1927.[6] To cope with this qualitatively different challenge, the Central Committee majority became more aggressive. What had been the "weakest link in the Party," one led by "misguided champions of a crooked and winding political line," became, in the official Party discourse, "a second party, one openly hostile to Bolshevism." "The opposition has recently come to regard the Party as its enemy," the Siberian press stated, "and is involved with the counterrevolution."[7] "If the opposition means what it says," Bukharin emphatically pointed out, "it will be led to the conclusion that the Soviet government has to be overthrown."[8] "The opposition is no longer in a twilight zone," argued a majoritarian as the confrontation intensified, "it has already entered the night!"[9]

It is difficult to exaggerate the consequences of the discursive shift that turned "deviators" into "counterrevolutionaries." "Straight-liners" (*priamolineinye*) and "deviators" (*uklonisty*) had much in common: they traveled along identical routes, and oppositionism was simply one of the most ill-advised, lengthy, and hazardous routes. Nothing, however, united straight-liners with counterrevolutionaries: their journeys moved in completely opposite directions.

The speeches Stalin made over the course of the discussion year allow us to view his changing evaluation of the opposition like a sort of time-lapse image. At the August 1927 Central Committee plenary session Stalin was already explaining that "the leaders of the opposition have sunk to unprecedented depths.... Formerly they strove to secure freedom for factional groups within our Party; now they are moving toward an outright split."[10] On November 23 he was even less inclined to compromise: "Two parties—the old Leninist party and the new Trotskyist party—cannot coexist. It is impossible to go on, comrades, because all boundaries have been overstepped."[11] Finally, in December, at the Fifteenth Congress, Stalin called on all conscious Communists to acknowledge that the opposition had become an "evil force" (*zlostnaia sila*).[12]

Early on, majoritarians were careful about these sorts of nuances and refrained from assigning evil intentions to the opposition: its actions were instead "inadvertent" (*neumyshlennye*) and "lacking in consciousness" (*nesoznatel'nye*). In 1923, when he charged the opposition with "putting itself at the forefront of the enemies of the working class," Stalin added a mild qualification: "objectively speaking."[13] "From the perspective of class analysis," stated *Bol'shevik*, the Party's central theoretical organ, "the opposition plays a counterrevolutionary role," though from the opposition's own, subjective point of view it was "imbued with the best revolutionary intentions."[14] It was only once discursive borders were realigned in the fall of 1927 that the official press attacked: "Trotsky consciously hopes to destabilize the Party"; this had transformed his followers into "virulent counterrevolutionaries."[15]

However heterogeneous in its origins, the opposition was said to have possessed a definite history of its own, a history as the Party's evil shadow. To arm comrades against temptation, official historians set about writing this history.[16] From the mid-1920s on, a torrent of tracts dedicated to tracing the genesis and growth of the opposition poured forth, among them Sorin's *The Party and the Opposition: On the Mainsprings of Oppositionist Movements* (1925), Gonikman's *Ten Years: Outline for a History of Trotskyism in the Bolshevik Party* (1928), and Sokolov's *The Party and the Opposition: A History of All the Oppositionist Streams and Groups in the Bolshevik Party from October to the Fifteenth Congress* (1928). Articles and brochures purported to teach Communists the methods advocated by Lenin in the struggle against heterodoxy.[17]

As they went about the work of meticulously identifying the historical landmarks along the opposition's march toward evil, official historians came to concur that the "domino effect of heterodoxy" had been initiated during the discussions of 1918–1920, had escalated during the discussions with Trotsky (1923–1924) and Zinoviev (1925–1926), and had risen to a shrill pitch with the formation of the United Opposition. In the view of Sol'ts, the road from degeneration to the enemy camp passed through three basic stages: "The first stage—opposition as a platform—amounts to timid complaints about the lack of information regarding disagreements within the Central Committee.... By the next stage Party factions come into existence. During the final stage—opposition as an anti-Party—a heterodoxy distinguishes itself sharply from the Party."[18] Bubnov charted a similar decline, "from the struggle at the congress to the organization of illegal factions ... and then ... to anti-Party demagogic tricks."[19]

According to the Central Committee majority, the United Opposition, which was busily absorbing remnants of old Party splinter groups, was becoming more and more extreme, more and more willing to violate Party regulations. Trotsky, and even the long-since-defeated extremists who challenged Lenin in 1919–1921, had more and more to say, leaders of the more moderate Leningrad opposition less and less. Worst of all were the former supporters of Workers' Opposition and Democratic Centralism (the Sapronovists who had signed the hypercritical Declaration of the Fifteen); they were closely followed by the Trotskyists (who had signed the more moderate Declaration of the Eighty-three).[20]

"Which way is the opposition going?" Bukharin wondered. "Toward Shliapnikovshchina, toward Medvedevshchina, toward complete liquidationism, driven by a lack of faith in socialist construction in our country. For now, the opposition is still in a transitional stage, named Trotskyism.... Neither Zinoviev nor Kamenev has a single independent thought of his own."[21] But Trotsky emphasized that the United Opposition was not a spineless, ad hoc political union under his thumb but a true ideological alliance. "Both wings of the opposition give absolutely identical answers to all the main questions, domestic and international," he stated in 1926. "This unanimity was achieved not as a result of compromises and mutual concessions but as a result of our common approach . . . to evaluating the lessons of recent years."[22]

Disputes over language were an important feature of the intra-Party struggle. Not only the meaning but also the pragmatics of most Bolshevik terms depended on the speaker. Ostensibly used as uninflected tools, words functioned as slogans. Of course, each side claimed the other was abusing language. Trotsky insisted in May 1927 that his taxonomy was direct and truthful: "I call things by their proper names; euphemisms would not help." By contrast, he claimed, the Central Committee was doing the opposite. Take Smilga's administrative exile to Khabarovsk: Trotsky was outraged that it was presented as a regular assignment. "You are deceiving the Party and playing a double game [*dvoinaia igra*]," he charged.[23] "There is nothing worse to a revolutionary party than duality, a discrepancy between words and deeds."[24]

The opposition applied quotation marks widely to indicate that the Central Committee majority was making a travesty of key Bolshevik terms: the official use of such terms as "dictatorship of the proletariat," "intra-Party democracy," and "discussion" is always indicated in its documents by setting them in quotation marks.[25] The majoritarian Iaroslavskii was amazed by such inversions. "If the Soviet state can no longer be regarded as the dictatorship of the proletariat, if soviets no longer deserve their name, if GPU is struggling not with the economic and political counterrevolution but with the lawful dissatisfaction of the workers, if the Red Army becomes a weapon of a Bonapartist coup—how can one remain a Party member?" For the opposition, he went on, "there is no Party, no Central Committee, only 'the Stalinist faction.'"[26] When the Central Committee minority charged Stalin's group with "political libel,"[27] the latter retorted that it was comments made by the opposition that were truly "libelous."[28]

Accusations flew back and forth between the rival camps. Use of the adjective "leftist" was the subject of an especially relentless dispute. All wanted to be described as standing "on the left"; no one wanted to be "on the right."[29] A key declaration of the United Opposition was, "A blow against us is a blow against the leftist, proletarian, Leninist wing of the Party." And its programmatic documents maintained that "Stalin's line consists of short zigzags to the left and long zigzags to the right."[30] Since Trotsky and Zinoviev fancied themselves the true left, they demanded that the Party apparatus "redirect its fire from the left to the right!"[31] Scorning such remarks, majoritarians referred to extreme leftism as "infantilism."[32] Others, who refused to give up any turf when leftist credentials were at stake, claimed that Trotsky actually stood to the right of the Central Committee, his leftism nothing more than a "demagogic masquerade" to cover up his essentially right-wing nature.[33] "'Leftist' in its form, 'radical' in its content," the Declaration of the Fifteen was said to be actually "the work of arch rightists."[34] Trotsky was even described as a "leftist rightist."[35]

Many writers used the term "faction" to describe the opposition. Complaining he was tired of this recurrent plague, Bukharin warned that "if factions are permitted, the next stage will be the legalization of other parties."[36] Because the term carried such a stench of political pollution, the United Opposition strongly objected to being called a faction. "The so-called factionalism of Trotsky and Zinoviev consisted of fighting for the rights that the Party statute gives to every comrade."[37] The opposition demanded that attention be paid to the political implications of linguistic usage: "Today's agenda should be not the ban on 'factions' and 'groupings'—this could lead to the liquidation of any critical thought in the Party—but the legalization of the discussion."[38]

Paradoxically, a majority position could be described as a faction.[39] "Concerned about the publicity and criticism its decisions would attract, the ruling group within the Central Committee turned itself into a faction," Radek stated in August 1926. "The local district committees are run . . . by small factionalist troikas."[40] Can a Central Committee majority be a faction? Trotsky wondered. "A stable organization with an unchanging membership, it is indeed a faction today." According to Trotsky, "the majority faction uses the apparatus to prevent the Party from finding out, through a democratic process, where the real majority is and where the real minority is."[41]

Much ink was spilled in the debates over who really supported "Party Unity" and who was the actual "schismatic" (raskol'nik).[42] In a letter to the Politburo dated April 1927, Zinoviev emphasized that the official talk about unity did not correspond to reality. "What we need is not an outward unity but a true unity."[43] "No Party unity is conceivable," wrote Trotsky, "without prior disagreements, criticisms, clashes of ideas."[44] Stalin's supporters found the opposition's notion of unity distressing. When Iaroslavskii reproduced a polemical tirade written by an oppositionist named Khar'kov, his editorial remark was telling: immediately after quoting "Comrades, the last events have proved the need for unity in the ranks of the opposition," he commented, "and not in the ranks of the Party!"[45] Trotsky replied on November 13, 1927, that whenever the Central Committee spoke of "Party unity," it was more appropriate to speak of "schism."[46] A few days earlier, Trotsky had celebrated a victory: "The banner of 'Party Unity' has been wrested from Stalinist hands. More and more comrades interpret the banner in the following way: 'Do Not Harass the Opposition,' 'Do Not Purge and Do Not Arrest Oppositionists.'"[47]

"Leninism" was another contested term. After pondering the source of those two great evils, "grouping" and "faction," Iaroslavskii ended by suggesting that problems began when this or that segment of the Party began to "reevaluate and revise Leninism."[48] But the opposition dismissed the Central Committee's claim to a monopoly over Lenin's legacy. Instead, it set up a contrast between "the Leninist and the Stalinist lines" and asked comrades to choose between the two.[49] "While the theorists of the Stalin-Bukharin school present themselves as orthodox Leninists," said Smirnov, "in reality they distort Lenin's teachings."[50] Trotsky could not agree more: "Leninist theory, practice, and tactics have been filed away. What remains is only the Leninist label." The oppositionists claimed Lenin's mantle for themselves. "Get under the banner of the old Bolshevik party, under the banner of Lenin—that is our call."[51] In May 1927 Trotsky was even more resolute: "We, and we alone, know how to teach Lenin's method now that he is no longer with us. We, and we alone, retain ideological continuity with revolutionary Bolshevism."[52] The supporters of Trotsky and Zinoviev preferred to call themselves "Bolshevik-Leninists."[53]

"Trotskyism" was a label rejected by the Central Committee minority until the bitter end.[54] In a speech given at the Central Committee plenary session (April 6–9, 1926), Trotsky complained that "accusations of semi-Trotskyism fly from right and left; the accusers easily turn into the accused.... Every deviation, even by a millimeter, is turned into a monstrosity by the mythmaking activity of the apparatus."[55] He added: "Due to an ironic twist of history, a crude variant of Leninism is presented here as a critique of 'Trotskyism,' ... a term that changes its meaning every day."[56] As late as May 1927, Trotsky continued to insist that he was not a Trotskyist: "Over one hundred old Bolsheviks—the original [korennye] founders of our Party—submitted a letter to the Central Committee expressing solidarity with the opposition's basic view. This alone should squelch any further talk of 'Trotskyism.'"[57] And Zinoviev was equally defiant: "The struggle against so-called 'Trotskyism' will run into a wall of old Bolsheviks."[58] On December 15, 1927, the opposition addressed the Komintern on this subject: "It is not true that we defend Trotskyism. Trotsky had already admitted ... that on all of the important issues, including the questions of permanent revolution and the peasantry, Lenin was correct while he himself was not. Stalin's group, however, will not publish this resolution and continues to refer to us as 'Trotskyists.'"[59]

With few occasional exceptions, the Central Committee's critics resisted the pejorative labels applied to them. A certain uniformity of political vocabulary among the Bolsheviks and the relative stability of definitions stemmed the tendency to turn defamatory words into sources of pride. Indeed, there was very little room for alternative identities in the Bolshevik universe: no Bolshevik would embrace "factionalism" or "Trotskyism" as his self-description.

Opposition in Tomsk

The United Opposition failed to inspire the hearts and minds of students in the capitals with the same fervency Trotsky had infused in this group only a few years earlier.[60] In the months leading up to the Fifteenth Party Congress, the Communist students of Moscow and Leningrad largely turned their backs on the opposition.

It was at this moment, when many students in the Soviet Union's largest cities were returning to the fold, that something quite extraordinary happened in Tomsk.

A city whose Party organizations had lain dormant throughout the previous discussions now learned that its students formed the bulwark of opposition in Siberia. Tomsk Technological Institute will serve as our case study as we look closely at how Trotskyism was attributed the form of the quintessential counterrevolutionary movement. It is hardly surprising that the institute played a central role in the discussion—it was a highly politicized place. Most of the local students (73 percent) were Party members—the local Party cell numbered 311 full members and 133 candidates.[61]

The intra-Party struggle in Tomsk, and the discourse that interpreted it, developed gradually. In 1926, when the United Opposition was formed and began to publicize its program in Siberia, the city remained largely calm.[62] By the middle of the following year, however, a proliferation of heterodox speeches compelled the embarrassed Tomsk Party leadership to begin a search for scapegoats. Throughout the month of September, Party chieftains enunciated a series of charges, laying the responsibility for "oppositionist outbursts" at the feet of "exiled oppositionists coming to us from the capitals." A report run in the local daily newspaper in September maintained that "in Tomsk district no. 1 there was not a single meeting at which it was not said, 'We do not need another discussion and the disturbance it causes to our work.'" But the oppositionists did not fade away, and soon the Party cell at the local Technological Institute had to be recognized as richly infected by the heterodox bacillus.

The events of the joint Central Committee and Central Control Commission plenary session from the summer of 1927 (July 29 to August 9) reverberated throughout Tomsk. The plenary session was choreographed to the sound of intensifying clashes among the leaders. Bukharin presented a series of theses drawn up by the Central Committee majority, Zinoviev the countertheses of the opposition. The mutual recriminations were especially harsh, with each side accusing the other of losing sight of the interests of the proletariat and the international revolution.[63] When it looked like the proposal to purge the leaders of the opposition from the Central Committee for their "undisciplined conduct" would pass, Trotsky and Zinoviev made a declaration of submission. Condemning factionalism, they asked in return for the "cessation of repressive measures against the opposition and an orderly preparation for the forthcoming Party Congress."[64]

Since access to the details about the plenary session's actions was highly restricted in the provinces, the Tomsk Party organization was soon abuzz with rumors and speculation. When the Siberian Party committee announced the commencement of the pre-congress discussion, the opposition at the Technological Institute "emerged from cover."[65] The occasion was the appearance of Liapin, the secretary of the circuit committee, sent to defend the Central Committee theses by reading a report entitled "On the Party and Opposition" on October 24.[66] In an opening address that lasted one hour and fifteen minutes, Liapin incessantly and intemperately attacked Trotsky and Zinoviev: "Wishing to force the Party to approve an unrestrained Discussion of the Party, the opposition has begun illegally distributing its platform. . . . Certainly, ideological disagreements have to be aired out. But it is sheer Tolstoyism to think that the discussion should be conducted in the spirit of some sort of classless objectivity. Our goal is to bring the Party together, not to cause its disintegration." Calling for a "barrier" against Trotskyism—"an ideological tendency we have to unmask"—Liapin wanted to see "Leninism exported to the ranks of the wavering. . . . Factionalism must be nipped in the bud."[67]

A newcomer to the scene, Liapin still hoped that the upcoming debates among students would not go beyond a circumspect examination of the record of the local Party organization.[68] But when he suggested that the cell go through the motions and second self-congratulating resolutions he was in for a big surprise.[69] Students complained that "we are refused the minutes of the August Central Committee plenary session" and demanded far more detailed information about the debates that had taken place in the Party's higher echelons.[70]

In a dazzling exhibition of veiled allusions, exercises in sophistry, and stubborn rhetorical repetitions, Kutuzov, the chairman of the institute's meeting, managed to tilt the discussion toward questions of global scope. Even as he insisted that it was essential to treat the official Party reporter with civility and not to knock his teeth in, Kutuzov drove Liapin into a corner implacably and remorselessly; his strategy involved prompting students to ask the most difficult questions. "Is our recognition of the pre-war debt not a concession to international capital?" Liapin was asked, and "Under what banner will the bourgeoisie launch its war against the Soviet Union?" Seizing the initiative from an increasingly flustered plenipotentiary, the followers of Kutuzov left Liapin's presentation in a shambles. Eight of the thirteen speeches delivered that evening were "oppositionist in character"; the "exchange of ideas," customarily ten minutes long, lasted far into the night.[71]

Reluctant to challenge the Central Committee majority openly and risk being labeled a subversive, Kutuzov had preferred to outflank Liapin rather than attack him directly. He proposed not a set of countertheses but a "supplement" to the official resolution. In a placatory gesture, he averred that "factionalism was abnormal" but urged the official reporter to concede that the "atmosphere in the Party is unhealthy: the rank and file do not know what the opposition's real opinions are."[72]

When Liapin's time at the institute drew to a close, Kutuzov and the opposition had come up short. The official resolution garnered 104 votes, there were 12 abstentions, and Kutuzov's supplement had won only 48 votes.[73] Still, the vote was a slap in the majoritarians' face and Kutuzov succeeded in tacking two remarks onto the winning resolution: "Comrade Liapin guarantees that the minutes of the August plenary session will be made available to our entire cell"; and "In the final tally,

Comrade Liapin counted the votes of the Party candidates"; this was a violation of Party regulations, since candidates were normally allowed to serve only in a consultative capacity.[74]

At the center of the internecine war that was to rend the institute over the next few months stood a protracted showdown between two of the institute's most distinguished Communists: Kutuzov and Klikunov. The former was the institute's deputy rector and a Communist since 1919; the latter, the secretary of the Party cell, had been a Communist since 1920.[75] Kutuzov's forcefulness and ebullience contrasted with Klikunov's ideological rigidity and caution. A man of unremitting ideological zeal and a master at captivating his audience, Kutuzov was not comfortable with the tasks of day-to-day politics; he occasionally behaved maladroitly and could not sustain the spell he cast while on the podium once he had stepped down. Shrewd in his use of the administrative mechanisms at his disposal, tirelessly active, Klikunov carefully engineered every vote so that his rival came up short.

It would be simplistic to present what happened between these two men as a battle for individual prestige. When they confronted each other, each was obliged to recognize the other not as a political opportunist, but as the bearer of an idea. The showdown between Kutuzov and Klikunov was played out according to a shared set of ideals. So sharp were the differences in the two men's loyalties and in their political opinions that the parallels between them are all the more striking. Both were determined to guarantee democratic discussion within the Party and to make sure that the bourgeoisie were not permitted to usurp the workers' voice; the two men were equally fascinated with eschatological time reckoning; and they shared a fervent admiration for Lenin, whom both saw as their ideal. Both associated with the same heroic tradition of the Siberian Bolsheviks; both acted as masters of Marxist theory; and both presented themselves as model fighters for the Communist cause.

Kutuzov had championed proletarian truth from the outset, and, having found himself in the minority in 1927, had no choice but to cast himself in the role of a martyr. Nor was his archrival's rhetoric devoid of the thrills and passions of self-sacrifice: Klikunov reiterated time and again his willingness to jeopardize his popularity among students for the greater good of alerting his people to the dangers of divisiveness. Inhabiting a single narrative structure, a single conceptual world, tellers of mutually commensurable stories about what they were doing, Klikunov and Kutuzov did not dispute the meaning of martyrdom. But who was the victim and who the perpetrator?

Once its two leaders entered open conflict, the institute became wracked by tensions. "The vote brought oppositionists into the daylight," Klikunov argued. "Those students more likely to hold forth in the corridor than in the auditorium revealed their true selves." Opinions split, however, over how political moods were to be gauged. A Civil War veteran and one of the institute's most illustrious students,

Filimonov, adduced a whole string of reasons to explain Klikunov's simplifications in interpreting student attitudes. Imagining he might still bridge the gulf between the two warring camps, he tried to show that "the vote was not clear-cut. At this stage of the discussion it is difficult to tell who is who. The indecisiveness of our cell should be attributed to the complexity of the issues rather than to comrades' covert oppositionism." According to Filimonov, "many students sided with Kutuzov because of the nervousness of the local Party organization. I, for example, believe the Central Committee's claim that our growth pattern is socialist and not capitalist, and yet at the same time I think that the Central Committee has made mistakes. Can anyone really be mistake-free?" Still, Filimonov agreed with Klikunov's doubts about comrades' "sincerity." He, too, described the atmosphere at the institute as "opaque. At Party meetings I feel as if I am in a theater. How could a handful of heterodox speeches have translated into so many oppositionist votes?"[76]

Liapin was inclined to believe that "students were organized beforehand to challenge my report. They had notes and newspaper clippings . . . and were familiar with the Declaration of the Eighty-three."[77] But not everyone was a conniving foe. Stunning the local leadership, Liapin accepted that "comrades such as Filimonov are indeed simply confused" and blamed the Tomsk Party apparatus for it. "The real culprit is Zimov [the secretary of the district Party committee]—he failed to sound out the local mood." The institute majoritarians, however, called Liapin's interpretation of Filimonov's hodgepodge naive. "Filimonov's ruses [ulavki], typical of the intelligentsia, are transparent. He is simply justifying his vacillation."[78]

If Filimonov's "convoluted" thinking provoked some disagreements, the workings of Kutuzov's soul inspired protracted debate. Early on, there were those who maintained that the deputy rector had simply "lost his way," while others saw him as a convinced heretic. Disdainfully rejecting Kutuzov's "posturing as the 'Hero of Our Times' [an allusion to Lermontov's Pechorin]," Klikunov baited his adversary: "If you disagree with the Party line, say so. Do not murmur, hiding around corners and throwing sand in our eyes!" The fact that Kutuzov was associated with an oppositionist program not only made an apostate of him but also implied that what he had cunningly entitled a "supplement" was in fact a full-blown subversive agenda prepared in advance of the discussion. This Kutuzov denied. "In the summer, I was a vacillator and did not vote for the opposition. Instead, I simply left the hall." Pinning down the precise moment of Kutuzov's lapse was important: since the discussion was the only period when politics could legitimately be debated, he needed to convince the Party that his unorthodox views had crystallized at the appropriate moment—otherwise he was nothing but a seasoned enemy waiting for a propitious moment to bare his fangs.

Whatever Kutuzov's position may have been in the early part of the year, by November the last mooring snapped and he took to referring to himself as an "all-around oppositionist." Following the tradition of using the number of signatories as the name for the opposition's programmatic documents, majoritarians dubbed Kutuzov's supplement to Liapin's resolution the "Program of the Forty-eight."[79] But Kutuzov did not mind. "All forty-eight of us have our heads on our shoulders," he stated rather defiantly. In the atmosphere of the time, this statement meant that Kutuzov had swung out of the majoritarian ideological orbit and into that of the amorphous heterodox galaxy.

What for Kutuzov was the culmination of a long and steep road to the truth appeared to his adversaries as the nadir of his spiritual decline: "Less than two weeks ago, Kutuzov was playing the part of an infant with unformed views. . . . Today he alleges that he has, to use his own words, 'matured and has fully articulated his oppositionist worldview.' When in his recent speeches he says the word 'we' he means 'the opposition.'" Kutuzov has unleashed "a frenzy of oppositionist agitation in our city," the local paper reported in November. "This guest performer is offering his insipid propaganda to one and all."[80]

Indeed, the fat was in the fire. During the two weeks following Liapin's report to the institute, the discussion picked up speed in Tomsk. A remarkable number of debates took place over a short period, and Party meetings were often separated by no more than one or two days. Since the institute's potentates could freely come and go from simultaneously convened meetings, the names of leading oppositionists such as Kutuzov, Nikolaev, Beliaev, Gorbatykh, and Grinevich turn up very often on the lists of key speakers. As the pitch of the rhetoric mounted on both sides, the chances for a peaceful discussion dwindled. All rules were discarded, all taboos broken, and the discussion that should have been urbanely conducted within strict statutory rules was headed for all-out conflict. By the end of November the oppositionists would remove themselves from the official Party organization. But not every student who sympathized with Kutuzov opted out and not all at once, and, as many of them would later claim, "not wholeheartedly." For a while, words went before deeds.

"It was on the institute itself, however, that the opposition concentrated its powers," according to editorials in the Tomsk newspaper. "There the opposition prepared to wage a decisive battle."[81] Anxious lest the battlefield be surrendered entirely to the enemy, the district leadership frequented student meetings, turning them into political and ideological contests. Between November 2 and November 15, the Party cell at the Technological Institute heard reports on the work of the Tomsk district committee, on the Five-Year Plan, and on Molotov's agricultural theses. At every meeting, Kutuzov was the co-reporter. The heterodox forces he gathered under his banner were indeed impressive: according to the official bulletin, sixty-six students took the floor during these meetings, thirty of them speaking in support of Trotsky and Zinoviev. Fifteen percent of the cell was now said to be firmly in the oppositionist camp.[82]

As part of its attempt to retain control over the grassroots organization, the district committee closely monitored Party meetings. Official spokesman refused to acknowledge the "'freedom of criticism' the arch-radicals are demanding. There is such a thing as an anti-Party criticism, a wicked criticism."[83] A member of the presidium kept a record of who said what for the Tomsk Party committee. By the standards of the previous discussions, these transcripts were quite detailed and they provided the basis for classifying cells as "orthodox," "heterodox," or "vacillating." A special circular from Moscow instructed the local Party authorities to collect the impromptu, scribbled notes sent to the presidium and divide them into three categories: statements in support of the opposition, statements in support of the Central Committee, and indeterminate statements.[84] The institute's oppositionists were furious, but the Tomsk circuit control commission insisted that this was a moderate countermeasure in the face of oppositionist efforts to coordinate a secret agenda, including plans to demand the right to deliver a co-report on every policy issue under consideration.[85]

The debate over how to debate went in circles. Information in the hands of Kutuzov confirmed that the conduct of the discussion was highly irregular: "supported by Party monies and aided by the Party apparatus, apparatchiks have convened separatist meetings, presently in full swing."[86] Their membership was being sifted through two or three times. Tickets were individually labeled and granted only to majoritarians. Secretaries were taught "how to hoot, how to whistle, how to push people out."[87] But the opposition's presentation of the state of affairs in the Party came under withering fire. Official spokespeople in Tomsk claimed it was Trotsky who violated Party norms. They trumpeted around the city how GPU agents raided the opposition's printing shop on the night of September 12–13 and arrested several men engaged in illegally reproducing the Platform of the Oppposition—a document asserting that the ruling faction honored none of its promises to ameliorate the workers' living conditions and demanding wage increases for the underpaid workers and tax relief for the village poor.[88] Klikunov announced that the distribution of the confiscated programs involved the collaboration of a Wrangel army officer.

With such fiery headlines in the backdrop, the meeting held at the Tomsk Technological Institute on November 3 was especially acrimonious. Among those in the audience were Zimin, who shouldered the burden of the opening address, and Liapin, "as well as other heavy and light artillery of the Tomsk Party organization." Received with a certain coldness, Klikunov was initially discountenanced. Soon, however, he pulled himself together. Outraged by the election of the "untrustworthy" Nikolaev to chair the meeting and certain that this was the first salvo in the opposition's elaborate plan "to take over the cell," Klikunov annulled the vote. "The Nikolaev-Kutuzov duo is quite incapable of objectively conducting the Party meeting," he announced. Liapin promptly congratulated his fellow majoritarian: "By attacking the minority leaders, Klikunov has taken the bull by its horns. This is doing things the Lenin way!"[89]

Nikolaev's dismissal as chairman, an apparent contravention of procedure, touched off an explosion at the Tomsk Technological Institute. Could a critical comrade participate in a discussion? If so, he had to be heard. But if he was an outright enemy after all, he had to be cast out at once. As a tremendous din of protest rose up in reaction to his action, Klikunov remained unmoved: "One is either with the Party or one is against the Party, and therefore outside it." Nikolaev's supporters, however, insisted that they were simply demanding "that the Central Committee frankly explain its policy." "Enlighten us, do not purge us!"[90] "I will not respond to slanderous allegations!" shouted Nikolaev at the top of his lungs. "I am not a factionalist, and I do not feel guilty." Others called Klikunov's disciplinary action "unprecedented sabotage." "Is Nikolaev not a Party member the same as anyone? Doesn't this mean that he could be the chairman of the meeting?"[91]

Since the previous summer the Tomsk Party organization had been wrestling with the issue of Party democracy. Everybody in the institute remembered how Ivanova, an "ardent oppositionist," had been wont to complain that "comrades in the city remain unaware of the issues disputed by the Party. If we really mean to understand what is at stake, we must familiarize ourselves with the oppositionist material." Ivanova entered passages from the suppressed oppositionist documents into students' minds. "Our Party," she read out, "has the misfortune of being barred from making . . . a collective decision about the future of the working class."[92] The Politburo banned the Platform of the United Opposition (September 1927) altogether, since disseminating it "might be perceived as a legalization of factions," but to the opposition, "it was clear as day that fear of our platform meant fear of the masses."[93]

To shore up its rhetoric, the opposition began to make clandestine reproductions of key documents, including "Lenin's Testament."[94] Stalin had initially succeeded in persuading Trotsky, Kamenev, and Zinoviev to deny the Testament's authenticity. But once they were pressed to the wall, they allowed their supporters to turn it against the Party leadership. "Considering that Lenin's Testament insists on Stalin's removal from the position of the general secretary," Trotsky noted, "no wonder that during house searches, the Testament is the first to be confiscated."[95] Tarasov, a Zinovievist exiled to Tomsk, saw no way around the conclusion that "the worst fears expressed in Lenin's Testament have been fully realized."[96] The decision to impose a ban on this key document had, he told his provincial listeners, prefigured the withdrawal of the plenary session's stenographic record. "Such controls on information are not new. . . . Clearly, the violator of all Bolshevik traditions is the present Central Committee, which interprets any attempt to discuss the issues as a 'schism.'"[97]

To judge by the speeches that were made at the Technological Institute, it looks like the opposition's emissaries to Tomsk acquired a vociferous following indeed. Beliaev, Kutuzov's comrade-in-arms, was much exercised by the problem of Party democracy during the discussion and used his turn at the podium to widen the scope of the attack on the cell's "authoritarian" secretary. "Our leadership is making a travesty of the democratic Party spirit of old—whoever speaks critically is seized immediately by the throat. There are individuals here who marched in step with the Party for a decade—who can seriously claim we suddenly went sour?"[98]

Other champions of Party democracy followed suit:

We are scrambling for information about what is going on. The newspapers give only a one-dimensional picture. . . . How are we supposed to determine who is right, when the motives behind the opposition's actions remain unclear? . . .

If the Party leadership is entangled in disagreements, should the Party battalions not know? The present situation is not so dangerous that those at the top should distrust those at the bottom. Under the prevailing conditions, our only guidance is the authority of Party leaders. But leaders can be found on both sides! Should we believe the Central Committee thanks to the merit of the intertwined figures of Rykov, Stalin, and Kalinin? When we see other great leaders—Zinoviev, Trotsky, and Kamenev—in the other camp, we cannot decide.[99]

Things were balanced on a knife edge. Some spoke of covert threats to purge oppositionist students, and this rumor led to another round of mutual recriminations.[100] When Liapin supported his demotion, Nikolaev almost recklessly referred to his "strategy of intimidation. For a single speech he relegated me to the opposition. Where is this 'Party democracy' Liapin is talking about?"[101]

The next speaker accused the plenipotentiary of having contradicted himself. "The Central Committee, Liapin tells us, contends that 'there is no reason to be afraid of a handful of oppositionists.' In the same breath, however, it adds that 'the opposition has enough manpower to lay the groundwork for the organization of a rival party.'" Whatever their numerical strength, stated another critic, "GPU actions will not be effective against resolute individuals." Only enlightenment could work. "Many comrades possessed of a revolutionary soul do not understand much in matters of theory. If we lose them, they will become a dangerous enemy."

A stock technique in oppositionist polemics involved suggesting that the secretiveness of the Tomsk district committee was an affront to official practices. If Party democracy and the growth of consciousness went hand in hand, how could authoritarian practices dovetail with Party regulations? Neudakhin—another prominent supporter of Kutuzov—raised some shrewd questions: "Why is our grassroots membership unacquainted with the stenographic reports of the Central Committee and Central Control Commission plenary sessions? If we do not study its Platform how can we fight criticisms point for point?"[102] Without a broader dissemination of information about Party affairs "it is impossible to conduct genuine soul-searching."[103]

The Bolsheviks had an ambivalent attitude toward publicity: as a vehicle of consciousness, information had to be available to all; at the same time, they feared that the enemy might distort information for its own sinister aims. Kutuzov's supporters granted that "it is for the good of the general public that certain speeches are not published," but they still wanted "all Communists to be able to read them." What reason could be cited for refusing to permit Communists to peruse the oppositionist Platform, if done secretly? They had been accepted to the Party; had they not proved themselves conscious enough to distinguish right from wrong? "When a similar dilemma arose during the trade union debate of 1920," students recalled, "an ingenious solution was found: a special brochure presenting different positions on the debated subject was circulated only among Party members."[104]

Since the Fourteenth Party Congress, stenographic reports of important Party meetings had not been reproduced in the press. Was this right? "In Moscow, Communists read reports—what about us?" Tomsk students wondered. "All last year we were able to follow the Central Committee line, but we were permitted to read only scattered phrases uttered by the opposition."[105] Kutuzov hammered away at the Tomsk leadership, demanding that it gave up its parochialism: "We need a page in the local newspapers devoted to general political issues, because our daily activities are linked to general politics. To justify not publishing a discussion sheet by claiming that no one here can address big issues—what kind of response is that? Even I could write something!"[106] In an attempt to steal some of Kutuzov's thunder, Klikunov announced that discussion sheets would be published. "It is not enough," he agreed, "simply to condemn the existence of factions; we should try to explain why they spring up." At this early stage of the discussion, both sides were willing to agree on the primacy of enlightenment over reprisal.[107]

A brilliant extemporaneous speaker, the still vacillating Filimonov raised the organizational issue. First he kowtowed to the dictates of Leninism, reminding everybody that "factionalism was forbidden by the Tenth Party Congress." What followed, however, appeared as considerably less orthodox.

No one voted for Liapin. He was simply appended to our cell on orders from above. Instead of teaching us to show initiative, he threatens us. . . . The principles of Democratic Centralism call for mass participation in the selection of the guiding organs. However, in our case, the slate of bureau candidates is usually parachuted in. When our cell was finally encouraged to elect our bureau on our own, we completely lost our heads. This shows that we do not think problems through and that our consciousness is dormant. We have to become accustomed to independent activity. . . . The practices of our cell are irregular—we do more talking than acting about democracy, and the number of issues we rubber-stamp is overwhelming.[108]

In dealing with this speech, we must resist certain interpretive temptations. It would never have occurred to Filimonov that the leadership should not command the Party or that a grassroots network possessed the mandate to formulate policy. Within the framework of democratic centralism, superior consciousness, not superior numbers, was the arbiter of legitimacy. Such aspects of decision making as whether power should evolve from the cell upward or devolve from the Central Committee downward were entirely beside the point. Filimonov was simply insisting that by curbing their spontaneity the Central Committee had retarded the spiritual growth of the rank and file. He questioned not the leadership's authoritarian guidance of the Party but its incorrect implementation of the principle of guidance.

When Grinevich took the floor, he seemed at first to be disassociating himself from Filimonov. "The speaker is wrong to highlight the fact that Liapin was not elected", he stated. "The Party heads have the right to assign plenipotentiaries." In the final analysis, however, Grinevich's argument was not that different. The real question to him was not who could nominate Liapin but "whether we will eventually endorse Liapin at the forthcoming Tomsk Circuit Party conference"—an implicit acknowledgment that he could still become the cell's true, organic representative. While at times there was no choice but to virtually drag the grass roots into the classless paradise, Liapin was certainly wrong, Grinevich maintained, to look down on students. "Politically we have matured, and today we can be persuaded only by reliable materials."[109] If the leaders could not recognize this, it must be that their consciousness was lagging; not the grass roots but the leadership of the Party was affected by "isolationism" and "elitism."

"Not just the opposition but the Central Committee itself is headed in the direction of factionalism," agreed Kutuzov. "Odd as it may sound, it is the Central Committee that has a schismatic policy." Of course, the majoritarians did not rush to embrace the suggestion that the United Opposition possessed a superior consciousness. For them, oppositionist arguments were shaped not on the anvil of History but in the crucible of the counterrevolution.[110] According to Zimov, Grinevich's demands to make Party documents widely accessible bespoke political illiteracy: "Who in his right mind would make public the fact that we extracted a billion rubles from the peasants, for example?"[111] The broad masses were not ready: "premature publicity would unleash 1921 all over again."[112]

Zimov insisted that "discontent with the framework of our Party democracy is a hallmark of Menshevism, not Bolshevism." Had the Mensheviks not wanted to bring anyone into the political process, happy to dilute the proletarian consciousness in a sea of petit bourgeois clamor? And had their willingness to liquidate underground organizations not resembled the opposition's desire to open the Central Committee's secret files to all?[113] But the opposition too had no interest in extending the democratic franchise beyond the conscious. Beliaev insisted that "by branding demands for freedom of expression in the Party as 'Menshevism,' Zimov encourages ignorance of the true nature of the Bolshevik-Leninist position." Beliaev did not defend the Menshevik right to speak. He simply wanted to convince the Central Committee that he, a seasoned Communist, could be trusted to distinguish Bolshevism from Menshevism on his own.[114]

The last thing anyone from either side of the intra-Party divide wanted to do was behave like a Menshevik. To do so would be to lose one's proletarian acumen, to slip into a petit bourgeois political realm, to give up the great victories of 1917 and the Civil War. The charge of degeneration implied a serious illness, a clouding of the mind by the economic forces set free by NEP—words one had said during the discussion became instantly meaningless. Everything revolved around progress, general and individual. The development of the country and the purification of souls ran along parallel lines. The two movements were supposed to be synchronized, reinforcing one another; souls developed only when socialist construction advanced; and, conversely, only mature souls shaped policies that would push such construction forward. Over the course of the debates the indices for a true revolutionary consciousness were articulated: thinking universally, setting up correct historical analogies, and eventually, in a combination of all of these, mastering the eschatological timetable.

Because Communists never ceased to mull over the downfall of previous revolutions and were convinced that History advanced through zigzags, Kutuzov and Klikunov alike were anxious to apply rejuvenating measures to the dictatorship of the proletariat. It is possible that the bourgeoisie will take advantage of the erosion of the proletarian base, kick aside the Soviet footstool and establish a Bonapartist system—this was the danger the opposition was ramming into the head of any Communist who would listen. "Let's call things by their real names," pleaded Nikolaev. "If Lenin spoke in the past about the degeneration of our Party, why are we afraid to mention the word now?"

A bit more understated, Kutuzov said similar things: "our leadership is unable to pull the country toward socialism."[115] "Thermidor killed the French Revolution," he declared. "Can it not be that the same might happen here?" Thermidorian danger was the danger of a capitalist victory "attained not by means of a military intervention of the world bourgeoisie but by means of the slow switching of the Soviet Power from the proletarian to the petit bourgeois rails."[116] Kutuzov then cited—to great effect—Trotsky's analogy between the Party leadership and the Thermidorians: "In France the Jacobins executed the Thermidorians, and then the tables turned and the Thermidorians went on to execute the Jacobins. Trotsky called on us to reflect on the parallels between the French and Russian Revolutions, bearing in mind the following question: 'In which chapter would you have us shot?'"[117] Kutuzov was not averse to admitting that Bolshevik violence had achieved "gigantic results" against "reactionary lost causes." But the best thinkers in the institute—

himself and the slighted Nikolaev—embodied historic progress, not historical backsliding, and therefore the analogy did not hold.[118]

Though the struggle for the soul of the institute was being waged in earnest, some holds were still barred. For example, Tomsk oppositionists had yet to identify their adversaries directly with reaction. To have done so would have been tantamount to abandoning all hope of reforming the Party from within.[119] Kutuzov would not participate in a sweeping condemnation of the Party's historical record and described the Thermidorian effect as no more than an "objective result" of the Central Committee's shortsightedness.[120] But, as Trotsky pointed out, "those who buried the French Republic did not set out to destroy Jacobinism either. They did so unwittingly, out of weariness and confusion. Thermidorians were Jacobins, but Jacobins who had moved to the right."[121]

Bitter charges such as these triggered in turn a series of disputes over "socialism in one country"—the keystone to Stalin's ideological vision.[122] Debates on the true meaning of Leninism came into sharp focus. Was Lenin properly seen as an international leader, or was he the savior of the Russian proletariat only? Or, asked more broadly, was the Russian Revolution universal or particular in scope? In agreement with Trotsky and Zinoviev that socialism in one country was a petit bourgeois notion, Kutuzov railed against it.[123] "This deviationist theory is Stalin's, not Lenin's!" he said. "We do not possess the basic necessities and so are unable to build socialism without the help of an international revolution."[124]

In an attempt to outflank Kutuzov's salvo, the majoritarians claimed that their plans for the country's development were at once better attuned to real conditions in the Soviet Union than those of their rivals and, in the last account, more mindful of the proletariat: while the opposition was exposing workers to materials not yet digestible, the Central Committee was offering gentle guidance. "If presented with an alternative banner reading something like 'We Cannot Build Socialism Alone!' would our toilers go on working? . . . Socialism in one country can be justified on psychological grounds, and may serve to protect workers from despair."[125] But Kutuzov dismissed with considerable asperity all attempts to open up new lines of thought in Communist political thinking. He saw socialism in one country as counterproductive. "Proletarians of other countries would ask themselves, 'Why should we bring about a revolution? Let them build socialism first and we will see whether it works.'"[126]

Kutuzov described the true Leninist as a universalist to the marrow of his bones, focused on international class struggle, and he attacked a degenerate Party leadership with its Russified Communism and prioritizing of the domestic front.[127] He blamed Stalin's isolationist credo for the recent debacles in foreign policy. Because of Stalin's belief in a "revolutionary coalition of the Chinese working class and the Chinese progressive bourgeoisie," China's Communist Party subordinated its plans to the direction of the Kuomintang and its leader, Chiang Kai-shek. The

April 1927 massacre of thousands of workers in Shanghai by Chiang Kai-shek's forces dealt an irreparable blow to the dream of a revolution in the East, vindicating the opposition's claim that the alliance of the Chinese working class with the Chinese bourgeoisie was a disastrous policy.[128] Stalin's errors in foreign policy became even more evident to Kutuzov when Britain broke off diplomatic relations with the Soviet Union, following a London police raid on the premises of the Soviet Trade Office (evidence of espionage was collected). Increasingly isolated, the Soviet Union had to prepare for an imminent confrontation with the imperialist powers long before it was ready.[129]

Furthermore, the opposition accused the Central Committee of ignoring the link between the international situation and its disastrous ramifications on the home front.[130] Having abandoned the path of international revolution, "our leadership cannot afford to antagonize the rich peasantry at home. As a result the proletariat is betrayed on yet another front. The continued existence of the peasant proprietor is preventing the final consolidation of socialism."[131] And what does the Central Committee do? "It suppresses criticisms of class differentiation in the countryside."[132] Time and again, students expressed anxiety over the rise of the village bourgeoisie. "Did Lenin not already tell us in 1923 that we have retreated enough? . . . Whoever claims that the kulaks' share in the village economy is small is anti-Leninist. Just look at the anarchy of the NEP market."[133]

Neudakhin returned to the connection between the domestic and the foreign aspects of the class struggle: "We have to curb not only the kulak but also his fellow traveler, the middle peasant. Who knows whom he will follow when war breaks out?"[134] The opposition argued that a war against the proletarian state will not be a regular war of one state against another: it must take the form of the war of the international bourgeoisie against the international proletariat. "Taking a class character, such a war will necessarily intensify the class war inside the warring sides, creating an internal front alongside the external one."[135]

"Who prevails over whom?" demanded Kutuzov. "Class struggle in the countryside remains crucial!" Unmistakably, Thermidorian degeneration was a real danger, but "all we do now is praise ourselves. This is so unlike Lenin, who was not loath to dwell on the less sunny aspects of our work." And then, to probe the shadows, Kutuzov revived the questions Lenin had posed not long before he died: "Who is driving our state machine?" and "Are we moving in the right direction?" "Who dictates to whom—the Party to the economy or the economy to the Party?"[136] Toward the end of the deliberations he declared the credo of the United Opposition: "The First Five-Year Plan does not directly address the transformation of NEP Russia into socialist Russia. We say: Speed up industrialization!"[137]

Though Kutuzov had captivated the audience, and though he commanded the unflinching loyalty of his cohort, his economic program was eventually voted down, 126 to 42. Kutuzov's two countertheses, "On the Village" and "On Foreign Policy," were defeated as well.[138] But the institute's opposition gave no thought to raising the white flag. The continued, acrimonious controversy over domestic and international policy only drove a wedge deeper and deeper between the two student cohorts. Factional lines were not only drawn—they were forged in proletarian iron.

Predictably, the discussion boiled down to the following question: Was it the Central Committee or the opposition that expressed the political will of the proletariat? Since the Tomsk Party higher-ups were in fact standing in for the new bourgeoisie, the opposition declared its voice to be the sole voice of the "betrayed workers."[139] "Our worst nightmare," said Neudakhin, "is coming true. The salaries of workers are dropping. The salaries of employees are rising." "Neudakhin is right," agreed another discussant. "As a result of the center's mistaken policy, the worker masses are discontent. While the workers say in plain language 'Increase our salaries!' all the Party does is shovel more and more empty promises down their throats."[140]

The opposition maintained that "the independent-minded Communist workers are being pushed out of the factories, and elements who serve their bosses and not socialism are sent to replace them."[141] Much criticism was leveled at the so-called triangle (treugol'nik), the triple-headed factory board consisting of production manager, trade union representative, and Party secretary.[142] "You rivet together the circumference of the triangle so tightly," Kutuzov sneered, "that workers cannot find a way out." An equally sarcastic Grinevich told Klikunov "not to worry. The edges of your beloved triangle are as sharp as they can be."[143] The transformation of the triangle "from worker's friend to worker's foe" stemmed from the "resurgence of severe bureaucratism in our country."[144] Taking the floor one after another, oppositionist speakers assailed "the worship of the specialist."[145] Iarygin complained about bureaucratic neglect and Lun' noted that students' economic plight had a political dimension.[146] Gorbatykh lambasted the apparatus's habit of squelching those who demanded their rights. Having arrived from Leningrad, he had learned much about this tyranny while observing it firsthand: "Hiring and firing is now wholly decided by the factory administration. Apparatchiks predominate, and workers can no longer go to the factory committee during working hours without the foreman's permission."[147]

The Central Committee's "Anniversary Manifesto" had proposed a seven-hour workday. There is no basis for the statement that the Party abandoned the working class, Stalin claimed.[148] But Kutuzov's followers called this a "demagogic idea" and talked about an "anniversary zigzag."[149] "Why is it that any argument against the seven-hour workday is immediately construed as unrest and sedition within the Party?" wondered Filimonov. "I, for example, question not the principle of a shortened workday but the chances to implement it in practice."[150] Nikolaev was adamant that "bureaucratism is a disease that has to be attacked not with resolutions and administrative measures but through the proletarianization of the apparatus."[151]

Bringing the issue closer to home, Beliaev complained that "even here, in the institute, workers have to endure professorial aloofness." Nothing was going to change so long as the gulf between mental labor and manual labor was not bridged. "It is expedient to dispatch university officials periodically to production."[152] Kutuzov made reference to the alarming lack of worker interest in Party enrollment. "Workers can be attracted only if we demonstrate to them that we can make a difference. As it is, they have tasted too much bureaucratism to identify with the Party." The data Kutuzov cited showed a recent decrease in the percentage of workers in the institute's own cell—from fifty-two to forty-eight. This corroborated the claim of the opposition that "instead of the 'Lenin levy' [Leninskii prizyv] we have the 'Stalin dropout' [Stalinskii otsev]."[153] The Party bureau, however, vigorously rejected the suggestion that the cell's proletarian composition had been diluted because of his bureaucratized leadership. "We actually increased the ratio of workers in our organization," Klikunov noted: "sixty-seven of the seventy workers who applied last year were enrolled."[154]

While the arguments about class purity wore on, the opposition crowed monotonously about the number of proletarians in its own ranks. When a count was officially made there was cause to crow all the louder: 55 percent of the Siberian oppositionists were "workers," many "from the bench."[155] The odds were even better in Kutuzov's institute cohort—forty-three workers and peasants and only sixteen members of the intelligentsia.[156] Such group portraits mystified the Central Committee supporters, who had grown accustomed to the idea that the opposition, unable to find support within the working class, relied on nonproletarian class groups such as kulaks, NEPmen, and the bourgeois intelligentsia. If the majoritarians were to have any hopes of salvaging their oft-repeated claim that the opposition expressed class alien interests, Klikunov had to argue quickly.

Sol'ts, an authority on such issues, produced a blueprint of how this could be done. "During the transitional period," he stated, "the unevenness of the working class allows certain layers within its boundaries to be turned into weapons in the hands of the petite bourgeoisie." Sol'ts mentioned the workers from the Izhevsk and Votkinsk factories fighting in the ranks of Kolchak and advised majoritarians to use the example to show that the weakest links in the Russian proletariat could be perverted. A dose of sociology refined the argument. That monstrosity called the "oppositionist worker" could, according to a Central Committee spokesman, "come either from the semi-peasant bottom or from the aristocratic top of the working class, but never from its core." The bottom was the group of workers who had just left the village. Unskilled and poorly paid, "these peasant-workers approach our industries with the assumption that they are ordinary exploiters from whom the maximum possible wage must be extracted."[157]

Skilled workers could also join the opposition in this interpretation. "Some of them have houses and businesses of their own; many once occupied responsible positions but have been demoted and dispatched to production. These disgruntled former bosses have embraced the opposition because they hold a personal grudge against the Party." Such words were aimed at the likes of Tarasov, the above-mentioned founder of the opposition in Tomsk, who had served on the Leningrad Control Commission before being accused of factionalism and exiled to Siberia.[158]

Whatever the exact class composition of the opposition, majoritarian theorists pointed out that "the Leninist Party never aspired to represent the entire working class." There are moments in history when the historical interests of the working class "clash with the inclinations, aspirations, and prejudices of those workers who have become overwhelmed by petit bourgeois influences." At such historical junctures, the Party, armed with Marxist analysis, "must wage a merciless struggle against workers' superstitions."[159]

Ultimately, the question of who represents the empirical working class had to be rephrased as who represents true workers, those workers who are aware of their messianic mission.[160] When Neudakhin expressed the hope that "comrades will speak in defense of workers' demands," he was repelled by majoritarian stalwarts: "We should like to ask who it is the workers need to be protected from after ten years of the dictatorship of the proletariat? From what opera, dear comrade, have you borrowed your lines? Neudakhin, your brains must have gone soft!" Filimonov and Goliakov rushed to the rescue. "Workers who support the official line remain illiterate," they argued. "Brainwashed and prone to approach things mechanically, they take orders from their undisputed master, Klikunov, who leads them, like lambs to slaughter, into thoughtless opposition-bashing."[161]

Sure of its support among the conscious proletariat, the opposition started fantasizing about non-Party workers acting as referees in the discussion. "The working masses are Archimedes' point," oppositionist speakers explained. "Whoever controls them controls the Party."[162] The time had come for Stalin to relinquish his monopoly on the voice of the workers. "Today almost the entire working class is keenly interested in ... what the opposition has to say."[163] Since the Party belonged to the working class, so the opposition declared, "all its affairs should be working-class affairs as well. It is only natural that the discussion should overflow Party boundaries and become the business of workers in general." This line of thought had important implications: when the opposition stated that it was obliged to obey the Party line "only so long as the working class itself demands it," it was hinting at the possibility of dissociating the working class from the Party. Such openings permitted Kutuzov to smash through the theoretical obstacles that had prevented a direct appeal to non-Party workers. He stood ready to violate that sacred precept that only the Bolshevik party, as historically constituted, could speak in the name of the proletariat.[164]

A Black Mass

At some time in late 1927, the United Opposition decided to go over the Party's head and appeal directly to the working class.[165] Leaders of the opposition explained that "workers have to meet in private apartments to discuss the Party's situation, because they cannot hear the opposition at open meetings." Striking a celebratory tone, they declared that "the Party has returned to its tradition of collective thinking, which involves consulting the man in the workshop."[166]

Could the remnants of the Democratic Centralism and the Workers' Opposition be proven correct in recommending the use of independent organizations as magnets to attract dissatisfied workers—something these groupings had been doing for some years now? The Declaration of the Fifteen supported an attempt to circumvent the Central Committee already in June: "The fact that Stalin's people increasingly look for the support of the petite bourgeoisie against the workers dictates the course of the future struggle. . . . The attempt at restoration of the Bolshevik party must be replaced with efforts to organize a new party."[167]

At first Radek, Trotsky's right-hand man, fretted over collaboration with diehard oppositionists, remembered for their willingness to attack Lenin and their claim that the Central Committee under his leadership neglected the true proletarian for the Party boss. "It was a dangerous idea," Radek stated. The adoption of secessionist rhetoric, he feared, would veil a crucial difference between the anarchist extremists and authentic Bolshevik-Leninists.[168] Trotsky found the ex–"democratic centralists" equally worrisome: their talk of insurrection against the Party apparatus was, according to Trotsky, an "epidemic": Smirnov and Sapronov had gone too far and become an "ultra-leftist" threat that threatened to "twist the neck of the Revolution."[169]

Indeed, Trotsky was not exactly an enthusiast for a second party. At the Thirteenth Party Congress (1924), he had vowed to preserve unity: "Comrades, none of us wishes to be or can be right when against the Party. In the last instance the Party is always right, because it is the only historical instrument in the hands of the working class. . . . The English have a saying: 'My country, right or wrong.' We may say, and with much greater justice: 'My party, right or wrong.'"[170] Three years later, Trotsky appeared to be adhering to his old position. In August, he declared that he "decisively condemns any attempts to create a second party in the Soviet Union, a disastrous idea."[171] Protesting the "poisonous accusation that we want to create 'two parties,'" his supporters stated in September that "we believe that Party policy can be corrected from the inside."[172]

But in October Trotsky had begun undergoing something like a change of heart, albeit a very tentative one at first: he claimed that Lenin's ban on factions had been designed for a party in which freedom of expression was guaranteed, and that "in a muzzled organization, discontent and dissent by necessity tend to assume factionalist forms."[173] Stating in November 1927 that "It is too late to talk about Party unity because the Party machine has fallen into the hands of Thermidorian forces," Trotsky explicitly endorsed the radical program: given current conditions, the creation of a second party seemed necessary.[174]

How could those who joined the ranks of the opposition be sure that they were assisting in rehabilitating the proletarian party and not in forming some sort of bourgeois organization? As it turned out, everything depended on a precise eschatological time reckoning. Only the oppositionist who called for a new party at the appropriate moment could be considered a true Bolshevik-Leninist. If his demand reverberated when the Bolshevik party was still "healthy," his motives were counterrevolutionary. Conversely, apathy and political paralysis at the moment when a party had fallen on hard times were tokens of degeneration, attributes of an apparatchik who might well be benefiting from the situation.

Discussions of a second party revealed divisions within the United Opposition. Such relative newcomers to oppositionism as the supporters of Zinoviev and Kamenev retained their belief in the sanctity of Party unity, and the former questioned Trotsky's eschatological time line. Trotsky had elevated the New Course Discussion to the status of a seminal event that had shaken the Party mass from its dogmatic slumber. "Hundreds, no, thousands of revolutionaries previously keeping in line with the Leninist Central Committee started to think independently in 1923. It was then that they learned to use proper Marxist methods to assess events, to take revolutionary initiative, and to criticize [the current leadership]."[175]

The Zinovievist history of oppositionist consciousness was much shorter. Here nothing was said about an epic Trotskyist struggle, during which the righteous opposition graduated from a low-key challenge to the Party apparatus during the New Course Discussion to an all-out attack on the entire Party today.[176] There could not be any such talk, because Zinoviev and Kamenev had played no role in attacks on Stalin until the controversies of 1925–1926—to emphasize a history that began before that would have been embarrassing. For a long time the leaders of the Leningrad opposition labored to differentiate their faction from the insurrectionist tradition and moved to present their own, moderate, but nonetheless critical, solutions to the questions of the hour. Zinoviev declared that "the time to legalize factions has not yet come, and will not come during the dictatorship of the proletariat."[177]

The tension between the two main factions comprising the United Opposition may have faded a bit in the autumn of 1927 but it never disappeared. Many Trotskyists suspected that the Zinovievists were fair-weather oppositionists, cowards who had opportunistically appraised the political landscape and done what was necessary to survive.[178] The Zinovievists, in turn, could not quite rid themselves of the suspicion that the Trotskyists were cut from the same cloth as the overzealous adherents to "Workers' Opposition" and "Democratic Centralism."

Be that as it may, the Trotskyists and Zinovievists were able to join forces in October and November 1927 and create the skeleton of an autonomous organization. This was the United Opposition's boldest hour: it is estimated that in the month preceding the Fifteenth Party Congress, about fifteen thousand Party members attended oppositionist gatherings. Zinoviev confirmed that oppositionists "drank tea" together from time to time. Trotsky coined a euphemism of his own for such gatherings: "extraordinary conversations" (*chrezvychainye besedy*). Both of them explained to the Komintern: "In view of the fact that Stalin's Party secretaries convene secretly . . . we have no choice but to organize separate convocations of our own. Only pathetic philistines would give up preparation for a Party congress!" (September 1927).[179]

With the Party congress fast approaching, the oppositionists organized clandestine meetings, set up underground printing shops, and raided workers' cells.[180] Two of the secret meetings held in Moscow on October 25 and 29 were presided over by Kamenev; Zinoviev delivered a speech at another "non-Party gathering" on the Day of the Red Press; and Trotsky chaired an underground convention held on the outskirts of the capital on October 29. Serge described a Leningrad oppositionist gathering he attended as a model of revolutionary purity: "A poor dining room was filled with about fifty people listening to Zinoviev. . . . At the other end of the table sat Trotsky. It was simple and moving to see men of the proletarian dictatorship, yesterday still powerful, returning thus to the quarters of the poor and speaking here as men to men and looking for support and for comrades."[181]

In the eyes of the opposition, the status of the groups that met remained vague, perhaps deliberately so: whereas for at least some of the Trotskyists they spelled the inauguration of a new party, for the Zinovievists, they represented only the welcome consolidation of a faction within the extant Bolshevik organization. Thanks to this ambiguity it was not unusual for two separate bodies—one Trotskyist, the other Zinovievist—to preside over a single meeting. Such a meeting was held in early November in the private apartment of Smilga, a prominent leader of the Leningrad opposition.[182] A clear division of responsibilities meant that though the groups had worked out a united front, they retained their distinct identities. The Trotskyists were entrusted with the political and technical aspects of oppositionist work (i.e., the organization of clandestine cells), the Zinovievists with propaganda. This arrangement permitted the Zinovievists to go on maintaining that they were a faction struggling to be heard while the Trotskyist extremists were the real secessionists.[183]

Within Communist circles, the legitimacy of oppositionist meetings was hotly contested. When an undercover Stalinist who infiltrated one clandestine meeting called their work "part of the effort to piece together a new, non-Leninist, Menshevik-Trotskyist party," the oppositionists inverted this interpretation: "when representatives of the Central Control Commission arrived and told us to disperse, we invited them to participate in the debates. Only when they proved disruptive did we throw them out."[184]

Smirnov collected the threats that majoritarian leaders issued: "Whoever tries to go against the Party will end up in jail" (Tomskii); "We will knock the spirit of Sapronovshchina out of workers" (Uglanov); "The Party will make short shrift of the opposition [*mokrogo mesta ne ostavim*]" (Bukharin)."[185] But the opposition insisted it had no fear. "Even when purged, we will continue living the life of the Party, serving it much more loyally than many Party careerists and philistines."[186] Trotsky elaborated this point in October: "Reprisals only strengthen our cadres: . . . Physical pressure will wreck against the rocks of our revolutionary courage."[187] "Purge oppositionists in the hundreds, in the thousands," he boasted a month later. "You will not make them give up the cause."[188]

"It might well happen," Zinoviev told his followers, "that a number of oppositionist groups will be placed outside the Party for a while. Even without a Party card they will have to stick to Lenin's teaching."[189] Other oppositionists were even willing to offer the Central Committee a taste of its own medicine: "The oppositionist group is presently active in forming the . . . true Communist party of the future."[190] "Soon it will be us purging you!"[191] Serge confirmed that in the oppositionist milieu Party cards had become quite meaningless: "A woman worker sitting cross-legged on the floor [during a high-profile oppositionist gathering] asked suddenly, 'And what if we are expelled from the Party?' 'Nothing can prevent Communist proletarians from being Communists,' was Trotsky's answer. Half-smilingly, Zinoviev explained that we were entering an epoch when many of those expelled and partly expelled from the Party would be more worthy of the name of Bolshevik than the Party secretaries." Now that "many of the purged were politically superior to their purgers," members of the opposition came to see being expelled from the corrupt Party as a mark of distinction rather than of disgrace.[192]

According to the official view of events, the opposition "increasingly assumed the shape of a new, Trotskyist party."[193] An oppositionist acquaintance told Mikoian, a Central Committee member and the commissar of trade, that a faction is not a second party. "But what is the difference?" Mikoian wondered, "if you have your own platform, your own view on all issues?"[194] "You are not factionists," Rudzutak sardonically conceded. "You are reactionaries. Your activity has nothing to do with factionist struggle . . . and everything to do with an all-out struggle against the Party, against the Soviet state."[195] By organizing its own national center in Moscow as well as local committees in several provincial cities, the opposition employed "unprecedented methods."[196] According to the Central Committee narrative, "The arch-leftists and the Trotskyists . . . coordinated their organizations, calling them 'centers of literature and propaganda.'"[197] This was a clear "break with Leninism,"[198] an open apostasy.[199]

The Tomsk Party organization was horrified: "An entire counterrevolutionary organization has been set running." "They are trying to undermine the Party!" commented the local daily newspaper.[200] The Siberian GPU unmasked two underground oppositionist groups in Omsk, one "factionalist-Trotskyist" and the other "syndicalist-counterrevolutionary."[201] An intercepted letter from an extremist "group" to a more moderate "faction" included the following admonition: "Your methods of struggle are too parliamentarian and do not fit true Bolsheviks." In response to a question—"What sense does it make to grab power if power is in the hands of the working class anyway?"—the group explained that "parliamentary prattle" (*govoril'nia*) was useless. "Be more resolute," the extremists recklessly suggested, "and join us in toppling the government."[202]

Noting that "the Omsk Trotskyist group had ignored the anarchist essence of the Miasnikov program and formed an alliance with the remnants of the Workers' Opposition anyway," Liapin beseeched the students of Tomsk not to follow such an example. The groups in Omsk, he warned, "have recommended that should war break out we should not defend ourselves from the bourgeoisie and, adding insult to injury, they are agitating against GPU."[203] But his entreaties went unheard. The autumn of 1927 saw the founding of a local center in Tomsk. It appears to have been Tarasov who received the directive to organize an underground oppositionist group in the city; it was typically he who received communications from the opposition's headquarters, such as copies of the Declaration of the Eighty-three, a pirated copy of an article by Trotsky on the Chinese debacle, and, of course, Lenin's Testament. To copy these documents, Gorbatykh, one of Kutuzov's most trustworthy assistants at the institute, smuggled an illegal typewriter in from Leningrad.[204]

A number of conspiratorial meetings took place in Kutuzov's apartment. In addition to the rector, those regularly in attendance included Nikolaev, Beliaev, and Gorbatykh—all die-hard oppositionists. (Tarasov was arrested in November.)[205] Another locus of oppositionist activity was Goliakov's room in the dormitories: Kurkov and Sidorenko brought copies of Lenin's Testament there and the oppositionist program was also available. The majority of those initiated into the activities of the Tomsk Centre appear to have come from the Tomsk Technological Institute: forty-five out of sixty-two "oppositionist activists" were classified as "students." Additional evidence points in the same direction: some consultations were held before classes, and the oppositionist program was widely circulated in the dormitories (referred to as the "monastery").[206]

Siberia's opposition groups replicated the organizational structure of the Communist Party as well as its basic mode of operation—or so GPU informers kept saying:

Each oppositionist group draws up a statute and keeps track of its cell's membership. It also copies the Party's method of supporting itself, including the use of a mutual assistance fund founded on an income-rated deduction from members' salaries. . . . Individuals permitted to read documents have to pay two rubles "to cover expenses." Oppositionist speakers are in the habit of lecturing to raise money; 30 percent of their speaking fees go to the organization's funds.

Furthermore, the opposition emulated the Party's method of recruitment.

New members are attracted by disseminating heterodox material among the "trustworthy." Individuals are indoctrinated and written proclamations are read aloud. In some groups new members are inducted during general meetings.

Perhaps more significantly, the opposition imitated the Bolshevik method of policy deliberation.

Some groups regularly conduct "general meetings." Others meet on what they call "Party day." An agenda is drawn up in advance, and includes "reports from localities." . . . For example, the following issues were to be discussed at the group meeting of October 15, 1927: (1) reports from localities; (2) our factionalist work; (3) deliberation of our platform.

The Siberian oppositionist groups created their own troikas, a circuit committee, and found candidates for positions in the future state apparatus under their control.[207]

As if this mimicking of the Party's organizational principles was not enough, GPU also learned that oppositionist groups did not shy away from emulating the Party's conspiratorial methods. "Secret documents reproduced for internal circulation only and passwords are used to ensure that those present at the meetings have passed muster." The same was true of propaganda techniques: an editorial board was named to draft articles. All its members had to contribute pieces. In other words, something like a propaganda department was set up. "Finally, to top it off, the opposition even attempted to organize its own version of the official youth movement. 'It drafted an anti-Leninist Komsomol program, which was the program of a new Trotskyist youth league.'"[208]

Many of the passages from these informants' reports could as easily be minutes from a perfectly orthodox cell. So why were the resemblances between the opposition and the Party structures so palpably appalling to the GPU informers? Would one not expect the organizational affinities between the two camps to function as a mitigating factor?

Or maybe we ought to think of the opposition's new rituals as a Bolshevik Black Mass? An affair of contrary rites and ceremonies during which prayers were recited backwards, the Black Mass was, or so the Catholic Church believed, the chief liturgical service of those who worshipped the devil.[209] Satan himself presided personally over "this foul travesty of the holiest mysteries," which began with an invocation of the Devil and continued with a kind of general confession, which meant acknowledging any good the penitent might have done; as penance he was enjoined to utter some foul blasphemy or to violate some precept of the church. Among the other satanic practices were "diabolical sacraments imitating the baptism and the supper of our Lord." It was the calculated inversions of Christian practice that gave the Black Mass its fundamentally heretical nature. Completely independent rituals (such as those found in idolatry) would not have carried the same sting. Those who devote themselves to the service of evil "imitate in all respects the worship of Almighty God . . . so that they worship and praise him [Satan] eternally, just as we worship the true God."[210]

Of course, the object of investigation here is not the reality of oppositionist activity, but rather its perception or misperception by Klikunov and his followers. No matter what Tomsk oppositionists may have thought of themselves, they were perceived as subversive agents mocking the Party, and—this point is crucial—GPU acted on this perception. We will never understand why the opposition was repressed so brutally unless we take seriously the grid through which majoritarians viewed reality, a grid that attributed to the opposition demonic intentions and practices.[211]

Let us look once more at the practices of what the Catholic officials called "devil worshippers." The worst of the lot were the Cathars, usually presented in sources as the sect that performed the blackest of masses. Their inversion of Christian rituals seems to have attracted believers due to structural similarities with what disenchanted Christians knew best. To ensnare potential converts the Cathars had to reproduce the promises of salvation the official church was making. It did naive people "good to hear the Church denounced because of her departure from the perfect way," Catholic priests lamented; the language of the denunciation was seductively close to that of Christian ritual. The heretics' scheme to dispossess the Church demanded that they present themselves before the people as the true servants of God.[212]

The Central Committee majority and the opposition had also entered into an intense rivalry to see who could win more souls from the same congregation. The Party techniques adopted by oppositionist cells made them dangerous in the eyes of the majoritarians, and the Siberian Control Commission grew extremely uneasy as it learned of efforts by local underground groups to measure the susceptibility of the working class to oppositionist propaganda. The Omsk oppositionist center called itself the "worker-oppositionist group."[213] In one case, Stalin's secret agents reported, the center had undertaken a study of the living and working conditions of the local miners; in another case, its agitator was dispatched to Semipalatinsk when word filtered in of a strike planned by local workers; in a third case, the center sought advice on agitation from the opposition leaders in Moscow when it caught wind of rumors that a workers' coup was imminent.[214]

Official reports made the opposition out to be especially conniving. "They do not slumber. Conducting a subtle, deceitful politics, it seeks out our weak spots."[215] In Siberia, workers were softened up before being hit with the pitch: "Recruitment is by and large attempted over a bottle of beer or vodka." The majoritarians feared that segments of the opposition were imbued with the "ideas of Miasnikovshchina, this relapse of the workers' opposition, which styled itself as a proletarian group." And as they circulated petitions, oppositionists informed workers that "GPU activities target workers who are unhappy with the rule of Party bureaucrats and who want to be permitted to hear speeches by Trotsky, Zinoviev, and Radek."[216]

Then the city Party committee learned that the oppositionists had set up what they called a "Communist printing shop" and set about distributing "heterodox chicanery" in the Tomsk factories. One of the tracts intercepted by GPU was said to aim at "exploiting workers' naiveté." Entitled "An Appeal to Working-Class Comrades," this pamphlet read:

Comrade workers!
Our platform is the platform of the proletarian opposition. Stalin and Bukharin are trampling Lenin's name and flourishing at your expense!

To discredit this text, the official press promptly unmasked its anonymous author, a certain Ivashevich, identifying him as a "Left Socialist-Revolutionary." "What kind of proclamation," demanded the Tomsk daily, "can a Left SR write? Needless to say, it is not likely to be one in which the Soviet power is praised!" Every worker was expected to know that in 1918 the Left SRs had betrayed the Revolution by staging an uprising that had seriously jeopardized the Bolshevik government.[217]

Incensed that former members of social democratic parties and expelled Bolsheviks were allowed to participate actively in oppositionist groups, the Siberian Party organization did everything possible to "expose their true face." The local control commission made much of the presence of two erstwhile Anarchists among those implicated with Ivashevich in the activities of the illegal printing shop. Furthermore, the Tomsk Centre was found to harbor individuals such as Ivanova, Alekseevskii, and Vinogradova; the sinister intention of these "three Trotskyist moles remained unexpressed until Tarasov apparently instructed all undercover oppositionists to emerge from hiding." While Siberian authorities reiterated time and again that the opposition was courting discredited individuals, the opposition claimed that the "outsiders" in question evinced enough consciousness "to be included in our ranks."[218]

The Central Committee majority had to counter yet another oppositionist ruse, namely the pretense that by struggling against the Thermidorian regime it was perpetuating the heroic revolutionary tradition. Reminding his audience that he had once been "a young and unknown revolutionary," Trotsky suggested that the opposition was reviving Bolshevism's insurrectionary habits.[219] "Let's Recreate Lenin's Party!" urged oppositionist leaflets, and "Let's Organize an Underground According to the Methods We Used in 1907–11."[220] What troubled majoritarians about this was that while the opposition employed a language familiar from the revolutionary epoch, the ends to which this inflammatory language was put were not at all familiar. This was not about the glorification of the Bolshevik Revolution but its destruction by the epigones of petit bourgeois parties.

GPU claimed that it had obtained reliable information that the opposition denied the epoch-making significance of 1917 and that it indeed intended to conduct another, "truly proletarian" revolution. The United Opposition denied this. Kamenev, Zinoviev, and Trotsky argued in unison in August 1927 that "in applying the term 'insurgents' [povstanniki] to us Stalin's faction wants to legitimize the extirpation of the opposition."[221] In November, Kamenev clarified yet again that "the suspicions that we took the road of 'rebellion' and 'mutiny' are delirious."[222] Even the much radicalized Trotsky insisted that "the ascription to the opposition of putschist, adventurist, and rebellious goals—the apparatus seems to be ascribing to us at least the embryo of a desire to provoke another civil war—is a lie that does not do justice to our Marxist, Leninist, and Bolshevik convictions."[223]

But the Central Committee insisted that evidence was growing that the radical wing of the opposition was preparing a revolt against the Soviet power, which it had come to see as "nothing but a monstrous Stalinist dictatorship."[224] To prove its point, it evinced seditious leaflets that reached its offices. "Applaud Trotskyism!" one such leaflet reportedly demanded. "Away with the Soviet power!" brayed another.[225] A leaflet circulated in Siberian universities stated that the Party's best workers are being thrown in jail by the Oprichniks, the servants of Ivan the Terrible who helped him slaughter the Russian aristocracy in the sixteenth century, "and now languish in the torture chambers of the new Moscow tsar." The leaflet continued: "Those who are Leninists in their souls must close ranks and shout, 'Away with Bonaparte! Away with the Oprichnina! . . . Our numbers are growing and the throne of the tsar in Moscow named Stalin is shaking!'"[226]

The inversions of the Black Mass resonate with the GPU descriptions of an opposition girding its loins for insurrection. Because the model for these new warriors was the glorious pre-revolutionary Bolshevik underground, secrecy was emphasized: "The first Omsk Oppositionist group employed cabalistic stratagems to conceal the locations of its meeting places. . . . Harking back to the methods developed in Omsk during the struggle with Kolchakovshchina, the second Omsk oppositionist group dug itself even deeper underground. Discipline is reinforced by the threat of physical violence . . . . 'Traitors,' it is said, 'will be drowned in the Om.'" Conspiracy was paramount. A group member knew only the members of the "trio" or the "quintet" to which he himself belonged. "During the meetings, pickets are posted. Sensitive documents are reproduced in basements and attics by hectograph or typewriter."[227]

The discovery that oppositionists were using a cipher amazed GPU. Among the letters they drew on to prove the use of code was this one from one Siberian Oppositionist group to another:

Got your letter. Answered the first one. Very happy all goes well. Regards to Boria. How is your little brother? Did things work out? All here is as usual. Meet our friends seldom. They have all dispersed. How is the frost? Here it is chilly. After what we wrote last, no further news.

The letter also mentioned "illnesses" and "deaths," as well as the teasingly enigmatic "gathering of berries." All mystery disappeared once GPU offered a lexicon of the oppositionist code:

"Boria," "little brother"—nicknames;

"go to the forest to gather berries"—convoke a meeting;

"frosts"—Control Commission measures against the opposition;

"chills"—hiatus in the suppression of the opposition;

"fell ill"—became disillusioned with oppositionist work;

"died"—left the ranks of the opposition.[228]

With this as a guide, the text became transparent. It concerned underground activities, the measures GPU had taken against them, and the response of the oppositionist grass roots to repressive measures.

Informants concealed in the ranks of the Tomsk opposition reported that an insurrection would soon break out. In the best Bolshevik tradition, preparations were said to be conducted at night. "Ivashevich boasted that the opposition's activity was brilliantly concealed: 'No one knows what transpires in any oppositionist district but his own.'" An office dispatching illegal literature was set up, and Iakovlev from the Technological Institute was put to work there. Illegal materials were arriving from Novosibirsk, according to some testimony, sent by Smirnov himself. The planning of the insurrection was meticulous, and a range of contingency plans was drawn up. At one point Ivashevich received a secret assignment: "'Wait around the corner from the Workers' Palace at five o'clock in the evening. You will be picked up.'" When this particular underground action was cancelled, "a special messenger was sent to notify him."[229]

According to the same source, Tarasov expounded to his squeamish associate Taranov, the disgraced head of the GPU transport department (who was in direct contact with Volkov, Trotsky's son-in-law) the following plan for an uprising: "Our immediate mission is to knock off the leadership of one or more Party districts and circuit committees and get hold of local power. We will use such strategies as work stoppages and seizures of factories, followed by a general strike under oppositionist banners throughout Siberia." Having infiltrated military units from Novorossiysk to Cheliabinsk, the insurgents were also to have the army at their disposal.[230] Ultimately the opposition planned to announce to the Communist dignitaries: "Well, comrades, your time has come. This is the end of your reign!"

When the scandalized Taranov reproved Tarasov and told him that such activities were "anti-Soviet," Tarasov punched him in the nose. (Taranov tattled the whole affair to the authorities.) When the majoritarians saw that the opposition believed the insurrection would actually "redeem" (*spaset*) the Revolution they answered with a religious coin of their own and described the opposition's values system as "sacrilegious" (*sviatotatstvo*). In their eyes, Tarasov was "defiling" (*oporochit'*) the Party line.[231]

Obviously, there was little new in the United Opposition mirroring the official organizational structure in 1927. We have seen the Central Committee supporters doing something very similar two years earlier, when they were in a temporary minority in Leningrad. It seems that certain institutional practices cannot be identified with loyalism or oppositionism: the Bolshevik political discourse was one, and the institutional culture it bred was one as well. Whatever side was in a minority, it organized a parallel structure, serving as a leverage to convince true Bolsheviks—however defined—that it was their only legitimate representative.

Cast Beyond the Pale

There was a feeling in Siberia that the opposition's brash militancy would soon crumble. The Tomsk Party committee eagerly anticipated communications from Moscow that would permit it to set restraints on its challengers. Finally the news arrived: during the October 21–23 plenary session, Trotsky and Zinoviev had been charged with "undermining the unity of the Party" and had been purged from the Central Committee.[232]

The Tomsk city Party committee was preparing grounds for the final delegitimation of the opposition and "organizational conclusions" (read: purge). A rhetorical annihilation had to come first, and there was no better occasion for that than the Tomsk's Seventh District Party Conference convened in early November. Fortified by visions of a triumphant Stalin curbing heterodoxy, speakers at this conference, ostensibly convened to elect delegates to the upcoming Circuit Party Conference, turned against Kutuzovists in a mounting ecstasy of indignation. The opposition was nothing but a malignant tumor on the body of the Party, Klikunov argued, and the district committee, which appreciated him more with each passing day, saw to it that the following questions appeared on the agenda: "Why is it wrong to have two parties? How long can the Party tolerate oppositionists in its ranks?"[233] A complete unanimity seemed unlikely, however, since among the 143 delegates in attendance, a substantial minority of 24 delegates were classified as "oppositionist"—including 8 from the Tomsk Technological Institute. They showed themselves uncowed—Kutuzov sharp and often cuttingly ironical; Nikolaev impassioned; Grinevich and Gorbatykh calm and intent upon seeing their arguments duly recorded.[234]

Generally, Tomsk oppositionists argued, "we must be cautious in the wake of the removal of Trotsky and Zinoviev from the Central Committee. Expulsion of revolutionary leaders who enjoy prestige among workers can backfire." Or: "We cannot treat Trotsky and Zinoviev as if they were identical to Miasnikov." Particularly harsh words were reserved for the local press: "Our daily paper should not rely on Voroshilov when he says that Kamenev and Zinoviev were traitors before October. As to Trotsky, yes, it is true that he constantly makes mistakes. We have not forgotten the speeches he made during the New Course Discussion. But Trotsky is one of our leaders and we cannot simply erase him from our ranks." "Personally," confessed Filimonov, "I will find it hard to part with the likes of Rakovskii, Zinoviev, and Trotsky."[235]

All in all, however, only ten of the speeches given at the conference sympathized with the opposition. The majority accepted the official suggestion that disciplinary action be imposed:

"When they transgressed the limits of Party discipline, the leaders of the opposition debased themselves—they became counterrevolutionary";

"At the Komintern plenary session, Trotsky called for the creation of a new Central Committee. For that alone he deserved to be purged";

"The Party has stepped over such mountainous authorities as Plekhanov—by comparison, Trotsky and Zinoviev are dwarfs";

"As a worker, I feel compelled to say, 'Enough is enough!' Thanks to Trotsky we made it through the Civil War, but the time has come to say goodbye."[236]

When Kutuzov complained about the atmosphere of hostility toward the opposition, Klikunov chose to take his remarks as a compliment. And the suggestion that heterodox comrades had never before been purged was absurd.

On the contrary, it was the opposition's activities that were without precedent in the history of the Bolshevik Party. . . . Their unlawful conduct included the creation of a separate and distinct apparatus, separate and distinct committees, separate and distinct circles—in short, a counter-Party. . . . In the face of such blatant preparations for the creation of a new, Trotskyist party, one ideologically and organizationally hostile to Lenin's party, we have no choice but to move from educational, preventive measures to immediate, harsh, and merciless reprisal.[237]

Taking its lead from Klikunov, the conference endorsed a series of proposals made by the Siberian Control Commission for the punishment of the local "agitators" and "factionalists."[238] Kutuzov's proposal to "refrain from purges," and the five amendments to the official resolution he presented were all rejected. One of the last acts of the conference was the election of a new district committee bureau: Klikunov and his supporters were assigned prominent positions.[239]

Meanwhile, more news filtered in from the capitals. Local papers reported that on November 7, Trotsky and Zinoviev had exploited the tenth anniversary of the Revolution to attempt a direct appeal to the working class. The opposition had planned to march as a distinct group during the celebrations. At a crucial moment it would unfurl banners bearing such slogans as "Long Live the Leninist Central Committee!" "Long Live the Real Workers' Democracy!" "Fight Opportunism!" "Fight the Schism!" Alerted to the plans, GPU quickly crushed this alternative demonstration and squads of majoritarians broke into Smilga's apartment and tore up the portraits of Trotsky, Kamenev, and Zinoviev which the opposition meant to display to the columns of parading workers.[240] Descriptions of the opposition's behavior during the parade in the Tomsk press emphasized furtive and shadowy acts. "Instead of welcoming the millions of celebrating workers at the tribune above Lenin's mausoleum," a locus associated with transparency and light, "the opposition launched its sortie by popping out of narrow alleys." The article jubilantly announced that "the conspiracy was crushed."[241]

In the oppositionist counternarrative the Central Committee supporters appeared in the capacity of a "fascist gang"—this was an analogy to Italy and Germany, where Communist leaders suffered physical attacks from rightist nationalists. This was how Arkhipov, a Moscow oppositionist, described the events of November 7: "When the car carrying the leaders of the international revolution drove by, the fascist members of our cell hurled apples, bread batons, and every piece of junk under their hands at it."[242] The opposition denounced such actions to the Central Control Commission: "How dare the 'Party vigilantes' mock and defile the portraits of Lenin and his closest associates, Zinoviev and Trotsky!?"[243]

But the Central Committee was utterly shocked by the opposition's "illegal demonstration" and issued a directive urging provincial organizations "to expel without hesitation all Communists who oppose Party policy at non-Party meetings" on November 11. A few days later, Trotsky and Zinoviev were purged from the Party altogether "for undermining the dictatorship of the proletariat."[244] The signal was unmistakable, and the Tomsk circuit control commission promptly expelled thirteen of Tomsk's most prominent violators of discipline. "Though we did our best to cure the opposition, the proverb 'Only the grave can cure the hunchback' has again been proven correct."[245]

The Tomsk Circuit Committee Party Conference, which met on November 20, did not send a single heterodox delegate to the Party Congress. The opposition was furious: "Has a single ordinary worker been elected? No: everybody was nominated by the apparatus. Our people sit in GPU jails." The discussion had not even officially concluded when the delegates to the circuit conference were selected. Indeed, in the Tomsk Technological Institute, official reports on various aspects of Party policy continued through late November, even though the cell had long since dispatched its representatives to the regional conference. This reversal of order fueled the opposition's claim that the "Fifteenth Party Congress does not represent the will of the Party."[246] Besides, noted a Communist who insisted he was not an oppositionist, "what is the point in having a discussion if the authors of the countertheses, Trotsky and Zinoviev, are purged in advance?"[247]

Be that as it may, the results of the discussion were carefully tallied and published in the official press: 724,066 comrades voted for the theses of the Central Committee (99.3 percent); 4,120 comrades voted for the opposition (0.5 percent); and 2,676 comrades abstained (0.2 percent). In Siberia, the countertheses of the opposition received a meager 0.4 percent of the vote—slightly below the national average. "More importantly," stated a Siberian journal, "the discussion brought our oppositionist comrades out of hiding"; identified, they could now be brought under influence.[248]

For the longest time the oppositionists believed that their fortunes could be reversed. Hugely outnumbered at Party meetings, they still hoped to win significant unofficial support for their policy documents. "If we get thirty thousand signatures," Zinoviev explained during the summer, "they won't be able to stop us from stating our views at the congress."[249] On the same occasion he tried to rally his supporters: "Contrary to the suggestion from Stalin that defeating the opposition is simply a question of removing its 'leadership group,' the Party will soon realize that it is dealing not only with Zinoviev, Trotsky, and Vuilovich.... Anyone glancing at the list of signatories will say to himself, 'Hundreds of comrades with prerevolutionary standing can't have set their names under the oppositionist banner unless the opposition reflects a legitimate way of thinking.'"[250]

These signatures served as a counterbalance to the official Party membership records. Inverting the orthodoxy, the United Opposition suggested that only its adherents were true Bolsheviks—in fact, they were heroes. "Those who dare to sign oppositionist statements prove themselves true revolutionaries," Zinoviev passionately argued. "Each and every one of them is a political figure in his own right and not just a serial number."[251] Trotsky was also proud of those who linked their fate with the opposition: "The first quality of every revolutionary is the courage to swim against the current, the courage to stand up for the cause even under the harshest circumstances." "We will stand to the end for something we believe is true," the United Opposition proudly stated.[252]

Zinoviev urged all who had signed oppositionist statements to read them aloud at Party meetings and, when possible, to attract additional converts.[253] Here is a typical statement added to the "Declaration of the Eighty-three":

In keeping with the righteous discipline of the Leninist Party, I hereby affix my signature to the statement of May 25.

Ia. Poznanskii, Party member since 1904, [Party card] no. 0019773[254]

And here is a more verbose Communist:

The declaration of the Old Bolsheviks addresses a range of issues, such as the English-Russian Committee, the Chinese Revolution, internal politics, the intra-Party regime, the evident deviation of the leading kernel of the Central Committee to the right and its departure from Lenin's path. Having familiarized myself with the text of the declaration, I deem it my duty, the duty of every revolutionary and every Party member, to adhere to it.

D. Bluvberg, Party member since 1924, [Party card] no. 676032[255]

But when June and July flickered past and no more than 820 had signed, Iaroslavskii laughed in Zinoviev's face. "In one day," he boasted, "and in Moscow alone, we will get ten, twenty, thirty times as many signatures." A bolder, unidentified speaker cried out, "One hundred times as many!"[256] Even when the opposition opened the way for new Party members to sign, the total never rose above five thousand.[257] But Trotsky and Zinoviev refused to believe that their cause was weak: "We cannot, and do not want to inflate our numbers. Our strength lies in our correct ideological line. Future events will prove us correct."[258]

In the autumn the opposition ran another polling campaign, this time signing Party members to its Platform. Again, the idea was to impress the Central Committee majority with the number of its adherents, and again, the result was dissatisfying: not that many comrades were willing to sign a document that was declared illegal from every pulpit. At first, it was rumored that 4,000 comrades signed the Platform in only four days in Moscow and Leningrad, but when the materials were carefully examined by the oppositionists themselves, it turned out that there were barely 1,000 signatures. (In the next few weeks this number increased to some 5,000–6,000 signatures, but these numbers were still far below what was expected and hoped for.)[259] Furthermore, if the campaign to collect signatures on the Declaration was "democratic"—everyone who signed it had read it—this was not always the case with the Platform campaign. In the provinces, it was not always possible to obtain a copy of the Platform, and many signed without reading it, acting out of respect for leaders who authorized it. In some places the number of such blind signatures was almost 30 percent, leading prominent oppositionists to admit to unfair pressure from Trotsky and Zinoviev.[260]

Interestingly enough, majoritarians agreed that support for the opposition ran deeper than the list of signatures indicated and that many comrades simply refrained from speaking openly.[261] When Stalin noted in 1928 that "about six thousand votes were cast against the theses of the Central Committee prior to the Fifteenth Party Congress," he was immediately corrected: "Ten thousand votes!" Yes, Stalin agreed, "as many as twenty thousand supporters of the opposition may have abstained from voting altogether."[262] What worried Stalin was that so many oppositionists remained undercover.

The letter written by a member of the Moscow Komsomol named Feigin to

Ordzhonikidze late in 1927, the product of concerns much the same as Stalin's, shows how the Bolsheviks measured political support.

Nothing but sheer arrogance can explain the certainty of some comrades that . . . everyone wants to knock the teeth out of the opposition because everyone is consciously and confidently supporting the line of the Central Committee one hundred percent. . . . There are many who support the Central Committee simply because the majority reached certain decisions that, they say to themselves, must be accepted. . . . Others support the Central Committee out of fear. . . .

Let me give you an example: this week we celebrated the anniversary of the Moscow Komsomol. Ter-Vaganian, the head of the Zamoskvoretsk Komsomol organization, wanted to speak, but comrades would not let him because he is an oppositionist. Then we listened to a concert and, at midnight, a movie was shown—[Eisenstein's] *October*, featuring Trotsky in the role of Trotsky. Trotsky was shown at Brest Litovsk, at the Kazan' front, and so on. Each time he appeared on the screen, the audience applauded fervently. We stayed there until three in the morning, trying to figure out why they booed Ter-Vaganian but applauded Trotsky's appearances in the movie. Should we assign it to the sense they had of safety in darkness? I think not. There is no doubt in my mind that the same people who cheered Trotsky's appearance on-screen would not have let him speak had he appeared in the flesh five hours earlier.

In Feigin's analysis, the opposition's electoral defeat could not be interpreted straightforwardly as a victory of firm Bolshevik consciousness. Comrades were confused, reticent to come to grips with Trotsky's betrayal. "Of course, duality [*dvoistvennost'*] does not characterize everybody but certainly is typical of many," he summarized.[263]

But the Central Committee majority was eager to seal the victory. Convened after a year-long delay, the Fifteenth Party Congress had its first session on December 2, 1927. The leaders of the opposition had been excluded from the proceedings, and they now debated their next move. "Depriving the leaders of the opposition from the right to present their views—this is Stalin's 'democracy,'" Trotsky sneered.[264] Kamenev was also defiant: "Are we being ordered to forswear our convictions overnight?"[265]

The few token oppositionists who managed to attend the congress tried to preserve their dignity, but the Central Committee insisted on humiliation. Levity is an excellent index of the growing hostility: during the congress there was nothing lighthearted about the laughter that greeted the opposition—it was purely contemptuous and mean. When Kamenev wondered whether "you would believe our word of honor," for example, his opponents laughed at him.[266] Minin, the Zinovievist rector of Leningrad's Communist University in 1925, insisted that the Central Committee majority was not blameless. "We are in the midst of a crisis that has gone on for two years now, and there is no end in sight."[267] Stalin's lieutenants rejected this as mere rubbish. To Leonov, the delegate from the Caucasus, Minin was like a "watch that stopped two years ago. [Laughter.] This is the Fifteenth Party Congress, not the Fourteenth Party Congress!"[268] Rundin from the Urals was even more sarcastic: "A very 'judicious' [*umnyi*] but very mischievous [*bludnyi*] cat has just addressed us." His wisecrack was rewarded with snickering and giggling.[269]

All of the leaders of the opposition were depicted as ridiculous, each in his own way. Trotsky was ridiculous because of his belligerence. "When the opposition needs a warrior type, a stallion, it sends out Trotsky," Tomskii noted. "He is brandishing his sword and shield; his mane is flapping in the wind." Kamenev was devious and sweet-talking, like a diplomat. "When they want to make peace, they put him in the forefront." Finally, there was the pathetic Zinoviev, "When they need someone to shed tears, they parade Zinoviev." This too provoked laughter.[270]

When oppositionist delegates claimed that "we were pushed onto the oppositionist path by our profound belief in the Leninist character of our views," the majority jeered. Their "hypocritical statement" that they had ceased "all factionalist activity" reminded Rudzutak of the parrot who yelled, as the cat was dragging it from its cage, "If we must take this trip then so be it [*ekhat' tak ekhat'*]."[271]

Encouraged by the delegates rocking in their seats, Rutzutak leapt to satirize the leaders of the opposition:

You may recall that when a number of speakers suggested [in 1923] that a compromise with the opposition was imperative, Kamenev compared the opposition to a multicolored, fluffy tail. "If we kiss and make up with this tail," Kamenev stated, "the kiss will not be too savory." . . . Why don't we do what we've always done, first chop off the tail, and then kiss it and make up. I believe Kamenev is quite an expert in the area of tail-kissing by now. [Applause and laughter.] I think that during these last two years, besides landing on the tail, his kisses have also gone a bit below it. [Applause.]

The image of Kamenev kissing the opposition's ass was pleasantly malicious, and Stalin's young cohort compared favorably with sycophants like the former head of the Moscow Soviet. "No, I think that today we will take a different approach," Rutzutak concluded. "We will chop off the tail and we will neither kiss it nor will we ask to make up."

Evdokimov, Zinoviev's erstwhile collaborator, made a last-ditch effort to contest the legitimacy of the purge. "Comrades, I want to say a few words about what the working class really wants. Those on both sides of this quarrel—"

But Skrypnik interrupted him: "What do you mean by 'sides'?" The Party Congress was hardly an arena for legalistic disputations.[272]

Beside himself, Evdokimov abandoned his calm tone: "We must not lie to ourselves!" he yelled at the delegates. But his opponents, an overwhelming majority, gave him a dose of truth: "You know what the working class really wants? To see you out!" The levity had turned sardonic. Humor became derogatory, completely indistinguishable from malice.

Evdokimov made one final effort to hold his ground. "The working class does not want the majority to present impossible demands to the minority, forcing the latter into a position where it cannot tolerate the congress's decisions." But Stalin's people simply laughed. "So this is why you organized an underground?"

According to Rykov, workers were the first to use brute force against the opposition. "After Zinoviev saw for himself what swimming against the proletarian current of the Moika River means [laughter], he came running to us with his conciliatory speeches."[273] Tomskii's similar fusion of rhetorical violence and derision elicited a lively response.

We have seen how Moscow workers "applauded" the opposition. Do you always flee when applauded? . . . "We feared," the oppositionists explain, "that we would be dizzied as the support of the workers rocked us to and fro." And why did workers throw galoshes and cucumbers at you? Oh yeah, because they couldn't find any flowers. A bit more sympathy of this kind, Comrade Evdokimov, and I'm afraid you'll have to be hospitalized.

This speech was met with bouts of laughter throughout.[274]

The era of truces was over. While most of the oppositionist leaders would have settled for an honorable retreat, Stalin demanded their unconditional surrender. "We have only one set of terms," Stalin told the congress. "The opposition must give up its arms wholly and entirely—I mean ideologically and organizationally."[275] Rykov wondered, "What would have happened if the opposition had attempted to rally a few hundred followers in Red Square during Lenin's time, with banners reading 'Long Live the Workers' Opposition,' 'Away with the Central Committee'?" The response from the crowd was prompt: "We would have shot them." When similar threats had been made during the Tenth Party Congress, they were clearly nothing but hot air. Now, less than seven years later, the threats were dead serious.[276]

Majoritarian fierceness drew legitimation from the tumultuous events at the plenary session of the Central Committee that met a week before the Party congress opened. Morbid tenseness was in the air and shameless abuse was hurled at the opposition. Perhaps there was little new in egging on the chairman to silence the oppositionist speakers. But flinging objects at the speaker—this was an innovation from the autumn of 1927. Nikolai Kubiak, a Central Committee secretary, threw a glass at Trotsky, who stood at the podium. And Iaroslavskii grabbed the heavy volume of the First Five-Year Plan and threw it at the oppositionist leader, missing his head by inches. "Unable to persuade people with the contents of this volume, you surely can knock them over with it!" Trotsky commented, but his irony was lost on the enraged majoritarian audience. Demonization took another step ahead: violent rhetoric was replaced with violent action, albeit still largely symbolic.[277]

The congress declared the opposition "an anti-Leninist second party . . . which capitulated to the bourgeoisie." Adherence to the opposition was pronounced "incompatible with membership in the ranks of the Bolshevik party," so the Central Control Commission set up a commission of sixty-five delegates, chaired by Ordzhonikidze, to recommend a series of measures to be taken. The principal recommendation the commission ultimately offered was simple: "oppositionists were to recant or they would find themselves outside the Party." Trotsky regarded such measures as "an attempt to turn comrades into self-denying renegades by means of a direct administrative pressure coming from a rigged congress."[278] "True discussion," his followers had been saying for few weeks now, "will commence only after the congress is over."[279]

On December 10, only a week after he had struck a seemingly indomitable pose, Kamenev unequivocally submitted to the decisions of the congress, "painful as they may be." He soberly assessed the situation. "We stand before two roads and must choose one. One of these roads is that of a second party. . . . For us this road is forbidden, ruled out by our principles, by all of Lenin's teachings on the dictatorship of the proletariat. And then there is the second road, which involves full and complete submission to the Party. We have chosen this road because of a profound conviction that a correct Leninist policy can triumph only within and through our Party, and no such triumph is possible outside the Party and by opposing it."[280] Every word uttered by Kamenev and Zinoviev from this point on expressed their will to trim their sails closest to the wind. "The experience of two years of factionalist struggle," stated their joint recantation, "proved without any doubt that not only was the second party alternative a mistake, but so was a long-lived faction."[281]

Bukharin congratulated the moderate leaders of the opposition for their foresight: "The iron curtain of History was falling, and you stepped out of its way just in time." Obstinate in his defiance of the Central Committee, Trotsky was no less confident that time was on his side, however. "Expel us!" he challenged his tormentors. "You will not expel us from History!"[282]

As the "intransigent [neprimirimye]" refused to so much as consider recanting, the United Opposition was pulled apart at the seams.[283] On the same day that Kamenev and Zinoviev sent their statement of surrender to the congress, a trio of more resilient oppositionists announced that their consciences would not allow them to submit. "For us to refrain from advocating our views," wrote Rakovskii, Radek, and Muralov, "would be a renunciation of . . . our most elementary duty toward the Party and the working class."[284] Lashevich said the same, only without restraining himself: "I spit on the Fifteenth Party Congress. If reprisals intensify we will move underground. I have already been in exile [under the tsar], and penal servitude does not scare me, either."[285] Also unbowed was the Democratic Centralist wing of the United Opposition, with Smirnov at the head. They sneeringly described the congress as a "gathering of Stalinist potentates."[286]

A number of Siberian Trotskyists expressed resolve to "form a detachment and hide in the forest."[287] There is a small group of oppositionists that remains obstinate, commented Kalashnikov, the chairman of the Siberian Control Commission. "This group has become, to all intents and purposes, anti-Soviet, and it must be treated accordingly."[288] But while these exceptions were significant, the vast majority of the Siberian oppositionists followed Kamenev and Zinoviev. Kutuzov's erstwhile ideological brethren declared flatly: "We are quitting the opposition in conformity with the resolutions of the Fifteenth Party Congress."[289] Tomsk newspapers described comrades who, "having realized that a Party split was in the offing," had their signatures collectively removed from the oppositionist platform.[290]

On January 2, 1928, 1,250 Party members from Tomsk met to discuss the rulings of the Fifteenth Party Congress; there was standing room only in the city's largest movie theater. One speaker expressed the hope that "the decisions made by the Party Congress have opened oppositionists' eyes and cooled their ardor," and went on to lay blame at the feet of those "big fellows [bol'shye liudi]" who had raised the pitch of the discussion in Tomsk.[291]

Repentant oppositionists took the floor to announce that they had renounced their opinions. One of them ventured a ritualized self-humiliation:

I know the platform I distributed got into the hands of our enemies, and thus I unconsciously assisted the counterrevolutionary element that reared its head during the discussion. The activities of the opposition contributed to the foreign campaign against us and brought us closer to war. I did all the ignoble things our leaders told us to do, and it is too late to repent. The Party cannot and will not believe us.

Schismatics were obliged to declare before the entire Tomsk Party organization that "we were wrong and the Party was right."[292]

With great pomp, repentant oppositionists added their signatures to printed copies of the congress's resolutions. The meeting ended amid resonant thanks to the Party for "settling accounts with the opposition in a truly Bolshevik manner." Every measure voted on passed unanimously—"or, to be more precise," wrote one observer, "the local opposition did not participate in the deliberations and, toward the end of the proceedings, unobtrusively took its leave." Only one hand was raised to oppose the suggestion that all confirmed oppositionists be immediately purged, "but even that hand was immediately lowered as though its owner hoped not to be noticed." The atmosphere of the meeting may be gauged from the following note, which was sent to the presidium: "Who is this type sitting here next to me? When the speaker condemned the opposition, he murmured: 'You cannot put everyone in jail. Besides, incarceration is a bourgeois form of punishment.'"[293]

To make things easier for the naive oppositionists, the decisions of the Fifteenth Congress were "reformulated in popular terms understandable to everyone," to be gone over in specially organized political grammar circles.[294] At the Tomsk Technological Institute the working through of the issues was declared "the most important of the second trimester's tasks."[295] Oppositionists despised such practices: "Those who work through decisions imposed from the top instead of using their brains and hearts . . . replace a living Party with a charade."[296]

Despite the fact that the institute's organized opposition folded its banners, not every adherent renounced the opposition's platform. "Though I have cast down my arms in the organizational realm", announced Kutuzov, "I cannot do the same in the ideological realm. A number of congressional decisions do not square with my views."[297] As he took up the martyr's cross—Kutuzov knew full well how he would be repaid for his protracted defiance—he was following a path blazed by Khristian Rakovskii, a prominent Trotskyist who insisted that the "expression of oppositionist views was compatible with Party regulations."[298]

The sequel surprised no one. In the winter of 1928, Kutuzov and his closest collaborators—Osokin, Parkhomov, Taskaev, and others—were arraigned before the Tomsk Control Commission and purged from the Party.[299] Following a dramatic vote in an unfortunately undocumented meeting that took place in January or February 1928, they were all also kicked out of the institute.[300] In the months to come, how one had voted on Kutuzov's expulsion and whether one attended the "farewell banquet" Kutuzov threw before going into exile served to identify the last die-hards of oppositionism.[301]

31. "Masses after the Leaders . . ." The workers wield banners: "Long Live the Party's Central Committee"; "Away with the Oppositionist-Trotskyists"; "For Leninism, for the Line of the Central Committee." Bottom: Trotsky: "You see, I told you that the masses push behind us. We barely have the time to show the way. . . . We can barely grease our soles. . ." *Sovetskaia Sibir'*, no. 266, November 20, 1927.

32. "The Oppositionist Luminaries." Above: Rakovskii (extreme left): "He said lots of rubbish at the Moscow conference on the question of war"; Preobrazhenskii (extreme right): "Where his crooked road will get us: 'New Economics'—the current Bible of the Opposition." Below: Tomskii stated at the Party Congress: "When the opposition needs a warrior type, a stallion, it sends out Trotsky. He is brandishing his sword and shield; his mane is flapping in the wind. When they want to make peace, they put Kamenev in the forefront. When they need someone to shed tears, they parade Zinoviev." *Rabochaia gazeta*, no. 283, December 11, 1927.

33. *(left)* "Bluffing." From the Opposition's tiny rowboat holding Trotsky, Kamenev, and Zinoviev, Trotsky yells to Stalin and Rykov atop a huge ship: "Give in or we will break you in two!" The opposition is too tiny to make good on its threat and bring about a Party schism. *Rabochaia gazeta*, no. 282, December 10, 1927.

34. *(right)* A drawing by Belotskii from the sixth day of the Fifteenth Party Congress (December 7, 1927) depicting the oppositionist speaker N. Muralov jeered by the audience: "Nikolai Ivanovich, shame on you! Drop Trotsky's cheat sheet!" "Comrades, if someone said you had killed your own wife, eaten up your own grandfather, torn off the head of your grandmother, how would you feel?" Muralov said at the congress, supposedly at Trotsky's request. "How could I prove this did not happen?" Outrageous charges were made against the opposition that were very difficult to disprove, because the Central Committee controlled the Party press and insisted that the burden of proof was on the opposition. Muralov was a member of the Central Control Commission (removed in 1927) as well as the rector of the Timiriazev Agricultural Academy. Belotskii was a Party member since 1918 and a functionary of the Commissariat of Foreign Affairs since 1925. RGASPI, f. 74, op. 2, d. 168, l. 50.

35. "Unanimously!" "Are they voting for the Opposition's Resolution or for giving the speaker additional time?" *Krokodil*, 1927, no. 54, p. 9 (drawing by D. Mel'nikov).

ВЫЛЕТ

Рис. К. Елисеева

Троцкисты Серебряков и Преображенский исключены из ВКП(б) за раскольническую фракционную работу.

ТРОЦКИЙ: — Гляди-ка! Птенцы-то уже оперились и вылетели!..
ЗИНОВЬЕВ: — Из гнезда?
ТРОЦКИЙ: — Нет, из партии.

36. "Out of the Nest." "The Trotskyists Serebriakov and Preobrazhenskii are purged from the Party for schismatic, factionist activity." Trotsky: "Just look! The fledglings grew feathers and left!" Zinoviev: "The nest?" Trotsky: "No, the Party." *Krokodil*, 1927, no. 42, p. 4 (drawing by K. Eliseev).

НЕОПРОВЕРЖИМОЕ ДОКАЗАТЕЛЬСТВО

Рис. К. Елисеева

САМ (глава семьи):— Мы были правы,— яблоки нам бросали гнилые, калоши рваные... А что из этого следует? Что материальное положение рабочего класса тяжело,— как мы и говорил.

37. "Incontrovertible Proof." "Sam (the head of the family): We were right, the apples thrown at us were rotten, the galoshes torn. . . . And what follows from this? That the material condition of the working class is indeed grave—as we argued." Sam is Trotsky, who twists reality to convince his wife (Zinoviev) that the working class is behind him. *Krokodil*, 1927, no. 43, p. 9 (drawing by K. Eliseev).

38. "We Are Tired of This Music!" The organ-grinder is Trotsky; Zinoviev, again as a female, is the singer; and Kamenev is the parrot. Below: "We play and play, but no one is coming!" *Krokodil*, 1927, no. 44, p. 1 (drawing by K. Eliseev).

39. "Oppositionist Ward No. 1; The Chronically Ill." History of Kamenev's illness: "oppositionist fever, recurrence of the outburst of 1917"; history of Zinoviev's illness: "oppositionist fever, recurrence of the outburst of 1917"; history of Trotsky's illness: "oppositionist fever, permanent outbursts since 1923." The opposition is still medicalized and presumably can be healed. But the illness is unremitting and the Central Committee speaks in terms of constitutional propensity to oppositionism. The boundary between recurring illness and criminal recidivism became very thin as the 1920s progressed. *Krokodil*, 1926, no. 43, p. 5.

40. "In the Illegal Typography."
—"Well, you got the cipher?! Got everything?"
—"Almost everything. Three letters are missing, VKP [the Party's acronym]."
Radek and Kamenev are in the front, Trotsky is in the back. *Krokodil*, 1927, no. 44, p. 4
(drawing by K. Eliseev).

41. "By the oppressive will of all-party chief policeman, Stalin." The jail is called the Party apparatus (RKP is the acronym on the prison bars). In his boot Stalin keeps the resolution of the Party congress, and he is trampling on the banner of intra-Party democracy. His hunting dog is "Iaroslavka," whose collar reads "Central Control Commission." This cartoon targeting Stalin and Iaroslavski was printed in one of the opposition's underground typographies. Only the contours of the drawing were reproduced and the images were supposed to be colored by the recipients and distributed as widely as possible. The cartoon is signed with the pseudonym "Ovod" ("The Gadfly"), the title of a novel by E. Voinich that was popular among the radical intelligentsia; its hero was a revolutionary who paid with his life for the cause. RGASPI, f. 74, op. 2, d. 170, l. 99.

The Oppositionist as a Personality Type

If in the early 1920s a modicum of political heterodoxy was still compatible with Party affiliation, and the term "oppositionism" was not yet applied to each and every expression of political dissent, by the end of the decade heterodoxy had been turned into an immutable personality trait. Among all the shifting political labels—Trotskyist, Zinovievist, Bukharinist—oppositionism was essentialized and made retroactive. Now the Party believed that there was an essential, true self hiding behind one's public self-presentation. But while the oppositionist became increasingly imbued with an essential character, no one had yet suggested a necessary link between him and counterrevolution. There was always an impetus to psychologize errant behavior, to purge, not to kill.

42. "Incompatible with Membership." "Your heart is moved to the right, you are limping on your right leg. Clearly not ready for attack." This is an example of Party hermeneutics; the Party reads one's heart and knows what is in it: in this case an individual is diagnosed as a Rightist oppositionist. *Krokodil*, 1930, no. 26–27, p. 17.

43. "Opportunist Barometer." "His usual position is 'variable' but he is very sensitive to the pressures of the petit bourgeois atmosphere, moving to the left and the right." This cartoon and the one below make fun of the oppositionists' constant vacillations (*shataniia*), a psychological condition induced by a divided will. *Krokodil*, 1930, no. 10, p. 1.

44. "I envy this pendulum: sixty swings a minute and no one accuses him of deviationism!" *Krokodil*, 1930, no. 39, p. 1.

45. "A Somnambulist Walking on the Right Side."
"I will tell you a secret, The moon is good to me,
At night I go to factionist meetings, And in the morning I remember nothing."
Krokodil, 1930, no. 36.

46. "This is what I call a double-dealer! An entire faction in one individual!" While a model Communist possessed monumental spiritual wholeness, the public and private identities of the double-dealer were worlds apart. In order to infiltrate the brotherhood of the elect, ardent oppositionists were in the habit of feigning submission to the general line—they wanted to remain in the Party at all costs, though this meant deceit and hiding their true faces, so that they could betray it at the most appropriate moment. The oppositionist double-dealer appears here in the image of the Indian God Shiva with his many limbs, each going in its own direction. *Krokodil*, 1930, no. 36, p. 17.

47. "No Success!" An oppositionist circus, a place where one cannot believe one's eyes, was the antipode of the Bolshevik steady and reliable Party organization. Everyone is jumping from the right to the left and back, twisting and turning like snakes. This expresses the oppositionist type, vacillating and changing sides. *Krokodil*, 1930, no. 16.

Keeping the House in Order

The systematic and often repeated cleansing of membership commonly known as "purges" (*chistki*) or "verifications" (*proverki*) was a cornerstone of the Party's attempt to ensure the purity of its ranks.

48. "Party Record Keeping." Below: "Incoming, Outgoing." The Party is carefully watching its membership. Workers come in, petit bourgeois interlopers go out. *Krokodil*, 1924, no. 9, p. 16 (drawing by K. Rotov).

Необходимое мероприятие.

49. "Purge." Below: "A Necessary Enterprise." A rank-and-file Party member, dressed as a worker, is sweeping the Party floor of oppositionist banners and resolution proposals (and eventually, the oppositionists themselves). If the efforts to create the New Man were typically addressed through construction metaphors, the tenacious attacks on oppositionists were seen as a grand cleansing campaign. *Krasnoe znamia*, no. 259, November 13, 1927 (drawing by Mazhericher).

50. "A Conversation with the Party Card." A petit-bourgeois-looking Communist is sorrowfully parting with his Party card. *Krokodil*, 1929, no. 8, p. 1.

INQUISITION, COMMUNIST STYLE

Housecleaning

After the Fifteenth Party Congress, Party members at the Tomsk Technological Institute had to do a lot of soul-searching. The "ideological health" of the Party cell there had been sorely compromised, and Moscow was obliged to initiate harsh disciplinary actions.

On April 4, 1928, the new bureau and the representatives of the control commission convened behind closed doors to talk things over. L'vov, a new emissary from the center, scolded the local Party representatives: "You woke up too late, and the Tomsk Control Commission had to go to battle against the opposition practically unaided." Other speakers took up L'vov's theme. "It took two whole months before the institute was finally shaken into confronting the opposition." "The district committee left the institute to stew in its own juice." Anxious to preserve its authority, the beleaguered local leadership had to close ranks fast. Rushing to Klikunov's defense, the bigwigs declared: "It is not true that the heads of the institute missed the moment when comrades started drifting away. They simply witnessed no incidents of outright factionalism "until quite late in the autumn." Klikunov mournfully reviewed the events: "The discussion—by far the most important event of the last year—lapsed into deviance and then into an intra-Party struggle. We wanted to emerge from it with honor, but this proved difficult."[1]

But the books on the opposition were not yet closed. Before adjourning, the leaders of the Technological Institute resolved to follow the recommendation issued by the Central Control Committee and conduct a verification of their Party organization. The verification would take place in several stages. First, an unexceptionable troika, including Fel'belbaum, Obrazov, and of course Klikunov, conducted a preliminary investigation.[2] Every Communist whose name appeared on the "list of oppositionists" prominently posted by the institute's bureau was strongly advised to submit a "letter of recantation" as soon as possible.[3]

The troika carefully inspected the recantations that started coming in already last November, comparing their contents with evidence collected by Tiul'kin and the circuit control commission. Once that comparison had been carried out, students were interrogated in person by the entire bureau. Finally, towards late April, the bureau's recommendations were set before the institute's Party cell. Since the old bureau had been accused of "intimidating the grass-roots membership," the district committee warned its successor to "report to the cell in detail. Recommendations must not be rubber-stamped." Grass-roots democracy was something Klikunov was committed to. And cell meetings held during the verification were to be closed; dirty laundry was not to be aired in public.[4]

The Bolshevik hermeneutical discourse underwent a number of important changes following the investigation of 1924: most ideological dissent was increasingly labeled "oppositionism," now a clear-cut term of opprobrium. The Party had recognized the United Opposition as a dangerous cabal, and the Central Committee had spoken: no mercy would be shown to those who challenge the Party's monopoly on truth. Although oppositionism retained a marked ethical component, the investigation of 1928 had a more narrow political character now—students were asked less about their parents and their everyday life and more about whom they supported during the discussion and why. Heterodoxy received a strong temporal dimension: the defendants were evaluated in terms of their long-term political behavior, and those who relapsed were good candidates to be considered inveterate oppositionists.

The instructions of the Central Control Commission constructed procedures and vocabulary that combined to form a new field of knowledge around oppositionism, a knowledge that was bound up with operations of power and representation. While the official discourse concerning political heterodoxy overlapped and interwove with the Bolshevik moral, theoretical, and legal discourses, oppositionism had begun to represent itself as a field of inquiry that was separate and authoritative. The Bolshevik hermeneutics had to fine-tune its inquiry into an erring soul.

A certain clearing up of the Party's position vis-à-vis the opposition following the resolutions of the Fifteenth Party Congress does not mean that the tension between two discursive constructions, the oppositionist as mistaken friend and the oppositionist as subversive foe, was completely resolved. In one way, the verification commission clung to many of the previous discourses surrounding deviation, articulated around the notion that oppositionists were confused comrades, unable to fully account for their actions. This drove Klikunov and his underlings to treat the interogatees as objects of knowledge, identified and characterized as ill, degenerate, or swayed by circumstance. But insofar as the verification process assumed a comrade challenging official categories and offering views of his own, the hermeneutical discourse tended to construct autonomous, self-conscious oppositionists. Such tension between the construction of objects of knowledge and subjects within knowledge made the outcome of the interrogation, at least in some cases, unpredictable, despite the guidance of the Tomsk Control Commission and the GPU as to how each case must be resolved.

The verification commission did not have to exercise absolute power to be effective. It sufficed that the ritual dictated the terms by which students understood their own selves and inculcated desirable reactions to ideological deviance.[5] At least in theory an affair internal to the Party cell in question, the verification pulled students into hermeneutical discourse, where power primarily operated not from an exterior source against the student's will, but inculcated the notions of individuality and autonomy and shaped interogatees as freely confessing subjects. Examination of the ways in which the official discourse placed recalcitrant students into particular kinds of identities should not ignore the possibilities of evasion or subversion on the part of the defendants. In the pages below I frame the performance of subjectivity by each interrogated student as a contest between the official discourse and alternative modes of Bolshevik speech, and seek not only to show how effective was the new discourse on the opposition but also to call attention to the agency allowed to the defendants, and the tactics they utilized to save their Party cards.[6]

In a typical interrogation, the purgers focused on the nature of the oppositionist's doctrinal disagreements with the Party and on his possible complicity in underground activities. Wayward Communists were divided into three categories: "suspect"—students who had voted for the opposition; "inclined towards the opposition"—students who had appended their signature to a copy of the Platform; and "outright oppositionists"—students who had tried to convert others to Trotskyism. The better to seduce others, such students typically presented their illegal actions as heroic "self-denial" (samootverzhennost'). Sometimes they had done little but "flirt" (zaigryvat') with other Communists to "confuse" (sbivat' s tolku) them. But at other times they had gone as far as "wining over some of them to their cause" (sagitirovat'), "drafting them" (zaverbovat') into the heterodox army.[7]

Within the third category, students were ranked according to how intimate they had become with leading insurrectionists. Links with Tarasov, for example, who was a center-based oppositionist, were more incriminating than links with Kutuzov, who was only a local celebrity. But links with Kutuzov were more incriminating than links with individuals such as Nikolaev or Gorsunov, whose activities had primarily been confined to the institute. Anyone categorized as an "outright oppositionist" could safely expect to be purged. But those who escaped the worst of the three categorizations might hope for a lighter sentence.[8]

To be sure, most of the students summoned for interviews continued to debate the meaning of oppositionism. Some called those who proselytized for factional freedom true oppositionists; others contended that only membership in the Tomsk Centre made one an outright heretic. According to Beliaev, "a true oppositionist is anyone who had signed the Platform, had organizational ties with the opposition, and conducted active [propaganda] work on its behalf."[9] None of those questioned was willing to admit that voting for the countertheses made one a heretic. All this, however, was little but a rearguard struggle: once the supreme Party authorities had censured Kutuzov's actions, his supporters, large and small, were at Klikunov's mercy.

When forgiveness was sought, the obvious truth was that repentance would carry far more weight than forensic disputation. When the number of Tomsk oppositionists who defiantly clung to martyrdom was counted in April 1928, the fingers of one hand more than sufficed. And the Kutuzovists' continuous endorsement of countertheses was an outrage, for the discussion was now seen as a battle that had spilled out of the Party, closer to a class war than to a regulated procedure. The defendants themselves understood that while some confusion on this score had been excusable a few months back, they were expected to understand now that their rivals had been in the right all along. Many pleas were based on the distinction between past and present understandings of oppositionism: we are loyal comrades who acted wrongly but in good faith, and the proof lies in the realization we made once we were shown the truth; we admitted that we were mistaken and ought to be absolved.

The system of codes and meanings structuring the activity of the verification commission is more important to our purposes than the actual doctrinal disagreements. The interrogators did more than continuously shift back and forth between student's communications and the official dogma. They listened to the latter's account of his actions and thoughts, and their attention was drawn now this way, now that. Certain themes stood out, certain pieces did not fit together. Gradually the purgers' intuition about the defendant crystallized. As they went along deciphering the defendant's testimony piece by piece, some underlying processes in the latter's political behavior emerged. The interrogators began to have a sense of what had been confessed sincerely, what had been distorted, and what had been completely omitted, and this awareness shaped their thoughts concerning possible remedy or censure.

Gorbatykh's interrogation was by the book. Two damning admissions were squeezed out of the defendant during a prolonged investigation: "I have voted on all issues with Kutuzov," Gorbatykh confessed; and "I have read almost all oppositionist literature." These violations pulverized Gorbatykh's initial self-presentation as an innocent lamb. Without further ado, the bureau moved to examine his ties to the Tomsk Centre.

Q: Did you attend illegal meetings at Kutuzov's?

GORBATYKH: Yes. . . . I talked there to Gorsunov and Pishchal'ko. I usually arrived towards the end of the meetings when only the leaders remained; I never talked to non-Party.

Q: Did you attend the illegal meeting at which Nikolaev's candidacy for chairman was discussed?

GORBATYKH: I do not remember.

Q: What was said at the first meeting?

GORBATYKH: That we had to widen the scope of our work. . . . Kutuzov said we had to take over the cell. I disagreed. . . .

Q: What was said at the second meeting?

GORBATYKH: That we should make an appeal to non-Party workers.

Gorbatykh's testimony up to this point had been quite damaging. And his unconvincing recourse to a weak memory feebly sheltered his great sin: he had joined Nikolaev and Kutuzov in their attempt to take over the cell the previous November. Another crime he would not admit to was the spreading of oppositionist documents outside the institute. Gorbatykh claimed he was never personally charged with any special assignments, "only engaged in agitation."

The temporal framework of the defendant's vacillations was established with astounding care:

Q: When did you come under the influence of Leningrad? . . .

GORBATYKH: I have been vacillating since late October or early November.

Q: When and how did you realize that the opposition was wrong?

GORBATYKH: I cut myself off from the opposition on December 1. . . . [At the time,] I faced a dilemma: I had to either tell the Party everything or degenerate further. . . . As soon as I left the hospital [Gorbatykh fell ill during the winter] I notified the bureau that I had signed the Platform.

December 1—the day Gorbatykh's Communist consciousness resurfaced—coincided with the opening date of the Fifteenth Party Congress. By retracing his change of heart to this event, the defendant hoped to impress upon his interrogators that he had been a mere doubter whose mind was in sync with the Party's timekeeping.

Having finished its direct questioning, the bureau, as was its habit, began to deliberate the case. Different members espoused different reconstructions of Gorbatykh's inner world. Speaking out of turn and at times interrupting each other, verification referees voiced their opinions. But Fel'belbaum clearly spoke for the majority when he noted that "Gorbatykh appears to be shielding his collaborators. The only oppositionists he names are those he knows have already been punished." Krasnikov was also harsh on the defendant:

In Gorbatykh we have a factionalist of the first rank, of refined Leningrad vintage. I cannot believe he signed a copy of the Platform without reading it all. Gorbatykh used all his strength to shove a wedge into the cracks that opened up within the Party. For all we know he is vacillating right now. Contrary to what he says, he must still think that the opposition is in the right.... An overt oppositionist like Gorbatykh will return to his old habits at the first opportunity.

Only Klikunov seemed inclined to clemency. "Gorbatykh," he maintained, "is not as dedicated an oppositionist as some of you seem to think. He was simply hoodwinked by local oppositionist leaders." Eventually, however, Klikunov joined the rest of the bureau in recommending that "Gorbatykh be purged as an oppositionist."

Now it was up to the institute cell to decide Gorbatykh's fate—this was part and parcel of the verification process—and the issue became far more controversial as his political dependability was assessed. A number of speakers believed the defendant redeemable, and one of them explained: "If we load Gorbatykh with public work he is capable of mending his ways." But even those who knew Gorbatykh well ended by condemning him. "Gorbatykh's pretense of habitude is a typical oppositionist ploy," detractors argued. "He is not so easily confused. He is not a vacillator but a convinced oppositionist." The control commission's overseer had tipped the scales. "Gorbatykh," Tiul'kin said, "should confess what it was that he brought from Leningrad. He told us 'I brought a sewing machine' but the truth is that he brought a typewriter."[10]

Sincerity was the ultimate touchstone for recantations, and here Gorbatykh was found lacking. Klikunov drove home this point: "When it is time to assign censure, sincerity must weigh heavily in the consideration. This is by no means secondary to social position or revolutionary merit."[11] "Comrades ought to know," the verification commission stated in no uncertain terms, "that sincerity is absolutely indispensable if oppositionist tendencies are to be brought to light and uprooted for good."[12] If a student truly repented and spoke openly he might have a relatively untainted soul; after all, he had supported the opposition "mechanically," and had quite possibly been "brainwashed" (vnushenie). If insincere, a defendant would give himself away by being "indirect" (nepriamolineinyi) and feigning "dimwittedness" (neponiatlivost').

Suspicion of "insincerity" alone sufficed to have Andrievskii, whose only sin was a single vote in favor of Kutuzov's thesis on agricultural policy, put on the bureau's blacklist. "I have no idea why I come across as a doubter," averred Andrievskii. "Oppositionists avoided me because they were convinced that I supported the Party majority." But Klikunov had noted something contrived in the defendant's conduct. Acknowledging that "formally, Andrievskii is clean," the secretary recalled how he and Andrievskii had "tried to trip each other up. It was as if we were members of different camps. What prompted Andrievskii to go back and forth and to engage in diplomatic maneuvers is a mystery to me. He must have been holding something back, avoiding an open exchange of opinions." So Andrievskii failed the sincerity test and was reprimanded—heavy censure considering how trifle was his actual infraction.[13]

Looking into the Soul Within

First and foremost, verification took place in a tribunal of conscience. The commission employed the hermeneutics of the soul as a crucial tool: this body of theory and practice permitted Klikunov and his friends to determine who was injurious to the brotherhood of the elect and who was not, which defense pleas were insubstantial and which solid. A picturesque catalogue of Bolshevik hermeneutical stratagems, the verification protocols list Communist sins coupled with appropriate apologias and punishments. During the commission's deliberations a series of provisional sketches of oppositionist consciousness were tried out.

While legalistic terminology peppers the transcripts, the process was not centrally an investigation of facts.[14] After all, by the time the verification had begun there were few details the authorities did not know about student violations of Party discipline: the GPU and the circuit control commission sources had kept them well informed. Who wanted to waste his time quizzing oppositionists on topics with which they were already conversant?[15]

Turning into something like an ethical contest, Averin's case gives us insight into the verification as in inquiry into the soul. To excuse a momentary "loss of self" (namely, his vote in favor of Kutuzov's supplement), he invoked the authority of a protector with a solid reputation: "Comrade L'vov [the Party plenipotentiary] told me himself that since I realized that I lost my way during the discussion and since I have already came to self-awareness, my recantation is supererogatory."

A Komsomol member, however, testified against the defendant. "I read excerpts from the Program at Averin's apartment," his accuser maintained. "Others present, most of them non-Party individuals, debated the Program." An outraged Averin responded with complete denial, claiming he had no knowledge whatsoever of the opposition's secret meetings. "In any case", he added, "Ivanova would not have trusted me with such information."

As the questioning continued it became more and more evident that the investigation was not concerned with unearthing new and concrete details. Dominating the proceedings was a showdown between the moral qualities of the defendant and his detractor. To exonerate himself, Averin demanded a "confrontation" (*ochnaia stavka*). This ritual, a cornerstone of the Bolshevik hermeneutics of the soul, had little to do with the production of evidence—no one ever bothered to substantiate earlier claims. The face-off generally took the form of mutually contradictory claims and counterclaims and amounted to nothing less than a moral duel. The Party arbiter was expected to evaluate the various testimonies, make good use of his soul-reading skills, and determine who had spoken the truth and who had lied.

To judge from the verdict in Averin's case—"severely reprimanded for concealment of oppositionist activity"—the confrontation did not go as he had hoped.[16]

The interrogators wanted to penetrate into the oppositionist's subjective state—outward behavior did not concern them so much.[17] Students whose actions might have been enough to convict them of sedition were forgiven when the significance of what they were doing had been lost on them, while students who committed lesser crimes were heavily censured when it could be established that they had "consciously harmed the Party."[18]

If the Party apparatus had set up the verification only to collect bare evidence, it would have made all the necessary inquiries as promptly as possible and would have doggedly followed up fresh tracks. In fact, it did nothing of the kind. The Central Control Committee clearly instructed Party organizations to let several months elapse before commencing verification.[19] The passage of time served a range of purposes, and important among them was the provision of Party hermeneuts with a chance to observe the suspect for a while. Only the test of time would determine whether that oppositionist recantation was in earnest.

Throughout the previous autumn, the student-worker Panov had been a pugnacious and outspoken oppositionist—was he really capable of the radical ideological about-face he now said he had accomplished? "A couple of us who looked into the question cannot understand what could possibly push someone like a Panov to join the opposition," Obrazov noted. "Equally strange was his total capitulation, which was sudden and seemingly left no ragged edges." Other hermeneuts, however, reckoned they could explain "Panov's rapid recovery without difficulty. Once he had filled some gaps in his reading, Panov became convinced he had erred."[20]

Because the object of the interrogation was the self, whatever testimony the oppositionists gave, no matter how clear or how utterly factual, had to be interpreted. Imagine a defendant who speaks highly of Kutuzov, boldly declaring that he had behaved righteously during the discussion. Immediately, two opposite readings of such testimony were possible: this is indeed an irredeemable oppositionist, or this is a steadfast individual whose willingness to pay the price for his convictions justifies sympathy and possibly even forgiveness. Or imagine one who confessed to what he now admits were terrible crimes: he had associated with oppositionist leaders and devoured illegal leaflets. Here, too, the verification commission had to choose between two interpretations: either here was a duplicitous criminal, whose contrived candor was a wicked ploy, or here was a repentant and reformed man whose forthright confession proved his sincere commitment to the Party. No interrogator claimed infallible understanding of the defendant's heart. Although a verdict would have to be reached eventually, no evidence could ever constitute a final proof of guilt or innocence.

Only a subtle hermeneutical investigation of the soul could elicit the kind of self-revelation that distinguished, at least tentatively, a doubter from a here-

tic. "Doubt" (*somnenie*) and "heresy" (*inakomyslie*) were subjective states, not easily grasped through external, objective indices. Doubt signified a lapse of Party
consciousness. Though certainly a negative mental condition opening the soul to
temptation, it might quickly be remedied with the aid of proper "working through."
Heresy, on the other hand, grew out of positive conviction, indicated irreversibility,
and was hopeless.[21]

Heresy has a long history in the Western tradition. When the Greeks used
the word they meant "choice," "election," and "decision or purposive effort." This accounts for the Christian use of the term to mean "school" or "received opinion"—all
of which, like the pagan term, emphasized the idea of the free choice of a doctrine.[22]
In the Middle Ages, heresy was defined as an openly taught and pertinaciously defended opinion that violated the accepted interpretation of the scriptures. Christians deemed an opinion "heretical" only when it was the blasted fruit of wicked
will. He who gave up his unsavory views once shown the error of his ways was simply a repentant dissenter.[23] The true heretic was an individual "whose will was stubborn, refusing to bow before superior wisdom and legitimate authority."[24]

The inveterate oppositionist was one who, unpersuaded by any sort of enlightenment, challenged the Party—clearly he and the heretic of medieval Christianity
were twin souls. An oppositionist became a counterrevolutionary only if he held to
his beliefs steadfastly, despite recurrent clarifications by supreme Party organs. Just
as one could not be a heretic without the Church, so one could not be an oppositionist without a Party Congress to interpret the Party line. Should an oppositionist continue to defend his unacceptable ideological stance after the strictures of the
Party Congress, he would be guilty of a persistent thought crime.[25]

The language employed by the verification commission at the Tomsk Technological Institute made fine distinctions between a range of mental states, and Communist hermeneutics provided a rich psychological vocabulary to map the road
to sin and redemption. The oppositionist set out on his travels with "vacillation"
(*kolebanie*) stamped on his Party card: if he "lost his way" (*zabludilsia*) it was because of "flaws in the consciousness" (*nedostatok soznaniia*) or "character weakness"
(*slabost' kharaktera*). Such an individual was "undeveloped" (*nerazvityi*), "decadent"
(*upadochnyi*), "untempered" (*nevyderzhannyi*), "unstable" (*neustoichivyi*), "indecisive"
(*nereshitel'nyi*), or "wavering" (*nepostoiannyi*). The "skeptic" (*malover*) was "prone to
plunging into a morass" (*vvalivatsa v kashu*). At times it was said of an oppositionist
that he had "lost his mind" (*svikhnulsia*). Some "deviated" (*otklonilsia*), while worse
cases "retreated" (*otstupilsia*) from the Communist truth. The latter "fell shamefully"
(*pozorno upali*)—when the Russian Communists spoke of falling it had the same
religious connotations as in English. Losing faith in the Party could be injurious: a
soul that was "rugged" (*s sherokhovatostiami*) "wandered" (*kochevala*) between ideological camps.

If one wanted to earn redemption, one had to step into the spotlight. Doubts had to be revealed and murky thoughts "cleared up" (*proiasnitsia*). A heterodox comrade who took the time to "look about" (*osmotret'sia*) usually "opened his eyes" (*prozrel*), regained his sense of self (*prishel v sebia*) and reversed his earlier opinions (*otdumalsia*). The best way to recuperate was to "air" (*ventilirovat'*) and "think through" (*promozgovat'*) ideological issues. At the end of the journey, the repentant oppositionist confessed. A moral experience, his recovery was described either as "correction" (*ispravlenie*) or as "healing" (*ozdorovlenie*), both processes assuming a total "renunciation" (*otreshenie*) of heterodoxy.[26] Not all oppositionists, however, could be saved. While some had only been touched by heterodoxy a bit, the "convinced" (*ubezhdennyi*) and the "virulent" (*iaryi*) oppositionists were "incorrigible" (*neispravimyi*). Their souls were described as thoroughly "ignoble" (*gnusnye*) or even "abominable" (*merzkie*).

Perhaps the case of Samoilov will allow us to get an idea of how the connection between outward behavior and intentions had to be unraveled. For all of the questions Samoilov had to answer about his actions, his interrogators were really after the subjective story. How could a welder's assistant like him become an oppositionist? asked a puzzled interrogator. Samoilov broke into a long narrative.

It was Kutuzov who led me astray by casting a false light on the circumstances and force-feeding me illegal materials. These unscrupulous methods convinced me that the opposition must be right. . . . I did not seek advice from the cell's bureau because I had my own opinions. "If leaders as prominent as Kamenev and Zinoviev have taken these sorts of measures," I said to myself, "the opposition must be right." . . . Soon, however, I changed my mind. Furthermore, I had elected not to propagate heterodox opinions because I was never fully convinced that the opposition was right.

Samoilov's presentation, which examined the experiential aspects of his fall and even included a short soliloquy, made out his involvement in the Tomsk Centre to be little but the misguided actions of one blindly loyal to a few famous revolutionary leaders.

So much for Samoilov's version. His auditors came up with their own interpretations, and soon the bureau had polarized around two quite different views: either he was an old Trotskyist, fully aware of his malfeasance, or he was a befuddled worker, a temporary convert to the least virulent type of heterodoxy. The interrogators played out the rope and hoped the defendant might hang himself. "What was it you said when opposition documents were shown to you?" Samoilov was asked. "That the Platform must be kept secret," he answered. In this scenario, Samoilov knew Kutuzov was trying to win supporters for the opposition, but not that he was "circulating leaflets around the institute." The defendant named names, recalling that Parkhomov had recruited him into the Tomsk Centre. "I did not ask who the other members were and attended no illegal meetings."

When the bureau had run out of questions, opinion was still split over

Samoilov's true self. Klikunov, one of the more sympathetic questioners, urged his colleagues to "take into account that no one made Samoilov submit a recantation. . . . We never suspected him of factionalist activity. Nor did his last name appear on any of the lists of opposition members." According to Klikunov, Samoilov had turned himself in even though he had not been caught in anything, the action of a truly repentant comrade.

Overall, however, the hermeneutical evidence argued against such indulgence. "Samoilov's attitude," declared Obrazov, "is a grave example of thoughtlessness, aggravated by an insincere confession." He went on to rebut the cell's secretary at length. "The motivations Samoilov reports are too opaque and convoluted; he is not telling the truth. Who would believe that he became an oppositionist by entrusting himself to a piece of paper [i.e., the Platform]? It is obvious that he must have subscribed deeply to oppositionist ideas before that. Samoilov's impulsiveness suggests that he is easily led astray. The rust of oppositionism is eating at him."

Obrazov saw no merit in Klikunov's point that since Samoilov's recantation was voluntary it had to be sincere. It must have been a calculated step: "Samoilov realized that we would eventually learn of the part he played in oppositionism."

Could Samoilov be somehow redeemed after all? That depended on whether he was a Zinovievist (healable) or a Trotskyist (irremediably heterodox). When asked whether he had any previous record of insubordination, the defendant had portrayed himself as an adherent of the Leningrad Opposition: "I remember talking with friends in an excursion wagon and expressing support for the countertheses Zinoviev submitted to the Fourteenth Party Congress." As Samoilov well knew, Zinoviev was the cutoff figure between deviation and counterrevolution: Samoilov could safely trace his heterodoxy to 1925 but no earlier. "Only gradually did it dawn on me that the opposition was wrong," he said. "But Zinoviev's recantation to the Politburo certainly clinched it." Samoilov insisted that his oppositionist trajectory paralleled Zinoviev's and that, like his leader, he had recanted after the Fifteenth Party Congress said its word.

His interrogators ultimately agreed not to go in this case beyond a "severe reprimand."[27]

Pastoral Care

At the center of the verification a dialogue took place between the lapsed comrade and his interrogators. At first glance, the confrontational aspect of the dialogue leaps to eye: while the oppositionist typically tried to minimize his guilt, the interrogators assumed that it lay deeper. The aggressiveness of the encounter was underlined by the praise heaped on "tested" (*iskushennye*) Communist heresiologists for "cracking the oppositionists open" (*raskusit'*) and determining their spiritual "kernel" (*nutro*).[28]

In spite of the stiffening of penalties and the wider employment of the new inquisitorial procedure, Party experts still insisted that proceedings against oppositionists be conducted not from a zeal for vengeance but out of the wish to correct an erring comrade. To ensure the spiritual health of the Party, the verification had to be endowed with pastoral power. "This form of power," Michel Foucault writes, "cannot be exercised without knowing the inside of people's minds, without exploring their souls, without making them reveal their innermost secrets. It implies a knowledge of the conscience and an ability to direct it."[29] The intent of the Bolshevik pastoral strategy was inner desire, not mere outward conformity. Overall, this was a shaping and a subjection of consciousness that aimed not to force a comrade to obey, but rather to cultivate the sincere wish to obey. Pastoral power did not rule out coercion, understood as something like parental correction. In the enterprise of the verification commission, free choice and compulsion were not mutually exclusive. In the long enlightenment to which it subjected its members, the Party could use a measure of constraint precisely with the goal of bringing about internal moral progress.[30]

Gosunov's case illustrates the strong current of patience and instruction that could be applied to a dissenting worker by sensitive interrogators, as well as the limitations of such a charitable approach. His persona left the verification commission deeply affected. Interrogators could not agree: Could Gorsunov be healed within the walls of the institute? If so, pastoral care could be brought to bear. If not, there was no choice but to expel him. Klikunov opened the interrogation by briefly reviewing the history of the case. Earlier, he reminded the commission, "we were inclined to forgive Gorsunov, since we believed that he had voted for the opposition unthinkingly. Now, however, we have learned that he frequented Kutuzov's apartment . . . as late as this January." Some touchy issues had to be ferreted out.

Gorsunov testified that Kutuzov wanted to get some notes back before leaving Tomsk, "so I went over to deliver them. But that was all—we did not discuss political issues." Yes, he met with Kurkov and Goliakov and they gave him the Platform to sign. "I did not turn them in because I thought I was doing the right thing for the Revolution." So belated a confession to contacts with the Tomsk Centre more than justified a purge. But here pastoral care began to assert itself.

Pigilev, for example, did not believe a worker could become a lost soul in six months. "Although the Fifteenth Party Congress instructed us to expel someone like Gorsunov for oppositionism, we are also told to take the concrete individual into account. Gorsunov is politically immature. . . . We have to make a study of how the Tomsk opposition came into being if we are to understand what happened to him." Fel'belbaum chimed in with Pigilev: "Though Gorsunov lacked the courage to report his connections, I too am convinced that he did not understand the basic nature of the opposition."

But the defendant wriggled and kept wriggling, clearly dodged repeated queries about the composition of the Tomsk Centre, and the accusation of "insincerity" did not go away. Obrazov expressed grim satisfaction at being able to revisit the case: "Gorsunov thinks the opposition is more precious than the Party. He submitted his recantation because he was told to do so. Having committed an anti-Party crime, he was happy to escape serious punishment." Just as tough on the defendant, Klikunov was convinced that Gorsunov's embrace of the official Central Committee position was carefully thought out. "At the first interrogation, I dared Gorsunov to be sincere but he told us nothing about the oppositionist literature. Mind you, Gorsunov has told us in his own words that he signed the Platform 'consciously.'"

Pigilev suggested asking Gorsunov "whether he supported Zinoviev's or Trotsky's point of view"—a litmus test supposed to distinguish between doubters and die-hard heretics.[31] But the defendant only grumbled in response. "I have no idea what is the difference between them."

In his closing statement, Gorsunov insisted that his recantation was absolutely full. As one who had left oppositionism far behind, he cast an objective glance at his former, tainted self: "My own view is that I did deceive the bureau, but I was not competent on the issues." By a vote of five to three the bureau elected to believe Gorsunov's story and the defendant got away with a "severe reprimand." Pastoral power appeared to have gotten the upper hand.

A month later, however, Gorsunov had to be arraigned before the verification commission once more. His third appearance was due to "hoodwinking the bureau, not once but twice." During previous interrogations he had concealed his participation in important illegal meetings—it turned out that he had been privy to the most subversive activities of the Tomsk Centre. Obrazov and Klikunov finally won: indulgence was set aside and a measure of proletarian wrath administered.[32]

On the whole, however, the verification commission was reluctant to declare too many erring comrades as lost souls. Klikunov preferred to describe them as uprooted workers: "victimized by separation from their native milieu, they miss the factory."[33]

Kamkov, for example, was regarded as typical of those who succumbed to their "petit bourgeois academic surroundings." When they asked themselves why "this worker showed himself indifferent when cracks appeared in our organization," his interrogators could only hypothesize that while studying at the institute the defendant "must have sunk into some sort of despondency." Klikunov testified that Kamkov "comes from a disciplined family. Unfortunately, he had not yet been properly tested in struggles."

The defendant jumped on the bandwagon:

My demand to see the August plenary session's stenographic report, which I now regret, must have been triggered by an alienation from the working class. I thought the discussion was nothing but a simple exchange of opinions. When I voted to grant Kutuzov more time to speak I was thinking that once the opposition had been allowed to express itself the majority would snatch away Kutuzov's last trump cards. As soon as I realized that by calling for publicity I was actually encouraging internecine warfare, I adopted the Central Committee's position without any misgivings.

Poor, misguided Kamkov! His name was removed from the official list of oppositionists.[34]

To be sure, erring comrades were bound to give up their views at the sound of authoritative rebuke. But the interrogators were obliged to correct legitimately: even when invested with institutional power authorities could be severely reprimanded for censuring comrades without rendering them an adequate explanation. The Party was supposed to bring doubters back into the fold, not to stigmatize them. "Every Party member should feel free to approach the Central Committee for explanations if he is unclear on things or has doubts or is wavering on issues. We must help a comrade dispel doubts and vacillations, save a comrade from doubts and vacillations, return a comrade to the correct Bolshevik path. A doubting comrade must be helped, not censored."[35] The use of cynical words that denied the soul-healing aims of the verification process provoked outbursts—language associated with police work, for example. Students complained that "bureau members use a non-Communist terminology, including such words as 'detective' [*syshchik*], 'shadowing' [*slezhka*], 'interrogation' [*dopros*]. Such language must not be used in the context of verification work."[36]

Indeed, insofar as interrogators and interogatees shared a common interest—the accurate diagnosis of ailments of consciousness—the process of verification resembled the working of a conventional court of law less than it did a surprisingly gentle inquisition. Unlike the image we have of a harsh and intolerant investigation of heresies, in the ideal inquisition, as envisaged by the medieval Church, the confessor was supposed to have "much the same relation to the suspect as a solicitor or counsel has to a modern defendant"—ecclesiastical writers insisted that proceedings against heretics be conducted "not because of a zeal for righteous vengeance but because of a loving compulsion to correct an erring brother."[37] Similarly, the great task of the verification commission was the healing of the wounds of heterodoxy, so that a Communist spirit might reverberate again in comrades' souls.

The Weight of the Past

No one who entered the room where sat the interrogators was a stranger. Class origins deeply influenced the commission's assessment of the character and reliability of each student.

Students with roots in the countryside who came before the verification commission were fond of suggesting that the legacy of village life deprived them of the sort of political self-awareness possessed by all deliberate schismatics. They needed enlightenment and healing, not the Party's punishing hand. This was the line taken by Zuev, who passed himself off as an uncouth and impulsive peasant who had signed the oppositionist Platform out of sheer foolishness. "My support for Kutuzov," granted Zuev, "was a grave and thoughtless mistake that necessitated my appearance here." Alternating between supplication and defiance, the defendant sounded his appeals in a variety of discordant notes. When pressured a bit, he allowed that "even now I still think our policy is a bit too soft. My opinions on issues," he hastened to add upon seeing so many eyebrows raised, "may well stem from my short-sightedness."

The image of the rube suffered a great test when Obrazov, a member of the Party bureau, spoke. "Politically, Zuev is fairly well developed. It is unlikely that he joined the opposition out of ignorance. As we all know, Goliakov, with whom Zuev lived, possessed illegal literature—does anyone believe that Zuev did not read it?" Volokhov, also a bureau member, added a temporal dimension to Obrazov's damaging reconstruction of the defendant's self: "I noticed a heterodox inclination in Zuev quite some time ago. He used to be afflicted by the typical oppositionist longing to be a hero and a martyr." By the time Obrazov and Volokhov were done with him, Zuev no longer resembled an innocent doubter; he had become a devoted oppositionist.

Other interrogators were concerned that "when the Party was faced with an internal split, Zuev followed his emotions, not his mind." Paradoxically, it was this particular type of indictment that the defendant had hoped for: he could only benefit from the charge that he was weak-willed and emotional, a typically obtuse peasant who, much as he tried, had yet to overcome the gullibility so typical of his class. Speaking next, Klikunov claimed that "Zuev should not behave like a child and justify his [dissenting] vote by a 'wish to get on the nerves of the official reporter.'" This was a stern rebuke, but Zuev was breathing more and more freely: somebody with an immature political outlook—so Klikunov described him—could not be a counterrevolutionary. In the final scene of his performance as village idiot, the defendant flaunted his political infantilism: "I read only *Pravda*, and even that irregularly. Since I failed to keep in touch with *Bol'shevik*, I was bound to remain uninformed." Styling himself as one of the flock and sorely ignorant, Zuev was sure to recover following "immersion in public work."[38]

On the face of it, Grinevich, a bookish student, was Zuev's opposite. His learned, intransigent speeches stimulated heterodox moods. Should this member of the intelligentsia be purged despite the fact that he clearly had no links with the Tomsk Centre? Klikunov leaned towards clemency: "Not a single oppositionist testified to having any ties to Grinevich." Others saw it differently. "An oppositionist kernel lingers in Grinevich even today," stated one of the interrogators. "He still believes that it was the Central Committee that broke away from the Party!"

When the interrogation gathered momentum and Grinevich depicted his attitude towards Kutuzov as "personal sympathy, no more," his detractors pressed on: "Did Kutuzov attempt to assign you missions?" No, he said, "we talked in late October or early November—I do not remember exactly when. In any case, I refused." Grinevich claimed he "fully realizes that he cannot eschew responsibility by pleading political ignorance." He saw himself as an ideologist at least as sophisticated as Kutuzov and implied that his theoretical background had rendered him immune to oppositionist machinations. "I was not influenced by Kutuzov," he insisted. "I think he has a thing or two to learn from me, himself." Surprisingly, Grinevich's intelligentsia background saved him: not swayed by Kutuzov's charisma, he could not be categorized as a full-blown heretic.

Just as members of all classes could attain the light, so could members of all classes succumb to evil temptations. To be sure, workers were spared whenever possible. When Obrazov rather pedantically reminded his colleagues that "the Fifteenth Party Congress clearly stated that oppositionists cannot remain in the Party," Klikunov shrugged it off: "Did the congress not also tell us to be careful with workers?"[39] The healthy instincts of workers and their natural affinity with the Party were supposed to be strong antidotes to wrongheaded propaganda. But if suspected of illegal activity, workers were censured on equal footing with peasants and the intelligentsia.

Kurkov, a worker-oppositionist, was haunted by his crimes. Not only had "he voted for Kutuzov's countertheses throughout the discussion," he had been close to the leaders of the Tomsk Centre. When he essayed the line that had helped so many escape serious punishment and presented himself as a confused worker, his defense slammed into a brick wall.

The interrogators grilled Kurkov for the longest time: "Did you think that the disagreements within the Party were programmatic or tactical?" "Did you think the Platform corresponds to reality?" "How can you think that it was 'not a great crime' to sign the Platform when you are fully aware that it undercuts the line of the Central Committee?" Kurkov explained that he thought the discussion was "a power struggle within the Party" and he did not see enough cause to rebuke the opposition. "I had no ties with Kutuzov and company."

Goliakov, however, was merely a personal friend.

I used to visit his apartment, though seldom, and only to read some literature. . . . It was there that I familiarized myself with Lenin's Testament. It was Goliakov who twice gave me copies of the Platform—"Just to read," as he phrased it. . . . I had little understanding of theory, believed every word of the Platform and signed the document unthinkingly . . . drawing a false analogy to the Brest-Litovsk peace treaty. I used to think that the Platform [just like Lenin's outward capitulation to German demands in 1918] was a tactical maneuver. . . . Bear in mind that Goliakov did not tell me that he was carrying out factionalist work—clearly they did not consider me one of them.

All of Kurkov's attempts to portray his entry into opposition work as hesitant and partial fell on deaf ears. "Kurkov's answers are convoluted," noted Fel'belbaum. "This makes it difficult to determine whether he is a confirmed oppositionist or merely succumbed temporarily. It is hard to believe that a worker would change his opinions under the impression of local, fleeting circumstances."

Then those well disposed to Kurkov began to speak. Obrazov attempted to demonstrate that the defendant's spiritual malady had followed the series of mishaps that commonly befell uncouth workers.

I believe that in Kurkov's case the formation of an oppositionist outlook went from the particular to the general. He generalized the small irregularities he encountered in his specific environment. The philistine buzz all around him, the talk about the aberrations in the economic and political situation—these took their toll. Subsequently, when he came across the Platform, Kurkov mistook it for a pseudo-corroboration of the sorts of petty criticisms he had been hearing. Kurkov had always been a disciplined and firm comrade. . . . I am sure that he is sincere when he claims that his oppositionist delusion was temporary.

If he had come to oppositionism recently, by way of induction, not deduction, and had always been open about his convictions, Kurkov could not have entertained abstract heterodox ideas.

Resourceful and bold, this apologia did not go over well. Other interrogators were displeased with what they perceived as Obrazov's excessive gentleness in questioning and leniency in interpretation. If the mind of a worker might have been muddled a few months earlier, it had to be crystal clear by now. But not only could Kurkov not recall whether he had signed the Platform before or after he had seen the stenographic report of the Fifteenth Party Congress (if after, his guilt would have been enormous), "his words today were . . . illogical and riddled with holes. If the oppositionists let him read the Platform, they must have imagined that he shared their views."

Volkov chose to turn the defendant's autobiography against him: "We have listened as Kurkov told us that he was a collectivist from a young age. Shouldn't that sort of individual mull things over in the most thorough way before signing anything?" This was only a gentle prelude to the soaring crescendo of Volkov's invective: "I cannot believe that Kurkov would sign the Platform without absorbing its content in full. Kurkov's recantation is a document directly drawn from the world of diplomacy: he writes that 'signing the Platform is, in itself, a crime.' But when it comes time to answer our questions, he says just the opposite." According to Klikunov, Kurkov was "one of those individuals who pick up on small irregularities and at a convenient moment fling them in the Party's face without any concrete proof. His contention that he signed the Platform out of loyalty to the leaders of the opposition is a smoke screen. It is Kurkov's fault that he signed a Menshevik platform; in so doing he acted like a member of a different party."

"Most of those here believe that I am hiding something," declared Kurkov when given a final chance to exonerate himself. "Well, I can only repeat that I have fully recanted all of my mistakes. Experience taught me that I had taken a false path."

His judges had a lot of trouble reaching a verdict. Initially Kurkov was purged as "ideologically unstable"; after appeal, however, his censure was commuted to a "severe reprimand."[40]

Party veterans were supposed to be immune from temptation even more than workers. Steadfastly siding with the Reds during the difficult years of 1917–1921, they were supposed to serve as an example to the rest. But such lofty expectations were not always met. Consider the case of Umanets, a Civil War combatant. As they posed their questions, the disappointment of the interrogators grew ever more palpable: "It is strange that a Communist of such stature failed to take a clear stand during our tumultuous meetings." In an unusually long apology, Umanets questioned the very idea that "someone like me, who proved himself during the numerous ordeals at the fronts, be accused of 'indecisiveness' and 'neutrality.' Had I really been a convinced oppositionist, I would have joined in Moscow and signed the Platform there. Was I not criticized by the mutineers [buntovshchiki] at the cell meetings?" Far from happy with the defendant's "non-Party tone," the verification commission unanimously recommended that he be reprimanded as "undisciplined."[41]

Then there was Podborskii, another decorated Civil War hero, whose ties to the leadership of the Tomsk Centre puzzled the verification commission. Podborskii admitted that he had been in the habit of visiting Kutuzov's apartment. Asked how, "personal sympathies aside, could Kutuzov be sure you would not turn him in?" he answered: "I do not know. I've never been inside his head." Something had to be said, however, for the part Podborskii had played in doing away with Kutuzov. No one could deny that his sacrifice had been impressive, and Podborskii had made much of it. He had voted to expel Kutuzov "with great reluctance: I felt a great personal sympathy for him."

If in the case of Kutuzov, Podborskii's mind had overcome his heart, Trotsky was a different matter: the defendant could not bring himself to renounce the leader for the life of him: "The purge of Trotsky has been hard for me to take. I cannot agree with this measure." The interrogators eventually spared Podborskii, concluding that his continuing loyalty to Trotsky was shared by many overzealous veterans who had been dazzled by the military commissar's heroic passion.[42]

Podborskii was always mentioned in the same breath with his close friend Filimonov—one of the most outspoken oppositionists in the institute. Both men had distinguished military backgrounds, but when the verification commission considered Filimonov's Civil War record, it ran into difficulties. His autobiography amounted to a catalogue of a seemingly endless series of exploits: the defendant had fought on the Baikal front, the Northern front, and the Southern front; he also served as an adjutant in a Red battalion, superintended a military region, and worked as an activist in the cultural department of the Red Army.

This was all most respectable. But there was a catch: Filimonov was mobilized by Kolchak in Irkutsk. "I served as a scribe, but for [only] a month and a half," he confessed. "In 1920 I joined the Red Army because it needed fresh recruits; at the time about 150–160 students volunteered, but only twelve or thirteen of us actually ended up enlisting." This was the archetypal journey of a Siberian worker who was drafted into the enemy forces only to rebel and emerge at last an ardent Bolshevik. At the same time, the events in this narrative could easily be presented in a different light: Filimonov was so susceptible to denunciations that he opportunistically switched sides only when it seemed clear that the Reds would prevail. His interrogators could not exclude the possibility that the defendant had converted to political heterodoxy long before, under the influence of Trotsky's New Course.

Q: How did you behave during the previous discussions?

FILIMONOV: I always sided with the majority.

Q: So what made you vacillate now?

FILIMONOV: I gradually came to have some doubts, thanks to such abnormalities as the minuscule number of elected Party positions. . . . It is not that I oppose regimentation in the right places, but we should not overdo it. I had hoped that by openly raising these issues I might make the situation healthier.

Here was a strikingly original line of defense, one that defied all expectations. Filimonov brashly inverted established meanings, interpreting his frequent attacks on the district committee's authoritarianism as proofs of loyalism, not heterodoxy. Crucial to his presentation was the word "democracy," long employed as a key slogan not only by the oppositionists but also by the majoritarians. According to Filimonov, to defend Party democracy meant to side not with the opposition but with the Central Committee majority.

The confessors abetted this ingenious self-presentation with a no less ingenious diagnosis. Was it not possible, suggested Obrazov, that Filimonov's contributions to the discussion had reflected not his real thoughts but the desire to enliven the debate and enhance the consciousness of all those present? "Filimonov is a very sensitive comrade. The diatribes he contributed to the discussion were meant to bring out the internal potential of the many Party members who had returned from practical work with doubts induced by the distortions they had encountered in their everyday lives." Perhaps it was best to think of Filimonov as an oppositionist vaccine, a hint of heterodoxy that permitted the body to build up its defenses. Fundamentally, Obrazov was suggesting that everything Filimonov had said was, like some children's game, the reverse of what he sincerely thought. Those who thought Filimonov was one of them, the inveterate oppositionists, were soon unmasked. And gullible students drawn by oppositionists' rhetorical skills experienced the shock of their lives when they discovered that the object of their adoration did not mean what he said. Once the example of Filimonov had taught these impressionable youngsters something about how to identify empty talk, they became immune to heresy. Pivnev embraced Obrazov's view that what Filimonov really did during the discussion was to shoulder the thankless task of a Central Committee provocateur. As "an individual with a direct and open character who always agreed with the Party," Filimonov in this reconstruction sacrificed his personal prestige for the cause, "losing face not only in the eyes of the majority but also in the eyes of the minority."

Though clearly some took it quite seriously, this interpretation of Filimonov's conduct was ultimately rejected. Klikunov proved that the defendant, regardless of his motives, had harmed at least one student, "Comrade Podborskii," who had taken Filimonov at his word. Once he had heard Filimonov praise oppositionist literature, Podborskii no longer valued Party discipline, and very nearly became a Trotskyist.

Before voting on the case, the cell decided to investigate a long-standing denunciation asserting that Filimonov had served as Kolchak's staff captain. If verified, this detail would have destroyed the claims of those who would invert the apparent meaning of Filimonov's inflammatory speeches, and Filimonov would have been taken at face value and branded a counterrevolutionary.

When Filimonov failed to report for the new hearing, it looked quite bad.[43] His final hearing took place at the Tomsk circuit control commission, and we can only guess that it did not turn out too well.

Sooner or later the problem of the oppositionist's relationship to the text of his confession must be tackled. Many historians would argue that within the constraints created by the framework and categories of verification, Kurkov, Podborskii, and Filimonov fended for themselves as best they could, using the official language for their own ends. Such an interpretation invites a cynical reading of the records: oppositionists never sincerely embraced the language of ideological enlightenment, only used it to save their Party cards. The defendant becomes here an individual who confronts the verification commission as a set of verbal possibilities that he tries to manipulate in order to maximize his chances of survival. But cultural historians have powerfully critiqued such a perspective, reminding us that intentions cannot exist outside of language. Leigh Gilmore adds that identity does not exist prior to confession, patiently waiting for the moment of revelation, but rather that it is "the space from which confession issues," and that space is always already structured by the dominant discourse.[44]

It would be hard to make of the oppositionist confessions an expression of a single mind possessing all the logical and rhetorical unity the defendant imposes on it. Like David Harlan, I do not believe that a writer can stand outside his own universe of discourse. A yearning for the presence of the speakers, "a presence that seems to shimmer just beneath the surface of the text but a presence that is, in fact, always deferred, always elsewhere, always already absent," may be futile.[45] The meanings oppositionists gave to their lives cannot be separated from the prevailing discursive mechanisms of their time and place, because it was these that constituted them as historical actors in the first place, imbuing them with their worldview, their interests, their fears—everything that made them who they were.

A Dialogue?

The work of the verification commission was not a simple projection of existing relations in the Tomsk Party organization but a transfiguration of power: Klikunov was triumphant and the opposition publicly humiliated. Along with disgrace, Kutuzov's supporters had to contend with the implicit yet palpable threat of dispatch to the control commission, not to mention the more direct means of coercion at the Party's disposal: purge, exile, even arrest. But coercion remained behind the scenes, as the work of the verification commission meant translating power into discourse; if ideological domination took the form of naked oppression it could damage the Party's legitimacy.

A crucial aspect of the translation of authority into language involved defining the issues: the verification commission posed the questions and the defendants had to answer. Some might plead ignorance, but students who remained completely silent were flouting the Party's authority. The truth would remain concealed to all who failed to pose questions and deliberate them openly; once those questions had been answered the truth had a form and a binding force.

Of course, we must learn to disentangle the different threads that form the textual fabric of verification transcripts. Following the methodology outlined by Carlo Ginzburg, I read such documents as the product of an utterly unbalanced interrelationship, trying, by way of deciphering them, "to catch, behind the smooth surface of the text, a subtle interplay of treats and fears, of attacks and withdrawals."[46] My understanding of how the interrogation worked invites an emphasis on a symptomatic reading. A "reading against the grain" interprets omissions, distortions, and insinuations. Trying to pin down the narratological strategy employed by the various speakers is interesting because the protocol seems always to reveal certain slippages.[47]

To what extent can we describe the 1928 interrogations as a dialogue? Of course, the positions of the speaking figures were unequal. Pastoral care aside, gross inequalities in terms of real and symbolic power explain why the verification commission was usually successful in eliciting the confessions it sought. The interrogations appear repetitive and monologic because the defendants' answers often no more than echoed the questions of Klikunov and his underlings.[48]

But the interrogation of a bitter critic of the Tomsk Party organization such as Filatov lacked the highly ritualistic quality seen in other interrogations. The case gives us a rare opportunity not only to outline the construction of discourse, but also to demonstrate the agency heterodox students demanded for themselves. Challenging the intrinsic opposition of orthodoxy and oppositionism, Filatov demarcated a position for himself that was circumscribed by neither side, although negotiating both. For a brief but tantalizing moment, he allowed himself to break free from the strict codes of official categorization.

During this interrogation, the defendant refused to acknowledge his prosecutors. He moved beyond quarreling about the actual contents of the narrative and questioned the verification commission's authority to construct narratives in the first place. Filatov was doing more than just subverting the official language: he was speaking in a dialect of his own, a Bolshevik language, to be sure, but different from its official variant. Precisely because it is a record of misunderstandings, obstacles, and conflicts, the record of Filatov's interrogation contains more traces of the agency of the defendant than any interrogation examined above. We also find here traces of an especially thick nonverbal subtext: silences, evasions, and denials were all prominent enough despite the work of the official who edited the stenographic report. Paradoxically, difficulties in communication permitted the appearance of a real dialogue, an unresolved clash of distinct, conflicting voices.[49]

The beginning was modest. A Party member since 1920, Filatov insisted that his reservations regarding official policy were minor. His was not a doctrinal quarrel with Stalin and Bukharin but a disagreement with local bigwigs over the sale of vodka and the housing crisis. During the discussion, he jeered at the local leadership: "You say that accommodations in Tomsk are fine. Then why are students being charged ten to fifteen rubles for a room?" Quoting the Declaration of the Fifteen to the effect that "the housing norm for workers is much lower than the urban average,"[50] Filatov wanted to see a direct proletarian action: "Many houses in Tomsk are privately owned. Why shouldn't the district committee requisition them?" "Compensate the owners with henhouses!" he added sardonically.

Questioning Filatov six months later, the verification commission wanted to know what he made of official housing policy now. "Can [negligent] attitudes be widespread among the Party leadership?" Filatov would not go that far: "I don't approach the issue that way and I never did."

On most issues, the defendant was similarly submissive. He accepted the Five-Year Plan and claimed he had no complaints about Party democracy. Paradoxically, Filatov's answers provoked the greatest suspicions precisely because they were quite innocuous. "This is not the first time that Filatov has had to answer our questions," Fel'belbaum pointed out. "His story today is identical to the story he told us at the previous meeting, word for word; he must have prepared set answers and is keeping to them." Instead of accepting the hermeneutical framework that one divulges one's innermost thoughts, Filatov simply said, in effect, I know what you want me to say and here I am saying it. By distancing himself from what was happening he hinted that the interrogation was a ritual; as he went through the motions he implied that the event was utterly hollow.

Belittling himself, Filatov consistently avoided the big issues. "International politics is too complex, and it is not for me to critique it." "What do you think about the peasant issue?" "I had my doubts, but then I asked myself: Do I, someone who never worked in a village, have the right to judge the policy of the Central Committee on the subject?" Undermining official language with his empty echo, Filatov claimed moral and epistemological superiority.

Rather than an evaluation of a soul, the interrogation became a contest over the authority of the verification commission. His confessors wanted to extract more and more depositions and personal revelations from Filatov. Then someone like Fel'belbaum would be able to show that even on his own premises, the defendant was in error. At the moment, he complained, "Filatov does not care about the Central Committee." But Filatov spoke only when he was certain of the subtext: since he had manifestly failed to prove that he was a legitimate Bolshevik, he was reluctant to say too much lest his confessions contextualize it in a way unsuitable to him. Ever more evasive, he blamed his "inability to penetrate the issues" and allowed the interrogators to monopolize the transcript.

Some defendants filled the interrogators' ears; Filatov made them strain. What bothered the control commission most was that the suspect apparently believed that silence or meaningless concessions could save him. "This case is more complex that the earlier ones," Tiul'kin noted. "Something is fishy here. No one would join the opposition for the reasons Filatov gave."

As the atmosphere of the interrogation heated up, the authenticity of Filatov's arguments was flatly denied. Obrazov excoriated him in a blistering tone: "One can easily see how insincere these oppositionists are. Filatov obfuscates the issues. . . . When I asked him whether he agrees with how the control commission presents things, he answered, 'Yes and No.'" Karasov declared, "No Communist can be of two minds [*dvoiakovmysliashchii*]!"

Was it clear to the defendant that full confession, far from being a sure way to indictment, was his only chance for forgiveness? "Can I remain in the Party?" Filatov asked aloud. "If I am considered an oppositionist I should be purged." The whole point, however, was that he never been a true "oppositionist." Filatov carefully avoided stereotypes: he recognized the narrative his interrogators tried to impose and refused to provide grounds for making it stick. Constantly undercutting the distinction the verification commission drew between those who opposed and those who supported the Central Committee, Filatov insisted he was no more sympathetic with Kutuzov than he was with Klikunov. "I specified my points of dissent—they are personal." His praising of heterodoxy was markedly detached. "I thought that by confronting the Central Committee the opposition could straighten out the Party line."

To resolve the standoff between Filatov and the verification commission, some common ground had to be found. Yet, as it proceeded, the interrogation increasingly resembled a game of hide-and-seek. While Filatov admitted that he had erred, he also showed himself quite capable of flouting Central Committee guidelines, even going so far as to question official sources of information. "I got the impression that the press was not giving accurate information on the numerical strength of the opposition. *Pravda* no longer prints the truth."

A scandalized Krasnikov rose to protest. "What a lack of trust in the official press! Filatov simply mistrusts our state!"

The commission took an interest in Filatov's views on a range of additional issues. "In your opinion," he was asked, "was the Fifteenth Party Congress fairly elected?" Though he replied in the affirmative, his testimony was doubted. At his wit's end, Obrazov snarled at the defendant: "Filatov, we have rock-solid proof that you believe the Fifteenth Party Congress was rigged. You are lying to the Party, which is pure insolence! Shame on you!" But Filatov would not budge: he demanded a confrontation with any witness who contradicted his statements.

Questions continued to pelt him like vindictive hail.

Q: What did you think of the opposition's October demonstration in Moscow? Did it suggest to you a breakdown in political leadership?

FILATOV: When I read about it in the papers I did not believe [the story]. Later I received letters from friends in Moscow [corroborating it]. Nothing good could come from that kind of demonstration. It harmed the opposition.

It was as if Filatov were discussing a third party, something utterly unrelated to himself. Yes, he condemned the opposition, but its behavior did not reflect on him. Even when he drew upon the loyalist narrative almost verbatim the defendant was vague about whether he was endorsing it. Quotations were not necessarily tokens of identification; they could also have been a parody. Considering Filatov's general attitude, the closer the quotation, the more pointed the parody. To quote almost out of context was a very effective way to disappoint the verification commission's generic expectations and thus emphasize one's ambivalence towards the Party line.

By appearing as someone who was disclosing his views, Filatov seemingly took steps towards accepting the premise that he was supposed to reveal his true thoughts. Now it was up to the verification commission to persuade him of its authority to diagnose what ailed him and attempt to heal him. Fel'belbaum made this point clearly: "As one listens to Filatov one realizes that he barely understands what he wants from the Party himself. . . . What we really must do is eradicate his mistaken oppositionist opinions and direct a comrade who has lost his way to the right path."

But what could be done with one who never mentioned Trotsky or any other source of inspiration, who admitted he read the Platform and yet insisted he refused to sign it? Things came to a head when the name of Iakovlev, an enemy of the Central Committee who had already been apprehended by GPU, burst upon the proceedings. This was to prove Filatov's most damaging association, and his interrogators immediately recognized its value. Haltingly at first, the defendant began to give voice to his bitterness: "I am accused here of being Iakovlev's friend. But Iakovlev can't have been a counterrevolutionary! . . . During the revolutionary days, he was a good worker. Later he became a good Communist. We met again in Tomsk, and up until the recent events we used to exchange opinions. Iakovlev's arrest was a shock to me."

Filatov was quite capable of attacking heterodoxy: it was said that he had demanded the execution of four local oppositionists considered anti-Leninist. But this case was different. Filatov insisted that he and Iakovlev were willing to play by the rules, but when the authorities silenced them, they left them no alternative but to develop a separate (if not necessarily antithetical) identity. This was a case of self-fulfilling prophesy: as soon as Klikunov labeled them oppositionists they were forced to assume an oppositionist identity.

"I am ready to vouch for Iakovlev [*vziat' na poruki*]," Filatov stated. He had such faith in his friend that he invoked a curious Bolshevik practice—soul sponsoring. When a Party member maintained the sort of faith in a fallen comrade that Filatov had in Iakovlev, he could declare it his personal responsibility to drag that comrade out of the gutter. The enterprise had real risks, as the sponsor could find himself cast into the gutter alongside his protégé. Filatov knew the risks, but his friend was "falsely accused" and he did not flinch. "By the way," he added, "there are other Communists who wanted to vouch for Iakovlev—Kalkiner, for example, and yet no one regards Kalkiner as an oppositionist." Noting that vouching for a comrade "is an old tradition among Siberian artisans," Filatov declared his readiness to pay the price: "Put me in jail if you like!"

When he stood up for Iakovlev, Filatov insisted on the difference between his worldview and that of his confessors. This rekindled the war over language, reducing the gains Klikunov had made over the course of the interrogation to nil. Filatov constructed a political identity for himself (as a proletarian fighter) outside the official institutions responsible for the elaboration of political truth. In his version of reality, he and Iakovlev were workers to the marrow of their bones, dedicated to the proletarian cause. Neither was an "oppositionist." He might as well have said it thus: by oppressing us you dilute the energies of the Bolshevik camp and actually obstruct the Revolution. In his discussion of Iakovlev, Filatov made two analogies, between the old Bolshevik martyrs and Iakovlev (and, by extension, himself), as well as between the tsarist gendarmes and the verification commission. The defendant's dichotomy, martyr versus persecutor, had nothing to do with the dichotomy Klikunov tried to establish, orthodoxy versus heterodoxy.

The basic question was again the meaning of democratic centralism: could there be a direct link between a Bolshevik and the proletarian truth, or were Party institutions a necessary intermediary? Filatov was not that arrogant: he was alert for weaknesses and pitfalls in his thinking and was willing to relinquish them. Yet he ignored a fundamental point dear to his interrogators: a Communist could not place himself outside the Party's ideological apparatus.

Filatov's veiled jeers at Party institutions earned him no friends on the commission. "This is your last chance to admit that you lied when you stated that you did not know about Iakovlev's escapades," he was told. It was said that Iakovlev himself had admitted printing seditious materials. "Then we have a contradiction here," Filatov responded. "L'vov [the emissary from the center] said Iakovlev never admitted doing such a thing. You say he did. I cannot make heads or tails of it."

Tiul'kin consulted the archive and offered a timely clarification: "Iakovlev confessed everything to us on February 25, 1928." "You forget that a Communist cannot see the GPU as a tsarist plague or a torture chamber!" Fel'belbaum commented acidly. Klikunov closed the lid on the defendant: "Filatov, you are just like Iakovlev. The difference between the two of you is that the GPU got its hands on Iakovlev, whereas you sneaked away. Actually you are worse than Iakovlev!" Worse because, while Iakovlev had at least confessed, Filatov merrily continued his dissimulations.

Left with no choice, Fel'belbaum and Klikunov transposed a text fundamentally repugnant to them into another, more acceptable key. Attempts to get Filatov to cooperate in his inculpation were abandoned. He was declared incapable of independent thought, obliging the verification commission to speak for him. Taking the theoretical high ground, the members of the commission seldom flatly contradicted Filatov. Instead they offered generalizations. Klikunov listened to the defendant, compared his words and deeds to those of other deviants (such as Iakovlev), and the desired result was eventually obtained: a heretical self that could be held accountable.

While Filatov denied his Trotskyist sympathies, too much of what he was saying and doing resembled what other Trotskyists were doing. "Filatov is clearly an oppositionist," Klikunov concluded. "He speaks of only vodka and houses but consistently votes with the opposition."

Tiul'kin made a last effort to convince the defendant to embrace this diagnosis: "Filatov should tell us in his closing statement why he is an oppositionist." But Filatov held out: "You label me a taciturn individual and claim that I continue to harbor oppositionist moods. . . . But you cannot treat me as an oppositionist." Then he turned to address those present: "You will soon vote: consider whether purging me would be for the good."

Much to the consternation of Tiul'kin and Klikunov, Filatov was not one inch closer to playing the role they had prepared for him. The tiniest recantation, the tiniest undermining of his outlook, would have spelled the destruction of his self—official language flowing in to fill up the vacuum. Re-creating himself in the official language, the defendant would have legitimized the verdict. But Filatov refused to don the oppositionist mantle, and in this respect he stood alone among the interrogatees.

Through the verdict he received—on the strength of 150 grassroots votes (against 20 who preferred a severe reprimand) Filatov was purged—and even more importantly, through the transcript of his interrogation, Filatov was fixed as an oppositionist.[51] His future behavior would be understood through the written record of his personal evaluations. The power of validation and categorization was located in such texts, as Tiul'kin's references to the protocols of the control commissions make clear.

The verification commission attempted to bring the inchoate deposition of Filatov under the official control of certified knowledge through various techniques of interpretative stitching such as contextualization, nomination, and generalization. Klikunov's interrogation style was designed to set up a mark of distinction between Party orthodoxy and Party heterodoxy and to police this mark repeatedly in order to ascertain his mastery over students. By insisting that he produce a proposition of the type "I am an oppositionist," Klikunov, Fel'belbaum, and Tiul'kin aimed to insert Filatov into a prescribed order of words and things. They aimed, though the extraction of a confession, to immobilize the speaking subject and force a system of meaning upon him. Filatov, on the other hand, tried to modify the linguistic system permeating the work of the verification commission to his advantage.[52] The proliferation of interpretations set in motion by Filatov's speech did not set up an asymptotical progression towards elucidation of his state of consciousness. Rather, they worked as a series of alibis and evasions that obfuscated the questions of intention and guilt. A number of interventions made by his aberrant voice modified the classificatory system that attempted to subjugate him.

Filatov's act of resistance must be sought not so much in the manifest contents of his language—this tended to be similar in the transcripts of the verification commission—but in his withdrawal from the meanings of his depositions just as he was uttering them. The only linguistic traces that remain of this withdrawing subject are those indices which indicate rote repetition or evasive silence. The incessant alterations produced by Filatov's speech perverted the meaning of the interrogation ritual and undermined the Party's control over revolutionary meanings.

A careful scrutiny of the transcript of Filatov's interrogation also points to the vanishing point of classificatory enterprise, the result of his peculiar indifference or resistance with regard to official games of interpretation. If in the previous sections my task was to isolate the constraining structures that informed the activity of the Party's interpretative machinery at Tomsk, here I was more concerned to qualify the omnipotence of these coercive structures by pointing to the disruptions that a seemingly incompetent speech operated on them. Through a chain of rhetorical devices, Filatov's voice unsettled the discursive construct though which certified Party hermeneuts assigned him his identity. His problematization of the division between authorized knowledge and ignorance and between significant and insignificant utterances showed that some—albeit very limited—room for maneuver was still open to the defendant.

Double-Dealers

In order to infiltrate the brotherhood of the elect, ardent oppositionists were in the habit of feigning submission to the general line—or so said the Central Control Commission. Undercover agents reported the cynical formula they had supposedly heard spoken by members of the opposition: "We must remain in the Party at all costs, though this means deceit and hiding our true faces."[53] Those who practiced such insidious behavior were guilty of "double-dealing" (*dvurushnichestvo*). Trickery and lies were the double-dealer's main weapons.[54] In one widely publicized set of recantations, a number of oppositionists confessed that the opposition's center had instructed them in the fine art of deceit: "Never cast an opposing vote, the better to avoid suspicion. If your oppositionism is exposed, deny all responsibility."[55] On another occasion, oppositionists were told to "vote for the Central Committee resolutions until your hand falls off, while all the time you are swelling our ranks."[56] Iaroslavskii intercepted instructions received by Leningrad Trotskyists: "Refrain from speaking openly, . . . make sure we are trusted and get ourselves elected as delegates to the Fifteenth Party Congress. Then the vote will tell."[57]

This was allegedly a cloak which the oppositionists found convenient to wear, a union of scary cant and wildest fanaticism, a tactic in a grand strategy of exposing members to little risk while quietly increasing membership.[58] According to Rykov, "the central committee of the Trotskyist party decided to preserve the oppositionists' legal status within our party in order to mask their unlawful activity."[59] What the oppositionists really wanted, in this scenario, was "to form their own apparatus, extending all the way from the oppositionist district committee below to an oppositionist Central Committee above."[60] "We insincerely spoke against the formation of a second party," confessed two Siberian "double-dealers," "only because the Party was practically split anyway. We believed the Central Committee line would soon prove bankrupt, opening the way for the opposition's takeover."[61]

While a model Communist possessed monumental spiritual wholeness, the double-dealer was split between his inner and outer self; his public and private identities were worlds apart.[62] The trouble with double-dealing was not just the actual split between their outer and inner selves but the fact that they were conscious of this split and that their outer self was therefore absolutely contrived. To be sure, the petit bourgeois also privileged the private self over the public self. Only in private, secluded in his rooms, he sought to express his authentic self. But such an individual was simply unaware of the merits of collectivism. Adroitly applied enlightenment would surely pull him out of his decadence. Not so the double-dealer. An interloper into the brotherhood of the elect, he knew everything there was to know. His oppositionist cell was not a relic of the bourgeois past but a vibrant Trotskyist organization. Looking into the future rather than the past, influenced by sinister intentions, not ignorance, double-dealers were most dangerous practitioners of the oppositionist Black Mass.

Though the heads of the Tomsk Party organization routinely boasted that impostors had rarely fooled them, the specter of double-dealing haunted the Technological Institute. When the verification commission began its work, it revealed at every turn a gnawing anxiety; counterrevolution seemed to be hiding under a variety of sometimes very unpredictable masks.

Klikunov, for example, strongly suspected that Kazantsev was two-faced. After all, Kazantsev had been present at Kutuzov's farewell banquet, though he tried to mitigate this offense by insisting that the affair had been nothing but an innocuous get-together: "no toasts or speeches were made." The interrogators thought it unlikely that the defendant had evaded Kutuzov's wooing. "Yeah, yeah," went a lampoon of the defense's claims, "Kazantsev used to come to Kutuzov's apartment, see illegal literature but, you see, he was not curious enough to so much as touch it. Who is going to believe that?!"

Challenges came thick and fast: "Who believes that one on good terms with Kutuzov, such as Kazantsev, saw nothing of his agitation?" Behind Kazantsev's disciplined facade, said Rezhenov, "I smell an oppositionist. We can rest assured, comrades, that Kazantsev will attack us again in the future."

A skilled discussant, Kazantsev proved quite capable of responding. If interrogators contended that he was an instrument of the Devil, he presented himself as an innocent lamb on which demons had descended. "Of course, Kutuzov and I talked. How could I oppose him, given my weak theoretical preparation?" Though Kazantsev escaped censure, he was warned that "if in the future he compromised himself again, the cell would treat the offense very strictly."[63]

Another student suspected of being a double-dealer was Lun', who had repeatedly criticized Party policy the previous fall. Suspicions intensified when Lun' stated, "I did not have a deep understanding and would never have ventured to discuss sensitive issues." "Comrade Lun'," his interrogators sarcastically noted, "does not strike us as the sort of person who would poke his nose in things he does not understand [*ne znaia brodu suetsia v vodu*]"—he must have known what he was doing.

The defendant's Baptist background had put his interrogators on the alert. Baptists were generally seen as a more serious challenge to Communism than Orthodox Christians. Traditional faith was mechanical, and once enlightened an Orthodox Christian lost his superstitions. Sectarians, by contrast, possessed a fully developed worldview of their own.[64] Because they too had been persecuted by the authorities of the old regime, they appeared as freedom fighters and were hard to expose. Christians who recognized the justice of Communism in the domain of social life were considered more harmful and dangerous than Christians who openly approved a restoration of the tsarist regime because they were likely to advance a well-thought-out alternative to the Communist method of attaining equality.[65]

Lun's affiliation with the opposition confirmed deeply seated suspicions towards Baptists: his conversion, it was feared, might have been faked and he could be an interloper. Popkov diagnosed Lun' as "developed but inclined to rapid self-transformations." This was a highly abnormal predicament—the more "developed" a Communist was the less volatile his consciousness was supposed to be. Unless, of course, Lun' was a counterrevolutionary hiding behind a Communist mask. Had he received the standard instructions regarding the need to camouflage his real views? Such instructions could explain why Lun' endorsed one position one day and its opposite the next.

"At the present I have no doubts or disagreements with the Party," declared Lun'. "Everything is clear to me." The defendant insisted he was no longer a Baptist. "It took me so long to join the Party because I had religious scruples. But eventually, after taking Liadov's course [at Sverdlov Communist University in Moscow], I lost my faith." To fend off the suggestion that his recent oppositionist outburst had religious motives, Lun' referred to his conversion to Communism as a clear and distinct occurrence, brought about through the overwhelming influence of one of the great ideologists of atheism.

Reluctantly, the interrogators had to accept the defendant's own presentation of his self. There was too little evidence to back up suspicions: the defendant was "outspoken in his criticisms of the Central Committee while at the institute, but never outside it," that is, Lun' never violated Party regulations and approached workers directly with sensitive questions. Though he had been unable to prove his case, Popkov still felt that Lun' was a double-dealer, and ought at least to be "reprimanded" so that there would be a record for future reference. His pleas were in vain; Lun' got off with a warning.[66]

Two Inveterate Counterrevolutionaries

No one on the verification commission wanted to portray the institute as a center of counterrevolution. A standard formulation was that "overt ideological oppositionists have but seldom got in and set up among students" and when they had done so, they had made a short blaze and gone out in a snuff. Those few bad seeds, it was usually added, "are no longer with us"; the GPU had already identified and arrested them. Despite these confident assertions, a few heretics were still found hiding within the institute walls in the spring of 1928.

A great deal of effort was invested in drawing up the set of criteria according to which hopeless heretics were identified, and rabid counterrevolutionaries were those who displayed a persistent heterodox consciousness. Only outright and unrenounced oppositionism warranted absolute excommunication and possible arrest.

The most obvious oppositionists turned counterrevolutionaries were the Trotskyists. Once Trotsky had rejected the decisions of the Fifteenth Party Congress, a consensus emerged in the higher echelons of the Party that his followers (unlike the followers of Kamenev and Zinoviev) "completed their transformation from an anti-Party group into an underground anti-Soviet organization."[67] The path chosen by the Trotskyist opposition, Tomsk authorities stated during the verification, forced the Party to move from "preventive" (*predupreditel'nye*) and "educational" (*vospitatel'nye*) measures to "harsh" (*surovye*) and "decisive" (*reshitel'nye*) steps that would put an end to subversive activities.[68] The GPU had warned already the previous summer that "we will not be able to maintain national order unless the Party authorizes us to arrest oppositionists." The protocol of the Central Control Commission from September 13, 1927, referred to those who met with the Wrangel's officer as "Communists who participate in a counterrevolutionary organization."[69] Agreeing that "oppositionist criminality knows no limits," the Party leadership informed GPU that Trotskyists were henceforth fair game.[70] Characteristically, when a GPU collegium took up the "case of the citizen Lev Davidovich Trotsky" in January 1929, it invoked the 58th paragraph of the penal code, the paragraph addressing "counterrevolutionary activity."[71] Some oppositionists were amazed: "[comrades were] held by the GPU based on article 58-4, which means counterrevolutionism! We are talking about 'participation in an organization that set itself the aim of toppling Soviet Power,' and punishment can only be one: execution and confiscation of property."[72]

All of this meant that the odds of Beliaev's survival in the university were slim.[73] Ever since his service in the Red Army, Beliaev had borne an admiration for Trotsky, and in the days of the verification, that put him squarely in the heretical camp. Aggravating his crime, Beliaev had befriended such untouchable oppositionists as Goliakov and Kutuzov. By the time he got to the interrogation chamber, his confessors had grave doubts about the sincerity of so devout a Trotskyist.

Q: Do you think you are guilty?

BELIAEV: Since I fueled the opposition's fire, to some extent, I am. . . .

Q: Do you agree with the characterization of Trotsky as a counterrevolutionary?

BELIAEV: When Trotsky allied himself with foreign rightists he was working against the Party. But I still can't call Trotsky our resolute enemy since in the past he proved himself a talented military trailblazer.

This sort of loyalty to the head of the opposition would have undermined almost any defense argument. After all, only those who repented could be forgiven, and as Trotsky showed no sign of repenting, his disciple could not be expected to go down on bended knee any time soon.

Obrazov took the lead in baiting Beliaev:

Once his veil of deceit is penetrated, I can see a convinced oppositionist. Beliaev did a good job mastering the repertoire of the opposition. The opposition conducts its work behind closed doors these days and Beliaev does the same. Students have told me that they are tired of his proselytizing. It is impossible to reeducate Beliaev: everywhere one finds signs that he does not believe that the Congress reached the right resolutions.

Completing a series of cruel rhetorical pirouettes, Obrazov drew a parallel between the fall of two Civil War heroes, big Trotsky and little Beliaev. "Why is Beliaev with the opposition?" he wondered. "Perhaps because the world of small revolutionary deeds is not to his liking?" Perhaps he is unable to assimilate that world to the world of his heroic memories. "This becomes especially evident when Beliaev talks about Trotsky."

Klikunov picked up where Obrazov left off. Trotsky and Beliaev, the two "orators of the Revolution," had been borne into the counterrevolutionary camp on the wings of their penchant for flowery eloquence.

During the discussion Beliaev did not allow anyone to say a word. He does the same today. His propaganda activity can be described as "wild." This is no exaggeration! A number of comrades—and we have no reason to doubt their words—said he called members of the Politburo names that I cannot bring myself to repeat [*iazyk ne povorachivaetsia*]. Whatever good points Beliaev could claim before the Revolution, the more recent damage he has done has completely erased them. His conduct during the discussion was precisely what the Party might have expected from a member of a rival camp ready to take up arms.

Ruzhenkov commented that "while Beliaev describes himself as 'objectively speaking, a quiet oppositionist,' his actions prove he is of the ardent ilk. He has yet to cease distributing illegal literature in the student dormitories even now!"

When he was finally allowed to speak, Beliaev did his best to respond to these reproaches. In order to counter the implicit accusation of counterrevolutionism, he tried to show that he was making a distinction between Trotsky and Trotskyism:

I haven't tried to subvert anyone. My respect for Trotsky is solely based on his importance as a military figure who proved himself during the Civil War. This does not mean I share Trotsky's current views. . . . As far as Trotsky's purge from the Party goes, I have not concealed my view on that from the Control Commission: I believe it was wrong to purge the leader of the opposition before the Congress was even convened. However, once the Congress resolved to purge Trotsky I was satisfied that this was indeed the will of the Party. . . . Someone here said that I was "unreformable" and that I cannot be re-educated. On the contrary, I have already become aware of my mistakes and have abandoned the oppositionist outlook.

Such protestations saw Beliaev through the first stage of the verification by the skin of his teeth. The bureau was split almost evenly: while six votes were cast for purging, seven votes, displaying a modicum of clemency, went for severe reprimand. "Although Beliaev should not preach to us or oppose the bureau," explained the advocates of pastoral care, "we, at the same time, do not have to insist that he call Trotsky a 'counterrevolutionary.' Purging Beliaev would be too cruel."

Beliaev's good fortune was short-lived. Early on in the cell's verification, Klikunov reported that he had received a letter of denunciation stating that the defendant "is still working for the opposition." "Flaunting the label 'oppositionist,'" Beliaev reportedly "called the adherents of the Party line 'Central Committee spies.'"

"Be specific, Klikunov!" Beliaev was yelling during the hearings at the general cell level. He was determined to learn the names of his denouncers.

Klikunov shrewdly replied: "I am only speaking for another member of the bureau. If the audience so chooses, I will divulge the identity of our source."

"No!" voices roared back. "No need to!"

Beliaev braced himself before another attack, this time led by rank-and-file hermeneuts. "Did you consider yourself an oppositionist?" "My only fault was voting for the countertheses," Beliaev answered. But comments he had made in the past seemed to disprove his statement.

Q: You used to say that [the election of members of] the circuit conference and the Congress were rigged. How do you reconcile what you are saying now with what you said then?

BELIAEV: Very simply. I am a member of the Party, and since a majority of the Party members arrived at a decision during the Congress I have to obey it.

Q: Do you recall saying to me in the theater, "Allow us to convert you to our faith"?

BELIAEV: It is true that at the time I was with Kutuzov and Goliakov. But those words were facetious.

Following a few more rounds, during which he continued to be soundly beaten, the stakes turned decisively against the defendant. One after the other, students excoriated Beliaev for the diversionary tactics he had employed during the discussion. For this and for his unswerving devotion to Trotsky, they demanded harsh punishment.

DUTOV: I used to meet Beliaev often in the company of Kutuzov as they came to the dormitories to brainwash young students. I have the impression that Beliaev was a zealous oppositionist. We have to purge him.

KHROMOV: I remember that Beliaev condemned the expulsion of Trotsky from the Party. We must purge him. . . .

KOLKOV: Beliaev is an ideological oppositionist. All of his philosophizing about who should be considered an oppositionist and who should not is moot. We have to purge him. . . .

BULKIN: I and Beliaev used to live together in the dormitories and I was paired with him in the same study group for the working through of the resolutions of the Fifteenth Party Congress. My impression is that Beliaev has been insincere. We should purge him.

"Purge him" resounded with the insistence of an incantation.

The defendant begged for more time; "you can always chase me out of the Party. But why not give Beliaev a chance to shoulder responsibility and see whether he is sincere or not?" When he spoke of himself in the third person, he made of himself a type. If clemency was shown, it would not be about Beliaev the individual but about the contribution Bolsheviks with his experience could make to the Revolution.

But the mood of the cell was harsh. Klikunov even apologized for the soft sentence recommended by the bureau: "We too consider Beliaev an oppositionist, and our vote was close. Beliaev still considers Trotsky's purge a mistake!"

"I no longer think so!" Beliaev interjected.

But he was doomed. While 68 students sided with the bureau's recommendation, 143 students voted for expulsion.

When small fry like Beliaev were being purged, what could Nikolaev, the most infamous oppositionist to undergo verification, expect? He knew that he was going to be portrayed as one of the institute well-poisoners—it will be remembered that but for the intervention of the district committee, Nikolaev would have wrought a Kutuzovist victory at a crucial cell meeting—and indeed Nikolaev was obliged to submit no fewer than three letters of recantation. When the first two recantations, those of November 27 and December 22, 1927, were described as shallow, Nikolaev had added a third. Though this letter, written jointly with Gorbatykh, finally conceded Nikolaev's organizational ties to the opposition, it too was criticized. "Don't you know that you cannot submit a collective recantation?" he was asked. "Other letters which bore only my signature were sent to the circuit control commission." An exception had been made for two miners, Paskho and Makerenko, who voted for Kutuzov; electing to interrogate them together, the verification commission suggested that neither could have possessed an autonomous political consciousness.[74] Nikolaev, by contrast, would certainly be interviewed by himself—this reflected the interrogator's preconception that the defendant was a conscious individual who had to be held fully responsible for his seditious actions.[75]

At the outset, the defendant was asked, largely pro forma, about his oppositionist convictions. Nikolaev explained that while in the past he had been angered by aspects of the official labor policy, "Iaroslavskii's explanations in *Pravda* had satisfied him completely." But this was of little moment. It was obvious to all present that the real issue was not Nikolaev's political stance but his connection to the Tomsk Centre; the interrogation quickly moved in that direction:

Q: How did you hook up with Kutuzov?

NIKOLAEV: Kutuzov told me about an article by Trotsky on the British-Russian committee, so I took a look at it. . . .

Q: What would you say now about your second recantation, in which you denied all organizational ties to the opposition?

NIKOLAEV: I [still insist that I] was not a member of a faction. And I did not attend Kutuzov's banquet. . . . I knew nothing about the print shop and nothing about the distribution of the oppositionist leaflets.

A number of bureau members claimed that Nikolaev was an insolent scoundrel: his ideological about-face and his alliance with Kutuzov—which shocked Obrazov—were taken as illustrations of his slickness. "As late as last summer, Nikolaev betrayed no traces of what was in store. When fall rolled around, however, he revealed his ardent oppositionism." Karasov too saw the defendant as a counter-revolutionary in disguise: "Nikolaev was very active during the entire discussion. But his recantation is craftily couched in language that plays down his oppositionist ardor."

Nikolaev's rhetorical skills attracted heavy fire. Brandishing ideas borrowed from Kutuzov, he was described as "swaying the mass of students with his endless hodgepodge of phrases and thereby obtaining a following." A duplicitous sweet-talker was "all the more dangerous in our university milieu."

A somewhat more kindhearted diagnosis, attributing to Nikolaev only a passive, semiconscious oppositionism, competed with Obrazov's version. "My impression used to be that Nikolaev tended to be swept away by his own rhetoric," Fel'belbaum tentatively suggested. "While I sometimes thought Nikolaev possessed a mature consciousness, at other times I believed he could not be in full control." In Fel'belbaum's interpretation Nikolaev was less a source of noxious heresies than their conduit. Other caring confessors believed in the sincerity of Nikolaev's repentance. "We should consider our verdict very carefully. In his final recantation, Nikolaev told us everything down to the smallest details. Remember that he never signed the Platform . . . and that he submitted his first recantation before the Congress had even met."

But the majority sided with Klikunov, against clemency. Nikolaev had dragged down too many good Communist souls to be let off. The cell's secretary conveyed the anguish with which he had observed the seduction of innocent comrades by the defendant's enticing words. "For example," he recalled. "It was Nikolaev who cast the influence of the opposition over Gorbatykh." It was quite possible that the latter had acted all unawares, but Nikolaev, "an important leader in the eyes of many oppositionists," must have acted quite deliberately.

When it comes to Nikolaev, we are dealing with a committed oppositionist. What lingers in my mind is Nikolaev's comment: "So, you think we are oppositionists, don't you?" There and then I realized that he must be one of them. I recall that as early as August Kutuzov was proposing "to applaud Lev Davidovich [Trotsky]." He was Kutuzov's right hand all along—Nikolaev must have known what was on Kutuzov's mind. Some time after that, Kutuzov did not even try to deny that he and Nikolaev had devised a strategy to take over our cell.

The last part of Klikunov's harangue boiled down to the following logical deduction: Kutuzov admitted he was a Trotskyist; Nikolaev, knowing full well what Kutuzov stood for, collaborated with him; ergo, Nikolaev was a Trotskyist himself. On top of that, added Klikunov, he was an insurrectionist plotter: "At great risk to myself, I had to intervene and annul Nikolaev's subversive election as a meeting chair. When things started to look bad, Nikolaev had taken the first step in distancing himself from the opposition by submitting a first, very succinct, recantation—that had been in November." By December, Nikolaev was willing to divulge more details. Even then he persevered in his oppositionist activities, insincere to the core. Klikunov's chronology was damning—as soon as the opposition's fortunes waned, Nikolaev transformed himself from an open counterrevolutionary into a double-dealer.

Klikunov's lengthy tirade had shaken him, but Nikolaev summoned his nerve and again stood before the bureau to defend himself. "Klikunov wrongly calls me a leader of the opposition. I was not, nor will I ever be one. Yes, my speech attracted votes for the opposition. But isn't that the whole point of giving a speech?" In this final apology Nikolaev attempted no wholesale denial of his past sins; instead, he labored to convince his auditors that he had repented. "My gradual retreat from the opposition was motivated by second thoughts and doubts," rather than tactical calculation. As to his dangerous rhetorical skill, Nikolaev hoped to persuade the bureau that he had used it not to corrupt good Communists but, quite the contrary, to bring them back into the fold: "Klikunov, you say I took advantage of Gorbatykh. But in fact it was I who persuaded Gorbatykh to follow my example and leave the opposition."

When his case was passed along to the cell, Nikolaev wanted his last recantation read aloud for all to hear. Klikunov warned that the text was very long. A compromise was suggested by Krasnikov: "Let's just go over the parts where Nikolaev confesses his organizational ties to the opposition." But the idea that Klikunov, his arch-enemy, would be the editor of his recantation was anathema to Nikolaev: "As an individual on the verge of his political death, I want my recantation read in full. You comrades have to know all the details before you decide what to do with me."

Klikunov gave in. He read the letter in its entirety and announced that "the bureau recommends purging Nikolaev, who is a mature oppositionist and an active factionalist." Nikolaev replied by declaring that he had recently made promising strides towards purifying his consciousness:

Since I was not sincere in my first two recantations, I can rightly be considered a provocateur. But the gradual progress noticeable when the three recantations are compared finds its explanation in the psychological change I underwent. We all are familiar with such processes. I am sincere now and my departure from the opposition is complete. The task now is to smother and obliterate all doubts within us. We made a mistake, but we deserve a chance to rectify it.

Should one moment of doubt make us unworthy of the Party? A whole array of important comrades were mistaken on a variety of issues and yet now they contribute to the Party. Recall 1917, when Rykov and Nogin left the government disagreeing with the decision to shut down the bourgeois press. We, of course, cannot guarantee we will never make mistakes in the future. But who among us is infallible?!

Neudakhin, another serious oppositionist present in the hall, jumped on the opportunity to turn Nikolaev's marvelously executed apology into a blueprint for a general narrative of oppositionist recantation. "I can tell you that when Nikolaev declares his departure from the opposition he speaks the truth," Neudakhin emphatically stated. "Being once an oppositionist myself I know what I am talking about."

This argument addressed a crucial dilemma, one lying at the heart of the hermeneutics of the soul: Who is the better Communist, he who has never sinned, or he who has sinned and repented? Loosening his argument from its Christian matrix, Neudakhin was invoking something like Augustine's famous "God doth joy more over one sinner that repenteth than over ninety and nine persons that need no repentance." Neudakhin slyly suggested that the eternally immaculate comrade had simply never had to wrestle with temptation. In fact, his untested consciousness might be quite shaky. Someone like Nikolaev, by contrast, had been tempted, had succumbed, and now that he had recovered might be immune to oppositionism forever. Neudakhin's defense was a tour de force, and his central point was the refutation of Klikunov's proverbial assertion that once a sinner, always a sinner. Only he, Neudakhin, whose experience had resembled Nikolaev's, could identify with the defendant's predicament and fairly judge him. This was a bold attempt on Neudakhin's part to crown himself a master hermeneut.

Startled by this sophistry, the sinless Klikunov hastened to disqualify Neudakhin's unorthodox hermeneutics. The confessor and the confessed, Klikunov was emphatic about that, should never be confounded:

These days everybody says, "Oh, we were mistaken." Rykov was mistaken. Nogin was mistaken. So why cannot our little Nikolaev be mistaken? This is a worthless way of going about it! You, Nikolaev, know perfectly well that you harmed the Party. Now you can only twist and turn. You should have asked to be purged, adding that you would do all in your power to prove you were worthy of readmission.

Having launched every weapon in his arsenal at the defendant, who after all had almost cost him the leadership of the cell, Klikunov finally carried the day: only one meek voice proposed a "severe reprimand with a warning"; 134 students voted for a "purge" and at last Nikolaev encountered the "political death" he had so dreaded.

Condemned as a dangerous Trotskyist, Nikolaev was purged, but escaped arrest. Not yet, anyway. Not in 1928. Even when heretics were identified, the ax did not fall too swiftly. Only after they had been given many chances to vanquish their doubts and had utterly failed to find the truth, were oppositionist "backsliders" (retsidivisty) classified as irredeemable counterrevolutionaries. In any case, the verification commissions, like all Communist tribunals of conscience, had a mandate to diagnose, not to punish; meting out justice was the prerogative of the juridical apparatus. Just as the medieval inquisitor could not burn a heretic himself but had to hand him over to the secular authorities, so the punishing of counterrevolutionary acts was left to the discretion of GPU-NKVD.

The Ghost of the United Opposition

The adherents to opposition could hardly slip right back into Soviet society, and they would hardly be forgiven and welcomed by the Party they had betrayed. Keenly aware of stains in peoples' biographies the Soviet government referred to a number of categories of individuals as "formers" (byvshie).[76] The most famous "formers" were the potentates of the old regime, "nobles," "tsarist policemen," and "servants of the cult." With time, former Communists were added to, albeit never completely fused with, this category.

Ever on the alert, the Central Committee issued a top secret circular concerning "purged Party members" in 1922. Every move formers made was to be reported by the provincial committees according to the set of questions provided with the circular: "What are the career patterns of ex-Communists?" "Do they have a demoralizing effect on Party members or on non-Party activists?" "Do they express interest in rejoining the Party?"[77] The GPU warned that "formers believe it is they who are the real Communists, not those who possess token Party cards." Furthermore, authorities observed that they tended to form unsavory alliances: "The formers are joining with the Mensheviks and Socialist Revolutionaries to oppose Party policy directly or indirectly. Because these dissidents have considerable experience as agitators and organizers, they are capable of sowing seeds of dissension among untested Party members."[78]

While it had to be allowed that some individuals had been purged because of their undeveloped consciousness, nothing of the sort could be said about the conscientious objectors who were expelled because they formulated principled criticisms of Party policies. We have seen that since 1926 at the latest, the Party apparatus was obliged to prepare special personnel files on oppositionists, including a summary of their actions during the various discussions. Even when returned to the Party rolls, they always constituted a group apart.

The issue of former oppositionists came into sharp relief not too long after the Fifteenth Party Congress was over. Alarmed by the crisis in the procurement of wheat in the winter of 1927–1928 and the ensuing shortfalls in urban provisioning, the Central Committee decided to break with the moderate policies it had only recently so zealously defended and launch an all-out war against the kulak. This sudden radicalization of Party policy looked to the banished Trotskyists like a tacit adoption of their political vision. In his "Appeal to All Oppositionist Comrades" Preobrazhenskii stated: "There was a time when we were constantly battling against the mistakes of the majority. Recent developments, however, have rendered unnecessary our independent existence."[79] Vrachev, a staunch adherent of Trotsky who was in prison for oppositionist activity, confessed to his wife on May 29, 1929, that he was "surprised and delighted by the scale of the Five-Year Plan . . . and overtaken by the pathos of social construction." A month later he could no longer tolerate "to be a prisoner in our own country and under our own power, . . . especially now, when our disagreements with the Party diminish with an unprecedented speed" (July 2, 1928).[80]

In April–July 1929, the Central Control Committee received letters from about 500 "factionalists," among them Radek, Smilga, Serebriakov, and Drobnis, expressing desire to resume working with the Party. Many of those who had played active roles in the United Opposition were reinstated.[81] But when Party authorities received a number of anonymous letters wondering: "Is it not time to co-opt Trotsky into the Politburo?" Stalin instructed that "the struggle against Trotskyism must continue." The Central Committee majority refused to acknowledge any affinity between its recent policy swing and the old platform of the United Opposition.[82]

No sooner had the Tomsk Technical Institute's oppositionists been driven from the flock than they began a mass return. In October 1928, a mere six months after the conclusion of the verification, the Tomsk bureau was informed that "at this time most of our oppositionists have recovered their Party cards." Adapting to the new climate, the institute welcomed oppositionists back and even "entrusted them with positions of responsibility."[83] But they remained the Party's prodigal sons, and were far from becoming its vindicated heroes. When two Kutuzovists won seats on the bureau, the Tomsk district committee commented censoriously that "under the guise of Party democracy a grave mistake has been allowed to happen." It immediately passed a resolution barring on principle all ex-Leftists from occupying important administrative positions. The recent elections were annulled, votes recast, and a new and improved bureau elected. "Considering that Trotskyists have recently begun to raise their heads," the members of the newly constituted bureau clamored, "we do not think we should have waited for a special resolution by the district committee [to kick them out]. Formers [byvshie] are politically unstable elements who cannot contribute to the implementation of the Party line."

This brief skirmish in the autumn of 1928 was only a prelude to what was to come in the following year: the issue exploded with full force during the national Party purge in November 1929. For a time, with what they perceived as a favorable ideological wind at their backs, former oppositionists clearly enjoyed a boost in confidence. Not only had arch-heretics, including even Kutuzov, been rehabilitated, but fresh recruits were joining the heterodox contingent, oppositionists who had arrived at the institute after the discussion and verification were already over. Even more dramatic was the transformation of the political leadership of the institute. In a truly amazing turn of events, Klikunov found himself unmasked as an officer in Kolchak's army, or so claimed his foes. Deeply disturbed, his friends blamed the fall of their mentor on the vengeful Trotskyists. Obrazov, for example, was certain that a coterie within the institute collected whatever incriminating material they could find concerning their erstwhile persecutors and waited for the appropriate moment to take vengeance. "Some among our oppositionists try to manipulate comrades' mistakes for political gains," he said.

Former oppositionists would have none of this. "To the extent that we do stick together," said Grinevich, "it is because we need to protect ourselves. There have been innumerable cases of captious objections to us." The emergence of the "Right"—a legitimate political catchword that could now be bandied about—assisted the leftists.[84] "It was the Rightists," Kurkov maintained, who were clinging together—he was referring to Klikunov and the rest of the crew that had assailed the United Opposition: "When denunciations against any of the Rightists were received local potentates hushed them up." An effective unmasker of the rightist deviationists during the 1929 purge, Kurkov flatly rejected the notion that he was motivated by vindictiveness. "I went around denouncing so many students because I know all kinds of things about all kinds of people. This action of mine has nothing to do with oppositionism and is perfectly legitimate." As to what he jeeringly called the "mutual defense pact," Gorbatykh called all references to it "empty talk. When my turn to be interrogated came and no less than fourteen detractors attacked me, two among them were actually former oppositionists! Conversely, onetime oppositionists were among those I myself denounced. My stance depended solely on the character of the individual under scrutiny."[85]

Convinced that the Party had become much more tolerant of Leftist phraseology, Kochkurov raised the stakes. "If one must speak of 'nepotism' in our cell, it would be better to consider not the conduct of formers but the work of the purge commission itself: there nepotism really flourished. How else could a group of Kolchak volunteers have stayed on at the institute!?"[86]

Compelling and eloquent as Kochkurov's tirade was, it was eclipsed by the address delivered by Matveev, who had only recently enrolled at the institute. "Nowadays our cell is the site of a bitter 'class struggle' between the employee-Rightists [Klikunov and company] and the worker-Leftists [Kutuzov and his supporters]." The bias displayed by the purge commission—its leniency towards Rightists and excessive harshness towards Leftists—had cast the institute's rightward swing into sharp relief. By describing himself and other former oppositionists as "Leftist partisans of proletarian causes," Matveev clearly meant to rehabilitate the United Opposition. And he righteously stated: "Since we have been accepted back into the Party, we former Leftists should be treated as equals. Instead, public organizations needle us. Such practices are likely to prompt workers to say: 'Here are our Party cards. Take them and run the Party by yourselves!'"[87] Matveev was proposing a radical refashioning of the history of the United Opposition. The events of the last year, he argued, proved that apologies were due from Klikunov and not Kutuzov.

It did not take long for bureau members to recognize the gravity of the situation and they launched an immediate and pugnacious refutation. If Matveev saw the former oppositionists as working-class martyrs, the majoritarians knew perfectly well that they were heretics. "It is my duty to denounce Matveev here as a Trotskyist," Kashkin promptly declared. This label was damaging: during a meeting held in March 1928 students stated unequivocally: "It is difficult to imagine a revolutionary sinking lower than the renegade Trotsky."[88] When a speaker asserted that "Matveev's speech repeats Trotsky's phrases word for word," the righteous champion of the United Opposition was immediately in trouble. "This student has not succeeded in cutting his ties with the opposition," declared Fel'belbaum. "Rather, he is dodging the issue of Trotskyism, not so much in terms of what he formally says as in terms of what his gut really craves." Soskin, who often set the tone for the bureau, proposed that, "to judge from his attitude, Matveev is precisely the sort of Trotskyist the Party does not usually reinstate."[89]

Matveev's attempts to "draw undue advantages" by mentioning workers was said to "hide a Leftist deviation." Usatov, who voiced this appraisal, rejected the very possibility of a class struggle within the brotherhood of the elect: "Who could dream up so wrongheaded a notion as employee-Communists clashing with worker-Communists?" "Class struggle in the Party!" someone protested. "What kind of rubbish is this?" "Enough with *makhaevshchina* [intelligentsia baiting]?" another voice stated. "A mistaken worker is not untouchable," a third joined in. Particularly galling was Matveev's depiction of the 1928 suppression of the opposition as "Rightist"—it drew heavy fire. "Klikunov represented no particular class," intoned Kaziukin authoritatively. "By combating the opposition he did exactly what any decent leader would have done." An outmaneuvered Matveev had no choice but to surrender. "It was rash of me to suggest that workers might discard their cards; let me take it back."[90]

Ex-Leftists had failed in their bid to establish themselves as the new epitome of Communist consciousness. The time had come to deal with a fundamental question: Did formers deserve equal rights in the Communist brotherhood? Soskin was convinced that "for the time being the suspicion in which we have held former oppositionists has to be prolonged." The next speaker, Brusnikin, was also adamant that "it is up to the formers to prove themselves first." To his mind, the real question was not, as Matveev would have it, whether the Party had created conditions favorable for former oppositionists, "but whether the formers successfully completed their self-education." A vocal group of speakers was convinced that "Party work can be assigned only to those comrades who had never showed any vacillation."[91]

In the final account, the former oppositionists' attempt to reshape the Party history of the United Opposition backfired; now the sincerity of each and every recantation seemed doubtful. Kaziukin saw Matveev as a mere mouthpiece for more prominent heretics intent on probing a shadowy region. "To target Matveev is to aim at a decoy. We should aim at Kutuzov instead."

Hoping to salvage something from the debacle, Kutuzov finally spoke up. "I am being stalked," he whined, a shadow of his former self. "All kinds of things are wrongly attributed to me—for example, the suggestion that I support Matveev." Back-pedaling, Kutuzov made no plea for the rehabilitation of former oppositionists—he wanted only to be dissociated from them: "People say that my return to the Party was insincere. But didn't I submit a recantation a month after my expulsion declaring my departure from the opposition? Didn't I vote for the resolution criticizing Trotsky's performances abroad?"

The leaders of the Tomsk Technological Institute managed to shake off the charge of "Rightism" and, by branding their "Leftist" foes "Trotskyist double-dealers," forced them to revert to their degraded status of lapsed comrades. Kaziukin offered a triumphant version of the events: "The former oppositionists had not dared come out into the open. As they changed their stripes to cozy up to the Party, the would-be Leftists went to the other extreme—Rightism." "Kutuzov's return to the Party was quite insincere," Brusnikin avowed. "All he has done is cover up for oppositionists."[92]

Though the Party's shift leftward had seemed auspicious for Kutuzov's brand of radicalism, the United Opposition, or its ghost, lost yet another round to the Central Committee. The truth is that the ex-oppositionists never stood much of a chance: the opposition was still tainted. When charges of heterodoxy were leveled, ideological issues came a distant second; contravention of the Party line, for whatever reason and with whatever merit, overshadowed everything else. The Party's message was clear, strong, and unequivocal: political loyalty and discipline—the organizational principles that safeguarded the continuity of the Leninist revelation—came before all ideological disputes.

THE OPPOSITION DEMONIZED

The Bolshevik discourse was permeated by values steeped in eschatology that resonate with the Judeo-Christian tradition. Among these values was the belief in the singularity of truth as well as in a modern version of salvation that, the Bolsheviks thought, could be attained by steering each individual into a conscious accordance with truth. The authority of the Central Committee and the long-standing expectation that the Party Congress would be able to adjudicate disputes cannot be understood outside these institutions' claims to possess the keys to this unique truth.

The political and ideological tensions between factions within the Bolshevik party during the 1920s stemmed in large part from clashes over the right to interpret the truth, to determine what, for example, "unity," "consciousness," and "true Leninism" stood for. Striving for a revolution in the human self and the creation of the New Man, the contestation of the revolutionary project cannot be reduced to a set of personal incompatibilities in the Bolshevik leadership. Politics and ethics were constantly intermixed: intra-Party debates had to do with the uses of the hermeneutics of the soul—the ubiquitous attempt by each and every Bolshevik faction to position itself as the one most conscious and therefore best capable of interpreting comrades' trustworthiness, commitment to the Revolution, and moral potential.

Taking a moral stance, opting for a self-conscious, theoretically informed articulation of its program, and claiming the right to speak in the name of the proletariat, the opposition challenged Party leadership. There was good dose of courage in this step, something Trotsky and Zinoviev never tired of emphasizing. But taking the oppositionists at their word and viewing them as victims can be somewhat misleading. The Trotskyists and the Stalinists held in common many assumptions about the meaning and structure of politics—a shared discourse that became especially evident when we examined the strategies of defense that oppositionists employed during the various Party verifications. Seen from this perspective, the opposition emerges as having been neither heroic nor much of an "opposition" in the literal sense of the word, but rather the other side of the Stalinist coin.

327

Why then such a brutal struggle between Siamese twins? What are its origins and how did it evolve? How did the opposition come to epitomize ideological danger and, ultimately, treason?[1] Intersecting yet analytically distinct, two vectors describe the process that produced the "opposition problem." The first vector was shaped by the power of the Central Committee to define a category and to subsume individuals under this definition. Those who refused to bow to the official line were labeled "vacillators," "deviationists," and finally "oppositionists." The second vector was defined by the more or less autonomous behavior of the comrades so labeled. At first, Party members who insisted on pursuing their own, heterodox ideas created a set of political identities for themselves—for example, "champions of the workers' democracy," "true Bolsheviks," and "Bolshevik-Leninists," but eventually they accepted the label "oppositionism," turning it into something of their own—a source of pride, not shame.

These discursive transformations did not occur in a day. During the New Course Discussion (1923–1924) "oppositionism" appeared in quotation marks. Discussants identified with this or that platform, this or that Party leader. None of them described himself or herself as a steadfast heretic. The oppositionist identity was still shunned during the Discussion with Zinoviev, when Leningrad students described themselves as "true Leninists"; dangerous oppositionists were the others, primarily the defeated Trotskyists. But the Central Committee's control over political coinage increased in the aftermath of the Fourteenth Party Congress.

The following exchange, which took place in 1926, shows how the threshold for heresy was lowered after Kirov took over control of the Leningrad Communist University. After Pozern had completed his report on Party policy at the university, Rudnyi, a member of the local bureau, noted that the new rector "had failed to acknowledge properly . . . the difficulties involved in the construction of socialism." What is interesting in this debate is not the familiar arguments between optimists and pessimists regarding Soviet economic performance, but Rudnyi's insistence on his right to criticize without being castigated. "Comrades, you will probably find my speech utterly oppositionist, yet I think it my Party duty to say what I think." No less telling was his fellow students' determination to deny him this right. "What are Rudnyi's tactics?" Shabanov wondered. "Instead of speaking firmly, Rudnyi pretends to vacillate, to be less than consistent. 'I am not an oppositionist,' he says. 'I just want to offer some criticism.' This is an ideological coward . . . hiding his head under his wing."

Another student, Anfalov, also demanded that Rudnyi speak plainly: "We must make Rudnyi eat his words. 'Do not preen your feathers,' we must tell him, 'but call yourself plainly an oppositionist.'"

A stricter concept of oppositionism was shaping up, and it involved a conspiracy, a cabal. "We still have oppositionists in our university," Anfalov noted. "Even now they say, 'One day you'll see that we're right.' We were told that during the summer practicum these students approached Sarkis and wanted to 'exchange information.' They whisper in each others' ears [*oni shushukaiutsia*]."[2] Anfalov faulted his oppositionist counterparts with going through the motions of Party procedures but purposefully mocking them all along, and he hastened to pay them back in kind. In his eyes, much like the Black Mass, the oppositionist performance of Party rituals was a carnivalesque inversion of the good and true form that he, and the Stalinists, embodied.

For the longest time, Trotsky and his followers rejected "opposition" as a term that could be applied to themselves. The platform of the Bolshevik-Leninists repudiated this identity: "For many months now a poisonous polemical campaign has been waged against the opinions of Bolsheviks; they have been labeled 'the opposition.' . . . In reality, this so-called opposition is the Leninist current in the Party."[3] But sometime in 1927 a positive oppositionist identity began to emerge. "What is an opposition?" Trotsky asked. "The opposition is the leftist, Leninist, proletarian wing of the Party. It is the Party minority that strives to influence the Party, especially its proletarian kernel."[4] Note how in the language of Smirnov, Sapronov, and other old-timers the word "opposition," quite positive in its connotation, included all Bolsheviks united by an entrenched anxiety about the future of the Revolution. "Deeply rooted in the working-class component of our Party the oppositionist movement . . . protests the squandering of October's achievements."[5] Here "opposition" is uncoupled from its usual companions "faction" and "grouping," which were seen as more fitting for Stalin and his men, and attached to a "movement" (*dvizhenie*)—the legitimate expression of the working class's political will.

If for the Trotskyists, oppositionism became a designation of uncompromised revolutionary conscience, the determination to hold to one's individual truth, for the Central Committee's majority this was a clear term of opprobrium, a marker of the enemy within.

Humor, now mocking, even sardonic, reflected the growing vilification of the opposition and the identification of its leadership with imperialist powers outside the Soviet Union. Consider the feuilleton a certain Nikishev from Moscow sent to *Rabochaia gazeta* in March 1929. Entitled "History Laughs!" the feuilleton ridiculed Trotsky as someone whose true face has finally been exposed.

HISTORY LAUGHS!

Reflections on a Portrait of Trotsky . . .

Before me hangs a portrait of Trotsky in a Red Army helmet, with a large, brilliant Red Army star, Trotsky of the Civil War days, collaborator with Il'ich and the Party.

How strange the associations made by the human mind: for some reason I remember an amusing little scene from the Red Corner in a certain factory, where a prankster had placed a Red Army helmet on . . . a scarecrow representing Chamberlain. The times are changing. "Mister" Chamberlain has not yet had the chance to adorn his magisterial

forehead with a Red Army helmet and turn in his "Mister" for the more familiar sobri-
quet "Comrade."

Yet all the same, HISTORY LAUGHS.

Trotsky, who is depicted in a Red Army helmet, who wrote . . . whole tomes on Party
ethics, today stands in Constantinople . . . and expresses his RESPECT for the president
of the Turkish Republic, sells for one thousand dollars his *The Truth About the USSR* to
the bourgeois press. He shakes the hands of the butchers of the workers. Surely he is already in a top hat and smoking jacket. . . . So, speak up, comrades, will we be surprised if
the newspaper brings us news that Trotsky is a candidate for some Afghan throne . . . or
. . . the English Ministry of Interior Affairs? No, I don't think we will be surprised at all.

For, HISTORY LAUGHS![6]

History, the feuilletonist tells us, always progresses. The time will come when
the bourgeois will convert to the Marxist point of view and even England, the cradle of capitalism, will become Red. Chamberlain, or one of his successors, will don
a proletarian hat. For now, history had already exposed Trotsky and his cronies.
Trotsky has become a traitor. The emphasis on clothing is important: clothes make
the man, but they can also serve as a camouflage. For the longest time, Trotsky's
Civil War dress was identified with revolutionary attire. But the recent exchange of
a Red Army helmet for a top hat and smoking jacket leaves no doubt; he has gone
bourgeois.

The feuilletonist realized that Trotsky had not suddenly become an enemy.
Rather, he had never been anything else. "Your rebirth is too sudden, 'Mister'
Trotsky, you spend too little time on changing your headgear!" the feuilletonist remarks sardonically. What he sees might not be a true spiritual transformation but a
mask falling off. History laughs because the enemy stands naked before the working class.

The overflowing of sarcasm in the piece must be connected to the marked im-
provement in the Party's hermeneutical capacities. In a sublime eschatological irony,
Trotsky's constant changing of masks inadvertently strengthened the hermeneutical acumen of the Party. With each new peak in the intra-Party struggle, the Party's own history (the history of the good), as well as the history of the opposition
(the history of evil), were freshly reinterpreted. In the early 1920s, Trotsky might
have been more or less successful in duping the Party into believing he was moving
toward the light. Following the launching of the Five-Year Plan and the unprecedented growth in comrades' consciousness, his actual activity on behalf of reaction
was clear for everyone to see. Nikishev's laughter was the laughter of a self-assured
hermeneut who knew he would never be tempted by Trotskyist propaganda again,
never take oppositionists for well-meaning, if mistaken, friends.

As collectivization and industrialization were launched, the official press all
around the country trumpeted the message that the dreams of the Soviet toilers

would soon become reality. The final victory, however, was still one step away as long as not every single oppositionist had been finally exposed and defeated.

The responsibility to penetrate the inner self of each and every comrade and expose oppositionists was enormous. The seizure of all the important leverages of power by official hermeneuts of the soul made them able to meet this enormous task: they were fully in command of the Party bureaucracy, the newspaper, the judiciary, and most important, the internal security apparatus. More that just a set of institutional controls was at stake. The elusive ways of seeing things, talking about things and doing things, were equally important. We have seen how an object— in this case "the oppositionist"—was identified; how the evaluation of his state of mind was gradually transformed: from an "erring comrade" in the early 1920s to a "degenerate" in the middle of the decade to a "wrecker" toward its end; and, finally, how punitive strategies were adjusted: from rhetorical embattling to correcting and healing and finally to purging and isolating.

Subtle but important changes in hermeneutics of the self prepared the ground for the denigration of oppositionists so that their physical annihilation would later become possible. An epochal shift in culpability from the body to the soul goes to the heart of the book's main thesis: Stalin's consolidation of power coincided and was in large ways dependent on the essentialization of the opposition and its transformation into a personality trait. Through the campaign against oppositionism, what the Central Committee and the Central Control Commission were aiming at was no longer the act but the heterodox subject behind the act, a certain will that manifested its intrinsically wicked character. If before, oppositionism had retained some internal gradations and shades of meaning, now its various manifestations— Medvedevshchina, Zinovievshchina, Trotskyism—were definitely all hewn from the same stone.

By the late 1920s, the official discourse had come to identify the opposition as a malevolent pseudo-community and designed ways to neutralize its adherents. Though many oppositionists were readmitted into the Party, and though most of them were allowed to take second-tier positions in economic management during the Second Five-Year Plan, the anti-oppositionist know-how was not forgotten. While the template demonizing Trotskyists and Zinovievists would remain dormant until 1935–1936, it was easily reactivated when Stalin decided to do away with the remnants of the old oppositions once and for all.

With the onset of messianic times and the growing expectations that Communists would be ever more self-conscious, hermeneutics of the soul became a very difficult métier. Each time the NKVD announced that another conspiracy was just discovered, more potentates were condemned as failed hermeneuts, unable, or unwilling, to see through the enemy. One such person was Karklin, a Party member since 1902, who at one point served as the deputy chairman of the Supreme Court of the Russian republic. Later the chair of Leninism at the Omsk Veterinarian Institute and the secretary of the Party Control Commission in Krym, Karklin was arrested in January 1938 and charged as a Trotskyist and a counterrevolutionary terrorist—synonyms by the standards of the time. For ten months Karklin refused to admit to anything, but eventually he broke down and confessed that he had been recruited in 1933 into an anti-Soviet organization by the first secretary of the Krym regional Party committee, Semenov. In October 17, 1939, the Military Tribunal Collegium of the Black Sea Navy condemned him to ten years in prison on the basis of his confession alone. The verdict read in part, "a member of a Rightist-Trotskyist terrorist counterrevolutionary organization, Karklin . . . prevented the uncovering of enemies . . . thus allowing them to persevere in the Party ranks."[7]

Former employees of the judiciary such as Karklin were among the first to be condemned because, setting the moral standards and declaring themselves to be the best readers of human souls, they were held personally responsible for breakdowns in vigilance. In his appeal to the military collegium of the Supreme Court from October 22, 1939, Karklin did not claim innocence—he admitted his failure in unmasking Trotskyists working around him and asked only that his punishment be softened. Like so many Bolsheviks whose names appear in the pages above, he could not, would not wrest himself from the official discourse even when the violence of the Great Purge was evident to everyone. In a further appeal to Ul'rich, the chairman of the military collegium from March 25, 1940, Karklin concluded on a pathetic note: "I am old. But my belief in our Party, in our government, is boundless." But the military collegium left the verdict intact; Karklin slaved away in the Gulag where he died on September 12, 1942.[8]

Karklin was just one of thousands of old Bolsheviks sharing this fate and would not have merited a special mention here if not for one special circumstance—this was the man who presided over Malinovskii's trial of 1918 and signed the death verdict. Of course, Malinovskii was a real agent provocateur, working at the service of the tsarist Okhrana and betraying scores of Bolsheviks, while Karklin maintained that "in reality, I committed no crimes"—a claim that was upheld by Khrushchev's jurors who rehabilitated him in 1956.[9] Nor did Karklin have real links to any opposition whatsoever during the 1920s, as he told his tormentors repeatedly. And yet interest in factual accuracy should not prevent us from seeing the very real effects of the Communist discourse on treason and double-dealing, however phantasmagoric. Whether oppositionist or not in biographical terms, victims of the Great Purge died as oppositionists.

No one described, rightly or wrongly, as an oppositionist remained in the Party past 1935, and few lived past 1938. The Party's propaganda apparatus subsumed everyone accused by the NKVD under the category of agents provocateurs and declared them ubiquitous, highly dangerous, and difficult to recognize. The specter of the intimate enemy, he Judas, he Malinovskii, he Trotsky, was raised high.

NOTES

The following abbreviations are used in the notes.

BSE
vols.   *Bol'shaia sovetskaia entsiklopediia* [Great Soviet Encyclopedia], 1st ed., 65
        (Moscow, 1926–1947)

Deiateli SSSR   *Deiateli SSSR i revoliutsionnogo dvizheniia Rossii: Entsiklopedicheskii slovar'*
                  (Moscow: Sov. entsiklopediia, 1989)

PANO   Partiinyi arkhiv Novosibirskoi oblasti

PATO   Partiinyi arkhiv Tomskoi oblasti

PSS   V. Lenin, *Polnoe sobranie sochinenii*, 5th ed. (Moscow, 1963–1977)

RGASPI Rossiiskii gosudarstvennyi arkhiv sotsial'no politicheskoi istorii

TsGA IPD   Tsentral'nyi gosudarstvennyi arkhiv istoriko politicheskikh dokumentov

TsGAODM   Tsentral'nyi gosudarstvennyi arkhiv obshchestvennykh dvizhenii g.
          Moskvy

Prologue: The First Intimate Enemy

1. R. Wilcox, "The Secret Police of the Old Regime," *Fortnightly Review* 108 (December 1917); and V. Zhilinskii, "Organizatsiia i zhizn' okhrannogo otdeleniia vo vremena tsarskoi vlasti," *Golos minuvshego*, no. 9–10, September–October, 1917; A. Vassilyev, *The Ochrana: The Russian Secret Police* (London, 1930); C. Bobrovskaya, *Provocateurs I Have Known* (London, n.d.).

2. *Delo provokatora Malinovskogo* (Moscow: Respublika, 1992), p. 154. For provocateurs in the Bolshevik camp see "Provokatory sredi Bol'shevikov," *Byloe*, vol. 1, book 46 (1933).

3. N. Krupskaia, *Vospominaniia o Lenine* (Moscow, 1989), pp. 222–23. Malinovskii was not the only agent provocateur whose actions were uncovered following the fall of the tsarist regime, nor the only such agent tried in 1918. VTsIK's Supreme Tribunal condemned, among others, Romanov, Sokolov, Lobov, Poskrebukhin, Leonov, Regekampf-Zlatkin, and Popov; all were found guilty, just like Malinovskii, of "betraying workers' centers at the peak of their activity, thus inflicting a cruel blow to the revolutionary cause." Romanov, a member of the Social Democratic Party since 1906, was drafted by the Okhrana in 1910 and given the cover name "Pelageia." As a delegate of the Central Industrial Region, he

participated in the activity of the Prague Party Conference in January 1912. On his tip, the members of the Bolshevik illegal conference in Ozerki at the outskirts of Petrograd were arrested. Sokolov, named in police correspondence "Konduktor," also collaborated closely with the Okhrana; Sokolov participated in the activities of the Fifth London Congress of the Social Democratic Party in 1907. On his tips, Krylenko (Malinovskii's chief prosecutor) and other Bolshevik activists were arrested. In April 1912, there were fifty-five secret agents active in revolutionary organizations on the payroll of the Moscow Okhrana alone. N. Smirnov, *Repressirovannoe pravosudie* (Moscow: "Gelios ARV," 2001), pp. 101–2.

4. I. Rozental', *Provokator: Roman Malinovskii; sud'ba i vremia* (Moscow: ROSSPEN, 1996), p. 199.

5. *Delo provokatora Malinovskogo*, p. 181.

6. B. Erenfel'd, "Delo Malinovskogo," *Voprosy istorii*, no. 7 (1965), p. 107.

7. *Delo provokatora Malinovskogo*, pp. 175–78.

8. *Zhizn' dlia vsekh* (St. Petersburg, 1910), no. 2, pp. 103–4.

9. *Golosa istorii*, vyp. 2 (Moscow, 1992), pp. 31–32.

10. *Delo provokatora Malinovskogo*, p. 162.

11. Ibid., p. 146.

12. N. Krylenko, "Delo provokatora Malinovskogo," in *Za piat' let, 1918–1923* (Moscow, 1923), p. 321.

13. F. Bulkin, *Na zare profdvizheniia: Istoriia Peterburgskogo soiuza metallistov, 1906–1914* (Leningrad, 1924), p. 184.

14. *Delo provokatora Malinovskogo*, p. 207.

15. Ibid., pp. 138, 207–8.

16. F. Samoilov, *Po sledam minuvshego* (Moscow, 1934), p. 320.

17. Voronskii, *Za zhivoi i mertvoi vodoi* (Moscow, 1934), p. 516; "Protokoly VI (Prazh-skoi) Vserossiiskoi konferentsii RSDRP," *Voprosy istorii KPSS*, no. 7 (1988), pp. 53–54.

18. L. Germanov, "Iz partiinoi zhizni v 1910 godu," *Proletarskaia revoliutsiia*, 1922, no. 5, pp. 231–32. D. Sverchkov, *Na zare revoliutsii* (Moscow-Petrograd, 1924), p. 312.

19. P. Zavarzin, *Zhandarmy i bol'sheviki* (Paris, 1930,), pp. 195–96.

20. *Delo provokatora Malinovskogo*, p. 140.

21. Smirnov, *Repressirovannoe pravosudie*, p. 103.

22. *Delo provokatora Malinovskogo*, pp. 159, 216.

23. Ibid., p. 217.

24. Ibid., pp. 156–57.

25. Smirnov, *Repressirovannoe pravosudie*, p. 104.

26. For Lenin's relations with Malinovskii, a subject of much speculation, see B. Wolfe, "Lenin and the Agent Provocateur Malinovsky," *Russian Review* 5 (Autumn 1945), pp. 49–69; D. Anin, "Lenin and Malinovsky," *Survey* 21, no. 4 (Autumn 1975).

27. *Delo provokatora Malinovskogo*, pp. 140–41.

28. Ibid., p. 143.

29. Ibid., p. 211.

30. Ibid., p. 164.

31. Ibid., p. 147.

32. A. Kiselev, "V iiule 1914 goda," *Proletarskaia revoliutsiia*, 1924, no. 7, pp. 41–42.

33. *Delo provokatora Malinovskogo*, p. 189.

34. Smirnov, *Repressirovannoe pravosudie*, p. 105.

35. *Delo provokatora Malinovskogo*, p. 147.

36. Ibid., p. 152.

37. Smirnov, *Repressirovannoe pravosudie*, p. 105.

38. G. Zinoviev, "Vospominania. Malinovskii," *Izvestiia TsK KPSS* 1989, no. 6, p. 198; V. Kraevskii, "Iz vospominanii o Lenine," *Pechat' i revoliutsiia* (Moscow, 1922), no. 1–2, p. 5.

39. For conflicting opinions regarding Malinovskii's possible provocation before the revelations of 1917, see "Iz epistoliarnogo naslediia N. I. Bukharina," *Izvestiia TsK KPSS* 1989, no. 4, pp. 206–7; "Perepiska TsK RSDRP s mestnymi partiinymi organizatsiiami v gody novogo revoliutsionnogo pod"ema," *Istoricheskii arkhiv*, 1957, no. 1, p. 37.

40. V. I. Lenin, *Neizvestnye dokumenty: 1891–1922 gg.* (Moscow: ROSSPEN, 2000), pp. 190–96.

41. *Delo provokatora Malinovskogo*, p. 217.

42. Kraevskii, "Iz vospominanii o Lenine," *Pechat' i revoliutsiia*, no. 1–2, pp. 6–7; Rozental', *Provokator*, p. 177.

43. *Delo provokatora Malinovskogo*, pp. 148, 218.

44. Ibid., pp. 148–49.

45. I. Halfin, *Terror in My Soul: Communist Autobiographies on Trial* (Cambridge, Mass.: Harvard University Press, 2003), pp. 7–42.

46. *Delo provokatora Malinovskogo*, p. 230.

47. J. Hazard, "Soviet Law: The Bridge Years, 1917–1920," in *Russian Law: Historical and Political Perspectives*, ed. William E. Butler (Leyden: A. W. Sijthoff, 1977), p. 241.

48. V. Viktorov, *Bez grifa "sekretno"* (Moscow, 1990), pp. 95–96.

49. N. Krylenko, *Obvinitel'nye rechi po naibolee krupnym politicheskim protsessam* (Moscow, 1937), pp. 305–6.

50. V. Viktorov, *Bez grifa "sekretno,"* pp. 97–98.

51. *Delo provokatora Malinovskogo*, p. 187.

52. Ibid., p. 226.

53. Ibid., p. 229.

54. Ibid., p. 142.

55. Ibid., pp. 193–94.

56. Ibid., pp. 232–33.

57. Ibid., p. 234.

58. Ibid., p. 201.

59. Ibid., p. 235.

60. Ibid., p. 220.

61. Ibid., p. 153.

62. Ibid., p. 221.

63. Ibid., p. 219.

64. Ibid., p. 149.

65. Ibid., pp. 221–22.

66. Ibid., p. 230.

67. Smirnov, *Repressirovannoe pravosudie*, p. 108.

Introduction: Individual Truth and Party Truth

1. A. Iakovlev (ed.), *Reabilitatsiia: Politicheskie protsessy 30kh–50kh godov* (Moscow: Izdatel'stvo politicheskoi literatury, 1991), pp. 192–93; A. Kirilina, *Neizvestnyi Kirov* (Saint Petersburg: Izdatel'skii dom "Neva"; Moscow: Izd-vo "OLMA-PRESS," 2001), p. 363.

2. *Rabochaia oppozitsiia: Materialy i dokumenty, 1920–1926 gg.* (Moscow: Gosizdat, 1926), p. 169.

3. *Iz arkhiva L. O. Dan* (Amsterdam, 1987), pp. 101–4.

4. *Tainy natsional'noi politiki TsK RKP: Stenograficheskii otchet sekretnogo IV soveshchaniia TsK RKP* (1923; reprint, Moscow, 1992), p. 63.

5. TsGAODM, f. 64, op. 1, d. 78, l. 140b; V. I. Lenin, *Polnoe sobranie sochinenii*, 5th ed. (Moscow, 1963–1977) (henceforth *PSS*), vol. 19, p. 308; Khlevniuk et al. (eds.), *Stalinskoe politbiuro v 30-e gody, sbornik dokumentov* (Moscow, 1995), pp. 101–2; *Pod znamenem marksizma*, no. 8–9 (1923), pp. 285–86.

6. For self-revelation in the revolutionary context, see P. Holquist, "State Violence as Technique: The Logic of Violence in Soviet Totalitarianism," in *Landscaping the Human Garden*, ed. Amir Weiner (Stanford: Stanford University Press, 2003); and O. Kharkhordin, *The Collective and the Individual in Russia: A Study of Practices* (Berkeley: University of California Press, 1999), pp. 175–77.

7. TsGAODM, f. 67, op. 1, d. 97, l. 130b; f. 80, op. 1, d. 58, l. 22; f. 1614, op. 1, d. 40, l. 10b.

8. *Pis'ma vo vlast', 1917–1927* (Moscow: ROSSPEN, 1998), pp. 446–47.

9. E. Kviring, *Zachatki revizii Leninizma u Preobrazhenskogo* (Khar'kov: Chervonoi Shliakh, 1924), p. 3.

10. V. Kovalev, *Dva stalinskikh narkoma* (Moscow: Progress, 1995), p. 137.

11. Ibid.

12. J. Cassiday, *The Enemy on Trial* (DeKalb: Northern Illinois University Press, 2000), pp. 163, 180–81.

13. For the Party courts as a modern inquisition, see H. Dewar, *The Modern Inquisition* (London: A. Wingate, 1953); B. Lewytzkyi, *Die rote Inquisition* (Frankfurt, 1967).

14. L. Shapiro, *The Communist Party of the Soviet Union*, 2nd ed. (London: Eyre and Spottiswoode, 1970), p. 284.

15. M. David-Fox, *Revolution of the Mind: Higher Learning among the Bolsheviks, 1918–1929* (Ithaca: Cornell University Press, 1997), p. 231.

16. Whatever comparison of Christian with Bolshevik ritual I suggest serves an analytical and not a historical function. My reference to the Black Mass throughout is no more than a heuristic device intended to evoke images familiar to the reader. For example, the claim that oppositionist rituals were perceived by the loyalists as a Black Mass should be understood as an attempt to flesh out the meaning Bolsheviks invested in their organizational structure by analogy to the Church model in which the community of the believers could embody itself in one and only one institution. This claim is, then, not an invitation to seek the origins of the attitude of the Party apparatus towards the oppositionists in the attitude of the Orthodox Church towards heretics. If the history of the secularization process or the index of cultural borrowings within the Western tradition were the center of my discussion, Christianity would have served as a source of Bolshevism. Yet I do not suppose, or suggest, that Christianity was in some sense a primary phenomenon while Bolshevism was its derivative. Instead, I use examples from Christianity to approach an

archetype of eschatological thinking as such, and thereby to elucidate the implications of my argument that Bolshevism was an eschatological movement.

17. V. Serge, *Memoirs of a Revolutionary, 1901–1941* (Oxford, 1951), p. 233; I. Deutscher, *The Prophet Outcast: Trotsky, 1929–1940* (London: Oxford University Press, 1963), pp. 84–91.

18. *Deviatyi s"ezd RKP(b), Mart–Aprel' 1920 goda: Stenograficheskii otchet* (Moscow, 1968), pp. 85, 167.

19. L. Trotski, *Nashi politicheskie zadachi* (Zheneva, 1904), p. 71.

20. Ibid., pp. 71–72.

21. *Desiatyi s"ezd RKP(b), Mart 1921: Stenograficheskii otchet* (Moscow, 1968), p. 61.

22. L. Kamenev, *Stat'i i rechi*, vol. 10 (Moscow: Gosizdat, 1927), pp. 18–19.

23. L. Trotsky, *The New Course*, trans. and ed. Max Shachtman (New York: New International, 1943), p. 94.

24. *Chetyrnadtsatyi s"ezd VKP(b): Stenograficheskii otchet* (Moscow, 1926), pp. 165–66.

25. I. Smilga, *Na povorote* (Moscow: Gosizdat, 1921), p. 11.

26. TsGA IPD, f. 1816, op. 2, d. 5094, ll. 113–15.

27. A. Slepkov, *Platforma oppozitsionnogo likvidatorstva* (Moscow-Leningrad: Gosizdat, 1926), p. 60.

28. E. Iaroslavskii, *Novoe i staroe v novoi oppozitsii* (Moscow-Leningrad: Gosizdat, 1927), p. 7.

29. V. Rogovin, *Vlast' i oppozitsii* (Moscow, 1993), p. 6.

30. A. Gusev, "Levokommunisticheskaia oppozitsiia v SSSR v kontse 20-kh godov," *Obshchestvennaia istoriia*, vol. 1 (1996), p. 96.

31. R. Daniels, *The Conscience of the Revolution: Communist Opposition in Soviet Russia* (Cambridge, Mass.: Harvard University Press, 1960), p. 207.

32. I. Deutscher, *The Prophet Unarmed: Trotsky, 1921–1929* (London: Oxford University Press, 1959), p. 288.

33. For problematizations of context relevent to my argument, see J. Derrida, "Signature, Event, Context," *Glyph* 1 (1977), pp. 185–86; Bakhtin, *Art and Answerability: Early Philosophical Essays by M. M. Bakhtin* (Austin: University of Texas Press, 1990), p. 87.

34. See, for example, Lewis H. Siegelbaum and Ronald Grigor Suny (eds.), *Making Workers Soviet* (Ithaca: Cornell University Press, 1995).

35. A. Walicki, *Marxism and the Leap to the Kingdom of Freedom: The Rise and Fall of the Communist Utopia* (Stanford: Stanford University Press, 1995); L. Kolakowski, "Marxist Roots of Stalinism," in *Stalinism: Essays in Historical Interpretation*, ed. R. Tucker (New York: Norton, 1977).

36. There are a number of excellent Party histories, for example, T. Rigby, *Communist Party Membership in the U.S.S.R., 1917–1967* (Princeton: Princeton University Press, 1968); G. Gill, *The Origins of the Stalinist Political System* (Cambridge: Cambridge University Press, 1990).

37. My view of the subject relies on the work of Michel Foucault, especially his theoretical statements collected in *Power*, ed. James D. Faubion, trans. Robert Hurley and others (New York: New Press, 2000).

38. C. Bell, *Ritual Theory, Ritual Practice* (New York: Oxford University Press, 1992), p. 221.

338   ■   NOTES TO PAGES 29–31

39. N. Rose, *Inventing Our Selves: Psychology, Power, and Personhood* (Cambridge: Cambridge University Press, 1996), p. 176.

40. For politics as an exercise in symbolic power, see P. Bourdieu, *Language and Symbolic Power* (Cambridge, Mass.: Harvard University Press, 1991), p. 111.

41. For the poetics of self fashioning, see I. Lotman, "The Poetics of Everyday Behavior in Eighteenth-Century Russian Culture," *The Semiotics of Russian Cultural History* (Ithaca: Cornell University Press, 1985), pp. 74–81; For the poetics of the Stalinist rituals, see L. Siegelbaum, "'Dear Comrade, You Ask What We Need': Socialist Paternalism and Soviet Rural 'Notables' in the mid 1930s," *Slavic Review* 57 (1998).

42. S. Kotkin, *Magnetic Mountain: Stalinism as a Civilization* (Berkeley: University of California Press, 1995), pp. 198–237.

43. J. Butler, *Excitable Speech: A Politics of the Performative* (New York: Routledge, 1997), p. 161.

44. For the subject of posturing in the context of the Soviet 1920s, see G. Alexopoulos, "Portrait of a Con Artist as a Soviet Man," *Slavic Review* 57, no. 4 (1998); S. Fitzpatrick, "The World of Ostap Bender: Soviet Confidence Men in the Stalin Period," *Slavic Review* 61, no. 3 (2002).

45. Rose, *Inventing Our Selves*, p. 189.

46. C. Morris, *The Discovery of the Individual* (London: SPCK, 1972), pp. 7–8.

47. M. Foucault, *Technologies of the Self* (Amherst: University of Massachusetts Press, 1988); C. Taylor, *The Sources of the Self: The Making of the Modern Identity* (Cambridge, Mass.: Harvard University Press, 1989).

48. N. Werth, *Être communiste en URSS sous Stalin* (Paris: Gallimard-Julliard, 1981).

49. In the field of Soviet history, this new theoretical framework became available just as the Party archives were opened to serious research. S. Fitzpatrick, "Lives under Fire. Autobiographical Narratives and their Challenges in Stalin's Russia," *Die Russia et d'ailleurs: Melanges Marc Ferro* (Paris, 1995); J. Hellbeck, "Fashioning the Stalinist Soul: The Diary of Stepan Podlubnyi, 1831–1838," *Jahrbücher für Geschichte Osteuropas*, no. 3 (1996); J. Hellbeck, "Writing the Self in the Time of Terror: Alexander Afinogenov's Diary of 1937," in *Self and Story in Russian History*, ed. L. Engelstein and S. Sandler (Ithaca: Cornell University Press, 2000); C. Pennetier and B. Pudal (eds.), *Autobiographies, autocritiques, aveux dans le monde communiste* (Paris, 2002).

50. For the notion of "discourse" see the discussion in D. Macdonell, *Theories of Discourse: An Introduction* (Oxford: Blackwell, 1986).

51. Many scholars have contributed to the study of Bolshevik political biography; I will not be adding my name to that impressive roster. In addition to the numerous biographies of Trotsky, see also S. Cohen, *Bukharin and the Bolshevik Revolution: A Political Biography, 1888–1938* (London: Wildwood House, 1971); A. Senin, *A. I. Rykov: Stranitsy zhizni* (Moscow: izd. MGU, 1993); O. Gorelov, *Tsurtsvang Mikhaila Tomskogo* (Moscow: ROSSPEN, 2000).

52. R. Coward and F. Ellis, *Language and Materialism: Development in Semiology and the Theory of the Subject* (London: Routledge and Kegan Paul, 1977), p. 133.

Chapter 1: Oppositionism as a Malady of the Mind

1. Rossiiskii gosudarstvennyi arkhiv sotsial'no politicheskoi istorii (henceforth, RGASPI), f. 45, op. 1, d. 31, l. 39.

2. *Dvenadtsatyi s"ezd RKP(b)*, 17–25 Aprelia 1923 goda: *Stenograficheskii otchet* (Moscow: Gospolitizdat, 1968), pp. 152–53.

3. *Dvenadtsatyi s"ezd RKP(b)*, pp. 116–17.

4. For contemporary discussion of the Bolshevik language, see P. Chernykh, "O novykh slovakh," *Etnograficheskii biulleten'* (Irkutsk) no. 3 (March 1923); A. Selishchev, *Revoliutsiia i iazyk* (Moscow, 1925); N. Prianishnikov, "Otrazhenie revoliutsii v iazyke," *Krasnyi ural*, nos. 96, 113, 114 (1926).

5. For the application of the concept of "public sphere" to the Soviet Union, see D. Beyrau, "Macht und Öffentliche Räume im Sozialismus: Einführung," *Jahrbücher für Geschichte Osteuropas* 50, no. 2 (2000), pp. 161–62; G. Rittersporn, M. Rolf, and J. Behrends, "Open Spaces and Public Realm: Thoughts on the Public Sphere in Soviet-Type Systems," in *Sphären von Öffentlichkeit in Gesellschaften sowjetischen Typs* (Frankfurt: Peter Lang, 2003).

6. RGASPI, f. 45, op. 1, d. 28, l. 118; TsGAODM, f. 1660, op. 1, d. 58, l. 190b.

7. The concept of secular ritual is helpful here. S. Moore and B. Myerhoff, "Secular Ritual: Forms and Meanings," in *Secular Ritual*, ed. S. Moore and B. Myerhoff (Assen: Van Gorcum, 1977); C. Geertz, *The Interpretation of Cultures* (New York: Basic Books, 1973); S. Wilentz (ed.), *Rites of Power: Symbolism, Ritual and Politics since the Middle Ages* (Philadelphia: University of Pennsylvania Press, 1985).

8. The Tenth Party Congress received petitions expressing hope that "the congress will unanimously accept Lenin's theses." RGASPI, f. 45, op. 1, d. 31, l. 18.

9. For a recent discussion of these themes, see A. Getty, "*Samokritika* Rituals in the Stalinist Central Committee, 1933–38," *Russian Review* 58 (1999), pp. 49–51.

10. RGASPI, f. 45, op. 1, d. 1, l. 8. TsGAODM, f. 3, op. 8, d. 92, l. 10; TsGAODM, f. 64, op. 1, d. 78, l. 5.

11. *Dvenadtsatyi s"ezd RKP(b)*, pp. 116–17. "Discussion" refers to the specific Party institution that Trotsky defined as "deliberation of general political issues by Party members." Trotsky, *Nashi politicheskie*, p. 63.

12. Lenin, *PSS*, vol. 8, p. 113.

13. A. Lazovskii, *Zadachi professional'nykh soiuzov* (Moscow, 1921), p. 14.

14. The congress met from ten in the morning until ten in the evening, with an intermission from three to six. A. Mitrofanov, "Vladimir Il'ich na XI s"ezde RKP(b)," *Voprosy istorii KPSS*, no. 4 (1968), p. 104.

15. *Deviatyi s"ezd*, pp. 203–4. Direct democracy did not figure in the Bolshevik plan: Lenin believed that representative institutions must be maintained, and that only the liberal division of labor between the legislative and the executive must be abolished. The grass roots were enjoined to petition the congress but not to instruct it. Petitioning assumed that the delegate was so completely possessed of the full authority of the proletariat that he must be solicited, never commanded, by the particular comrades that dispatched him to Moscow. He or she spoke for the general interest of the Revolution and not merely for the grassroots organization that elected him or her as its representative. The Tenth Party Congress received petitions urging general solutions to the problems besetting the

young republic ("show the way to the emancipation of the working class from hunger and cold," "correct the development of the national economy," etc.). Instructing assumed that the delegate represented was a trusted agent of the electors who voted for him, and such narrow-minded advocacy of a particular interest was generally believed to violate revolutionary universalism. When regional peculiarities were mentioned in grassroots petitions to the congress, this was done not with hope for a specific redress but in order to show what specific contribution a given locality can make to the universal cause. While instructions might have transformed the congress into a battlefield where opposing interests struggled for supremacy, there was scarcely a divide in the Bolshevik mind sharper than the one between delegates at a Party congress and the utilitarian-minded constituencies taking part in the parliamentarian game. *Desiatyi s"ezd RKP(b), Mart 1921: Stenograficheskii otchet* (Moscow, 1968), pp. 779–85.

16. Party members could appeal Central Committee decisions to the congress. RGASPI, f. 99, op. 1, d. 7, l. 22.

17. TsGAODM, f. 3, op. 6, d. 2, l. 18.

18. *Desiatyi s"ezd RKP(b), Mart 1921 goda* (Moscow, 1963), pp. 102–3.

19. *Dvenadtsatyi s"ezd RKP(b)*, p. 227.

20. *Desiatyi s"ezd RKP(b)*, p. 499.

21. *Vos'moi s"ezd RKP(b)*, p. 26.

22. *Dvenadtsatyi s"ezd RKP(b)*, pp. 104–5.

23. *Deviataia konferentsiia RKP(b), Sentiabr' 1920g: Protokoly* (Moscow, 1972), p. 150.

24. *Desiatyi s"ezd RKP(b)*, p. 309.

25. R. Kowalski, *The Bolshevik Party in Conflict: The Left Communist Opposition of 1918* (Pittsburgh: University of Pittsburgh Press, 1991); A. Siderov, "Ekonomicheskaia programma oktiabria i diskussiia s levymi kommunistami o zadachakh sotsialisticheskogo stroitel'stva," *Proletarskaia revoliutsiia*, 1929, no. 6, pp. 26–75; L. Stupochenko, "Brestkie dni," *Proletarskaia revoliutsiia*, no. 4 (16) (1923), pp. 94–111.

26. *Deviatyi s"ezd*, p. 28.

27. A. Bubnov, VKP(b), *BSE* (Moscow, 1930), vol. 11, pp. 471–72; *Leninskie printsipy partiinogo rukovodstva massami v pervye gody stroitel'stva sovetskogo obshchestva, 1917–1923* (Moscow: Mysl', 1967), p. 175; RGASPI, f. 17, op. 71, d. 4, l. 290b; f. 45, op. 1, d. 1, l. 65.

28. R. Daniels, *The Conscience of the Revolution: Communist Opposition in Soviet Russia* (Cambridge, Mass.: Harvard University Press, 1960), p. 95; L. Schapiro, *The Origin of the Communist Autocracy: Political Opposition in the Soviet State, First Phase, 1917–1922*, 2nd ed. (London: Macmillan, 1977), p. 223; R. Service, *The Bolshevik Party in Revolution: A Study in Organisational Change, 1917–1923* (London: Macmillan, 1979), pp. 130–31; *Deiateli SSSR i revoliutsionnogo dvizheniia Rossii: entsiklopedicheskii slovar'* (Moscow: Sov. entsiklopediia, 1989), pp. 569–73; 649–50.

29. N. Osinskii, *Stroitel'stvo sotsializma* (Moscow, 1918), p. 38.

30. *Pravda*, December 26, 1920.

31. *Pravda*, January 15, 1919.

32. *Vos'moi s"ezd RKP(b)*, p. 170.

33. *Vos'maia konferentsiia RKP(b), December 1919 goda: Protokoly* (Moscow, 1961), p. 42.

34. *Deviatyi s"ezd*, pp. 94–96.

35. According to the regulations, every group that had forty signatures had a right for a co-report, RGASPI, f. 45, op. 1, d. 1, l. 33.

36. *Deviatyi s"ezd RKP(b), Mart–Aprel' 1920 goda: Stenograficheskii otchet* (Moscow, 1968), pp. 52–53.

37. *Izvestiia TsK*, 23, September 23, 1920, p. 1.

38. A. Bubnov, "VKP(b)", pp. 470–71; RGSASPI, f. 17, op. 71, d. 1, l. 14. TsGAODM, f. 67, op. 1, d. 97, l. 23. S. Spencer, "A Political Biography of Alexander Shliapnikov," Ph.D. thesis, Oxford University, 1981; Schapiro, *Origin of the Communist Autocracy*, pp. 221–22; Daniels, *Conscience of the Revolution*, pp. 125–26; Service, *Bolshevik Party*, p. 133; M. Vasser, "Bor'ba Kommunisticheskoi partii protiv antileninskoi rabochei oppozitsii' i ee raznovidnostei v pervye gody nepa, X-XII s'ezdy partii," *Vestnik Moskovskogo universiteta*, 1957, no. 4, pp. 174–76.

39. RGASPI, f. 17, op. 71, d. 1, l. 2.

40. B. Allen, "Alexander Shliapnikov and the Origins of the Workers' Opposition, March 1919–April 1920," *Jahrbücher für Geschichte Osteuropas*, no. 1 (2005), pp. 11–12.

41. A. Kollontai, *Diplomaticheskie dnevniki 1922–1940* (Moscow: Academia, 2001), vol. 1, p. 16.

42. A. Kollontai, *Rabochaia oppozitsiia* (Moscow, 1921), p. 9.

43. RGASPI, f. 17, op. 84, d. 217, l. 7; f. 99, op. 1, d. 7, l. 19; l. 12.

44. TsGAODM, f. 1614, op. 1, d. 40, l. 1; f. 1673, op. 1, d. 48, l. 11.

45. RGASPI, f. 17, op. 71, d. 3, l. 4. TsGAODM, f. 67, op. 1, d. 97, l. 3. For the official rebuttals of the Workers' Opposition claim see Trotskii, *Sochineniia*, 21 vols. (Moscow: Gosizdat, 1924–27), vol. 15, pp. 218–21.

46. *Desiatyi s"ezd RKP(b)*, p. 387. *Arkhiv Trotskogo*, vol. 3, l. 95; vol. 4, p. 75. PATO, f. 17, op. 1, d. 1065, ll. 8–9, 54–55.

47. *Sed'moi ekstrennyi s"ezd RKP(b)*, p. 60.

48. T. Liudvinskaia, "Iz istorii bor'by za edinstvo partii v 1920–1921 gg." *Istoricheskii arkhiv*, no. 2 (1960), pp. 165–66; *Pravda*, January 19, 1921; *Izvestiia VTsIK*, January 29, 1921; TsGAODM, f. 1614, op. 1, d. 40, l. 5.

49. *Deviatyi s"ezd RKP(b), Mart–Aprel' 1920 goda* (Moscow, 1960), p. 178.

50. *Deviatyi s"ezd*, p. 203. Trotsky criticized "separatist attitudes" and Lenin "could not tolerate" erroneous opinions. Trotsky, *Sochineniia* vol. 3; *Leninskii sbornik*, vol. 4 (1925), p. 6.

51. *Deviatyi s"ezd*, p. 178.

52. *Deviatyi s"ezd*, pp. 242–43.

53. "'. . . Sudorozhno tsepliaiutsia za ortodoksiiu . . .'. Neizvestnoe pis'mo A. V. Lunacharskogo L. B. Krasinu," *Kommunist*, no. 12 (1991), p. 104.

54. *Odinnadtsatyi s"ezd RKP(b), Mart–Aprel' 1922 goda: Stenograficheskii otchet* (Moscow, 1966), pp. 188–89.

55. RGASPI, f. 45, op. 1, d. 1, l. 67; PATO, f. 17, op. 1, d. 749, l. 155. In the early 1920s the discussion sheet came out more or less regularly before Party congresses as a separate publication; later on it was to become a part of *Pravda*. Discussion sheets were known before the revolution too, see Lenin, *PSS*, vol. 20, pp. 334–35.

56. *Deviataia konferentsiia RKP(b)*, p. 149.

57. TsGAODM, f. 3, op. 4, d. 32, l. 21; f. 67, op. 1, d. 97, l. 1; f. 1614, op. 1, d. 40, l. 1; I. Smilga, *Na povorote* (Moscow: Gosizdat, 1921), p. 21; Zinoviev, *Sochineniia*, vol. 6, pp. 490–91.

58. Daniels, *Conscience of the Revolution*, p. 164.

59. *Desiatyi s"ezd RKP(b)*, p. 299.

60. *Odinnadtsatyi s"ezd RKP(b)*, pp. 465–66.

61. *Desiatyi s"ezd RKP(b)*, p. 397; I. Smilga, *Na povorote*, p. 11; TsGAODM, f. 1660, op. 1, d. 58, l. 30b. RGASPI, f. 17, op. 84, d. 217, l. 4.

62. *Desiatyi s"ezd RKP(b)*, p. 327.

63. *Desiatyi s"ezd RKP(b)*, p. 289.

64. *Desiatyi s"ezd RKP(b)*, p. 258. See I. Smilga, *Na povorote*.

65. O. Obichkin, *Kratkii ocherk istorii ustava KPSS* (Moscow, 1986).

66. "Each assembly," Larin stated at the Eleventh Party Congress, "establishes its own rules of conduct, its own constitution. According to the constitution of the Party Congress, delegates must be allowed to speak for and against every motion that was introduced. Yet, when I requested the right to speak, the chairman, instead of fulfilling his duty, asked the delegates to vote on whether they want to listen to what I have to say." Larin argued that this was an "unjustified alteration of the regulations," and his view eventually prevailed. *Odinnadtsatyi s"ezd RKP(b)*, p. 281.

67. TsGAODM, f. 1614, op. 1, d. 40, l. 10b.

68. *Desiatyi s"ezd RKP(b)*, pp. 304–5.

69. *Desiatyi s"ezd RKP(b)*, p. 243.

70. *Desiatyi s"ezd RKP(b)*, p. 523.

71. RGASPI, f. 45, op. 1, d. 1, ll. 56, 60. The supporters of workers' opposition constituted two-thirds of the Samara provincial Party committee, RGASPI, f. 17, op. 3, d. 882, ll. 10–11. See also *Kommuna* (Samara), October 15 and 29, 1920; November 10 and 30, 1920. *Izvestiia Samarskogo partiinogo komiteta RKP(b)*, 1921, no. 13, p. 17.

72. *Pravda*, December 12, 1920; *Izvestiia TsK VKP(b)*, no. 26, December 20, 1920; RGASPI, f. 17, op. 2, d. 55, l. 1. The Central Committee's decision to convene the Tenth Party Congress was promulgated in December 1920, almost two months ahead of the event, and the electoral system was worked out: one delegate with voting rights was sent to Moscow per thousand Party members. *Izvestiia TsK VKP(b)*, no. 27, January 27, 1921; RGASPI, f. 45, op. 1, d. 1, l. 58; d. 27, ll. 1–7; RGASPI, f. 17, op. 71, d. 79, l. 1; f. 45, op. 1, d. 1, l. 68. TsGAODM, f. 64, op. 1, d. 74, l. 17; f. 1614, op. 1, d. 40, l. 1.

73. TsGAODM, f. 1673, op. 1, d. 48, l. 10b; L. Trotsky, *Rol' i zadachi professional'nykh soiuzov* (Moscow: iz. Tsenkhrana, 1920); Daniels, *Conscience of the Revolution*, pp. 132–33. Shapiro, *Origin of the Communist Autocracy*, pp. 284–85.

74. TsGAODM, f. 67, op. 1, d. 97, l. 2. *O roli professional'nykh soiuzov v proizvodstve* (Moscow, 1921); N. Bukharin, *O zadachakh profsoiuzov* (Petrograd, 1921); A. Mikoian, *Mysli i vospominaniia o Lenine* (Moscow, 1970), p. 124.

75. *Partiia i soiuzy* (Petrograd, 1921); L. Trotskii, *O zadachakh profsoiuzov: Doklad prochitannyi na sobranii 30 dekabria 1920 goda* (Moscow, 1921); G. Zinoviev, *Spor o professional'nykh soiuzakh* (Petrograd, 1921); Ia. Bronin, "Platforma tov. Bukharina v profsoiuznoi diskussii," *Proletarskaia revoliutsiia*, no. 95 (1929), pp. 13–35.

76. TsGAODM, f. 1614, op. 1, d. 40, l. 10b; *Platforma Shliapnikova i Medvedeva* (Moscow, 1927).

77. Lenin, *PSS*, vol. 42, pp. 205, 207, 221.

78. *Desiatyi s"ezd RKP(b)*, p. 846.

79. A. Lazovskii, *Zadachi professional'nykh soiuzov* (Moscow, 1921), p. 1.

80. A. Vitkin, *Razgrom Kommunisticheskoi partiei trotskizma i drugikh antileninskikh grupp* (Leningrad: izd. LGU, 1966), p. 27.

81. G. Taranenko, *Bor'ba Moskovskoi partiinoi organizatsii za ukreplenie edinstva i splochenie partiinykh riadov v period mezhdu X i XIII s"ezdami RKP(b)* (Moscow, 1969).

82. *Pravda*, January 19, 1921; *Desiatyi s"ezd RKP(b)*, pp. 803, 871.

83. *Moskovskaia gubernskaia konferentsiia RKP(b): Kratkii otchet i rezoliutsii* (Moscow, 1921), p. 5; Taranenko, *Bor'ba Moskovskoi partiinoi organizatsii*, p. 12.

84. RGASPI, f. 17, op. 3, d. 131, l. 1; Service, *Bolshevik Party*, p. 150.

85. *Ural'skii rabochii*, February 11 and 13, 1921; *Izvestiia Ekaterinburgskogo gubkoma RKP(b)*, 1921, no. 1–2. Only 34 delegates voted for Trotsky, the co-reporter, and only 14 voted for the candidate of the Workers' Opposition, a certain Shur. The votes elsewhere in the country were similar. At the Riazan' Provincial Party Conference "the Ten" received 33 votes, the Workers' Opposition 15. At the Ivanovo-Voznesensk Provincial Party Conference "the Ten" received 99 votes, Trotsky 12, and Workers' Opposition 7 votes. *Pravda*, February 24, 1921. *Izvestiia Ivanovo-Voznesenskogo Partiinogo kommitteta RKP*, 1921, no. 3–4, p. 15.

86. The Eight Samara Provincial Party Conference dispatched three supporters of Shliapnikov to the Tenth Party Congress (Milonov, Sirotin, and Manevich). *Izvestiia Samarskogo partiinogo komiteta RKP(b)*, 1922, no. 2 (30), p. 1. *Desiatyi s"ezd RKP(b)*, p. 866 note 65; *Odinnadtsatyi s"ezd RKP(b)*, p. 54.

87. *Desiatyi s"ezd RKP(b)*, p. 524.

88. *Desiatyi s"ezd RKP(b)*, p. 384.

89. *Pravda*, February 5, 1921. TsGAODM, f. 64, op. 1, d. 74, l. 30b. I. Smilga, *Na povorote*, p. 21. *Desiatyi s"ezd RKP(b)*, p. 833. When the Ekaterinburg provincial Party committee tried to suggest that the use of clearly defined platforms might needlessly lead to the "intensification of intraparty disputes" it was strongly criticized. *Ural'skii rabochii*, January 16 and February 11, 13, 22, and 24, 1921. When Workers' Opposition in Vladimir published its platform despite the fact it was voted down by the local provincial committee, Bukharin was amused: "It is fashionable these days to publish even theses that were rejected." *Rabochaia oppozitsiia*, p. 87.

90. *Reabilitatsiia*, pp. 106–7.

91. RGASPI, f. 45, op. 1, d. 3, l. 20.

92. *Desiatyi s"ezd RKP(b)*, p. 3.

93. *Desiatyi s"ezd RKP(b)*, p. 524.

94. *Desiatyi s"ezd RKP(b)*, p. 4.

95. RGASPI, f. 17, op. 71, d. 1, l. 2–3; f. 45, op. 1, d. 1, l. 7. TsGAODM, f. 64, op. 1, d. 74, l. 30b; f. 67, op. 1, d. 97, l. 20b.

96. Lenin, *PSS*, vol. 41, p. 27.

97. G. Vinokur, *Kul'tura iazyka* (Moscow, 1925), pp. 60–61.

98. TsGAODM, f. 3, op. 4, d. 32, l. 35.

99. RGASPI, f. 45, op. 1, d. 1, l. 17. For the changes the Bolshevik party underwent during these years, see J. Adelman, "The Development of the Soviet Party Apparat in the Civil War: Center, Localities, and National Areas," *Russian History* 1982, no. 9.

100. N. Popov, "O sotsial'nom sostave RKP(b) i o Leninskom prizyve," *Krasnaia nov'* 1924, no. 3, pp. 310–11.

101. *Pravda*, January 21 and 29, 1921; *Kommunisticheskii trud*, March 8, 1921.

102. *Desiatyi s"ezd RKP(b)*, pp. 520–21.

103. R. Pethybridge, "Concern for Bolshevik Ideological Predominance at the Start of NEP," *Russian Review* 41 (1982), pp. 445–53.

104. *Desiatyi s"ezd RKP(b)*, p. 333.

105. TsGAODM, f. 64, op. 1, d. 74, l. 2; f. 1660, op. 1, d. 58, l. 30b.

106. *Leninskii sbornik* 35, p. 155; R. Eideman, *Bor'ba s kulatskim povstanchistvom i banditizmom* (Khar'kov, 1921); N. Denisov, "Sibirskii banditizm," *Krasnaia armiia*, no. 9 (1921); A. Filimonov, "Melkoburzhuaznaia kontrrevoliutsiia pri perekhode k nepu," *Istoricheskii zhurnal*, no. 4 (1938).

107. *Desiatyi s"ezd RKP(b)*, p. 230.

108. *Desiatyi s"ezd RKP(b)*, pp. 304–5.

109. *Desiatyi s"ezd RKP(b)*, p. 394.

110. *Desiatyi s"ezd RKP(b)*, pp. 539–40.

111. *Desiatyi s"ezd RKP(b)*, p. 540.

112. RGASPI, f. 45, op. 1, d. 1, l. 73.

113. For the support of the resolution at the grassroots level see RGASPI, f. 17, op. 3, d. 397, l. 84; d. 389, l. 171; TsGA IPD, f. 16, op. 4, d. 4184, l. 5; d. 4195, l. 8.

114. *Desiatyi s"ezd RKP(b)*, pp. 571–73.

115. I. Deutscher, *The Prophet Armed* (New York: Oxford University Press, 1954), pp. 518–19.

116. *Desiatyi s"ezd RKP(b)*, pp. 571–76.

117. *Desiatyi s"ezd RKP(b)*, pp. 534, 524–26.

118. I. Smilga, *Na povorote*, p. 23.

119. TsGAODM, f. 1660, op. 1, d. 58, l. 6.

120. I. Smilga, *Na povorote*, p. 21.

121. A. Lazovskii, *Zadachi professional'nykh soiuzov* (Moscow, 1921), p. 14. RGASPI, f. 17, op. 71, d. 1, l. 11. RGASPI, f. 17, op. 2, d. 685, l. 95.

122. RGASPI, f. 17, op. 2, d. 104, ll. 60, 73.

123. RGASPI, f. 17, op. 71, d. 3, l. 5.

124. *Leningradskaia pravda*, December 15, 1923.

125. A. Selishchev, *Iazyk revoliutsionnoi epokhi. Iz nabliudenii nad russkim iazykom poslednikh let (1917–1926)* (Moscow, 1928), pp. 99–100.

126. *Sed'moi ekstrennyi s"ezd RKP(b)*, p. 69.

127. *Sed'moi ekstrennyi s"ezd RKP(b)*, p. 72.

128. PANO, f. 1, op. 1, d. 819, l. 2.

129. RGASPI, f. 17, op. 71, d. 1, l. 12. *Proletarskaia diktatura*, no. 1, September 21, 1919, p. 4; *Metallist i gorniak*, November 30, 1920.

130. G. Zinov'ev, "Skol'ko 'marksizmov' sushchestvuet na svete?" *Bol'shevik*, no. 16 (1928), p. 28.

131. This was a position accepted by most Russian Social Democrats. The Menshevik theorist, Iulii Martov, for example, wanted nothing to do with "mechanical combination of contradictory tendencies" or "mechanical superiority of one faction over another." *Luch'* (Petrograd), November 19, 1917; *Vpered*, December 15, 1917.

132. *Desiatyi s"ezd RKP(b)*, pp. 305–6.

133. *Desiatyi s"ezd RKP(b)*, p. 268.

134. *Desiatyi s"ezd RKP(b)*, p. 538.

135. *Desiatyi s"ezd RKP(b)*, p. 538.

136. At the elections to the Central Committee held at the Tenth Party Congress, Shliapnikov received 354 votes and Kutuzov 380. The votes cast in favor of Lenin (479),

Stalin (458), and Trotsky (452) were not much higher. RGASPI, f. 45, op. 1, d. 29, l. 12; Zinoviev, *Sochineniia*, vol. 6, pp. 624–25.

137. *Odinnadtsatyi s"ezd RKP(b)*, p. 451.

138. *Desiatyi s"ezd RKP(b)*, p. 75. But Shliapnikov could also sound more conciliatory, as in *Metallist*, no. 3–4 (April–May 1921), p. 1.

139. *Desiatyi s"ezd RKP(b)*, p. 527.

140. *Desiatyi s"ezd RKP(b)*, p. 524.

141. RGASPI, f. 17, op. 71, d. 1, l. 12.

142. *Desiatyi s"ezd RKP(b)*, p. 531.

143. *Desiatyi s"ezd RKP(b)*, pp. 528–29. For such a notion of unity see the trade union press that tended to support the Workers' Opposition, e.g., *Rabochii metallist*, no. 9, May 12, 1921; *Kommunisticheskii trud*, June 6, 1921.

144. *Odinnadtsatyi s"ezd RKP(b)*, pp. 191–93.

145. TsGAODM, f. 67, op. 1, d. 97, l. 3. For arguments in favor of workers' "spontaneous initiative," see *Metallist i gorniak*, October 10, 1920; *Proletarskaia diktatura*, no. 11, February 8, 1920.

146. *Desiatyi s"ezd RKP(b)*, pp. 528–29.

147. RGASPI, f. 17, op. 71, d. 1, l. 6. *Desiatyi s"ezd RKP(b)*, pp. 236–37.

148. *Desiatyi s"ezd RKP(b)*, pp. 91–92.

149. *Desiatyi s"ezd RKP(b)*, p. 317.

150. K. Kreibikh, "Poslednii mogikane 'rabochei oppozitsii v RKP(b)," *Kommunisticheskii internatsional* 1922, no. 1, p. 55.

151. *Desiatyi s"ezd RKP(b)*, p. 283. RGASPI, f. 17, op. 71, d. 1, l. 3.

152. E. Iaroslavskii, *Za edinstvo VKP(b)*, p. 18.

153. *Desiatyi s"ezd RKP(b)*, p. 384.

154. Stalin, *Sochineniia*, vol. 5, p. 106.

155. Iaroslavskii, *Za edinstvo VKP(b)*, p. 18.

156. *Leninskii sbornik*, vol. 36, p. 174.

157. *Desiatyi s"ezd*, pp. 574–75.

158. V. Vorovskii, *K istorii marksizma v Rossii* (Moscow, 1923); M. Liadov, *Kak nachala skladyvatsa Rossiiskaia kommuinisticheskaia partiia* (Moscow, 1926); V. Nevskii, *Istoriia RKP(b)* (Leningrad, 1926).

159. *Vos'moi s"ezd RKP(b)*, p. 102. For the key role of science in Bolshevism, see L. Graham, *Science and Philosophy in the Soviet Union* (London: Allen Lane, 1966); Z. Jordan, *The Evolution of Dialectical Materialism: A Philosophical and Sociological Analysis* (New York, 1967); R. Zapata, *Luttes philosophiques en U.S.S.R., 1922–1931* (Paris: Presses universitaires de France, 1983). Pseudoscience was an important accusation. See talk about the "so-called scientific argumentation of Trotsky," *Krasnyi Altai*, November 30, 1924.

160. S. Legezo, "Osoznanie stikhiinogo," *Oktiabr' mysli*, no. 1 (1924), pp. 30–31; S. Krivtsov, "Problema stikhiinosti i soznatel'nosti v leninizme," *Pod znamenem marksizma*, no. 1 (1929), pp. 1–2.

161. G. Zinoviev, *Bezpartiinyi ili Kommunist* (Odessa, 1920), p. 7. A. Polan, *Lenin and the End of Politics* (Berkeley: University of California Press, 1984), pp. 72–79.

162. S. Schwarz, *Lenine et le mouvement syndical* (Paris, 1935).

163. *Deviatyi s"ezd RKP(b)*, p. 221; TsGAODM, f. 3, op. 4, d. 32, l. 22.

164. *Deviataia konferentsiia RKP(b)*, p. 172.

165. TsGAODM, f. 67, op. 1, d. 97, l. 2.

166. *Desiatyi s"ezd RKP(b)*, p. 271.

167. *Desiatyi s"ezd RKP(b)*, p. 299.

168. TsGAODM, f. 1614, op. 1, d. 40, l. 5; f. 1660, op. 1, d. 58, l. 10.

169. *Desiatyi s"ezd RKP(b)*, p. 271.

170. *Desiatyi s"ezd RKP(b)*, pp. 75–76.

171. *Dvenadtsatyi s"ezd RKP(b)*, pp. 673–74.

172. *Rabochaia oppozitsiia*, p. 6.

173. RGASPI, f. 45, op. 1, d. 1, l. 26.

174. *Odinnadtsatyi s"ezd RKP(b)*, p. 388.

175. G. Zinoviev, *Nepravil'noe vo vzgliadakh rabochei oppozitsii na rol' profsoiuzov* (Tashkent, 1921), p. 7.

176. *Desiatyi s"ezd RKP(b)*, p. 380. See also Zinoviev, *Sochineniia*, vol. 6 (Moscow, 1929), pp. 420, 460; D. Riazanov, *Zadachi profsoiuzov do i v epokhu diktatury proletariata* (Moscow: Moskovskii rabochii, 1922), pp. 79, 95.

177. R. Williams, "The Russian Revolution and the End of Time, 1900–1940," *Jahrbücher für Geschichte Osteuropas*, no. 3 (1995), pp. 389–401.

178. I. Halfin, *From Darkness to Light: Class, Consciousness, and Salvation in Revolutionary Russia* (Pittsburgh: University of Pittsburgh Press, 2000), p. 40.

179. G. Carleton, "Genre in Socialist Realism," *Slavic Review* 53 (1994), p. 1002.

180. *Rabochaia oppozitsiia*, p. 5.

181. *Dvenadtsatyi s"ezd RKP(b)*, pp. 621–22.

182. *Deviataia konferentsiia RKP(b)*, p. 152.

183. O. Cullmann, *Salvation in History* (New York: Harper and Row, 1967), pp. 182–83.

184. *Deviataia konferentsiia RKP(b)*, pp. 260–61.

185. *Desiatyi s"ezd RKP(b)*, p. 396.

186. *Desiatyi s"ezd RKP(b)*, pp. 520–21.

187. Stalin, *Sochineniia*, vol. 4, p. 306.

188. *Deviatyi s"ezd RKP(b)*, p. 114.

189. *Dvenadtsatyi s"ezd RKP(b)*, p. 28.

190. TsGAODM, f. 64, op. 1, d. 78, l. 8; f. 1614, op. 1, d. 40, l. 8; f. 1673, op. 1, d. 48, l. 8; K. Radek, *O biurokratizme i bor'be s nim* (n.p., 1921), pp. 2–3; I. Smilga, *Vosstanovitel'nyi protsess: Stat'i i rechi* (Moscow, 1927).

191. TsGA IPD, f. 80, op. 1, d. 62, l. 42.

192. R. Pethybridge, *One Step Backwards, Two Steps Forward: Soviet Society and Politics in the New Economic Policy* (Oxford: Clarendon Press, 1990).

193. *Odinnadtsatyi s"ezd RKP(b)*, p. 130. *The Trotsky Papers, 1917–1922*, ed. J. Meijer, vol. 2 (The Hague: Mouton, 1971), pp. 578, 660.

194. *Dvenadtsatyi s"ezd RKP(b)*, p. 367.

195. *Dvenadtsatyi s"ezd RKP(b)*, p. 223.

196. *Odinnatsataia vserossiiskaia koferentsiia VKP(b), 19–22 Dekabria 1921 goda: Stenograficheskii otchet* (Rostov-on-Don: Gosizdat, 1922), pp. 17–18.

197. For Shliapnikov's apprehensive attitude towards the impact of NEP on the working class see B. Allen, "The Evolution of Communist Party Control over Trade Unions: Alexander Shliapnikov and the Trade Unions in May 1921," *Revolutionary Russia* 15 (2002), p. 77.

198. *Kommunist* (Baku), November 7, 1920; Stalin, *Sochineniia*, p. 388. *Odinnadtsatyi s"ezd RKP(b)*, p. 274. *Izvestiia TsK*, March 1922, p. 70. L. Trotsky, *Novaia ekonomicheskaia politika Sovetskoi Rossii i perspektivy mirovoi revoliutsii* (Moscow, 1923).

199. *Desiatyi s"ezd RKP(b)*, p. 520.

200. My work corresponds with the so-called Begriffsgeschichte methodology developed by R. Kosselleck and his research team. *Geschichtliche Grundbegriffe: Historisches Lexikon zur politisch-sozialen Sprache in Deutschland*, ed. Otto Brunner, Werner Conze, and Reinhart Koselleck (Stuttgart: E. Klett, c. 1972).

201. Not only did the various factions challenging the Party line not tend to unite, but they were often more critical of each other than of the Central Committee majority. In 1921, Medvedev from the Workers' Opposition claimed that "Democratic Centralists are petit-bourgeois. They ask us to join in but our answer is, 'Stay away! While we have some disagreements with someone like Trotsky, your position is abhorrent to us in principle.'" TsGAODM, f. 67, op. 1, d. 97, l. 40b. Democratic Centralists, on their part, supported the ban on factions as a means to do the Workers' Opposition in. When they maintained that purging deviant Central Committee members such as Shliapnikov or Kutuzov was perfectly legitimate, even Lenin felt obliged to cull their ardor. "Our Party regulations do not allow the Central Committee to purge its own members. Since he has said the contrary, the spokesman for the Group for Democratic Centralism clearly has no idea what he is talking about. No type of centralism, no type of democracy, can tolerate a Central Committee empowered to purge its own members—this is an extraordinary measure unprecedented in the history of our party." *Desiatyi s"ezd RKP(b)*, pp. 98–99, 537.

202. For a prerevolutionary, neutral use of the term "opposition" by Trotsky see *Sochineniia*, vol. 2 (Moscow-Leningrad, 1925), p. 124.

203. Thus Robert Daniels argues in terms of the "history of the Communist Opposition" and searches for reasons for the failure of the "Communist Opposition movement in Russia"; Leonard Shapiro writes about "the opposition" and the "opposition movements" in relation to 1919–1921; and E. H. Carr mentions the "opposition campaign" from 1923. In writing about "successive confrontations between shifting official majorities and dissenting oppositions" Steven Cohen is a bit more cautious (hence the plural) but he too ignores the discursive process through which the opposition was consolidated into a continuous entity. Daniels, *Conscience of the Revolution*, pp. 3, 398. Shapiro, *Origin of the Communist Autocracy*, pp. 240, 299; E. Carr, *The Interregnum, 1923–24* (London: Macmillan, 1954), p. 324; S. Cohen, *Bukharin and the Bolshevik Revolution: A Political Biography, 1888–1938* (New York: Knopf, 1973), p. 126.

204. In Lenin's prerevolutionary vocabulary, there were various terms describing intra-Party splinter formations. In addition to the familiar terms such as "groups" and "currents" he also talked about "directions" (*napravleniia*) and "shades" (*ottenki*) in the Party. Lenin, *PSS*, vol. 8, p. 333; vol. 9, pp. 4, 20, 50; vol. 14, p. 170. From time to time, Lenin also mentioned "circles" (*kruzhki*), invoking the much discussed problem of *kruzhkovshchina*— the detachment of the revolutionary intelligentsia from social reality and its penchant for scholastic debating in close circles. Lenin, *PSS*, vol. 8, p. 202. The connection between the "circles" of the self-righteous intelligentsia and the opposition within the Bolshevik ranks was made after 1917 as well, albeit very rarely. "Everyone now wants to be in some sort of an opposition," Smilga noted before the Tenth Party Congress. "Apparently Party circles [*kruzhki*] are in fashion again." I. Smilga, *Na povorote*, p. 22. For the term "*kruzhkovshchina*"

see L. Haimson, "Introduction," in *The Making of Three Russian Revolutionaries: Voices from the Menshevik Past*, ed. L. Haimson, Z. Galili, and R. Wortman (Cambridge: Cambridge University Press, 1987), as well as A. K. Wildman, "The Russian Intelligentsia of the 1890's," *American Slavic and East European Review* 19 (April 1960), pp. 157–58. For the preservation of the circle after the revolution see B. Walker, *Maximilian Voloshin and the Russian Literary Circle: Culture and Survival in Revolutionary Times* (Bloomington: Indiana University Press, 2005).

205. *Deviatyi s"ezd RKP(b)*, pp. 147, 226.

206. *Deviatyi s"ezd RKP(b)*, p. 154. Impressed by some vociferous "currents"—another designation for the nonconformists—Lenin was willing to permit them a degree of representation on the Central Committee. Trotsky dismissed the idea of a Central Committee "based on the principle of a Noah's ark," but he did not object to having "activists connected to various currents on board." *Deviatyi s"ezd RKP(b)*, p. 201. Stalin used soft language when he talked in 1921 about Trotsky's "mistakes" (*oshibki*); so did Iaroslavskii when he talked about Shliapnikov's mistakes. Stalin, *Sochineniia*, vol. 5, p. 7. B. Belkin, "'Rabochaia oppozitsiia,' Post Scriptum," *Oni ne molchali*, ed. A. Afanas'ev (Moscow: Politizdat, 1991), p. 53.

207. *Deviatyi s"ezd RKP(b)*, p. 212.

208. *Odinnadtsatyi s"ezd RKP(b)*, p. 45.

209. RGASPI, f. 17, op. 2, d. 104, l. 60. TsGAODM, f. 3, op. 6, d. 2, l. 167. Before the Revolution, Lenin conceived of the Bolsheviks as a "faction" within the Russian Social Democratic Party. He talked in terms of "our faction," and said, "What brings a faction together is not a common place of activity, common language, or any other objective state of affairs, but by a specific set of opinions on party questions" (*PSS*, vol. 19, pp. 40, 51; vol. 20, p. 342). In the prerevolutionary years, Lenin did not see anything necessarily wrong in the existence of factions. "The Bolsheviks would have dispersed their faction in January 1910 if other factions had done the same," he wrote at one point. Lenin referred to the "factionist struggle" but, in his prerevolutionary eyes, this was a normal state of affairs; history was supposed to prove his faction was on the right track (*PSS*, vol. 20, p. 302; vol. 19, pp. 198, 412).

210. TsGA IPD, f. 258, op. 1, d. 46, ll. 10–11; RGASPI, f. 17, op. 71, d. 3, l. 4.

211. *Rabochaia Moskva*, December 18 and 19, 1923; *Sovetskaia Sibir'*, January 31, 1924. RGASPI, f. 17, op. 2, d. 104, l. 58; d. 685, l. 95.

212. *Desiatyi s"ezd RKP(b)*, p. 396.

213. *Odinnadtsatyi s"ezd RKP(b)*, p. 703.

214. *Desiatyi s"ezd RKP(b)*, p. 540.

215. *Dvenadtsatyi s"ezd RKP(b)*, p. 819.

216. *Bol'shevitskoe rukovodstvo*, p. 296.

217. *Izvestiia TsK KPSS*, 1989, no. 10, p. 65; TsGAODM, f. 3., op. 8, d. 92, l. 30; f. 1660, op. 1, d. 58, l. 6. RGASPI, f. 17, op. 2, d. 104, l. 59. For Lenin's early use of "group" and "grouping" see Lenin, *PSS*, vol. 8, pp. 94, 199, 202. For his dismissive "groupings for an hour" see *PSS*, vol. 25, p. 220.

218. While "factions" were forbidden in the Siberian Party organization in the early 1920s, "ideological groupings" were allowed. V. Demidov, *Politicheskaia bor'ba oppozitsii v Sibiri, 1922–1929* (Novosibirsk, 1994), p. 28.

219. *Desiatyi s"ezd RKP(b)*, p. 122.

220. Trotsky claimed in 1921 that Shilapnikov suffers from a syndicalist "deviation." TsGAODM, f. 67, op. 1, d. 97, l. 10b. Shliapnikov retorted that Trotsky's platform contains at least two "deviations." TsGAODM, f. 1614, op. 1, d. 40, l. 5. See also the prerevolutionary Lenin's use of "digression" (*uklonenie*). Lenin, *PSS*, vol. 19, p. 199.

221. *Desiatyi s"ezd RKP(b)*, p. 518.

222. *Desiatyi s"ezd RKP(b)*, p. 518.

223. Stalin, *Sochineniia*, vol. 5, p. 193.

224. *Desiatyi s"ezd RKP(b)*, pp. 520–21, 535, 537.

225. For the comparison of the Party line with "rails" (*rel'sy*) see PANO, f. 2, op. 1, d. 1924, l. 456. For the term, "orthodoxy," used by Lunacharskii in a private letter from May 1924, see "'. . . Sudorozhno tsepliaiutsia za ortodoksiiu . . .' Neizvestnoe pis'mo A. V. Lunacharskogo L. B. Krasinu," *Kommunist*, no. 12 (1991), p. 103.

226. *Desiatyi s"ezd RKP(b)*, pp. 258–59.

227. *Desiatyi s"ezd RKP(b)*, pp. 102–3.

228. *Desiatyi s"ezd RKP(b)*, pp. 528–29.

229. *Desiatyi s"ezd RKP(b)*, p. 385.

230. *Desiatyi s"ezd RKP(b)*, pp. 520–21.

231. *Desiatyi s"ezd RKP(b)*, pp. 532–33.

232. Slepkov talked about the so-called "leftist" nature of the "Workers' Opposition." A. Slepkov, *Put' rabochei oppozitsii* (Moscow: Pravda i Bednota, 1926), p. 50. By 1930, Stalin could talk about the "leftist-rightist bloc." Stalin, *Sochineniia*, vol. 13, p. 44.

233. PANO, f. 2, op. 1, d. 51, l. 18.

234. I. Smilga, *Na povorote*, p. 17.

235. A. Slepkov, "Ob 'uklonakh' i putiakh vozmozhnogo pererozhdeniia," *Bol'shevik*, no. 3–4 (May 1924), p. 23. Note that when Stalin wrote about the "left" and the "leftist danger" in 1922, he always used quotation marks. This was not done when he mentioned the right. Stalin, *Sochineniia*, vol. 5, p. 310, 317. Lenin talked about the "right wing" in the Party long before 1917, see Lenin, *PSS*, vol. 8, p. 334.

236. *Desiatyi s"ezd RKP(b)*, p. 309.

237. *Bol'shevistskoe rukovodstvo: Perepiska 1912–1927*, ed. A.V. Kvashonkin et al. (Moscow: ROSSPEN, 1996).

238. *Deviataia konferentsiia RKP(b)*, p. 180.

239. *Dvenadtsatyi s"ezd RKP(b)*, pp. 215–16.

240. For "heresies" see Lenin, *PSS*, vol. 10, p. 396; For the use of the term "heterodoxy" (*inakomyslie*) see RGASPI, f. 17, op. 71, d. 1, l. 10; *Desiatyi s"ezd RKP(b)*, p. 101; A. Shliapnikov, "O demonstrativnoi atake i pravoi opasnosti v partii," *Bol'shevik*, no. 17 (1926), p. 73. The term "heresy" was used by Krasin, *Dvenadtsatyi s"ezd RKP(b)*, p. 125. Kemenev talked about "heretic-Marxists" (*eretiki-marksisty*), but he had Mensheviks in mind. L. Kamenev, "Literaturnoe nasledstvo i sobranie sochinenii Vladimira Il'icha," *Leninskii sbornik* 1 (Moscow-Leningrad, 1924), p. 5.

241. Supporters of the Workers' Opposition were included on the purge commissions with the explicit goal of making sure that the generally undisciplined were expelled and not those who ever said anything in criticism of the Central Committee. *Izvestiia TsK RKP(b)*, no. 33, pp. 39–40.

242. I was able to find only one example of Lenin's usage of the term "opposition" before the Revolution, dating to 1904. *PSS*, vol. 8, p. 135.

243. *Sed'moi ekstrennyi s"ezd RKP(b)*, March 1918 (Moscow, 1962), p. 73.

244. *Sed'moi ekstrennyi s"ezd RKP(b)*, p. 45.

245. *Vos'moi s"ezd RKP(b)*, pp. 325, 219.

246. *Vos'moi s"ezd RKP(b)*, p. 215; I. Iurenev, *Nashi nastroeniia: K voprosu o preodolenii elementov upadka v RKP(b)* (Kursk, 1920), p. 38.

247. A. Miasnikov, *Za partiiu (K krizisu partii)* (n.p.: Gosizdat, 1921), p. 38.

248. *Vos'moi s"ezd RKP(b)*, p. 211.

249. *Desiatyi s"ezd RKP(b)*, p. 315.

250. *Desiatyi s"ezd RKP(b)*, p. 99.

251. *Desiatyi s"ezd RKP(b)*, p. 78.

252. *Vos'moi s"ezd RKP(b), Mart 1919 goda: Protokoly* (Moscow: Politicheskaia literatura, 1959), pp. 171–72.

253. *Vos'moi s"ezd RKP(b)*, p. 319.

254. *Deviatyi s"ezd RKP(b)*, p. 278. For the term "rivals" (*protivniki*) see also TsGA-ODM, f. 67, op. 1, d. 97, l. 40b.

255. *Deviatyi s"ezd RKP(b)*, p. 178.

256. *Deviataia konferentsiia RKP(b)*, p. 141.

257. *Deviataia konferentsiia RKP(b)*, p. 156.

258. *Desiatyi s"ezd RKP(b)*, p. 118.

259. RGASPI, f. 45, op. 1, d. 4, l. 2.

260. TsGAODM, f. 3, op. 4, d. 32, l. 34.

261. *Desiatyi s"ezd RKP(b)*, p. 261.

262. In this connection Danishevskii mentioned Sapozhkov, who "turned his criticism of soviet politics into an uprising with arms in hand last summer [1920]." *Desiatyi s"ezd RKP(b)*, p. 285.

263. *Desiatyi s"ezd RKP(b)*, p. 113.

264. *Pravda*, March 22, 1921; TsGAODM, f. 67, op. 1, d. 97, l. 2.

265. *Deviatyi s"ezd RKP(b)*, p. 88. The terms "squabble" (*skloka*) and "spat" (*driazga*) can be found in early Lenin, *PSS*, vol. 9, p. 19.

266. *Deviataia konferentsiia RKP(b)*, p. 146.

267. PANO, f. 1, op. 3, d. 44, ll. 151–52.

268. *Odinnadtsatyi s"ezd RKP(b)*, p. 371.

269. *Dvenadtsatyi s"ezd RKP(b)*, p. 245.

270. *Odinnadtsatyi s"ezd RKP(b)*, pp. 401–3.

271. *Dvenadtsatyi s"ezd RKP(b)*, p. 141.

272. *Dvenadtsatyi s"ezd RKP(b)*, pp. 104–5.

273. *Dvenadtsatyi s"ezd RKP(b)*, p. 102.

274. RGASPI, f. 17, op. 71, d. 3, l. 4.

275. *Dvenadtsatyi s"ezd RKP(b)*, p. 152.

276. *Desiatyi s"ezd RKP(b)*, p. 115.

277. I. Smilga, *Na povorote*, p. 22; *Desiatyi s"ezd RKP(b)*, pp. 258–59. In May 1921, the Central Committee accused Shliapnikov of "intriguing" against Tomskii. RGASPI, f. 17, op. 84, d. 217, l. 214.

278. *Desiatyi s"ezd RKP(b)*, p. 262. Emphasis added.

279. *Desiatyi s"ezd RKP(b)*, p. 27.

280. *Desiatyi s"ezd RKP(b)*, p. 312.

281. *Desiatyi s"ezd RKP(b)*, p. 83.

282. *Desiatyi s"ezd RKP(b)*, pp. 309, 308.

283. TsGAODM, f. 67, op. 1, d. 97, l. 10b; *Deviataia konferentsiia RKP(b)*, p. 175.

284. Smilga talked about "the worker-Communists' oppositionist moods," I. Smilga, *Na povorote*, p. 24.

285. In 1924, Lunacharskii still spoke about the "so-called majority and the so-called opposition." "'. . . Sudorozhno tsepliaiutsia za ortodoksiiu . . .' Neizvestnoe pis'mo A. V. Lunacharskogo L. B. Krasinu," *Kommunist*, no. 12 (1991), p. 104.

286. Some dissenting alliances, most prominently, Democratic Centralists, did not choose to have "opposition" as part of their names. Clearly, in 1920–1921 there was no sustained effort to unite all critics of the Central Committee on the lexical level.

287. *Desiatyi s"ezd RKP(b)*, p. 393.

288. *Desiatyi s"ezd RKP(b)*, p. 274.

289. *Desiatyi s"ezd RKP(b)*, p. 248.

290. *Desiatyi s"ezd RKP(b)*, p. 91.

291. *Desiatyi s"ezd RKP(b)*, p. 395.

292. *Desiatyi s"ezd RKP(b)*, p. 396.

293. *Deviatyi s"ezd RKP(b)*, p. 204.

294. In 1921, Lozovskii talked about the "theses whose author is Nogin," not about Nogism or Noginshchina. A. Lazovskii, *Zadachi professional'nykh soiuzov* (Moscow, 1921), p. 12.

295. *Tainy natsional'noi politikii TsK RKP, stenograficheskii otchet sekretnogo iv soveshchaniia TsK RKP, 1923 goda* (Moscow, 1923, reprint, 1992), p. 17. When the ending *-shchina* was added, the opposition was identified as a wicked force, e.g. Rafailovshchina, TsGAODM, f. 3, op. 8, d. 92, l. 18; Miasnikovshchina, RGASPI, f. 17, op. 2, d. 685, l. 88; Ossovshchina, *Proletarskaia revoliutsiia* 1931, no. 6, p. 85; Sapronovshchina, *Arkhiv Trotskogo*, vol. 4, p. 274. In 1924, Workers' Opposition was renamed "Medvedevshchina." A. Slepkov, "Put' rabochei oppozitsii," *Put' rabochei oppozitsii* (Moscow: Pravda i Bednota, 1926), p. 63.

296. *Sed'moi ekstrennyi s"ezd RKP(b)*, p. 68.

297. *Desiatyi s"ezd RKP(b)*, p. 391.

298. *Desiatyi s"ezd RKP(b)*, p. 393. Bukharin described the 1921 discussion as a "struggle between different tendencies [*tendentsii*] in our Party, where points of view are determined by specific spheres of experience." He attributed clashes at the congress to occasional differences in personal experience. *Desiatyi s"ezd RKP(b)*, p. 230.

299. RGASPI, f. 45, op. 1, d. 1, l. 72.

300. *Desiatyi s"ezd RKP(b)*, p. 352.

301. For background on the medicalization of politics in the Russian context see Daniel Beer, "'The Hygiene of Souls': Languages of Illness and Contagion in Late Imperial and Early Soviet Russia," Ph.D. diss., University of Cambridge, 2002.

302. TsGAODM, f. 67, op. 1, d. 97, l. 6; I. Smilga, *Na povorote*, p. 24; *Izvestiia Sibbiuro TsK KRP(b)*, 1923, no. 65–66, p. 4; V. Kuibyshev, "Itogi plenuma TsKK," *Biulleten' TsKK RKP(b) i NK R-KI SSSR* 22 (November 15, 1924), p. 5.

303. TsGAODM, f. 3, op. 4, d. 32, l. 56.

304. *Vos'moi s"ezd RKP(b)*, p. 106.

305. *Deviataia konferentsiia RKP(b)*, p. 171.

306. *Deviataia konferentsiia RKP(b)*, p. 155.

307. *Odinnadtsatyi s"ezd RKP(b)*, p. 461.

308. *Desiatyi s"ezd RKP(b)*, p. 99.

309. *Vos'moi s"ezd RKP(b)*, p. 173.

310. *Deviataia konferentsiia RKP(b)*, p. 188.

311. *Deviataia konferentsiia RKP(b)*, p. 181.

312. *Odinnadtsatyi s"ezd RKP(b)*, pp. 116–17.

313. RGASPI, f. 17, op. 71, d. 1, l. 12; d. 89, ll. 10–11; op. 85, d. 222, l. 159; TsGAODM, f. 67, op. 1, d. 97, l. 60b; Smilga, *Na povorote*, p. 23; *Leningradskaia pravda*, December 5, 1923. [So'lts], "Pravaia opasnost' v nashei partii," *Put' rabochei oppozitsii* (Moscow, 1926), p. 3. *Komsomol'skaia pravda*, September 19, 1926.

314. S. Gilman, "Political Theory and Degeneration: From Left to Right, from Up to Down," in *Degeneration: The Dark Side of Progress*, ed. J. E. Chamberlin and S. Gilman (New York: Columbia University Press, 1985), p. 168.

315. TsGAODM, f. 3, op. 4, d. 32, l. 34. *Komsomol'skaia pravda*, March 1, 1927; See also the usage in the prerevolutionary Marxist pamphlet, V. Posse, *Vyrozhdenie i vozrozhdenie* (St. Petersburg, 1913).

316. K. Marx and F. Engels, *Selected Correspondence* (Moscow, 1965), p. 172.

317. For the reception of Darwin in early 1920s Russia see S. Iu. Semkovskii, *Chto takoe Marksizm (Darvin i Marks)* (Khar'kov, 1922); G. Broido, "Darvinizm i Marksizm," *Pechat' i revoliutsiia* 3 (1923); G. Daian, "Darvinizm i Marksizm," *Sputnik Kommunista*, no. 21 (1923).

318. *Dvenadtsatyi s"ezd RKP(b)*, p. 343.

319. *Odinnadtsatyi s"ezd RKP(b)*, p. 464. In Bolshevik formulations about "pollution" (*zagriaznenie*) the differences between medical pollution (a literary reading of the term) and sociopolitical pollution (a metaphorical reading of the term) sometimes faded away. While health measures were said to be necessary, the language of prophylaxis was highly ambiguous: was it supposed to be read directly, through the medical lens, or was it a euphemism for a political purge? At the Ninth Party Congress Lutovinov mentioned that: "Though Moscow is being cleansed these days, much pollution remains." By "cleansing" he appears to have been referring principally to the Hygiene Commission's campaign for prophylaxis against infectious diseases (March 10–13, 1920), but the speaker seemed to think that such a campaign might prepare the way for the extirpation of erroneous opinion in the metalworkers' trade union. *Deviatyi s"ezd VKP(b)*, p. 246, note 93; p. 605.

320. *Desiatyi s"ezd RKP(b)*, p. 803.

321. *Odinnadtsatyi s"ezd RKP(b)*, p. 46.

322. *Desiatyi s"ezd RKP(b)*, p. 284.

323. *Desiatyi s"ezd RKP(b)*, p. 72.

324. TsGAODM, f. 67, op. 1, d. 97, l. 4. And Bubnov had prescriptions that would "refresh" (*osvezhit'*) the Party ranks. TsGAODM, f. 67, op. 1, d. 97, l. 60b.

325. *Deviataia konferentsiia RKP(b)*, p. 174.

326. *Odinnadtsatyi s"ezd RKP(b)*, p. 198. A little later she spoke of a "lymphatic Party, its activity decreased, suffering from dearth of critical thought." *Odinnadtsatyi s"ezd RKP(b)*, p. 200.

327. RGASPI, f. 17, op. 71, d. 3, l. 4; f. 613, op. 1, d. 3, ll. 83, 138. Already at the Ninth Party Congress, Sapronov claimed that "denial of the right to criticize" explained "such ugly phenomena as the mass exits of workers from the Party." *Deviataia konferentsiia RKP(b)*,

p. 160. According to official statistics, 17,796 comrades voluntarily left the Party in the first half of 1921 (about 2.5 percent). *Deviatyi s"ezd RKP(b)*, p. 648. In the first few months following the introduction of NEP, 1,215 comrades departed from the Ekaterinburg Party organization. *Izvestiia Ekaterinburgskogo gubkoma RKP(b)* (1921) no. 11, pp. 42–43. About 5 percent of the Liven district Party organization (Orel province) left the Party around the same time, *Vestnik Orlovskogo gubkoma RKP(b)* 1922, no. 2, p. 27.

328. *Odinnadtsatyi s"ezd RKP(b)*, p. 119.

329. *Odinnadtsatyi s"ezd RKP(b)*, p. 128.

330. *Odinnadtsatyi s"ezd RKP(b)*, p. 438.

331. *Odinnadtsatyi s"ezd RKP(b)*, p. 205.

332. *Deviataia konferentsiia RKP(b)*, pp. 182–84.

333. *Deviataia konferentsiia RKP(b)*, p. 163.

334. *Desiatyi s"ezd RKP(b)*, p. 118.

335. *Odinnadtsatyi s"ezd RKP(b)*, p. 455.

336. *Dvenadtsatyi s"ezd RKP(b)*, p. 350.

337. TsGAODM, f. 1673, op. 1, d. 48, l. 11. *Znamia Kommunista* 1924, no. 7, p. 2.

338. *Desiatyi s"ezd RKP(b)*, p. 295.

339. Lenin, *PSS*, vol. 41, pp. 394, 541.

340. *Dvenadtsatyi s"ezd RKP(b)*, p. 221.

341. *Desiatyi s"ezd RKP(b)*, p. 83. Stalin, *Sochineniia*, vol. 5, p. 8.

342. *Desiatyi s"ezd RKP(b)*, p. 324.

343. *Odinnadtsatyi s"ezd RKP(b)*, pp. 23–25.

344. *Deviatyi s"ezd RKP(b)*, pp. 77, 85.

345. [*Odinnatsataia] vserossiiskaia konferentsiia VKP(b), 19–22 Dekabria 1921 goda: Stenograficheskii otchet* (Rostov-on-Don: Gosizdat, 1922), pp. 75–76.

346. *Pravda*, March 25, 1921.

347. *Odinnadtsatyi s"ezd RKP(b)*, pp. 23–25.

348. *Desiatyi s"ezd RKP(b)*, p. 380.

349. *Desiatyi s"ezd RKP(b)*, pp. 380, 258–59.

350. *Deviataia konferentsiia RKP(b)*, p. 147. *Odinnadtsatyi s"ezd RKP(b)*, p. 455.

Chapter 2: Killing with Words

1. Zinoviev repeatedly claimed during the 1920s that he felt very close to Lenin. The Germans dispatched them into Russia after the fall of the Romanov dynasty in the same sealed train with the (correct) hope that they would undermine the tsar's war effort. Kamenev and Stalin, who were in Siberian exile at that time, received the news about the February Revolution in a village in the Tukhansk region. Stranded in this remote corner of the Russian empire, the two used to sing duets together. Having heard about the February Revolution, they made their way back to Petrograd in the same train car. (Kamenev was one of only eight Bolsheviks who addressed Stalin with the informal "ty" into the 1930s.) Such stories of everyday intimacy can be multiplied at will. A member of the Petrograd soviet and the RSDR(P) committee in the spring of 1917, Petr Zalutskii, who will crop up in the pages below a number of times, shared a room with Molotov in an apartment in Petrogradskaia storona; the adjacent room was occupied by Stalin. Smilga, another hero of

this book, and his wife lived in a third room in the same apartment. All those Bolsheviks lived in a commune, sharing their income and cooking together. N. Zen'kovich, *Samye zakrytye liudi* (Moscow:"Ol'ma Press," 2002), pp. 229, 231.

2. TsGAODM, f. 3, op. 4, d. 32, l. 24.

3. There were warnings, however, that laughter could serve the counterrevolution. Ia. Shafir,"Pochemu my ne umeem smeiat'sia," *Krasnaia pechat'* 17 (1923), p. 8.

4. *Deviataia konferentsiia RKP(b)* (Moscow, 1972), p. 106.

5. TsGAODM, f. 3, op. 6, d. 2, l. 37."Lenin's voice sounded special, as if it was coming from the most inner recesses of his soul [*iz samikh glubin ego dushi*]," noted Mitrofanov, a delegate from Nizhni Novgorod. A. Mitrofanov,"Vladimir Il'ich na XI s"ezde RKP(b)," *Voprosy istorii KPSS*, no. 4 (1968), p. 105.

6. *Desiatyi s"ezd RKP(b)*, *Mart 1921: Stenograficheskii otchet* (Moscow, 1968), p. 301.

7. *Dvenadtsatyi s"ezd RKP(b)*, *17–25 Aprelia 1923 goda: Stenograficheskii otchet* (Moscow: Gospolitizdat, 1968), p. 162.

8. *Deviatyi s"ezd RKP(b)*, *Mart–Aprel' 1920 goda* (Moscow, 1960), p. 69.

9. *Desiatyi s"ezd RKP(b)*, pp. 520–21.

10. *Desiatyi s"ezd RKP(b)*, p. 306.

11. *Odinnadtsatyi s"ezd RKP(b)*, *Mart–Aprel' 1922 goda: Stenograficheskii otchet* (Moscow: Gospolitizdat, 1966), p. 197. *Desiatyi s"ezd RKP(b)*, p. 78.

12. *Dvenadtsatyi s"ezd RKP(b)*, pp. 116–17.

13. *Deviataia konferentsiia RKP(b)* (Moscow, 1972), p. 40.

14. *Desiatyi s"ezd RKP(b)*, pp. 41, 69.

15. RGASPI, f. 45, op. 1, d. 1, l. 72; I. Smilga, *Na povorote* (Moscow: Gosizdat, 1921), p. 3.

16. *Desiatyi s"ezd RKP(b)*, p. 63.

17. *Desiatyi s"ezd RKP(b)*, pp. 126, 89, 92.

18. RGASPI, f. 99, op. 1, d. 7, l. 20.

19. *Desiatyi s"ezd RKP(b)*, p. 50.

20. *Desiatyi s"ezd RKP(b)*, p. 152.

21. *Desiatyi s"ezd RKP(b)*, p. 126. Were threats a jest, or should they be taken at face value? Strongly objecting to the Brest treaty in 1918, members of the Left Opposition reportedly intended to arrest Lenin. When Lenin was told about the scheme to substitute him with Piatakov he"laughed his head off." *Bol'shevistskoe rukovodstvo: Perepiska 1912–1927*, ed. A. V. Kvashonkin et al. (Moscow: ROSSPEN, 1996), pp. 290–92. Belen'kii assured the Ninth Party Congress two years later that his threats were as frolicsome as the threats made by the Left Opposition against Lenin."When a squabble broke out at the Moscow Party committee I adopted an ironic tone suggesting that some of our comrades must be shot. Anyone with a head on his shoulders knows that I was not sincerely advocating the introduction of the death penalty into the Party." *Deviataia konferentsiia RKP(b)*, p. 201. When Lozovskii, whose time was about to expire at the Fourteenth Party Congress, remarked,"A sword is hovering about his head," the chairman calmed him down at once: "Not a sword, only a bell." At this stage, threats were funny. *Odinnadtsatyi s"ezd RKP(b)*, p. 261.

22. *Desiatyi s"ezd RKP(b)*, p. 73.

23. *The Trotsky Papers*, *1917–1922*, ed. J. Meijer (The Hague: Mouton, 1971), vol. 2, pp. 694–96; RGASPI, f. 17, op. 3, d. 135, l. 17.

24. *Desiatyi s"ezd RKP(b)*, pp. 123–24.

25. *Desiatyi s"ezd RKP(b)*, p. 386.

26. Kisilev was a member of the presidium of the Central Control Commission. *Deiateli SSSR*, pp. 191–94.

27. *Desiatyi s"ezd RKP(b)*, pp. 543–44.

28. *Odinnadtsatyi s"ezd RKP(b)*, pp. 23–25.

29. *Leninskii sbornik*, vol. 36, p. 24; For disciplinary measures against Shliapnikov see *Izvestiia TsK RKP(b)*, no. 33, p. 42; RGASPI, f. 99, op. 1, d. 3, ll. 29–30.

30. *Odinnadtsatyi s"ezd RKP(b)*, p. 102.

31. *Odinnadtsatyi s"ezd RKP(b)*, pp. 24–25, 148.

32. *Odinnadtsatyi s"ezd RKP(b)*, p. 141.

33. *Desiatyi s"ezd RKP(b)*, pp. 28–29.

34. *Odinnadtsatyi s"ezd RKP(b)*, p. 141.

35. *Odinnadtsatyi s"ezd RKP(b)*, p. 102.

36. *Odinnadtsatyi s"ezd RKP(b)*, p. 148.

37. RGASPI, f. 17, op. 2, d. 69, l. 1; TsGAODM, f. 3, op. 8, d. 92, l. 100b. Freud was perhaps the first to connect laughter to violence. He presents laughter as a mechanism through which soldiers release their energy once they are notified that the battle they prepared themselves for was cancelled at the last moment. Real violence is substituted here by metaphoric violence. S. Freud, "Jokes and Their Relations to the Unconscious," *The Standard Edition of the Complete Psychological Works of Sigmund Freud*, trans. James Strachey, 24 vols. (London: Hogarth Press, 1953–1974), vol. 8, pp. 147, 151. Alan Dundes also sees humor as "socially sanctioned outlet." A. Dundes, *Cracking Jokes: Studies of Sick Humor Cycles and Stereotypes* (Berkeley: Ten Speed Press, 1987), p. vii.

38. Maevich, "Iumor i satira," *Zhurnalist* 4 (1923); A. Lezhnev, "Na puti k vozrozhdeniiu satiry," *Literaturnaia gazeta*, April 22, 1929; Lunacharskii, "Budem smeiat'sia," *Sobranie sochinenii v vos'mi tomakh* (Moscow, 1964), vol. 3, p. 78; Lunacharskii, "O smekhe," *Sobranie sochinenii v vos'mi tomakh*, vol. 8, pp. 538.

39. The Soviet humorists were instructed to avoid all ambiguity. Ia. Shafir, "K voprosu o satiristicheskom romane," *Pechat' i revoliutsiia* 12 (1929), p. 31.

40. V. Garros, "Moscou 1936–1938: Les Rires de la Terreur," *De Russie et d'ailleurs, Mélanges Marc Ferro* (Paris, 1995), pp. 72, 80.

41. The show trials are sometimes presented as rituals with a humoristic aspect. See B. Grois, "Totalitarizm karnavala," *Bakhtinskii sbornik* 3 (Moscow: Labirinth, 1997), pp. 76–80.

42. For humor as play, see S. Gusev and G. Tul'chinskii, *Problema ponimaniia v filosofii* (Moscow, 1985), pp. 172–73; G. Nodia, "Chelovek smeiushchiisia v kontekste filosofii kul'tury," in *Filosofiia, kul'tura, chelovek* (Tbilisi, 1988), pp. 47–52; A. Kozintsev, *Smekh: Istoki i funktsii* (St. Petersburg, 2002).

43. *Desiatyi s"ezd RKP(b)*, p. 126.

44. *Odinnadtsatyi s"ezd RKP(b)*, p. 148.

45. A Mitrofanov, Vladimir Il'ich na XI s"ezde RKP(b), *Vorposy istorii KPSS*, no. 4 (1968), p. 106.

46. For jokes, a very famous genre in Soviet history, see D. Shturman and S. Tiktin, *Sovetskii Soiuz v zerkale politicheskogo anekdota* (London: Overseas Publication Ltd., 1985), pp. 183–84; S. Graham, "A Cultural Analysis of the Russo-Soviet Anekdot," Ph.D. dissertation, University of Pittsburgh, 2003.

47. For the history of the Soviet satire see L. Ershov, *Sovetskaia satiristicheskaia proza 20-kh godov* (Moscow-Leningrad: Izdatel'stvo Akademii nauk SSSR, 1960); E. Ozmitel', *Sovetskaia satira: Seminarii* (Moscow-Leningrad: Prosveshchenie, 1964).

48. *Vos'moi s"ezd RKP(b)*, p. 219.

49. Of course, the stenographic reports are a blunt instrument with which to gauge the emotions in the hall during Party congresses. Laughter mentioned in the text could signify a range of possible reactions on the part of the audience—derision, embarrassment, nervousness, or genuine amusement. It is difficult to tell whether the Bolsheviks' laughter was deeply felt or conventional and utilitarian, and the political and discursive contexts of laughing must be taken into account. I study laughter here as a ritual of collective behavior and not necessarily a spontaneous expression of individual emotion. Accordingly, what I am tracking in this essay is a formal change in Bolshevik rituals—the way in which Party members were obliged publicly to behave—rather than a substantial change in how comrades actually felt. For a review of literature on laughter and other emotions as a subject of historical inquiry, see B. Rosenwein, "Worrying about Emotions in History," *American Historical Review* 107, no. 3 (2002). For a theory of cognitive emotions from Aristotle on, see S. Leighton, "Aristotle and the Emotions," in *Essays on Aristotle's Rhetoric*, ed. Amélie Oksenberg Rorty (Berkeley: University of California Press, 1996); and W. W. Fortenbaugh, *Aristotle on Emotion: A Contribution to Philosophical Psychology, Rhetoric, Poetics, Politics, and Ethics* (London: Duckworth, 2002). For the view of emotions as discursively constructed, see Rom Harré (ed.), *The Social Construction of Emotions* (Oxford: Blackwell, 1986). In recent years the historian William M. Reddy developed the concept of "emotional regimes," which can shed light on the emotional responses of the Bolshevik leadership as well. See his "Emotional Liberty: Politics and History in the Anthropology of Emotions," *Cultural Anthropology* 14 (May 1999) pp. 256–88; and "Sentimentalism and Its Erasure: The Role of Emotions in the Era of the French Revolution," *Journal of Modern History* 72 (March 2000): 109–52.

50. *Dvenadtsatyi s"ezd RKP(b)*, p. 186.

51. *Dvenadtsatyi s"ezd RKP(b)*, pp. 133–34.

52. *Dvenadtsatyi s"ezd RKP(b)*, p. 222.

53. *Dvenadtsatyi s"ezd RKP(b)*, p. 148.

54. Ia. El'sberg, *Voprosy teorii satiry* (Moscow, 1960); D. Nikolaev, *Smekh—oruzhie satiry* (Moscow, 1962).

55. *Odinnadtsatyi s"ezd RKP(b)*, pp. 145–47.

56. *Dvenadtsatyi s"ezd RKP(b)*, pp. 152–53, 215.

57. *Dvenadtsatyi s"ezd RKP(b)*, p. 113.

58. *Dvenadtsatyi s"ezd RKP(b)*, p. 111.

59. Ia. Rokitianskii, "Tragicheskaia sud'ba akademika D. B. Riazanova," *Novaia i noveishaia istoriia*, no. 2 (1992), pp. 107–48; *Deiateli SSSR*, pp. 688–89.

60. *Odinnadtsatyi s"ezd RKP(b)*, p. 203.

61. *Odinnadtsatyi s"ezd RKP(b)*, p. 79.

62. *Odinnadtsatyi s"ezd RKP(b)*, p. 204. The proceedings of the Fourth Congress of the Metalworkers' Union in May 1921 developed into a battle between the Communist faction of the union and the Politburo of the Party's Central Committee. B. Allen, "Alexander Shliapnikov and the Origins of the Workers' Opposition, March 1919–April 1920," *Jahrbücher für Geschichte Osteuropas*, no. 1 (2005), pp. 91–92. Riazanov's unauthorized

resolution was passed at the Fourth Congress of the Union of the Metal Workers (May 1921) and he was subsequently banned by the Central Committee from any further work in the trade unions. RGASPI, f. 17, op. 2, d. 65 (May 18, 1921). For details on the case see J. Sorenson, *The Life and Death of Soviet Trade Unionism, 1917–1928* (New York: Atherton, 1969), pp. 167–68.

63. *Desiatyi s"ezd RKP(b)*, p. 360.

64. *Desiatyi s"ezd RKP(b)*, p. 85.

65. *Desiatyi s"ezd RKP(b)*, pp. 75, 331.

66. *VII ekstrennyi s"ezd RKP(b)*, p. 39. *Dvenadtsatyi s"ezd RKP(b)*, p. 651.

67. *Desiatyi s"ezd RKP(b)*, pp. 379, 886.

68. *Vos'moi s"ezd RKP(b)*, p. 184. A few years later Lazovskii used the same violent metaphor when he talked about "blood-spilling discussions [*diskussirovali s krovoprolitiem*]" occurring until the moment the Party Congress made its decision. A. Lazovskii, *Zadachi professional'nykh soiuzov* (Moscow, 1921), p. 14.

69. *Desiatyi s"ezd RKP(b)*, p. 286.

70. *Pravda*, November 30, 1920.

71. *Desiatyi s"ezd RKP(b)*, p. 135.

72. *Desiatyi s"ezd RKP(b)*, p. 397.

73. For the grotesque as a historical problem, see A. Gurevich, "K istorii groteska: 'Verkh' i 'niz' v srednevekovoi latinskoi literature," *Izvestiia AN SSSR* 1975, ser. Lit. I iaz., vol. 34, no. 4; M. Bakhtin, *Tvorchestvo Fransua Rable i narodnaia kul'tura srednevekov'ia i renessansa* (Moscow, 1994), pp. 24–27.

74. *Desiatyi s"ezd RKP(b)*, p. 331.

75. R. Aron, "Ideology and Totalitarianism," *Survey* 23 (1977–78); L. Kolakowski, "Communism as a Cultural Formation," *Survey* 29 (1985).

76. Lunacharskii, "Budem smeiat'sia!" *Sobranie sochinenii*, vol. 3, pp. 76–79.

77. RGASPI, f. 99, op. 1, d. 7, l. 20.

78. TsGAODM, f. 67, op. 1, d. 97, l. 20b.

79. *Desiatyi s"ezd RKP(b)*, pp. 305–6.

80. *Desiatyi s"ezd RKP(b)*, p. 330.

81. A. Kollontai, *Rabochaia oppozitsiia* (Moscow, 1921), p. 36.

82. *Desiatyi s"ezd RKP(b)*, p. 117.

83. *Desiatyi s"ezd RKP(b)*, p. 379.

84. RGASPI, f. 45, op. 1, d. 28, l. 31; S. E. Rabinovich, "Delegaty 10-go s"ezda R.K.P. (b), pod Kronshtadtom v 1921 godu," *Krasnaia letopis'*, no. 2 (41), pp. 22–55.

85. L. Trotskii, *Kak vooruzhalas' revoliutsiia*, vol. 1 (Moscow, 1924), p. 207; The Kronshtadt mutiny was described as Menshevik and thus counterrevolutionary. N. Boldin, "Men'sheviki v kronshtadtskom miatezhe," *Krasnaia letopis'*, no. 3 (1931), pp. 5–31.

86. *Desiatyi s"ezd RKP(b)*, p. 115.

87. *Odinnadtsatyi s"ezd RKP(b)*, pp. 23–25.

88. RGASPI, f. 17, op. 71, d. 1, l. 14.

89. *Desiatyi s"ezd RKP(b)*, p. 115.

90. For talk about the "so-called 'workers' opposition'" see TsGAODM, f. 67, op. 1, d. 97, l. 10b.

91. *Dvenadtsatyi s"ezd RKP(b)*, p. 221.

92. *Dvenadtsatyi s"ezd RKP(b)*, p. 346.

93. But the monologization of laugher did not necessarily mean it disappeared. E. Lozowy, "Satire et Histoire: L'article encyclopedique de Bakhtine sur la Satire dans le Contexte de la Critique Litteraire Sovietique des Annes 1920s et 1930," *Canadian-American Slavic Studies* 35 (2001), p. 382.

94. *Dvenadtsatyi s"ezd RKP(b)*, p. 135.

95. *Odinnadtsatyi s"ezd RKP(b)*, p. 149.

96. *Odinnadtsatyi s"ezd RKP(b)*, p. 46.

97. *Odinnadtsatyi s"ezd RKP(b)*, p. 187.

98. *Odinnadtsatyi s"ezd RKP(b)*, p. 646.

99. RGASPI, f. 17, op. 71, d. 1, l. 7; TsGAODM, f. 1660, op. 1, d. 58, l. 6. *Odinnadtsatyi s"ezd RKP(b)*, p. 578.

100. *Odinnadtsatyi s"ezd RKP(b)*, p. 148.

101. *Odinnadtsatyi s"ezd RKP(b)*, p. 104.

102. *Odinnadtsatyi s"ezd RKP(b)*, p. 451.

103. *Desiatyi s"ezd RKP(b)*, p. 310; *Odinnadtsatyi s"ezd RKP(b)*, p. 394.

104. *Odinnadtsatyi s"ezd RKP(b)*, p. 194.

105. RGASPI, f. 17, op. 71, d. 1, l. 10. TsGAODM, f. 67, op. 1, d. 97, l. 4.

106. *Odinnadtsatyi s"ezd RKP(b)*, pp. 130–31.

107. *Izvestiia TsK RKP(b)* no. 32, August 6, 1921.

108. *Odinnadtsatyi s"ezd RKP(b)*, p. 452. And Radek complained about the "teeth breaking [*zubodrobitel'naia*]" attitude towards the opposition. *RKP(b), Vnutripartiinaia bor'ba v dvadtsatye gody: Dokumenty i materialy 1923 g.* (Moscow: ROSSPEN, 2004), p. 406.

109. *Dvenadtsatyi s"ezd RKP(b)*, pp. 104–5.

110. *Dvenadtsatyi s"ezd RKP(b)*, pp. 116–17.

111. *Dvenadtsatyi s"ezd RKP(b)*, p. 220.

112. *Dvenadtsatyi s"ezd RKP(b)*, p. 200.

113. *Dvenadtsatyi s"ezd RKP(b)*, pp. 188–90. Disillusioned with the growth of bureaucracy in the Party, the crestfallen Lutovinov committed suicide the following year. Allen, "Alexander Shliapnikov," p. 18, note 82.

114. *Desiatyi s"ezd RKP(b)*, p. 27.

115. E. Iaroslavskii, *Za edinstvo VKP(b)* (Moscow-Leningrad, 1927), pp. 55–56.

116. TsGAODM, f. 67, op. 1, d. 97, l. 130b.

117. TsGA IPD, f. 138, op. 1, d. 2, l. 6. Note the verb *dochistit'*, TsGA IPD, f. 138, op. 1, d. 1g, l. 27.

118. *Bol'shevitskoe rukovodstvo*, p. 240.

119. RGASPI, f. 17, op. 2, d. 104, ll. 58, 73; d. 685, l. 95; op. 71, d. 3, l. 5.

120. *Dvenadtsatyi s"ezd RKP(b)*, pp. 152–53.

121. *Dvenadtsatyi s"ezd RKP(b)*, p. 153.

122. *Dvenadtsatyi s"ezd RKP(b)*, p. 138. In criticizing the supporters of Trotsky in 1923, Safarov distanced himself from hermeneutical judgments: "What we need is not 'moral suspicion' [*moral'noe zapodazrivanie*] . . . but a Marxist, sociological analysis." *Za partiiu. Za leninizm* (Petrograd, 1924), p. 111.

123. *Dvenadtsatyi s"ezd RKP(b)*, p. 155.

124. *Dvenadtsatyi s"ezd RKP(b)*, p. 160.

125. *Dvenadtsatyi s"ezd RKP(b)*, p. 138.

126. *Dvenadtsatyi s"ezd RKP(b)*, pp. 152–53.

127. *Dvenadtsatyi s"ezd RKP(b)*, p. 220.

128. RGASPI, f. 17, op. 71, d. 3, l. 4; d. 79, l. 1. TsGAODM, f. 3., op. 8, d. 92, l. 10.

129. PANO, f. 2, op. 1, d. 1860, l. 244.

130. *Deviataia konferentsiia RKP(b)*, p. 160.

131. *Deviataia konferentsiia RKP(b)*, p. 188.

132. *Deviataia konferentsiia RKP(b)*, p. 167.

133. *Deviataia konferentsiia RKP(b)*, p. 151.

134. *Pravda*, March 25, 1921.

135. *Odinnadtsatyi s"ezd RKP(b)*, p. 646.

136. *Desiatyi s"ezd RKP(b)*, p. 240.

137. *Dvenadtsatyi s"ezd RKP(b)*, p. 102.

138. *Odinnadtsatyi s"ezd RKP(b)*, p. 54.

139. RGASPI, f. 17, op. 3, d. 882, l. 12.

140. RGASPI, f. 613, op. 1, d. 6, l. 108.

141. *Odinnadtsatyi s"ezd RKP(b)*, p. 54.

142. RGASPI f. 17, op. 71, d. 79, l. 1.

143. *Odinnadtsatyi s"ezd RKP(b)*, p. 175.

144. *Odinnadtsatyi s"ezd RKP(b)*, pp. 155–56.

145. "O chistkakh partii v 20–30kh godakh," *Izvestiia TsK KPSS*, no. 2 (1990).

146. RGASPI, f. 613, op. 1, d. 3, l. 3; TsGAODM, f. 3, op. 4, d. 32, l. 1; TsGAODM, f. 1614, op. 1, d. 40, l. 7; *The Trotsky Papers, 1917–1922*, vol. 2, pp. 648–50.

147. *Desiatyi s"ezd RKP(b)*, p. 268.

148. Lenin, *PSS*, vol. 25, p. 79.

149. *Desiatyi s"ezd RKP(b)*, p. 310.

150. *Desiatyi s"ezd RKP(b)*, pp. 102–3.

151. *Desiatyi s"ezd RKP(b)*, p. 318.

152. *Odinnadtsatyi s"ezd RKP(b)*, p. 394.

153. But as long as the opposition respected Party regulations, its members could not legitimately be purged. In 1921, when the first comprehensive Party purge meant the expulsion of every fourth Communist, the Central Committee explicitly prohibited action against the "heterodox" (*inakomysliashchie*). Supporters of Workers' Opposition were included on the purge commissions with the explicit goal of making sure that the generally undisciplined were expelled and not those who ever said anything in criticism of the Central Committee. RGASPI, f. 613, op. 1, d. 3, l. 9. *Izvestiia TsK RKP(b)*, no. 33, pp. 39–40.

154. *Desiatyi s"ezd RKP(b)*, p. 319. Who exactly should be purged was a bone of contention between the various heterodox groupings as well. Maksimovskii from the Democratic Centralists disagreed with the Workers' Opposition criteria: "In dividing the Party into proletarian and nonproletarian halves and in suggesting that the latter half should be purged, the 'Workers' Opposition' introduces cleavages into our ranks." Ignatov answered, warning the intelligentsia-prone Democratic Centralists: "We want to clean the Party from class alien elements who did not absorb proletarian psychology." *Desiatyi s"ezd RKP(b)*, p. 318.

155. *Izvestiia TsK RKP(b)*, no. 33, pp. 39–40.

156. "Iz polozheniia o kontrol'nykh komissiiakh vsem paertiinym organizatsiiam RKP," *Izvestiia TsK RKP(b)*, December 20, 1920. "Tsentral'nye kontrol'nye organy partii," *Izvestiia TsK KPSS*, no. 5 (1990).

157. TsGAODM, f. 3, op. 1, d. 216. The antecedents of the Bolshevik courts of honor can be found in Lenin's suggestion from 1904 to institute an arbitration tribunal inside the Party: "In the interest of clearing the atmosphere and relieving comrades from dealing with seriously ill comrades and their pranks we should copy a rule from the regulations of the German Social Democratic Workers Party into our book: The party affiliation of an individual guilty of grave violation of the party program or of a honorless act [*bezchestnyi postupok*] is decided by an arbitration tribunal [*treteiskii sud*]. Half the judges on the tribunal are nominated by those who suggest expulsion, the other half by the guilty part; the chairman of the tribunal is nominated by the Party's governing body. The decision of this tribunal can be appealed to the control commission or to the Party congress." According to Lenin, if introduced, such a rule was to become a good weapon of struggle against those who throw accusations (or spread rumors) lightly. Lenin, *PSS*, vol. 8, pp. 413–14. For the Civil War Party courts of honor see O. Khakhordin, *The Collective and the Individual in Russia: A Study of Practices* (Berkeley: University of California Press, 1999), pp. 39–40.

158. *Deviataia konferentsiia RKP(b)*, p. 149.

159. *Deviataia konferentsiia RKP(b)*, p. 153.

160. TsGAODM, f. 3, op. 2, d. 18, l. 5. TsGAODM, f. 3, op. 4, d. 32, l. 32.

161. *Desiatyi s"ezd RKP(b)*, p. 65.

162. *Dvenadtsatyi s"ezd RKP(b)*, p. 80.

163. *Odinnadtsatyi s"ezd RKP(b)*, p. 182.

164. *Odinnadtsatyi s"ezd RKP(b)*, p. 207.

165. RGASPI, f. 613, op. 3, d. 161, l. 30. *Odinnadtsatyi s"ezd RKP(b)*, p. 207.

166. *Odinnadtsatyi s"ezd RKP(b)*, p. 686. [*Pravda*, March 17, 1922].

167. For Lenin's relation to the Central Control Commission see E. Rees, *State Control in Soviet Russia* (Houndmills: Macmillan, 1987), pp. 64–65.

168. *Odinnadtsatyi s"ezd RKP(b)*, p. 208.

169. *Odinnadtsatyi s"ezd RKP(b)*, p. 694. See also RGASPI, f. 17, op. 3, d. 131, l. 1; f. 613, op. 1, d. 3, ll. 3, 5, 14.

170. TsGA IPD, f. 197 , op. 1, d. 115, ll. 112–113; d. 117, l. 30; PANO, f. 2, op. 1, d. 24, l. 59; f. 17, op. 1, d. 1065, ll. 60–61.

171. RGASPI, f. 613, op. 1, d. 6, l. 79. *TsKK-RKI v osnovnykh postanovleniiakh partii* (Moscow-Leningrad: Godizdat, 1927), pp. 3–22.

172. TsGA IPD, f. 197, op. 1, d. 725, ll. 169–71; RGASPI, f. 17, op. 85, d. 222, ll. 60–62.

173. RGASPI, f. 45, op. 1, d. 28, l. 99.

174. *Dvenadtsatyi s"ezd RKP(b)*, pp. 243–44.

175. *Dvenadtsatyi s"ezd RKP(b)*, p. 248.

176. RGASPI, f. 45, op. 1, d. 29, ll. 6–7. Within limits, Party control commissions could utilize the services of the state's legal apparatus. Authorized to subpoena all documents they needed, control commissions had the right to shoulder comrades working in the investigation departments of the courts with certain tasks (not as part of the official job of the latter, however, but as a "Party duty"). The relation between control commissions and regular Party bodies was also complex. Members of the local control commissions could not be placed on the provincial Party committees or assume any other administrative posi-

tions in the Party structure. "No comrade can execute a task and oversee its execution at one and the same time," the Party regulations explained. *Desiatyi s"ezd RKP(b)*, pp. 64–65. Nevertheless, the Central Control Commission conducted a joint plenary sessions with the Central Committee throughout the 1920s. RGASPI, f. 67, op. 1, d. 1, ll. 1–2. *Odinnadtsatyi s"ezd RKP(b)*, pp. 695–96. *Dvenadtsatyi s"ezd RKP(b)*, p. 637.

177. TsGAODM, f. 3, op. 5, d. 32, ll. 133–34; *Biulleten' TsKK RKP(b) i NK R-KI SSSR* 23 (March 15, 1925), p. 15.

178. *Odinnadtsatyi s"ezd RKP(b)*, pp. 506–8.

179. *Odinnadtsatyi s"ezd RKP(b)*, p. 699.

180. *Desiatyi s"ezd RKP(b)*, p. 59.

181. *Leninskii sbornik*, vol. 20, p. 47.

182. *Odinnadtsatyi s"ezd RKP(b)*, p. 196.

183. *Odinnadtsatyi s"ezd RKP(b)*, pp. 176, 196.

184. RGASPI, f. 17, op. 2, d. 65, l. 18; A Mitrofanov, "Vladimir Il'ich na XI s"ezde RKP(b)," *Voprosy istorii KPSS*, no. 4 (1968), p. 107; E. H. Carr, *The Bolshevik Revolution, 1917–1923* (London: Macmillan, 1951), vol. 2, pp. 324–25; Schapiro, *Origin of the Communist Autocracy*, pp. 324–25.

185. *Izvestiia TsK*, no. 32 (August 6, 1921), pp. 2–3.

186. *Odinnadtsatyi s"ezd RKP(b)*, pp. 281–82.

187. *Odinnadtsatyi s"ezd RKP(b)*, pp. 203–4.

188. *Odinnadtsatyi s"ezd RKP(b)*, p. 203.

189. *Odinnadtsatyi s"ezd RKP(b)*, p. 179.

190. *Odinnadtsatyi s"ezd RKP(b)*, p. 179.

191. *Leninskii sbornik*, vol. 36, p. 137.

192. RGASPI, f. 17, op. 2, d. 104, l. 60; d. 685, l. 95.

193. K. Kreibikh, "Poslednie mogikane 'rabochei oppozitsii v RKP(b)'," *Kommunisticheskii internatsional* (1922), no. 1, p. 55.

194. RGASPI, f. 17, op. 71, d. 3, l. 3.

195. *Odinnadtsatyi s"ezd RKP(b)*, pp. 707–8, 753.

196. Shliapnikov denied he ever claimed his house was searched. "I only said that the messenger who carried a letter for me was arrested and that I perceived that as a lack of trust." RGASPI, f. 17, op. 71, d. 1, l. 8.

197. *Izvestiia TsK*, March 1922, pp. 69–70.

198. *Izvestiia TsK*, March 1922, p. 70; *Odinnadtsatyi s"ezd RKP(b)*, pp. 707–8.

199. *Odinnadtsatyi s"ezd RKP(b)*, p. 131. RGASPI, f. 17, op. 71, d. 1, ll. 1, 130b.

200. *Odinnadtsatyi s"ezd RKP(b)*, pp. 707–8.

201. *Odinnadtsatyi s"ezd RKP(b)*, p. 579.

202. *Odinnadtsatyi s"ezd RKP(b)*, pp. 703, 708.

203. *Odinnadtsatyi s"ezd RKP(b)*, p. 174.

204. *Odinnadtsatyi s"ezd RKP(b)*, p. 196.

205. *Odinnadtsatyi s"ezd RKP(b)*, p. 195.

206. *Odinnadtsatyi s"ezd RKP(b)*, p. 189.

207. *Odinnadtsatyi s"ezd RKP(b)*, pp. 188–89.

208. TsGAODM, f. 3, op. 8, d. 92, l. 32.

209. *Odinnadtsatyi s"ezd RKP(b)*, p. 189.

210. *Odinnadtsatyi s"ezd RKP(b)*, p. 193.

211. RGASPI, f. 17, op. 71, d. 3, l. 1.

212. *Odinnadtsatyi s"ezd RKP(b)*, pp. 191–93.

213. *Odinnadtsatyi s"ezd RKP(b)*, p. 205.

214. *Odinnadtsatyi s"ezd RKP(b)*, p. 709.

215. *Odinnadtsatyi s"ezd RKP(b)*, p. 176.

216. *Rabochaia oppozitsiia*, p. 152.

217. *Odinnadtsatyi s"ezd RKP(b)*, pp. 703–4.

218. *Odinnadtsatyi s"ezd RKP(b)*, p. 709. M. Vasser, "Razgrom anarkho-sindikalis-ticheskogo uklona v partii," *Voprosy istorii KPSS*, no. 3 (1962), p. 75.

219. *Odinnadtsatyi s"ezd RKP(b)*, pp. 703–4.

220. Whether the leaders of Workers' Opposition crossed the boundary of Party acceptability and deserved to be purged was a cause for repeated debate. Already on August 9, 1921, Lenin proposed to show Shliapnikov the door for "systematic violation of Party discipline," but his motion came one vote short of the necessary two-thirds majority (17 to 10). *Odinnadtsatyi s"ezd RKP(b)*, pp. 710, 173, 704. Arguing that opinion could not be used as grounds for a purge, Kollontai protested the purge of Mitin and Kuznetsov in 1922, "though no crime has been committed." Stalin, Dzerzhinskii, Sol'ts, and others sitting on the special commission insisted, however, that the two Workers' Oppositionists were to leave the Party not because of their opinions but because they had violated Party discipline. *Odinnadtsatyi s"ezd RKP(b)*, p. 200.

221. This group was further divided into two cohorts according to the degree of remorse: those who regretted their mistakes were carefully distinguished from those who were unwilling to make such statements. *Odinnadtsatyi s"ezd RKP(b)*, pp. 708–9.

222. *Odinnadtsatyi s"ezd RKP(b)*, p. 709.

223. *Odinnadtsatyi s"ezd RKP(b)*, pp. 176–77.

224. *Desiatyi s"ezd RKP(b)*, p. 324.

225. *Desiatyi s"ezd RKP(b)*, pp. 266–67.

226. *Desiatyi s"ezd RKP(b)*, p. 531.

227. *Odinnadtsatyi s"ezd RKP(b)*, p. 194.

228. *Pravda*, December 19 and 30, 1923; "Vozzvanie gruppy 'Rabochaia pravda,'" *Sotsialisticheskii vestnik*, no. 49 (1923), pp. 12–14.

229. RGASPI, f. 17, op. 82, d. 182, l. 99; On the social composition of Workers' Truth, see B. Belkin, "'Rabochaia oppozitsiia', Post Scriptum," ed. A. Afanas'ev, *Oni ne molchali* (Moscow: Politizdat, 1991), p. 52.

230. E. Iaroslavskii, *Za edinstvo VKP(b)*, p. 64.

231. N. Bukharin, "Dezertiry proletarskoi revoliutsii. Gruppa Rabochaia Pravda," *Pravda*, March 25, 1923.

232. RGASPI, f. 17, op. 71, d. 4, l. 30b.

233. RGASPI, f. 17, op. 71, d. 81, ll. 1–23; "Obrashchenie gruppy 'Rabochaia pravda' k XII s"ezdu RKP," *Sotsialisticheskii vestnik*, no. 65 (1923), pp. 13–14.

234. RGASPI, f. 17, op. 71, d. 4, l. 10b.

235. *Dvenadtsatyi s"ezd RKP(b)*, pp. 346, 792. N. Karev, "O gruppe 'rabochaia pravda,'" *Bol'shevik*, July 15, 1924, pp. 31–33.

236. Iaroslavskii, *Za edinstvo VKP(b)*, pp. 76, 64–65.

237. *Neizvestnyi Bogdanov: v 3-kh knigakh / A. A. Bogdanov (Malinovskii)*, ed. G. Bordiugov (Moscow: "AIRO-XX", 1995), vol. I, pp. 52–57.

238. "Delo A. A. Bogdanova (Malinovskogo)," *Voprosy istorii*, no. 9 (1994), pp. 14–15; *Neizvestnyii Bogdanov: v 3-kh knigakh / A. A. Bogdanov (Malinovskii)*, ed. G. Bordiugov. (Moscow: "AIRO-XX", 1995), vol. 2, p. 209.

239. RGASPI, f. 259, op. 1, d. 2, ll. 11–12.

240. RGASPI, f. 17, op. 84, d. 327, ll. 17–18.

241. Iaroslavskii, *Za edinstvo VKP(b)*, pp. 60–61.

242. L. Smirnov, "Iz istorii bor'by V. I. Lenina, partii bol'shevikov protiv Bogdanovskoi 'Organizatsionnoi nauki,'" *Nauchnye doklady vysshei shkoly (fisolofskie nauki)*, no. 3 (1966), pp. 89–90.

243. *Izvestiia TsK RKP(b)*, no. 9–10 (1923). TsGA IPD, f. 197, op. 1, d. 725, ll. 167, 169.

244. G. Ustinov, *Krushenie partii levykh es-erov* (Moscow, 1918); I. Vardin "Ot melkobur-zhuaznoi kontr-revoliutsii k restavratsii kapitalizma (Partiia menshevikov posle oktiabria)," in *Za piat' let, 1917–1922, Sbornik, TsK RKP* (Moscow, 1922). Zinoviev spoke against the resurgent anti-Soviet parties and tendencies at the Twelfth Party Conference in August 1922. G. Zinov'ev, *Ob antisovetskikh partiiakh i techeniiak. (Rech' na vserossiiskoi konferentsii R.K.P. s prilozheniem rezoliutsii)* (Moscow, 1922).

245. *Za partiiu: Za leninizm* (Petrograd, 1924), pp. 70–71.

246. *Dvenadtsatyi s"ezd RKP(b)*, p. 792.

247. *Za partiiu: Za leninizm*, pp. 70–71.

248. *Desiatyi s"ezd RKP(b)*, p. 77.

249. *Dvenadtsatyi s"ezd RKP(b)*, p. 792.

250. E. Iaroslavskii, *Za edinstvo VKP(b)*, p. 58.

251. E. Iaroslavskii, *Za edinstvo VKP(b)*, pp. 56–57, 59. *Dvenadtsatyi s"ezd RKP(b)*, p. 346.

252. The Black Mass metaphors were not the exclusive property of the Central Committee majority. Consider the terms of political analysis by an ultra-radical activist who conceived of himself as standing to the left of the Workers' Truth, let alone the Central Committee, both hopelessly petit bourgeois in his eyes. Since the Central Committee was clearly beyond the pale, most of the ire fell actually on the oppositionist fringe. "Of course, the Workers' Truth is not stupid enough to say up front, 'We work for the bourgeoisie.' What worker would follow them if they did? Workers would have understood right away that these are the old Menshevik-SR-Kadet tunes [*pogudki*]." But the Russian workers will not remain naive and gullible forever. "Do you, my Communist comrades, think that the endless repetition of the word 'revolution' will allow you to hide your reactionary and counterrevolutionary aims? During the last six years the working class of Russia has seen so many counterrevolutionaries that your ploy will not fool it; the working class knows who is who." The agenda of this anonymous, radical pamphleteer was not to create an alternative to Communism but to return Communism to its pristine values. "Under the prevailing conditions [read: NEP] the creation of a worker Communist group that is organizationally free from the Bolshevik party but fully accepts the party's regulations and platform is objectively unavoidable. Such a group will emerge despite the wild resistance of the ruling party and the soviet and trade union bureaucracies." RGASPI, f. 17, op. 71, d. 4, ll. 30–31.

253. TsGAODM, f. 3, op. 6, d. 2, l. 14. Daniels, *Conscience of the Revolution*, p. 204.

254. RGASPI, f. 17, op. 71, d. 3, l. 1. For background see R. Sinigaglia, *Miasnikov e la revoluzione russa* (Milan, 1973); R. Medvedev, "O tragicheskoi sud'be G. I. Miasnikova

i ego sem'i," in *Politicheskii dnevnik, 1965–1970* (Amsterdam, 1975), pp. 58–60; P. Avrich, "Bolshevik Opposition to Lenin: G. T. Miasnikov and the Workers' Group," *Russian Review* 43 (1984).

255. For Miasnikov's stance during the Civil War see *Shestoi vserossiiskii chrezvychainyi s"ezd sovetov rabochikh, krest'ianskikh, kazach'ikh i krasnoarmeiskikh deputatov: Stenograficheskii otchet* (Moscow, 1919), p. 188. On his alleged ties with the Workers' Opposition see *BSE*, vol. 47, pp. 760–61.

256. *Diskussionnyi material (Tezisy tov. Miasnikova, pis'mo tov). Lenina, otvet emu, postanovlenie Org. biuro Ts.K. i rezoliutsiia motovilikhintsev* (Perm, 1921); *Odinnadtsatyi s"ezd RKP(b)*, p. 646.

257. *Leninskii sbornik*, vol. 36, p. 299; A. Berkman, *Letters from Russian Prisons* (New York, 1925), pp. 85–86.

258. G. Miasnikov, "To zhe, da ne to," in G. Zinoviev (ed.), *Partiia i soiuzy (K diskussii o role i zadachakh profsoiuzov)* (Petrograd, 1921), pp. 282–83. M. Vasser, "Razgrom anarkho-sindikalisticheskogo uklona v partii," *Voprosy istorii KPSS*, no. 3 (1962), p. 76.

259. TsGIA IPD, f. 16, op. 4, d. 4169, l. 1. *Odinnadtsatyi s"ezd RKP(b)*, p. 710.

260. *Izvestiia TsK RKP(b)* 1922, no. 39, p. 11. "GPU o 'rabochei gruppe' RKP(b)," *Sotsialisticheskii vestnik*, July 6, 1924, pp. 9–10. The charge that Miasnikov was a former SR did not appear until later. See B. Pismanika, "Rabochaia gruppa" ('Miasnikovshchina'), *Proletarskaia revoliutsiia* 1931, no. 6, p. 85.

261. *Dvenadtsatyi s"ezd RKP(b)*, p. 221. "Zamechatel'nyi document," *Sotsialisticheskii vestnik*, February 23, 1922.

262. V. Sorin, *Rabochaia gruppa "Miasnikovshchina"* (Moscow: Izd. Mk RKP, 1924), p. 63; A. Tiskhov, *Pervyi chekist* (Moscow, 1968), pp. 121–22. For Miasnikov's complaints to the Central Committee about his arrest see RGASPI, f. 82, op. 2, d. 177, l. 33.

263. Deutscher, *The Prophet Outcast*, p. 108.

264. *Dvenadtsatyi s"ezd RKP(b)*, p. 847.

265. According to some sources, the Workers' Group included no more than 200 members during the peak of its activity. Even after GPU arrests and reprisals, there remained 28 individuals who continued to adhere to it. M. Vasser, "Razgrom anarkho-sindikalisticheskogo uklona v partii," *Voprosy istorii KPSS*, no. 3 (1962), p. 77.

266. E. Iaroslavskii, *Za edinstvo VKP(b)*, p. 63.

267. *Dvenadtsatyi s"ezd RKP(b)*, p. 189.

268. RGASPI, f. 17, op. 84, d. 327, l. 99.

269. *Dvenadtsatyi s"ezd RKP(b)*, p. 159, 52.

270. *Dvenadtsatyi s"ezd RKP(b)*, p. 223.

271. *Dvenadtsatyi s"ezd RKP(b)*, pp. 189, 120, 159.

272. The fact that the Party treated splinter groups as nascent counterrevolutionary formations does not mean that the participants of these groups regarded themselves as non-Bolsheviks. Kuznestov, one of the leaders of the Workers' Group, rejected the label of counterrevolutionary and was arrested by the GPU in the summer of 1923, a time when few Bolsheviks received such treatment. The Central Committee perceived him as someone who, in calling for a Party schism, violated a major taboo. Kuznetsov himself, however, maintained he was loyal to Bolshevik values. His remonstrations about the reprisals against his group suggest he could not break out of the Party framework. It is particularly

noteworthy that he demanded that the Bolsheviks find moral fault in him and not just purge him on legal grounds. Sitting in the GPU jail in the autumn of 1923, Kuznetsov wrote, "I will not deny that the creation of Workers' Group violated the decisions of Party congresses. It is also true that a Temporary Central Organizational Bureau was formed. I admit my guilt here and realize I was mistaken. . . . But this is the formal aspect of things. And what is the moral basis for the charges against me? Are we guilty that, having similar attitudes towards the workers' experience of poverty, suffering, coercion and injustice . . . we were morally in agreement with each other?" *RKP(b) i vnutrepartiinaiia bor'ba v dvadtsatye gody* (Moscow, 2004), p. 94.

273. *Dvenadtsatyi s"ezd RKP(b)*, pp. 221, 223.

274. *Dvenadtsatyi s"ezd RKP(b)*, pp. 223, 224.

275. *Dvenadtsatyi s"ezd RKP(b)*, p. 238.

276. *Dvenadtsatyi s"ezd RKP(b)*, p. 238.

277. PATO, f. 17, op. 1, d. 43, ll. 8, 22.

278. J. Ali, "Aspects of the RKP(b) Secretariat, March 1919 to April 1922," *Soviet Studies* 3 (1974); N. Rosenfeldt, "'The Consistory of the Communist Church': The Origins and Development of Stalin's Secret Chancellery," *Russian History* 1982, no. 2–3.

279. TsGA IPD, f. 24, op. 2b, d. 1428, l. 222; f. 197, op. 1., d. 722, ll. 22–31; d. 1133, ll. 35–37; f. 566, op. 1, d. 280, ll. 13–17; d. 276, l. 128.

280. *Desiatyi s"ezd RKP(b)*, pp. 544–45.

281. *Desiatyi s"ezd RKP(b)*, pp. 773–74.

282. *Desiatyi s"ezd RKP(b)*, p. 90.

283. RGASPI, f. 17, op. 71, d. 1, l. 1.

284. Lenin used the language of moral correction on other occasions as well. There are those unhappy "characters [*natury*]" whose criticisms are always venomous, he said about Sosnovskii. And in July 1922 he insisted on the exile of the Menshevik Rozhkov because "it is impossible to correct him." Lenin, *PSS*, vol. 42, p. 272. RGASPI, f. 2, op. 2, d. 1338, l. 1. Nor was the hermeneutical gaze Lenin's sole prerogative. In 1913, Trotsky bemoaned the "terrible moral decline" of Khrustalev, his predecessor as the head of the Petersburg Soviet during the First Russian Revolution. Taking a patronizing tone, Trotsky insisted he never publicly "defamed" (*shel'movat'*) Khrustalev but treated him as a victim of his "psychological depravity." And Khrustalev was not irredeemable: Trotsky insisted on "retaining him in our milieu provided he will walk in step with us." L. Trotsky, *Sochineniia*, vol. 2 (Moscow-Leningrad, 1925), p. 514. Or consider Ordzhonikidze's view of Bukharin's character, expressed in a private letter to Voroshilov dated June 26, 1929: "Surprisingly, Bukharin turned out to be an indecent [*neprilichnyi*] individual. He does everything he can to create the impression that he is being wronged and at the same time he is ready to cover everybody else with shit." *Sovetskoe rukovodstvo: Perepiska; 1928–1941* (Moscow: ROSSPEN, 1999), p. 80.

285. *Odinnadtsatyi s"ezd RKP(b)*, p. 144.

286. A. Mitrofanov, Vladimir Il'ich na XI s"ezde RKP(b), *Voprosy istorii KPSS*, no. 4 (1968), p. 106.

287. *Odinnadtsatyi s"ezd RKP(b)*, pp. 145–47.

288. "Pis'ma N. I. Bukharina," *Voprosy istorii KPSS*, no. 11 (1988), p. 49. "Byla li otkrovennoi ispoved'? Materialy partiinoi chistki N. I. Bukharina v 1933 godu," *Voprosy istorii KPSS*, no. 3 (1991), pp. 45, 49, 56.

289. *Desiatyi s'ezd RKP(b): Stenographicheskii otchet* (Moscow, 1963), p. 61.

290. TsGAODM, f. 67, op. 1, d. 97, l. 130b; TsGAODM, f. 80, op. 1, d. 58, l. 22; TsGIA IPD, f. 408, op. 1, d. 1175, l. 91.

291. Lenin, *PSS*, vol. 45, p. 474. L. Trotsky, *The Suppressed Testament of Lenin* (New York, 1935), pp. 11–12; Stalin, *Sochineniia*, vol. 10, pp. 175–76. See also B. Bazhanov, *Vospominaniia byvshego sekretaria Stalina* (Moscow, 1990), pp. 105–6; L. Trotskii, "Zaveshchanie Lenina," *Portrety revoliutsionerov* (Moscow, 1991), pp. 267–68; "Opaseniia V. I. po adressu t. Stalina ne opravdalis," Obsuzhdenie na XIII s'ezde RKP(b) Leninskogo pis'ma s'ezdu 1924 g. *Istoricheskii arkhiv*, no. 1 (2005).

292. For such an approach see Service, *Lenin*, pp. 282–86, and E. G. Plimak, *Politicheskoe zaveshchanie V. I. Lenina: Istoki, sushchnost', vypolnenie* (Moscow, 1989).

293. *Arkhiv Trotskogo*, vol. 1, pp. 73–74.

294. For Sultangaliev's biography see Mirsaid Sultan-Galiev, *Stat'i, vystupleniia, dokumenty* (Kazan', 1992), pp. 386–87; A. Lemercier-Quélquejay, *Ch. Sultan Galiev: Le père de la révolution tiers-mondiste* (Paris, 1986), pp. 9–11; R. Landa, "Mirsaid Sultan-Galiev," *Voprosy istorii*, no. 8 (1999), p. 53.

295. "O Tak nazyvaemoi Sultangalievskoi kontrrevoliutsionnoi organizatsii," *Izvestiia TsK KPSS* 1990, no. 10, p. 76.

296. *Tainy natsional'noi politikii TsK RKP, stenograficheskii otchet sekretnogo iv soveshchaniia TsK RKP, 1923 goda* (Moscow, 1923; reprint, 1992), pp. 18, 22.

297. "O Tak nazyvaemoi Sultangalievskoi kontrrevoliutsionnoi organizatsii," *Izvestiia TsK KPSS* 1990, no. 10, pp. 79–80.

298. *Tainy natsional'noi politiki TsK RKP*, p. 21.

299. *Tainy natsional'noi politiki TsK RKP*, pp. 43, 52, 23.

300. *Tainy natsional'noi politiki TsK RKP*, p. 50.

301. *Tainy natsional'noi politiki TsK RKP*, pp. 74, 98.

302. *Tainy natsional'noi politiki TsK RKP*, pp. 39–40.

303. *Tainy natsional'noi politiki TsK RKP*, p. 20.

304. *Delo provokatora Malinovskogo*, pp. 220, 280, note 225.

305. *Tainy natsional'noi politiki TsK RKP*, p. 32.

306. *Tainy natsional'noi politiki TsK RKP*, pp. 55–56.

307. *Tainy natsional'noi politiki TsK RKP*, pp. 71–72.

308. *Tainy natsional'noi politiki TsK RKP*, pp. 36–37.

309. *Tainy natsional'noi politiki TsK RKP*, p. 39.

310. *Tainy natsional'noi politiki TsK RKP*, pp. 38–39.

311. *Tainy natsional'noi politiki TsK RKP*, p. 60.

312. *Tainy natsional'noi politiki TsK RKP*, pp. 59, 60.

313. *Tainy natsional'noi politiki TsK RKP*, p. 63.

314. *Tainy natsional'noi politiki TsK RKP*, p. 21.

315. *Tainy natsional'noi politiki TsK RKP*, p. 87.

316. *Tainy natsional'noi politiki TsK RKP*, pp. 23, 82. Stalin concurred: Sultangaliev admitted more sins than we had documentation on, confessed his guilt fully, and repented. Stalin, *Sochineniia*, vol. 5, p. 305.

317. *Tainy natsional'noi politiki TsK RKP*, pp. 88, 23.

318. "O tak nazyvaemoi Sultangalievskoi kontrrevoliutsionnoi organizatsii," pp. 80–86; quote, p. 80.

Chapter 3: Healing Oppositionist Souls

1. TsGAODM, f. 3, op. 6, d. 2, l. 2.

2. *Leninizm ili trotskizm* (Iaroslavl', 1925), p. 7.

3. *Dvenadtsatyi s"ezd RKP(b), 17–25 Aprelia 1923 goda: Stenograficheskii otchet* (Moscow: Gospolitizdat, 1968), pp. 89, 223.

4. For the succession struggle see M. Eastman, *Since Lenin Died* (London, 1925); and A. D'Agostino, *Soviet Succession Struggles* (Boston: Allen and Unwin, 1988).

5. For his early attempt to present himself as the closest to Lenin, see L. Trotskii, *O Lenine: Materialy dlia biografa* (Moscow, 1924).

6. A. Barmine, *One Who Survived* (New York: G. P. Putnam's Sons, 1945), p. 212.

7. *Pravda*, March 14, 1923; *Pechat' i revoliutsiia* 4 (1924), p. 162.

8. A. Lunacharskii, K. Radek, L. Trotskii, *Siluety: Politicheskie portrety* (Moscow, 1991), pp. 349–51.

9. B. Kolonitskii, "'Revolutionary Names': Russian Personal Names and the Political Consciousness in the 1920s and 1930s," *Revolutionary Russia* 6 (1993), p. 222.

10. R. Daniels, *The Conscience of the Revolution: Communist Opposition in Soviet Russia* (Cambridge, Mass.: Harvard University Press, 1960), pp. 173–74; *RKP(b) i vnutrepartiinaia bor'ba v dvadtsatye gody* (Moscow: ROSSPEN, 2004), p. 129. The honorary presidium of the Eleventh Moscow Provincial Party Conference from January 10, 1924, included Lenin, Zinoviev, Stalin, and Trotsky—the order in which these names appeared gives us a sense of the Party's hierarchy days before Lenin's death. TsGAODM, f. 3, op. 6, d. 2, l. 3.

11. *La Russie vers la socialisme: La discussion dans le parti communiste de l'USSR* (Paris, 1926), p. 45.

12. TsGAODM, f. 88, op. 1, d. 169, l. 139.

13. Demian Bednyi ridiculed the cult of the leader in the following poem: *Chei tut grekh? Obshchii grekh / —Rasplodili idolopoklonnikov! / Vozhdei, kak gribov posle dozhdia! / Dali razvitsia samomneniiam ogromnym, / Same na nikh pal'tsem tykali, / A teper' zakhnykali.* "Whose sin is that? / Everybody's sin / We bred idol worshippers! / Leaders like mushrooms after the rain! / We allowed enormous egos to flourish / We pointed at them with a finger / And now we begin winning." *Pravda*, January 11, 1924.

14. One might see in the number of projected volumes a peculiar hierarchy of revolutionary truth telling: Lenin's oeuvre amounted to thirty volumes, Trotsky's to twenty-three, and Kamenev's to only fifteen. Stalin's collected writings would have to wait for the 1930s. Kamenev stated: "If we want to be on alert regarding Trotsky we must 'study' Trotsky not only based on what he includes in his collected writings but also what he chooses to omit." L. Kamenev, "Leninizm ili trotskizm," *Pod Leninskim znamenem*, no. 3 (1924), p. 44.

15. TsGAODM, f. 3, op. 4, d. 32, l. 2. V. Sorin, *Rabochaia gruppa "Miasnikovshchina"* (Moscow: Izd. MKRKP, 1924), pp. 3–4. K. Murphy, "Opposition at the Local Level: A Case Study of the Hammer and Sickle Factory," *Europe-Asia Studies* 53, no. 2 (2001), p. 332.

16. E. H. Carr, *The Interregnum, 1923–24* (London: Macmillan, 1960), pp. 93–94.

17. RGASPI, f. 17, op. 2, d. 685, l. 34. TsGAODM, f. 3, op. 6, d. 2, l. 67.

18. Daniels, *Conscience of the Revolution*, pp. 218–19. RGASPI, f. 17, op. 2, d. 104, l. 67.

19. *RKP(b) i vnutrepartiinaia bor'ba v dvadtsastye gody* (Moscow: ROSSPEN, 2004), pp. 154, 166. Towards 1923, about every second secretary of a provincial Party committee

was nominated or "recommended" by the Central Committee. This allowed Stalin to
assume control over the secretarial hierarchy and control the provincial Party apparatus.
RKP(b) i vnutrepartiinaiia bor'ba v dvadtsastye gody (Moscow: ROSSPEN, 2004), p. 186.

20. *Pravda*, December 13, 1923. RGASPI, f. 17, op. 2, d. 104, l. 52.

21. B. Knei-Paz, *The Social and Political Thought of Leon Trotsky* (Oxford: Oxford
University Press, 1978), pp. 367–441.

22. R. Service, *The Bolshevik Party in Revolution: A Study in Organisational Change,
1917–1923* (London: Macmillan, 1979), pp. 188–90.

23. Daniels, *Conscience of the Revolution*, p. 223.

24. For the history of the animosity between Trotsky and Zinoviev see *Petrogradskaia
Pravda*, January 18, 1921.

25. *Pravda*, December 18, 1923. *Izvestiia TsK KPSS* 1991, no. 3, p. 202; PATO, f. 1, op. 1, d.
109, l. 110.

26. TsGAODM, f. 3, op. 4, d. 32, l. 19.

27. Carr, *The Interregnum*, p. 312. M. David-Fox, *Revolution of the Mind: Higher Learning
among the Bolsheviks, 1918–1929* (Ithaca: Cornell University Press, 1997), p. 97.

28. In January 1924, the opposition was supported by forty Moscow student cells, the
Central Committee by twenty-two; the opposition may have claimed up to two-thirds
of the student cells. D. Hincks, "Support for the Opposition in Moscow in the Party
Discussion of 1923–24," *Soviet Studies* 44 (1992), p. 141.

29. *Kommunist* (Khar'kov), December 25, 1923. TsGAODM, f. 3, op. 5, d. 2, l. 200; f. 88,
op. 1, d. 170, l. 1060b. *Rabochaia Moskva*, December 30, 1923; A. Bubnov, BSE, 1st ed. vol. 1,
p. 498; V. Vilkova (ed.), *The Struggle for Power: Russia in 1923* (Amherst, N.Y.: Prometheus
Books, 1996), pp. 264–81.

30. *Svod uzakonenii Rossiiskoi federatsii sovetskikh respublik* (SU RSFSR), 1921, no. 12,
pp. 79, 83. L. Ivanova, *U istokov sovetskoi istoricheskoi nauki (podgotovka kadrov istorikov-
marksistov 1917–1929)* (Moscow, 1968), pp. 138–39.

31. *Normal'nyi ustav kommuniversitetov* (Petrograd, 1923).

32. For an English translation of his biography see S. Kanatchikov, *A Radical Worker
in Tsarist Russia: The Autobiography of Semen Ivanovich Kanatchikov* (Stanford: Stanford
University Press, 1986). For a scholarly introduction see R. Zelnik, "The Fate of a Russian
Bebel: Semen I. Kanatchikov, 1905–1940," *Carl Beck Papers*, no. 1105 (1995); R. Hernandez,
"The Confessions of Semen Kanatchikov: A Bolshevik Memoir as Spiritual Autobiogra-
phy," *Russian Review* 60 (2001).

33. This formulation belongs to M. David-Fox, *Revolution of the Mind*, p. 100.

34. For how such circles operated see M. Rogov, "Ocherki Sverdlovii," *Molodaia gvardiia*,
no. 5 (1924), pp. 200–201.

35. TsGA IPD, f. 7, op. 2, d. 1242, ll. 4–5.

36. RGASPI, f. 17, op. 2, d. 104, l. 26; d. 109, ll. 5–6; d. 685, l. 72. Only Central Committee members were supposed to see the classified file with Trotsky's letters. RGASPI, f. 17,
op. 2, d. 685, l. 73.

37. *Sotsialisticheskii vestnik*, no. 11 (81), May 24, 1924; TsGA IPD, f. 197, op. 1, d. 117, ll.
33–35; d. 725, ll. 138, 141.

38. V. Demidov, *Politicheskaia bor'ba oppozitsii v sibiri, 1922–1929* (Novosibirsk, 1994),
p. 27.

39. TsGA IPD, f. 7, op. 2, d. 1242, l. 25.

40. TsGA IPD, f. 197, op. 1, d. 4b, l. 14.

41. *Leningradskaia pravda*, December 21, 1923. TsGA IPD, f. 197, op. 1, d. 4b, l. 1; TsGA IPD, f. 7, op. 2, d. 1242, 116ob–118.

42. Karpov was thus in agreement with someone like Radek, who insisted a few weeks earlier that the Politburo must meet Trotsky halfway. "The Party cannot afford today that any groups of comrades feel that they are constricted, unless we are talking about groups such as 'Workers' Truth' that collude against the Party." "Ia zaiavliaiu ... Ultimatum Karla Radeka chlenam Politbiuro TsK VKP(b)," *Istochnik*, no. 2 (1998).

43. *Leningradskaia pravda*, December 20, 1923.

44. P. Zalutskii, *O sovremennom trotskizme* (Leningrad: Priboi, 1925), p. 4.

45. *Leningradskaia pravda*, December 20, 1923. TsGA IPD, f. 7, op. 2, d. 1242, l. 121. S. Kanatchikov, "O likvidatorskikh nastroeniiakh nashei partii," *Za partiiu. Za leninizm* (Petrograd, 1924), p. 114; P. Zalutskii, *O sovremennom trotskizme* (Leningrad: Priboi, 1925), p. 29.

46. TsGA IPD, f. 197, op. 1, d. 725, l. 38; f. 7, op. 2, d. 1242, l. 118.

47. TsGAODM, f. 3, op. 4, d. 32, l. 4.

48. L. Trotsky, *The New Course*, trans. and ed. Max Shachtman (New York: New International, 1943), pp. 89–98; Daniels, *Conscience of the Revolution*, pp. 224–25.

49. TsGA IPD, f. 197, op. 1, d. 1141, ll. 1, 11.

50. TsGA IPD, f. 197, op. 1, d. 725, ll. 38–39.

51. TsGA IPD, f. 197, op. 1, d. 4b, l. 2.

52. TsGA IPD, f. 197, op. 1, d. 1141, l. 9.

53. *Dvenadtsatyi s"ezd RKP(b)*, p. 705.

54. TsGA IPD, f. 7, op. 2, d. 1242, l. 3.

55. TsGA IPD, f. 197, op. 1, d. 4b, l. 23.

56. TsGA IPD, f. 197, op. 1, d. 1141, l. 6.

57. TsGA IPD, f. 7, op. 2, d. 1242, 116ob–118.

58. TsGA IPD, f. 197, op. 1, d. 1141, l. 1.

59. TsGA IPD, f. 197, op. 1, d. 4b, ll. 2–3.

60. TsGA IPD, f. 197, op. 1, d. 725, ll. 37–38.

61. TsGAODM, f. 3, op. 6, d. 2, l. 26. *Pravda*, December 14, 1923.

62. *Pravda*, December 12, 1923. See also Rafail's ironic comparison of Stalin with "commander in chief." TsGAODM, f. 3, op. 4, d. 32, l. 18.

63. *Leningradskaia pravda*, December 15, 1923.

64. TsGA IPD, f. 197, op. 1, d. 725, ll. 37–38.

65. TsGA IPD, f. 197, op. 1, d. 1141, l. 16.

66. TsGA IPD, f. 197, op. 1, d. 1141, l. 17.

67. TsGA IPD, f. 197, op. 1, d. 4b, l. 14.

68. TsGA IPD, f. 197, op. 1, d. 1141, ll. 2–3, 18.

69. TsGA IPD, f. 7, op. 2, d. 1242, l. 119.

70. Nor was it clear whether Trotsky could be described as an oppositionist or a factionist. For the arguments, pro and contra, see RGASPI, f. 17, op. 2, d. 685, l. 51. TsGAODM, f. 88, op. 1, d. 170, l. 106.

71. TsGA IPD, f. 197, op. 1, d. 1141, ll. 6, 8.

72. TsGA IPD, f. 197, op. 1, d. 4b, l. 32.

73. TsGAODM, f. 3, op. 6, d. 2, ll. 20–21; op. 8, d. 92, l. 32.

74. David-Fox, *Revolution of the Mind*, p. 151.

75. TsGA IPD, f. 197, op. 1, d. 1141, l. 4.

76. *Za partiiu*, p. 49–50. TsGAODM, f. 3, op. 8, d. 92, l. 33.

77. TsGA IPD, f. 7, op. 2, d. 1242, 1160b–118. Trotsky was frequently described as a Menshevik in the official press, *Pravda*, December 20, 1923. *Rabochaia Moskva*, December 2, 1924.

78. *Leningradskaia pravda*, December 21, 1923.

79. TsGA IPD, f. 197, op. 1, d. 725, l. 38.

80. TsGA IPD, f. 7, op. 2, d. 1242, 1160b–118.

81. A. Kaktyn', *Novaia ekonomicheskaia politika i "nozhnitsy": Ocherednye zadachi ekonomicheskoi politiki* (Moscow, 1924). RGASPI, f. 17, op. 2, d. 104, l. 56; op. 71, d. 5, l. 1. *Izvestiia TsK KPSS* 1990, no. 7, p. 187. Daniels, *Conscience of the Revolution*, pp. 218–19.

82. *Pravda*, January 1, 1924; RGASPI, f. 17, op. 2, d. 104, l. 56; op. 71, d. 5, l. 1. *Izvestiia TsK KPSS* 1990, no. 7, p. 187. Eastman, *Since Lenin Died*, p. 37.

83. TsGA IPD, f. 197, op. 1, d. 725, l. 147.

84. TsGAODM, f. 3, op. 6, d. 2, l. 27.

85. RGASPI, f. 17, op. 2, d. 103, l. 8; TsGA IPD, f. 197, op. 1, d. 725, l. 148.

86. TsGA IPD, f. 197, op. 1, d. 725, ll. 146, 155. For related claims see RGASPI, f. 17, op. 2, d. 685, ll. 66, 77; TsGAODM, f. 88, op. 1, d. 170, l. 1070b.

87. TsGA IPD, f. 7, op. 2, d. 1242, l. 8; f. 197, op. 1, d. 1141, l. 18.

88. TsGA IPD, f. 197, op. 1, d. 4b, l. 1600b; d. 119, l. 880b.

89. *Leningradskaia pravda*, December 21, 1923.

90. TsGA IPD, f. 197, op. 1, d. 725, l. 154.

91. TsGA IPD, f. 197, op. 1, d. 725, l. 39.

92. TsGA IPD, f. 197, op. 1, d. 13, ll. 2–3.

93. The New Course Discussion ended in a decisive victory for the Central Committee majority. Described as "demagogic," the opposition had received between 1 and 10 percent of the vote, according to official sources. At the grassroots level, however, things may have looked a bit different. Sapronov claimed that when he attended a district Party conference in Moscow (the organizational tier immediately above the primary cells), the opposition obtained at least 36 percent of the vote, while at the provincial Party conference, the next tier, that percentage shrunk by half. Rather shrewdly, Sapronov surmised that, given the apparent diminution by half at each tier, the critics of the Central Committee must have won over a very convincing majority of Party members. *Trinadtsataia konferentsiia Rossiiskoi kommunisticheskoi partii (bol'shevikov)* (Moscow: Krasnaia nov', 1924), p. 131. TsGA IPD, f. 197, op. 1, d. 13, ll. 6–8; TsGAODM, f. 3, op. 6, d. 2, l. 3. *Izvestiia Sibbiuro Tsk KRP(b)*, 1923, no. 65–66, p. 4; *KPSS. Spravochnik* (Moscow, 1963), p. 193. A. Titov, "Borb'a kommunisticheskoi partii s trotskizmom v period diskussii 1923–24 gg," *Voprosy istorii KPSS*, no. 7 (1965), p. 50.

94. TsGA IPD, f. 7, op. 2, d. 1242, l. 8; f. 197, op. 1, d. 1141, l. 18.

95. *Trinadtsataia konferentsiia*, p. 201.

96. G. Zinov'ev, "O vuzovtsakh," *Iunyi kommunist*, no. 3 (1924); I. Stalin, "O partstroitel'stve", *Pod znamenem Kommunizma*, no. 1 (1924), pp. 104–10.

97. V. Ivanov, *Iz istorii bor'by partii protiv "levogo" opportunizma; Leningradskaia partiinaia organizatsiia v bor'be protiv trotskistko-zinovevskoii oppozitsii v 1925–1927 gg.* (Leningrad: Lenizdat, 1965), p. 54.

98. *Kommunisticheskaia Partiia Sovetskogo Soiuza v rezoliutsiiakh i resheniiakh s"ezdov, konferentsii i plenumov TsK*, 7th ed. (Moscow: Gosizdat, 1954), vol. 2, p. 511.

99. E. Troshchenko, "Vuzovskaia molodezh," in *Kakova zhe nasha molodezh* (Moscow, 1927), pp. 160–61.

100. TsGA IPD, f. 197, op. 1, d. 4b, l. 40.

101. *Itogi proverki chlenov i kandidatov RKP(b) neproizvodstvennykh iacheek* (Moscow, 1925), p. 5.

102. *Pravda*, March 27, 1924. *Sotsialisticheskii vestnik*, no. 11 (1924), pp. 8–14; A. Grebkov, "K proverke vuzovskikh i sovetskikh iacheek RKP(b)," *Student-proletarii* 1924, no. 5, p. 9.

103. TsGA IPD, f. 6, op. 1, d. 224, l. 173; *Sbornik materialov Leningradskogo komiteta RKP*, no. 8 (Leningrad, 1925), p. 74; TsGA IPD, f. 6, op. 1, d. 224, l. 173. Once the verification commissions had conducted their interviews, they forwarded students' personal files, Party cards, and protocols to the Leningrad Party Control Commission, a body that had been recently strengthened and better staffed. Kuibyshev, Sol'ts's replacement as the chairman of the Central Control Commission, noted its enormous contribution to "stamping out disagreements that undermine Party unity." *Dvenadtsatyi s"ezd RKP(b)*, p. 248; Kuibyshev, "Pervyi god raboty," *Voprosy sovetskogo khoziaistva i upravleniia*, April–May, 1924, p. 4; *Trinadtsataia konferentsiia*, p. 196.

104. *Pravda*, April 30, 1924.

105. N. Babenkova, "Ukreplenie partiacheek vuzov v pervyi period nepa," in *Studentchestvo v obshchestvenno-politicheskoi zhizni* (Moscow, 1979), p. 64.

106. B. Bazhanov, *Vospominania byvshego sekretaria Stalina* (Paris, 1980), pp. 33–34.

107. The commissar of education, Lunacharskii, described the purge in a private letter as the "extirpation of Party intelligentsia." "'. . . Sudorozhno tsepliaiutsia za ortodoksiiu . . .' Neizvestnoe pis'mo A. V. Lunacharskogo L. B. Krasinu," *Kommunist*, no. 12 (1991), p. 103.

108. TsGA IPD, f. 197, op. 1, d. 22, l. 3. TsGA IPD, f. 7, op. 2, d. 1242, l. 122.

109. This was not unusual for Communist universities. David-Fox, *Revolution of the Mind*, p. 149.

110. TsGA IPD, f. 197, op. 1, d. 12, l. 15.

111. TsGA IPD, f. 197, op. 1, d. 117, l. 37.

112. TsGA IPD, f. 197, op. 1, d. 117, l. 28.

113. TsGA IPD, f. 197, op. 1, d. 117, l. 30.

114. TsGA IPD, f. 197, op. 1, d. 115, l. 30.

115. *Dvenadtsatyi s"ezd RKP(b)*, p. 248.

116. *Itogi proverki*, pp. 123–39.

117. TsGA IPD, f. 197, op. 1, d. 119, l. 65.

118. TsGA IPD, f. 197, op. 1, d. 117, l. 33.

119. *Trinadtsataia konferentsiia*, pp. 201–2.

120. TsGA IPD, f. 197, op. 1, d. 116, ll. 67–68.

121. TsGA IPD, f. 197, op. 1, d. 116, ll. 67–68.

122. TsGA IPD, f. 197, op. 1, d. 119, l. 65ob.

123. TsGA IPD, f. 197, op. 1, d. 119, l. 59.

124. TsGA IPD, f. 197, op. 1, d. 117, l. 33.

125. TsGA IPD, f. 258, op. 1, d. 111, l. 43

126. TsGA IPD, f. 197, op. 1, d. 116, l. 65.

127. TsGA IPD, f. 197, op. 1, d. 116, l. 75.

128. Every personal evaluation endorsed by more than three votes had to be carefully registered, and occasionally a struggle broke out over minority opinions. Lobanova, for example, refused to sign the protocol because the circle had failed to include her criticisms of Chelyshev, fearing they "might compromise this student." Following Lobanova's appeal to the university Party bureau, the actions of the circle's presidium were described as "inadmissible" and bordering on "fraud" (*shulerstvo*). Eventually her minority opinion found its way to the table of the control commission. TsGA IPD, f. 197, op. 1, d. 12, l. 180b.

129. *Itogi proverki*, p. 30.

130. TsGA IPD, f. 197, op. 1, d. 117, l. 33.

131. TsGA IPD, f. 197, op. 1, d. 117.

132. TsGA IPD, f. 197, op. 1, d. 115, l. 22.

133. TsGA IPD, f. 197, op. 1, d. 116, ll. 77–78.

134. TsGA IPD, f. 197, op. 1, d. 116, l. 74.

135. TsGA IPD, f. 197, op. 1, d. 116, l. 75.

136. TsGA IPD, f. 197, op. 1, d. 116, ll. 83–84; TsGA IPD, op. 1, d. 117, ll. 760b–77.

137. TsGA IPD, f. 197, op. 1, d. 117, ll. 33–35.

138. TsGA IPD, f. 197, op. 1, d. 119, ll. 16–20.

139. TsGA IPD, f. 197, op. 1, d. 120, l. 4.

140. TsGA IPD, f. 197, op. 1, d. 119, l. 15.

141. TsGA IPD, f. 197, op. 1, d. 120, l. 4.

142. TsGA IPD, f. 197, op. 1, d. 119, ll. 880b-197.

143. TsGA IPD, f. 197, op. 1, d. 119, ll. 95, 97.

144. TsGA IPD, f. 197, op. 1, d. 120, l. 1280b.

145. TsGA IPD, f. 197, op. 1, d. 116, l. 72.

146. TsGA IPD, f. 197, op. 1, d. 116, l. 65.

147. TsGA IPD, f. 197, op. 1, d. 119, ll. 16–20.

148. TsGA IPD, f. 197, op. 1, d. 115, ll. 17–18.

149. TsGA IPD, f. 197, op. 1, d. 116, l. 75.

150. K. Geigner, *The Family in Soviet Russia* (Cambridge, Mass.: Harvard University Press, 1968), p. 63.

151. TsGA IPD, f. 197, op. 1, d. 117, l. 730b.

152. TsGA IPD, f. 197, op. 1, d. 116, l. 72.

153. TsGA IPD, f. 197, op. 1, d. 116, l. 70.

154. TsGA IPD, f. 197, op. 1, d. 116, l. 77.

155. TsGA IPD, f. 197, op. 1, d. 117, ll. 26–29.

156. G. Zinoviev, *Bol'shevizm ili trotskizm?* (Leningrad: Proletarii, 1925), p. 54.

157. TsGA IPD, f. 197, op. 1, d. 116, l. 730b.

158. TsGA IPD, f. 197, op. 1, d. 117, ll. 30–300b.

159. TsGA IPD f. 197, op. 1, d. 115, ll. 112–13.

160. The term used was petit bourgeois "enveloping" (*obvolakivanie*) and loss of Party spirit. *Leningradskaia pravda*, December 4, 1923. Another description was students "philistine deviation" (*meshchanskii uklon*), TsGA IPD, f. 258, op. 1, d. 42, l. 31.

161. TsGAODM, f. 88, op. 1, d. 169, l. 123.

162. TsGA IPD, f. 197, op. 1, d. 22, ll. 4–5.

163. TsGA IPD, f. 197, op. 1, d. 119, l. 65.

164. TsGA IPD, f. 197, op. 1, d. 115, l. 21.

165. TsGA IPD, f. K-601, op. 1a, d. 735, ll. 1–15.

166. TsGA IPD, f. 197, op. 1, d. 115, ll. 22–24, 119.

167. TsGA IPD, f. 197, op. 1, d. 115, l. 14.

168. TsGA IPD, f. 197, op. 1, d. 115, l. 16.

169. TsGA IPD, f. 197, op. 1, d. 115, ll. 14–15.

170. TsGAODM f. 1660, op. 1, d. 58, l. 5.

171. *Leningradskaia pravda*, December 4, 1923.

172. TsGA IPD, f. 197, op. 1, d. 116, ll. 77–78.

173. TsGA IPD, f. 197, op. 1, d. 115, ll. 23–24.

174. R. Williams, *The Other Bolsheviks: Lenin and His Critics, 1904–1914* (Bloomington: Indiana University Press, 1986), pp. 127–31; Z. Sochor, *Revolution and Culture: The Bogdanov-Lenin Controversy* (Ithaca: Cornell University Press, 1988); J. Biggart, "Alexander Bogdanov and the Theory of a 'New Class,'" *Russian Review* 49 (1990).

175. TsGA IPD, f. 197, op. 1, d. 13, l. 2

176. TsGA IPD, f. 197, op. 1, d. 13, ll. 2–3.

177. TsGA IPD, f. 197, op. 1, d. 725, ll. 166–67.

178. TsGA IPD, f. 197, op. 1, d. 725, ll. 167–69.

179. TsGA IPD, f. 197, op. 1, d. 725, l. 167.

180. TsGA IPD, f. 197, op. 1, d. 725, l. 169.

181. A. Udal'tsov, "K kritike teorii klassov A. A. Bogdanova," *Pod znamenem marksizma*, no. 7–8 (1922).

182. TsGA IPD, f. 197, op. 1, d. 725, l. 169.

183. E. Iaroslavskii, *Za edinstvo VKP(b)* (Moscow-Leningrad, 1927), p. 66.

184. Ibid., p. 65.

185. TsGA IPD, f. 197, op. 1, d. 725, ll. 167, 169.

186. TsGA IPD, f. 197, op. 1, d. 725, l. 169.

187. TsGA IPD, f. 197, op. 1, d. 725, l. 171.

188. TsGA IPD, f. 197, op. 1, d. 725, ll. 166–70.

189. TsGA IPD, f. 197, op. 1, d. 725, ll. 157–68.

190. TsGA IPD, f. 197, op. 1, d. 115, l. 16.

191. TsGA IPD, f. 197, op. 1, d. 117, l. 27.

192. TsGA IPD, f. 197, op. 1, d. 725, ll. 157–62.

193. TsGA IPD, f. 197, op. 1, d. 725, l. 159.

194. TsGA IPD, f. 197, op. 1, d. 725, l. 137.

195. TsGA IPD, f. 197, op. 1, d. 725, ll. 160–61.

196. TsGA IPD, f. 197, op. 1, d. 725, l. 137.

197. TsGA IPD, f. 197, op. 1, d. 725, l. 160.

198. TsGA IPD, f. 197, op. 1, d. 725, ll. 160–63.

199. *Trinadtsatyi s"ezd RKP(b)*, p. 193.

200. *Tinadstatyi s"ezd, RKP(b)*, p. 223.

201. L. Trotsky, *K istorii Russkoi revoliutsii* (Moscow, 1990), pp. 184–85.

202. K. Kirkizh, *Komsomol ili trotskizm* (Moscow, 1925), p. 32.

203. TsGAODM, f. 88, op. 1, d. 170, l. 106ob. *Izvestiia Sibbiuro TsK RKP(b)*, no. 67–68, p. 9. Service, *Bolshevik Party*, p. 192.

204. PANO, f. 1, op. 2, d. 353, ll. 33–34.

205. TsGA IPD, f. 984, op. 1, d. 244, l. 21.

Chapter 4: The Emergence of "Trotskyism" and "Zinovievism"

1. TsGAODM, f. 3, op. 6, d. 2, l. 57.

2. R. Tucker, *Stalin as Revolutionary, 1879–1929* (New York: Norton, 1973), p. 342.

3. L. Trotsky, *The Lessons of October* (New York: Pioneer Publishers, 1937), pp. 37, 52.

4. G. Zinoviev, *Bol'shevizm ili trotskizm?* (Leningrad: Proletarii, 1925), pp. 46–47.

5. *Doloi fraktsioznost'! Otvet TsK Partii tov. trotskomu* (Moscow: Glavpolitprosvet, 1924), p. 17.

6. *Za leninizm: Sbornik statei* (Moscow-Leningrad: Gosizdat, 1925), p. 93.

7. R. Daniels, *The Conscience of the Revolution: Communist Opposition in Soviet Russia* (Cambridge, Mass.: Harvard University Press, 1960), p. 243.

8. Tucker, *Stalin as Revolutionary*, p. 345.

9. L. Trotsky, *The Stalin School of Falsification* (New York: Pioneer Publishers, 1962), pp. 89–97.

10. *Izvestiia TsK RKP(b)* 1925, no. 1, pp. 2–3.

11. *Kommunist* 1988, no. 6, pp. 3–5; See also Stalin, *Sochineniia*, vol. 6, p. 357.

12. B. Kun, "Ideologicheskie osnovy trotskizma," *Kommunisticheskii internatsional* 1925, no. 1, p. 14; I. Variekis, *Vnutrpartiinye raznoglasiia: Otnoshenie partii k trotskizmu* (Moscow-Leningrad, 1925). The expression "Comrades Trotskyists" was used at the Tenth Party Congress. A. Potashev, *V. I. Lenin i L. D. Trotskii: Uroki ideinoi borb'y vnutri praviashchei partii* (Rostov-on-Don, 1992), p. 8. For the phrase "variety of Bolshevism" see Ia. Diman, *Partiia i oppozitsiia (trotskizm)* (Irkutsk, 1926), p. 8. For "variety of Menshevism" see Zinoviev, *Bol'shevizm ili trotskizm?* p. 35.

13. For references to Trotsky's criticism of Lenin's "apparatchina" see *Trotskii o Lenine i leninizme* (Moscow, 1926), pp. 57–88; Lenin's contemporary rebuttals were collected in *Lenin o Trotskom i trotskizme* (Moscow, 1925).

14. E. Iaroslavskii, "U istokov Men'shevizma," *L. D. Trotskii o partii v 1904 godu* (Moscow-Leningrad, 1928), pp. 15–16. For Lenin's harsh characterizations of Trotsky see also I. Nosov, *O trotskom i trotskizme* (Simferopol', 1924); E. Kviring, *Trotskizm—smes' levoi frazy s prakticheskim opportunizmom* (Artemovsk, 1924).

15. *Za leninizm*, pp. 103–4; "Trotskizm ili leninizm," in Stalin, *Sochineniia*, vol. 6 (Moscow, 1947), pp. 324–57.

16. *The Trotsky Papers, 1917–1922*, ed. J. Meijer (The Hague: Mouton, 1971), vol. 2, p. 642.

17. *Za leninizm*, p. 240. PATO, f. 1, op. 1, d. 128, l. 52.

18. Zinoviev, *Bol'shevizm ili trotskizm?* pp. 3, 35; L. Kamenev, "Leninizm ili trotskizm," *Pod leninskim znamenem*, no. 3 (1924), p. 37.

19. N. Bukharin, "Teoriia permanentnoi revoliutsii," *Za leninizm*, pp. 367, 372.

20. B. Babakhan, *Leninizm i trotskizm* (Kazan', 1925), p. 77. For additional denunications of Trotskyism, old and new, see N. Bukharin, *K voprosu o trotskizme* (Moscow, 1925); I. Stalin, *O trotskizme* (Moscow, 1925); G. Zinoviev and L. Kamenev, *O trotskizme* (Moscow, 1925); V. Sorin, *Uchenie Lenina o partii (Organizatsionnye osnovy bol'shevizma)* (Moscow, 1925).

21. *Sovetskaia sibir'*, December 13, 1924; *Krasnoe znamia*, December 14, 1924.

22. *Za leninizm*, pp. 102–6. *Rabochii put'*, January 16, 1925; *Sovetskaia sibir'*, January 20, 1925; For the paucity of facts in Stalin's charges against Trotsky see I. Struev, *Teoriia permanentnoi revoliutsii tov. Trotskogo* (Rostov-on-Don, 1925), pp. 40–41.

23. L. Trotsky, *The New Course*, trans. and ed. Max Shachtman (New York: New International, 1943), p. 52. Zinoviev, *Bol'shevizm ili Trotskizm?* p. 108.

24. I. Vareikis, *Vnutrepartiinye raznoglasiia: Otnoshenie partii i Trotskizma* (Moscow-Leningard: Gosizdat, 1925), p. 56; *Leninskoe i trotskistkoe ponimanie dvizhushchikh sil Russkoi revoliutsii* (Leningrad: Priboi, 1925), p. 28.

25. L. Schapiro, *The Communist Party of the Soviet Union* (New York: Random House, 1959), pp. 288–89.

26. Stalin, *Sochineniia*, vol. 6, p. 357.

27. Babakhan, *Leninizm i trotskizm*, p. 78.

28. L. Kamenev, "Leninizm ili trotskizm," *Pod Leninskim znamenem*, no. 3 (1924), p. 34.

29. Vareikis, *Vnutrepartiinye raznoglasiia*, p. 22.

30. L. Trotsky, *Moia zhizn'* (Moscow, 1990), vol. 2, p. 256.

31. Vareikis, *Vnutrepartiinye raznoglasiia*, p. 101.

32. *Arkhiv Trotskogo: Kommunisticheskaia oppozitsiia v SSSR, 1923–1927*, ed. Iu. Fel'shinskii (Moscow: Terra, 1990), vol. 1, p. 100.

33. *Arkhiv Trotskogo*, vol. 1, p. 116.

34. Vareikis, *Vnutrepartiinye raznoglasiia*, p. 19.

35. V. Molotov, *Ob urokakh Trotskizma* (Moscow-Leningrad: Gosizdat, 1925), p. 35.

36. *Leninizm ili trotskizm* (Iaroslavl', 1925), p. 6.

37. Sarkis, *Eshche ob odnom svoistve trotskizma* (Leningrad: Priboi, 1925), pp. 3–4.

38. See Kamenev's introduction to *Leninskii sbornik*, vol. 6 (1927).

39. Babakhan, *Leninizm i trotskizm*, p. 10.

40. *Za leninizm*, pp. 28–30, 60–62.

41. *Arkhiv Trotskogo*, vol. 1, pp. 115–16.

42. Vareikis, *Vnutrepartiinye raznoglasiia*, p. 21.

43. *Za leninizm*, pp. 102–6.

44. *Voprosy prepodavaniia leninizma, istorii VKP(b) i Kominterna* (Moscow, 1930), p. 231.

45. L. Kamenev, "Leninizm ili trotskizm," *Pod Leninskim znamenem*, no. 3 (1924), pp. 24, 34. *Rabochii put'*, January 10, 1924.

46. S. Gonikman, *Desiat' let: Ocherk istorii trotskizma v VKP(b)* (Khar'kov, 1928), pp. 4, 16. Trotsky was said to resemble Sukhanov, a prominent Menshevik. A. Shlikhter, *Na platforme sotsial-demokraticheskogo uklona* (Moscow-Leningard, 1927), p. 84.

47. K. Kirkizh, *Komsomol i trotskizm* (Khar'kov, 1925), p. 4

48. P. Zalutskii, *O sovremennom trotskizme* (Leningrad, Priboi, 1925), p. 31.

49. S. Kanatchikov, *Istoriia odnogo uklona* (Leningrad, 1924), p. 4.

50. Babakhan, *Leninizm i trotskizm*, p. 74.

51. Babakhan, *Leninizm i trotskizm*, p. 73.

52. F. Goloshchekin, *Protiv trotskizma* (n.p., 1925), p. 25. See also E. Kviring, *O literaturnoi polemike s tov: Trotskim* (Ekaterinoslav, 1924), p. 9.

53. G. Evdokimov, *V zashchitu partii* (Leningad: Priboi, 1924), p. 47.

54. Babakhan, *Leninizm i trotskizm*, p. 73.

55. Vareikis, *Vnutrepartiinye raznoglasiia*, p. 18.

56. I. Stalin, "Trotskizm ili leninizm," *Za leninizm*, p. 108.

57. *Doloi fraktioznost'!* (Moscow: Glavpolitprosvet, 1924), p. 6; "factionalist imagination," Zinoviev, *Bol'shevizm ili trotskizm?*, pp. 48–49.

58. Vareikis, *Vnutrepartiinye raznoglasiia*, p. 89.

59. Zinoviev, *Bol'shevizm ili trotskizm?* p. 54.

60. Babakhan, *Leninizm i trotskizm*, p. 78.

61. Vareikis, *Vnutrepartiinye raznoglasiia*, p. 22.

62. N. Bukharin, *K voprosu o trotskizme* (Moscow-Leningrad: Gosizdat, 1925), p. 8.

63. Ia. Diman, *Partiia i oppozitsiia (trotskizm)* (Irkutsk: Izdanie provinstial'nogo Partiinogo kommitteta VKP[b], 1926), pp. 61, 66.

64. G. Evdokimov, *V zashchitu partii* (Leningad: Priboi, 1924), p. 3.

65. G. Safarov, *Kommunisticheskaia partiia pri diktature proletariata* (Leningrad, 1925), p. 31.

66. Sarkis, *Eshche ob odnom svoistve trotskizma*, pp. 11–12.

67. Ibid.

68. Consider the balancing act performed by Zinoviev in treating the issue of Party seniority in his memoir from April 1933. Writing about "my life before I met V[ladimir] I[lich Lenin]," Zinoviev attributed to the founder of Bolshevism a decisive influence on his life. Mentioning Lenin by name and patronymic he alluded to their former closeness, thus reminding the Party that he, Zinoviev, is one of its co-founders. At the same time, Zinoviev refrained from speaking in terms of the "Leninist period," or about "Leninism," although he had authored books and articles with those terms in the title in the past and though the terms were in wide use at the time of writing. Instead, he wrote about "Stalin's period" (*Stalinskii period*) lest anyone suspect he did not acknowledge Stalin's individual seniority to him. Zinoviev had made a number of political lapses and thus had to start his Bolshevik life story from scratch, whereas Stalin's life, a life of absolute steadiness and purposefulness, was the name of an epoch. *Izvestiia TsK KPSS*, 1989, vol. 7, p. 177.

69. Daniels, *Conscience of the Revolution*, p. 247; Zinoviev, *Bol'shevizm ili trotskizm?* p. 15.

70. *Biulleten' XXI konferentsii Leningradskoi organizatsii VKP(b)*, no. 1, 1925 (Leningrad: Priboi, 1925), p. 11. What attitude the Party should take towards Trotsky was discussed in A. Stachinskii, *Politgramota*, 5th ed. (Moscow-Leningrad, 1925), p. 230; S. Shul'man (ed.), *Put' Bol'shevizma: Posobie dlia samoobrazovaniia nizovogo partiinogo i komsomol'skogo aktiva* (Moscow-Leningrad, 1926), pp. 253–75.

71. Stalin, *Sochineniia*, vol. 7, pp. 379–80.

72. RGASPI, f. 17, op. 2, d. 209, l. 5.

73. Babakhan, *Leninizm i trotskizm*, p. 89.

74. L. Kamenev, "Leninizm ili trotskizm," *Pod Leninskim znamenem*, no. 3 (1924), p. 41.

75. *Arkhiv Trotskogo*, vol. 1, pp. 172–73.

76. Vareikis, *Vnutrepartiinye raznoglasiia*, p. 21.

77. RGASPI, f. 89, op. 8, d. 442, l. 13.; TsGAODM, f. 478, op. 1, d. 10, l. 52. *Leningrad-skaia pravda*, November 21 and 28, 1924. Mnukhin, "Beglye vospominaniia. K 10-letiiu Sverdlovii", *X Let. 1918–1928: Kommunisticheskii universitet imeni Ia. M. Sverdlova* (Moscow, 1928), p. 323. In the summer of 1924, an informal "seven" (*semerka*)—Bukharin, Zinoviev, Kamenev, Rykov, Stalin, Tomskii, and Kuibyshev—was formed within the Politburo. This forum held preliminary deliberations and only then raised the issues in Trotsky's attendance. V. Nadtocheev, "'Triumvirat' ili 'Semerka'? Iz istorii vnutrepartiinoi bor'by v 1924–25 godakh," *Trudnye voprosy istorii. Poiski. Razmyshleniia. Novyi vzgliad n sobytiia I fakty*, ed. V. V. Zhuravlev (Moscow, 1991), pp. 68–70.

78. RGASPI, f. 89, op. 8, d. 442, l. 13.; TsGAODM, f. 478, op. 1, d. 10, l. 52.

79. *Sbornik materialov Leningradskogo komiteta RKP(b)*, vyp. 8, p. 92; TsGA IPD, f. 138, op. 1, d. 2, l. 1; S. Bliumental', "Chto dali perevybory biuro kollektivov?" *Pod znamemen kommunizma*, no. 1 (1924), p. 177; *Sbornik materialov Leningradskogo komiteta RKP*, vyp. 7 (Leningrad, 1924), pp. 102, 247, 229; *Sbornik materialov Leningradskogo komiteta RKP*, vyp. 8 (Leningrad, 1925), p. 29.

80. TsGA IPD, f. 16, op. 1, d. 5707, l. 6. TsGA IPD, f. 984, op. 1, d. 120, l. 8; "Chistka i leninskii prizyv," *Oktiabr' mysli* 1924, no. 3–4, p. 77.

81. TsGA IPD, f. 258, op. 1, d. 42, l. 54.

82. TsGA IPD, f. 16, op. 9, d. 9670, ll. 3–4.

83. TsGA IPD, f. 197, op. 1, d. 725, l. 173.

84. TsGA IPD, f. 197, op. 1, d. 725, l. 165; op. 1, d. 12, l. 6.

85. TsGA IPD, f. 197, op. 1, d. 725, l. 175.

86. *Krasnaia gazeta*, December 21, 1924.

87. V. Serge, *Memoirs of a Revolutionary, 1901–1941* (Oxford, 1951), p. 218.

88. "Studenchestvo v Leningrade," *Sotsialisticheskii vestnik*, no. 1 (1925), p. 14.

89. *Arkhiv Trotskogo*, vol. 3, p. 178.

90. Several histories of the "new opposition" appeared soon after the events, e.g., V. Tomskii, *Partiia i oppozitsiia* (Moscow, 1926); N. Bukharin, *K itogam diskussii* (Moscow, 1926); G. Zinoviev, *Nashi raznoglasiia* (Moscow, 1926); G. Safarov, "Kak bylo delo," in *Novaia oppozitsiia: Sbornik materialov o diskussii 1925 goda* (Leningrad: Priboi, 1926).

91. TsGAODM, f. 3, op. 6, d. 2, ll. 100–101.

92. *Chetyrnadtsatyi s"ezd VKP(b): Stenograficheskii otchet* (Moscow: Gosizdat, 1926), p. 44 (Stalin); Daniels, *Conscience of the Revolution*, pp. 258–59 (Molotov).

93. For Zinoviev's position see *Itogi XIV vsesoiuznoi partkonferentsii i II s"ezda sovetov SSSR* (Moscow: Moskovskii rabochii, 1925), pp. 1–12, as well as his *Leninizm i NEP* (Leningrad, 1926), p. 63. For Safarov's position see his "Vynuzhdennye zametki o goskapitalizme i pessimizme," *Leningradskaia pravda*, December 8, 1925; and Safarov, *Leninizm kak teoriia razvitiia proletarskoi revoliutsii* (Leningrad: Priboi, 1925), p. 12. Also very important in this connection was P. Zalutskii, *Zvenovye organizatory i ikh zadachi* (Moscow, 1926), p. 7.

94. For the early critiques of socialism in one country see G. Zinoviev, *Leninizm* (Moscow, 1926), pp. 322–23, as well as his *Nashi raznoglasiia* (Moscow, 1926), pp. 54–56. For the Central Committee rebuttal see I. Stalin, *Voprosy i otvety* (Moscow, 1925), pp. 10–12, 36–44; I. Stalin, *Voprosy leninizma* (Moscow, 1926), pp. 45–68; and N. Bukharin, *Put' k sotsializmu i roboche-krest'ianskii soiuz* (Moscow, 1925), N. Bukharin, *K itogam diskussii* (Moscow, 1926), pp. 30–32, 76–77. Zinoviev's alleged belief that the Soviet Union cannot overcome its economic backwardness was criticized in I. Zhirov, "V chem partiia usmotrela 'likvidatorskoe' bezverie v sotsialisticheskie puti nashego razvitiia," *Bol'shevik*, no. 1 (1926).

95. A. Zinoviev, *Filosofiia epokhi* (Leningrad, 1925), p. 12. For the importance of the struggle against bureaucracy see L. Kamenev, *Nashi dostizheniia, trudnosti i perespektivy* (Moscow, 1925), pp. 36–42; G. Zinoviev, *Polosa velikogo stroitel'stva* (Moscow, 1926). *Deviat' mesiatsev partiinogo stroitel'stva: Otchet raikoma Moskovsko-Narvskogo raiona Leningradskoi organizatsii RKP(b)* (Leningrad, 1925), pp. 3–4. See also G. Zinoviev, *Leninizm: Vvedenie v izuchenie leninizma* (Leningrad, 1925), pp. 260–72.

96. Daniels, *Conscience of the Revolution*, pp. 254–55.

97. For the debate on the regulation of the social growth of the Party, see Sarkis, *Shag*

vpered, dva shaga nazad (Moscow, 1926). The Central Committee majority responded with *Za liniiu partii* (Moscow, 1926); E. Smittern, "K itogam regulirovaniia rosta partii," *Bol'shevik*, no. 12, 1926.

98. *Bol'shevistskoe rukovodstvo: Perepiska 1912–1927*, ed. A. V. Kvashonkin et al. (Moscow: ROSSPEN, 1996), pp. 309–10.

99. N. Mandel'shtam, *Edinstvennaia i absoliutno edinaia partiia* (Moscow-Leningrad: Moskovskii rabochii, 1926), p. 12.

100. M. Tomskii, *Partiia i oppozitsiia* (Leningrad, 1926), p. 6.

101. Vareikis, *Vnutrepartiinye raznoglasiia*, p. 5; K. Bauman, *Osnovnye voprosy raznoglasii i resheniia XIV s"ezda* (Moscow-Leningrad, 1926), p. 5.

102. Daniels, *Conscience of the Revolution*, p. 255.

103. L. Shapiro, *The Communist Party of the Soviet Union* (New York: Random House, 1960), pp. 291–92.

104. *Leningradskaia pravda*, December 8, 1925.

105. *Stenograficheskii otchet XXII konferentsii Leningradskoi gubernskoi organizatsii RKP(b)*, Biulleten' no. 1, pp. 14, 18. The new opposition has been warning against the kulak danger since mid-1925, Iu. Larin, *Rost krest'ianskoi obshchestvennosti i ee ocherednye zadachi* (Moscow, 1925). The disbelief in the peasant as an ally of the worker was defined by Stalin as a "departure from Leninism," I. Stalin, *Voprosy leninizma*, pp. 115–26. Bukharin also called to preserve the worker-peasant alliance in N. Bukharin, *Put' k sotsializmu i raboche-krest'ianskii blok* (Moscow, 1925). The position of the Central Committee was also defended in the authoritative V. Molotov, *Politika partii v derevne* (Moscow, 1926); and Rykov, *Novaia obstanovka i zadacha partii* (Moscow, 1926), pp. 42–50.

106. *Piatnadtsatyi s"ezd VKP(b)*, p. 317; *Sovetskoe rukovodstvo: Perepiska; 1928–1941* (Moscow: ROSSPEN, 1999), p. 476.

107. TsGAODM f. 3, op. 44, d. 362, l. 1900b.

108. *Novaia oppozitsiia: Sbornik materialov o diskussii 1925 goda* (Leningrad: Priboi, 1926), p. 39.

109. *Pravda*, December 8, 1925.

110. *Leningradskaia pravda*, December 29, 1925.

111. *Leningradskaia pravda*, December 11, 1925.

112. *Novaia oppozitsiia*, pp. 46–47.

113. *Novaia oppozitsiia*, p. 66.

114. *Novaia oppozitsiia*, p. 52. *Krasnoe znamia*, December 20, 1925.

115. *Novaia oppozitsiia*, pp. 64, 34.

116. *Leningradskii kommunisticheskii universitet: Tri goda leninskoi ucheby, 1924–1927* (Leningrad, 1927), p. 19; *Leningradskaia pravda*, December 2, 1925; TsGA IPD, f. 197, op. 1, d. 725, l. 56.

117. RGASPI, f. 17, op. 2, d. 209, l. 6.

118. G. Bykov, "Piatnatstat' let kuznitsy bol'shevitskikh kadrov," *XV let Vsesoiuznogo Kommunisticheskogo sel'sko-khoziaistvennogo universiteta imeni I. V. Stalina* (Leningrad, 1933), pp. 45–46.

119. *Leningradskaia pravda*, December 11, 1925.

120. TsGA IPD, f. 197, op. 1, d. 725, l. 56.

121. TsGA IPD, f. 7, op. 1, d. 1898, l. 1.

122. *Leningradskaia pravda*, December 29, 1925; *Chetyrnadtsatyi s"ezd VKP(b)*, p. 503.

123. TsGA IPD, f. 7, op. 1, d. 1898, l. 1.

124. TsGA IPD, f. 7, op. 1, d. 1898, l. 3.

125. *Novaia oppozitsiia*, pp. 53, 79.

126. V. Ivanov, *Iz istorii bor'by partii protiv "levogo" opportunizma: Leningradskaia partiinaia organizatsiia v bor'be protiv trotskistko-zinovevskoii oppozitsii v 1925–1927 gg.* (Leningrad: Lenizdat, 1965), p. 101.

127. TsGAODM, f. 3, op. 44, d. 362, l. 191.

128. *Chetyrnadtsatyi s"ezd VKP(b)*, p. 949. Ivanov, *Iz istorii bor'by partii*, p. 115.

129. *Chetyrnadtsatyi s"ezd VKP(b)*, p. 7–8, Ivanov, *Iz istorii bor'by partii*, p. 104.

130. A. Kirilina, *Neizvestnyi Kirov* (Saint Petersburg: Izdatel'skii dom "Neva"; Moscow: Izd-vo "OLMA-PRESS," 2001), p. 102.

131. *Chetyrnadtsatyi s"ezd VKP(b)*, pp. 98, 109, 111, 430.

132. *Chetyrnadtsatyi s"ezd VKP(b)*, pp. 274–75.

133. *Chetyrnadtsatyi s"ezd VKP(b)*, pp. 504–8.

134. *Chetyrnadtsatyi s"ezd VKP(b)*, pp. 301–2. For the debate on Party democracy in connection with the 1925 discussion see N. Mandel'shtam, *Edinstvennaia i absoliutno edinaia partiia* (Moscow, 1926); M. Riutin, *Edinstvo partii i distsiplina* (Moscow, 1926); V. Astrov, "Pod otkos—k burzhuaznoi demokratii," in, *O pravoii opasnosti v nashei partii* (Moscow, 1926); Boreva, "O svobode fraktsii i gruppirovok," *Sputnik agitatora* 1926, no. 14–15; Mal'tsev, "Za edinstvo, za distsiplinu," *Sputnik agitatora* 1926, no. 16; Lavrentev, "Edinstvennaia, edinaia partiia," *Sputnik agitatora* 1926, no. 16.

135. *Chetyrnadtsatyi s"ezd VKP(b)*, pp. 523–24, 949.

136. *Chetyrnadtsatyi s"ezd VKP(b)*, pp. 531, 622.

137. *Novaia oppozitsiia*, p. 291.

138. Kirilina, *Neizvestnyi Kirov*, p. 100.

139. *Novaia oppozitsiia*, p. 4.

140. *Novaia oppozitsiia*, p. 10. E. Carr, *Socialism in One Country, 1924–1926* (New York: Macmillan, 1961), vol. 2, pp. 112–13.

141. M. Tomskii, *Partiia i oppozitsiia* (Leningrad, 1926), p. 9.

142. *Pravda*, December 31, 1925.

143. *Leningradskaia pravda*, December 9, 1925.

144. *Novaia oppozitsiia*, p. 339.

145. TsGA IPD, f. 16, op. 1, d. 157, ll. 88, 92.

146. Ivanov, *Iz istorii bor'by partii*, p. 117.

147. TsGAODM, f. 3., op. 8, d. 92, l. 100b.

148. TsGA IPD, f. 408, op. 1, d. 1175, ll. 82–83, 86.

149. TsGA IPD, f. 9, op. 1, d. 139, ll. 48–50.

150. TsGA IPD, f. 16, op. 1, d. 167, l. 25. TsGA IPD, f. 3, op. 1, d. 847, l. 114. Ivanov, *Iz istorii bor'by partii*, p. 122.

151. TsGA IPD, f. 16, op. 1, d. 7193, ll. 4–8; d. 7239, l. 230.

152. TsGA IPD, f. 16, op. 1, d. 157, ll. 90–92. V. Suzdal'tseva, "Bor'ba s Zinovievtsami i Trotskistami v Leningrade, 1925–27," *Klassovaia bor'ba*, no. 9 (1936), p. 18.

153. TsGA IPD, f. 7, op. 1, d. 163, l. 20.

154. The support for Zinoviev's leadership was never watertight even in Leningrad. The Tolmachev Military-Political Academy and the Military-Naval Academy were the first Party organizations to criticize the conduct of the Leningrad organization (December 20).

On December 21, the plenary session of the Vyborg district, the only one to take issue with the local potentates, criticized Leningrad's stance at the Congress. Ivanov, *Iz istorii bor'by partii*, p. 120.

155. Ivanov, *Iz istorii bor'by partii*, pp. 135–36.

156. Ibid., pp. 128–29.

157. TsGA IPD, f. 4000, op. 5, d. 3144, l. 5.

158. TsGA IPD, f. 9, op. 1, d. 1145, l. 149.

159. Ivanov, *Iz istorii bor'by partii*, p. 163.

160. "Vokrug s"ezda RKP (pis'mo iz Moskvy), *Sotsialisticheskii vestnik*, January 16, 1926.

161. *Chetyrnadtsatyi s"ezd VKP(b)*, pp. 242, 297.

162. Ivanov, *Iz istorii bor'by partii*, pp. 125–26.

163. TsGA IPD, f. 408, op. 1, d. 1175, ll. 67–68.

164. TsGA IPD, f. 408, op. 1, d. 1175, l. 86.

165. RGASPI, f. 17, op. 60, d. 745, ll. 110–11, cited after P. Konecny, *Builders and Deserters: Students, State and Community in Leningrad, 1917–1941* (Ithaca: McGill-Queen's University Press), pp. 108–9.

166. *Leningradskaia pravda*, December 28, 1925.

167. I. Skvortsov-Stepanov, *Izbrannye proizvedeniia*, 2 (1931), p. 329; F. Dzerzhinskii, *Izbrannye proizvedeniia*, 2 (1957), pp. 235–36; *Chetyrnadtsatyi s"ezd VKP(b)*, pp. 711–12.

168. *Leningradskaia organizatsiia i chetyrnadtsatyi s"ezd* (Moscow-Leningrad: Gosizdat, 1926), pp. 29–31. *Leningradskaia pravda*, December 30, 1925.

169. Kirilina, *Neizvestnyi Kirov*, p. 108.

170. RGASPI, f. 613, op. 3, d. 161, l. 3. TsGA IPD, f. 9, op. 1, d. 127, l. 1; f. 16, op. 1, d. 161a, l. 54.

171. Kirilina, *Neizvestnyi Kirov*, p. 110.

172. *Leningradskaia pravda*, December 31, 1925.

173. RGASPI, f. 613, op. 3, d. 161, l. 5.

174. *Chetyrnadtsatyi s"ezd VKP(b)*, p. 935; Ivanov, *Iz istorii bor'by partii*, p. 138.

175. RGASPI, f. 613, op. 3, d. 161, l. 9.

176. Ivanov, *Iz istorii bor'by partii*, p. 138.

177. TsGA IPD, f. 7, op. 2, d. 1898, ll. 23–24.

178. TsGA IPD, f. 408, op. 1, d. 1477, l. 106.

179. Bykov, "Piatnatsat' let kuznitsy bol'shevitskikh kadrov," p. 46.

180. TsGA IPD, f. 197, op. 1, d. 205, l. 80.

181. TsGA IPD, f. 197, op. 1, d. 725, l. 57.

182. *Leningradskaia pravda*, December 31, 1925.

183. *Moskovskaia pravda*, December 31, 1925.

184. TsGA IPD, f. 408, op. 1, d. 1175, l. 78; TsGA IPD, f. 197, op. 1, d. 211, l. 16.

185. Bykov, "Piatnatstat' let kuznitsy bol'shevitskikh kadrov," pp. 46–47.

186. TsGA IPD, f. 197, op. 1, d. 725, l. 570b.

187. TsGA IPD, f. 197, op. 1, d. 725, l. 570b.

188. TsGA IPD, f. 197, op. 1, d. 208, l. 1.

189. TsGA IPD, f. 197, op. 1, d. 725, l. 57.

190. TsGA IPD, f. 197, op. 1, d. 725, ll. 27–28.

191. TsGA IPD, f. 197, op. 1, d. 1007, l. 12.

192. TsGA IPD, f. 197, op. 1, d. 725, l. 29.

193. TsGA IPD, f. 197, op. 1, d. 725, l. 32.

194. TsGA IPD, f. 197, op. 1, d. 725, l. 32; d. 207, ll. 3–4.

195. TsGA IPD, f. 197, op. 1, d. 725, l. 31.

196. TsGA IPD, f. 197, op. 1, d. 725, l. 30.

197. TsGA IPD, f. 197, op. 1, d. 725, ll. 30, 32.

198. TsGA IPD, f. 197, op. 1, d. 725, l. 34.

199. Ivanov, *Iz istorii bor'by partii*, pp. 150–51.

200. Ibid., p. 152.

201. RGASPI f. 17, op. 2, d. 209, ll. 3–4.

202. RGASPI, f. 558, op. 1, df. 2751, ll. 37–39., cited after Kirilina, *Neizvestnyi Kirov*, p. 111.

203. *Bol'shevitskoe rukovodstvo*, p. 316.

204. *Leningradskaia pravda*, January 8, 1926; *VII s"ezd vsesoiuznogo Leninskogo Kommunisticheskogo Soiuza Molodezhi* (1926), p. 69; A. Mil'chakov, *Pervoe desiatiletie* (Moscow: Molodaia Gvardiia, 1959), pp. 159–60.

205. Carr, *Socialism in One Country*, vol. 2, p. 159.

206. *Leningradskaia organizatsiia i chetyrnadtsatyi s"ezd*, pp. 35–36; TsGA IPD, f. 7, op. 1, d. 163, l. 230b. *Novaia oppozitsiia*, p. 323.

207. *Krasnaia gazeta*, January 9, 1926. TsGA IPD, f. 7, op. 2, d. 1898, l. 18.

208. TsGA IPD, f. 7, op. 1, d. 180, l. 2.

209. *Novaia oppozitsiia*, p. 274.

210. *Leningradskaia pravda*, January 21, 1926. TsGA IPD, f. 197, op. 1., d. 1007, ll. 91–99; d. 994, l. 114.

211. TsGA IPD, f. 9, op. 1, d. 139, l. 9.

212. Ivanov, *Iz istorii bor'by partii*, p. 166. On the notion of "working through" (*prorabatyvat'*) see M. David-Fox, *Revolution of the Mind: Higher Learning Among the Bolsheviks, 1918–1929* (Ithaca: Cornell University Press, 1997), p. 173; O. Kharhordin, *The Collective and the Individual in Russia. A Study of Practices* (Berkeley: University of California Press, 1999), pp. 242–48.

213. Kirilina, *Neizvestnyi Kirov*, pp. 111–12.

214. TsGA IPD, f. 16, op. 1, d. 167, ll. 9–10.

215. TsGA IPD, f. 9, op. 1, d. 1145, l. 189. TsGA IPD, f. 9, op. 1, d. 139, l. 2.

216. Kirilina, *Neizvestnyi Kirov*, p. 116.

217. Kirilina, *Neizvestnyi Kirov*, p. 115–16.

218. TsGA IPD, f. 16, op. 1, d. 167, ll. 67–69.

219. *Leningradskaia organizatsiia i chetyrnadtsatyi s"ezd*, p. 59.

220. Ivanov, *Iz istorii bor'by partii*, p. 167.

221. TsGA IPD, f. 9, op. 1, d. 139, l. 34. TsGA IPD, f. 16, op. 1, d. 618, l. 166. *Leningradskaia pravda*, January 9, 1926, Ivanov, *Iz istorii bor'by partii*, p. 179.

222. TsGA IPD, f. 16, op. 1, d. 624, l. 34.

223. *Leningradskaia pravda*, January 7, 1926; January 5, 1926.

224. TsGA IPD, f. 16, op. 7, d. 7244, ll. 76–80.

225. *Novaia oppozitsiia: Sbornik materialov o diskussii 1925 goda* (Leningrad: Priboi, 1926), p. 271.

226. The letter is from February 6, 1926. *Bol'shevitskoe rukovodstvo*, p. 320.

227. Ivanov, *Iz istorii bor'by partii*, p. 186.

228. Ibid., p. 188.

229. Ibid., p. 147.

230. TsGA IPD, f. 197, op. 1, d. 208, l. 2.

231. TsGA IPD, f. 197, op. 1, d. 211, l. 17.

232. TsGA IPD, f. 197, op. 1, d. 725, l. 570b.

233. TsGA IPD, f. 197, op. 1, d. 207, l. 10b.

234. TsGA IPD, f. 197, op. 1, d. 208, l. 4.

235. "Otchetnaia kampaniia v Leningrade o rabotakh XIV partiinogo s"ezda (Beseda s sekretarem TsK VKP[b] tov. Molotovym)," in *Novaia oppozitsiia*, pp. 271–74; N. Ruban, "Bor'ba partii protiv trotskistsko-zinovevskoi oppozitsii," *Voprosy istorii KPSS*, no. 5 (1958), pp. 125–28; Daniels, *Conscience of the Revolution*, p. 270.

236. TsGA IPD, f. 207, op. 1, l. 3.

237. TsGA IPD, f. 197, op. 1, d. 207, ll. 3–4.

238. TsGA IPD, f. 7, op. 1, d. 191, l. 270b.

239. TsGA IPD, f. 7, op. 1, d. 204, l. 1; op. 2, d. 1898, l. 23.

240. TsGA IPD, f. 197, op. 1, d. 207, l. 7.

241. TsGA IPD, f. 7, op. 1, d. 191, l. 270b.

242. TsGA IPD, f. 16, op. 7, d. 7244, l. 504.

243. TsGA IPD, f. 7, op. 1, d. 191, l. 3.

244. TsGA IPD, f. 7, op. 1, d. 191, l. 220b.

245. TsGA IPD, f. 7, op. 1, d. 191, l. 210b.

246. TsGA IPD, f. 7, op. 1, d. 138, l. 11.

247. TsGA IPD, f. 408, op. 1, d. 1175, ll. 79–80.

248. TsGA IPD, f. 408, op. 1, d. 174, ll. 6–7.

249. *Pravda*, January 19, 1926; S. Kirov, *Izbrannye stat'i i rechi, 1912–1934* (Moscow-Leningrad, 1939), p. 69; I. Skvortsov-Stepanov, *Izbrannye proizvedeniia*, 2 (Moscow-Leningrad, 1931), pp. 327, 335.

250. *Bol'shevitskoe rukovodstvo*, pp. 314–15.

251. *Bol'shevitskoe rukovodstvo*, p. 318.

252. RGASPI, f. 3, op. 1, d. 3260, l. 2, cited after Ivanov, *Iz istorii bor'by partii*, p. 190.

253. C. Black, "Party Crisis and the Factory Shop Floor: *Krasnyi Putilovets* and the Leningrad Opposition, 1925–26," *Europe-Asia Studies* 46, no. 1 (1994), p. 119.

254. *Pravda*, January 22, 1926.

255. TsGA IPD, f. 7, op. 1, d. 191, l. 270b.

256. Black, "Party Crisis and the Factory Shop Floor," p. 118.

257. Ivanov, *Iz istorii bor'by partii*, p. 160.

258. *Leningradskaia pravda*, January 17, 1926. Ivanov, *Iz istorii bor'by partii*, pp. 158–59.

259. *Sergei Mironovich Kirov: Vospominaniia Leningradskikh rabochikh*, pp. 19–20; Ivanov, *Iz istorii bor'by partii* p. 161. RGASPI, f. 3, op. 1, d. 5218, l. 1.

260. *Leningradskaia pravda*, January 21, 1926; *Sergei Mironovich Kirov: Vospominaniia Leningradskikh rabochikh*, pp. 22–23; *Arkhiv Trotskogo*, vol. 1, pp. 172–73. Ivanov, *Iz istorii bor'by partii*, p. 194.

261. TsGA IPD, f. 16, op. 1, d. 178, l. 59.

262. *Novaia oppozitsiia*, p. 327.

263. *Novaia oppozitsiia*, p. 275. *Leningradskaia pravda*, January 29, 1926.

264. *Novaia oppozitsiia*, p. 272. Only 3.6 percent voted for the opposition in the districts.

Leningradskaia organizatsiia i chetyrnadtsatyi s"ezd, p. 83. The Central District was praised: above 98 percent approved the report.

265. *Novaia oppozitsiia*, p. 273.

266. V. Molotov, *Za partiiu* (Moscow-Leningrad: Gosizdat, 1927), p. 19; M. Riutin, *Edinstvo partii i distsiplina* (Moscow-Leningrad: Rabochii, 1926), p. 5.

267. *Novaia oppozitsiia*, pp. 334–35.

268. TsGA IPD, f. 197, op. 1, d. 1132, l. 47.

269. *Novaia oppozitsiia*, pp. 338, 339–41.

270. *Leningradskaia organizatsiia i chetyrnadtsatyi s"ezd* (Moscow-Leningrad, 1926), p. 88.

271. Ibid., p. 109.

272. Ibid., p. 106.

273. Ibid., p. 107.

274. M. Riumina, *Estetika smekha: Smekh kak virtual'naia real'nost'* (Moscow: URSS, 2003), pp. 36–37.

275. *Leningradskaia organizatsiia*, p. 173.

276. *Ibid*, p. 173.

277. TsGA IPD, f. 408, op. 1, d. 1175, ll. 75, 84.

278. TsGA IPD, f. 197, op. 1, d. 725, ll. 28, 59.

279. *Biulleten' TsKK VKP(b)—NK RKI SSSR i RSFSR*, 1927, no. 2–3, pp. 12–13; *Dva goda raboty TsKK-RKI. Otchet XV s"ezdu partii* (Moscow, 1927), pp. 3–4; *Pravda*, February 13 and 16, 1926; *Stenograficheskii otchet XXIII cherezvychainoi konferentsii Leningradskoi gubernskoi organizatsii VKP(b)* (Leningrad, 1926), p. 40.

280. TsGA IPD, f. 197, op. 1, d. 723, l. 15.

281. TsGA IPD, f. 197, op. 1, d. 723, l. 16.

282. TsGA IPD, f. 197, op. 1, d. 725, l. 31.

283. Ivanov, *Iz istorii bor'by partii*, p. 184.

284. TsGA IPD, f. 197, op. 1, d. 1132, l. 47.

285. TsGA IPD, f. 197, op. 1, d. 723, l. 15.

286. TsGA IPD, f. 197, op. 1, d. 723, l. 79ob.

287. TsGA IPD, f. 197, op. 1, d. 723, l. 24ob.

288. TsGA IPD, f. 197, op. 1, d. 723, ll. 25, 79.

289. TsGA IPD, f. 197, op. 1, d. 723, l. 24ob; TsGA IPD, f. 197, op. 1, d. 1448, ll. 89–97.

290. Although present as a nonvoting delegate Trotsky himself took no part in the controversies at the Fourteenth Party Congress and reportedly even thought of intervening on the side of Stalin. Daniels, *Conscience of the Revolution*, pp. 271–72.

291. TsGA IPD, f. 197, op. 1, d. 236, ll. 92–95.

292. TsGA IPD, f. 197, op. 1, d. 1132, ll. 93–94.

293. TsGA IPD, f. 197, op. 1, d. 723, ll. 71–73.

294. TsGA IPD, f. 197, op. 1, d. 4b, ll. 160ob.

295. TsGA IPD, f. 197, op. 1, d. 723, l. 81.

296. TsGA IPD, f. 197, op. 1, d. 723, ll. 71–73.

297. TsGA IPD, f. 16, op. 1, d. 618, l. 107.

298. TsGA IPD, f. 197, op. 1, d. 723, ll. 24ob, 25.

299. TsGA IPD, f. 197, op. 1, d. 723, ll. 48–49.

300. TsGA IPD, f. 197, op. 1, d. 723, ll. 20–21.

301. TsGA IPD, f. 197, op. 1, d. 723, l. 33.

302. PATO, f. 17, op. 1, d. 1065, l. 260b.

303. TsGA IPD, f. 197, op. 1, d. 723, l. 108.

304. TsGA IPD, f. 408, op. 1, d. 174, l. 95a.

305. Some Party members refused to submit a recantation, at great risk to themselves. Late in 1927 Leningrad Communist University's Lukin stated appositely: "I believe that the opposition is correct. To renounce it would be to renounce myself." When, in a related case of February 1928, a recantation was demanded of Pavel', this one-time student at the Leningrad Industrial Academy flatly refused. "A pragmatic person who cares only about his own well-being can easily submit a recantation just to emerge from the water dry. But would this really benefit the Party? I feel that I have nothing to recant: I was never a full oppositionist and it never crossed my mind at any time that the Party had degenerated." This sort of defiance elicited varied reactions. One of the interrogators, Fedorov, accepted that "a mistaken Communist should not be forced to renounce himself. Do we really want him to say something like 'I am not myself, nor is this horse mine [*ia ne ia i loshad' ne moia*]'?" Fedorov continued, "But since Pavel' was a member of the opposition since the Fourteenth Party Congress . . . he has to submit a written recantation. Otherwise he must remain on the list of the oppositionists and face the consequences." Bogomolov, another interrogator, concurred: "A spoken recantation can easily be violated later on. The Party needs something in writing from Pavel'." But Pavel' proved intransigent—"At the present I refuse to submit a recantation"—and was purged. *Reabilitatsiia*, p. 140; TsGA IPD, f. 1816, op. 2, d. 5093, ll. 137–38.

306. TsGA IPD, f. 197, op. 1, d. 723, l. 930b–94.

307. *Bol'shevitskoe rukovodstvo*, p. 349.

308. TsGA IPD, f. 197, op. 1, d. 725, l. 42.

309. TsGA IPD, f. 197, op. 1, d. 723, l. 14.

310. TsGA IPD, f. 197, op. 1, d. 723, l. 95.

311. TsGA IPD, f. 197, op. 1, d. 208, l. 1.

312. TsGA IPD, f. 3, op. 1, d. 847, ll. 122–26, cited in Ivanov, *Iz istorii bor'by partii*, p. 183.

313. Ivanov, *Iz istorii bor'by partii*, p. 184.

314. TsGA IPD, f. 4000, op. 6, d. 403, ll. 4–9; *Sergei Mironovich Kirov: Vospominaniia Leningradskikh rabochikh*, pp. 31–34; Ivanov, *Iz istorii bor'by partii*, p. 185.

Chapter 5: From a Weak Body to a Wicked Mind

1. *Kommunist* (Khar'kov), January 13, 1926.

2. *Rabochii put'*, August 3, 1926.

3. R. Daniels, *The Conscience of the Revolution: Communist Opposition in Soviet Russia* (Cambridge, Mass.: Harvard University Press, 1960), p. 309.

4. *Krasnoe znamia*, October 4, 1927.

5. *Krasnoe znamia*, October 16, 1927; A. Slepkov, *Oppozitsionnye techeniia vnutri VKP(b)* (Moscow-Leningrad, 1926), p. 4. Posle ob"edinennogo plenuma," *Na leninskom puti*, no. 1 (1927), p. 7; Gendin. p. 17; S. Syrtsov, "Avantiuristy," *Na leninskom puti*, no. 3 (1927), p. 21.

6. Stalin remarked on this change of attitude on the part of the opposition in the summer of 1926, when he noticed that the followers of Zinoviev continued to meet outside official party forums. He wrote to Molotov, Rykov, and Bukharin on June 25: "Until the ap-

pearance of Zinoviev's group, oppositionist currents (Tr[otsky], Work[ers'] Opp[osition], etc.) conducted themselves more or less loyally, more or less tolerably, but after the appearance of Zinov[iev's] group, opposition[ist] currents got impudent and begun breaking the rules." *Pis'ma I.V. Stalina V.M. Molotovu, 1925–1936 gg. : Sbornik dokumentov* [ed. L. Kosheleva et al.] (Moscow: "Rossiia molodaia," 1995), p. 72.

7. "Za chto iskliucheny iz partii Trotskii i Zinov'ev," *Na leninskom puti,* no. 4–5 (1927); RGASPI, f. 17, op. 85, d. 67, l. 1640b.

8. "Kak partiia otnositsia k shirokoi diskussii?," *Bol'shevik* 1927, no. 15–16, p. 8; S. Syrtsov, "Avantiuristy," *Na leninskom puti,* no. 3 (1927), p. 21.

9. B. Bak, "Vnepartiinye soiuzniki trotskistskoi oppozitsii," *Na leninskom puti,* no. 2 (1927), p. 13.

10. J. Stalin, *On Opposition* (Peking, 1974), pp. 840, 842.

11. Stalin, *Sochineniia,* vol. 10, p. 267.

12. "Itogi XV s'ezda," *Agitator,* no. 1 (1928), p. 5.

13. I. Stalin, *Eshche raz o sotsial-demokraticheskom uklone v nashei partii* (Moscow: gospolitizdat, 1927), p. 66.

14. M. Glebov, "Kto vedet sovremennuiu oppozitsiiu?" *Bol'shevik,* no. 22 (1927), p. 22. Earlier in the year, majoritarians still described the foes in medico-psychological terms as, "people suffering from factionalist madness [*fraktsionnoe beshenstvo*]." *Na leninskom puti,* 1927, no. 2, p. 5.

15. *Krasnoe znamia,* November 17, 1927.

16. PANO, f. 2, op. 1, d. 42, l. 18.

17. The opposition responded with a counternarrative. "Ignorant historians attempt to discredit us by making reference to our ideological struggle with Lenin," Shliapnikov, the leader of the Workers' Opposition, argued. "They do not understand the true motives of these struggles or their real political significance.... What made the intra-Party struggle of 1920–1922 different in comparison to today is that it was characterized by profound mutual respect." Trotsky and Zinoviev also maintained that the Party did not learn anything since Lenin's time, only unlearned some important things. In a letter to the executive committee of the Komintern they reminisced: "How were things done in Lenin's time? First, Party Congresses were convened exactly on time.... Second, Party members enjoyed the real possibility of publishing their suggestions, theses, platforms, and brochures in the Party press." For official histories of the opposition see V. Sorin, *Partiia i oppozitsiia: Iz istokov oppozitsionnykh techenii* (Moscow, 1925); Ia. Diman, *Partiia i oppozitsiia (trotskizm)* (Irkutsk, 1926); M. Sokolov, *Partiia i oppozitsiia: Istoriia vsekh oppozitsionnykh techenii i gruppirovok v VKP(b) ot oktiabria 1917 goda po XV s'ezd* (Rostov-on-Don , 1928); S. Gonikman, *Desiat' let: Ocherk istorii trotskizma v VKP(b)* (Khar'kov, 1928). See also I. Nosov, *O Trotskom i trotskizme* (Simferopol', 1924); E. Kviring, *Trotskizm—smes' levoi frazy s prakticheskim opportunizmom* (Artemovsk, 1924); A. Shlikher, *Na platforme sotsial-demokraticheskogo uklona* (Moscow-Leningrad, 1927); S. Pokrovskii, *Trotskizm prezhde i teper'* (Leningrad, 1927); Baranchikov, *Pravda li chto partiia dushit oppozitsiiu?* (Moscow-Leningrad, 1927); P. Boiarskii, *Pochemu trotskizm vernulsia k menshevizmu* (Moscow-Leningrad, 1928); L. P. Roshal', *Bol'shevistkaia partiinost' i trotskizm* (Moscow-Leningrad, 1928); A. Kuznetsov, *Partiia i oppozitsiia* (Moscow-Leningrad, 1928); A. Shestakov, *Partiia bol'shevikov i oppozitsiia* (Moscow-Leningrad, 1928) ; S. Gopner, *Za leninizm! za leninskuiu partiinost'!* (Khar'kov, 1927). For the opposition's counternarrative see A. Slepkov, "Put' rabochei

oppozitsii," *Put' rabocheii oppozitsii* (Moscow: Pravda i Bednota, 1926), p. 75; *Arkhiv Trotskogo: Kommunisticheskaia oppozitsiia v SSSR, 1923–1927*, ed. Iu. Felshtinskii (Moscow: Terra, 1990), vol. 4, p. 99.

18. I. Sol'ts, "Miasnikovshchina i trotskistskaia oppozitsiia," *Krasnaia pechat'*, no. 22 (1927), p. 9.

19. A. Bubnov, *Partiia i oppozitsiia 1925 goda* (Moscow: Voennyi vestnik, 1926), p. 3.

20. Iaroslavskii noted in April 1928 that Sapronovists were so radical that they criticized Trotsky "from the left." *Plenum TsKK sozyva XV s"ezda VKP(b), 2–5 aprelia 1928 goda* (Moscow, 1928), p. 247.

21. N. Bukharin, *Partiia i oppozitsionnyi blok* (Leningrad: Priboi, c. 1926), p. 69. Bubnov was equally dismissive of the last two: "Kamenev and Zinoviev have become Trotsky's ideological slaves." A. Bubnov, *Partiia i oppozitsiia 1925 goda*, p. 9.

22. *Arkhiv Trotskogo*, vol. 2, p. 70.

23. *Arkhiv Trotskogo*, vol. 3, pp. 46, 93.

24. *Arkhiv Trotskogo*, vol. 1, p. 233.

25. *Arkhiv Trotskogo*, vol. 1, pp. 212, 231; vol. 3, p. 60; vol. 4, p. 273.

26. E. Iaroslavskii, *Novoe i staroe v "novoi" oppozitsii* (Moscow-Leningrad, 1927), pp. 71, 72.

27. *Arkhiv Trotskogo*, vol. 4, p. 22.

28. *Oppozitsionnyi neomen'shevizm (O "novoi" platforme)* (Moscow: Bednota, 1927), p. 32.

29. RGASPI, f. 17, op. 85, d. 222, l. 113; PATO, f. 17, op. 1, d. 749, l. 156ob.

30. *Arkhiv Trotskogo*, vol. 3, p. 67; vol. 4, p. 116.

31. "Posle ob"edinennogo plenuma," *Na leninskom puti*, no. 1 (1927), p. 5; *Arkhiv Trotskogo*, vol. 4, p. 227.

32. S. Goner, *Za leninizm: Za leninskuiu partiinost'* (Khar'kov, 1927), p. 106; Zinoviev made similar claims when still in the majority. G. Zinoviev, *Mirovaia partiia leninizma* (Moscow, 1924), p. 19.

33. *Pravda*, July 30 and November 6, 1926.

34. *Oppozitsionnyi neomen'shevizm*, pp. 31–32.

35. S. Gonikman, *Istoriia VKP(b)* (Khar'kov, 1927), pp. 68–69.

36. N. Bukharin, *Partiia i oppozitsionnyi blok* (Leningrad: Priboi, c. 1926), pp. 60–61.

37. *Arkhiv Trotskogo*, vol. 4, p. 225.

38. *Arkhiv Trotskogo*, vol. 3, p. 183.

39. RGASPI, f. 17, op. 71, d. 85, ll. 1–2; op. 85, d. 222, l. 37.

40. *Arkhiv Trotskogo*, vol. 2, p. 41.

41. *Arkhiv Trotskogo*, vol. 2, p. 68. A similar effort was made to describe the Central Committee as a "current," another term normally associated with heterodoxy. Opposing the Bolshevik-Leninists were the "rightist current" (Rykov, Kalinin, and others) and the "centrist current" (Stalin, Molotov, and others)." *Arkhiv Trotskogo*, vol. 4, pp. 148, 151.

42. RGASPI, f. 17, op. 85, d. 67, l. 39.

43. *Arkhiv Trotskogo*, vol. 2, p. 235.

44. *Arkhiv Trotskogo*, vol. 2, p. 77.

45. E. Iaroslavskii, *Novoe i staroe*, p. 56.

46. *Arkhiv Trotskogo*, vol. 4, p. 264.

47. *Arkhiv Trotskogo*, vol. 4, p. 252.

48. E. Iaroslavskii, *Za edinstvo VKP(b)* (Moscow-Leningrad, 1927), p. 12.

49. TsGAODM, f. 3, op. 8, d. 92, l. 48.

50. *Arkhiv Trotskogo*, vol. 3, p. 195.

51. *Arkhiv Trotskogo*, vol. 3, p. 139.

52. *Arkhiv Trotskogo*, vol. 3, p. 58.

53. The implications of such claims did not escape Iaroslavskii, who wrote in a private letter to Ordzhonikidze dated October 4, 1927: "The opposition calls its new platform the 'Platform of the Bolshevik-Leninists.' Needless to say, this means that you and I are no longer Bolshevik-Leninists!" *Bol'shevitskoe rukovodstvo*, p. 349.

54. For the official use of "Trotskyism" see PANO, f. 2, op. 2, d. 56, l. 1. The term "Stalinists" was not used by the majoritarians at the time, probably because Stalin managed to preserve his reputation as a proponent of collective leadership, paying respects to the theoretical abilities of Bukharin. Only after Bukharin's reputation was shaken in 1928 do we find students at the Institute of Red Professors calling themselves "Stalinites" (*Stalintsy*) and not the harsher "Stalinists" (*Stalinisty*)." *Sovetskoe rukovodstvo: Perepiska; 1928–1941* (Moscow: ROSSPEN, 1999), p. 39.

55. *Arkhiv Trotskogo*, vol. 1, p. 211.

56. *Arkhiv Trotskogo*, vol. 2, pp. 90–91.

57. *Arkhiv Trotskogo*, vol. 3, p. 40.

58. *Arkhiv Trotskogo*, vol. 3, pp. 82–83.

59. *Arkhiv Trotskogo*, vol. 4, p. 173. F. Ksenofontov, *Osnovnye voprosy strategii i taktiki VKP(b)* (Moscow, 1927), p. 187. While "Trotskyism," understood as an anti-Leninist ideology, was in currency since 1925, the label "Trotskyists" came into wide use only in 1928–29, describing those oppositionists who refused to recant after the Fifteenth Party Congress. L. Ozerov, "Bor'ba partii s trotskizmom v 1928–1930gg.," *Voprosy istorii KPSS*, no. 3 (1968), pp. 48–49.

60. TsGAODM, f. 3, op. 44, d. 362, l. 272. But see the report on a substantial support of the opposition at the Moscow Institute of Red Professors. M. Shamberg, "Oppozitsionnyi blok i studenchestvo," *Krasnoe studenchestvo*, no. 8 (1926), pp. 4–5.

61. PATO, f. 17, op. 1, d. 952, l. 81.

62. *III Sibirskaia kraevaia partiinaia konferentsiia: Stenograficheskii otchet* (Novosibirsk, 1927), p. 276.

63. *Pravda*, October 17, 1926.

64. A. Meyer, "The War Scare of 1927," *Soviet Union. Union Sovietique* 5 (1978), p. 22.

65. PATO, f. 17, op. 1, d. 883, l. 29. During the New Course Discussion (1923), the Siberian Party leadership mostly supported the majority line. The Siberian Party bureau stated that the opposition should be regarded as "an organized crusade against Lenin's disciples" and urged Siberian Communists to endorse the Letter of the Petrograd Party Organization. The response of the Tomsk potentates was lukewarm. The head of the Tomsk propaganda department, Vol'fovich, doubted the "timeliness" and "expedience" of the strongly anti-Trotsky Letter of the Petrograd Organization, and the Tomsk Party leadership voted down the resolution in the condemnation of Trotsky proposed by the head of the provincial Party committee, Kalashnikov, largely on the strength of the students' votes. Once the decisions of the Thirteenth Party Congress became known, however, the resolutions of the Tomsk academic cells were amended in the proper majoritarian spirit. No massive purge took place in Tomsk: only 4 students were removed from the Party cell of the Tomsk Technological Institute (out of 107) during the verifica-

tion campaign of 1924–25. V. Zolotarev, "K istorii uchastiia komsomola sibiri v bor'be kommunisticheskoi partii za leninizm, protiv trotskizma (1924–1925)," *Sibir' i dal'nii vostok v period vosstanovleniia narodnogo khoziaistva*, no. 2 (Tomsk, 1963), p. 85; *Itogi proverki chlenov i kandidatov RKP(b) neproizvodstvennykh iacheek*, p. 87; PANO, f. 2, op. 2, d. 65, ll. 5–7, d. 39, ll. 238–241; d. 71, l. 32; d. 548, l. 120; d. 175, l. 6; d. 331, l. 70; PATO, f. 1, op. 1, d. 109, l. 110; f. 320, op. 1, d. 7, ll. 1, 13.

66. RGASPI, f. 17, op. 67, d. 187, l. 53.
67. PATO, f. 320, op. 1, d. 20, ll. 280b–29.
68. PATO, f. 320, op. 1, d. 20, l. 330b.
69. PATO, f. 17, op. 1, d. 1076, l. 260b.
70. RGASPI, f. 17, op. 67, d. 187, l. 53.
71. PATO, f. 17, op. 1, d. 883, ll. 240b-25; PATO, f. 17, op. 1, d. 749, l. 152; d. 883, l. 120b; O. Barabashev, "Zametki o voennoi opasnosti," *Na leninskom puti*, no. 4–5 (1927), pp. 15–21; and D. Charnyi, "Partiia i opasnost' voiny," *Na leninskom puti*, no. 4–5 (1927), pp. 61–66; B. Abramov, "Razgrom trotskistko-zinov'evskogo antipartiinogo bloka," *Voprosy istorii KPSS*, no. 6 (1959), pp. 42–43; A. Meyer, "The War Scare of 1927," *Soviet Union* 5 (1978), p. 22; I. Deutscher, *The Prophet Unarmed: Trotsky, 1921–1929* (London: Oxford University Press, 1959), pp. 349–50.
72. PATO, f. 17, op. 1, d. 883, ll. 10, 120b. Daniels, *Conscience of the Revolution*, p. 312.
73. *Krasnoe znamia*, January 17, 1928; RGASPI, f. 17, op. 67, d. 187, l. 53. PATO, f. 320, op. 1, d. 20, l. 33.
74. PATO, f. 320, op. 1, d. 20, l. 37.
75. A regular member of the "board of student affairs," Kutuzov was also the institute's representative at the circuit committee's academic council. PATO, f. 17, op. 1, d. 747, l. 38; d. 749, l. 160.
76. PATO, f. 17, op. 1, d. 883, ll. 260b–27.
77. RGASPI, f. 17, op. 67, d. 187, l. 53.
78. PATO, f. 17, op. 1, d. 320, l. 270b.
79. V. V. Demidov, *Politicheskaia bor'ba oppozitsii v sibiri, 1922–1929* (Novosibirsk, 1994), p. 94.
80. *Krasnoe znamia*, November 8 and 13, 1927.
81. *Krasnoe znamia*, November 19 and 22, 1927.
82. PATO, f. 17, op. 1, d. 883, ll. 100b–11.
83. E. Iaroslavskii, *Novoe i staroe v "novoi" oppozitsii*, p. 74.
84. RGASPI, f. 17, op. 85, d. 67, l. 59. B. Dvinskii, "Ob opyte izucheniia podavaemykh na sobraniiakh zapisok," *Izvestiia TsK VKP(b)*, no. 43–44 (1926), p. 3.
85. Deutscher, *The Prophet Unarmed*, p. 358; *Pravda*, September 29, *Partiia i oppozitsiia po dokumentam: Materialy k XV s"ezdu VKP(b)* (Moscow, 1927), p. 372; *Dva goda raboty TsKK RKI*, pp. 22–23; *Sotsialisticheskii vestnik* 1927, no. 19, p. 14.
86. In the summer, Trotsky jeered at the Central Committee claims of overwhelming popular support. "A comrade who does not want to participate in a compulsory vote, who escapes through the door, is stopped. 'You must vote as told!' the secretary says. Those who abstain enter his black list." Trotsky and Zinoviev repeatedly demanded that control commissions punish Party secretaries who "restrict minority rights," and their motion had some grassroots support. "We hear the voice of the accuser but not the voice of the accused," unidentified voices stated. "Without hearing the defense, how can we reach a verdict?" Or:

"Why is Trotsky not allowed to criticize Party decisions?" "Has a dictatorship formed itself in the Party?" The opposition claimed that spies were regularly sent to meetings to identify troublesome comrades; "our speakers are shouted down; Party secretaries threaten to have those who voted for the opposition expelled." Radek complained that comrades voted "hypocritically [*litsemerno*], just to avoid persecution. This state of things does not allow for a true, respectful majority to be established through the discussion process." According to Zinoviev's sources, majoritarian apparatchiks made outrageous statements in their July reports: "We are members of the same Party only nominally—the oppositionists cannot be considered true Communists"; "If we purge and possibly even arrest the leadership of the opposition it will lose popularity," and so on. Zinoviev complained that the Central Committee cynically emptied the discussion of all meaning. "Do you really think that if the opposition has the upper hand we will submit?" its supporters asked. "Never! . . . If outvoted, we will overthrow the new majority." *Arkhiv Trotskogo*, vol. 3, p. 103; vol. 4, p. 107 (Trotsky's and Zinoviev's complaints); RGASPI, f. 17, op. 85, d. 222, ll. 42–43 (grassroots); PATO, f. 17, op. 1, d. 883, l. 210b; l. 23 (spies); *Arkhiv Trotskogo*, vol. 2, p. 50 (Radek); *Arkhiv Trotskogo*, vol. 3, p. 185, 249–50 (Zinoviev).

87. *Arkhiv Trotskogo*, vol. 4, pp. 102, 236.

88. *Arkhiv Trotskogo*, vol. 4, p. 189.

89. PATO, f. 17, op. 1, d. 883, l. 10; f. 76, op. 1, d. 512, ll. 115–129; d. 749, l. 1520b.

90. PATO, f. 17, op. 1, d. 883, l. 90b. *Krasnoe znamia*, October 22 and 26, 1927.

91. PATO, f. 17, op. 1, d. 749, ll. 151–1510b, 159. Complaints against violations of Party democracy do not necessarily mean that the opposition had an alternative political culture. Kuzovnikov, a prominent oppositionist organizer from the Urals, left a rare testimony that reveals something of the oppositionist mode of operation. In November 1927, Kuzovnikov went to Moscow and attended a meeting of the United Opposition's leadership with the intention of expressing his disagreements with Trotsky's radical line. "I put my name down [in the agenda list] but my attitudes were well known so they did not let me speak." Luckily, there were others, perhaps even the majority, to voice misgivings similar to Kuzovnikov's to the effect that the opposition will lose its revolutionary legitimacy if it appeals directly to the working class. "When the mood began swinging against Trotsky, Ivan Smirnov intervened and decided to close discussions. Debates were terminated and I could not shed light on the realities in the Urals and present my point of view."

Immediately upon his return to Sverdlovsk, Kuzovnikov convened the local opposition-ists hoping to alert them to disagreements in Moscow's headquarters. Styling himself as the "de-facto head of the Urals oppositionist center," he expected to lead discussion and offer his own "political assessment" of the situation. To his surprise, however, Mrachkovskii, a national oppositionist leader, and his affiliates suggested that a certain Kholmovskii be the meetings' chair—a coup that Kuzovnikov described as a "game in democracy. . . . Almost all of our previous meetings were chaired by me," he explained, seeing no reason to bow to the vote that unseated him. It would be simplistic to present Kuzovnikov as a man of convenience, a democrat when the majority is with him and an authoritarian when the majority is against him. Kuzovnikov maintained that the ultimate referee in questions of politics should be theoretical acumen and not just numbers, and he expressed conviction that the truth was with him. Of course, Mrachkovskii and other Moscow legates shared the same epistemology, only in their view the truth was with them. Mrachkovskii told Kuzovnikov to leave Sverdlovsk at once, a relocation that suggests that the opposition had a strict cadre policy of its own, and a procedure not unlike the "relocation" practices of the Central Committee. Kuzovnikov had no intention of giving in. "I retorted that as the faction's secretary it is me who is the *khoziain*"—Stalin's informal title of the 1930s meaning, roughly, the lord of the household—"and that it is me who is in a position to ask him to leave. 'Don't speak to me like that!' I said to Mrachkovskii. 'If you insist on staying here we will not stop before any methods of physical reprisal against you,' Mrachkovskii replied." Kuzovnikov summarized: "this shows that nothing will stop them, especially as they know my character and my political line very well." But his ire against such unfair play did not stop him from denouncing his erstwhile comrades to the Ural Control Commission, though he was fully aware of the consequences. *Pravda*, November 23, 1927.

92. Deutscher, *The Prophet Unarmed*, pp. 349–50; Bak, "Vnepartiinye soiuzniki trotskistkoi oppozitsii," p. 15; O. Barabashev, "Zametki o voennoi opasnosti," *Na leninskom puti*, no. 4–5 (1927), pp. 15–21; D. Petrovskii, *Anglo-russkii komitet i oppozitsiia* (Moscow-Leningrad, 1927); B. Abramov, "Razgrom trotskistko-zinov'evskogo antipartiinogo bloka," *Voprosy istorii KPSS*, no. 6 (1959), pp. 42–43.

93. Carr, p. 32; *TsK-RKI v osnovnykh postanovleniiakh partii* (Moscow-Leningrad, 1927), p. 223; *Arkhiv Trotskogo*, vol. 4, p. 220. RGASPI, f. 17, op. 71, d. 89, l. 1.

94. RGASPI, f. 17, op. 71, d. 83, ll. 1–44. TsGAODM, f. 3., op. 8, d. 92, l. 3.

95. *Arkhiv Trotskogo*, vol. 4, p. 236.

96. *Arkhiv Trotskogo*, vol. 4, p. 150.

97. Unable to deflect all demands to learn about the Testament, Siberian potentates presented it in a truncated and somewhat distorted form: "Lenin wrote about essential, important mistakes by Kamenev, Zinoviev, Trotsky, and Bukharin." "The general secretary should resemble Stalin in all respects," he added, "only be more polite." This was not the only doctored version that circulated in Siberia. "Lenin's Testament," a local newspaper reported, "states that Stalin is a model Bolshevik. He has one shortcoming: he is sometimes coarse. . . . Trotsky is also a major figure but he has quirks." *Vlast' truda*, November 17 and 18, 1927; Demidov, *Politicheskaia bor'ba oppozitsii v sibiri*, p. 84. RGASPI, f. 17, op. 69, d. 25, l. 148.

98. PATO, f. 17, op. 1, d. 883, ll. 8, 26–28; For a majoritarian rebuttal, see, among others, A. Troitskii, "Delovoe obsuzhdenie ili diskussionnaia likhoradka?" *Molodoi bol'shevik*, no. 17 (1927); *Krasnoe znamia*, September 8 and November 13, 1927.

99. PATO, f. 17, op. 1, d. 749, l. 159; d. 883, ll. 8, 120b, 200b–21.

100. PATO, f. 17, op. 1, d. 883, l. 210b.

101. PATO, f. 17, op. 1, d. 749, l. 1520b.

102. PATO, f. 17, op. 1, d. 883, l. 90b.

103. PATO, f. 17, op. 1, d. 883, l. 8; d. 1065, l. 61.

104. The Trade Union Discussion was a mistake, the Central Committee answered. Besides, "Lenin believed that under the dictatorship of the proletariat a widescale discusion should be averted whenever possible." E. Iaroslavskii, *Protiv oppozitsii* (Moscow-Leningrad, 1928), pp. 315–20; V. Adoratskii, "V. I. Lenin v bor'be s oppozitsiei," *Kommunisticheskaia revoliutsiia 1927*, no. 21–22, pp. 12–13. The opposition bewailed the existence of "'specialists' in 'smashing' the opposition. . . . When a rare oppositionist text does appear in the press, it is invariably accompanied with an 'antidote' they prepared. . . . Forced to refute everything the opposition is claiming, the young theorists of the 'Bukharin school' pull sentences out

of the context, distort the authors' ideas through wicked and disingenuous interpretations, sometimes even falsifying quotations." *Arkhiv Trotskogo*, vol. 4, p. 87.

105. PATO, f. 320, op. 1, d. 20, l. 34.

106. PATO, f. 17, op. 1, d. 749, l. 155ob. RGASPI, f. 17, op. 71, d. 97, ll. 1–47.

107. PATO, f. 17, op. 1, d. 883, l. 10.

108. PATO, f. 17, op. 1, d. 883, ll. 210b-23; PATO, f. 320, op. 1, d. 20, l. 32; d. 883, l. 270b.

109. PATO, f. 17, op. 1, d. 883, ll. 23–230b.

110. The Siberian control commissions had already concluded in the summer of 1927 that the activity of the opposition "violates the Party regulations and assumes a counter-revolutionary character." PANO, f. 2, opo. 2, d. 234, l. 10.

111. PATO, f. 320, op. 1, d. 20, l. 33.

112. PATO, f. 320, op. 1, d. 20, l. 350b.

113. *Sovetskaia Sibir'*, December 7 and 16, 1924. See also *XV konferentsiia Vsesoivznoi Kommunisticheskoi partii (bol'shevikov), Stenograficheskii otchet* (Moscow, 1927), p. 814; N. Litvinov, "Oppozitsiia i Men'shevizm," *Molodoi kommunist*, no. 14 (1927); I. Baranchikov, *Kak oppozitsiia skatilas' k men'shevizmu* (Moscow-Leningrad, 1928); The opposition retorted that it was the Central Committee that "degenerated" and "declined towards Menshevism." RGASPI, f. 17, op. 85, d. 67, l. 1160b.

114. PATO, f. 17, op. 1, d. 749, l. 1520b., d. 749, l. 1560b; d. 883, l. 140b. PATO, f. 17, op. 1, d. 883, l. 25.

115. PATO, f. 320, op. 1, d. 20, l. 330b.

116. *Arkhiv Trotskogo*, vol. 3, p. 74.

117. *Arkiv Trotskogo*, vol. 3, p. 109; O. Matveev, "Proroki komsomol'skogo 'termidora,'" *Molodoi bol'shevik*, no. 22 (1927); Maretskii, "Tak nazyvaemyi 'Termidor' i opasnost' pererozhdeniia," *Pravda*, July 24 and 29, 1927.

118. PATO, f. 17, op. 1, d. 883, l. 94.

119. On this Stalin had been quite clear: "The rejection of the possibility that our Party can construct socialism in Russia equals the rejection of the historical timeliness [*zakono-mernost'*] of the October Revolution." *Pravda*, December 14, 1926. For the argument that the Thermidor theses implied a denial of the socialist nature of the October revolution, see "Itogi XV s'ezda," *Agitator*, no. 1 (1928), p. 6; O. Matveev, "Proroki komsomol'skogo 'termidora'"; Maretskii, "Tak nazyvaemyi 'Termidor' i opasnost' pererozhdeniia."

120. PATO, f. 17, op. 1, d. 883, l. 240b.

121. Deutscher, *The Prophet Unarmed*, p. 312.

122. TsGA IPD, f. 80, op. 1, d. 62, l. 42.

123. RGASPI, f. 17, op. 2, d. 317, l. 153.

124. PATO, f. 17, op. 1, d. 883, ll. 15–150b.

125. Offended by the opposition's venomous replacement of "socialism in one country" (*v odnoi strane*) with "socialism in one county" (*v odnom uezde*), the Klikunovists pointed out that this pun "had been borrowed from the pens of Hilferding and Kautsky, Lenin's notorious petit bourgeois critics." PATO, f. 17, op. 1, d. 883, l. 170b.

126. PATO, f. 320, op. 1, d. 20, ll. 26–29.

127. Here Kutuzov was directly drawing on the "Declaration of the Eighty-three."

128. RGASPI, f. 17, op. 71, d. 89, l. 16. TsGAODM, f. 3, op. 8, d. 92, ll. 3, 6. *Arkhiv Trotskogo*, vol. 3, pp. 244–48; vol. 4, p. 22. RGASPI, f. 17, op. 71, d. 88, ll. 1–99.

129. A. Shestakov, *Partiia bol'shevikov i oppozitsiia* (Moscow-Leningrad, 1928), pp. 17–18; PATO, f. 17, op. 1, d. 883, l. 26; f. 320, op. 1, d. 20, ll. 28–33; d. 883, l. 170b. Such fiery talk aroused majoritarians who matched the volatile language of their opponents. Mal'gin accused Kutuzov of having joined forces with class aliens: so intent was he on faulting the Soviet power that he had entirely failed to assign bourgeois foreign governments their share of the blame for the threats to the Soviet Union. As important as any discussion of policy was determining whose consciousness had caught up with the pace of history, and who was thinking in hopelessly retrograde terms. "The conjuncture we are presently facing has a tense international situation as its background," Mal'gin told Kutuzov. "Showing their ignorance of the significance of the present moment the oppositionists allow themselves to advance criticisms that reflect poorly on our international stature." The structure of this apparently simple set of propositions is revealing: Mal'gin could have said that "the current international situation is tense," or something of the sort, if he simply wanted to convey the idea of an imminent attack on the Soviet Union but he chose instead to subsume the concrete situation under a general, metahistorical framework. Communists like Mal'gin knew that the road to classless society was uneven, and at times counterrevolution would appear to be in the ascendant. Such times tested the dedication of all Communists. So the current war scare was part of the preordained ordeal, an ordeal for which all conscious Party members had to be prepared. Now, if Kutuzov wavered here, it was due to his weak will: he could not withstand the pressure of events. Kutuzov faltered because his hero, Trotsky, faltered: "When the victories of the October Revolution had to be guarded, Trotsky proved to be a tenacious orator. But now that we have been granted a respite, he has lost his historical perspicacity. The oppositionists stuffed their sweet little stomachs and lost touch." Indeed, throughout the proceedings, Kutuzov and his followers were accused of "defeatism" (*porazhenchestvo*). The subtext was the notorious analogy between Trotsky and Clemenceau. "At the beginning of the imperialist war," Trotsky explained, "the French bourgeoisie had at its head a blundering government, a government without rudder or sail. Refusing to back down even though German soldiers had come within eighty kilometers of Paris, Clemenceau waged a furious struggle against the government's flabbiness." Clemenceau, Trotsky asserted, had not "betrayed" his class, and went on to conclude that the "opposition should not identify the defence of the Soviet Union with the defence of Stalinism. Long live the socialist fatherland? Yes! Long live the Stalinist course? No!" Tomsk majoritarians were familiar with Molotov's rebuttal that "Trotsky's SR inspired statements . . . foreshadowed a wartime coup d'état." Daniels, *Conscience of the Revolution*, pp. 283–86. Deutscher, *The Prophet Unarmed*, pp. 349–50; Bak, "Vnepartiinye soiuzniki trotskistkoi oppozitsii," p. 15; O. Barabashev, "Zametki o voennoi opasnosti," *Na leninskom puti*, no. 4–5 (1927), pp. 1–21; and D. Charnyi, "Partiia i opasnost' voiny," *Na leninskom puti*, no. 4–5 (1927), pp. 61–66; D. Petrovskii, *Anglo-russkii komitet i oppozitsiia* (Moscow-Leningrad, 1927); B. Abramov, "Razgrom trotskistko-zinov'evskogo antiparti-inogo bloka," *Voprosy istorii KPSS*, no. 6 (1959), pp. 42–43. *Arkhiv Trotskogo*, vol. 3, p. 222; vol. 4, pp. 179–84. PATO, f. 17, op. 1, d. 883, l. 150b; f. 320, op. 1, d. 20, ll. 310b–32.

130. PATO, f. 17, op. 1, d. 883, l. 31.

131. PATO, f. 17, op. 1, d. 749, l. 1520b; d. 883, ll. 14, 150b-16; f. 320, op. 1, d. 20, l. 31.

132. *Arkhiv Trotskogo*, vol. 3, p. 64.

133. PATO, f. 17, op. 1, d. 883, ll. 14, 180b–19.

134. PATO, f. 17, op. 1, d. 883, ll. 19–20. The debate on the kulak question was especially poignant in Siberia; G. Safarov, "Nastuplenie kapitala v sibirskoi dervene (Krichashchie fakty)," *Bol'shevik*, no. 15–16, 1927; S. Syrtsov, "Neudachnoe vystuplenie tov. Safarova," *Bol'shevik*, no. 15–16, 1927. *Sovetskaia sibir'*, November 30, 1926; January 12, 1927; March, 4, 1927.

135. *Arkhiv Trotskogo*, vol. 3, p. 134. *K diskussii o rabote v derevne* (Novosibirsk, 1927), pp. 27–28.

136. PATO, f. 17, op. 1, d. 883, l. 140b. Kutuznov was citing here from the Declaration of the Fifteen, *Arkhiv Trotskogo*, vol. 4, p. 110.

137. PATO, f. 17, op. 1, d. 749, ll. 153, 158. *Arkhiv Trotskogo*, vol. 4, pp. 133–34.

138. PATO, f. 17, op. 1, d. 749, l. 1580b; d. 883, l. 32.

139. PATO, f. 17, op. 1, d. 749, l. 1590b; f. 320, op. 1, d. 20, l. 300b; PATO, f. 17, op. 1, d. 883, l. 14

140. PATO, f. 17, op. 1, d. 883, ll. 95–96.

141. *Arkhiv Trotskogo*, vol. 3, p. 66.

142. *Arkhiv Trotskogo*, vol. 2, p. 41.

143. PATO, f. 17, op. 1, d. 749, l. 151.

144. For the general terms of the debate on the condition of the working class, see Daniels, *Conscience of the Revolution*, 314; For the discussion of the issue in Tomsk, see *Krasnoe znamia*, October 28, 1927; PATO, f. 320, op. 1, d. 20, l. 32; d. 749, ll. 157–60.

145. PATO, f. 17, op. 1, d. 749, l. 1530b.

146. Demidov, *Politicheskaia bor'ba oppozitsii v sibiri*, p. 94.

147. PATO, f. 17, op. 1, d. 883, l. 18; d. 1065, l. 28.

148. RGASPI, f. 17, op. 71, d. 89, l. 9; op. 85, d. 222, l. 157.

149. *Arkhiv Trotskogo*, vol. 4, pp. 215–16.

150. PATO, f. 17, op. 1, d. 883, ll. 27–28.

151. PATO, f. 17, op. 1, d. 749, l. 152.

152. PATO, f. 17, op. 1, d. 883, l. 18; d. 1065, l. 28.

153. *Arkhiv Trotskogo*, vol. 4, p. 146.

154. PATO, f. 17, op. 1, d. 749, ll. 1510b–152, 156, 160; d. 1076, 883, l. 27.

155. PATO, f. 17, op. 1, d. 1065, l. 66.

156. That the opposition boasted of its proletarian makeup, seeing in it an important source of Bolshevik legitimacy, is evident from Serge's testimony regarding Leningrad: "Our circle [consisted of] two old Bolshevik workers . . . ; X——, an unassuming man, formerly the organizer of a Party printing shop, who had been dropped from various sinecures because of his excessive integrity and who, ten years after the seizure of power, was living as poorly as he always had, pale and bony under his faded cloth cap; [and] Fedorov, a huge red-haired fellow, splendidly strapping, with an open face fit for a barbarian warrior—he was a factory worker. Even our two or three students . . . were of working class origins." V. Serge, *Memoirs of a Revolutionary, 1901–1941* (Oxford, 1951), p. 207.

157. Bak, "Vnepartiinye soiuzniki trotskistkoi oppozitsii," pp. 12–17.

158. A. Gendin, "Itogi preds"ezdovskoi diskussii v sibiri," *Na leninkom puti*, no. 6 (1927), pp. 17–18; I. Koz'min, *Oppozitsiia v sibiri* (Novosibirsk, 1928), pp. 6–8. RGASPI, f. 17, op. 85, d. 67, l. 23. *Pravda*, November 1, 1927.

159. M. Brudnyi, "Nashi raznoglasiia i neodnorodnost' proletariata," *Bol'shevik*, no. 19–20

(1927), pp. 53–54, 61; Sol'ts, "Miasnikovshchina i trotskistskaia oppozitsiia," p. 12; "S novymi silami," Bol'shevik, no. 1 (1928), p. 3.

160. RGASPI, f. 17, op. 85, d. 67, l. 23. Pravda, November 1, 1927.

161. Krasnoe znamia, November 19, 1927; Koz'min, Oppozitsiia v sibiri, p. 20.

162. Arkhiv Trotskogo, vol. 4, p. 77.

163. "Inache byt' ne mozhet," Bol'shevik (1927), no. 23–24, pp. 4–5.

164. PATO, f. 17, op. 1, d. 883, l. 24; f. 320, op. 1, d. 20, ll. 320b, 330b; PATO, f. 17, op. 1, d. 883, l. 29.

165. "Moia rabota v oppozitsionnoi gruppe. Iz zapisok trotskista N. N. Gavrilova," Pamiat'. Istoricheskii sbornik (Paris, 1980), pp. 389–90.

166. Arkhiv Trotskogo, vol. 4, p. 236.

167. Arkhiv Trotskogo, vol. 3, p. 207.

168. Serge, Memoirs of a Revolutionary, p. 221. Arkhiv Trotskogo, vol. 4, p. 79.

169. A. Gusev, "Levokummunisticheskaia oppozitsiia v SSSR v kontse 20-kh godov," Obshchestvennaia istoriia, vol. 1 (1996), p. 99.

170. Trinadtsatyi s"ezd RKP(b), pp. 165–66.

171. Arkhiv Trotskogo, vol. 4, p. 69.

172. Arkhiv Trotskogo, vol. 4, pp. 149, 174.

173. Deutscher, The Prophet Unarmed, p. 291.

174. Bak, "Vnepartiinye soiuzniki trotskistkoi oppozitsii," p. 13; Deutscher, The Prophet Unarmed, pp. 293, 378, Serge, Memoirs of a Revolutionary, p. 234.

175. Trotskii, Moia zhizn' (Moscow, 1991), pp. 502, 504.

176. Trotsky affirmed the infallibility of a general line of 1917–1923, a period when he was a majoritarian. The Serge-Trotsky Papers, ed. D. Cotterill (London: Pluto Press, 1994), p. 199.

177. Bak, "Vnepartiinye soiuzniki trotskistkoi oppozitsii," p. 10; Deutcher, The Prophet Unarmed, p. 292. RGASPI, f. 17, op. 71, d. 89, l. 13.

178. Arkhiv Trotskogo, vol. 3, pp. 178–79.

179. Arkhiv Trotskogo, vol. 2, p. 187; vol. 4, pp. 265, 107.

180. RGASPI, f. 17, op. 85, d. 222, l. 159; d. 67, l. 590b. TSAODM, f. 3, op. 8, d. 92, ll. 44–45; f. 80, op. 1, d. 276, l. 12; op. 44, d. 362, ll. 142, 2710b.

181. Trinadtsataia konferentsiia RKP(b) (Moscow, 1924), pp. 93–101.

182. Piatnadtsatyi s"ezd VKP(b), dekabr' 1927 goda: Stenograficheskii otchet (Moscow: Gospolitizdat, 1961–1962), p. 292.

183. Gusev, "Levokummunisticheskaia oppozitsiia," p. 94.

184. Krasnoe znamia, November 11, 1927. It will be wrong to conclude that the Party apparatus objected to oppositionist gathering and the rank and file was somehow sympathetic to them. In fact, sympathy and antipathy towards oppositionist activities crisscrossed the Party. Writing on behalf of his female friend, too confused or shy to step forward, Stepanykh, a Moscow Communist, sent the following denunciation to the Bauman Party committee (Moscow) on December, 8, 1927. "A group of students are in the habit of convening factionalist, oppositionist meetings at Kolokolnik Alley No. 19, Apt. 3. Varvara Solov'eva accidentally found herself at one such meeting on December 2, 1927; six individuals were in attendance. Everything in the meeting was mysterious [tainstvenno]: [the leader's] name was just 'Peter' [clearly a pseudonym]. My friend was interviewed and then one of the attendants expressed a reservation in her regard, 'Well, she is not an

oppositionist.' [But others believed] 'she will not stand in our way.' Eventually, they lost all shame and suggested she 'sit for a while and listen.' After the meeting, a certain 'Zverev' gave her a leaflet, *Mensheviks against Stalin*, although he knew she was a member of the Komsomol. He also promised to get additional materials, 'with data' for her, but Varvara has not seen him since. The majority of the attending were not Party members, and 'Peter' expressed his regret in this regard." The author of the letter is a forerunner of the Stalinist vigilante; he expresses the usual majoritarian concerns: the opposition conducts its work in secrecy, disseminates seditious propaganda, and does not respect the boundary between the Party and the non-Party. TsGAODM, f. 3, op. 8, d. 92, l. 5.

185. *Arkhiv Trotskogo*, vol. 4, p. 274.

186. *Arkhiv Trotskogo*, vol. 4, p. 149.

187. *Arkhiv Trotskogo*, vol. 4, pp. 222–23.

188. *Arkhiv Trotskogo*, vol. 4, p. 269.

189. RGASPI, f. 17, op. 71, d. 89, l. 13.

190. TsGAODM, f. 3, op. 8, d. 92, ll. 56–57.

191. *Bol'shevitskoe rukovodstvo*, p. 349. On November 11, the Central Committee resolved that factionalist meetings will be dispersed by force. The opposition officially stated on November 14 that it would put an end to the links between the working class and its leadership "because we do not want to assist Stalin in organizing brawls that, in Khark'kov for example, were accompanied by revolver shots." *Arkhiv Trotskogo*, vol. 4, pp. 263, 266, 268.

192. Serge is quoted in Deutscher, *The Prophet Unarmed*, pp. 368–69.

193. *Tsifry i fakty protiv likvidatorov i pererozhdentsev* (Leningrad: Priboi, 1927), pp. 9–10.

194. *Piatnadtsatyi s"ezd VKP(b)*, p. 385.

195. Ibid., p. 219.

196. Serge, *Memoirs of a Revolutionary*, pp. 210, 212; Demidov, *Politicheskaia bor'ba oppozitsii v sibiri*, pp. 77–79; P. Broue, "Les trotskystes en Union sovietique, 1929–1938," *Cahiers Leon Trotsky*, no. 6 (1980), p. 11.

197. E. Iaroslavskii, *Novoe i staroe v "novol" oppozitsii*, pp. 56–57.

198. N. Mandel'shtam, *Edinstvennaia i absoliutno edinaia partiia* (Moscow-Leningrad: Moskovskii rabochii, 1926), p. 25; A. Bubnov, *Partiia i oppozitsiia 1925 goda*, p. 28.

199. [So'lts], "Pravaia opasnost' v nashei partii," *Put' rabochei oppozitsii* (Moscow: Pravda i bednota, 1926), p. 3.

200. *Krasnoe znamia*, October 1, 1927; I. Stepichev, "Bor'ba KPSS s Trotskistko-Zinov'evskim antipartiinym blokom v 1926–1927gg", *Iz istorii partiinykh organizatsii vostochnoi sibiri* (Irkutsk, 1962), p. 13. PATO, f. 320, op. 1, d. 20, ll. 310b, 330b.

201. Mogila, p. 63.

202. A. Gendon, "Itogi preds"ezdovskoi diskussii v sibire," *Na leninskom puti*, no. 6 (1927), p. 19; Sol'ts, "Miasnikovshchina i trotskistskaia oppozitsiia," p. 15.

203. *Na leninskom puti*, no. 1 (1927), p. 29; Koz'min, *Oppozitsiia v sibiri*, pp. 13–14. Kuklin, the head of the Leningrad propaganda department under Zinoviev, and El'tsin, Trotsky's envoy from Moscow, came to Siberia to organize an oppositionist center. Radek, who spent some time in Tomsk, may also have been instrumental in helped local oppositionists establish ties with Trotsky. Demidov, *Politicheskaia bor'ba oppozitsii v sibiri*, pp. 83, 122.

204. I. Moletotov, *Sibkraikom: Pariinoe stroitel'stvo v Sibiri 1924–1930 gg* (Novosibirsk:

Nauka, Sib. otd-nie, 1978), p. 227; PATO, f. 17, op. 1, d. 1065, l. 61. The following numbers can be adduced to measure the size of the ultra-radical oppositionist cells in Siberia: the Tomsk Group, 62 members; the Irkutsk Group, 45 members; the Second Omsk Group, 13 members; the Third Omsk Group, 4 members; (the First Omsk Group, number unknown). PANO, f. 2, op. 1, d. 1308, l. 738. Endowed with "abnormal political consciousness and considerable organizational skill," oppositionists such as Gorbatykh had been dispatched from the cities to gull the innocent provincials. "Hardened during past struggles against the Central Committee" such individuals were reckoned to be "much more sophisticated than their provincial sympathizers." Indeed, the Siberian Control Commission singled out "overt" (*iavnye*) oppositionists as especially dangerous. TsGAODM, f. 3, op. 8, d. 92, l. 13. *SibKK-RKI: Otchet o rabote Aprel' 1927–Octiabr' 1928 IV Sibirskoi kraevoi partkonferentsii* (Novosibirsk, 1928), p. 41; PANO, f. 2, op. 1, d. 24, l. 59. Bak, "Vnepartiinye soiuzniki trotskistkoi oppozitsii," p. 11; Koz'min, *Oppozitsiia v sibiri*, p. 7.

205. *Rabochii put'*, October 21, 1927.

206. *Krasnoe znamia*, January 17, 1928; PATO, f. 17, op. 1, d. 1065, ll. 8, 10, 24, 280b–29, 610b–62; f. 320, op. 1, d. 20, l. 280b.

207. PANO, f. 6, op. 4, d. 26, l. 18.

208. Koz'min, *Oppozitsiia v sibiri*, pp. 11–12; See also *Pravda*, October 16, November 1, and November 27, 1927; *Izvestiia TsK VKP(b)* (1927), no. 42–43, p. 2; Stepichev, *Bor'ba KPSS s Trotskistko-Zinov'evskim antipartiinym blokom*, pp. 15–16. TsGAODM, f. 3, op. 8, d. 92, l. 61.

209. H. Rhodes, *The Satanic Mass* (New York: Rider, 1954), p. 24. Possibly the oldest account that exhibits the Black Mass's narratological structure is Tacitus's rendition of the Exodus. When his country was stricken by a plague, so the story goes, the Egyptian king consulted the oracle and learned that he must banish the Hebrews. Moses led the Hebrews to the promised land and established a capital in the holy city of Jerusalem. To solidify his spiritual authority, Moses invented a new religion that reverses all Eyptian rites and customs: "The Jews regard as profane all that we hold sacred; on the other hand, they permit all we abhor." In the temple of the Hebrews, the priests consecrate the donkey and sacrifice a ram to its statue, "apparently in derision of Ammon"; they also sacrifice a bull "because the Egyptians worship Apis." The Egyptian story Tacitus narrates is an exact inversion of the biblical one. If according to the Egyptians, the Jews are lepers, in the Bible the Egyptians are defamed as inhuman slave torturers. Tacitus, *Histories*, 5.3–5; M. Stern, *Greek and Latin Authors on Jews and Judaism*, 3 vols. (Jerusalem, 1974–1984), vol. 1, pp. 419–21. The logic of the Black Mass was at play during the struggle over the right to wield proletarian symbols in 1917; revolutionaries of various stripes claimed that they, and only they, were entitled to the red flag, and accused their opponents of besmirching this sacred symbol. The Anarchist-Communist leaflet from September 30, 1917, is worthy of Tacitus: "Instead of the red flag which our new 'tormentors' hold in hand they should be wielding a broom with dog's head on it." In hoisting red flags on their ships, the rebels of Kronshtadt similarly emphasized that they were more entitled to revolutionary symbols than the Bolsheviks. A leaflet of the Petrograd Workers' Organization published in April 1921 stated: "Kronshtadt rebelled not for the sake of the counterrevolution, but in order to wrestle the glorious Red Banner from the hands of the Party that soiled it with people's blood." *Anarkhisty*, vol. 2, p. 59; B. Kolonitskii, *Simvoly vlasti i bor'ba za vlast* (St. Petersburg, 2001), p. 284.

210. M. Summers, *History of Witchcraft and Demonology* (London: K. Paul, Trench,

Trubner and Co., 1926), pp. 146, 154–56. M. Griffin, "Devil Worship," *New Catholic Encyclopedia*, vol. 4 (London, 1967), p. 829.

211. The present reconstruction of oppositionist ritual is based on unfriendly, official testimony—none of the available sources shed much light on how Kutuzov and his followers themselves perceived their organization. Indeed, sources that would elucidate the oppositionists' own self-image are scarce. Interestingly, however, when Nadezhda Ioffe, an ardent follower of Trotsky, described oppositionist activity in the Plekhanov Institute of People's Economy where she studied in 1927, she presented the oppositionist attempt to mirror official institutions as "natural." "We did approximately what revolutionaries did in the tsarist underground," she recalled. "We organized groups of sympathizers at the factories and in the schools; we issued leaflets and distributed them.... The strongest Opposition group was in our Plekhanov Institute. We naturally established contacts with young workers, and due to this I became acquainted with many of their representatives. Their real names were not used. At one of those meetings I got to know Roman, one of the leaders of a 'group of five.' Somewhat later, I met for the second time with the man by the name of Roman. He said that in order to coordinate the work, a Moscow Komsomol Center had been formed, and the general opinion was that I should be sent there from our region. Soon, I was at the first session of the center. I don't remember how many people were there. Probably about ten or fifteen, but perhaps there were more. In any case, all the regions of Moscow were represented. We exchanged information—who among us was connected with what number of people and in what form. As far as I remember, no minutes of the meeting were taken. Nevertheless, a few years later, at one of my interrogations, the investigator read me a very detailed account of the sessions of the Moscow Center." *Back in Time: My Life, My Fate, My Epoch; The Memoirs of Nadezhda A. Joffe*, trans. F. Choate (Oak Park: Labor Publications, 1995), p. 67.

The testimony of the aforementioned Kuzovnikov, a Trotskyist leader of some stature in the Urals, is one of the few contemporary sources that can tell us something about the oppositionists' own self-understanding. True, Kuzovnikov's is not a pristine oppositionist voice: disillusioned and outraged, he had just cut his ties with the opposition. Yet the stenographic report of his speech before the Ural control commission is reproduced unedited. From time to time Kuzovnikov still reasserted his oppositionism, for example, when he refused to disclose secret apartments, identities of certain people, etc.

Broadly speaking, this testimony corroborates what emerges from Ioffe's memoir: the opposition was the Party's Siamese twin, a rival organization but one that could not disassociate itself from its other half. Kuzovnikov was the first to admit that, "what is extant is not a faction but a certain party. This party had not yet had a national congress but it does have a central committee; it convenes national party conferences and has its own apparatus in the provinces." Whenever something important happened, the oppositionist membership convened and leading activists reported. Such a plenary session could involve the narrow leadership (5–7 individuals) or the entire local cadres (about 25–30 individuals), depending on the circumstances. The regional center consisted of a "five [*piaterka*], activists assigned by our illegal regional center, ... and plenipotentiaries [*polnomochenye*] at every single district. At the grassroots level we have circles [*kruzhki*], whose activity is methodically guided by a program.... We have our own Ural theses covering all the issues." Additional trappings of a Bolshevik organization were in place. "We collected members dues; while some paid 10, 20, 30 kopeks, others paid a ruble ... based on the system of our Commissariat of Supplies: the richer the guy, the more he gives. . . . We also had an archive (including all the printed materials we received, the Declaration of 46, and other documents) and a typography; typing machines and a hectograph were located in a certain apartment."

The more Kuzovnikov said, the more evident it became that the opposition's organizational mentality corresponded with the official one. If the Central Committee worried that the Party was insufficiently homogeneous, so did the opposition. "Our faction, our Trotskyist party, did not have a unanimous leadership," Kuzovnikov reported, still noticeably upset. "We had Sapronovists and Shliapnikovists, and so on; they would come and go—musical chairs." Even the opposition's core was "never monolithic. The Zinovievists not only kept their own organizational center, but also their own political doctrine. . . . In addition, there was a Workers' Opposition center in the Urals, although at some point "it split in two and some of the guys joined the Trotskyist faction." Much like the official party, the opposition feared a "schism" (*raskol*). Much like the official party, it imposed "a most strict discipline [*strozhaishaia distsiplina*]" to avoid it. "We had a principle: if unanimity is absent on a certain issue, the center cannot raise that issue sharply lest a schism would occur." At the peak of the United Opposition's activity, discipline prevailed. Thus when major disagreements between groups intensified before the plenary session of the Komintern, Trotsky was able to enforce his position that the opposition must emerge from hiding. "It was decided that though we do not abide by the Party discipline we must abide by our own and the majority at the 'Central Committee' was ours, Trotskyist."

Following standard Bolshevik practice in yet another crucial domain, the oppositionist apparatus—and we saw that there clearly was one—monitored comrades' consciousness. The term "vacillations" (*kolebaniia*) cropped up frequently in Kuzovnikov's testimony, though here one doubted the opposition and possibly considered defection to the official political line. The opposition's effort in dispelling doubts and keeping comrades in its ranks paralleled similar efforts on the part of the Central Committee regarding its own following. Take the example of Evdokimov, Zinoviev's underling. "There was a period when Evdokimov vacillated gravely and leaned towards Leningrad workers [regarding by the opposition as insufficiently conscious]. Trotsky pressured Zinoviev, and Zinoviev pressured Evdokimov in turn, and the latter was eventually corrected." Evdokimov did nothing that would give the official Party committee reason to suspect that he vacillates [and to attempt to lure him to its side]. And what about Kuzovnikov himself? Making a confession, he had to testify to his own consciousness, its past and its present. Standing firmly on Trotskyist positions, he said, "I had no vacillations" during the New Course discussion of 1923. When Kuzovnikov began losing his faith, oppositionist hermeneuts such as Mrachkovskii and Beloborodov (the latter, an old supporter of Trotsky, was the person who signed the execution order for the tsar and his family) claimed that "I lost my bearings [*sdreifil*]" and that "in essence, I have already become a supporter of Stalin." This was a hermeneutical diagnosis that would not have shamed the Central Control Commission.

Questions of conversion and tally of loyal souls clearly preoccupied the oppositionist organization in the Urals. "We kept lists of our faction membership, together with personal evaluations [*kharkateristiki*], and appraisals [*otsenki*] of each and every one among us." In addition, there was a list of sympathizers Kuzovnikov kept, even though at some point a directive came to destroy it.

At first sight, a gulf had opened up between oppositionists and the Party in the fall of 1927, and Kuzovnikov became a carrier of an independent political identity, one often antagonistic to the official Party. When he boasted "receiving the GPU secret reports even before you [the control commission] and the Party branches did—their dissemination was coordinated with us," he spoke in terms of "us" and "you." The disjuncture between an oppositionist and a loyalist identity was even more glaring in the following statement: "We had a number of people in the presidium of the control commission. These were not your people—some of them were vacillating, others, sympathetic to us, helped us quite actively." And yet, it would be a simplification to regard the opposition as simply a splinter party. Using the official acronym—VKP(b)—when discussing "the decision of the Central Committee of the VKP(b) to remove our most active guys," Kuzovnikov distanced himself from the ruling party. Criticizing the opposition's move underground as "a method of struggle that goes against the Leninist teaching," he embraced it again. To be sure, Kuzovnikov numbered himself with a distinct political body—he called it the "Trotskyist party" a number of times, spoke about "our Central Committee" and "we, the Trotskyists," within this Central Committee—but this was a parasite party, one that could exist only in and through the official party organization. Hence his confusing use of the pronoun "we", sometimes referring to various oppositionist bodies, other times to the official party personnel. When Kuzovnikov stated that "activization . . . cost us our party cards" it was not altogether unclear in what organization he lost membership. "When I was isolated from the party our guys lost faith. They kept asking, 'How will we go on with our work without you?' 'Who will make speeches?' . . . Who will put in effect the 'preliminary understandings' [*predvaritel'nye sgovory*] regarding what and who to vote for before every meeting?" Communists were the enemy and a war was going on; "our leads in the apparatus enabled us to maneuver and determine what would be the force of a strike prepared against us and where it would take place." But one could not just enroll into an independent Trotskyist party; to be an oppositionist one had to be a Communist first. When Kuzovnikov emphasized that "even that member of a regional committee who knows the location of all the secret apartments and meeting places is not aware of the location of the typography, so that in case he switches to the side of the adversary [*protivnik*] he will betray only that part of the apparatus he himself was responsible for," he added a most curious comment: "You know about all that from your illegal work in the Bolshevik party." It was as if he wanted to emphasize that the opposition and the Party had an identical root. *Pravda*, November 23, 1927.

212. Rhodes, *The Satanic Mass*, pp. 24, 30.

213. Demidov, *Politicheskaia bor'ba oppozitsii v sibiri*, p. 77.

214. RGASPI, f. 17, op. 67, d. 370, l. 38; op. 69, d. 25, l. 148.

215. TsGAODM, f. 3, op. 8, d. 92, ll. 1–2.

216. *Sovetskaia sibir'*, October 28, 1927; *Krasnoe znamia*, January 17, 1928; Koz'min, *Oppozitsiia v sibiri*, p. 11; N. Gavrilov, "Moia rabota v oppozitsionnoi gruppe: Iz zapisok trotskista N. N. Gavrilova," *Pamiat': Istoricheskii sbornik, Pamiat'* (Paris, 1980), p. 389.

217. *Krasnoe znamia*, January 17 and March 17, 1928.

218. Bak, "Vnepartiinye soiuzniki trotskistkoi oppozitsii," p. 13.

219. Deutscher, *The Prophet Unarmed*, p. 368.

220. TsGAODM, f. 3, op. 8, d. 92, l. 55; *XV s"ezd RKP(b): Stenograficheskii otchet* (Moscow, 1928), p. 497.

221. *Arkhiv Trotskogo*, vol. 4, p. 49.

222. *Arkhiv Trotskogo*, vol. 4, p. 262.

223. *Arkhiv Trotskogo*, vol. 4, p. 267.

224. A. Slepkov, "Kak reagirovala oppozitsiia na resheniia XVgo s'ezda," *Bol'shevik*, no. 3–4 (1928), p. 23.

225. *XV s'ezd RKP(b): Stenographicheskii otchet* (Moscow, 1928), p. 494. RGASPI, f. 17, op. 67, d. 370, l. 38; op. 69, d. 25, l. 148. During 1927, the press reported about at least two underground oppositionist cells that were uncovered in Siberia. In May 1927, the GPU obtained the *Collective Appeal* to Maksimov, former member of the Workers' Opposition and now a functionary in the state apparatus. The document was seized during an apparently accidental search of the belongings of Krylov, a "drunk and rowdy" train conductor who was associated with oppositionists. The text of the appeal read, in part: "Rumors circulate among workers that the mutiny is imminent. . . . Please advise us, dictate to us, give us something to raise the spirits of the international masses with." On May 20, Krylov confessed to his participation in an "underground" oppositionist organization in the infamous Moscow jail, Lublianka. Demidov, *Politicheskaia bor'ba oppozitsii v sibiri*, p. 78. On November 29, 1927, another Siberian oppositionist underground was uncovered. This was how the story was reported in *Pravda*: "A bunch of railways workers, all Party members, noted that oppositionists are gathering in one particular apartment and decided to find out what is going on." Breaking their way in—"no one would open the door to them"—the workers found thirteen oppositionists present and Kuklin, a staunch Zinovievist, presiding over the meeting: "the underground oppositionists, discomfited by the sudden visit, tried to insinuate that this was just a friendly get-together. They even fetched a samovar but it turned out to be cold and empty of water." *Pravda*, December 4, 1927.

226. N. Zaretskii, *Klassovaia bor'ba v sibirskikh vuzakh* (Novosibirsk, 1929), p. 72.

227. Koz'min, *Oppozitsiia v sibiri*, pp. 11–12.

228. N. Filatov, "Omskie oppozitsionery," *Sovetskaia sibir'*, October 15, 1927; Zinoviev was refered to as "Zlatovratskii"; Party as "Patriot," etc. *Dva goda raboty TsKK i RKI SSSR: Otchet XV s'ezdu partii* (Moscow, 1927), p. 5; To be sure, not all oppositionists were willing to rise against the Soviet government with arms in hand in the late 1920s. Okudzhava, Kosior, and Rakovskii deemed it "the duty of the opposition to dissuade the working class from methods of struggle such as strikes. Strikes harm the country's economy and, eventually, the workers themselves." *Biulleten' oppozitsii*, no. 6 (1929), p. 3.

229. Demidov, *Politicheskaia bor'ba oppozitsii v sibiri*, p. 95.

230. *Rabochii put'*, September 22, 1927.

231. M. Zaitsev, "S kem i kuda idet oppozitsiia," *Na leninskom puti*, no. 1 (1927). Koz'min, *Oppozitsiia v sibiri*, p. 23. PATO, f. 320, op. 1, d. 20, l. 31.

232. Daniels, *Conscience of the Revolution*, p. 316; Deutscher, *The Prophet Unarmed*, p. 379.

233. PATO, f. 320, op. 1, d. 20, l. 36ob.

234. PATO, f. 17, op. 1, d. 749, l. 157.

235. A. V. "Kak raz"iasniat' resheniia plemuma TsK i TsKK sredi bezpartiinykh," *Agitator*, no. 1 (1927); PATO, f. 17, op. 1, d. 749, ll. 151–59; d. 883, l. 30.

236. PATO, f. 320, op. 1, d. 20, l. 36ob. When Trotsky himself heard of such insinuations he claimed these were the backward, anti-Semitic layers of the working class that were speaking: "workers are egged on by Stalin's anti-opposition campaign to make demands . . . in the Black Hundred style." During a street fight in Leningrad that led to the death of

a student who spoke in support of Trotsky, the attacking gang members indeed egged each other on with, "This Judas, Trotsky, sold our Lenin!" Following the events at the November 7 demonstration, an oppositionist complained to the control commission, "a Black Hundreder yelled at the top of his lungs, 'Away with the Jews, Trotsky and Zinoviev.' When a female supporter of Trotsky retorted with, 'Away with provocateurs and anti-Semites!' she was beaten by hooligans who shouted, 'hit the Trotskyists.'" Note how threats were literalized: from the verbal, "away with . . ." to actual beating. The majoritarians conceded that anti-Semitic allusions abounded during the discussion with the United Opposition, and the fact that its leaders, Trotsky, Kamenev, and Zinoviev, were Jews certainly did not go unnoticed. Iaroslavskii mentioned a peasant Communist saying: "Trotsky could not be a Communist. His very nationality shows he must live off speculation." Speculation here could be read literally as a reference to the economic activity of the Jews or metaphorically, as reference to the supposedly fickle and disloyal political behavior of Jewish Communists. "Political speculation exists!" an anonymous voice exclaimed during one of the Moscow gatherings. "I am against the opposition because the majority in the Central Committee are Israelites [*Izraili*]," another voice followed suit. The opposition's attack on the village allowed for the following metonymic chain to form in the majoritarian grassroots rhetoric: anti-Stalin, anti-kulak, anti-Russian. Thus workers from the Bogatyr factory offered the following commentary to political events at the Fifteenth Party Congress: "this is a quarrel between the Jews and the Russians. Those who persecute Stalin and Bukharin . . . fear the kulak. The kulak is a muzhik, so the Jews are afraid of him." *Arkhiv Trotskogo*, vol. 3, pp. 98, 122 ("Black Hundred style"); TsGA IPD, f. K-598, op. 1, d. 70, ll. 39–40 ("Judas"); *Piatnadtsatyi s"ezd VKP(b)*, p. 397 ("speculation"); RGASPI, f. 17, op. 71, d. 80, l. 9 ("Israelites"); RGASPI, f. 17, op. 85, d. 67, l. 27 ("muzhiks"); RGASPI, f. 17, op. 71, d. 80, l. 9 ("violence").

237. *Krasnoe znamia*, November 2, 11, 13, 17, 1927; PATO, f. 17, op. 1, d. 749, l. 161. Many oppositionists still believed in the fairness of Party institutions, or, at least, made rhetorical gestures to emphasize that they expected the control commission to curb their delegitimation. Vrachev, a Bolshevik military specialist and an ardent Trotskyist, denounced Beseden, the Krasnaia Presnia district committee's official reporter, to the Moscow control commission on October 3, 1927. What raised Vrachev's ire were the words of the reporter to the effect that "You, oppositionists, got yourselves involved with the counterrevolution." Vrachev was insulted and angry at the provocation. "I immediately demanded that the words of the reporter will be written down into the protocol and notified the cell that I will ask the Party's controlling organs to censure the reporter." It is quite possible that Vrachev was gesturing, not acting. After all, he admitted that "what the reporter said must have been based on the notorious statements by the Politburo and the Central Control Commission." Nevertheless, it is noteworthy that he still "deemed it [his] Communist duty to bring comrade Beseden to a Party trial." The Moscow Control Commission ignored Vrachev's denunciation and later on in the year purged him from the Party. Increasingly, the control commissions were seen as a tool in Stalin's hand, so much so that their anti-oppositionist bias was described in underground oppositionist leaflets as a form of "facism." RGASPI, f. 17, op. 71, d. 80, l. 10. M. David-Fox, *Revolution of the Mind: Higher Learning among the Bolsheviks, 1918–1929* (Ithaca: Cornell University Press, 1997), p. 116.

238. PATO, f. 17, op. 1, d. 1065, ll. 25, 60.

239. PATO, f. 320, op. 1, d. 20, l. 360b.

240. TsGAODM, f. 3, op. 8, d. 92, l. 52. *Arkhiv Trotskogo*, vol. 4, 258–59; Daniels, *Conscience of the Revolution*, p. 316.

241. *Pravda*, November 10, 1927; *Krasnoe znamia*, November 10 and 15, 1927.

242. *Arkhiv Trotskogo*, vol. 4, p. 260.

243. *Arkhiv Trotskogo*, vol. 4, p. 257. Kamenev admitted that unfolding banners that were not approved by Party institutions could be regarded as "violation of discipline" but claimed that the banners themselves contained nothing anti-Soviet. Besides, with banners such as "Away with the Opposition" carried through the Red Square a number of times, "the Central Committee took the intra-Party debates to the street anyway." *Arkhiv Trotskogo*, vol. 4, p. 262.

244. *Izvestiia TsK VKP(b)*, no. 42–43 (1927), pp. 1–2. *Pravda*, November 15, 1927. RGASPI, f. 17, op. 69, d. 26, l. 117. According to the official sources, in the period intervening between the Fourteenth and the Fifteenth Party Congresses, 2,031 Communists were censored for "factionalism"; 14 percent of them classified as "students." *XV s'ezd RKP(b)*, p. 496.

245. *Krasnoe znamia*, October 26, November 23–24, 1927; PATO, f. 17, op. 1, d. 749, l. 1540b; f. 320, op. 1, d. 20, l. 350b; Ingulov, pp. 7–8.

246. "Posle ob"edinennogo plenary sessiona," *Na leninskom puti*, no. 1 (1927), p. 6.

247. PANO, f. 2, op. 1, d. 1859, l. 161.

248. *Pravda*, November 10, 1927; *Sovestskaia Sibir'*, November 10–13, 1927; Koz'min, *Oppozitsiia v sibiri*, p. 9; Gendin, p. 17; *Izvestiia TsK VKP(b)*, no. 45–46 (1927), p. 2.

249. *Arkhiv Trotskogo*, vol. 3, p. 86.

250. *Arkhiv Trotskogo*, vol. 3, pp. 82–83.

251. *Arkhiv Trotskogo*, vol. 3, p. 85.

252. *Arkhiv Trotskogo*, vol. 3, pp. 102–3; vol. 4, p. 50.

253. RGASPI, f. 17, op. 71, d. 12, ll. 1–86.

254. *Arkhiv Trotskogo*, vol. 3, l. 95.

255. RGASPI, f. 17, op. 71, d. 7, l. 111.

256. RGASPI, f. 17, op. 2, d. 317, l. 50.

257. According to Radek's information, 2,500 individuals signed the Declaration of the Eighty-three (August 12, 1927). *Arkhiv Trotskogo*, vol. 4, p. 75.

258. *Arkhiv Trotskogo*, vol. 3, pp. 82–83.

259. Deutscher, *The Prophet Unarmed*, pp. 367, 370.

260. *Pravda*, November 23, 1927.

261. PATO, f. 76, op. 1, d. 33, l. 28. According to Belen'kii, an oppositionist activist from Irkutsk, one third of the local Party organization supported the opposition. *Vlast' truda*, November 10, 1927; *Sovetskaia Sibir'*, November 11, 1927. For an attempt to measure the popularity of the United Opposition see K. Murphy, "Opposition at the Local Level: A Case Study of the Hammer and Sickle Factory," *Europe-Asia Studies* 53, no. 2 (2001), p. 347.

262. *Pravda*, November 24, 1928.

263. *Bol'shevitskoe rukovodstvo: Perepiska. 1912–1927* (Moscow: ROSSPEN, 1996), pp. 355–56. Lunacharskii was skeptical of reprisals against the opposition for similar reasons. "This only pushes the opposition into hiding, but does not break it," he noted. "'Sudorozhno tsepliaiutsia za ortodoksiiu . . .' Neizvestnoe pis'mo A. V. Lunacharskogo L. B. Krasinu," *Kommunist*, no. 12 (1991), p. 104. How Bubnov, the head of the Red Army's political brunch, discussed student grumbling at the Tolmachev Military-Political Acad-

emy in Leningrad tells us about the fear of surreptitious oppositionists. "The hell with all this hash-hashing [*shushukania*], group meetings, supposedly insignificant correspondence, pseudo-scientific chatting [*boltovnia*], silences and rumors [*krivotolki*]—they are absolutely intolerable," he wrote to Voroshilov in a private letter of September 11, 1928. According to Bubnov, attitudes that remained concealed were dangerous because their fermentation went unchecked. Informants told him that the local opposition plans to strengthen itself first and then "emerge into the open towards the end of the year." Embittered against the Central Committee, the student Evseev, for example, "cannot wait to reveal himself [*proiavit' sebia otkryto*]." In a follow-up letter of November 4, 1928, Bubnov continued bashing "worthless folks" who attack the Central Committee "from blind corners. . . . Take Ratnek, who sat still during the discussion at the Moscow Military Academy, kept quiet as a blockhead [*churban*], and then suddenly launched himself. He must have waited for the most opportune moment—what a scumbag!" *Sovetskoe rukovodstvo: Perepiska*, pp. 42–43, 56.

264. *Arkhiv Trotskogo*, vol. 4, p. 227.

265. *Piatnadtsatyi s"ezd VKP(b)*, pp. 68–82.

266. *Piatnadtsatyi s"ezd VKP(b)*, p. 284.

267. *Piatnadtsatyi s"ezd VKP(b)*, p. 235.

268. *Piatnadtsatyi s"ezd VKP(b)*, p. 331.

269. *Piatnadtsatyi s"ezd VKP(b)*, pp. 235–36.

270. *Piatnadtsatyi s"ezd VKP(b)*, p. 333.

271. *Piatnadtsatyi s"ezd VKP(b)*, pp. 219–20.

272. *Piatnadtsatyi s"ezd VKP(b)*, p. 260.

273. *Piatnadtsatyi s"ezd VKP(b)*, p. 293.

274. *Piatnadtsatyi s"ezd VKP(b)*, p. 332.

275. *Piatnadtsatyi s"ezd VKP(b)*, pp. 68–82.

276. *Piatnadtsatyi s"ezd VKP(b)*, p. 291.

277. N. Zen'kovich, *Samye zakrytye liudi* (Moscow: "Ol'ma Press," 2002), pp. 285, 689.

278. *Arkhiv Trotskogo*, vol. 4, p. 238.

279. TsGAODM, f. 3, op. 8, d. 92, l. 45.

280. *Piatnadtsatyi s"ezd VKP(b)*, p. 262; Daniels, *Conscience of the Revolution*, pp. 319–20.

281. Daniels, *Conscience of the Revolution*, p. 318.

282. *XV s"ezd RKP(b): Stenographicheskii otchet* (Moscow, 1928), pp. 352–53.

283. Demidov, *Politicheskaia bor'ba oppozitsii v sibiri*, p. 126.

284. Serge, *Memoirs of a Revolutionary*, p. 232; V. Volkogonov, *Trotskii* (Moscow, 1992), vol. 2, p. 83.

285. PANO, f. 6, op. 4, d. 22, l. 49.

286. *XV s"ezd RKP(b): Stenographicheskii otchet* (Moscow, 1928), pp. 1286–87. For tensions between the supporters of Smirnov (Democratic Centralists) and the Trotskyists see *Sputnik kommunista* (1929), no. 1–2, p. 12.

287. Demidov, *Politicheskaia bor'ba oppozitsii v sibiri*, p. 93.

288. *IV plenary session SibK. 10–13 marta 1928 g.* (Novosibirsk, 1928), pp. 5–6.

289. Gusev, "Levokummunisticheskaia oppozitsiia," p. 98.

290. *Vlast' truda*, February 10 and March 11, 1928; *Sovetskaia sibir'*, May 15, 1928; Gendon, "Itogi preds"ezdovskoi diskussii v sibire," *Na leninskom puti*, no. 6 (1927), p. 22; E. Iaroslavskii, *Za poslednei chertoi: Trotskistkaia oppozitsiia posle XV s"ezda* (Moscow-

Leningrad, 1930), p. 64. This was a continuation of a trend set in the autumn of 1927, after the Party's control commissions began purging oppositionists. If in August–September the Central Committee received less than one hundred declarations of "severance of ties with the opposition," in October–November the corresponding number climbed to 518. *Izvestiia TsK VKP(b)*, no. 45–46 (1927), p. 6.

291. *Krasnoe znamia*, January 5, 11, 17, 1928; Glebov, "Kto vedet sovremennuiu oppozitsiiu?" p. 39; PATO, f. 17, op. 1, d. 883, ll. 90–96, 153.

292. PATO, f. 320, op. 1, d. 20, l. 280b.

293. PATO, f. 17, op. 1, d. 883, l. 92.

294. The following excerpt from a stenographic report gives an inkling as to how one such "working through" of the issues evolved in Tomsk in the winter of 1927–28: "Q: Why was the opposition forbidden from publishing its platform and contesting the Central Committee's theses? A: Because the Central Committee maintains that the opposition is a tiny bunch [*kuchka*] and that its platform is Menshevik. Q: What about the opposition's argument that the Central Committee is starting to do only now what the opposition was advocating long ago—attack the kulak? A: The opposition can come up with all kinds of things. The Party pressed the kulak and the NEPman all that time so they have nothing left. But to kill [*umertvit'*] them was deemed unadvisable at the time because our agriculture and industry were weak. Now times have changed, and attacks on the kulak and NEPman can be launched.... Q: Is it possible to build socialism in one country? A: (collective) There are difficulties, but we can and will build socialism. Special opinion of comrade Riazanov: We can build socialism only after international revolution." PATO, f. 17, op. 1, d. 883, ll. 90–96.

295. "Itogi XV s"ezda," *Agitator*, no. 1 (1928), p. 3. PATO, f. 17, op. 1, d. 1065, p. 17.

296. *Arkhiv Trotskogo*, vol. 3, pp. 77–78.

297. *Krasnoe znamia*, January 17, 1928; PATO, f. 17, op. 1, d. 883, ll. 90–96.

298. Daniels, *Conscience of the Revolution*, p. 319.

299. *Krasnoe znamia*, January 6, 1928.

300. PATO, f. 17, op. 1, d. 1065, ll. 4, 25; PATO, f. 17, op. 1, d. 1076. l. 24.

301. PATO, f. 17, op. 1, d. 1065, l. 28.

Chapter 6: Inquisition, Communist Style

1. PATO, f. 17, op. 1, d. 1065, l. 28.

2. PATO, f. 17, op. 1, d. 1065, ll. 25–27.

3. PATO, f. 17, op. 1, d. 1065, l. 260b.

4. PATO, f. 17, op. 1, d. 1076, l. 27.

5. My discussion here is informed here by the superb J. H. Arnold, *Inquisition and Power: Catharism and the Confessing Subject in Medieval Languedoc* (Philadelphia: University of Pennsylvania Press, 2001).

6. M. de Certeau, *The Practice of Everyday Life* (Berkeley: University of California Press, 2002), pp. 29–42.

7. PATO, f. 17, op. 1, d. 1065, ll. 9–11, 30–31, 67.

8. All in all, the verification commission working at Tomsk Technological Institute implicated 59 students in oppositionism. Five students were purged, 13 reprimanded, and 9

warned. Nine students came out clean and 23 cases were transferred to the Tomsk control commission. PATO, f. 17, op. 1, d. 1065, l. 60.

9. Tomsk students were not receiving especially harsh treatment: as a result of the work of verification commissions across the country, 2,270 Communists were purged from the Party for "factionalism" from December 1927 until June 1, 1928 (another 3,098 Communists declared their "departure" from the opposition during the same time period). From the Fifteenth Party Congress until February 1, 1930, the Party's control commissions purged 7,300 oppositionists (3,110 were subsequently reinstated). Citing these data, Ordzhonikidze, the head of the Central Control Commission, boasted before the Sixteenth Party Congress (1929), "Nothing has remained out of the Trotskyist Opposition!" *Biulleten' TsK VKP(b)—NK RKI SSSR i RSFSR*, no. 6 (1928), p. 31. *Bol'shevik*, no. 4 (1929), p. 28; *XVI s"ezd VKP(b)* (Moscow, 1930), p. 323. PATO, f. 17, op. 1, d. 1065, ll. 59–60.

10. PATO, f. 17, op. 1, d. 1065, ll. 8–13, 60–62.

11. Texts found to contain "ambiguity" (*dvumysel*) were investigated by the Tomsk control commission. PATO, f. 17, op. 1, d. 1065, l. 4. TsGA IPD, f. 408, op. 1, d. 1175, l. 59.

12. PATO, f. 17, op. 1, d. 1065, l. 4.

13. PATO, f. 17, op. 1, d. 1065, ll. 26–29, 66–67.

14. Shliapnikov protested before the Politburo in 1926 against the "policelike questioning" (*politseiskie voprosy*) of the oppositionists by the control commissions. B. Belkin, "'Rabochaia oppozitsiia,' Post Scriptum," in *Oni ne molchali*, ed. A. Afanas'ev (Moscow: Politizdat, 1991), p. 55.

15. TsGA IPD, f. 197, op. 1, d. 732, l. 41.

16. PATO, f. 17, op. 1, d. 1065, ll. 54–57, 60–62.

17. Borer was accused of having shielded oppositionists by choosing to omit all record of unorthodox votes from the official record. To get at his state of mind, the commission posed a counterfactual question: "What resolution would you have voted for if you could have?" Borer made an effort to assure his interrogators that he had been a majoritarian at heart: "During the Discussion I spoke [in favor of certain ideas Kutuzov had] simply to display my independent-mindedness." The commission was unconvinced: "Borer doubtlessly would have voted for the opposition had he been a full Party member"; the verdict was all about disposition and not at all concerned with actual conduct. "He is lying from A to Z when he denies having been an ardent oppositionist." PATO, f. 17, op. 1, d. 1065, ll. 8–13.

18. Identical sins did not necessarily entail identical censures. The verification commission rejected a formal system of retribution. Having received a "reprimand" from the bureau, the worker Kostyliuk, for example, complained the censure was undeservingly strict. "My only lapse," he stated, "was my support of the opposition's demand to see secret Party documents published. My awe before the authority of Kamenev and Zinoviev motivated my step." When the cell requested an explanation as to "why for similar misdemeanors other oppositionists got only a warning" the bureau acknowledged that strictures were dealt according to the expectations from this or that comrade. Kostyliuk, for example, "was an old-timer in our cell; as such he should have been more disciplined." PATO, f. 17, op. 1, d. 1065, ll. 8–13, 66–67.

19. RGASPI, f. 17, op. 71, d. 80, l. 51. I. Koz'min, "XV s"ezd o trotskistkoi oppozitsii," *Agitator*, no. 1 (1928).

20. PATO, f. 17, op. 1, d. 1065, ll. 4, 33–37.

21. S. Kotkin, *Magnetic Mountain: Stalinism as a Civilization* (Berkeley: University of California Press, 1995), pp. 335–36.

22. K. Rudolf, "Heresy," *Encyclopedia of Religions* (1987), vol. 6, p. 270.

23. G. Buckley, "Sin of Heresy," in *New Catholic Encyclopedia* (New York: McGraw-Hill, 1967–1989), vol. 6, p. 1069.

24. This definition, by Robert Grosseteste (d. 1253), is quoted after E. Peters, *Inquisition* (London: Collier Macmillan, 1988), p. 42.

25. H. Schiler, "Hairesis," *Theological Dictionary of the New Testament*, ed. G. Kittel (Grand Rapids, Mich.: Eerdmans, 1964), vol. 1, pp. 182–83.

26. Few oppositionists wished the ominous title of a heretic upon themselves. Recanting, they typically did their best to show that their inner thoughts were characteristic of "doubters" who had succeeded in fully purging counterrevolutionary thoughts from their head. The poetics of a recantation letter was derivative of the confessional structure of the Communist autobiography. The recantation focused on the spiritual history of the oppositionist's consciousness. Unlike the autobiography, with its single account of conversion to Communism, the oppositionist's recantation often narrated the story of no less than three quasi-conversions. By virtue of the narrator's already being a Communist, the first, original conversion, not necessarily spelled out, was always in the background. Succumbing to the temptation of the opposition represented the second conversion, a conversion to heterodoxy. Explaining and somehow justifying this lapse was not easy. The author typically claimed that his doubting state of mind was shallow and fleeting and soon was transcended. The third conversion, which the oppositionist's recantation usually dwelt on, allowed the narrator to claim he had made his way back to the Party's bosom. Terminating his recent spiritual tribulation, it was the story of how Communist orthodoxy was embraced again. In his autobiography from April 1933, Zinoviev wrote about "three discrete lives comprising my former life [*tri tselykh zhizni v svoei predydushchei zhizni*]": youth, before he met Lenin and was converted by him to Bolshevism, "the period of work together with Ilich," and the "period of Stalin." *Izvestiia TsK KPSS*, 1989, vol. 7, p. 177.

27. PATO, f. 17, op. 1, d. 1065, ll. 8–13, 60–62. The oppositionism of Firsov could be traced back to the New Course Discussion with Trotsky. In the fall of 1923 he served on the bureau of the workers' faculty at the Tomsk University, where a "squabble" was unearthed. Headed by a certain Riadozubov, a faction of students, Firsov among them, critiqued the leadership of the cell, earning the title "Trotskyists." Obrazov maintained that "oppositionist attitudes lingered in Firsov from then until now." Asked whether he supported Riadozubov, Firsov claimed that "at the time I was neutral. But it was me who took all the heat [*a raskhlebyvat' vsiu kashu prishlos' mne*]." Once interrogators ascertained that the defendant did not try to convert anyone to oppositionism, Firsov was issued a "warning" only. PATO, f. 17, op. 1, d. 1065, ll. 33–37.

28. RGASPI, f. 17, op. 85, d. 67, l. 59.

29. M. Foucault, "The Subject as Power," in H. Dreyfus and P. Rabinow, *Michel Foucault, Beyond Structuralism and Hermeneutics* (Chicago: University of Chicago Press, 1982), pp. 214–15.

30. Pastoral care saved the outspoken oppositionist Kochkurov from a certain purge. Kochkurov was deemed to be "clearly unprepared to combine academic studies with theoretical development. . . . He gave little thought to where Kutuzovshchina might lead the Party." But this was a worker, and censure had to be applied judiciously. "Our general

impression," his benefactors said in his defense, "is that Kochkurov has been thoroughly brainwashed. . . . Something came over him [ego chto to zakhlestnulo].'I can't understand what's going on with me,' he would say." Clearly, Kochkurov had "lost his mind" (poterial golovu) the past autumn. But a hardened worker such as him deserved a second chance. "The lad is sincere," the proponents of pastoral care concluded. "He has learned his lesson, and in the future he'll think twice." PATO, f. 17, op. 1, d. 1065, ll. 8–13.

31. TsGAODM, f. 3, op. 8, d. 92, l. 10.

32. PATO, f. 17, op. 1, d. 1065, ll. 8–13, 26–29, 60–62. Just like Gorshunov, Popkov was suspected of being close to the arrested Goliakov—the two shared the same room in the dormitories—but his defense was much more successful. "Having known Goliakov since 1920, as a regular vacillator I swallowed none of his baits," Popkov assured the verification commission. "I found out Goliakov does factionalist work when everyone else already knew about it," so he did not bother to denounce him. Laptev believed the defendant: "I know Popkov: he might have agreed with Goliakov on some of the issues but for most part he took Goliakov to task for the latter's instability [nepostoianstvo]." PATO, f. 17, op. 1, d. 1065, ll. 33–37.

33. PATO, f. 17, op. 1, d. 1076, l. 25.

34. PATO, f. 17, op. 1, d. 1065, ll. 26–29.

35. *Stalinskoe politburo v 30-e gody*, pp. 104–5.

36. TsGA IPD, f. 197, op. 1, d. 732, l. 41.

37. H. Rhodes, *The Satanic Mass* (New York: Rider, 1954), p. 40 ("modern defendant"); Peters, *Inquisition*, p. 56 ("erring brother").

38. PATO, f. 17, op. 1, d. 1065, ll. 8–13.

39. PATO, f. 17, op. 1, d. 1065, ll. 12–13.

40. PATO, f. 17, op. 1, d. 1065, ll. 8–13, 26–29, 60–62.

41. PATO, f. 17, op. 1, d. 1065, ll. 54–57.

42. PATO, f. 17, op. 1, d. 1065, ll. 8–13, 60–62.

43. PATO, f. 17, op. 1, d. 1065, ll. 54–57. The best way to expose a double-dealer was to trace his political conduct over time, and the inquiry into the case of Labutin, a student with another vulnerable biography, makes this point evident. Interrogators imagined that Labutin was in spiritual cahoots with the opposition, and that he had concealed his heterodoxy because his previous record of insubordination had gotten him into enough trouble. There had been a time when he had abruptly exited the Party. His next departure had been involuntary: following the New Course Discussion, he was purged. Klikunov thought that "Labutin refrained from voting for the countertheses not because he was convinced by the Central Committee majority position, but simply because of cowardice." The bureau suggested that the verification commission of 1928 simply adopt the characterization of Labutin offered by its predecessors in 1924: this was "an alien element and a sponger." Though the Central Control Commission had absolved Labutin of this charge at the time, Labutin's more recent heterodoxy suggested that the regional verification commission had seen through his protests. "I think that the doubts expressed by Labutin during the last Discussion are the logical conclusion of a whole chain of vacillations and uncertainties," stated Klikunov. "We have to teach Labutin once and for all." Obrazov was also convinced that "Labutin was an oppositionist from day one."

Though he was tightly hemmed in, Labutin did not surrender: "You misunderstood my vacillations. A "worker and the son of a worker," he voted for the opposition (on the issue of democracy) "only because I wanted to see the unpublished materials." As for his other wrongdoing, opposing Kutuzov's expulsion from the institute, he explained that, "if Kutuzov had been purged and thrown into the workers' milieu, he could have caused even more damage. Workers are more naive regarding the maneuvers of the likes of Kutuzov because they have yet to be exposed to the temptations of the opposition." In other words, his vote for Kutuzov had not been a vote for Kutuzov at all. But even such a touching display of concern for the protection of workers' consciousness could not secure Labutin's acquittal. "One can hardly speak of Labutin as having a worker's psychology," commented Obrazov. "In 1917, I worked in the northern forest along with Labutin, but I never saw him hanging out with the young workers. He preferred to move in the intelligentsia circles." Despite Labutin's protestations ("At the time I was an activist in the Union of Socialist Youth, which was made up entirely of workers"), Obrazov would not relent: Where were all those members of the Union of Socialist Youth during the coup against Soviet power in Siberia, he wanted to know. "They went to Kolchak." Eventually, the verification commission passed Labutin's file along to the Tomsk circuit control commission, requesting that the supervisory body "clarify the facts regarding Labutin's past." The outcome of this investigation is unknown. PATO, f. 17, op. 1, d. 1065, ll. 33–37.

44. L. Gilmore, "Policing the Truth: Confession, Gender, and Autobiographical Authority," in *Autobiography and Postmodernism*, ed. K. Ashley, L. Gilmore, and G. Peters (Amherst: University of Massachusetts Press, 1994), p. 54.

45. D. Harlan, "Intellectual History and the Return of Literature," *Americal Historical Review*, vol. 94 (1989), pp. 591–92.

46. C. Ginzburg, *Myths, Emblems, Clues* (London: Hutchinson Radius, 1990), p. 160.

47. G. Spivak, "Subaltern Studies: Deconstructing Historiography," in *Selected Subaltern Studies*, ed. R. Guha and G. Spivak (New York: Oxford University Press, 1988), pp. 3–32.

48. Ginzburg, *Myths, Emblems, Clues*, p. 160.

49. Ibid., pp. 162–64.

50. *Arkhiv Trotskogo: Kommunisticheskaiia oppozitsiia v SSSR, 1923–1927*, ed. Iu. Felshtinskii (Moscow: Terra, 1990), vol. 4, p. 119.

51. PATO, f. 17, op. 1, d. 1065, ll. 60–62.

52. My approach here follows M. de Certeau, *The Writing of History* (New York: Columbia University Press, 1988), p. 257.

53. *KPSS v rezoliutsiiakh i resheniiakh*, vol. 4, p. 74.

54. A. Slepkov, "Kak reagirovala opozitsiia na resheniia XV s"ezda," *Bol'shevik*, no. 3–4 (1928), pp. 19–31.

55. *Partiia i oppozitsiia po dokumentam: Materialy k XV s"ezdu VKP(b)*, vyp. 2 (Moscow, 1927).

56. *Bol'shevik*, no. 19–20 (1926), p. 17.

57. *Arkhiv Trotskogo*, vol. 2, pp. 180.

58. RGASPI, f. 17, op. 2, d. 441, ll. 118–19.

59. *Piatnadtsatyi s'ezd VKP(b), dekabr' 1927 goda: Stenograficheskii otchet* (Moscow: Gospolitizdat, 1961–1962), p. 290.

60. "Itogi XV s"ezda," *Agitator*, no. 1 (1928), p. 7.

61. A. Gendon, "Itogi preds"ezdovskoi diskussii v sibire," *Na leninskom puti*, no. 6 (1927), p. 20.

62. K. Clark, *The Soviet Novel: History as Ritual* (Chicago: University of Chicago Press, 1985), p. 187.

63. PATO, f. 17, op. 1, d. 1065, ll. 26–29.

64. PATO, f. 17, op. 1, d. 1065, ll. 33–37, 66–67.

65. N. Berdiaev, *The Origins of Russian Communism* (New York, 1937), p. 202.

66. Ibid.

67. Stalin, *Sochineniia*, vol. 11, p. 314.

68. PATO, f. 320, op. 1, d. 20, l. 360b.

69. *Arkhiv Trotskogo*, vol. 4, p. 205.

70. RGASPI, f. 17, op. 71, d. 80, l. 17. "Za gran' sovetskoi legal'nosti," *Molodoi bol'shevik*, no. 22 (1927); Partiets, "Raskol'nicheskii put' oppozitsii," *Sputnik agitatora*, no. 13 (1927); *Sotsialisticheskii vestnik*, July 2, 1927, p. 12.

71. V. Serge, *Memoirs of a Revolutionary, 1901–1941* (Oxford, 1951), p. 233; V. Morgun, "Ne sklonivshii golovy," *Krasnoe znamia*, January 22, 1989. For the next stages in the demonization of Trotskyists see: E. Iaroslavskii, "Vcherashnii i zavtrashnii den' trotskistov," *Bol'shevik* 1929, no. 2, p. 17; A. Griunberg, *O trotskizme i trotskistakh* (Moscow, 1931). Iakov Bliumkin, Mirbach's assassin and a revolutionary of some fame, was sentenced to death shortly thereafter for daring to communicate with Trotsky. Though by the 1930s such a sentence would become routine, it was a shocking punishment at the time. I. Deutscher, *The Prophet Outcast: Trotsky, 1929–1940* (London: Oxford University Press, 1963), pp. 84–91.

72. RGASPI, f. 17, op. 85, d. 222, l. 37.

73. PATO, f. 17, op. 1, d. 1065, ll. 59–62.

74. As punishment, the two young worker-students were assigned public service "so that their minds could be adequately aired out." PATO, f. 17, op. 1, d. 1065, ll. 8–13.

75. Nikolaev did not have a sound social background he could fall back on. An orphan, he was raised by his two grandmothers, one a "petit bourgeois," the other a backward peasant. Still, the defendant showed his mettle in fashioning himself as a working class protector. When asked whether he was ever censured by the Party before, Nikolaev told the bureau that the control commission demoted his status to candidate for one year for supporting Omelich, a railroad worker who got in trouble for beating up his manager. He could not have acted any differently. Omelich's act of defiance symbolized to Nikolaev "the working class throwing a punch at the mug of Russian bureaucracy." Usanov corroborated the self-image the defendant was projecting: "Nikolaev was very active among railroad workers. He never alienated himself from the proletariat . . . so his recantation must be sincere." Yet this line of defense was scuttled by Zimov from the Tomsk district committee—and this is a rare case where the deliberation process at the level of the cell was circumvented by the Party higher-ups. Unable to see a leading oppositionist getting off the hook, he cited mysterious materials he saw at the GPU or the Tomsk Control Commission's offices: "I cannot reveal much except that this Omelich, on whose behalf Nikolaev interceded, was unmasked as an undercover provocateur and was purged from the Party."

76. *Izvestiia TsK KPSS*, no. 10 (1989), p. 68.

77. TsGA IPD, f. 138, op. 1, d. 1g, l. 12.

78. TsGA IPD, f. 258, op. 1, d. 14, l. 60; PANO, f. 1, op. 2, d. 241, l. 182.

79. RGASPI, f. 17, op. 71, d. 114, ll. 1–12. A. Gusev, "Levokummunisticheskaia oppozit-siia v SSSR v kontse 20-kh godov," *Obshchestvennaia istoriia*, vol. 1 (1996), p. 90.

80. RGASPI, f. 17, op. 71, d. 80, l. 23.

81. *Biulleten' TsK VKP(b)—NK RKI SSSR i RSFSR*, no. 4–5 (1929), p. 52. V. V. Demidov, *Politicheskaia bor'ba oppozitsii v sibiri, 1922–1929* (Novosibirsk, 1994), p. 133. The terms for the opposition's return into the Party were heatedly debated throughout 1928–29. Every word in every document was carefully weighed and the process had all the trappings of diplomatic negotiation. Judging by the time Stalin and the rest of the majoritarian leadership invested in reading and editing recantations until they assumed satisfactory shape, the Party treated its contrition rituals with utmost seriousness. Recantations had to be full and sincere and both sides excluded simulation: acting against all considerations of utility, the oppositionists agreed to renege on some of their beliefs but not on others, and the majoritarians insisted on certain formulas but made sure that those formulas would come from the renegades themselves. The oppositionists needed time to work on themselves if their recantations were to be worth the paper they were written on. Radek put it nicely in a letter to Piatakov from the beginning of 1928: "One cannot 'sincerely' capitulate too quickly. When I capitulate, perhaps in the not-too-distant future, I will do so 'sincerely' and 'openly' [*iskrenno i otkryto*]." In a year, a substantial progress was achieved. Iaroslavskii reported to Ordzhonikidze on July 29, 1929, that whereas Serebriakov and Drobnis "made acceptable recantations, the troika—Radek, Smilga, and Preobr[azhenskii] recanted *without* removing their signatures [from the oppositionist Platform] or denouncing their mistakes. Later they agreed to introduce these two points so I could send the text to Stalin, who, together with Molotov, introduced fresh corrections . . . ; Radek and Preobr[azhenskii] were today in my office and said they cannot agree to these new corrections so the issue in their regard drags on. If you ask me, this is a shame. There is no need to demand that they described the policy of the Party and the Central Committee from 1925–27 as *invariably correct*—we did make serious mistakes. [Stalin's doggedness] delays the departure of Smirnov [from the opposition]—he would surely have long recanted otherwise. Willy nilly, about 100–200 individuals would have parted ways with the Trotskyists—and these are not the worst revolutionaries I can think of" [italics in the original]." From July until the end of October 1929 the group of I. N. Smirnov continued drafting one recantation after another. First, they admitted their mistakes but also continued to criticize aspects of Central Committee policy and demanded that Trotsky be returned into the country. Gradually giving in, they revised their statements. Finally, Stalin was satisfied. On October 29, 1929, the Politburo resolved "to regard the recantation of I. N. Smirnov as acceptable [*priemlimoe*]." A. Gratsiozi, *A New, Peculiar State: Explorations in Soviet History, 1917–1937* (London: Praeger, 2000), p. 59, note 14 (Radek); *Sovetskoe rukovodstvo: Perepiska; 1928–1941* (Moscow: ROSSPEN, 1999), p. 81; *Izvestiia Tsk KPSS*, no. 6 (1991), pp. 74–76 (Smirnov).

The center of a Communist's life was supposed to be outside his individual self, and he had to draw meanings from the Party and its Central Committee. The trouble with oppositionism was not the challenge to the official line per se but its demand for certain spiritual autonomy. While doubt was an attitude that did not fully depend on the subject's will, a doubter had to know that whenever he questioned the Party line, he was engulfed by an illness. Remedy had to be sought in Party institutions, the only source of care and restitution, and launching a recantation was telling the Party what the symptoms were and letting it administer its spiritual cure. Iurii Piatakov, a major Soviet economic planner and a Trotskyist during the recent Discussion, stated famously in 1928 that "I am ready to sacrifice my pride and self-esteem and everything else. I know that ordinary people cannot make any instantaneous change, any reversal or amputation of their convictions. . . . Steeped in the idea of violence, we, the Bolsheviks, however, know how to direct it against ourselves. If the Party so demands and if it is necessary and important for the Party, I can by an act of will put out of my head in twenty-four hours ideas that I have cherished for years . . . reorient myself and come to agree with the Party inwardly, with my whole mind. . . , This sort of violence against the self is acutely painful, but such violence with the aim of breaking oneself so as to be in full accord with the Party constitutes the essence of a truly principled Bolshevik Communist. . . . Giving up life, shooting oneself through the head, are mere trifles compared with this other manifestation of will. . . . Yes, I shall consider black something that I considered to be white, since outside the Party, outside accord with it, there is no life for me." The influence of Piatakov's stance is evident from the correspondence between two mid-tier oppositionists, Golubenko and Livshits, both purged from the Party early in 1928 and sent to work in a minor capacity to the Far East. Golubenko wrote to Livshits from Chita on March 4: "Dear Iasha! Having read yesterday the recantation of Iurii [Piatakov], I hasten to exchange views with you about this and ask: what do we do next? Iurii's recantation comes as no surprise, especially after our conversation with him in Moscow. [Piatakov urged them to admit their mistakes and accept the resolutions of the Fifteenth Party Congress.] I agree with Iurii and made a firm decision to recant. To wait now and shun the Party while remaining loyal to the cause means to subject yourself to political death." The metaphor of "political death" (*politicheskaia smert'*) is important here, begging the question of the relation between political and real death in Bolshevism. Whereas in order to realize one's true self an individual had to shoulder the responsibilities of a Party member, a life lost to the Party was a life aborted. The person absolutely unable to identify with the official line had no right to exist. In the 1920s, Bolshevik misfits were given a second and a third chance to reform, to complete their life's journey and become good Party members, but during the Great Purge the names of Golubenko and Livshits will be dug out again with dire consequences. But in the meantime, in 1928, Golubenko saw "only one option—to return into the Party and become an active fighter in our mutual political struggle." Livshits concurred and in March 1928 the two officially recanted. On May 23, 1928, Golubenko wrote again to the same addressee: "Iasha, surely you read the newspapers and have noticed that a number of recantations went in recently, some full (Sarkis and others), other partial (Radek, Vuilovich, Safarov). . . . Think what you like, but in my view it is our gullibility and traditional trustworthiness that pushed us into uncharted water. The result is unnecessary, needless mental pain. One could live with that, but the temporary political death is inexcusable. We both took steps for self-resurrection [*voskreshenie sebia*] and hope for Party reinstatement, but the outcome could have been different. Let's learn our lesson. I, specifically, made all kinds of observations and will not be so susceptible to [oppositionist] feelings and sympathies in the future." N. Valentinov, "Sut' bolshevizma v izobrazhenii Iu. Piatakova," *Novyi zhurnal*, no. 52 (New York, 1958), p. 148 (Piatakov); *Sovetskoe rukovodstvo: Perepiska*, p. 344 (Golubenko and Livshits).

82. Demidov, *Politicheskaia bor'ba oppozitsii v sibiri*, pp. 124–25. I. Longuet, "L'Opposition de gauche en 1928–1929," *Cahiers de Leon Trotsky* 53 (1994), pp. 33–35.

83. PATO, f. 17, op. 1, d. 1076, l. 11.

84. *Sovetskaia sibir'*, October 25, 1928.

85. PATO, f. 17, op. 1, d. 1059, l. 253.

86. PATO, f. 17, op. 1, d. 1059, l. 252.

87. PATO, f. 17, op. 1, d. 1059, ll. 251, 254.

88. These castigations of Trotsky replicated the official line; see E. Iaroslavskii, "Eshche raz o mistere Trotskom," *Pravda*, March 22, 1929; and T. Bell, "Trotskii—sovetnik pravitel'stva ego velichestva," *Pravda*, March 22, 1929.

89. PATO, f. 17, op. 1, d. 1059, l. 252.

90. PATO, f. 17, op. 1, d. 1076, l. 24.

91. PATO, f. 17, op. 1, d. 1059, ll. 252–54.

92. PATO, f. 17, op. 1, d. 1050, ll. 251–54.

Epilogue: The Opposition Demonized

1. The term "treason" (*predatel'stvo*) appeared frequently in 1929–1931 in connection to the wrecking of industry. Though at this state the traitors were non-Party engineers and not former oppositionists, a constant effort was made to connect oppositionists (especially Rykov and Bukharin) with the bourgeois traitors. Another important step was made toward the unification of the various forms of evil. K. Levin, *Partiia i predateli* (Moscow: Molodaia gvardiia, 1931); N. Bliskavitskii (ed.), *Shpiony i vrediteli pered proletarskim sudom: Pokazaniia Ramzina* (Moscow-Leningrad: OGIZ-Moskovskii rabochii, 1930). K. Radek, *Portrety vreditelei* (Moscow: OGIZ-Moskovskii rabochii, 1931).

2. TSGA IPD, f. 197, op. 1, d. 725, l. 66.

3. *Arkhiv Trotskogo*, vol. 4, pp. 148, 151.

4. *Arkhiv Trotskogo*, vol. 4, p. 264.

5. *Arkhiv Trotskogo*, vol. 4, p. 274.

6. RGASPI, f. 6120, op. 1, d. 234, l. 10, cited after M. Lenoe, "Readers Response in the Soviet Press Campaign against the Trotsky-Zinoviev Opposition, 1926–28," *Russian History/Histoire Russe* 24, no. 1–2 (1997), pp. 101–2.

7. N. Smirnov, *Repressirovannoe pravosudie* (Moscow: "Gelios ARV," 2001), p. 115.

8. Ibid., pp. 113–15.

9. Ibid. p. 116.

INDEX

Page numbers in italics refer to illustrations.